500 BEST-EVER RECIPES

500 BEST-EVER RECIPES

A superb collection of all-time favourite dishes, from family meals
to special occasions, with clear instructions and 520 colour
photographs for great results

EDITED BY

MARTHA DAY

HERMES
HOUSE

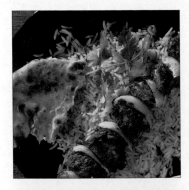

This edition is published by Hermes House, an imprint of Anness Publishing Ltd, Blaby Road, Wigston, Leicestershire LE18 4SE

Email: info@anness.com

Web: www.hermeshouse.com; www.annesspublishing.com

If you like the images in this book and would like to investigate using them for publishing, promotions or advertising, please visit our website www.practicalpictures.com for more information.

Publisher: Joanna Lorenz
Editorial Director: Helen Sudell
Editors: Simona Hill and Elizabeth Woodland
Design: SMI
Photographers: Karl Adamson, Edward Allwright, Steve Baxter, James Duncan, Michelle Garrett, Amanda Heywood, Don Last, Patrick McLeavy, Michael Michaels
Additional photography: Sopexa UK
Recipes: Carla Capalbo, Maxine Clark, Frances Cleary, Carole Clements, Roz Denny, Christine France, Sarah Gates, Shirley Gill, Rosamund Grant, Sue Maggs, Annie Nichols, Jenny Stacey, Liz Trigg, Hilaire Walden, Laura Washburn, Steven Wheeler, Elizabeth Wolf-Cohen
Food for Photography: Joanne Craig, Wendy Lee, Jenny Shapter, Jane Stevenson, Elizabeth Wolf-Cohen
Home Economists: Carla Capalbo, Jenny Shapter
Stylists: Madeleine Brehaut, Carla Capalbo, Michelle Garrett, Hilary Guy, Amanda Heywood, Blake Minton, Kirsty Rawlings, Rebecca Sturrock, Fiona Tillett
Production Controller: Pirong Wang

ETHICAL TRADING POLICY
At Anness Publishing we believe that business should be conducted in an ethical and ecologically sustainable way, with respect for the environment and a proper regard to the replacement of the natural resources we employ.
As a publisher, we use a lot of wood pulp in high-quality paper for printing, and that wood commonly comes from spruce trees. We are therefore currently growing more than 750,000 trees in three Scottish forest plantations. The forests we manage contain more than 3.5 times the number of trees employed each year in making paper for the books we manufacture.
Because of this ongoing ecological investment programme, you, as our customer, can have the pleasure and reassurance of knowing that a tree is being cultivated on your behalf to naturally replace the materials used to make the book you are holding. For further information about this scheme, go to www.annesspublishing.com/trees

© Anness Publishing Ltd 2006, 2011

A CIP catalogue record for this book is available from the British Library.

Previously published as *Five Hundred All-Time Great Recipes*

PUBLISHER'S NOTE
Although the advice and information in this book are believed to be accurate and true at the time of going to press, neither the authors nor the publisher can accept any legal responsibility or liability for any errors or omissions that may have been made nor for any inaccuracies nor for any loss, harm or injury that comes about from following instructions or advice in this book.

Main front cover image shows *Roast Pork with Sage & Onion* – for recipe, see page p110.

Notes

Bracketed terms are intended for American readers.

For all recipes, quantities are given in both metric and imperial measures and, where appropriate, in standard cups and spoons. Follow one set, but not a mixture, because they are not interchangeable.

Standard spoon and cup measures are level.
1 tsp = 5ml, 1 tbsp = 15ml, 1 cup = 250ml/8fl oz.

Australian standard tablespoons are 20ml. Australian readers should use 3 tsp in place of 1 tbsp for measuring small quantities.

American pints are 16fl oz/2 cups. American readers should use 20fl oz/2½ cups in place of 1 pint when measuring liquids.

Electric oven temperatures in this book are for conventional ovens. When using a fan oven, the temperature will probably need to be reduced by about 10–20°C/20–40°F. Since ovens vary, you should check with your manufacturer's instruction book for guidance.

The nutritional analysis given for each recipe is calculated per portion (i.e. serving or item), unless otherwise stated. If the recipe gives a range, such as Serves 4–6, then the nutritional analysis will be for the smaller portion size, i.e. serves 6. The analysis does not include optional ingredients, such as salt added to taste.

Medium (US large) eggs are used unless otherwise stated.

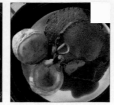

Contents

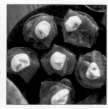

Introduction

In the modern world's quest for innovation and new taste sensations, it's easy to forget just how delicious and fulfilling a classic recipe can be. This volume contains a definitive selection of best-ever recipes that will serve as an essential reference point for beginners and as a timely reminder to the experienced cook when planning the perfect meal.

These cosmopolitan creations have gained world-wide status through their harmonious balance of fresh ingredients, herbs and spices. Stemming from justified popularity in their homelands, they have attained universal appeal as part of the international chef's repertoire. Even more appealing is the fact that many traditional recipes are based on a natural nutritional equilibrium which was taken for granted before the days of "fast food" and a high intake of saturated fats. Many of these dishes excel when analysed in the light of today's vogue for healthy eating. Others are unashamedly sinful (chocoholics, beware!).

The dishes presented in this book are tailored to every season and every event: you can mix and match cooking styles and influences to suit the mood and the occasion, not to mention your pocket. There is a fine selection of hearty soups such as Red Pepper Soup with Lime, which are satisfying enough for a light meal yet attractive enough to serve at an impressive dinner party.

Sophisticated appetizers include Smoked Salmon and Dill Blinis or Chicken Liver Pâté with Marsala, Avocados with Tangy Topping or Pears and Stilton.

Fish and shellfish are increasingly popular in today's health-conscious society. Flavoursome taste sensations such as Smoked Trout with Cucumber or Grilled Fresh Sardines are classic

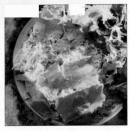

dishes that will always provide a light, fresh main course to tantalize your tastebuds.

Present directions in menu planning may point away from a truly carnivorous way of life, yet there are many occasions when a mouthwatering meat course will win the day. This volume will arm you with the confidence and conviction needed to present a perfect Roast Beef with Yorkshire Pudding or a melting Cottage Pie. Also included is a variety of more unusual dishes such as Duck with Chestnut Sauce, a simple yet impressive dinner party offering, and economical yet nutritious main courses that will appeal to adults and children alike, such as Sausage and Bean Ragoût. Whether we choose western fare such as Tuna Fishcake Bites or an exotic Kashmir Coconut Fish Curry, these recipes are characterized by a distinctive depth of flavour created by a judicious blend of herbs and spices.

The vegetable dishes in this book are mouthwatering concoctions that can be prepared at short notice for an accompaniment or for a complete, well-balanced meal. Some are long-standing favourites of vegetarian fare, such as Chickpea Stew; others are innovative versions of world-famous dishes, such as a Vegetables with Lentil Bolognese, which combines a colourful appearance with satisfying texture and harmonious flavours.

To finish, the moment that many have been waiting for: the dessert course. These dishes range from light, fluffy mousses and cool, super-smooth ices to the richest trifles, and dream desserts made from fruit, cream and chocolate.

This collection of recipes has been drawn together from the combined talents of some of the world's most respected cooks and food writers. With the help of this authoritative guide, your cooking will not only withstand the scrutiny of your most demanding critic – be it yourself or a fierce rival – but will win them over in style.

Leek, Potato & Rocket Soup

Rocket, with its distinctive peppery taste, is wonderful in this filling soup. Serve it hot with ciabatta croûtons.

Serves 4–6
50g/2oz/4 tbsp butter
1 onion, chopped
3 leeks, chopped
2 potatoes, diced
900ml/1½ pints/3¾ cups light chicken stock
2 large handfuls rocket (arugula), coarsely chopped
150ml/¼ pint/⅔ cup double (heavy) cream
salt and ground black pepper
garlic-flavoured ciabatta croûtons, to serve

1 Melt the butter in a large heavy pan over low heat. Add the onion, leeks and potatoes and stir until all the vegetable pieces are well coated in butter.

2 Cover with a tight-fitting lid and cook for about 15 minutes, until the vegetables are just beginning to soften but do not let them colour. Pour in the stock, bring to the boil and cover again with the lid, then simmer for a further 20 minutes, until the vegetables are tender.

3 Press the soup through a sieve (strainer) or food mill and return to the rinsed-out pan. (When puréeing the soup, don't use a blender or food processor, as these will give the soup a gluey texture.) Add the chopped rocket, stir in and cook gently for about 5 minutes.

4 Stir in the cream, then season to taste with salt and pepper. Reheat gently but do not boil. Ladle the soup into warmed soup bowls, sprinkle a few ciabatta croûtons into each one and serve immediately.

> **Cook's Tip**
> To make the croûtons, cut the bread into 1cm/½ in cubes, without the crust if you wish, and either fry or bake in a roasting pan in oil until golden and crunchy.

Carrot & Coriander Soup

Use a good home-made stock for this soup – it adds a far greater depth of flavour than stock made from cubes or powder. The latter may also have an unhealthily high salt content.

Serves 4
50g/2oz/4 tbsp butter
2 leeks, sliced
450g/1lb carrots, sliced
15ml/1 tbsp ground coriander
1.2 litres/2 pints/5 cups chicken stock
150ml/¼ pint/⅔ cup Greek (US strained plain) yogurt
salt and ground black pepper
30–45ml/2–3 tbsp chopped fresh coriander (cilantro), to garnish

1 Melt the butter in a large pan over low heat. Add the leeks and carrots and stir well, coating the vegetables with the butter. Cover with a tight-fitting lid and cook for about 10 minutes, until the vegetables are just beginning to soften but do not let them colour.

2 Stir in the ground coriander and cook for about 1 minute. Pour in the stock and season to taste with salt and pepper. Bring to the boil, cover and simmer for about 20 minutes, until the leeks and carrots are tender.

3 Leave to cool slightly, then ladle the soup into a blender, in batches if necessary, and process until smooth. Return the soup to the pan and add about 30ml/2 tbsp of the yogurt, then taste the soup and adjust the seasoning again to taste. Reheat gently but do not boil.

4 Ladle the soup into bowls and put a spoonful of the remaining yogurt in the centre of each. Sprinkle with the coriander and serve immediately.

> **Variation**
> For a vegetarian version of this soup, substitute a good-quality vegetable stock for the chicken stock

Coriander Energy 195kcal/807kJ; Protein 4.6g; Carbohydrate 12.3g, of which sugars 11.1g; Fat 14.9g, of which saturates 8.7g; Cholesterol 27mg; Calcium 108mg; Fibre 4.6g; Sodium 132mg.
Rocket Energy 245kcal/1015kJ; Protein 3g; Carbohydrate 11.9g, of which sugars 3.7g; Fat 20.9g, of which saturates 12.8g; Cholesterol 52mg; Calcium 54mg; Fibre 2.7g; Sodium 75mg.

Tomato & Basil Soup

In the summer, when tomatoes are both plentiful and inexpensive, this is a lovely soup to make.

Serves 4
30ml/2 tbsp olive oil
1 onion, chopped
2.5ml/½ tsp caster (superfine) sugar
1 carrot, finely chopped
1 potato, finely chopped
1 garlic clove, crushed
675g/1½lb ripe tomatoes, coarsely chopped

5ml/1 tsp tomato purée (paste)
1 bay leaf
1 thyme sprig
1 oregano sprig
4 fresh basil leaves, coarsely torn
300ml/½ pint/1¼ cups light chicken or vegetable stock
2–3 pieces sun-dried tomatoes in oil, drained
30ml/2 tbsp shredded fresh basil leaves
salt and ground black pepper

1 Heat the oil in a large pan over low heat. Add the onion, sprinkle with the sugar and cook gently for 5 minutes.

2 Add the chopped carrot and potato, stir well, then cover the pan with a tight-fitting lid and cook gently for a further 10 minutes, until the vegetables are beginning to soften but do not let them colour.

3 Stir in the garlic, tomatoes, tomato purée, bay leaf, thyme, oregano, torn basil leaves and stock and season to taste with salt and pepper. Cover the pan again with the lid and simmer gently for 25–30 minutes, or until the vegetables are tender.

4 Remove the pan from the heat and press the soup through a sieve (strainer) or food mill to extract all the skins and seeds. Taste the soup and season again with salt and pepper.

5 Return the soup to the rinsed-out pan and reheat gently, then ladle into four warmed soup bowls. Finely chop the sun-dried tomatoes and mix with a little of the oil from the jar. Add a spoonful to each serving, then sprinkle the shredded basil over the top and serve immediately.

Corn & Shellfish Chowder

"Chowder" comes from the French word *chaudron*, meaning a large pot in which the soup is cooked.

Serves 4
25g/1oz/2 tbsp butter
1 small onion, chopped
350g/12oz can corn, drained
600ml/1 pint/2½ cups milk
2 spring onions (scallions), finely chopped

115g/4oz/1 cup peeled, cooked prawns (shrimp)
175g/6oz can white crab meat, drained and flaked
150ml/¼ pint/⅔ cup single (light) cream
pinch of cayenne pepper
salt and ground black pepper
4 whole prawns in the shell, to garnish

1 Melt the butter in a large, heavy pan over medium heat. Add the onion and cook, stirring occasionally, for 4–5 minutes, until softened.

2 Reserve 30ml/2 tbsp of the corn for the garnish and add the remainder to the pan, then pour in the milk. Bring the soup to the boil, then reduce the heat to low, cover the pan with a tight-fitting lid and simmer gently for 5 minutes.

3 Ladle the soup into a blender or food processor, in batches if necessary, and process until smooth.

4 Return the soup to the rinsed-out pan and stir in the spring onions, prawns, crab meat, cream and cayenne pepper. Reheat gently over low heat, stirring occasionally. Do not let the soup come to the boil.

5 Meanwhile, place the reserved corn kernels in a small frying pan without oil and dry-fry over a medium heat until golden and toasted.

6 When the soup is hot, season to taste with salt and pepper and ladle it into warmed soup bowls. Garnish each bowl with a sprinkling of the toasted corn kernels and a whole prawn and serve immediately.

Basil Energy 129kcal/538kJ; Protein 2.2g; Carbohydrate 13.4g, of which sugars 9.2g; Fat 7.8g, of which saturates 1.3g; Cholesterol 0mg; Calcium 26mg; Fibre 3g; Sodium 30mg.
Corn Energy 359kcal/1506kJ; Protein 22.2g; Carbohydrate 32.5g, of which sugars 17.3g; Fat 16.5g, of which saturates 9.7g; Cholesterol 130mg; Calcium 299mg; Fibre 1.5g; Sodium 646mg.

Spiced Parsnip Soup

This pale, creamy-textured soup is given a special touch with an aromatic garlic and mustard seed garnish.

Serves 4–6
40g/1½oz/3 tbsp butter
1 onion, chopped
675g/1½lb parsnips, diced
5ml/1 tsp ground coriander
2.5ml/½ tsp ground cumin
2.5ml/½ tsp ground turmeric
1.5ml/¼ tsp chilli powder
1.2 litres/2 pints/5 cups chicken
    stock
150ml/¼ pint/⅔ cup single
    (light) cream
15ml/1 tbsp sunflower oil
1 garlic clove, cut into
    julienne strips
10ml/2 tsp yellow mustard seeds
salt and ground black pepper

1 Melt the butter in a large pan over medium heat. Add the onion and parsnips and cook gently, stirring occasionally, for about 3 minutes.

2 Stir in the spices and cook for 1 minute more. Add the stock, season to taste with salt and pepper and bring to the boil, then reduce the heat. Cover with a tight-fitting lid and simmer for about 45 minutes, until the parsnips are tender.

3 Cool slightly, then ladle the soup into a blender and process until smooth. Return the soup to the rinsed-out pan, add the cream and heat through gently over low heat.

4 Heat the oil in a small pan, add the julienne strips of garlic and yellow mustard seeds and cook briskly, stirring occasionally, until the garlic is beginning to brown and the mustard seeds start to pop and splutter. Remove the pan from the heat.

5 Ladle the soup into warmed soup bowls and pour a little of the hot spice mixture over each. Serve immediately.

Variation
Crushed coriander seeds may be substituted for the mustard seeds in the garnish.

Pumpkin Soup

The flavour of this soup will develop and improve if it is made a day in advance.

Serves 4–6
900g/2lb pumpkin
45ml/3 tbsp olive oil
2 onions, chopped
2 celery sticks, chopped
450g/1lb tomatoes, chopped
1.5 litres/2½ pints/6¼ cups
    vegetable stock
30ml/2 tbsp tomato
    purée (paste)
1 bouquet garni
2–3 rashers (strips) streaky
    (fatty) bacon, crisply fried
    and crumbled
30ml/2 tbsp chopped fresh flat
    leaf parsley
salt and ground black pepper

1 With a sharp knife cut the pumpkin into thin slices, discarding the skin and seeds.

2 Heat the olive oil in a large pan over medium heat. Add the onions and celery and cook, stirring occasionally, for about 5 minutes, until the vegetables are beginning to soften but do not let them colour.

3. Add the pumpkin slices and tomatoes and cook, stirring occasionally, for a further 5 minutes.

4 Add the vegetable stock, tomato purée and bouquet garni to the pan and season with salt and pepper. Bring the soup to the boil, then reduce the heat to low, cover with a tight-fitting lid and simmer gently for 45 minutes.

5 Leave the soup to cool slightly, then remove and discard the bouquet garni. Ladle the soup into a food processor or blender, in batches if necessary, and process until smooth.

6 Press the soup through a sieve (strainer) and return it to the rinsed-out pan. Reheat gently, then taste and season again if necessary. Ladle the soup into warmed soup bowls. Sprinkle each serving with the crisp bacon and chopped parsley and serve immediately.

Parsnip Energy 187kcal/780kJ; Protein 3g; Carbohydrate 14.8g, of which sugars 7g; Fat 13.3g, of which saturates 7g; Cholesterol 28mg; Calcium 70mg; Fibre 5.2g; Sodium 59mg.
Pumpkin Energy 136kcal/565kJ; Protein 4.6g; Carbohydrate 7.2g, of which sugars 6.2g; Fat 10g, of which saturates 2.4g; Cholesterol 11mg; Calcium 58mg; Fibre 2.6g; Sodium 235mg.

Jerusalem Artichoke Soup

Topped with saffron cream, this unusual soup is wonderful to serve on a chilly winter's day.

900ml/1½ pints/3¾ cups chicken stock
150ml/¼ pint/⅔ cup milk
150ml/¼ pint/⅔ cup double (heavy) cream
large pinch of saffron powder
salt and ground black pepper
chopped fresh chives, to garnish

Serves 4
50g/2oz/4 tbsp butter
1 onion, chopped
450g/1lb Jerusalem artichokes, peeled and cut into chunks

1 Melt the butter in a large heavy pan over medium heat. Add the onion and cook, stirring occasionally, for 5–8 minutes, until softened but not browned.

2 Add the artichokes to the pan and stir until coated in the butter. Reduce the heat to low, cover the pan with a tight-fitting lid and cook gently for 10–15 minutes but do not let the artichokes brown. Pour in the stock and milk, then cover the pan again and simmer gently for about 15 minutes. Leave the soup to cool slightly, then ladle it into a food processor or blender, in batches if necessary, and process until smooth.

3 Strain the soup back into the rinsed-out pan. Add half the cream, season to taste with salt and pepper and reheat gently.

4 Lightly whip the remaining cream and saffron powder. Ladle the soup into warmed soup bowls and put a spoonful of saffron cream in the centre of each. Sprinkle with the chopped chives and serve immediately.

Cook's Tip
The flesh of Jerusalem artichokes discolours when it is exposed to the air. Fill a bowl with cold water and add about 30ml/2 tbsp lemon juice. As you peel the artichokes drop them into the acidulated water to prevent them from turning brown.

Broccoli & Stilton Soup

A really easy, but deliciously rich, soup – choose something simple for the main course, such as plainly cooked meat, poultry or fish.

1 leek, white part only, chopped
1 small potato, diced
600ml/1 pint/2½ cups hot chicken stock
300ml/½ pint/1¼ cups milk
45ml/3 tbsp double (heavy) cream
115g/4oz Stilton cheese, rind removed, crumbled
salt and ground black pepper

Serves 4
350g/12oz/3 cups broccoli florets
25g/1oz/2 tbsp butter
1 onion, chopped

1 Discard any tough stems from the broccoli florets. Set aside two small florets for the garnish.

2 Melt the butter in a large pan over medium heat. Add the onion and leek and cook, stirring occasionally, for 5–8 minutes, until softened but not coloured.

3 Add the broccoli and potato and pour in the stock. Cover the pan with a tight-fitting lid, reduce the heat to low and simmer for 15–20 minutes, until the vegetables are tender.

4 Leave the soup to cool slightly, then ladle it into a food processor or blender and process until smooth. Strain through a sieve (strainer) back into the rinsed-out pan.

5 Add the milk and cream, season to taste with salt and pepper and reheat gently. When the soup is hot stir in the cheese until it just melts, then remove the pan from the heat. Do not let it come to the boil.

6 Meanwhile, blanch the reserved broccoli florets in lightly salted, boiling water for 1–2 minutes, then drain and cut them vertically into thin slices.

7 Ladle the soup into warmed soup bowls and garnish each with the sliced broccoli florets and a generous grinding of black pepper. Serve immediately.

Artichoke Energy 310kcal/1277kJ; Protein 2.7g; Carbohydrate 4.7g, of which sugars 4.3g; Fat 31.3g, of which saturates 19.4g; Cholesterol 80mg; Calcium 116mg; Fibre 1.5g; Sodium 168mg.
Stilton Energy 312kcal/1296kJ; Protein 14.4g; Carbohydrate 11.3g, of which sugars 6.8g; Fat 23.3g, of which saturates 14.7g; Cholesterol 60mg; Calcium 251mg; Fibre 3.3g; Sodium 310mg.

Minestrone with Pesto

This hearty, Italian mixed vegetable soup is a great way to use up any leftover vegetables you may have.

Serves 4
30ml/2 tbsp olive oil
2 garlic cloves, crushed
1 onion, sliced
225g/8oz/2 cups diced
  lean bacon
2 small courgettes (zucchini),
  quartered and sliced
50g/2oz/1¹/₂ cups green
  beans, chopped
2 small carrots, diced
2 celery sticks, finely chopped

1 bouquet garni
50g/2oz/¹/₂ cup short-cut
  macaroni or other soup pasta
50g/2oz/¹/₂ cup frozen peas
200g/7oz can red kidney beans,
  drained and rinsed
50g/2oz/1 cup shredded
  green cabbage
4 tomatoes, peeled and seeded
salt and ground black pepper

For the toasts
8 slices French bread
15ml/1 tbsp ready-made
  pesto sauce
15ml/1 tbsp freshly grated
  Parmesan cheese

1 Heat the oil in a large pan over low heat. Add the garlic and onion and cook, stirring occasionally, for 5 minutes, until just softened but not coloured.

2 Add the bacon, courgettes, green beans, carrots and celery to the pan and stir-fry for a further 3 minutes.

3 Pour 1.2 litres/2 pints/5 cups water over the vegetables and add the bouquet garni. Cover the pan with a tight-fitting lid and simmer for 25 minutes.

4 Add the macaroni, peas and kidney beans and cook for a further 8 minutes. Then add the cabbage and tomatoes and cook for 5 minutes more, until all the vegetables and the pasta are tender.

5 To make the toasts, spread the bread slices with the pesto, sprinkle a little Parmesan over each one and gently brown under a hot grill (broiler). Remove and discard the bouquet garni from the soup, season to taste and serve with the toasts.

French Onion Soup

Onion soup comes in many different guises from light, smooth and creamy to this rich, dark brown version – the absolute classic recipe from France.

Serves 4
25g/1oz/2 tbsp butter
15ml/1 tbsp sunflower oil
3 large onions, thinly sliced
5ml/1 tsp soft dark brown sugar
15g/¹/₂ oz/1 tbsp plain (all-
  purpose) flour

2 x 300g/10oz cans condensed
  beef consommé
30ml/2 tbsp medium sherry
10ml/2 tsp Worcestershire sauce
8 slices French bread
15ml/1 tbsp French coarse-
  grained mustard
75g/3oz Gruyère cheese, grated
salt and ground black pepper
15ml/1 tbsp chopped fresh flat
  leaf parsley, to garnish

1 Heat the butter and oil in a large pan over low heat. Add the onions and brown sugar and cook gently, stirring occasionally, for at least 20 minutes, until the onions start to turn golden brown and caramelize. (Depending on the variety, you may need to cook them for longer.)

2 Stir in the flour and cook, stirring constantly, for a further 2 minutes. Pour in the consommé and stir in two cans of water, then add the sherry and Worcestershire sauce. Season with salt and pepper, cover the pan with a tight-fitting lid and simmer gently for a further 25–30 minutes.

3 Preheat the grill (broiler) and, just before you are ready to serve, toast the bread lightly on both sides. Spread one side of each slice with the mustard and top with the grated cheese. Grill (broil) the toasts until the cheese has melted and is bubbling and golden.

4 Ladle the soup into warmed soup bowls. Place two slices of toasted bread on top of each bowl of soup and sprinkle with chopped fresh parsley to garnish. Alternatively, place the toasted bread in the base of the bowls and ladle the soup over them, then garnish with the parsley. Serve immediately.

Minestrone Energy 570kcal/2396kJ; Protein 26.9g; Carbohydrate 72.8g, of which sugars 12.5g; Fat 21g, of which saturates 6g; Cholesterol 35mg; Calcium 247mg; Fibre 9g; Sodium 1635mg.
Onion Energy 415kcal/1745kJ; Protein 13g; Carbohydrate 61.6g, of which sugars 12.6g; Fat 14.1g, of which saturates 6.7g; Cholesterol 25mg; Calcium 240mg; Fibre 4.1g; Sodium 1022mg.

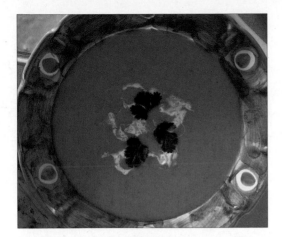

Curried Parsnip Soup

The spices in this soup impart a delicious, mild curry flavour redolent of the days of the British Raj.

Serves 4

25g/1oz/2 tbsp butter
1 garlic clove, crushed
1 onion, chopped
5ml/1 tsp ground cumin
5ml/1 tsp ground coriander
450g/1lb (about 4) parsnips,
   sliced
10ml/2 tsp medium curry paste
450ml/³/4 pint/scant 2 cups
   chicken or vegetable stock
450ml/³/4 pint/scant 2 cups milk
60ml/4 tbsp sour cream
good squeeze of lemon juice
salt and ground black pepper
fresh coriander (cilantro) sprigs,
   to garnish
garlic and coriander naan bread,
   to serve

1 Heat the butter in a large pan over medium heat. Add the garlic and onion and cook, stirring occasionally, for 4–5 minutes, until lightly golden. Stir in the cumin and coriander and cook, stirring frequently, for a further 1–2 minutes.

2 Add the parsnips and stir until well coated with the butter, then stir in the curry paste, followed by the stock. Bring to the boil, then reduce the heat to low, cover the pan with a tight-fitting lid and simmer gently for 15 minutes, until the parsnips are tender.

3 Leave the soup to cool slightly, then ladle it into a blender or food processor, in batches if necessary, and process to a smooth purée.

4 Return the soup to the rinsed-out pan and stir in the milk. Heat gently for 2–3 minutes, then stir in 30ml/2 tbsp of the sour cream and lemon juice to taste. Season to taste with salt and pepper.

5 Ladle the soup into warmed bowls and top each serving with a spoonful of the remaining sour cream. Garnish with the coriander sprigs and serve immediately accompanied by the warmed, spicy naan bread.

Red Pepper Soup with Lime

The beautiful rich red colour of this soup makes it a very attractive appetizer or light lunch.

Serves 4–6

5ml/1 tsp olive oil
4 fresh red (bell) peppers, seeded
   and chopped
1 large onion, chopped
1 garlic clove, crushed
1 small red chilli, sliced
45ml/3 tbsp tomato
   purée (paste)
juice and finely grated rind of
   1 lime
900ml/1¹/2 pints/3¹/4 cups
   chicken stock
salt and ground black pepper
shreds of lime rind, to garnish

1 Heat the oil in a pan over low heat. Add the peppers and onion, cover with a tight-fitting lid and cook, shaking the pan occasionally, for about 5 minutes, until softened.

2 Stir in the garlic, then add the chilli and tomato purée. Stir in half the stock and bring to the boil. Cover the pan again and simmer for 10 minutes.

3 Leave to cool slightly, then ladle the soup into a food processor or blender, in batches if necessary, and process to a purée. Return it to the rinsed-out pan, stir in the remaining stock, the lime rind and juice and season to taste with salt and pepper.

4 Bring the soup back to the boil, then ladle it into warmed soup bowls. Sprinkle each bowl with a few shreds of lime rind and serve immediately.

Cook's Tip
Small, pointed chillies are usually hotter than the larger, blunt ones. If you prefer a milder flavour, halve the chilli lengthways and scrape out the seeds and surrounding membrane with the blade of the knife before slicing. Most of the heat of chilli is concentrated in this membrane. Wash your hands well after handling it and avoid touching your eyes.

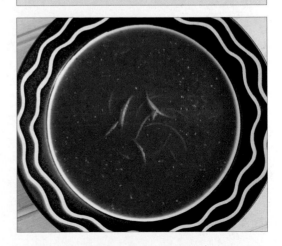

Parsnip Energy 207kcal/865kJ; Protein 6.5g; Carbohydrate 21.2g, of which sugars 13.2g; Fat 11.3g, of which saturates 6.6g; Cholesterol 29mg; Calcium 200mg; Fibre 5.4g; Sodium 104mg.
Red Pepper Energy 66kcal/274kJ; Protein 2.2g; Carbohydrate 12.5g, of which sugars 11g; Fat 1.1g, of which saturates 0.2g; Cholesterol 0mg; Calcium 25mg; Fibre 2.8g; Sodium 24mg.

Thai-style Corn Soup

This is a very quick and easy soup. If you are using frozen prawns, thaw them before adding to the soup.

Serves 4

2.5ml/½ tsp sesame or
   sunflower oil
2 spring onions (scallions),
   thinly sliced
1 garlic clove, crushed
600ml/1 pint/2½ cups chicken
   stock
425g/15oz can cream-style corn
225g/8oz/2 cups cooked, peeled
   prawns (shrimp)
5ml/1 tsp green chilli paste or
   chilli sauce (optional)
salt and ground black pepper
fresh coriander (cilantro) leaves,
   to garnish

1 Heat the oil in a large, heavy pan over medium heat. Add the spring onions and garlic and cook for about 1 minute, until softened but not browned.

2 Stir in the chicken stock, cream-style corn, prawns and chilli paste or sauce, if using. Bring the soup just to the boil, stirring occasionally, then remove the pan from the heat.

3 Season the soup to taste with salt and pepper, ladle it into warmed soup bowls, sprinkle with fresh coriander leaves to garnish and serve immediately.

Variations

• For a Chinese version of this soup add 5ml/1 tsp grated fresh root ginger to the pan with the spring onions (scallions) and garlic in step 1 and substitute finely shredded, cooked chicken for the prawns (shrimp) in step 2. Garnish the soup with rings of spring onion, using the green part only.
• For a more pungent version add 10ml/2 tsp grated galangal or fresh root ginger and 1 lemon grass stalk, cut into 2.5cm/1in lengths, to the pan with the spring onions and garlic in step 1. Remove and discard the pieces of lemon grass before ladling the soup into bowls. Serve with a sweet chilli sauce or a chilli relish handed separately.

Haddock & Broccoli Chowder

This hearty soup makes a meal in itself when served with crusty bread.

Serves 4

4 spring onions (scallions), sliced
450g/1lb new potatoes, diced
300ml/½ pint/1¼ cups fish stock
300ml/½ pint/1¼ cups milk
1 bay leaf
225g/8oz/2 cups broccoli
   florets, sliced
450g/1lb smoked haddock
   fillets, skinned
200g/7oz can corn, drained
ground black pepper
chopped spring onions, to garnish

1 Place the spring onions and potatoes in a pan and add the stock, milk and bay leaf. Bring to the boil, reduce the heat, cover and simmer for 10 minutes.

2 Add the broccoli. Cut the fish into bitesize chunks and add to the pan with the corn. Season with pepper, then cover again and simmer until the fish is cooked through.

3 Remove and discard the bay leaf, sprinkle the chopped spring onions over the soup and serve immediately.

Cock-a-leekie Soup

This healthy main course soup has a sweet touch.

Serves 4–6

1.5kg/3lb chicken
1 bouquet garni
4 leeks, thickly sliced
8–12 ready-to-eat prunes
salt and pepper

1 Simmer the chicken in a covered pan with 1.2 litres/2 pints/ 5 cups water and the bouquet garni for 40 minutes. Add the leeks and prunes and simmer for a further 20 minutes.

2 Discard the bouquet garni. Remove the chicken, discard the skin and bones and chop the flesh. Return the chicken to the pan and season to taste. Reheat the soup and serve.

Corn Soup Energy 177kcal/751kJ; Protein 13.1g; Carbohydrate 28.4g, of which sugars 10.4g; Fat 2g, of which saturates 0.3g; Cholesterol 110mg; Calcium 51mg; Fibre 1.6g; Sodium 394mg.
Haddock Energy 276kcal/1172kJ; Protein 30g; Carbohydrate 36g, of which sugars 10.7g; Fat 2.4g, of which saturates 0.6g; Cholesterol 43mg; Calcium 161mg; Fibre 3.5g; Sodium 1041mg.
Cock-a-leekie Energy 281kcal/1189kJ; Protein 24g; Carbohydrate 39.8g, of which sugars 38.4g; Fat 3.9g, of which saturates 0.9g; Cholesterol 92mg; Calcium 88mg; Fibre 10.1g; Sodium 94mg.

Green Pea & Mint Soup

This soup is equally delicious lightly chilled. Stir in the swirl of cream just before serving.

Serves 4

50g/2oz/4 tbsp butter
4 spring onions
    (scallions), chopped
450g/1lb/4 cups fresh or
    frozen peas
600ml/1 pint/2½ cups chicken or
    vegetable stock
2 large fresh mint sprigs
600ml/1 pint/2½ cups milk
pinch of sugar (optional)
salt and ground black pepper
single (light) cream and small
    fresh mint sprigs, to garnish

1 Heat the butter in a large pan over low heat. Add the spring onions and cook, stirring occasionally, for 3–5 minutes, until just softened but not coloured.

2 Stir the peas into the pan, add the stock and mint and bring to the boil. Cover and simmer very gently for about 30 minutes for fresh peas or 15 minutes if you are using frozen peas, until the peas are very tender. Remove about 45ml/3 tbsp of the peas using a slotted spoon and reserve for the garnish.

3 Leave the soup to cook slightly, then ladle it into a food processor or blender, add the milk and process until smooth. Return the soup to the rinsed-out pan and reheat gently. Season to taste with salt and pepper, adding a pinch of sugar if you like.

4 Ladle the soup into warmed bowls. Swirl a little cream into each, then garnish with mint and the reserved peas.

> **Cook's Tip**
> Fresh peas are increasingly available during the summer months from grocers and supermarkets. The time and effort of podding them are well worthwhile, as they impart a unique flavour to this delicious, vibrant soup.

Beetroot & Apricot Swirl

This soup is most attractive if you swirl together the two coloured purées, but mix them together if you prefer.

Serves 4

4 large cooked beetroot (beets),
    coarsely chopped
1 small onion, coarsely chopped
600ml/1 pint/2½ cups chicken
    stock
200g/7oz ready-to-eat
    dried apricots
250ml/8fl oz/1 cup orange juice
salt and ground black pepper

1 Place the beetroot and half of the onion in a pan with the stock. Bring to the boil, then reduce the heat, cover with a tight-fitting lid and simmer for about 10 minutes. Leave to cool slightly, then ladle the mixture into a food processor or blender, in batches if necessary, and process until smooth. Return to the rinsed-out pan and set aside.

2 Place the remaining onion in another pan with the apricots and orange juice, cover and simmer gently over low heat for about 15 minutes, until tender. Leave to cool slightly, then ladle the mixture into a food processor or blender and process until smooth. Return to the rinsed-out pan.

3 Gently reheat both purées. Season to taste with salt and pepper, then swirl the mixtures together in warmed individual soup bowls to create a marbled effect. Serve immediately.

> **Cook's Tip**
> Beetroot (beets) are widely available ready cooked. To cook your own, first rinse them well under cold running water and trim the stalks to about 2.5cm/1in above the beetroot. Do not peel or cut off the long roots as this will cause the colour to bleed away. Place the beetroot in a pan, add enough water to cover and bring to the boil. Lower the heat, cover and simmer for about 1 hour, until tender. Drain, then peel the beetroot with your fingers when cool enough to handle.

Green Pea Energy 242kcal/1012kJ; Protein 12.1g; Carbohydrate 18.3g, of which sugars 10.5g; Fat 13.9g, of which saturates 8.4g; Cholesterol 36mg; Calcium 226mg; Fibre 5.9g; Sodium 247mg.
Beetroot Swirl Energy 138kcal/587kJ; Protein 4g; Carbohydrate 31.4g, of which sugars 30.8g; Fat 0.5g, of which saturates 0g; Cholesterol 0mg; Calcium 63mg; Fibre 5.1g; Sodium 79mg.

Thai-style Chicken Soup

Like most Thai soups this one is quick and easy to prepare and may be served as a first course, a snack or a light lunch.

Serves 4

15ml/1 tbsp vegetable oil
1 garlic clove, finely chopped
2 x 175g/6oz boned chicken breast portions, skinned and chopped
2.5ml/½ tsp ground turmeric
1.5ml/¼ tsp hot chilli powder
75ml/5 tbsp coconut cream
900ml/1½ pints/3¾ cups hot chicken stock

30ml/2 tbsp lemon or lime juice
30ml/2 tbsp crunchy peanut butter
50g/2oz thread egg noodles, broken into small pieces
15ml/1 tbsp finely chopped spring onions (scallions)
15ml/1 tbsp chopped fresh coriander (cilantro)
salt and ground black pepper
30ml/2 tbsp desiccated (dry unsweetened shredded) coconut and ½ red chilli, seeded and finely chopped, to garnish

1 Heat the oil in a large, heavy pan over medium heat. Add the garlic and stir-fry for 1 minute, until lightly golden. Add the chicken, turmeric and chilli powder and stir-fry for a further 3–4 minutes.

2 Mix together the coconut cream and chicken stock until thoroughly combined and pour into the pan. Add the lemon or lime juice, peanut butter and egg noodles and bring to the boil, stirring constantly. Lower the heat, cover and simmer gently for 15 minutes.

3 Add the spring onions and coriander, season to taste with salt and pepper and cook for a further 5 minutes.

4 Meanwhile, heat a small frying pan, add the coconut and chilli and dry-fry, stirring constantly, for 2–3 minutes, until the coconut is lightly browned.

5 Ladle the soup into warmed soup bowls and sprinkle the coconut and chilli garnish over each. Serve immediately.

New England Pumpkin Soup

For a smooth-textured soup, process all the mixture in a food processor or blender.

Serves 4

25g/1oz/2 tbsp butter
1 onion, finely chopped
1 garlic clove, crushed
15g/½ oz/1 tbsp plain (all-purpose) flour
pinch of grated nutmeg
2.5ml/½ tsp ground cinnamon
350g/12oz pumpkin, seeded, peeled and diced

600ml/1 pint/2½ cups chicken stock
150ml/¼ pint/⅔ cup freshly squeezed orange juice
5ml/1 tsp brown sugar

For the croûtons

15ml/1 tbsp vegetable oil
2 slices multigrain bread, crusts removed
30ml/2 tbsp sunflower seeds
salt and ground black pepper

1 Melt the butter in a large pan over low heat. Add the onion and garlic and cook, stirring occasionally, for 4–5 minutes, until softened but not coloured.

2 Stir in the flour, nutmeg, cinnamon and pumpkin, then cover the pan and cook gently, stirring occasionally, for 6 minutes.

3 Add the chicken stock, orange juice and brown sugar. Cover the pan again, and bring to the boil, then simmer for 20 minutes until the pumpkin has softened.

4 Leave to cool slightly, then ladle half the mixture into a blender or food processor and process until smooth. Return the soup to the pan with the remaining chunky mixture. Season to taste and heat through, stirring constantly.

5 To make the croûtons, heat the oil in a frying pan, cut the bread into cubes and gently fry until just beginning to brown. Add the sunflower seeds and fry for 1–2 minutes. Drain the croûtons on kitchen paper. Serve the soup hot, garnished with a few of the croûtons sprinkled over the top and the remaining croûtons separately.

Thai Chicken Soup Energy 342kcal/1425kJ; Protein 25.7g; Carbohydrate 11.6g, of which sugars 2.4g; Fat 21.7g, of which saturates 13g; Cholesterol 65mg; Calcium 40mg; Fibre 1.4g; Sodium 111mg.
Pumpkin Soup Energy 189kcal/788kJ; Protein 4.1g; Carbohydrate 17.1g, of which sugars 6.4g; Fat 12.1g, of which saturates 4.1g; Cholesterol 13mg; Calcium 76mg; Fibre 2.2g; Sodium 109mg.

Split Pea & Courgette Soup

Rich and satisfying, this tasty and nutritious soup is ideal to serve on a chilly winter's day. Served with crusty bread it's perfect for lunch.

Serves 4
175g/6oz/1 cup yellow split peas
5ml/1 tsp sunflower oil
1 large onion, finely chopped
2 courgettes (zucchini), finely diced
900ml/1½ pints/3¾ cups chicken stock
2.5ml/½ tsp ground turmeric
salt and ground black pepper
warm crusty bread, to serve

1 Place the split peas in a bowl, cover with cold water and leave to soak for several hours or overnight. Drain, rinse in cold water and drain again.

2 Heat the oil in a pan over low heat. Add the onion, cover the pan with a tight-fitting lid and cook for about 8 minutes, until softened but not coloured.

3 Reserve a handful of diced courgettes and add the remainder to the pan. Increase the heat to medium and cook, stirring constantly, for 2–3 minutes.

4 Add the chicken stock and turmeric to the pan and bring to the boil. Reduce the heat to low, cover and simmer gently for 30–40 minutes, or until the split peas are tender. Season to taste with salt and pepper.

5 When the soup is almost ready, bring a large pan of water to the boil, add the reserved diced courgettes and cook for 1 minute, then drain and add to the soup before serving hot with warm crusty bread.

Cook's Tip
For a quicker alternative, use split red lentils for this soup. They do not require presoaking and cook very quickly. Adjust the amount of chicken stock used, if you need to.

Mediterranean Tomato Soup

Children will love this soup – especially if you use fancy pasta such as alphabet or animal shapes.

Serves 4
675g/1½lb ripe plum tomatoes
1 onion, quartered
1 celery stick
1 garlic clove
15ml/1 tbsp olive oil
450ml/¾ pint/scant 2 cups chicken stock
15ml/2 tbsp tomato purée (paste)
50g/2oz/½ cup small pasta shapes
salt and ground black pepper
fresh coriander (cilantro) or parsley sprigs, to garnish

1 Place the tomatoes, onion, celery and garlic in a pan with the olive oil. Cover with a tight-fitting lid and cook over low heat, shaking the pan occasionally, for 40–45 minutes, until the vegetables become very soft.

2 Leave to cool slightly, then spoon the vegetables into a food processor or blender and process until smooth. Press through a sieve (strainer) to remove the tomato seeds and skins, then return to the rinsed-out pan.

3 Stir in the stock and tomato purée and bring to the boil. Add the pasta and simmer gently for about 8 minutes, or until the pasta is tender. Season with salt and pepper to taste.

4 Ladle the soup into warmed soup bowls, sprinkle with coriander or parsley to garnish and serve immediately.

Cook's Tip
Plum tomatoes are best for this soup as they have a rich flavour and are less watery than some other varieties. They also have fewer seeds. However other types of tomato can be used, especially if they have been sun-ripened on the vine, which produces a delicious sweetness. Tomatoes that have ripened after picking are really not suitable but if you have to use them, add a good pinch of sugar at the beginning of step 3.

Split Pea Energy 182kcal/769kJ; Protein 12.2g; Carbohydrate 31.5g, of which sugars 6.1g; Fat 1.7g, of which saturates 0.2g; Cholesterol 0mg; Calcium 54mg; Fibre 3.7g; Sodium 19mg.
Tomato Energy 105kcal/444kJ; Protein 3.1g; Carbohydrate 16.3g, of which sugars 7.1g; Fat 3.5g, of which saturates 0.6g; Cholesterol 0mg; Calcium 23mg; Fibre 2.5g; Sodium 30mg.

White Bean Soup

Small white lima beans or pinto beans work well in this soup, or try butter beans for a change.

Serves 6

350g/12oz/1½ cups dried cannellini or other white beans
1 bay leaf
75ml/5 tbsp olive oil
1 onion, finely chopped
1 carrot, finely chopped
1 celery stick, finely chopped
3 tomatoes, peeled and finely chopped
2 garlic cloves, finely chopped
5ml/1 tsp fresh thyme leaves or 2.5ml/½ tsp dried thyme
750ml/1¼ pints/3 cups boiling water
salt and ground black pepper
extra virgin olive oil, to serve

1 Pick over the beans carefully, discarding any stones or other particles. Place the beans in a large bowl, add cold water to cover and leave to soak overnight. Drain well.

2 Place the beans in a large pan, add water to cover, bring to the boil and cook for 20 minutes. Drain, return the beans to the pan, cover with cold water and bring to the boil again. Add the bay leaf and cook 1–2 hours, until the beans are tender. Drain again. Remove and discard the bay leaf.

3 Spoon about three-quarters of the beans into a food processor or blender and process to a purée. Alternatively, pass through a food mill, adding a little water if necessary.

4 Heat the oil in a large pan over medium heat. Add the onion and cook, stirring occasionally, for about 5 minutes, until softened but not coloured. Add the carrot and celery and cook, stirring occasionally, for a further 5 minutes.

5 Stir in the tomatoes, garlic and fresh or dried thyme. Cook, stirring frequently, for 6–8 minutes more.

6 Pour in the boiling water. Stir in the beans and the bean purée and season to taste with salt and pepper. Simmer for 10–15 minutes. Ladle into warmed soup bowls, drizzle with a little extra virgin olive oil and serve immediately.

Fish Soup

For extra flavour use some smoked fish in this soup and rub the bread with a garlic clove before toasting.

Serves 6

90ml/6 tbsp olive oil, plus extra to serve
1 onion, finely chopped
1 celery stick, chopped
1 carrot, chopped
60ml/4 tbsp chopped fresh flat leaf parsley
175ml/6fl oz/¾ cup dry white wine
3 tomatoes, peeled and chopped
2 garlic cloves, finely chopped
1.5 litres/2½ pints/6¼ cups boiling water
900g/2¼lb mixed fish fillets such as coley (pollock), rock salmon (huss), whiting, red mullet, red snapper or cod
salt and ground black pepper
French bread, to serve

1 Heat the oil in a large pan over low heat. Add the onion and cook, stirring occasionally, for about 5 minutes, until just softened but not coloured.

2 Stir in the celery and carrot and cook, stirring occasionally for a further 5 minutes. Add the parsley.

3 Pour in the wine, increase the heat to medium and cook until it has reduced by about half. Stir in the tomatoes and garlic and cook, stirring occasionally, for 3–4 minutes. Pour in the boiling water and bring back to the boil, then lower the heat and simmer for 15 minutes.

4 Add the fish fillets and simmer for 10–15 minutes, or until they are tender. Season to taste with salt and pepper.

5 Remove the fish from the soup with a slotted spoon. Discard the skin and any bones, then place the flesh in a food processor with the rest of the soup and process until smooth. Taste again for seasoning. If the soup is too thick, add a little more water.

6 To serve, heat the soup to simmering. Toast the rounds of bread and sprinkle with olive oil. Place two or three in each soup plate before ladling the soup over them.

Bean Energy 249kcal/1050kJ; Protein 13.3g; Carbohydrate 28g, of which sugars 3.7g; Fat 10.2g, of which saturates 1.5g; Cholesterol 0mg; Calcium 66mg; Fibre 9.9g; Sodium 20mg.
Fish Energy 255kcal/1064kJ; Protein 28.1g; Carbohydrate 3.6g, of which sugars 3.3g; Fat 12.3g, of which saturates 1.8g; Cholesterol 69mg; Calcium 27mg; Fibre 1g; Sodium 102mg.

Barley & Vegetable Soup

This soup comes from the Alto Adige region in Italy's mountainous north. Not only tasty, it is thick, nourishing and warming.

Serves 6–8

225g/8oz/1 cup pearl barley
2 litres/3½ pints/8 cups beef
   stock or water, or a
   combination of both
45ml/3 tbsp olive oil
2 carrots, finely chopped
2 celery sticks, finely chopped
1 leek, thinly sliced
1 large potato, finely chopped
115g/4oz/½ cup diced ham
1 bay leaf
45ml/3 tbsp chopped
   fresh parsley
1 small fresh rosemary sprig
salt and ground black pepper
freshly grated Parmesan cheese,
   to serve

1 Pick over the barley and discard any stones or other particles. Wash the barley in cold water, then place it in a bowl, add cold water to cover and leave to soak for at least 3 hours.

2 Drain the barley and place it in a large pan with the stock or water. Bring to the boil, lower the heat and simmer for 1 hour. Skim off any scum.

3 Stir in the oil, carrots, celery, leek, potato and ham and add the bay leaf, parsley and rosemary. If necessary, add more water; the ingredients should be covered by at least 2.5cm/1in. Bring to the boil, then simmer for 1–1½ hours, or until the vegetables and barley are very tender.

4 Season to taste with salt and pepper. Ladle the soup into warmed soup bowls and serve immediately with grated Parmesan cheese for sprinkling.

> **Cook's Tip**
> For extra flavour you could substitute a small ham bone for the diced ham. Shortly before serving remove the bone, cut off the meat and return it to the soup.

Pasta & Dried Bean Soup

In Italy this soup is made with dried or fresh beans and served hot or at room temperature.

Serves 4–6

300g/11oz/1¼ cups dried
   borlotti or cannellini beans
400g/14oz can chopped plum
   tomatoes, with their juice
3 garlic cloves, crushed
2 bay leaves
90ml/6 tbsp olive oil, plus extra
   to serve
750ml/1¼ pints/3 cups water
10ml/2 tsp salt
200g/7oz/scant 2 cups ditalini or
   other small pasta
45ml/3 tbsp chopped fresh flat
   leaf parsley
ground black pepper
freshly grated Parmesan cheese,
   to serve

1 Place the beans in a bowl, add cold water to cover and leave to soak overnight. Drain the beans, rinse and drain well again.

2 Place the beans in a large pan and add water to cover. Bring to the boil and cook for 10 minutes. Drain, rinse and drain again, then return them to the pan. Add enough water to cover them by 2.5cm/1in. Stir in the tomatoes with their can juice, the garlic, bay leaves and olive oil and season with pepper. Bring to the boil, then lower the heat and simmer for 1½–2 hours, or until the beans are tender. Add more water during cooking if necessary to keep the beans covered.

3 Remove and discard the bay leaves. Pass about half of the bean mixture through a food mill or process to a purée in a food processor. Stir the purée into the pan with the remaining bean mixture. Add the measured water and bring the soup to the boil.

4 Add the salt and pasta. Stir, then cook until the pasta is just tender. Stir in the parsley.

5 Remove the pan from the heat and leave to stand for at least 10 minutes. Ladle the soup into warmed soup bowls and serve with extra olive oil for drizzling and grated Parmesan cheese for sprinkling.

Barley Energy 181kcal/762kJ; Protein 5.7g; Carbohydrate 29.4g, of which sugars 1.7g; Fat 5.3g, of which saturates 0.8g; Cholesterol 8mg; Calcium 27mg; Fibre 1g; Sodium 188mg.
Pasta Energy 360kcal/1518kJ; Protein 15.7g; Carbohydrate 49g, of which sugars 4.6g; Fat 12.6g, of which saturates 1.8g; Cholesterol 0mg; Calcium 78mg; Fibre 9.9g; Sodium 346mg.

Pasta & Lentil Soup

Small brown lentils are usually used in this wholesome soup, but green lentils may be substituted.

Serves 4–6

225g/8oz/1 cup dried brown or green lentils
90ml/6 tbsp olive oil
50g/2oz/¼ cup finely diced ham or salt pork
1 onion, finely chopped
1 celery stick, finely chopped
1 carrot, finely chopped
2 litres/3½ pints/8 cups chicken stock or water
1 fresh sage leaf
1 fresh thyme sprig or 1.5ml/ ¼ tsp dried thyme
175g/6oz/2½ cups ditalini or other small soup pasta
salt and ground black pepper
crusty bread, to serve

1 Carefully check the lentils for small stones. Place them in a bowl, add cold water to cover and leave to soak for 2–3 hours. Drain, rinse and drain well again.

2 Heat the olive oil in a large, heavy pan over low heat, Add the ham or salt pork and cook, stirring occasionally, for 2–3 minutes.

3 Add the onion and cook gently, stirring occasionally, for about 5 minutes until softened but not coloured.

4 Stir in the celery and carrot and cook, stirring frequently, for a further 5 minutes. Add the lentils and stir to coat them evenly in the cooking fats.

5 Pour in the stock or water and add the sage and thyme. Increase the heat to medium and bring the soup to the boil. Lower the heat, cover the pan and simmer gently for about 1 hour, or until the lentils are tender. Season to taste with salt and pepper.

6 Stir in the pasta, increase the heat to medium and cook for about 10 minutes, until it is just tender. Remove the pan from the heat and leave to stand for a few minutes. Ladle the soup into warmed soup bowls and serve with crusty bread.

Pasta & Chickpea Soup

The addition of a fresh rosemary sprig creates a typically Mediterranean flavour in this soup.

Serves 4–6

200g/7oz/generous 1 cup dried chickpeas
3 garlic cloves, peeled
1 bay leaf
90ml/6 tbsp olive oil
50g/2oz/¼ cup diced salt pork, pancetta or bacon
1 fresh rosemary sprig
600ml/1 pint/2½ cups water
150g/5oz/1¼ cups ditalini or other short hollow pasta
salt and ground black pepper
freshly grated Parmesan cheese, to serve (optional)

1 Place the chickpeas in a bowl, add cold water to cover and leave to soak overnight. Drain, rinse well and drain again.

2 Place the chickpeas in a large pan, add water to cover and bring to the boil. Cook for 15 minutes, then drain, rinse and drain again. Return the chickpeas to the pan. Add water to cover, one garlic clove, the bay leaf, half the olive oil and a pinch of pepper. Bring to the boil, then lower the heat and simmer for about 2 hours, until tender. Add more boiling water if necessary to keep the chickpeas covered.

3 Remove and discard the bay leaf. Pass about half the chickpeas through a food mill or process in a food processor with a little cooking liquid. Return the purée to the pan with the rest of the chickpeas and the remaining cooking water.

4 Heat the remaining olive oil in a frying pan. Add the pork, pancetta or bacon, rosemary and the remaining garlic cloves and cook gently, stirring frequently, until just golden. Remove and discard the rosemary and garlic.

5 Stir the meat with its flavoured oil into the chickpea mixture. Add the measured water and bring to the boil. Season to taste with salt and pepper. Stir in the pasta, and cook for about 10 minutes until it is just tender. Ladle the soup into warmed soup bowls and serve immediately with grated Parmesan cheese, if you like.

Pasta Energy 334kcal/1405kJ; Protein 14.2g; Carbohydrate 44.3g, of which sugars 3.2g; Fat 12.3g, of which saturates 1.8g; Cholesterol 5mg; Calcium 34mg; Fibre 3.1g; Sodium 120mg.
Chickpea Energy 309kcal/1297kJ; Protein 11.5g; Carbohydrate 35.1g, of which sugars 1.7g; Fat 14.6g, of which saturates 2.3g; Cholesterol 4mg; Calcium 60mg; Fibre 4.3g; Sodium 142mg.

Scotch Broth

Sustaining and warming, this
traditional Scottish soup
makes a delicious winter
dish anywhere in the world.

Serves 6–8
900g/2lb lean neck (US shoulder)
   of lamb, cut into large even-
   size chunks
1.75 litres/3 pints/7¹/₂ cups water

1 large onion, chopped
50g/2oz/¹/₄ cup pearl barley
1 bouquet garni
1 large carrot, chopped
1 turnip, chopped
3 leeks, chopped
¹/₂ small white cabbage, shredded
salt and ground black pepper
chopped fresh parsley,
   to garnish

1 Put the lamb and measured water into a large pan and bring
to the boil over medium heat. Skim off the scum, then stir in
the onion, barley and bouquet garni.

2 Bring the soup back to the boil, lower the heat, partly cover
the pan and simmer gently for 1 hour.

3 Add the carrot, turnip, leeks and cabbage and season to taste
with salt and pepper. Bring back to the boil, partly cover the
pan again and simmer gently for about 35 minutes, until the
vegetables are tender.

4 Remove and discard any surplus fat that has risen to the top
of the soup, then ladle into warmed soup bowls, sprinkle with
chopped parsley and serve immediately.

Cook's Tip
*Lamb stock is too strongly flavoured for general use but ideal
for making this soup. Put 1.3kg/3lb shoulder and/or breast
bones of lamb into a large pan, add 2.75 litres/5 pints/11¹/₂
cups water and bring to the boil. Skim off the scum, then lower
the heat and simmer for 45 minutes. Skim again and
add 2 coarsely chopped carrots, 2 coarsely chopped onions,
1 bouquet garni, 1 bay leaf and 6 black peppercorns. Simmer
for a further 2 hours, then strain and chill.*

Leek & Potato Soup

This classic combination is a
perennial favourite with
adults and children alike. It's
a great winter warmer after
a vigorous walk.

Serves 4
50g/2oz/4 tbsp butter
2 leeks, chopped

1 small onion, finely chopped
350g/12oz potatoes, chopped
900ml/1¹/₂ pints/3³/₄ cups
   chicken or vegetable stock
salt and ground black pepper
warm crusty bread and butter,
   to serve (optional)

1 Heat 25g/1oz/2 tbsp of the butter in a large pan over low
heat. Add the leeks and onion and cook, stirring occasionally, for
about 7 minutes, until softened but not coloured.

2 Add the chopped potatoes to the pan and cook, stirring
occasionally, for 2–3 minutes. Add the chicken or vegetable
stock and bring to the boil. Lower the heat, cover the pan with
a tight-fitting lid and simmer gently for 30–35 minutes, until all
the vegetables are very tender.

3 Season to taste with salt and pepper. Remove the pan from
the heat and stir in the remaining butter in small pieces until
completely melted. Ladle the soup into warmed soup bowls
and serve immediately with warm crusty bread and butter, if
you like.

Cook's Tips
*• If you prefer a smoother textured soup, press the mixture
through a sieve (strainer), using the base of a soup ladle, or
pass it through a food mill. Never use a food processor or
blender to purée potatoes as the starch in the vegetable will be
broken down and will create an unpleasant gluey consistency.
• Carrots make a great addition to this soup, providing extra
sweetness and bright colour. Simply add three or four sliced or
diced carrots with the potatoes in step 2. You don't need to
increase the quantity of stock.*

Leek & Potato Energy 182kcal/759kJ; Protein 3.4g; Carbohydrate 18.3g, of which sugars 4.3g; Fat 11.1g, of which saturates 6.7g; Cholesterol 27mg; Calcium 35mg; Fibre 3.3g; Sodium 88mg.
Scotch Broth Energy 267kcal/1118kJ; Protein 24.7g; Carbohydrate 12.9g, of which sugars 6.2g; Fat 13.3g, of which saturates 5.9g; Cholesterol 86mg; Calcium 58mg; Fibre 3.2g; Sodium 106mg.

Country Vegetable Soup

To ring the changes with this soup, vary the vegetables according to what you like and what vegetables are in season.

Serves 4

50g/2oz/4 tbsp butter
1 onion, chopped
2 leeks, sliced
2 celery sticks, sliced
2 carrots, sliced
2 small turnips, chopped
4 ripe tomatoes, peeled and chopped
1 litre/1¾ pints/4 cups chicken or vegetable stock
1 bouquet garni
115g/4oz/1 cup green beans, chopped
salt and ground black pepper
chopped fresh herbs such as tarragon, thyme, chives and parsley, to garnish

1 Melt the butter in a large, heavy pan over low heat. Add the onion and leeks and cook gently, stirring occasionally, for about 8 minutes, until softened but not coloured.

2 Add the celery, carrots and turnips and cook, stirring occasionally, for 3–4 minutes. Stir in the tomatoes and stock, add the bouquet garni and simmer the vegetables gently for about 20 minutes.

3 Add the beans to the soup and continue to cook until all the vegetables are tender. Season to taste with salt and pepper.

4 Ladle the soup into warmed soup bowls, garnish with chopped fresh herbs and serve immediately.

> **Cook's Tip**
> You can use the cooking water from a wide variety of vegetables and pulses as a flavoursome, easy and economical vegetable stock. Equally, vegetable peelings work well. Carrots, cauliflower, broccoli, green beans, leeks, lettuce, mushrooms, onions and potatoes are all good choices, but you should be light-handed with cabbage and members of the cabbage family, such as Brussels sprouts.

Split Pea & Bacon Soup

This soup is also called "London Particular", named after the notorious city fogs of the nineteenth century. The fogs, in turn, were named "pea-soupers".

Serves 4

15g/½ oz/1 tbsp butter
115g/4oz/⅔ cup chopped smoked lean back bacon
1 large onion, chopped
1 carrot, chopped
1 celery stick, chopped
75g/3oz/scant ½ cup split peas
1.2 litres/2 pints/5 cups chicken stock
2 thick slices firm bread, buttered and with crusts removed
2 rashers (strips) streaky (fatty) bacon
salt and ground black pepper

1 Melt the butter in a pan over medium heat. Add the back bacon and cook until the fat runs. Stir in the onion, carrot and celery and cook for 2–3 minutes.

2 Add the split peas, followed by the stock. Bring to the boil, stirring occasionally, then lower the heat, cover with a tight-fitting lid and simmer for 45–60 minutes.

3 Meanwhile, preheat the oven to 180°C/350°F/Gas 4. Place the bread on a baking sheet and bake for about 20 minutes, until crisp and brown, then cut into dice.

4 Grill (broil) the streaky bacon under a preheated grill (broiler) until very crisp, then chop finely.

5 When the soup is ready, season to taste and ladle into warmed soup bowls. Sprinkle each serving with the chopped bacon and croûtons and serve immediately.

> **Cook's Tip**
> For additional flavour you could spread the bread with herb or garlic butter before baking in the oven. Alternatively, you could sprinkle the bread slices with freshly grated Parmesan cheese and bake until it is golden and bubbling.

Vegetable Energy 160kcal/665kJ; Protein 3.6g; Carbohydrate 11.5g, of which sugars 10g; Fat 11.4g, of which saturates 6.8g; Cholesterol 27mg; Calcium 72mg; Fibre 5.4g; Sodium 106mg.
Pea & Bacon Energy 171kcal/710kJ; Protein 8.3g; Carbohydrate 9.9g, of which sugars 3.1g; Fat 11.2g, of which saturates 4.8g; Cholesterol 31mg; Calcium 31mg; Fibre 1.1g; Sodium 705mg.

Smoked Haddock & Potato Soup

This Scottish soup's traditional name is "cullen skink". A "cullen" is a town's port district and "skink" means stock or broth.

Serves 6

350g/12oz finnan haddock
   (smoked haddock)
1 onion, chopped
1 bouquet garni
900ml/1½ pints/3¾ cups water
500g/1¼lb potatoes, quartered
600ml/1 pint/2½ cups milk
40g/1½oz/3 tbsp butter
salt and ground black pepper
chopped fresh chives, to garnish
crusty bread, to serve (optional)

1 Put the haddock, onion, bouquet garni and measured water into a large pan and bring to the boil. Skim the scum from the surface, then cover the pan with a tight-fitting lid. Lower the heat and poach gently for 10–15 minutes, or until the haddock flakes easily.

2 Remove the poached fish from the pan using a fish slice or slotted spatula and remove the skin and bones. Flake the flesh and reserve. Return the skin and bones to the pan and simmer, uncovered, for 30 minutes.

3 Strain the fish stock and return to the rinsed-out pan, then add the potatoes and simmer for about 25 minutes, or until tender. Remove the potatoes from the pan using a slotted spoon. Add the milk to the pan and bring to the boil.

4 Meanwhile, mash the potatoes with the butter, then whisk into the milk in the pan until thick and creamy. Add the flaked fish to the pan and adjust the seasoning. Sprinkle with chopped chives, ladle into warmed soup bowls and serve immediately with crusty bread, if you like.

> **Cook's Tip**
> Try to find traditionally smoked fish, which is quite a pale colour, rather than chemically processed haddock, which has been dyed a bright yellow.

Mulligatawny Soup

Choose red split lentils for the best colour, although green or brown lentils could also be used.

Serves 4

50g/2oz/4 tbsp butter or 60ml/
   4 tbsp vegetable oil
2 large chicken pieces (about
   350g/12oz each)
1 onion, chopped
1 carrot, chopped
1 small turnip, chopped
about 15ml/1 tbsp curry powder,
   to taste
4 cloves
6 black peppercorns,
   lightly crushed
50g/2oz/¼ cup lentils
900ml/1½ pints/3¾ cups
   chicken stock
40g/1½oz/¼ cup sultanas
   (golden raisins)
salt and ground black pepper

1 Heat the butter or oil in a large pan over medium-high heat. Add the chicken and cook, turning occasionally, for about 10 minutes, until golden brown all over. Using tongs, transfer the chicken to a plate.

2 Lower the heat, add the onion, carrot and turnip and cook, stirring occasionally, for about 10 minutes, until softened and lightly coloured. Stir in the curry powder, cloves and peppercorns and cook for 1–2 minutes, then add the lentils.

3 Pour the stock into the pan, bring to the boil, then add the sultanas. Return the chicken to the pan together with any juices from the plate. Lower the heat, cover and simmer gently for about 1¼ hours.

4 Remove the chicken from the pan and discard the skin and bones. Chop the flesh into bitesize chunks, return to the soup and reheat. Season to taste with salt and pepper. Ladle the soup into warmed soup plates and serve immediately.

> **Cook's Tip**
> Use a good quality curry powder, which will add subtle flavour as well as heat to this spicy soup.

Haddock Energy 205kcal/864kJ; Protein 16.1g; Carbohydrate 19g, of which sugars 6.4g; Fat 7.8g, of which saturates 4.7g Cholesterol 41mg; Calcium 137mg; Fibre 1g; Sodium 132mg.
Mulligatawny Energy 513kcal/2136kJ; Protein 35.8g; Carbohydrate 17.3g, of which sugars 10.1g; Fat 33.9g, of which saturates 12.9g; Cholesterol 219mg; Calcium 42mg; Fibre 1.8g; Sodium 229mg.

Spinach, Bacon & Prawn Salad

Serve this hot salad with plenty of crusty bread to mop up the delicious juices.

Serves 4
105ml/7 tbsp olive oil
30ml/2 tbsp sherry vinegar
2 garlic cloves, finely chopped
5ml/1 tsp Dijon mustard

12 cooked king prawns (jumbo shrimp), in the shell
115g/4oz rindless streaky (fatty) bacon, cut into strips
115g/4oz/2 cups fresh young spinach leaves
½ head oak leaf lettuce, coarsely torn
salt and ground black pepper

1 To make the dressing, whisk together 90ml/6 tbsp of the olive oil with the vinegar, garlic and mustard in a small pan and season to taste with salt and pepper. Heat gently, whisking constantly, until slightly thickened, then remove from the heat and keep warm.

2 Carefully remove the heads and peel the prawns, leaving their tails intact. Cut along the back of each prawn and remove the dark vein. Set the prawns aside until needed.

3 Heat the remaining oil in a frying pan over medium heat. Add the bacon and cook, stirring occasionally, until golden and crisp. Add the prawns and stir-fry for a few minutes until warmed through.

4 Meanwhile, arrange the spinach leaves and lettuce leaves on four individual serving plates.

5 Spoon the bacon and prawns on to the leaves, then pour the hot dressing over them. Serve immediately.

> **Cook's Tip**
> *Sherry vinegar lends its pungent, nutty flavour to this delicious salad. It is readily available in large supermarkets or delicatessens. However, ordinary red or white wine vinegar could be used instead if you like.*

Smoked Haddock Pâté

This easily prepared pâté is made with Arbroath Smokies, small haddock which have been salted and hot-smoked.

Serves 6
butter, for greasing
3 large Arbroath Smokies (about 225g/8oz each) or other smoked haddock

275g/10oz/1¼ cups medium-fat soft (farmer's) cheese
3 eggs, lightly beaten
30–45ml/2–3 tbsp lemon juice
ground black pepper
fresh chervil sprigs, to garnish
lemon wedges and lettuce leaves, to serve

1 Preheat the oven to 160°C/325°F/Gas 3. Generously grease six individual ramekins with butter.

2 Place the fish in an ovenproof dish and heat through in the oven for 10 minutes. Carefully remove and discard the skin and bones from the fish, then flake the flesh into a bowl.

3 Mash the fish with a fork and gradually work in the cheese, then the eggs. Add the lemon juice and season with black pepper to taste.

4 Divide the fish mixture among the six ramekins and place in a roasting pan. Pour hot water into the roasting pan to come about halfway up the sides of the dishes. Bake for 30 minutes, until just set.

5 Leave to cool for 2–3 minutes, then run a knife point around the edge of each dish and invert on to a warmed plate. Garnish with fresh chervil sprigs and serve immediately with the lemon wedges and lettuce.

> **Variation**
> *This pâté is also tasty made with hot-smoked trout fillets. You can then omit the initial cooking in step 2.*

Pâté Energy 253kcal/1049kJ; Protein 17.9g; Carbohydrate 1.4g, of which sugars 1.4g; Fat 19.6g, of which saturates 6.6g; Cholesterol 151mg; Calcium 46mg; Fibre 0g; Sodium 527mg.
Salad Energy 320kcal/1325kJ; Protein 18.8g; Carbohydrate 0.9g, of which sugars 0.9g; Fat 26.8g, of which saturates 5.3g; Cholesterol 165mg; Calcium 117mg; Fibre 0.8g; Sodium 546mg.

Hot Tomato & Mozzarella Salad

A quick, easy appetizer with a Mediterranean flavour.

Serves 4
450g/1lb plum tomatoes, sliced
225g/8oz mozzarella cheese
1 red onion, chopped
4–6 pieces sun-dried tomatoes in oil, drained and chopped

60ml/4 tbsp olive oil
5ml/1 tsp red wine vinegar
2.5ml/½ tsp Dijon mustard
60ml/4 tbsp mixed chopped fresh herbs such as basil, parsley, oregano and chives
salt and ground black pepper
fresh herb sprigs, to garnish (optional)

1 Arrange the sliced tomatoes and mozzarella in circles in four shallow flameproof dishes. Sprinkle with the onion and sun-dried tomatoes. Whisk together the olive oil, vinegar, mustard, chopped herbs and seasoning. Pour over the salads.

2 Place the salads under a hot grill (broiler) for 4–5 minutes, until the mozzarella starts to melt. Grind over plenty of black pepper and serve garnished with fresh herb sprigs, if you like.

Devilled Kidneys

This tangy dish makes an impressive appetizer.

Serves 4
10ml/2tsp Worcestershire sauce
15ml/1 tbsp English (hot) mustard
15ml/1 tbsp lemon juice

15ml/1 tbsp tomato purée (paste)
40g/1½oz/3 tbsp butter
1 shallot, chopped
8 prepared lamb's kidneys
salt and cayenne pepper
chopped fresh parsley, to garnish

1 Mix together the Worcestershire sauce, mustard, lemon juice and tomato purée in a bowl. Season with cayenne and salt.

2 Melt the butter in a frying pan and cook the shallot for 5 minutes. Stir in the kidneys and cook for 3 minutes on each side. Coat with the sauce and serve, sprinkled with parsley.

Asparagus with Tarragon Butter

Eating fresh asparagus with your fingers is correct but messy, so serve this dish with finger bowls.

Serves 4
500g/1¼lb fresh asparagus
115g/4oz/½ cup butter

30ml/2 tbsp chopped fresh tarragon
15ml/1 tbsp chopped fresh flat leaf parsley
grated rind of ½ lemon
15ml/1 tbsp lemon juice
salt and ground black pepper

1 Trim off the woody ends from the asparagus spears, then tie the spears into four equal bundles.

2 Pour water into a large frying pan to a depth of about 2.5cm/1in and bring to the boil. Add the bundles of asparagus, cover with a lid and cook for 6–8 minutes, until the asparagus is tender but still firm. Drain well and discard the strings.

3 Arrange the asparagus spears on four warmed serving plates. Make the tarragon butter by creaming together the remaining ingredients. Heat the flavoured butter gently until just melted, then pour it over the asparagus. Serve immediately.

Cook's Tip
Frugal – and clever – cooks waste nothing. Add the trimmed woody ends of the asparagus spears to the cooking water and reserve the water when you drain the spears. Discard the woody ends. Use the cooking water to flavour home-made soups, such as asparagus or green pea soup.

Variation
You can also serve the asparagus with parsley and orange butter. Use 45ml/3 tbsp finely chopped fresh flat leaf parsley instead of the tarragon, substitute 10ml/2 tsp orange rind for the lemon rind and use orange instead of lemon juice.

Salad Energy 301kcal/1250kJ; Protein 11.8g; Carbohydrate 6.2g, of which sugars 5.9g; Fat 25.7g, of which saturates 9.9g; Cholesterol 33mg; Calcium 219mg; Fibre 1.8g; Sodium 237mg.
Kidneys Energy 140kcal/584kJ; Protein 10.8g; Carbohydrate 2.3g, of which sugars 1.9g; Fat 9.9g, of which saturates 5.7g; Cholesterol 210mg; Calcium 24mg; Fibre 24g; Sodium 191mg.
Asparagus Energy 249kcal/1022kJ; Protein 4.1g; Carbohydrate 3g, of which sugars 2.8g; Fat 24.5g, of which saturates 15.1g; Cholesterol 61mg; Calcium 59mg; Fibre 2.6g; Sodium 179mg.

Egg & Tomato Salad with Crab

You could also adjust the quantities in this tasty salad to make a quick, light and healthy weekday meal.

Serves 4
1 round (butterhead) lettuce
2 x 200g/7oz cans crab
   meat, drained
4 hard-boiled eggs, sliced
16 cherry tomatoes, halved
½ green (bell) pepper, seeded
   and thinly sliced
6 pitted black olives, sliced

For the dressing
45ml/3 tbsp chilli sauce
250g/8fl oz/1 cup mayonnaise
10ml/2 tsp freshly squeezed
   lemon juice
½ green pepper, seeded and
   finely chopped
5ml/1 tsp prepared horseradish
5ml/1 tsp Worcestershire sauce

1 First make the dressing. Place all the ingredients in a bowl and mix well with a balloon whisk. Cover with clear film (plastic wrap) and set aside in a cool place until required.

2 Line four plates with the lettuce leaves. Divide the crab meat among them, mounding it up in the centre of each plate. Arrange the slices of egg around the outside with the tomato halves on top.

3 Spoon a little of the dressing over the crab meat. Arrange the green pepper slices on top and sprinkle with the olives. Serve immediately with the remaining dressing handed separately.

Variations
• Use freshly cooked or thawed frozen crab meat instead of canned.
• Substitute well-drained, canned tuna for the crab meat.
• Use peeled cooked prawns (shrimp) instead of crab meat, but try to avoid frozen ones as the texture can be woolly.
• Use 16 whole quail's eggs, boiled for 1½ minutes, then cooled and shelled, instead of sliced hard-boiled eggs.

Stuffed Mushrooms

These flavoursome mushrooms may also be served as an accompaniment to a main course.

Serves 4
25g/1oz/2 tbsp butter, plus extra
   for greasing and brushing
275g/10oz spinach,
   stalks removed

400g/14oz medium
   cap mushrooms
25g/1oz bacon, chopped
½ small onion, chopped
75g/5 tbsp double (heavy) cream
about 60ml/4 tbsp grated
   Cheddar cheese
30ml/2 tbsp fresh breadcrumbs
salt and ground black pepper
fresh parsley sprigs, to garnish

1 Preheat the oven to 190°C/375°F/Gas 5. Grease an ovenproof dish with butter. Wash but do not dry the spinach. Place it in a pan, cover and cook, stirring occasionally, for 4–5 minutes, until just wilted.

2 Place the spinach in a colander and squeeze out as much liquid as possible, then chop finely. Snap the stalks from the mushrooms and chop the stalks finely.

3 Melt the butter in a pan. Add the bacon, onion and mushroom stalks and cook for about 5 minutes. Stir in the spinach, cook for a few seconds, then remove the pan from the heat. Stir in the cream and season to taste with salt and pepper.

4 Brush the mushroom caps with melted butter, then place, gills uppermost, in a single layer in the prepared dish.

5 Divide the spinach mixture among the mushrooms. Mix together the cheese and breadcrumbs and sprinkle over the mushrooms, then bake for about 20 minutes until the mushrooms are tender. Serve warm, garnished with parsley.

Cook's Tip
Squeeze out all the excess water from the cooked spinach, otherwise the stuffing will be too soggy.

Salad Energy 608kcal/2515kJ; Protein 25.9g; Carbohydrate 4.8g, of which sugars 4.5g; Fat 54.2g, of which saturates 9g; Cholesterol 309mg; Calcium 171mg; Fibre 1.3g; Sodium 1018mg.
Mushrooms Energy 281kcal/1166kJ; Protein 9.9g; Carbohydrate 8.9g, of which sugars 2.7g; Fat 22.8g, of which saturates 13.5g; Cholesterol 58mg; Calcium 258mg; Fibre 2.9g; Sodium 388mg.

Pears & Stilton

Firm juicy pears and piquant cheese are a truly magical combination in this summer appetizer – a perfect start to an al fresco meal.

Serves 4
4 ripe pears
75g/3oz blue Stilton cheese
50g/2oz/3 tbsp curd
    (farmer's) cheese

salt and ground black pepper
fresh watercress sprigs or mizuna,
    to garnish

For the dressing
45ml/3 tbsp light olive oil
15ml/1 tbsp lemon juice
10ml/2 tsp toasted poppy seeds

1 First make the dressing. Place the olive oil, lemon juice and poppy seeds in a screw-topped jar and season with salt and pepper. Close the lid and shake well until combined.

2 Cut the pears in half lengthways, then scoop out the cores and cut away the calyx from the rounded end.

3 Beat together the Stilton, curd cheese and a little pepper. Divide this mixture among the cavities in the pears. Arrange the filled pear halves on individual plates.

4 Shake the dressing to mix it again, then spoon it over the pears. Serve garnished with watercress or mizuna.

Cook's Tip
The pears should be lightly chilled in the refrigerator before they are used in this dish.

Variation
Stilton is the classic British blue cheese used in this classic British dish but you could use blue Cheshire, Roquefort or Gorgonzola instead.

Potted Shrimp

Sometimes the simplest recipes are the best and this classic English appetizer has stood the test of time and remains very popular.

Serves 4
225g/8oz/2 cups shelled shrimp

225g/8oz/1 cup butter
pinch of ground mace
salt and cayenne pepper
fresh dill sprigs, to garnish
lemon wedges and thin slices
    of brown bread and butter,
    to serve

1 Chop a quarter of the shrimp. Melt half the butter over low heat, carefully skimming off any foam that rises to the surface.

2 Stir the chopped and whole shrimp and the mace into the pan, season to taste with salt and cayenne pepper and heat gently without boiling. Pour the shrimp and butter mixture into four individual pots or ramekins and set aside to cool.

3 Heat the remaining butter in a clean small pan, then carefully spoon the clear butter over the shrimp, leaving the sediment behind in the pan.

4 Leave until the butter is almost set, then place a dill sprig in the centre of each pot. Leave to set completely, then cover and chill in the refrigerator.

5 Remove the potted shrimps from the refrigerator about 30 minutes before serving to bring to room temperature. Serve with lemon wedges and thin slices of brown bread and butter.

Cook's Tip
This dish is traditionally prepared with the tiny European brown shrimp found off the east coast of England. They have a incomparably delicate flavour but are very boring to peel. You can substitute small prawns (US small to medium shrimp) if you like. In that case, chop between a third and half the shellfish in step 1.

Pears Energy 243kcal/1007kJ; Protein 7.2g; Carbohydrate 15.5g, of which sugars 15.5g; Fat 17.2g, of which saturates 6.4g; Cholesterol 21mg; Calcium 109mg; Fibre 3.5g; Sodium 208mg.
Shrimp Energy 461kcal/1901kJ; Protein 10.3g; Carbohydrate 0.4g, of which sugars 0.4g; Fat 46.6g, of which saturates 29.4g; Cholesterol 230mg; Calcium 55mg; Fibre 0g; Sodium 448mg.

Garlic Prawns in Filo Tartlets

Tartlets made with crisp layers of filo pastry and filled with garlic prawns make a tempting, attractive and unusual appetizer.

Serves 4
For the tartlets
50g/2oz/4 tbsp butter, melted
2–3 large sheets filo pastry

For the filling
115g/4oz/½ cup butter
2–3 garlic cloves, crushed
1 fresh red chilli, seeded
    and chopped
350g/12oz/3 cups peeled,
    cooked prawns (shrimp)
30ml/2 tbsp chopped fresh
    parsley or chives
salt and ground black pepper

1 Preheat the oven to 200°C/400°F/Gas 6. Brush four individual 7.5cm/3in flan tins (pans) with melted butter.

2 Cut the filo pastry into twelve 10cm/4in squares and brush with the melted butter.

3 Place three squares of pastry inside each tin, overlapping them at slight angles and carefully frilling the edges and points while forming a good hollow in each centre. Bake the pastry for 10–15 minutes, until crisp and golden. Cool slightly and remove from the tins.

4 To make the filling, melt the butter in a large frying pan over medium-low heat. Add the garlic, chilli and prawns and cook, stirring frequently, for 1–2 minutes to warm through. Stir in the parsley or chives and season to taste with salt and pepper.

5 Using a spoon, divide the prawn filling among the tartlets and serve immediately.

Cook's Tips
• If using frozen filo pastry, leave it to thaw thoroughly first but keep it covered to prevent it from drying out.
• If using fresh filo pastry rather than frozen, wrap and freeze any leftover sheets for future use.

Leek Terrine with Deli Meats

This attractive appetizer is surprisingly simple yet looks really spectacular. For best results it should be made a day ahead.

Serves 6
20–24 small young leeks
about 225g/8oz mixed sliced
    meats, such as prosciutto,
    coppa and pancetta
50g/2oz/½ cup walnuts, toasted
    and chopped
salt and ground black pepper

For the dressing
60ml/4 tbsp walnut oil
60ml/4 tbsp olive oil
30ml/2 tbsp white wine vinegar
5ml/1 tsp wholegrain mustard

1 Cut off the roots and most of the green part from the leeks. Wash them thoroughly under cold running water.

2 Bring a large pan of salted water to the boil. Add the leeks, bring the water back to the boil, then simmer for 6–8 minutes, until the leeks are just tender. Drain well.

3 Fill a 450g/1lb loaf tin (pan) with the leeks, placing them alternately head to tail and sprinkling each layer as you go with salt and pepper.

4 Put another loaf tin inside the first and gently press down on the leeks. Carefully invert both tins and let any water drain out. Place one or two weights on top of the tins and chill the terrine for at least 4 hours or overnight.

5 To make the dressing, whisk together the walnut and olive oils, vinegar and mustard in a small bowl. Season to taste.

6 Carefully turn out the terrine on to a board and cut into slices using a large, sharp knife. Lay the slices of leek terrine on serving plates and arrange the slices of meat beside them.

7 Spoon the dressing over the slices of terrine and sprinkle the chopped walnuts over the top. Serve immediately.

Terrine Energy 232kcal/962kJ; Protein 10.5g; Carbohydrate 3.3g, of which sugars 2.6g; Fat 19.7g, of which saturates 2.4g; Cholesterol 22mg; Calcium 37mg; Fibre 2.4g; Sodium 453mg.
Tartlets Energy 440kcal/1825kJ; Protein 17.6g; Carbohydrate 15g, of which sugars 0.7g; Fat 34.8g, of which saturates 21.6g; Cholesterol 259mg; Calcium 118mg; Fibre 1g; Sodium 419mg.

Smoked Salmon & Dill Blinis

Blinis, small pancakes of Russian origin, are so easy to make, yet they make a sophisticated dinner party appetizer and great canapés.

Serves 4

115g/4oz/1 cup buckwheat flour
115g/4oz/1 cup plain (all-purpose) flour
pinch of salt
15ml/1 tbsp easy-blend (rapid-rise) dried yeast
2 eggs
350ml/12fl oz/1½ cups warm milk
15ml/1 tbsp melted butter, plus extra for pan-frying
150ml/¼ pint/⅔ cup crème fraîche or sour cream
45ml/3 tbsp chopped fresh dill
225g/8oz smoked salmon, thinly sliced
fresh dill sprigs, to garnish

1 Mix together the buckwheat and plain flours in a large bowl with the salt. Sprinkle in the yeast and mix well. Separate one of the eggs. Whisk together the whole egg and the yolk, the warm milk and the melted butter.

2 Pour the egg mixture on to the flour mixture. Beat well to form a smooth batter. Cover with clear film (plastic wrap) and leave to rise in a warm place for 1–2 hours.

3 Whisk the remaining egg white in a large, grease-free bowl until stiff peaks form, then gently fold into the batter.

4 Preheat a heavy frying pan or griddle and brush with melted butter. Drop tablespoons of the batter on to the pan, spacing them well apart. Cook for about 40 seconds, until bubbles appear on the surface.

5 Flip over the blinis and cook for 30 seconds on the other side. Wrap in foil and keep warm in a low oven. Repeat with the remaining mixture, buttering the pan each time.

6 Combine the crème fraîche or sour cream and chopped dill. Top the blinis with slices of smoked salmon and and a spoonful of dill cream. Garnish with dill sprigs and serve immediately.

Celeriac Fritters with Mustard Dip

The contrast of the hot, crisp fritters and the cold mustard dip makes this a very tasty combination.

Serves 4

1 egg
115g/4oz/1 cup ground almonds
45ml/3 tbsp freshly grated Parmesan cheese
45ml/3 tbsp chopped fresh flat leaf parsley
1 celeriac (about 450g/1lb)
squeeze of lemon juice
oil, for deep-frying
salt and ground black pepper
sea salt flakes, for sprinkling

For the mustard dip

150ml/¼ pint/⅔ cup sour cream
15–30ml/1–2 tbsp wholegrain mustard

1 Beat the egg well and pour into a shallow dish. Mix together the almonds, grated Parmesan and parsley in a separate dish. Season to taste, then set aside.

2 Peel and cut the celeriac into strips about 1cm/½in wide and 5cm/2in long. Immediately drop the strips into a bowl of water with a little lemon juice added to prevent them from becoming discoloured.

3 Heat the oil in a deep-fat fryer to 180°C/350°F or until a cube of day-old bread browns in 30 seconds. Drain and then pat dry half the celeriac strips. Dip them into the beaten egg, then into the ground almond mixture, making sure that the pieces are coated completely and evenly.

4 Deep-fry the celeriac fritters, a few at a time, for about 2–3 minutes, until golden. Drain on kitchen paper and keep warm while you cook the remainder.

5 To make the mustard dip, mix together the sour cream, mustard and salt to taste. Spoon into a small serving bowl.

6 Heap the celeriac fritters on to warmed individual serving plates. Sprinkle with sea salt flakes and serve immediately with the mustard dip.

Blinis Energy 557kcal/2328kJ; Protein 26.3g; Carbohydrate 51.8g, of which sugars 5.5g; Fat 28.8g, of which saturates 16.3g; Cholesterol 178mg; Calcium 197mg; Fibre 1.5g; Sodium 1185mg.
Fritters Energy 434kcal/1796kJ; Protein 14g; Carbohydrate 4.6g, of which sugars 3.8g; Fat 40.2g, of which saturates 10g; Cholesterol 81mg; Calcium 297mg; Fibre 3.6g; Sodium 288mg.

Chicken Liver Pâté with Marsala

This is a really quick and simple pâté to make, yet it has a delicious – and quite sophisticated – flavour.

Serves 4
350g/12oz chicken livers, thawed
   if frozen

225g/8oz/1 cup butter
2 garlic cloves, crushed
15ml/1 tbsp Marsala
5ml/1 tsp chopped sage
salt and ground black pepper
8 fresh sage leaves, to garnish
Melba toast, to serve

1 Pick over the chicken livers, then rinse and pat dry with kitchen paper. Melt 25g/1oz/2 tbsp of the butter in a frying pan over medium heat. Add the chicken livers and garlic and cook, stirring occasionally, for about 5 minutes, or until they are firm but still pink in their centres.

2 Transfer the livers to a food processor or blender using a slotted spoon. Add the Marsala and chopped sage.

3 Melt 150g/5oz/generous ½ cup of the remaining butter in the frying pan, stirring to loosen any sediment, then pour into the food processor or blender and process until smooth. Season well with salt and pepper.

4 Spoon the pâté into four individual pots and smooth the surface. Melt the remaining butter in a separate pan and pour it over the pâtés. Garnish with sage leaves and chill in the refrigerator until set. Serve with triangles of Melba toast.

> **Cook's Tip**
> To make Melba toast, first remove the crusts from medium-sliced white bread. Toast on both sides in a toaster or under the grill (broiler), until golden. Remove the toast and, using a sharp, serrated knife, cut horizontally through each slice to make two very thin slices. Cut each slice into quarters and toast the uncooked sides under the grill until golden and curling. Cool on a rack and store in an airtight container.

Salmon Rillettes

A variation on the classic French pork rillette, this appetizer is easier and less time consuming to make than the original.

Serves 6
350g/12oz salmon fillets
175g/6oz/¾ cup butter
1 leek, white part only,
   finely chopped

1 celery stick, finely chopped
1 bay leaf
150ml/¼ pint/⅔ cup dry
   white wine
115g/4oz smoked
   salmon trimmings
large pinch of ground mace
60ml/4 tbsp fromage frais
   (low-fat cream cheese)
salt and ground black pepper
salad leaves, to serve

1 Lightly season the salmon with salt and pepper. Melt 25g/1oz/2 tbsp of the butter in a frying pan over low heat. Add the celery and leek and cook, stirring occasionally, for about 5 minutes. Add the salmon and bay leaf and pour in the wine. Cover with a tight-fitting lid and cook for about 15 minutes, until the fish is tender. Set the salmon aside.

2 Strain the cooking liquid into another pan, bring to the boil and cook until reduced to 30ml/2 tbsp. Leave to cool.

3 Melt 50g/2oz/4 tbsp of the remaining butter in another pan and gently cook the smoked salmon until it turns pale pink. Leave to cool.

4 Remove the skin and any bones from the salmon fillets. Flake the flesh into a bowl and add the reduced cooking liquid. Beat in the remaining butter, the mace and fromage frais. Break up the smoked salmon trimmings and fold into the mixture with the pan juices. Taste and adjust the seasoning.

5 Spoon the salmon mixture into a dish or terrine and smooth the surface. Cover and chill in the refrigerator.

6 To serve the salmon rillettes, shape the mixture into oval quenelles using two dessert spoons and arrange on individual plates with the salad leaves.

Chicken Energy 507kcal/2090kJ; Protein 16g; Carbohydrate 1g, of which sugars 0.6g; Fat 48.3g, of which saturates 29.9g; Cholesterol 452mg; Calcium 18mg; Fibre 0.1g; Sodium 408mg.
Salmon Energy 373kcal/1542kJ; Protein 17.4g; Carbohydrate 1.2g, of which sugars 1g; Fat 31.4g, of which saturates 16.5g; Cholesterol 98mg; Calcium 33mg; Fibre 0.7g; Sodium 568mg.

Mexican Dip with Chips

This appetizer also makes a fabulous snack to serve with pre-dinner drinks.

Serves 4
2 avocados
juice of 1 lime
1/2 small onion, finely chopped
1/2 red chilli, seeded and
   finely chopped
3 tomatoes, peeled, seeded and
   finely diced
30ml/2 tbsp chopped fresh
   coriander (cilantro)

30ml/2 tbsp sour cream
salt and ground black pepper
15 ml/1 tbsp sour cream and
   a pinch of cayenne pepper,
   to garnish

For the chips
150g/5oz bag tortilla chips
30ml/2 tbsp finely grated mature
   (sharp) Cheddar cheese
1.5ml/1/4 tsp chilli powder
10ml/2 tsp chopped fresh parsley

1 Halve and stone (pit) the avocados and scoop the flesh with a spoon, scraping the shells well. Place the flesh in a blender or food processor with the remaining dip ingredients, reserving the sour cream and cayenne pepper for the garnish. Process until fairly smooth. Transfer to a bowl, cover with clear film (plastic wrap) and chill in the refrigerator until required.

2 To make the chips, preheat the grill (broiler), then spread out the tortilla chips on a baking sheet. Mix the grated cheese with the chilli powder, sprinkle over the chips and grill (broil) for 1–2 minutes, until the cheese has melted.

3 Remove the avocado dip from the refrigerator, top with the sour cream and sprinkle with cayenne pepper. Serve the bowl on a plate surrounded by the tortilla chips, garnished with the chopped fresh parsley.

> **Cook's Tip**
> You can omit the fresh chilli and the chilli powder if you prefer the dip to have a milder flavour or you are planning to serve it to young children.

French Goat's Cheese Salad

The deep, tangy flavours of this salad would also make it satisfying enough for a light meal, if you wished.

Serves 4
200g/7oz bag prepared mixed
   salad leaves including some soft
   and bitter varieties
4 rashers (strips) rindless lean
   back bacon
16 thin slices French bread
115g/4oz/1/2 cup full-fat
   goat's cheese

For the dressing
60ml/4 tbsp olive oil
15ml/1 tbsp tarragon vinegar
10ml/2 tsp walnut oil
5ml/1 tsp Dijon mustard
5ml/1 tsp wholegrain mustard
salt and ground black pepper

1 Preheat the grill (broiler). Rinse and dry the salad leaves, then arrange them in four individual serving bowls. Set aside in a cool place but not the refrigerator.

2 To make the dressing, pout the olive oil, vinegar, walnut oil and both types of mustard in a screw-top jar. Close the lid and shake well until combined. Season and set aside until required.

3 Lay the bacon rashers flat on a board, then stretch them using the back of a knife. Cut each rasher into four pieces. Roll up each piece up and secure with a wooden cocktail stick (toothpick). Grill (broil) for about 2–3 minutes, until golden on one side of the rolls.

4 Meanwhile, slice the goat's cheese into eight and halve each slice. Top each slice of bread with a piece of goat's cheese and place under the grill. Turn over the bacon rolls and continue cooking with the goat's cheese toasts until the cheese is golden and bubbling and the bacon rolls are cooked through.

5 Arrange the bacon rolls and toasts on top of the prepared salad leaves. Shake the dressing well again to mix and spoon a little of it over each serving. Serve immediately.

Dip Energy 332kcal/1385kJ; Protein 6.6g; Carbohydrate 27.3g, of which sugars 4.2g; Fat 22.3g, of which saturates 6.2g; Cholesterol 12mg; Calcium 133mg; Fibre 4.9g; Sodium 390mg.
Salad Energy 498kcal/2087kJ; Protein 19.6g; Carbohydrate 48.9g, of which sugars 3.5g; Fat 26.3g, of which saturates 8.8g; Cholesterol 40mg; Calcium 230mg; Fibre 3.2g; Sodium 1152mg.

Tomato & Cheese Tarts

These crisp little tartlets are easier to make than they look and are best eaten fresh from the oven.

Serves 4
2 sheets filo pastry

1 egg white
115g/4oz/½ cup low-fat soft
    (farmer's) cheese
handful of fresh basil leaves
3 small tomatoes, sliced
salt and ground black pepper

1 Preheat the oven to 200°C/400°F/Gas 5. Brush the sheets of filo pastry lightly with egg white and, using a sharp knife, cut into sixteen 10cm/4in squares.

2 Layer the squares in pairs in eight patty tins (muffin pans). Spoon the cheese into the pastry cases (pie shells). Season with salt and ground black pepper and top with basil leaves.

3 Arrange the tomato slices on the tartlets, season with salt and pepper and bake for 10–12 minutes, until golden. Serve warm or at room temperature.

Cook's Tip
Filo pastry can be made at home but the process is quite laborious and takes a long time. It is much easier to buy chilled or frozen ready-made dough. The sheets should be kept covered until you are working on them. Brushing with melted butter, oil or egg white before baking makes sure that the layers are crisp.

Variations
• *Substitute crumbled goat's cheese or feta for the soft (farmer's) cheese or cut a goat's cheese log into eight slices.*
• *Use four red and four yellow cherry tomatoes, halved and in two-colour pairs, to decorate the tops of these tartlets.*
• *Sprinkle the tartlets with chopped fresh chives when they have been assembled.*

Chinese Garlic Mushrooms

High in protein and low in fat, marinated tofu makes an unusual stuffing for these baked mushroom caps.

Serves 4
8 large open mushrooms
3 spring onions (scallions), sliced

1 garlic clove, crushed
30ml/2 tbsp oyster sauce
5g/10oz packet marinated
    tofu, diced
200g/7oz can corn, drained
10ml/2 tsp sesame oil
salt and ground black pepper

1 Preheat the oven to 200°C/400°F/Gas 6. Finely chop the mushroom stalks and mix with the next three ingredients.

2 Stir in the diced marinated tofu and corn, season well, then spoon the filling into the mushroom caps.

3 Brush the edges of the mushrooms with the sesame oil. Place them in an ovenproof dish and bake for 12–15 minutes, until the mushrooms are just tender, then serve immediately.

Ricotta & Borlotti Bean Pâté

A lovely, light yet full-flavoured vegetarian pâté.

Serves 4
400g/14oz can borlotti beans,
    drained and rinsed
175g/6oz/¾ cup ricotta cheese

1 garlic clove
60ml/4 tbsp melted butter
juice of ½ lemon
30ml/2 tbsp chopped
    fresh parsley
15ml/1 tbsp chopped fresh thyme
salt and ground black pepper

1 Put the beans, ricotta, garlic, butter and lemon juice in a food processor or blender and process. Add the parsley and thyme, season with salt and pepper and process again.

2 Spoon into a serving dish or four lightly oiled and base-lined ramekins. Chill. Garnish with salad leaves and serve with warm crusty bread or toast.

Mushrooms Energy 86kcal/361kJ; Protein 7.9g; Carbohydrate 4g, of which sugars 3.2g; Fat 4.4g, of which saturates 0.6g; Cholesterol 0mg; Calcium 268mg; Fibre 2.2g; Sodium 701mg.
Pâté Energy 290kcal/1208kJ; Protein 11g; Carbohydrate 19.3g, of which sugars 5.1g; Fat 19.3g, of which saturates 11.9g; Cholesterol 50mg; Calcium 74mg; Fibre 6.2g; Sodium 481mg.
Tarts Energy 118kcal/497kJ; Protein 7.3g; Carbohydrate 17.9g, of which sugars 3.6g; Fat 2.8g, of which saturates 1.6g; Cholesterol 7mg; Calcium 65mg; Fibre 1.3g; Sodium 149mg.

Avocados with Tangy Topping

Lightly grilled with a tasty topping of red onions and cheese, this dish makes a delightful appetizer.

Serves 4
15ml/1 tbsp sunflower oil
1 small red onion, sliced
1 garlic clove, crushed

dash of Worcestershire sauce
2 ripe avocados, halved and stoned (pitted)
2 small tomatoes, sliced
15ml/1 tbsp chopped fresh basil, marjoram or parsley
50g/2oz Lancashire or mozzarella cheese, sliced
salt and ground black pepper

1 Heat the oil in a frying pan over low heat. Add the onion and garlic and cook, stirring occasionally, for about 5 minutes, until just softened. Shake in a little Worcestershire sauce.

2 Preheat the grill (broiler). Place the avocado halves on the grill (broiling) pan and spoon the onion mixture into the centres. Divide the tomato slices and fresh herbs among the four halves and top with the cheese.

3 Season well with salt and pepper and grill (broil) until the cheese melts and starts to brown.

Chilled Avocado Salad

This simple appetizer makes a delightful change from avocados with vinaigrette.

Serves 4
2 avocados
juice of 1 lemon

300ml/1/2 pint/1 1/4 cups Greek (US strained plain) yogurt
2 garlic cloves, crushed
2 orange (bell) pepper, seeded and diced
salt and ground black pepper

1 Peel, halve and stone (pit) the avocados. Dice the flesh and toss with the lemon juice. Mix together the yogurt and garlic, season and fold in the avocados. Place in a serving dish, sprinkle with the orange peppers and chill before serving.

Bruschetta with Goat's Cheese

Simple to prepare in advance, this tempting dish can be served as an appetizer or as part of a finger buffet.

Serves 4–6
For the tapenade
400g/14oz black olives, pitted and finely chopped
50g/2oz sun-dried tomatoes in oil, drained and chopped
30ml/2 tbsp capers, rinsed and chopped
15ml/1 tbsp green peppercorns, in brine, crushed

2 garlic cloves, crushed
45ml/3 tbsp chopped fresh basil
45–60ml/3–4 tbsp olive oil
salt and ground black pepper

For the bases
12 slices ciabatta or other crusty bread
olive oil, for brushing
2 garlic cloves, halved
115g/4oz/1/2 cup soft goat's cheese or other full-fat soft cheese
mixed fresh herb sprigs, to garnish

1 To make the tapenade, mix all the tapenade ingredients together and check the seasoning. It should not need too much. Leave to marinate overnight, if possible.

2 To make the bruschetta, toast both sides of the bread lightly until golden. Brush one side of each slice with with oil and then rub with the garlic cloves. Set aside until ready to serve.

3 Spread the bruschetta with the cheese, fluffing it up with a fork, and spoon the tapenade on top. Garnish with sprigs of mixed fresh herbs.

> **Cook's Tips**
> • Grill the bruschetta on a barbecue for a delicious smoky flavour if you are making this appetizer in the summer.
> • Basil loses its characteristic flavour when dried – fresh basil is infinitely better. If the fresh herb is not available, you could substitute 15ml/1 tbsp good-quality pesto without sacrificing the flavour.

Avocados Energy 162kcal/668kJ; Protein 3.6g; Carbohydrate 2.9g, of which sugars 1.9g; Fat 15.1g, of which saturates 4.1g; Cholesterol 7mg; Calcium 56mg; Fibre 2.2g; Sodium 55mg.
Salad Energy 264kcal/1094kJ; Protein 7.7g; Carbohydrate 9.8g, of which sugars 7.3g; Fat 22.5g, of which saturates 7.1g; Cholesterol 0mg; Calcium 129mg; Fibre 4.3g; Sodium 62mg.
Bruschetta Energy 288kcal/1197kJ; Protein 8.1g; Carbohydrate 17.8g, of which sugars 1.5g; Fat 20.9g, of which saturates 5.8g; Cholesterol 18mg; Calcium 107mg; Fibre 2.8g; Sodium 1795mg.

Grilled Garlic Mussels

Use a combination of fresh herbs, such as oregano, basil and flat leaf parsley.

Serves 4
1.5kg/3–3¹/₂lb fresh mussels
120ml/4fl oz/¹/₂ cup dry
    white wine
50g/2oz/4 tbsp butter
2 shallots, finely chopped

2 garlic cloves, crushed
50g/2oz/¹/₂ cup dried
    white breadcrumbs
60ml/4 tbsp mixed chopped
    fresh herbs
30ml/2 tbsp freshly grated
    Parmesan cheese
salt and ground black pepper
fresh basil leaves, to garnish

1 Scrub the mussels well under cold running water. Remove the "beards" and discard any mussels with damaged shells or that do not shut immediately when sharply tapped.

2 Place in a large, heavy pan with the wine. Cover with a tight-fitting lid and cook over high heat, shaking the pan occasionally for 5–8 minutes, until the mussels have opened.

3 Strain the mussels and reserve the cooking liquid. Discard any mussels that remain closed. Leave them to cool slightly, then remove and discard the top half of each shell.

4 Melt the butter in a pan over low heat. Add the shallots and cook, stirring occasionally, for 5 minutes, until softened. Add the garlic and cook for 1–2 minutes. Add the breadcrumbs and cook, stirring until lightly browned. Remove the pan from the heat and stir in the herbs. Moisten with a little of the reserved mussel liquid, then season to taste with salt and pepper.

5 Spoon the breadcrumb mixture over the mussels and arrange on baking sheets. Sprinkle with the grated Parmesan.

6 Cook the mussels under a hot grill (broiler), in batches, for about 2 minutes, until the topping is crisp and golden brown. Keep the cooked mussels warm in a low oven while grilling (broiling) the remainder. Garnish with fresh basil leaves and serve immediately.

Nut Patties with Mango Relish

These spicy vegetarian patties can be made in advance, if you like, and reheated just before serving.

Serves 4–6
butter, for greasing
175g/6oz/1¹/₂ cups roasted
    and salted cashew nuts,
    finely chopped
175g/6oz/1¹/₂ cups walnuts,
    finely chopped
1 small onion, finely chopped
1 garlic clove, crushed
1 green chilli, seeded
    and chopped
5ml/1 tsp ground cumin
10ml/2 tsp ground coriander

2 carrots, coarsely grated
50g/2oz/1 cup fresh white
    breadcrumbs
30ml/2 tbsp chopped fresh
    coriander (cilantro)
15ml/1 tbsp lemon juice
1–2 eggs, lightly beaten
salt and ground black pepper
fresh coriander sprigs, to garnish

For the relish
1 large ripe mango, cut into
    small dice
1 small onion, cut into slivers
5ml/1 tsp grated fresh root ginger
pinch of salt
15ml/1 tbsp sesame oil
5ml/1 tsp black mustard seeds

1 Preheat the oven to 180°C/350°F/Gas 4. Lightly grease a baking sheet with butter.

2 Mix together the cashews, walnuts, onion, garlic, chilli, cumin, ground coriander, carrots, breadcrumbs and chopped coriander in a bowl and season with salt and pepper.

3 Sprinkle the lemon juice over the mixture and add enough of the beaten egg to bind it together. Using your hands, shape the mixture into twelve balls, then flatten slightly into round patties. Place them on the prepared baking sheet and bake for about 25 minutes, until golden brown.

4 To make the relish, mix together the mango, onion, fresh root ginger and salt. Heat the oil in a small frying pan, add the mustard seeds and cook for a few seconds until they pop and give off their aroma. Stir the seeds into the mango mixture and transfer the relish to a serving bowl. Serve with the nut patties, garnished with coriander sprigs.

Mussels Energy 289kcal/1211kJ; Protein 24g; Carbohydrate 10g, of which sugars 0.6g; Fat 15.2g, of which saturates 8.4g; Cholesterol 79mg; Calcium 333mg; Fibre 0.3g; Sodium 490mg.
Patties Energy 464kcal/1926kJ; Protein 12.8g; Carbohydrate 19.3g, of which sugars 8.4g; Fat 37.9g, of which saturates 5.2g; Cholesterol 32mg; Calcium 66mg; Fibre 3.5g; Sodium 167mg.

Dim Sum

A popular Chinese snack, these tiny dumplings are now fashionable in many specialist restaurants.

Serves 4
For the dough
150g/5oz/1¼ cups plain (all-purpose) flour
50ml/2fl oz/¼ cup boiling water
25ml/1½ tbsp cold water
7.5ml/½ tsp vegetable oil

For the filling
75g/3oz minced (ground) pork

45ml/3 tbsp chopped canned bamboo shoots
7.5ml/½ tsp light soy sauce, plus extra to serve
5ml/1 tsp dry sherry
5ml/1 tsp demerara (raw) sugar
2.5ml/½ tsp sesame oil
5ml/1 tsp cornflour (cornstarch)

To serve
mixed fresh lettuce leaves such as iceberg, frisée or Webbs
spring onion (scallion) curls
sliced red chilli
prawn (shrimp) crackers

1 To make the dough, sift the flour into a bowl. Stir in the boiling water, then the cold water together with the oil. Mix to form a ball and knead until smooth. Divide the mixture into sixteen equal pieces and shape into rounds.

2 For the filling, mix together the pork, bamboo shoots, soy sauce, sherry, sugar and oil. Then stir in the cornflour.

3 Place a little of the filling in the centre of each dim sum round. Carefully pinch the edges of the dough together to form little "purses".

4 Line a steamer with a damp dish towel. Place the dim sum in the steamer and steam for 5–10 minutes. Serve immediately on a bed of lettuce with soy sauce, spring onion curls, sliced red chilli and prawn crackers.

> **Variation**
> As an alternative filling, substitute cooked, peeled prawns (shrimp) for the pork.

Sesame Prawn Toasts

Serve about four of these delicious toasts per person with a soy sauce for dipping.

Serves 6
175g/6oz/1½ cups cooked, peeled prawns (shrimp)
2 spring onions (scallions), finely chopped
2.5cm/1in piece fresh root ginger, peeled and grated

2 garlic cloves, crushed
30ml/2 tbsp cornflour (cornstarch)
10ml/2 tsp soy sauce, plus extra for dipping
6 slices day-old bread from a small loaf, without crusts
40g/1½ oz sesame seeds
about 600ml/1 pint/2½ cups vegetable oil, for deep-frying

1 Place the prawns, spring onions, ginger and garlic cloves into a food processor fitted with a metal blade. Add the cornflour and soy sauce and process the mixture into a paste.

2 Spread the bread slices evenly with the paste and cut into triangles. Sprinkle with the sesame seeds, making sure they stick to the bread. Chill in the refrigerator for 30 minutes.

3 Heat the vegetable oil in a deep-fryer or large, heavy pan to 190°C/375°F or until a cube of day-old bread browns in 30 seconds. Using a slotted spoon, lower the toasts, in batches, into the oil, sesame-seed side down, and fry for 2–3 minutes, turning them over for the last minute. Remove with a slotted spoon and drain on absorbent kitchen paper. Keep the toasts warm while frying the remainder.

4 Place the toasts on individual dishes and serve immediately with little bowls of soy sauce for dipping.

> **Cook's Tip**
> Chinese soy sauce may be either light or dark. The former has a stronger flavour, while the latter is sweeter and is often used in cooking to give a richer colour to dishes. Light soy sauce is most usually used as a condiment and for dipping.

Dim Sum Energy 183kcal/773kJ; Protein 7.2g; Carbohydrate 31.5g, of which sugars 1.8g; Fat 3.8g, of which saturates 0.9g; Cholesterol 12mg; Calcium 55mg; Fibre 1.2g; Sodium 148mg.
Prawn Toasts Energy 207kcal/865kJ; Protein 8.7g; Carbohydrate 17.4g, of which sugars 1g; Fat 11.9g, of which saturates 1.5g; Cholesterol 57mg; Calcium 98mg; Fibre 1g; Sodium 427mg.

Golden Cheese Puffs

Serve these deep-fried puffs – called *aigrettes* in France – with a fruity chutney and a green salad.

Makes 8
50g/2oz/½ cup plain (all-
   purpose) flour
15g/½oz/1 tbsp butter
1 egg
1 egg yolk
50g/2oz/½ cup finely grated
   mature (sharp) Cheddar cheese
15ml/1 tbsp freshly grated
   Parmesan cheese
2.5ml/½ tsp mustard powder
pinch of cayenne pepper
vegetable oil, for deep-frying
salt and ground black pepper
mango chutney and green salad,
   to serve

1 Sift the flour on to a square of greaseproof (waxed) paper and set aside. Place the butter and 150ml/⅔ pint/⅔ cup water in a pan and heat gently until the butter has melted.

2 Bring the liquid to the boil and tip in the flour all at once. Remove the pan from the heat and stir well with a wooden spoon until the mixture begins to leave the sides of the pan and forms a ball. Leave to cool slightly.

3 Beat the egg and egg yolk together in a bowl with a fork and then gradually add to the mixture in the pan, beating well after each addition.

4 Stir the Cheddar and Parmesan cheeses, mustard powder and cayenne pepper into the mixture and season to taste with salt and pepper.

5 Heat the vegetable oil in a deep-fryer or large, heavy pan to 190°C/375°F, or until a cube of day-old bread browns in 30 seconds. Drop four spoonfuls of the cheese mixture into the oil at a time and deep-fry for 2–3 minutes, until golden. Remove with a slotted spoon, drain on kitchen paper and keep hot in the oven while cooking the remaining mixture.

6 Serve two puffs per person with a spoonful of mango chutney and green salad.

English Ploughman's Pâté

This is a contemporary interpretation of the traditional ploughman's lunch – bread, cheese and a variety of pickles.

Serves 4
50g/2oz/3 tbsp full-fat
   soft (farmer's) cheese
50g/2oz/½ cup grated Caerphilly
   or other crumbly white cheese
50g/2oz/½ cup grated Double
   Gloucester or other mellow,
   semi-hard cheese
4 pickled silverskin onions,
   drained and finely chopped
15ml/1 tbsp apricot chutney
30ml/2 tbsp butter, melted
30ml/2 tbsp chopped fresh chives
4 slices soft-grain bread
salt and ground black pepper
watercress or rocket (arugula) and
   cherry tomatoes, to serve

1 Mix together the soft cheese, grated cheeses, pickled onions, chutney and butter in a bowl and season lightly with salt and ground black pepper.

2 Spoon the mixture on to a sheet of greaseproof (waxed) paper and roll up into a cylinder, smoothing the mixture into a roll with your hands. Scrunch the ends of the paper together and twist them to seal. Place in the freezer for about 30 minutes, until the roll is just firm.

3 Spread the chives on a plate, then unwrap the chilled cheese pâté. Roll it in the chives until evenly coated. Wrap in clear film (plastic wrap) and chill for 10 minutes in the refrigerator.

4 Preheat the grill (broiler). Lightly toast the bread on both sides. Cut off the crusts and slice each piece in half horizontally to make two very thin slices. Cut each half into two triangles. Grill (broil) again, untoasted side up, until golden and curled at the edges.

5 Slice the pâté into rounds with a sharp knife and serve three or four rounds per person with the toast, watercress or rocket and cherry tomatoes.

Pâté Energy 288kcal/1200kJ; Protein 10.6g; Carbohydrate 18.7g, of which sugars 5.1g; Fat 19g, of which saturates 11.9g; Cholesterol 52mg; Calcium 267mg; Fibre 1.3g; Sodium 511mg.
Cheese Puffs Energy 162kcal/669kJ; Protein 3.5g; Carbohydrate 5.8g, of which sugars 0g; Fat 13.9g, of which saturates 4.1g; Cholesterol 61mg; Calcium 77mg; Fibre 0g; Sodium 90mg.

Kansas City Fritters

Crisp bacon and vegetable fritters are served with a spicy tomato salsa.

Makes 8
200g/7oz/1¾ cups canned corn, drained well
2 eggs, separated
75g/3oz/¾ cup plain (all-purpose) flour
75ml/5 tbsp milk
1 small courgette (zucchini), grated
2 rashers (strips) rindless lean back bacon, diced
2 spring onions (scallions), finely chopped

large pinch of cayenne pepper
45ml/3 tbsp sunflower oil
salt and ground black pepper
fresh coriander (cilantro) sprigs, to garnish

For the salsa
3 tomatoes, peeled, seeded and diced
½ small red (bell) pepper, seeded and diced
½ small onion, diced
15ml/1 tbsp lemon juice
15ml/1 tbsp chopped fresh coriander
dash of Tabasco sauce

1 To make the salsa, mix all the ingredients together in a bowl and season to taste with salt and pepper. Cover with clear film (plastic wrap) and chill until required.

2 Empty the corn into another bowl and mix in the egg yolks. Add the flour and blend in with a wooden spoon. When the mixture thickens, gradually blend in the milk.

3 Stir in the courgette, bacon, spring onions and cayenne pepper and season with salt and pepper. Whisk the egg whites in a grease-free bowl until stiff peaks form. Gently fold into the corn batter mixture.

4 Heat the oil in a large frying pan and place four spoonfuls of the mixture into it. Cook over a medium heat for 2–3 minutes on each side, until golden. Drain on kitchen paper and keep warm in the oven while cooking the remaining four fritters.

5 Serve two fritters each, garnished with coriander sprigs and a spoonful of the chilled tomato salsa.

Spinach & Cheese Dumplings

These tasty little dumplings are known as *gnocchi* in Italy, where they are extremely popular, especially in the northern regions.

Serves 4
butter, for greasing
40g/1½oz/½ cup freshly grated Parmesan cheese
175g/6oz cold mashed potato
75g/3oz/½ cup semolina
115g/4oz/1 cup frozen leaf spinach, thawed, squeezed out and chopped

115g/4oz/½ cup ricotta cheese
30ml/2 tbsp beaten egg
2.5ml/½ tsp salt
large pinch of grated nutmeg
pinch of ground black pepper
fresh basil sprigs, to garnish

For the butter sauce
75g/3oz/6 tbsp butter
5ml/1 tsp grated lemon rind
15ml/1 tbsp lemon juice
15ml/1 tbsp chopped fresh basil

1 Preheat the oven to 150°C/300°F/Gas 2. Lightly grease a flameproof dish with butter and place it in the oven to warm. Set aside 30ml/2 tbsp of the Parmesan cheese. Place the remainder in a bowl, add the potato, semolina, spinach, ricotta, beaten egg, salt, nutmeg and pepper and mix well.

2 Take walnut-size pieces of the mixture and roll each one back and forth along the prongs of a fork until ridged. Make 28 dumplings in this way. Preheat the grill (broiler).

3 Bring a large pan of water to the boil, reduce to a simmer and drop in the dumplings. As they cook they will rise to the surface; this takes about 2 minutes, then simmer for 1 minute more. Transfer the dumplings to the prepared dish.

4 Sprinkle the dumplings with the Parmesan cheese and grill under high heat for 2 minutes, or until lightly browned.

5 Meanwhile, heat the butter in a pan and stir in the lemon rind, lemon juice and basil. Season to taste with salt and pepper. Pour some of this butter over each portion and serve immediately, garnished with basil sprigs.

Fritters Energy 152kcal/636kJ; Protein 5.3g; Carbohydrate 17.2g, of which sugars 5.6g; Fat 7.4g, of which saturates 1.5g; Cholesterol 51mg; Calcium 42mg; Fibre 1.5g; Sodium 190mg.
Dumplings Energy 432kcal/1796kJ; Protein 18.2g; Carbohydrate 23.1g, of which sugars 2g; Fat 30.3g, of which saturates 18.2g; Cholesterol 126mg; Calcium 381mg; Fibre 1.4g; Sodium 465mg.

Tricolor Salad

This can be a simple appetizer if served on individual salad plates, or part of a light buffet meal laid out on a platter.

Serves 4–6
1 small red onion, thinly sliced
6 large full-flavoured tomatoes
extra virgin olive oil, to drizzle
50g/2oz rocket (arugula) or watercress, chopped
175g/6oz mozzarella cheese, thinly sliced
salt and ground black pepper
30ml/2 tbsp pine nuts, to garnish (optional)

1 Soak the onion slices in a bowl of cold water for about 30 minutes, then drain and pat dry with kitchen paper.

2 Cut a cross in the tops of the tomatoes, place in a heatproof bowl and pour boiling water over them. Leave for 1 minute, then drain and peel off the skins. Remove the cores and slice the flesh. Arrange half the sliced tomatoes on a large platter or divide them among small plates.

3 Drizzle liberally with olive oil, then layer with half the chopped rocket or watercress and half the soaked onion slices, seasoning well with salt and pepper. Add half the mozzarella, then drizzle with more olive oil and season again.

4 Repeat with the remaining tomato slices, salad leaves, onion slices, mozzarella and olive oil.

5 Season well to finish and complete with some olive oil and a good sprinkling of pine nuts, if using. Cover the salad with clear film (plastic wrap) and chill in the refrigerator for at least 2 hours before serving.

> **Cook's Tip**
> When lightly salted, tomatoes make their own dressing with their natural juices. The sharpness of the rocket (arugula) or watercress offsets them wonderfully.

Minted Melon Salad

Use two different varieties of melon in this salad, such as Charentais and Galia or Ogen.

Serves 4
2 ripe melons
fresh mint sprigs, to garnish

For the dressing
30ml/2 tbsp coarsely chopped fresh mint
5ml/1 tsp caster (superfine) sugar
30ml/2 tbsp raspberry vinegar
90ml/6 tbsp extra virgin olive oil
salt and ground black pepper

1 Halve the melons, then scoop out the seeds using a dessertspoon. Cut the melons into thin wedges using a large sharp knife and remove the skins.

2 Arrange the two different varieties of melon wedges alternately among four individual serving plates.

3 To make the dressing, whisk together the mint, sugar, vinegar and olive oil n a small bowl and season to taste with salt and pepper. Alternatively, put them in a screw-top jar, close the lid and shake well until combined.

4 Spoon the mint dressing over the melon wedges and garnish with mint sprigs. Chill in the refrigerator for about 15 minutes before serving.

> **Cook's Tip**
> You can make raspberry vinegar yourself by steeping the fresh fruit in wine vinegar and then straining it. Steeping another batch of fruit in the same vinegar intensifies the flavour.

> **Variation**
> You could also try an orange-fleshed Cantaloupe with a pale green Ogen, or choose a small white-fleshed Honeydew for a different variation.

Tricolor Energy 98kcal/408kJ; Protein 6.5g; Carbohydrate 4g, of which sugars 3.8g; Fat 6.3g, of which saturates 4.1g; Cholesterol 17mg; Calcium 129mg; Fibre 1.3g; Sodium 136mg.
Melon Energy 218kcal/904kJ; Protein 1.7g; Carbohydrate 15.7g, of which sugars 15.1g; Fat 16.8g, of which saturates 2.4g; Cholesterol 0mg; Calcium 59mg; Fibre 1g; Sodium 80mg.

Garlic Mushrooms

Serve these on toast for a quick, tasty appetizer or pop them into ramekins and serve with slices of warm crusty bread.

Serves 4
450g/1lb button (white)
    mushrooms, sliced if large
45ml/3 tbsp olive oil
45ml/3 tbsp stock or water
30ml/2 tbsp dry sherry (optional)
3 garlic cloves, crushed
115g/4oz/1/2 cup low-fat
    soft (farmer's) cheese
30ml/2 tbsp chopped
    fresh parsley
15ml/1 tbsp chopped fresh chives
salt and ground black pepper
toast or bread, to serve

1 Put the mushrooms into a large pan with the olive oil, stock or water and sherry, if using. Heat until the liquid is bubbling, then cover the pan with a tight-fitting lid and simmer gently for about 5 minutes.

2 Add the crushed garlic and stir well to mix. Cook for a further 2 minutes. Remove the mushrooms with a slotted spoon and set them aside. Cook the liquid until it reduces to about 30ml/2 tbsp. Remove the pan from the heat and stir in the soft cheese, parsley and chives.

3 Stir the mixture well until the cheese has completely melted, then return the mushrooms to the pan and stir so that they become coated with the cheese mixture. Season to taste with salt and pepper.

4 Pile the mushrooms on to thick slabs of hot toast and serve immediately. Alternatively, spoon them into four ramekins and serve accompanied by slices of crusty bread.

> **Cook's Tip**
> Use a mixture of different types of mushrooms for this dish, if you like. Shiitake mushrooms, if you can find them, will give this appetizer a particularly rich flavour. Oyster mushrooms, on the other hand, offer an interesting texture.

Vegetables with Tahini

This colourful appetizer is easily prepared in advance. For an al fresco meal, you could grill the vegetables on a barbecue.

Serves 4
2 red, green or yellow (bell)
    peppers, seeded and quartered
2 courgettes (zucchini),
    halved lengthways
2 small aubergines
    (eggplants), degorged and
    halved lengthways
1 fennel bulb, quartered
olive oil, for brushing
115g/4oz halloumi cheese, sliced
salt and ground black pepper
warm pitta or naan bread,
    to serve

For the tahini cream
225g/8oz tahini paste
1 garlic clove, crushed
30ml/2 tbsp olive oil
30ml/2 tbsp freshly squeezed
    lemon juice
120ml/4fl oz/1/2 cup cold water

1 Preheat the grill (broiler) or barbecue until hot. Brush the vegetables with the olive oil and cook until just browned, turning once. (If the peppers blacken and blister, don't worry. The skins can be peeled off when they are cool enough to handle.) Cook the vegetables until just softened.

2 Place all the vegetables in a shallow dish and season to taste with salt and pepper. Leave to cool slightly. They are best served warm rather than hot.

3 Meanwhile, brush the cheese slices with olive oil and grill (broil) these on both sides until they are just charred. Remove them from the grill (broiler) pan with a metal spatula.

4 To make the tahini cream, place all the ingredients, except the water, in a food processor or blender. Process for a few seconds to mix, then, with the motor still running, pour in the water and blend until smooth.

5 Place the vegetables and cheese slices on a platter and trickle over the tahini cream. Serve with plenty of warm pitta or naan bread while the cheese is still hot, as it will become rubbery as it cools down.

Mushrooms Energy 131kcal/542kJ; Protein 6.7g; Carbohydrate 1.8g, of which sugars 1.5g; Fat 11.3g, of which saturates 2.8g; Cholesterol 7mg; Calcium 65mg; Fibre 1.9g; Sodium 136mg.
Vegetables Energy 523kcal/2164kJ; Protein 19.1g; Carbohydrate 9.9g, of which sugars 9.1g; Fat 45.5g, of which saturates 9.7g; Cholesterol 17mg; Calcium 530mg; Fibre 9.1g; Sodium 136mg.

Haddock with Parsley Sauce

The parsley sauce is enriched with cream and an egg yolk in this simple supper dish.

Serves 4
4 haddock fillets (about 175g/
   6oz each)
50g/2oz/4 tbsp butter
150ml/¼ pint/⅔ cup milk
150ml/¼ pint/⅔ cup fish stock

1 bay leaf
20ml/4 tsp plain (all-
   purpose) flour
60ml/4 tbsp double
   (heavy) cream
1 egg yolk
45ml/3 tbsp chopped
   fresh parsley
grated rind and juice of ½ lemon
salt and ground black pepper

1 Place the fish in a frying pan, add half the butter, the milk, fish stock and bay leaf and season with salt and pepper. Bring to simmering point over medium-low heat. Lower the heat, cover the pan with a tight-fitting lid and poach the fish for 10–15 minutes, depending on the thickness of the fillets, until the fish is tender and the flesh just begins to flake.

2 Transfer the fish to a warmed serving plate with a slotted spoon, cover it and keep warm while you make the sauce.

3 Return the cooking liquid to the heat and bring to the boil, stirring constantly. Simmer for about 4 minutes, then remove and discard the bay leaf.

4 Melt the remaining butter in a pan, add the flour and cook, stirring constantly, for 1 minute. Remove from the heat and gradually stir in the fish cooking liquid. Return to the heat and bring to the boil, stirring constantly. Simmer for about 4 minutes, stirring frequently.

5 Remove the pan from the heat, blend the cream into the egg yolk, then stir into the sauce with the parsley. Reheat gently, stirring for a few minutes, but do not let it to boil. Remove from the heat, add the lemon juice and rind and season to taste with salt and pepper. Pour the sauce into a warmed sauceboat and serve immediately with the fish.

Pickled Herrings

A good basic pickled herring dish which is enhanced by the grainy mustard vinaigrette.

12 black peppercorns
2 bay leaves
4 cloves
2 small onions, sliced

Serves 4
4 fresh herrings, gutted
   and boned
150ml/¼ pint/⅔ cup white
   wine vinegar
2 tsp salt

For the dressing
1 tsp coarse grain mustard
3 tbsp olive oil
1 tbsp white wine vinegar
salt and ground black pepper

1 Preheat the oven to 160C°/325°F/Gas 3. Cut each fish into two fillets with a sharp knife.

2 Roll up the fillets tightly and place them in an ovenproof dish, closely packed together so that they can't unroll.

3 Pour the vinegar over the fish and add just enough water to cover them.

4 Add the salt, peppercorns, bay leaves, cloves and onions, cover and bake for 1 hour. Remove the fish from the oven and leave to cool in the liquid.

5. To make the dressing, put all the ingredients in a screw-top jar, close the lid and shake well to combine. Serve the fish with the dressing poured over the top.

Variation
Cook soused herrings in the same way, substituting malt vinegar for the wine vinegar, 5ml/1 tsp allspice for the peppercorns and 5ml/1 tsp pickling spice for the cloves and adding 5ml/1 tsp sugar to the mixture. Soused herrings are usually served cold – with or without the dressing from the recipe above – but may also be served hot with boiled potatoes.

Haddock Energy 317kcal/1332kJ; Protein 35.9g; Carbohydrate 8.5g, of which sugars 0.9g; Fat 15.9g, of which saturates 8.9g; Cholesterol 148mg; Calcium 85mg; Fibre 0.9g; Sodium 204mg.
Herrings Energy 231kcal/963kJ; Protein 12.5g; Carbohydrate 7.5g, of which sugars 7.5g; Fat 16.6g, of which saturates 1.2g; Cholesterol 32mg; Calcium 10mg; Fibre 0g; Sodium 623mg.

Fish & Chips

The traditional British combination of battered fish and thick-cut chips is served with lemon wedges.

Serves 4

115g/4oz/1 cup self-raising (self-rising) flour
150ml/¼ pint/⅔ cup water
675g/1½lb potatoes
675g/1½lb skinned cod fillet, cut into four
vegetable oil, for deep-frying
salt and ground black pepper
lemon wedges, to serve

1 Stir the flour and a pinch of salt together in a bowl, then form a well in the centre. Gradually pour into the water, whisking in the flour to make a smooth batter. Leave to stand for 30 minutes.

2 Cut the potatoes into strips about 1cm/½ in wide and 5cm/2in long. Place the potatoes in a colander, rinse in cold water, then drain and dry them well with kitchen paper.

3 Heat the oil in a deep-fat fryer or large heavy pan to 150°C/300°F, or until a cube of day-old bread browns in 50 seconds. Using the wire basket, lower the potatoes, in batches, into the oil and cook for 5–6 minutes, shaking the basket occasionally until the potatoes are soft but not browned. Remove the chips (French fries) from the oil and drain them thoroughly on kitchen paper.

4 Heat the oil in the fryer to 190°C/375°F, or until a cube of day old bread browns in 30 seconds. Season the fish with salt and pepper. Stir the batter, then dip the pieces of fish in turn into it, allowing the excess to drain off.

5 Working in two batches if necessary, lower the fish into the oil and fry for 6–8 minutes, until crisp and brown. Drain the fish on kitchen paper and keep warm.

6 Add the chips, in batches, to the oil and cook them for 2–3 minutes, until golden and crisp. Keep hot until ready to serve, then sprinkle with salt and serve with the fish, accompanied by lemon wedges.

Herrings in Oatmeal with Mustard

In this delicious dish, crunchy-coated herrings are served with a piquant mustard sauce.

Serves 4

about 15ml/1 tbsp Dijon mustard
about 7.5ml/1½ tsp tarragon vinegar
175ml/6fl oz/¾ cup thick mayonnaise
4 herrings (about 225g/8oz each), gutted
1 lemon, halved
115g/4oz/1 cup medium oatmeal
salt and ground black pepper

1 Beat the mustard and vinegar to taste into the mayonnaise. Chill lightly in the refrigerator.

2 Place one fish at a time on a chopping board, cut-side down and opened out. Press gently all along the backbone with your thumbs. Turn the fish over and carefully lift away the backbone and discard.

3 Squeeze lemon juice over both sides of each fish, then season with salt and ground black pepper. Fold the fish in half, skin-side outwards.

4 Preheat the grill (broiler) until fairly hot. Place the oatmeal on a shallow plate, then coat each herring evenly in the oatmeal, pressing it on gently with your fingers.

5 Place the herrings on a grill (broiler) rack and grill (broil) the fish for about 3–4 minutes on each side, until the skin is golden brown and crisp and the flesh flakes easily. Serve hot with the mustard sauce, served separately.

Variation
For extra flavour coarsely chop 4 rashers (strips) of streaky (fatty) bacon and dry-fry in a heavy frying pan over low heat until golden and crisp. Drain on kitchen paper. Sprinkle the bacon over the cooked fish before serving.

Herrings Energy 721kcal/2997kJ; Protein 35.3g; Carbohydrate 21.7g, of which sugars 0.6g; Fat 55.4g, of which saturates 10.6g; Cholesterol 109mg; Calcium 69mg; Fibre 2g; Sodium 476mg.
Fish & Chips Energy 820kcal/3429kJ; Protein 32.6g; Carbohydrate 71.2g, of which sugars 2.9g; Fat 40.5g, of which saturates 13g; Cholesterol 0mg; Calcium 132mg; Fibre 4.6g; Sodium 329mg.

Trout with Hazelnuts

The hazelnuts in this recipe make an interesting change from the almonds that are more often used.

Serves 4

50g/2oz/¹⁄₂ cup hazelnuts, chopped

65g/2¹⁄₂oz/5 tbsp butter
4 trout (about 275g/10oz each), gutted
30ml/2 tbsp lemon juice
salt and ground black pepper
lemon slices and fresh flat leaf parsley sprigs, to serve

1 Preheat the grill (broiler). Toast the nuts in a single layer, stirring frequently, until the skins split. Then transfer the nuts to a clean dish towel and rub to remove the skins. Leave the nuts to cool, then chop them coarsely.

2 Heat 50g/2oz/4 tbsp of the butter in a large frying pan. Season the trout inside and out with salt and pepper, then cook them, two at a time, for 12–15 minutes, turning once, until the trout are brown and the flesh flakes easily when tested with the point of a sharp kitchen knife.

3 Drain the cooked trout on kitchen paper, then transfer to a warm serving plate and keep warm while frying the remaining trout in the same way. (If your frying pan is large enough, you could, of course, cook the trout in one batch.)

4 Add the remaining butter to the frying pan and fry the hazelnuts until evenly browned. Stir the lemon juice into the pan and mix well, then quickly pour the buttery sauce over the trout and serve immediately, garnished with slices of lemon and flat leaf parsley sprigs.

Cook's Tip
You can use a microwave to prepare the nuts instead of the grill (broiler). Spread them out in a shallow microwave dish and leave uncovered. Cook on full power until the skins split, then remove the skins using a dish towel as described above.

Trout Wrapped in a Blanket

The "blanket" of bacon bastes the fish during cooking, keeping it moist and adding flavour at the same time.

Serves 4

butter, for greasing
juice of ¹⁄₂ lemon
4 trout (about 275g/10oz each), gutted

4 fresh thyme sprigs, plus extra to garnish
8 thin rashers (strips) rindless streaky (fatty) bacon
salt and ground black pepper
chopped fresh parsley, to garnish
lemon wedges, to serve

1 Preheat the oven to 200°C/400°F/Gas 6. Lightly grease a shallow ovenproof dish with butter.

2 Squeeze lemon juice over the skin and inside the cavity of each fish, season all over with salt and ground black pepper, then put a thyme sprig in each cavity.

3 Stretch each bacon rasher using the back of a knife, then wrap two rashers around each fish. Place the fish in the prepared dish, with the loose ends of bacon tucked underneath to prevent them from unwinding.

4 Bake the trout for 15–20 minutes, until the flesh flakes easily when tested with the point of a sharp knife and the bacon is crisp and beginning to brown.

5 Transfer the fish to warmed individual plates and serve immediately garnished with chopped parsley and sprigs of thyme and accompanied by lemon wedges.

Variation
Smoked streaky (fatty) bacon will impart a stronger flavour to the fish. If you like, use chopped fresh coriander (cilantro) in place of the parsley for the garnish.

With Hazelnuts Energy 414kcal/1723kJ; Protein 38.7g; Carbohydrate 0.9g, of which sugars 0.6g; Fat 28.4g, of which saturates 10.7g; Cholesterol 187mg; Calcium 78mg; Fibre 0.8g; Sodium 237mg.
In a blanket Energy 316kcal/1323kJ; Protein 42.8g; Carbohydrate 0.1g, of which sugars 0.1g; Fat 16g, of which saturates 4.8g; Cholesterol 176mg; Calcium 64mg; Fibre 0.1g; Sodium 611mg.

Smoked Trout Salad

Horseradish goes just as well with smoked trout as it does with roast beef. It combines well with yogurt to make a lovely dressing.

Serves 4

1 oak leaf or other red lettuce, such as lollo rosso
225g/8oz small ripe tomatoes, cut into thin wedges
1/2 cucumber, peeled and thinly sliced
4 smoked trout fillets, about 200g/7oz each, skinned and coarsely flaked

For the dressing

pinch of English (hot) mustard powder
15–20ml/3–4 tsp white wine vinegar
30ml/2 tbsp light olive oil
100ml/3 1/2fl oz/scant 1/2 cup natural (plain) yogurt
about 30ml/2 tbsp grated fresh or bottled horseradish
pinch of caster (superfine) sugar

1 To make the dressing, mix together the mustard powder and vinegar in a bowl, then gradually whisk in the olive oil, yogurt, grated horseradish and sugar. Set aside in a cool place for about 30 minutes.

2 Place the lettuce leaves in a large bowl. Stir the dressing again, then pour half of it over the leaves and toss lightly using two spoons.

3 Arrange the lettuce on four individual plates with the tomatoes, cucumber and trout. Spoon the remaining dressing over the salads and serve immediately.

> **Cook's Tips**
> • The addition of salt to the horseradish salad dressing should not be necessary because of the saltiness of the smoked trout fillets.
> • Look for natural, uncoloured smoked trout fillets — they should be a delicate cream colour.

Moroccan Fish Tagine

In Morocco *tagine* is the name of the large cooking pot used for this type of cooking, as well as the name of the dish.

Serves 4

2 garlic cloves, crushed
30ml/2 tbsp ground cumin
30ml/2 tbsp paprika
1 small fresh red chilli, seeded and finely chopped (optional)
30ml/2 tbsp tomato purée (paste)
60ml/4 tbsp lemon juice
4 whiting or cod steaks (about 175g/6oz each)
350g/12oz tomatoes, sliced
2 green (bell) peppers, seeded and thinly sliced
salt and ground black pepper
chopped fresh coriander (cilantro) or flat leaf parsley, to garnish

1 Mix together the garlic, cumin, paprika, chilli, if using, tomato purée and lemon juice in a bowl. Place the fish in a shallow dish and spread this mixture over it. Cover with clear film (plastic wrap) and chill in the refrigerator for about 30 minutes to let the flavours penetrate.

2 Preheat the oven to 200°C/400°F/Gas 6. Arrange half of the tomatoes and peppers in an ovenproof dish.

3 Cover with the fish, then arrange the remaining tomatoes and peppers on top. Cover the dish with foil and bake for about 45 minutes, until the fish is tender. Sprinkle with chopped coriander or parsley to serve.

> **Cook's Tips**
> • Try different white fish in this dish, such as hoki, hake, ling or pollack.
> • If you are preparing this dish for a dinner party, it can be assembled completely and stored in the refrigerator until you are ready to cook it.
> • Green (bell) peppers have a pleasing sharpness that goes well with this dish, but if you want to add more colour, substitute a red or yellow pepper for one of the green ones.

Trout Energy 303kcal/1268kJ; Protein 40.9g; Carbohydrate 4.4g, of which sugars 4.4g; Fat 13.7g, of which saturates 1g; Cholesterol 0mg; Calcium 81mg; Fibre 1g; Sodium 139mg.
Tagine Energy 174kcal/735kJ; Protein 33.7g; Carbohydrate 6.1g, of which sugars 5.9g; Fat 1.8g, of which saturates 0.4g; Cholesterol 81mg; Calcium 32mg; Fibre 2.5g; Sodium 135mg.

Prawn & Mint Salad

Using raw prawns makes all the difference to this salad, as the flavours marinate superbly into the prawns before cooking.

Serves 4
12 large raw prawns (shrimp)
15g/½ oz/1 tbsp unsalted (sweet) butter
15ml/1 tbsp Thai fish sauce
juice of 1 lime
45ml/3 tbsp thin coconut milk
2.5cm/1 in piece of fresh root ginger, peeled and grated
5ml/1 tsp caster (superfine) sugar
1 garlic clove, crushed
2 fresh red chillies, seeded and finely chopped
30ml/2 tbsp fresh mint leaves
ground black pepper
225g/8oz light green lettuce leaves, such as round (butterhead), to serve

1 Pull off the heads from the prawns and peel them, leaving the tails intact. Make a small cut along the back of each prawn and remove the dark vein with the point of the knife.

2 Melt the butter in a large frying pan over medium heat. Add the prawns and cook, turning and tossing frequently, for about 3 minutes, until they turn pink.

3 Mix the Thai fish sauce, lime juice, coconut milk, ginger, sugar, garlic, chillies and pepper together in a large bowl.

4 Add the warm prawns to the sauce and toss well, then add the mint leaves and toss again.

5 Make a bed of green lettuce leaves on each of four individual plates and divide the prawns and sauce among them. Serve the salads immediately.

Cook's Tip
For a really tropical touch, garnish this flavoursome salad with some shavings of fresh coconut (made using a vegetable peeler) or with grated papaya. Use slightly unripe fruit and peel and remove the seeds before grating.

Mackerel with Tomatoes & Pesto

This rich and oily fish contrasts superbly with the slight sharpness of the tomato sauce. The aromatic pesto is excellent drizzled over the fish.

Serves 4
For the pesto sauce
50g/2oz/½ cup pine nuts
30ml/2 tbsp fresh basil leaves
2 garlic cloves, crushed
30ml/2 tbsp freshly grated Parmesan cheese
150ml/¼ pint/⅔ cup extra virgin olive oil

For the fish
4 fresh mackerel, gutted
30ml/2 tbsp olive oil
115g/4oz onion, coarsely chopped
450g/1lb tomatoes, coarsely chopped
salt and ground black pepper

1 To make the pesto sauce, place the pine nuts, basil and garlic cloves in a food processor fitted with a metal blade. Process until the mixture forms a coarse paste. Add the Parmesan cheese and, with the motor still running, gradually add the oil. Set aside in a cool place until required.

2 Preheat the grill (broiler) until very hot. Season the mackerel well with salt and pepper, place on the grill (broiler) rack and cook for 10 minutes on each side.

3 Meanwhile, heat the olive oil in a large, heavy pan over low heat. Add the onion and cook, stirring occasionally, for about 5 minutes, until softened but not coloured.

4 Stir in the tomatoes and cook, stirring occasionally, for 5–10 minutes, until just pulpy. Spoon the tomato mixture on to warmed serving plates, add the fish and top each one with a spoonful of pesto sauce. Serve immediately.

Cook's Tip
The pesto sauce can be made ahead and stored in the refrigerator until needed. Soften it again before using. For red pesto sauce, add some puréed sun-dried tomatoes after the oil.

Prawn Salad Energy 76kcal/319kJ; Protein 9.3g; Carbohydrate 1.5g, of which sugars 1.5g; Fat 3.7g, of which saturates 2.1g; Cholesterol 106mg; Calcium 59mg; Fibre 0.5g; Sodium 132mg.
Mackerel Energy 759kcal/3145kJ; Protein 39.3g; Carbohydrate 6.3g, of which sugars 5.6g; Fat 64.2g, of which saturates 11.6g; Cholesterol 100mg; Calcium 126mg; Fibre 1.8g; Sodium 194mg.

Whitebait with Herb Sandwiches

Whitebait are the tiny fry of sprats or herring and are always served whole. Cayenne pepper makes them spicy hot.

Serves 4
unsalted (sweet) butter,
for spreading
6 slices multigrain bread
90ml/6 tbsp mixed chopped fresh
herbs, such as parsley, chervil
and chives

450g/1lb whitebait, thawed
if frozen
65g/2^1/$_2$ oz/scant ^{3}/$_4$ cup plain
(all-purpose) flour
15ml/1 tbsp chopped
fresh parsley
salt and cayenne pepper
groundnut (peanut) oil, for
deep-frying
lemon slices, to garnish

1 Butter the bread slices. Sprinkle the herbs over three of the slices, then top with the remaining slices of bread. Remove the crusts and cut each sandwich into eight triangles. Place them on a plate, cover with clear film (plastic wrap) and set aside in a cool place.

2 Rinse the whitebait thoroughly under cold running water. Drain and then pat dry on kitchen paper.

3 Put the flour, chopped parsley, salt and cayenne pepper in a large plastic bag and shake to mix. Add the whitebait, a few at a time, and toss gently in the seasoned flour, until lightly coated. Heat the oil in a deep-fat fryer or large, heavy pan to 180°C/350°F, or until a cube of day-old bread browns in 30 seconds.

4 Lower the fish into the hot oil, in batches, and cook for 2–3 minutes, until golden and crisp. Lift out of the oil and drain well on kitchen paper. Keep warm in the oven until all the fish are cooked.

5 Sprinkle the whitebait with salt and more cayenne pepper, if you like, and garnish with the lemon slices. Serve immediately with the herb sandwiches.

Mackerel with Mustard & Lemon

Mackerel must be really fresh to be enjoyed. Look for bright, firm-fleshed fish with iridescent scales and clear, unsunken eyes.

Serves 4
4 fresh mackerel (about
275g/10oz each), gutted
175–225g/6–8oz/1^1/$_2$–2 cups
spinach
salt and ground black pepper

For the mustard and lemon butter
115g/4oz/^{1}/$_2$ cup butter, melted
30ml/2 tbsp wholegrain mustard
grated rind of 1 lemon
30ml/2 tbsp lemon juice
45ml/3 tbsp chopped
fresh parsley

1 To prepare each mackerel, use a sharp knife to cut off the head just behind the gills, then cut along the belly so that the fish can be opened out flat.

2 Place the fish on a chopping board, skin-side up, and press firmly all along the backbone to loosen it.

3 Turn the fish over and carefully pull the bone away from the flesh. Remove the tail and cut each fish in half lengthways. Rinse under cold running water and pat dry with kitchen paper. Score the skin three or four times, then season the fish all over with salt and pepper. Preheat the grill (broiler).

4 To make the mustard and lemon butter, mix together the melted butter, mustard, lemon rind and juice and parsley. Season with salt and pepper.

5 Place the mackerel on a grill (broiler) rack. Brush a little of the flavoured butter over the mackerel and grill (broil), basting occasionally, for 5 minutes on each side, until cooked through.

6 Arrange the spinach leaves in the centres of four large plates. Place the mackerel on top. Heat the remaining mustard and lemon butter in a small pan until sizzling and pour it over the mackerel. Serve immediately.

Mackerel Energy 723kcal/2995kJ; Protein 44.7g; Carbohydrate 1.2g, of which sugars 1.1g; Fat 59.9g, of which saturates 22.5g; Cholesterol 181mg; Calcium 124mg; Fibre 1.4g; Sodium 369mg.
Whitebait Energy 776kcal/3222kJ; Protein 26.7g; Carbohydrate 27.7g, of which sugars 1.8g; Fat 62.9g, of which saturates 10.4g; Cholesterol 21mg; Calcium 1088mg; Fibre 2.3g; Sodium 569mg.

Sole Goujons with Lime Mayonnaise

This simple dish can be rustled up very quickly. It makes an excellent light lunch or supper.

Serves 4
675g/1½lb sole fillets, skinned
2 eggs, beaten
115g/4oz/2 cups fresh
  white breadcrumbs
vegetable oil, for deep-frying
salt and ground black pepper
lime wedges, to serve

For the lime mayonnaise
200ml/7fl oz/scant 1 cup
  mayonnaise
1 small garlic clove, crushed
10ml/2 tsp capers, rinsed
  and chopped
10ml/2 tsp chopped gherkins
finely grated rind of ½ lime
10ml/2 tsp lime juice
15ml/1 tbsp chopped fresh
  coriander (cilantro)

1 To make the lime mayonnaise, mix together the mayonnaise, garlic, capers, gherkins, lime rind and juice and chopped coriander in a bowl. Season to taste with salt and pepper. Transfer to a serving bowl, cover with clear film (plastic wrap) and chill in the refrigerator until required.

2 Cut the sole fillets into finger-length strips. Dip them first into the beaten eggs and then into the breadcrumbs.

3 Heat the oil in a deep-fat fryer or large, heavy pan to 180°C/350°F, or until a cube of day-old bread browns in 30 seconds. Add the fish, in batches, and cook until golden and crisp. Remove from the oil and drain well on kitchen paper.

4 Pile the goujons on to warmed serving plates and serve with the lime wedges for squeezing over. Serve the lime mayonnaise separately.

Cook's Tip
Make sure you use good quality mayonnaise for the sauce, or – better still – make your own. But remember that pregnant women, the elderly and the very young should not eat raw egg.

Spicy Fish Rösti

Serve these delicious fish patties crisp and hot for lunch or supper with a mixed green salad.

Serves 4
350g/12oz large, firm
  waxy potatoes
350g/12oz salmon fillet, skinned
3–4 spring onions (scallions),
  finely chopped
5ml/1 tsp grated fresh root ginger
30ml/2 tbsp chopped fresh
  coriander (cilantro)
10ml/2 tsp lemon juice
30–45ml/2–3 tbsp sunflower oil
salt and cayenne pepper
lemon wedges, to serve
fresh coriander sprigs, to garnish

1 Bring a pan of water to the boil, add the potatoes with their skins on and cook for about 10 minutes. Drain and leave to cool for a few minutes.

2 Meanwhile, finely chop the salmon and place in a bowl. Stir in the spring onions, ginger, chopped coriander and lemon juice. Season to taste with salt and cayenne pepper.

3 When the potatoes are cool enough to handle, peel off the skins and grate the flesh coarsely. Gently stir the grated potato into the fish mixture. Form the mixture into 12 patties, pressing the mixture together but leaving the edges slightly uneven.

4 Heat the oil in a large frying pan over medium heat. Add the fish rösti, a few at a time, and cook for 3 minutes on each side, until golden brown and crisp. Remove from the pan and drain on kitchen paper. Keep warm while you cook the remaining rösti. Serve hot with lemon wedges for squeezing over and garnished with sprigs of fresh coriander.

Variation
You can also make these tasty patties with cod or coley (pollock) fillet or with a mixture of 225g/8oz white fish fillet and 115g/4 oz salmon fillet.

Sole Energy 978kcal/4047kJ; Protein 26.8g; Carbohydrate 25.2g, of which sugars 2.4g; Fat 86.3g, of which saturates 11.1g; Cholesterol 127mg; Calcium 87mg; Fibre 0.1g; Sodium 546mg.
Rösti Energy 208kcal/870kJ; Protein 17.7g; Carbohydrate 14.4g, of which sugars 1.4g; Fat 9.2g, of which saturates 1.2g; Cholesterol 40mg; Calcium 17mg; Fibre 1g; Sodium 63mg.

Mediterranean Fish Rolls

Sun-dried tomatoes, pine nuts and anchovies make a flavoursome stuffing for the fish.

Serves 4

75g/3oz/6 tbsp butter, plus extra
   for greasing
4 plaice or flounder fillets (about
   225g/8oz each), skinned
1 small onion, chopped
1 celery stick, finely chopped
115g/4oz/2 cups fresh
   white breadcrumbs
45ml/3 tbsp chopped
   fresh parsley
30ml/2 tbsp pine nuts, toasted
3–4 pieces sun-dried tomatoes in
   oil, drained and chopped
50g/2oz can anchovy fillets,
   drained and chopped
75ml/5 tbsp fish stock
ground black pepper

1 Preheat the oven to 180°C/350°F/Gas 4. Grease a shallow, ovenproof dish with butter. Using a sharp knife, cut the fish fillets in half lengthways to make eight smaller fillets.

2 Melt the butter in a heavy pan over low heat. Add the onion and celery, cover with a tight-fitting lid and cook, stirring occasionally, for about 15 minutes, until the vegetables are very soft but not coloured.

3 Mix together the breadcrumbs, parsley, pine nuts, sun-dried tomatoes and anchovies in a bowl. Stir in the softened vegetables with the buttery pan juices and season to taste with pepper.

4 Divide the stuffing into eight equal portions. Taking one portion at a time, form the stuffing into balls, then roll up each one inside a fish fillet. Secure each roll with a wooden cocktail stick (toothpick).

5 Place the rolled-up fillets in the prepared dish. Pour the fish stock over them and cover the dish with buttered foil. Bake for about 20 minutes, or until the fish flakes easily with the point of a sharp knife. Remove and discard the cocktail sticks, transfer the fish rolls to warmed plates, drizzle a little of the cooking juices over them and serve immediately.

Salmon with Watercress Sauce

Adding the watercress right at the end of cooking retains much of its flavour and colour.

Serves 4

300ml/½ pint/1¼ cups crème
   fraîche
30ml/2 tbsp chopped
   fresh tarragon
25g/1oz/2 tbsp butter
15ml/1 tbsp sunflower oil
4 salmon fillets, skinned
1 garlic clove, crushed
120ml/4fl oz/½ cup dry
   white wine
1 bunch of watercress or
   rocket (arugula)
salt and ground black pepper
mixed lettuce salad, to
   serve (optional)

1 Gently heat the crème fraîche in a small pan until just it is beginning to boil. Remove the pan from the heat and stir in half the tarragon. Leave the herb cream to infuse (steep) while cooking the fish.

2 Heat the butter and oil in a heavy frying pan over medium heat. Add the salmon fillets and cook for 3–5 minutes on each side. Remove them from the pan and keep warm.

3 Add the garlic to the pan and cook for 1 minute, then pour in the wine and leave it to bubble until it has reduced to about 15ml/1 tbsp.

4 Meanwhile, strip the leaves off the watercress stalks and chop them finely. Discard any damaged leaves. (Save the watercress stalks for soup, if you like.) If using rocket, trim the stems and chop the leaves finely.

5 Strain the herb cream into the frying pan and cook, stirring constantly, for a few minutes, until the sauce has thickened. Stir in the remaining tarragon and watercress or rocket, then cook for a few minutes, until the leaves have wilted but are still bright green. Season to taste with salt and pepper. Place the salmon fillets on warmed plates, spoon the sauce over them and serve immediately. The dish may be accompanied by a mixed lettuce salad if you like.

Fish Rolls Energy 528kcal/2213kJ; Protein 45.9g; Carbohydrate 24.6g, of which sugars 2.8g; Fat 28.1g, of which saturates 11g; Cholesterol 142mg; Calcium 189mg; Fibre 1.3g; Sodium 1100mg.
Salmon 743kcal/3078kJ; Protein 43.3g; Carbohydrate 2.2g, of which sugars 2g; Fat 60.3g, of which saturates 27.8g; Cholesterol 198mg; Calcium 153mg; Fibre 0.6g; Sodium 164mg.

Warm Salmon Salad

This light salad is perfect in summer. Serve it as soon as it is ready, or the salad leaves will lose their colour.

Serves 4
450g/1lb salmon fillet
30ml/2 tbsp sesame oil
grated rind of ½ orange
juice of 1 orange
5ml/1 tsp Dijon mustard
15ml/1 tbsp chopped
   fresh tarragon

45ml/3 tbsp groundnut
   (peanut) oil
115g/4oz fine green beans,
   trimmed
175g/6oz mixed salad leaves,
   such as young spinach leaves,
   radicchio and frisée
15ml/1 tbsp toasted sesame
   seeds
salt and ground black pepper

1 Skin the salmon fillet, if this has not already been done by your fish supplier, and cut the flesh into bitesize pieces with a sharp knife. Set aside.

2 To make the dressing, mix together the sesame oil, orange rind and juice, mustard and chopped tarragon in a bowl and season to taste with salt and ground black pepper. Set aside.

3 Heat the groundnut oil in a heavy frying pan over medium heat. Add the pieces of salmon and cook, stirring occasionally, for 3–4 minutes, or until lightly browned on the outside but still tender on the inside.

4 While the salmon is cooking, blanch the green beans in a pan of boiling salted water for 5–6 minutes, until tender but still slightly crisp.

5 Add the dressing to the salmon, toss together gently and cook for 30 seconds. Remove the pan from the heat.

6 Arrange the salad leaves on serving plates. Drain the beans and toss them over the leaves. Spoon the salmon and its cooking juices over the top, sprinkle with the toasted sesame seeds and serve immediately.

Red Mullet with Fennel

The delicately flavoured, almost sweet flesh of the fish is beautifully complemented by the aniseed-like taste of fennel.

Serves 4
3 small fennel bulbs
60ml/4 tbsp olive oil

2 small onions, sliced
2–4 fresh basil leaves
4 small or 2 large red mullet or
   snapper, gutted
grated rind of ½ lemon
150ml/¼ pint/⅔ cup fish stock
50g/2oz/4 tbsp butter
juice of 1 lemon

1 Snip off the feathery fronds from the fennel bulbs, finely chop and reserve them for the garnish. Cut the fennel bulb into wedges, being careful to leave the layers attached at the root ends so that the pieces stay intact.

2 Heat the oil in a frying pan large enough to take the fish in a single layer. Add the wedges of fennel and the onions and cook over low heat, stirring occasionally, for 10–15 minutes, until softened and lightly browned.

3 Tuck a basil leaf inside the cavity of each fish, then place them on top of the vegetables. Sprinkle the lemon rind on top. Increase the heat to medium, pour in the stock and bring just to the boil. Lower the heat, cover with a tight-fitting lid and poach gently for 15–20 minutes, until the fish is tender.

4 Melt the butter in a small pan and, when it starts to sizzle and colour slightly, add the lemon juice. Pour the flavoured butter over the fish, sprinkle with the reserved fennel fronds and serve immediately.

Cook's Tip
Other fish with fine-flavoured flesh may also be cooked this way. These include sea bass, sea bream, porgy and goatfish. It's best to trim the fins of all types and it is essential with those that have sharp spines.

Salmon Energy 362kcal/1499kJ; Protein 24.3g; Carbohydrate 1.7g, of which sugars 1.4g; Fat 28.7g, of which saturates 5g; Cholesterol 56mg; Calcium 72mg; Fibre 1.3g; Sodium 53mg.
Red Mullet Energy 330kcal/1369kJ; Protein 20.7g; Carbohydrate 4.3g, of which sugars 3.6g; Fat 25.8g, of which saturates 8.1g; Cholesterol 27mg; Calcium 111mg; Fibre 3.4g; Sodium 190mg.

Sautéed Salmon with Cucumber

Cucumber is the classic accompaniment to salmon. Here it is served hot, but be careful not to overcook it.

Serves 4
450g/1lb salmon fillet
40g/1½oz/3 tbsp butter
2 spring onions
  (scallions), chopped
½ cucumber, seeded and cut
  into strips
60ml/4 tbsp dry white wine
120ml/4fl oz/½ cup crème
  fraîche
30ml/2 tbsp chopped fresh chives
2 tomatoes, peeled, seeded and
  diced
salt and ground black pepper

1 Skin the salmon fillet, if this has not already been done by your fish supplier. Using a very sharp knife cut the flesh into about 12 thin slices, then cut across into strips.

2 Melt the butter in a large frying pan over medium-low heat. Add the salmon and cook, stirring occasionally, for 1–2 minutes. Remove the salmon strips using a slotted spoon and set aside.

3 Add the spring onions to the pan and cook for 2 minutes. Stir in the cucumber and sauté for 1–2 minutes, until hot. Remove the cucumber and keep warm with the salmon.

4 Add the wine to the pan and let it bubble until well reduced. Stir in the cucumber, crème fraîche and half the chives and season to taste with salt and pepper. Return the salmon to the pan and warm through gently. Sprinkle the tomatoes and remaining chives over the top. Serve immediately.

> **Cook's Tip**
> To skin a fish fillet, place it on a chopping board with the tail end towards you. Hold a sharp knife at an angle down towards the skin. Cut between the skin and the flesh, keeping the blade as close to the skin as possible. As the flesh is cut away, grasp the skin firmly with your other hand and continue cutting. A little salt sprinkled on your fingers makes this task less slippery.

Tuna with Pan-fried Tomatoes

Meaty and filling tuna steaks are served here with juicy tomatoes and black olives.

Serves 2
2 tuna steaks (about 175g/
  6oz each)
90ml/6 tbsp olive oil
30ml/2 tbsp lemon juice
2 garlic cloves, chopped
5ml/1 tsp chopped fresh thyme
4 canned anchovy fillets, drained
  and chopped
225g/8oz plum tomatoes, halved
30ml/2 tbsp chopped
  fresh parsley
4–6 black olives, pitted
  and chopped
pinch of ground black pepper
crusty bread, to serve

1 Place the tuna steaks in a shallow, non-metallic dish. Mix 60ml/4 tbsp of the oil with the lemon juice, garlic, thyme, anchovies and black pepper in a jug (pitcher). Pour this mixture over the tuna, cover and leave to marinate for at least 1 hour.

2 Preheat the grill (broiler). Lift the tuna from the marinade and place on a grill (broiler) rack. Grill (broil) for 4 minutes on each side, or until the tuna feels firm to touch, basting with the marinade. Take care not to overcook.

3 Meanwhile, heat the remaining oil in a frying pan and cook the tomatoes for a maximum of 2 minutes on each side.

4 Divide the tomatoes equally between two serving plates and sprinkle the chopped parsley and olives over them. Top each with a tuna steak.

5 Add the remaining marinade to the pan juices and warm through. Pour over the tomatoes and tuna steaks and serve immediately with crusty bread for mopping up the juices.

> **Cook's Tip**
> If you are unable to find fresh tuna steaks, you could replace them with salmon fillets, if you like – just grill (broil) them for one or two minutes more on each side.

Tuna Energy 757kcal/3135kJ; Protein 32.8g; Carbohydrate 4.8g, of which sugars 4.5g; Fat 67.7g, of which saturates 18.8g; Cholesterol 130mg; Calcium 93mg; Fibre 2.4g; Sodium 1138mg.
Salmon Energy 412kcal/1709kJ; Protein 24.1g; Carbohydrate 3g, of which sugars 2.8g; Fat 32.8g, of which saturates 15.5g; Cholesterol 111mg; Calcium 54mg; Fibre 0.7g; Sodium 124mg.

Crunchy-topped Cod

It's easy to forget just how tasty and satisfying a simple, classic dish can be.

Serves 4
4 pieces cod fillet (about 115g/4oz each), skinned
2 tomatoes, sliced
50g/2oz/1 cup fresh wholemeal (whole-wheat) breadcrumbs
30ml/2 tbsp chopped fresh parsley
finely grated rind and juice of ½ lemon
5ml/1 tsp sunflower oil
salt and ground black pepper

1 Preheat the oven to 200°C/400°F/Gas 6. Arrange the cod fillets in a wide, ovenproof dish.

2 Arrange the tomato slices on top. Mix together the breadcrumbs, fresh parsley, lemon rind and juice and the oil in a bowl. Season to taste with salt and pepper.

3 Spoon the crumb mixture evenly over the fish, then bake for 15–20 minutes. Serve immediately.

Cook's Tip
Over-fishing of cod – and some other members of the cod family – has reached a critical level in many parts of the world with the result that some stocks have been completely fished-out. Conservation initiatives are having some remedial effect, so it is strongly advised to check that the cod we are buying comes from a sustainable source. Otherwise, we may lose this useful fish with its lovely, white flaky flesh. Other members of the cod family that have not been so popular in recent decades are becoming increasingly available and some would make very acceptable substitutes in this dish. For example, coley, known as pollock in the United States, has a good flavour but is a rather unappealing greyish colour. However, the crunchy topping in this recipe overcomes this drawback. The various types of ling also have a good flavour and a firm texture and this is also true of another lesser known cousin of cod called pollack (not to be confused with pollock).

Fish Balls in Tomato Sauce

This quick meal is a good choice for young children, as there are no bones.

Serves 4
450g/1lb hoki or other white fish fillets, skinned
60ml/4 tbsp fresh wholemeal (whole-wheat) breadcrumbs
30ml/2 tbsp chopped chives or spring onion (scallion)
400g/14oz can chopped tomatoes
50g/2oz button (white) mushrooms, sliced
salt and ground black pepper

1 Cut the fish fillets into chunks; place in a food processor. Add the breadcrumbs, chives or spring onion. Season and process until the fish is chopped, but still with some texture. Divide the fish mixture into about 16 even-sized pieces, then mould them into balls with your hands.

2 Place the tomatoes and mushrooms in a pan; cook over medium heat until boiling. Add the fish balls, cover and simmer for about 10 minutes until cooked. Serve hot.

Tuna & Corn Fish Cakes

These economical tuna fish cakes are quick to make.

Serves 4
300g/11oz/1½ cups mashed potato
200g/7oz can tuna, drained
115g/4oz/½ cup canned corn, drained
30ml/2 tbsp chopped fresh parsley
50g/2oz/1 cup fresh breadcrumbs
salt and ground black pepper

1 Place the mashed potato in a bowl and stir in the tuna, corn and parsley. Season to taste and shape into eight patties.

2 Press the fish cakes into the breadcrumbs to coat them lightly, then place on a baking sheet. Grill (broil) under medium heat until crisp and golden, turning once. Serve immediately.

Cod Energy 160kcal/674kJ; Protein 24.7g; Carbohydrate 11.3g, of which sugars 1.9g; Fat 2g, of which saturates 0.3g; Cholesterol 58mg; Calcium 31mg; Fibre 0.8g; Sodium 175mg.
Fish Balls Energy 167kcal/709kJ; Protein 21.7g; Carbohydrate 14.8g, of which sugars 3.5g; Fat 2.8g, of which saturates 0.5g; Cholesterol 0mg; Calcium 44mg; Fibre 1.5g; Sodium 221mg.
Fish Cakes Energy 231kcal/976kJ; Protein 17.5g; Carbohydrate 29.8g, of which sugars 4.4g; Fat 5.5g, of which saturates 0.9g; Cholesterol 25mg; Calcium 53mg; Fibre 2.1g; Sodium 330mg.

Cod Creole

Inspired by the cuisine of the Caribbean, this lightly spiced fish dish is both colourful and delicious, as well as being quick and easy to prepare.

Serves 4

450g/1lb cod fillets
15ml/1 tbsp lime or lemon juice
10ml/2 tsp olive oil
1 onion, finely chopped
1 green (bell) pepper, seeded and sliced
2.5ml/½ tsp cayenne pepper
2.5ml/½ tsp garlic salt
425g/14oz can chopped tomatoes
boiled rice or potatoes, to serve

1 Skin the cod fillets if this has not already been done by your fish supplier, then cut the flesh into bitesize chunks and sprinkle with the lime or lemon juice.

2 Heat the oil in a large, non-stick frying pan over low heat. Add the onion and green pepper and cook, stirring occasionally, for about 5 minutes, until softened. Add the cayenne pepper and garlic salt.

3 Stir in the cod and the chopped tomatoes, increase the heat to medium and bring to the boil. Lower the heat, cover and simmer for about 5 minutes, or until the fish flakes easily. Transfer the fish and sauce to warmed plates and serve immediately with boiled rice or potatoes.

> **Cook's Tip**
> *This flavoursome dish is surprisingly light in calories and low in fat, so if you are worried about your waistline or conscientious about a healthy diet, this would be an excellent choice. In addition, (bell) peppers are a good source of vitamin C, while tomatoes are rich in the antioxidant lycopene, which is thought to lower the risk of some cancers. Processed and cooked tomatoes – in this case, canned tomatoes – are an even richer source because processing or cooking them makes it easier for the body to absorb lycopene.*

Salmon Pasta with Parsley Sauce

The parsley sauce is prepared and added at the last moment to the salmon mixture and does not have to be cooked separately.

Serves 4

450g/1lb salmon fillet
225g/8oz/2 cups pasta, such as penne
175g/6oz cherry tomatoes, halved
150ml/¼ pint/⅔ cup crème fraîche or sour cream
45ml/3 tbsp finely chopped fresh parsley
finely grated rind of ½ orange
salt and ground black pepper

1 Skin the salmon if this has not already been done by your fish supplier and cut the flesh into bitesize pieces. Spread out the pieces of fish on a heatproof plate and cover with foil.

2 Bring a large pan of salted water to the boil, add the pasta and bring back to the boil. Place the plate of salmon on top of the pan and cook for 10–12 minutes, until the pasta is just tender and the salmon is cooked.

3 Set the plate of salmon aside, then drain the pasta and return it to the pan. Add the tomatoes and salmon to the pasta and toss well.

4 Mix together the crème fraîche or sour cream, parsley and orange rind in a bowl and season with pepper to taste. Add the parsley sauce to the salmon and pasta, toss again and serve hot or leave to cool to room temperature.

> **Variations**
> *• Sea trout, also known as salmon trout, would also be beautifully complemented by the parsley sauce in this recipe. Other, perhaps less obvious substitutes could be gurnard (US sea robin) fillets.*
> *• You could also try using trout fillets and substitute grated lemon rind for the orange.*

Cod Energy 144kcal/607kJ; Protein 22.1g; Carbohydrate 7.9g, of which sugars 7.4g; Fat 2.9g, of which saturates 0.5g; Cholesterol 52mg; Calcium 26mg; Fibre 2.2g; Sodium 81mg.
Salmon Energy 469kcal/1971kJ; Protein 31.2g; Carbohydrate 45.4g, of which sugars 5g; Fat 19.3g, of which saturates 6.1g; Cholesterol 56mg; Calcium 100mg; Fibre 2.8g; Sodium 75mg.

Monkfish with Mexican Salsa

It is rare to see whole monkfish on sale generally, as only the tail is eaten. Apart from its delicious flavour and meaty texture, the tail has the advantage of having no pinbones.

Serves 4
675g/1½lb monkfish tail
45ml/3 tbsp olive oil
30ml/2 tbsp lime juice
1 garlic clove, crushed
15ml/1 tbsp chopped fresh
  coriander (cilantro)
salt and ground black pepper
fresh coriander sprigs and lime
  slices, to garnish

For the salsa
4 tomatoes, seeded, peeled
  and diced
1 avocado, stoned (pitted), peeled
  and diced
½ red onion, chopped
1 green chilli, seeded
  and chopped
30ml/2 tbsp chopped
  fresh coriander
30ml/2 tbsp olive oil
15ml/1 tbsp lime juice

1 To make the salsa, mix all the salsa ingredients and leave to stand at room temperature for about 40 minutes.

2 Prepare the monkfish. Using a sharp knife, remove the pinkish-grey membrane. Cut the fillets from either side of the backbone, then cut each fillet in half to give four steaks.

3 Mix together the oil, lime juice, garlic and coriander in a shallow non-metallic dish and season with salt and pepper. Turn the monkfish several times to coat with the marinade, then cover the dish and leave to marinate in a cool place or in the refrigerator, for 30 minutes. Preheat the grill (broiler).

4 Remove the monkfish from the marinade and grill (broil) for 10–12 minutes, turning once and brushing frequently with the marinade until cooked through.

5 Serve the monkfish garnished with coriander sprigs and lime slices and accompanied by the salsa.

Seafood Crêpes

The combination of fresh and smoked haddock imparts a wonderful flavour to the crêpe filling.

Serves 4–6
12 ready-made crêpes
melted butter, for brushing

For the filling
225g/8oz smoked haddock fillet
225g/8oz fresh haddock fillet

300ml/½ pint/1¼ cups milk
150ml/¼ pint/⅔ cup single
  (light) cream
40g/1½oz/3 tbsp butter
40g/1½oz/3 tbsp plain (all-
  purpose) flour
pinch of freshly grated nutmeg
2 hard-boiled eggs, shelled
  and chopped
salt and ground black pepper
sprinkling of Gruyère cheese and
  curly salad leaves, to serve

1 To make the filling, put the smoked and fresh haddock fillets in a large pan, add the milk and bring just to the boil. Lower the heat, cover and poach for 6–8 minutes, until just tender. Lift out the fish with a slotted spoon and, when cool enough to handle, remove the skin and bones. Reserve the milk. Pour the cream into a measuring jug (cup), then strain enough milk into the jug to make it up to 450ml/¾ pint/scant 2 cups.

2 Melt the butter in a pan over low heat. Stir in the flour and cook, stirring constantly, for 1 minute. Gradually add the milk mixture, stirring constantly to make a smooth sauce. Cook for 2–3 minutes. Season to taste with salt, pepper and nutmeg. Flake the haddock and fold into the sauce with the eggs. Remove the pan from the heat and leave to cool.

3 Preheat the oven to 180°C/350°F/Gas 4. Divide the filling among the crêpes. Fold the sides of each crêpe into the centre, then roll them up to enclose the filling completely. Brush four or six individual ovenproof dishes with melted butter and arrange two or three filled crêpes in each, or grease one large dish for all the crêpes. Brush the crêpes with melted butter and cook for 15 minutes.

4 Sprinkle over the Gruyère and cook for a further 5 minutes. Serve hot with a few curly salad leaves.

Monkfish Energy 320kcal/1335kJ; Protein 31g; Carbohydrate 4.9g, of which sugars 4.2g; Fat 19.6g, of which saturates 3.3g; Cholesterol 27mg; Calcium 36mg; Fibre 2.3g; Sodium 46mg.
Seafood Energy 567kcal/2373kJ; Protein 24.9g; Carbohydrate 47.8g, of which sugars 20.1g; Fat 32.1g, of which saturates 7.1g; Cholesterol 118mg; Calcium 188mg; Fibre 1.2g; Sodium 445mg.

Herbed Fish Croquettes

Deep-fry with clean oil every time as the fish will flavour the oil and taint any other foods later fried in it.

Serves 4
450g/1lb plaice or flounder fillets
300ml/¹/₂ pint/1¹/₄ cups milk
450g/1lb cooked potatoes
1 fennel bulb, finely chopped
1 garlic clove, finely chopped
45ml/3 tbsp chopped fresh parsley
2 eggs
15g/¹/₂oz/1 tbsp unsalted (sweet) butter
225g/8oz/2 cups white breadcrumbs
30ml/2 tbsp sesame seeds
vegetable oil, for deep-frying
salt and ground black pepper

1 Put the fish fillets in a large pan, add the milk and bring just to the boil. Lower the heat, cover and poach gently for about 15 minutes, until the fish flakes easily with the tip of a knife. Remove the fillets with a slotted spoon and set aside until cool enough to handle. Reserve the milk.

2 Remove the skin and any bones from the fish and coarsely flake the flesh. Put the fish, potatoes, fennel, garlic, parsley, eggs and butter in a food processor fitted with a metal blade and process until thoroughly combined.

3 Add 30ml/2 tbsp of the reserved cooking milk, season to taste with salt and pepper and process briefly again.

4 Scrape the fish mixture into a bowl, cover with clear film (plastic wrap) and chill in the refrigerator for about 30 minutes.

5 Using your hands shape the fish mixture into 20 croquettes. Mix together the breadcrumbs and sesame seeds on a shallow plate. Roll the croquettes in the breadcrumb mixture to form a good coating.

6 Heat the oil in a large heavy pan to 180°C/350°F, or until a cube of day-old bread browns in 30 seconds. Deep-fry the croquettes, in batches, for about 4 minutes until golden brown. Drain well on kitchen paper and serve immediately.

Mixed Smoked Fish Kedgeree

An ideal breakfast dish on a cold weekend morning and a classic for brunch. Garnish with quartered hard-boiled eggs and season well.

Serves 6
450g/1lb mixed smoked fish such as smoked cod, smoked haddock and smoked mussels or oysters
300ml/¹/₂ pint/1¹/₄ cups milk
175g/6oz/scant 1 cup long grain rice
1 slice of lemon
50g/2oz/4 tbsp butter
5ml/1 tsp medium-hot curry powder
2.5ml/¹/₂ tsp freshly grated nutmeg
15ml/1 tbsp chopped fresh parsley
salt and ground black pepper
2 hard-boiled eggs, to garnish

1 Put the fish, but not the shellfish, in a large pan, add the milk and bring just to the boil. Lower the heat, cover and poach for 10 minutes, or until it flakes easily with the tip of a knife.

2 Remove the fish with a slotted spoon and set aside until cool enough to handle. Discard the milk. Remove the skin and any bones from the fish and flake the flesh. Mix with the smoked shellfish in a bowl and set aside.

3 Bring a pan of salted water to the boil, add the rice and slice of lemon and boil for 10 minutes, or according to the instructions on the packet, until just tender. Drain well and discard the lemon.

4 Melt the butter in a large frying pan and add the rice and fish. Shake the pan to mix all the ingredients together.

5 Stir in the curry powder, nutmeg, parsley and seasoning. Serve immediately, garnished with quartered eggs.

> **Cook's Tip**
> When flaking the fish, keep the pieces fairly large to give the dish a chunky consistency.

Croquettes Energy 625kcal/2627kJ; Protein 35.9g; Carbohydrate 63.3g, of which sugars 4.3g; Fat 27.3g, of which saturates 5.8g; Cholesterol 246mg; Calcium 252mg; Fibre 4.6g; Sodium 681mg.
Kedgeree Energy 250kcal/1044kJ; Protein 17.7g; Carbohydrate 25.8g, of which sugars 2.5g; Fat 8.3g, of which saturates 5g; Cholesterol 55mg; Calcium 79mg; Fibre 0.1g; Sodium 950mg.

Spanish-style Hake

Hugely popular in Spain, hake is an unfairly neglected fish in many other countries.

Serves 4

30ml/2 tbsp olive oil
25g/1oz/2 tbsp butter
1 onion, chopped
3 garlic cloves, crushed
15g/½oz/1 tbsp plain (all-purpose) flour
2.5ml/½ tsp paprika
4 hake steaks (about 175g/6oz each)
250g/8oz fine green beans, cut into 2.5cm/1in lengths
350ml/12fl oz/1½ cups fresh fish stock
150ml/¼ pint/⅔ cup dry white wine
30ml/2 tbsp dry sherry
15–20 live mussels, scrubbed and debearded
45ml/3 tbsp chopped fresh parsley
salt and ground black pepper
crusty bread, to serve

1 Heat the oil and butter in a sauté or frying pan over low heat. Add the onion and cook, stirring occasionally, for about 5 minutes, until softened but not coloured. Add the garlic and cook for 1 minute more.

2 Mix together the flour and paprika, then lightly dust the hake with the mixture, shaking off any excess. Push the sautéed onion and garlic to one side of the pan.

3 Add the hake steaks to the pan and cook until golden on both sides. Stir in the beans, stock, wine and sherry and season to taste with salt and pepper. Bring to the boil and cook for about 2 minutes.

4 Discard any mussels with broken shells or that do not shut immediately when sharply tapped. Add the mussels and parsley to the pan, cover with a tight-fitting lid and cook for 5–8 minutes, until the mussels have opened. Discard any mussels that have remained closed.

5 Divide the hake, mussels and vegetables among warmed, shallow soup bowls and serve immediately with crusty bread to mop up the juices.

Fish Goujons

Any white fish fillets can be used to make these goujons – you could try a mixture of haddock and cod.

Serves 4

60ml/4 tbsp mayonnaise
30ml/2 tbsp natural (plain) yogurt
grated rind of ½ lemon
squeeze of lemon juice
15ml/1 tbsp chopped fresh parsley
15ml/1 tbsp capers, drained and chopped
2 sole fillets (about 175g/6oz each)
2 plaice or flounder fillets (about 175g/6oz each)
1 egg
115g/4oz/2 cups fresh white breadcrumbs
15ml/1 tbsp sesame seeds
pinch of paprika
vegetable oil, for deep-frying
salt and ground black pepper
watercress or mizuna, to garnish
4 lemon wedges, to serve

1 To make the lemon mayonnaise, mix the mayonnaise, yogurt, lemon rind and juice, parsley and capers in a bowl. Cover with clear film (plastic wrap) and chill until required.

2 Skin the fish fillets if this has not already been done by your fish supplier and cut them into thin strips with a sharp knife.

3 Lightly beat the egg in a shallow bowl with a fork. Mix together the breadcrumbs, sesame seeds and paprika in another shallow bowl and season with salt and pepper.

4 Dip the fish strips, one at a time, first into the beaten egg, then into the breadcrumb mixture and toss until coated evenly. Lay on a clean plate.

5 Heat about 2.5cm/1in of vegetable oil in a frying pan to 180°C/350°F, or until a cube of day-old bread browns in 30 seconds. Add the fish strips, in batches, and cook for 2–3 minutes, until lightly golden brown all over.

6 Remove with a slotted spoon, drain on kitchen paper and keep warm while frying the remainder. Garnish with watercress or mizuna. Serve with lemon wedges and lemon mayonnaise.

Hake Energy 338kcal/1409kJ; Protein 35.6g; Carbohydrate 6.9g, of which sugars 2.7g; Fat 15.2g, of which saturates 4.7g; Cholesterol 62mg; Calcium 68mg; Fibre 1.7g; Sodium 264mg.
Goujons Energy 482kcal/1997kJ; Protein 8.1g; Carbohydrate 24.5g, of which sugars 1.6g; Fat 39.7g, of which saturates 4.9g; Cholesterol 31mg; Calcium 126mg; Fibre 0.1g; Sodium 486mg.

Pan-fried Garlic Sardines

Lightly fry a sliced garlic clove to garnish the fish. This dish could also be made with sprats or fresh anchovies, if available.

4 garlic cloves
finely grated rind of 2 lemons
30ml/2 tbsp chopped
   fresh parsley
salt and ground black pepper

Serves 4
1.2kg/2½lb fresh sardines
30ml/2 tbsp olive oil

For the tomato bread
8 slices crusty bread, toasted
2 large ripe beefsteak tomatoes

1 First, scale the sardines. Hold each fish by the tail under cold running water and run your other hand all along the body from tail to head to scrape off the scales. Cut off the fish heads if you like. Slit open the belly of each fish, using a sharp knife, and remove the guts with your fingers. Rinse the body cavities well under cold running water and pat dry with kitchen paper.

2 Heat the olive oil in a heavy frying pan over medium-low heat. Add the garlic cloves and cook, stirring frequently, for 1–2 minutes, until softened.

3 Add the sardines to the pan and cook, turning once, for 4–5 minutes until light golden brown. Sprinkle the lemon rind and parsley over the fish and season to taste with salt and black pepper.

4 Cut the tomatoes in half and rub them on to the toast. Discard the skins. Serve the sardines with the tomato toast.

> **Cook's Tips**
> • Scaling the sardines is, without question, a very messy and time-consuming business. However, the fish are so much nicer to eat when scaled that it is worth the effort. (Clear the discarded scales from the sink afterwards.)
> • Make sure you use very ripe beefsteak tomatoes for this dish so they will rub on to the toast easily.

Sea Bass en Papillote

Bring the unopened parcels to the table and let your guests uncover their own fish to release the delicious aroma of this dish.

130g/4½oz/generous
   ½ cup butter
450g/1lb spinach, coarse
   stalks removed
3 shallots, finely chopped
60ml/4 tbsp white wine
4 bay leaves
salt and ground black pepper

Serves 4
4 small sea bass, scaled, gutted
   and with fins trimmed

1 Preheat the oven to 180°C/350°F/Gas 4. Season both the inside and outside of the fish with salt and pepper.

2 Melt 50g/2oz/4 tbsp of the butter in a large, heavy pan over low heat. Add the spinach and cook gently, turning once or twice, until the spinach has broken down into a smooth purée. Remove from the heat and set aside to cool.

3 Melt another 50g/2oz/4 tbsp of the butter in a clean pan over low heat. Add the shallots and cook, stirring occasionally, for 5 minutes, until soft. Add to the spinach and leave to cool, then divide the spinach mixture among the cavities of the fish.

4 For each fish, fold a large sheet of greaseproof (waxed) paper in half, lay the fish on one half and cut around it to make a heart shape when opened out. The paper should be at least 5cm/2in larger all round than the fish. Remove the fish from the paper hearts.

5 Melt the remaining butter and brush a little on to the paper. Replace the fish and add 15ml/1 tbsp wine and a bay leaf to each parcel. Fold the other side of the paper over the fish and make small pleats to seal the two edges, starting at the curve of the heart. Brush the outsides with butter.

5 Transfer the parcels to a baking sheet and bake for 20–25 minutes, until the parcels are brown. Lift the parcels on to warmed plates with a metal spatula and serve immediately.

Sardines Energy 513kcal/2149kJ; Protein 47.4g; Carbohydrate 27.9g, of which sugars 4.5g; Fat 24.1g, of which saturates 5.8g; Cholesterol 0mg; Calcium 279mg; Fibre 2g; Sodium 504mg.
Sea Bass Energy 446kcal/1850kJ; Protein 35.2g; Carbohydrate 2.3g, of which sugars 2.1g; Fat 31.8g, of which saturates 17.7g; Cholesterol 201mg; Calcium 414mg; Fibre 2.4g; Sodium 469mg.

Chilli Prawns

This delightful, spicy combination makes a lovely light main course for an informal supper.

Serves 3–4

45ml/3 tbsp olive oil
2 shallots, chopped
2 garlic cloves, chopped
1 fresh red chilli, chopped
450g/1lb ripe tomatoes, peeled, seeded and chopped

15ml/1 tbsp tomato purée (paste)
1 bay leaf
1 fresh thyme sprig
90ml/6 tbsp dry white wine
450g/1lb/4 cups cooked peeled large prawns (shrimp)
salt and ground black pepper
coarsely torn fresh basil leaves, to garnish

1 Heat the olive oil in a pan over low heat. Add the shallots, garlic and chilli and cook, stirring occasionally, for about 5 minutes, until the shallots have softened and the garlic starts to brown.

2 Increase the heat to medium, add the tomatoes, tomato purée, bay leaf, thyme sprig and wine and season to taste with salt and pepper. Bring to the boil, then lower the heat and simmer gently, stirring occasionally, for about 10 minutes, until the sauce has thickened. Remove and discard the bay leaf and thyme sprig.

3 Stir the prawns into the sauce and heat through for a few minutes. Taste and adjust the seasoning if necessary. Sprinkle the basil leaves over the top and serve immediately.

Cook's Tip
Avoid buying frozen cooked prawns (shrimp), if possible, as they often have a soggy texture and poor flavour, especially if they have been peeled before freezing. If freshly cooked prawns are not available, then consider using raw prawns and cook them in the sauce a little longer or pan-fry or boil them until they change colour before adding them in step 3.

Scallops with Ginger

Scallops are at their best in winter. Rich and creamy, this dish is very simple to make and quite delicious.

Serves 4
8–12 shelled scallops
40g/1½oz/3 tbsp butter

2.5cm/1in piece fresh root ginger, finely chopped
1 bunch of spring onions (scallions), sliced diagonally
60ml/4 tbsp white vermouth
250ml/8fl oz/1 cup crème fraîche
salt and ground black pepper
chopped fresh parsley, to garnish

1 Remove the white muscle opposite the coral on each scallop if this has not already been done by your supplier. Separate the coral from the white part and cut the white part of the scallop in half horizontally. Reserve the corals.

2 Melt the butter in a frying pan over medium heat. Add the scallops, including the corals, and sauté for about 2 minutes until lightly browned. Take care not to overcook the scallops as this will toughen them.

3 Lift out the scallops with a slotted spoon and transfer to a warmed serving dish. Keep warm.

4 Add the ginger and spring onions to the pan and stir-fry for 2 minutes. Pour in the vermouth and leave to bubble until it has almost evaporated. Stir in the crème fraîche and cook for a few minutes until the sauce has thickened. Season to taste with salt and pepper.

5 Pour the sauce over the scallops, sprinkle with parsley and serve immediately.

Cook's Tip
The orange-coloured coral of the scallop is the roe and this, with the round, white adductor muscle, this comprises the edible part. In Europe the coral is regarded as a delicacy, although in the United States it is usually discarded.

Prawns Energy 202kcal/845kJ; Protein 21g; Carbohydrate 5.4g, of which sugars 5g; Fat 9.3g, of which saturates 1.4g; Cholesterol 219mg; Calcium 104mg; Fibre 1.5g; Sodium 234mg.
Scallops Energy 392kcal/1621kJ; Protein 13.6g; Carbohydrate 4.5g, of which sugars 2.5g; Fat 34.1g, of which saturates 22.4g; Cholesterol 115mg; Calcium 63mg; Fibre 0.4g; Sodium 168mg.

Cod with Spiced Red Lentils

This is a very tasty, filling and economical dish, with the added bonus of being a healthy option.

Serves 4

175g/6oz/³/₄ cup red lentils
1.25ml/¼ tsp ground turmeric
600ml/1 pint/2½ cups fish stock
450g/1lb cod fillets
30ml/2 tbsp vegetable oil
7.5ml/1½ tsp cumin seeds
15ml/1 tbsp grated fresh
   root ginger
2.5ml/½ tsp cayenne pepper
15ml/1 tbsp lemon or lime juice
30ml/2 tbsp chopped fresh
   coriander (cilantro)
pinch of salt, to taste
fresh coriander leaves and lemon
   or lime wedges, to garnish

1 Put the lentils in a pan with the turmeric and fish stock. Bring to the boil, then lower the heat, cover with a tight-fitting lid and simmer for 20–25 minutes, until the lentils are just tender. Remove from the heat, season with salt and set aside.

2 Meanwhile, skin the cod fillets if this has not already been done by your supplier and cut the flesh into large chunks with a sharp knife. Place the pieces on a plate, cover with clear film (plastic wrap) and store in the refrigerator until required.

3 Heat the oil in a small, heavy frying pan over medium-low heat. Add the cumin seeds and cook, stirring occasionally, until they begin to pop and give off their aroma, then add the grated ginger and cayenne pepper. Stir-fry the spices for a few seconds more, then pour the mixture on to the lentils. Add the lemon or lime juice and the chopped coriander and stir them gently into the mixture.

4 Lay the pieces of cod on top of the lentils, cover the pan and then cook gently over low heat for 10–15 minutes, or until the fish is tender and cooked through.

5 Spoon the cod and lentil mixture on to warmed individual plates. Sprinkle the the whole coriander leaves over the top and garnish each serving with one or two lemon or lime wedges. Serve immediately.

Smoked Trout Pilaff

Smoked trout might seem a rather unusual partner for rice, but if you try it, you will find that this is a winning combination.

Serves 4

225g/8oz/1¼ cups white
   basmati rice
40g/1½oz/3 tbsp butter
2 onions, sliced into rings
1 garlic clove, crushed
2 bay leaves
2 whole cloves
2 green cardamom pods
2 cinnamon sticks
5ml/1 tsp cumin seeds
4 smoked trout fillets, skinned
50g/2oz/½ cup slivered
   almonds, toasted
50g/2oz/generous ½ cup
   seedless raisins
30ml/2 tbsp chopped
   fresh parsley or
   coriander (cilantro)
mango chutney and poppadoms,
   to serve

1 Wash the rice thoroughly in several changes of water and, if there is time, leave to soak in cold water for 10–15 minutes. Drain well and set aside.

2 Melt the butter in a large pan over low heat. Add the onions and cook, stirring occasionally, for 10–20 minutes, until well browned.

3 Increase the heat, add the garlic, bay leaves, cloves, cardamom pods, cinnamon and cumin seeds and stir-fry for 1 minute.

4 Stir in the rice, then add 600ml/1 pint/2½ cups boiling water. Bring back to the boil, cover the pan with a tight-fitting lid, lower the heat and cook very gently for 20–25 minutes, until the water has been absorbed and the rice is tender.

5 Flake the smoked trout and add to the pan with the almonds and raisins. Fork through gently, then re-cover the pan and leave the smoked trout to warm in the rice for a few minutes.

6 Transfer the pilaff to warmed plates, sprinkle the parsley or coriander over the top and serve immediately with mango chutney and poppadoms.

Trout Energy 536kcal/2238kJ; Protein 27.8g; Carbohydrate 62.5g, of which sugars 14.9g; Fat 19.6g, of which saturates 5.8g; Cholesterol 21mg; Calcium 90mg; Fibre 2.8g; Sodium 130mg.
Cod Energy 279kcal/1174kJ; Protein 31g; Carbohydrate 24.6g, of which sugars 1.1g; Fat 6.9g, of which saturates 0.9g; Cholesterol 52mg; Calcium 33mg; Fibre 2.2g; Sodium 83mg.

Mediterranean Fish Stew

Use any combination of white fish you like in this tasty stew.

Serves 4

225g/8oz/2 cups cooked prawns (shrimp) in the shell
450g/1lb mixed white fish fillets, skinned and chopped (reserve skins for the stock)
45ml/3 tbsp olive oil
1 onion, chopped
1 leek, sliced
1 carrot, diced
1 garlic clove, chopped
2.5ml/½ tsp ground turmeric
150ml/¼ pint/⅔ cup dry white wine or (hard) cider
400g/14oz can chopped tomatoes
sprig of fresh parsley, thyme and fennel
1 bay leaf
small piece of orange rind
1 prepared squid, body cut into rings and tentacles chopped
12 fresh mussels, scrubbed
salt and ground black pepper
30–45ml/2–3 tbsp fresh Parmesan cheese shavings and fresh parsley, to garnish

For the rouille sauce
2 slices white bread, crusts removed
2 garlic cloves, crushed
½ fresh red chilli
15ml/1 tbsp tomato purée (paste)
45–60ml/3–4 tbsp olive oil

1 Remove the heads and peel the prawns, leaving the tails intact. Reserve the shells and devein the prawns. Make a stock by simmering the prawn shells and fish skins in 450ml/¾ pint/scant 2 cups water for 20 minutes. Strain and reserve.

2 Heat the oil in a large pan. Add the onion, leek, carrot and garlic and cook, stirring occasionally, for 6–7 minutes. Stir in the turmeric and add the wine, tomatoes, reserved stock, herbs and orange rind. Bring to the boil, cover and simmer for 20 minutes.

3 To make the rouille sauce, process all the sauce ingredients in a food processor or blender.

4 Add the fish and seafood to the pan and simmer for 5–6 minutes, until the mussels open. Remove the bay leaf and rind and season to taste. Serve with a spoonful of the rouille, garnished with Parmesan cheese and parsley.

Salmon with Herb Butter

Other fresh herbs could be used to flavour the butter – try mint, fennel, flat leaf parsley or oregano.

Serves 4

50g/2oz/4 tbsp butter, softened, plus extra for greasing
finely grated rind of ½ small lemon
15ml/1 tbsp lemon juice
15ml/1 tbsp chopped fresh dill
4 salmon steaks
2 lemon slices, halved
4 fresh dill sprigs
salt and ground black pepper

1 Place the butter, lemon rind, lemon juice and chopped dill in a small bowl, season with salt and pepper and mix together with a fork until thoroughly blended.

2 Spoon the butter on to a piece of greaseproof (waxed) paper and roll up, smoothing with your hands into a neat sausage shape. Twist the ends of the paper tightly, wrap in clear film (plastic wrap) and place in the freezer for about 20 minutes, until firm.

3 Meanwhile, preheat the oven to 190°C/375°F/Gas 5. Cut out four squares of foil each big enough to enclose a salmon steak and grease lightly with butter. Place a salmon steak in the centre of each square.

4 Remove the herb butter from the freezer, unwrap and slice into eight rounds. Place two rounds on top of each salmon steak, then place a halved lemon slice in the centre and a sprig of dill on top. Lift up the edges of the foil and crinkle them together until they are well sealed.

5 Lift the parcels on to a baking sheet and bake for about 20 minutes, until the fish is cooked through. (Loosen the top of one parcel to check, if necessary.)

6 Remove from the oven and transfer the unopened parcels to warmed plates with a fish slice or metal spatula. Open the parcels and slide the contents on to the plates with the cooking juices. Serve immediately.

Fish Stew Energy 505kcal/2112kJ; Protein 51.7g; Carbohydrate 15.8g, of which sugars 7.8g; Fat 23.8g, of which saturates 5.4g; Cholesterol 349mg; Calcium 252mg; Fibre 3.1g; Sodium 520mg.
Salmon Energy 364kcal/1511kJ; Protein 30.5g; Carbohydrate 0.2g, of which sugars 0.1g; Fat 26.8g, of which saturates 9.4g; Cholesterol 102mg; Calcium 39mg; Fibre 0.1g; Sodium 144mg.

Spanish Seafood Paella

Use monkfish instead of the cod, if you like, and add a red mullet or snapper cut into chunks.

Serves 4

60ml/4 tbsp olive oil
225g/8oz cod, skinned and cut into chunks
3 prepared baby squid, body cut into rings and tentacles chopped
1 onion, chopped
3 garlic cloves, finely chopped
1 red (bell) pepper, seeded and sliced
4 tomatoes, peeled and chopped

225g/8oz/1¼ cups Valencia or risotto rice
450ml/¾ pint/scant 2 cups fish stock
150ml/¼ pint/⅔ cup dry white wine
75g/3oz/¼ cup frozen peas
4–5 saffron threads, soaked in 30ml/2 tbsp hot water
115g/4oz/1 cup cooked peeled prawns (shrimp)
8 fresh mussels, scrubbed and debearded
salt and ground black pepper
15ml/1 tbsp chopped fresh parsley, to garnish
lemon wedges, to serve

1 Heat 30ml/2 tbsp of the olive oil in a heavy frying pan over medium heat. Add the cod and squid and stir-fry for 2 minutes. Transfer to a bowl.

2 Heat the remaining oil in the pan over low heat. Add the onion, garlic and red pepper and cook, stirring occasionally, for 6–7 minutes, until softened but not coloured.

3 Stir in the tomatoes and cook for a further 2 minutes, then add the rice, stirring to coat the grains with oil, and cook for 2–3 minutes more. Pour in the fish stock and wine and add the peas and saffron with its soaking water. Season to taste with salt and pepper.

4 Gently stir in the reserved cooked fish with all the juices, followed by the prawns. Push the mussels into the rice. Cover with a tight-fitting lid and cook over low heat for about 30 minutes, or until the stock has been absorbed. Remove from the heat, keep covered and leave to stand for 5 minutes. Sprinkle with parsley and serve with lemon wedges.

Spaghetti with Seafood Sauce

The tomato-based sauce in this dish is a traditional marinara, popular in Italy's coastal regions.

Serves 4

45ml/3 tbsp olive oil
1 onion, chopped
1 garlic clove, finely chopped
225g/8oz spaghetti
600ml/1 pint/2½ cups passata (bottled strained tomatoes)
15ml/1 tbsp tomato purée (paste)

5ml/1 tsp dried oregano
1 bay leaf
5ml/1 tsp sugar
225g/8 oz/2 cups cooked peeled prawns (shrimp)
175g/6oz cooked clam or cockle meat (rinsed well if canned or bottled)
15ml/1 tbsp lemon juice
45ml/3 tbsp chopped fresh parsley
25g/1oz/2 tbsp butter
salt and ground black pepper
4 cooked prawns, to garnish

1 Heat the olive oil in a large pan over low heat. Add the onion and garlic and cook, stirring occasionally, for 6–7 minutes, until softened but not coloured.

2 Meanwhile, cook the spaghetti in a large pan of boiling salted water for 10–12 minutes, or according to the instructions on the packet, until just tender.

3 Stir the passata, tomato purée, oregano, bay leaf and sugar into the onion mixture and season to taste with salt and pepper. Bring to the boil, then simmer for 2–3 minutes.

4 Add the prawns, clams or cockles, lemon juice and 30ml/2 tbsp of the parsley. Stir well, then cover and cook for a further 6–7 minutes.

5 Drain the spaghetti, return to the pan and add the butter. Using two large spoons, toss well to coat, then season with salt and pepper.

6 Divide the spaghetti among four warmed plates and top with the seafood sauce. Sprinkle with the remaining parsley, garnish with whole prawns and serve immediately.

Paella Energy 478kcal/1998kJ; Protein 29.8g; Carbohydrate 53.1g, of which sugars 6.9g; Fat 13.4g, of which saturates 2g; Cholesterol 198mg; Calcium 74mg; Fibre 2.1g; Sodium 181mg.
Spaghetti Energy 414kcal/1749kJ; Protein 28.3g; Carbohydrate 48.8g, of which sugars 7.8g; Fat 13.2g, of which saturates 3.5g; Cholesterol 198mg; Calcium 131mg; Fibre 2.9g; Sodium 1818mg.

Deep-fried Spicy Whitebait

This is a delicious British dish – serve these tiny fish very hot and crisp.

Serves 4
450g/1lb whitebait
40g/1½oz/3 tbsp plain (all-purpose) flour
5ml/1 tsp paprika
pinch of cayenne pepper
12 fresh parsley sprigs
vegetable oil, for deep-frying
salt and ground black pepper
4 lemon wedges, to garnish

1 If using frozen whitebait, thaw in the bag, then drain off any water. Spread out the fish on kitchen paper and pat dry.

2 Place the flour, paprika and cayenne in a large plastic bag and add salt and pepper. Add the whitebait, in batches, and shake gently until all the fish are lightly coated with the flour mixture. Transfer to a plate.

3 Heat about 5cm/2in of oil in a pan or deep-fat fryer to 190°C/375°F, or until a cube of day-old bread browns in about 30 seconds.

4 Add the whitebait, in batches, and deep-fry in the hot oil for 2–3 minutes, until the coating is lightly golden and crisp. Remove from the pan with a slotted spoon, drain on kitchen paper and keep warm in the oven while frying the remainder.

5 When all the whitebait is cooked, drop the sprigs of parsley into the hot oil (don't worry if the oil spits slightly) and deep-fry for a few seconds until crisp. Drain on kitchen paper. Serve the whitebait immediately, garnished with the deep-fried parsley sprigs and lemon wedges.

> **Cook's Tip**
> There are two varieties of paprika, sweet and hot. Sweet paprika is quite mild, while hot paprika is spicier (but not as spicy as cayenne). Always check the label when buying.

Garlic Chilli Prawns

In Spain *gambas al ajillo* are traditionally cooked in small earthenware dishes, but a frying pan is just as suitable.

Serves 4
60ml/4 tbsp olive oil
2–3 garlic cloves, finely chopped
½ –1 fresh red chilli, seeded and chopped
16 cooked Mediterranean prawns (large shrimp)
15ml/1 tbsp chopped fresh parsley
salt and ground black pepper
lemon wedges and French bread, to serve

1 Heat the olive oil in a large frying pan over medium heat. Add the garlic and chilli and stir-fry for 1 minute, until the garlic begins to turn brown.

2 Add the prawns and stir-fry for 3–4 minutes, coating them well with the flavoured oil.

3 Add the parsley, remove from the heat and place four prawns in each of four warmed bowls. Spoon the flavoured oil over them. Serve with lemon wedges for squeezing and French bread to mop up the juices.

Tapas Prawns

These succulent prawns are simply irresistible as part of a *tapas* or *mezze*.

Serves 4
30ml/2 tbsp olive oil
4 garlic cloves, finely chopped
900g/2lb raw Mediterranean prawns (large shrimp), peeled
40g/1½oz/3 tbsp butter
15ml/1 tbsp orange juice
chopped fresh parsley, to garnish

1 Heat the oil in a frying pan. Add the garlic cloves and cook for 1–2 minutes. Add the prawns and cook, turning gently, for 2 minutes. Stir in the butter and orange juice and cook until the prawns have changed colour. Sprinkle with chopped parsley.

Chilli Prawns Energy 157kcal/653kJ; Protein 13.3g; Carbohydrate 0.1g, of which sugars 0.1g; Fat 11.5g, of which saturates 1.7g; Cholesterol 146mg; Calcium 67mg; Fibre 0.2g; Sodium 144mg.
Tapas Prawns Energy 224kcal/928kJ; Protein 19.9g; Carbohydrate 1.4g, of which sugars 0.5g; Fat 15.3g, of which saturates 6.5g; Cholesterol 91mg; Calcium 127mg; Fibre 0.3g; Sodium 1434mg.
Whitebait Energy 591kcal/2446kJ; Protein 22g; Carbohydrate 6g, of which sugars 0.1g; Fat 53.5g, of which saturates 5g; Cholesterol 0mg; Calcium 968mg; Fibre 0.2g; Sodium 259mg.

Tuna Fishcake Bites

An updated version of a traditional British tea-time dish, these delicious, little fishcakes would also make an elegant appetizer.

Serves 4

675g/1½lb potatoes
knob (pat) of butter
2 hard-boiled eggs, chopped
3 spring onions
   (scallions), chopped
grated rind of ½ lemon
5ml/1 tsp lemon juice
30ml/2 tbsp chopped
   fresh parsley
200g/7oz can tuna in oil, drained
10ml/2 tsp capers, drained
   and chopped

2 eggs, lightly beaten
115g/4oz/2 cups fresh
   white breadcrumbs
sunflower oil, for pan-frying
salt and ground black pepper
green salad, to serve

For the tartare sauce
60ml/4 tbsp mayonnaise
15ml/1 tbsp natural (plain) yogurt
15ml/1 tbsp finely
   chopped gherkins
15ml/1 tbsp capers, drained
   and chopped
15ml/1 tbsp chopped
   fresh parsley

1 Cook the potatoes in boiling salted water for 25–30 minutes, until tender. Drain and mash with the butter.

2 Mix the hard-boiled eggs, spring onions, lemon rind and juice, parsley, tuna, capers and 15ml/1 tbsp of the beaten eggs into the cooled potato. Season to taste, then cover and chill.

3 Mix all the sauce ingredients together. Chill in the refrigerator.

4 Roll the fishcake mixture into about 24 balls. Dip these into the remaining beaten eggs and then roll gently in the breadcrumbs until evenly coated. Transfer to a plate.

5 Heat 90ml/6 tbsp of the oil in a frying pan. Add the fish balls, in batches, and cook over medium heat, turning two or three times, for about 4 minutes, until browned all over. Drain on kitchen paper and keep warm in the oven while frying the remainder. Serve with the tartare sauce and a salad.

Baked Fish Creole-style

Fish fillets cooked in a colourful pepper and tomato sauce are topped with a cheese crust.

Serves 4

15ml/1 tbsp sunflower oil
25g/1oz/2 tbsp butter, plus extra
   for greasing
1 onion, thinly sliced
1 garlic clove, chopped
1 red (bell) pepper, seeded, halved
   and sliced
1 green (bell) pepper, seeded,
   halved and sliced
400g/14oz can chopped
   tomatoes with basil

15ml/1 tbsp tomato
   purée (paste)
30ml/2 tbsp capers, drained
   and chopped
3–4 drops Tabasco sauce
4 tail end pieces cod or haddock
   fillets (about 175g/6oz
   each), skinned
6 basil leaves, shredded
45ml/3 tbsp fresh breadcrumbs
25g/1oz/¼ cup grated
   Cheddar cheese
10ml/2 tsp chopped fresh parsley
salt and ground black pepper
fresh basil sprigs, to garnish

1 Preheat the oven to 230°C/450°F/Gas 8. Heat the oil and half of the butter in a pan over low heat. Add the onion and cook, stirring occasionally, for about 6–7 minutes, until softened. Add the garlic, peppers, chopped tomatoes, tomato purée, capers and Tabasco and season to taste with salt and pepper. Cover and cook for 15 minutes, then uncover and simmer gently for 5 minutes to reduce slightly.

2 Grease an ovenproof dish, place the fish fillets in it, dot with the remaining butter and season lightly. Spoon the tomato and pepper sauce over the top and sprinkle with the shredded basil. Bake for about 10 minutes.

3 Meanwhile, mix together the breadcrumbs, cheese and parsley in a bowl. Remove the fish from the oven and sprinkle the cheese mixture over the top. Return to the oven and bake for about 10 minutes more. Let the fish stand for about a minute, then, using a fish slice or spatula, carefully transfer each topped fillet to warmed plates. Garnish with sprigs of fresh basil and serve immediately.

Baked Fish Energy 332kcal/1399kJ; Protein 38.1g; Carbohydrate 19.2g, of which sugars 10.2g; Fat 11.9g, of which saturates 5.4g; Cholesterol 82mg; Calcium 106mg; Fibre 3g; Sodium 308mg.
Fishcake Energy 567kcal/2380kJ; Protein 26.8g; Carbohydrate 54.5g, of which sugars 7.5g; Fat 28.4g, of which saturates 3.8g; Cholesterol 228mg; Calcium 111mg; Fibre 3g; Sodium 656mg.

Kashmir Coconut Fish Curry

The combination of spices in this dish give an interesting depth of flavour to the creamy curry sauce.

Serves 4

30ml/2 tbsp vegetable oil
2 onions, sliced
1 green (bell) pepper, seeded and sliced
1 garlic clove, crushed
1 dried chilli, seeded and chopped
5ml/1 tsp ground coriander
5ml/1 tsp ground cumin
2.5ml/½ tsp ground turmeric
2.5ml/½ tsp hot chilli powder
2.5ml/½ tsp garam masala

15g/½oz/1 tbsp plain (all-purpose) flour
300ml/½ pint/1¼ cups coconut cream
675g/1½lb haddock fillet, skinned and chopped
4 tomatoes, peeled, seeded and chopped
15ml/1 tbsp lemon juice
30ml/2 tbsp ground almonds
30ml/2 tbsp double (heavy) cream
fresh coriander (cilantro) sprigs, to garnish
naan bread and boiled rice, to serve

1 Heat the oil in a large pan over low heat. Add the onions, green pepper and garlic and cook, stirring occasionally, for 6–7 minutes, until the onions and pepper have softened but not coloured.

2 Stir in the dried chilli, ground coriander, cumin, turmeric, chilli powder, garam masala and flour and cook, stirring constantly, for 1 minute more.

3 Mix the coconut cream with 300ml/½ pint/1¼ cups boiling water and stir into the spicy vegetable mixture. Bring to the boil, cover with a tight-fitting lid and simmer gently for about 6 minutes.

4 Add the pieces of fish and the tomatoes, re-cover the pan and cook for 5–6 minutes, or until the fish has turned opaque and flakes easily with the tip of a knife. Uncover and gently stir in the lemon juice, ground almonds and cream and heat through for a few minutes. Season well, garnish with coriander and serve with naan bread and rice.

Mussels with Wine & Garlic

This famous French dish is traditionally known as *moules marinière*, and can be served as an appetizer or a main course.

Serves 4

1.75kg/4lb fresh mussels
15ml/1 tbsp olive oil
25g/1oz/2 tbsp butter

1 small onion or 2 shallots, finely chopped
2 garlic cloves, finely chopped
150ml/¼ pint/⅔ cup dry white wine
4 fresh parsley sprigs
ground black pepper
30ml/2 tbsp chopped fresh parsley, to garnish
French bread, to serve

1 Scrub the mussels under cold running water and pull off the beards. Discard any with broken shells or that do not shut immediately when sharply tapped.

2 Heat the oil and butter in a large pan over medium heat. Add the onion or shallots and garlic and cook, stirring occasionally, for 3–4 minutes.

3 Pour in the wine, add the parsley sprigs, stir well and bring to the boil. Add the mussels, cover with a tight-fitting lid and cook, shaking the pan occasionally, for 5–7 minutes, until the shells have opened. Discard any mussels that remain closed.

4 Transfer the mussels to warmed serving bowls with a slotted spoon. Strain the cooking juices through a fine strainer lined with muslin (cheesecloth) and spoon them over the shellfish. Sprinkle with the chopped parsley, season well with pepper and serve immediately with hot French bread.

> **Variation**
> This dish is served everywhere in France, but in the apple-growing region of Normandy it is made with (hard) cider rather than white wine. For a really rich dish, strain the cooking liquid into a pan, stir in 90ml/6 tbsp double (heavy) cream and cook for a few minutes before spooning over the mussels.

Curry Energy 496kcal/2068kJ; Protein 36.6g; Carbohydrate 18.9g, of which sugars 13.6g; Fat 31.1g, of which saturates 20.5g; Cholesterol 71mg; Calcium 75mg; Fibre 3.2g; Sodium 137mg.
Mussels Energy 224kcal/939kJ; Protein 20g; Carbohydrate 5.4g, of which sugars 1.1g; Fat 11g, of which saturates 4g; Cholesterol 83mg; Calcium 70mg; Fibre 0.2g; Sodium 460mg.

Thai Prawn Salad

This salad has the distinctive flavour of lemon grass, the bulbous grass used widely in South-east Asian cooking.

Serves 2

250g/9oz extra-large tiger prawns
  (jumbo shrimp), thawed
  if frozen
30ml/2 tbsp groundnut
  (peanut) oil
15ml/1 tbsp Thai fish sauce
30ml/2 tbsp lime juice
7.5ml/1½ tsp soft light
  brown sugar

1 small fresh red chilli,
  finely chopped
1 spring onion (scallion),
  finely chopped
1 small garlic clove, crushed
2.5cm/1in piece fresh lemon
  grass, finely chopped
30ml/2 tbsp chopped fresh
  coriander (cilantro)
45ml/3 tbsp dry white wine
8–12 Little Gem (Bibb) lettuce
  leaves, to serve
fresh coriander sprigs,
  to garnish

1 Remove the heads and peel the prawns. (Reserve the shells for making shellfish stock, if you like.) Make a shallow cut along the back of each prawn and remove the dark vein with the tip of the knife.

2 Heat the oil in a wok or heavy frying pan over medium heat. When it is very hot, add the prawns and stir-fry for 2–3 minutes, until they have changed colour. Be careful not to overcook them. Remove with a slotted spoon and drain on kitchen paper. Leave to cool.

3 Place the tiger prawns in a non-metallic bowl and add all the remaining ingredients except the lettuce and coriander sprigs. Stir thoroughly to combine and dissolve the sugar, cover with clear film (plastic wrap) and leave to marinate in the refrigerator for 2–3 hours, occasionally stirring and turning the prawns.

4 Arrange two or three of the lettuce leaves on each of four individual serving plates. Spoon the prawn salad and marinade on to the lettuce leaves. Garnish with fresh coriander sprigs and serve immediately.

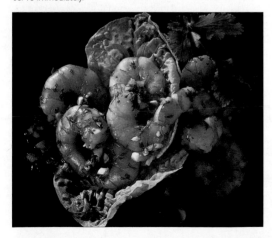

Cajun Spiced Fish

Fillets of fish are coated with an aromatic blend of herbs and spices and pan-fried in butter.

Serves 4

5ml/1 tsp dried thyme
5ml/1 tsp dried oregano
5ml/1 tsp ground black pepper
1.25ml/¼ tsp cayenne pepper
10ml/2 tsp paprika

2.5ml/½ tsp garlic salt
4 tail end pieces of cod fillet
  (about 175g/6oz each)
75g/3oz/6 tbsp butter
½ fresh red (bell) pepper, seeded
  and sliced
½ green (bell) pepper, seeded
  and sliced
fresh thyme sprigs, to garnish
grilled (broiled) tomatoes and
  sweet potato purée, to serve

1 Place the dried thyme, oregano, black pepper, cayenne, paprika and garlic salt in a bowl and mix well. Dip the fish fillets in the spice mixture until lightly coated.

2 Heat 25g/1oz/2 tbsp of the butter in a large frying pan over medium-low heat. Add the red and green peppers and cook, stirring occasionally, for 4–5 minutes, until softened. Remove the peppers and keep warm.

3 Add the remaining butter to the pan and heat until it is sizzling. Add the cod fillets and cook over medium heat for 3–4 minutes on each side, until browned and cooked.

4 Transfer the fish to a warmed serving dish, surround with the peppers and garnish with thyme sprigs. Serve the spiced fish with some grilled tomatoes and sweet potato purée.

Cook's Tip
Cajun cooking is a rural tradition that originated in Louisiana over 200 years ago. It is an immensely flexible cuisine based on home-grown crops, locally caught fish and any game that could be hunted. It is often confused with Creole cuisine, which evolved in the same region but was created for the rich. Creole includes French, Spanish and African influences.

Thai Prawn Energy 130kcal/546kJ; Protein 22.4g; Carbohydrate 4.7g, of which sugars 4.6g; Fat 0.9g, of which saturates 0.2g; Cholesterol 244mg; Calcium 112mg; Fibre 0.3g; Sodium 240mg.
Cajun Fish Energy 295kcal/1228kJ; Protein 32.7g; Carbohydrate 3g, of which sugars 2.9g; Fat 16.9g, of which saturates 10g; Cholesterol 120mg; Calcium 31mg; Fibre 0.9g; Sodium 222mg.

Golden Fish Pie

This lovely light pie with a crumpled filo pastry topping makes a delicious lunch or supper dish.

Serves 4–6
675g/1½lb white fish fillets
300ml/½ pint/1¼ cups milk
½ onion, thinly sliced
1 bay leaf
6 black peppercorns
115g/4oz/1 cup cooked peeled prawns (shrimp)
115g/4oz/½ cup butter
50g/2oz/½ cup plain (all-purpose) flour
300ml/½ pint/1¼ cups single (light) cream
75g/3oz/¾ cup grated Gruyère cheese
1 bunch watercress, leaves only, chopped
5ml/1 tsp Dijon mustard
5 sheets filo pastry
salt and ground black pepper

1 Place the fish in a pan, pour in the milk and add the onion, bay leaf and peppercorns. Bring to the boil, lower the heat, cover with a lid and simmer for 10–12 minutes, until the fish is almost tender. Lift out the fish with a slotted spatula and place on a chopping board. Strain and reserve the cooking liquid.

2 Remove the skin and any bones from the fish, then coarsely flake the flesh and place in a shallow, ovenproof dish. Sprinkle the prawns over the fish.

3 Melt 50g/2oz/4 tbsp of the butter in a pan. Stir in the flour and cook, stirring constantly, for 1 minute. Stir in the reserved cooking liquid and cream. Bring to the boil, stirring, then simmer for 2–3 minutes, until thickened. Remove from the heat and stir in the Gruyère, watercress and mustard. Season with salt and pepper. Pour the mixture over the fish and leave to cool.

4 Preheat the oven to 190°C/375°F/Gas 5, then melt the remaining butter. Brush one sheet of filo pastry with a little melted butter, then crumple up loosely and place on top of the filling. Repeat with the remaining filo sheets and melted butter until they are all used up and the pie is completely covered. Bake for 25–30 minutes, until the pastry is golden and crisp. Serve immediately.

Special Fish Pie

This fish pie is colourful, healthy and best of all, it is very simple to make.

Serves 4
350g/12oz haddock fillet
30ml/2 tbsp cornflour (cornstarch)
115g/4oz/1 cup cooked peeled prawns (shrimp)
200g/7oz can corn, drained
75g/3oz/scant 1 cup frozen peas
150ml/¼ pint/¾ cup skimmed milk
150ml/¼ pint/¾ cup low-fat fromage frais (farmer's cheese)
75g/3oz/1½ cups fresh wholemeal (whole-wheat) breadcrumbs
40g/1½ oz/generous ¼ cup grated reduced-fat Cheddar cheese
salt and ground black pepper
fresh vegetables, to serve

1 Preheat the oven to 190°C/375°F/Gas 5. Skin the haddock fillet if this has not already been done by your fish supplier and cut the flesh into bitesize pieces. Toss the pieces of fish in the cornflour to coat evenly.

2 Place the fish, prawns, corn and peas in an ovenproof dish. Beat together the milk and fromage frais in a bowl and season with salt and pepper. Pour the mixture into the dish.

3 Mix together the breadcrumbs and grated cheese, then spoon evenly over the top, pressing down gently with the back of the spoon.

4 Bake for 25–30 minutes, or until the topping is golden brown. Serve hot with fresh vegetables.

Variations
• For a slightly more economical version of this dish, omit the prawns (shrimp) and increase the quantity of haddock fillet to 450g/1lb.
• Substitute smoked haddock fillet for half the fresh fish.
• Use frozen or drained canned broad (fava) beans instead of the peas.

Golden Fish Energy 344kcal/1442kJ; Protein 32g; Carbohydrate 17.5g, of which sugars 3.8g; Fat 16.4g, of which saturates 9g; Cholesterol 129mg; Calcium 239mg; Fibre 0.8g; Sodium 246mg.
Special Fish Energy 329kcal/1394kJ; Protein 34.1g; Carbohydrate 41.2g, of which sugars 10g; Fat 4.3g, of which saturates 1.7g; Cholesterol 94mg; Calcium 228mg; Fibre 2g; Sodium 490mg.

Smoked Trout with Cucumber

Smoked trout provides an easy and delicious first course or light meal. Serve at room temperature for the best flavour.

Serves 4
1 large cucumber
60ml/4 tbsp crème fraîche or Greek (US strained plain) yogurt
15ml/1 tbsp chopped fresh dill
4 smoked trout fillets
salt and ground black pepper
fresh dill sprigs, to garnish
crusty wholemeal (whole-wheat) bread, to serve

1 Peel the cucumber, cut in half lengthways and scoop out the seeds using a teaspoon. Cut the flesh into tiny dice.

2 Put the cucumber in a colander set over a plate and sprinkle with salt. Leave to drain for at least 1 hour to draw out the excess moisture.

3 Rinse the cucumber well, then pat dry on kitchen paper. Transfer the diced cucumber to a bowl and stir in the crème fraîche or yogurt, chopped dill and some freshly ground pepper. Chill the cucumber salad for about 30 minutes.

4 Arrange the trout fillets on individual plates. Spoon the cucumber and dill salad on one side and grind over a little black pepper. Garnish the dish with dill sprigs and serve immediately with crusty bread.

> **Cook's Tip**
> *Trout is hot-smoked at a temperature of 75–100°C/ 167–212°F, which, in effect, cooks it at the same time. It, therefore, needs no further cooking. If you are planning to substitute another fish, make sure that it has also been hot-smoked, as, with the exception of salmon, most cold-smoked fish requires further cooking.*

Fishcakes

Home-made fish cakes are an underrated food which bear little resemblance to the store-bought type.

Serves 4
450g/1lb mixed white and smoked fish fillets, such as haddock or cod, flaked
450g/1lb cooked, mashed potatoes
25g/1oz/2 tbsp butter, diced
45ml/3 tbsp chopped fresh parsley
1 egg, separated
1 egg, beaten
about 50g/2oz/1 cup fine white breadcrumbs made with day-old bread
salt and pepper
vegetable oil, for pan-frying

1 Place the fish in a large pan, season with salt and pepper and pour in water just to cover. Bring to the boil, then lower the heat, cover and simmer for about 15 minutes, until the flesh flakes easily with the tip of a knife. Remove the fish with a slotted spatula and leave until cool enough to handle. Discard the cooking liquid.

2 Remove and discard the skin and any bones from the fish and flake the flesh. Place the potatoes in a bowl and beat in the fish, butter, parsley and egg yolk. Season to taste with pepper.

3 Divide the fish mixture into eight equal portions, then, with floured hands, form each into a flat patty. Beat the remaining egg white with the whole egg. Dip each fish cake first into the beaten egg, then in breadcrumbs.

4 Heat the oil in a frying pan over a medium heat. Add the fish cakes and cook for 3–5 minutes on each side, until crisp and golden. Serve immediately.

> **Cook's Tip**
> *Make smaller fishcakes to serve as an appetizer with a salad garnish. For a more luxurious version, make them with cooked fresh salmon or drained, canned red or pink salmon.*

Trout Energy 146kcal/606kJ; Protein 15.2g; Carbohydrate 1.1g, of which sugars 1g; Fat 8.9g, of which saturates 4.1g; Cholesterol 17mg; Calcium 25mg; Fibre 0.3g; Sodium 47mg.
Fishcakes Energy 399kcal/1670kJ; Protein 27.5g; Carbohydrate 28.2g, of which sugars 2.1g; Fat 20.4g, of which saturates 5.6g; Cholesterol 160mg; Calcium 71mg; Fibre 2g; Sodium 252mg.

Stuffed Fish Rolls

Plaice or flounder fillets are a good choice for families because they are economical, easy to cook and free of bones.

Serves 4
1 courgette (zucchini), grated
2 carrots, grated
60ml/4 tbsp fresh wholemeal (whole-wheat) breadcrumbs
15ml/1 tbsp lime or lemon juice
4 plaice or flounder fillets
salt and ground black pepper
new potatoes, to serve

1 Preheat the oven to 200°C/400°F/Gas 6. Mix together the courgette and carrots in a bowl. Stir in the breadcrumbs and lime juice and season with salt and pepper.

2 Lay the fish fillets, skin-side up, on a board and divide the stuffing among them, spreading it evenly.

3 Roll up to enclose the stuffing and place in an ovenproof dish. Cover and bake for about 30 minutes, or until the fish flakes easily. Serve immediately with new potatoes.

Cook's Tip
Flat fish, such as plaice and flounder, have one light- and one dark-skinned side. Most people consider the darker skin to be unappetizing and many dislike any sort of skin. The skin is very easy to remove. Make a small cut between the skin and the flesh at the tail end of the fillet, then dip your fingers in salt to stop them from slipping, take a firm hold of the skin and simply pull it away from the flesh in one piece. Spread the filling on to the side where the skin was.

Variation
Substitute 115g/4oz/1 cup finely chopped cooked, peeled prawns or drained, canned crab meat for the carrots to create a more sophisticated version of this dish.

Mackerel Kebabs with Parsley

Oily fish, such as mackerel, are ideal for grilling as they cook quickly and need no extra oil.

Serves 4
450g/1lb mackerel fillets
finely grated rind and juice of 1 lemon
45ml/3 tbsp chopped fresh parsley
12 cherry tomatoes
8 pitted black olives
salt and ground black pepper
boiled rice or noodles and green salad, to serve

1 Cut the fish into 4cm/1½ in chunks and place in a non-metallic bowl with half the lemon rind and juice and half the parsley and season with salt and pepper. Cover the bowl with clear film (plastic wrap) and leave to marinate in a cool place for about 30 minutes.

2 Preheat the grill (broiler). Thread the chunks of fish on to eight long wooden or metal skewers, alternating them with the cherry tomatoes and olives. Grill (broil) the kebabs, turning occasionally, for 3–4 minutes, until the fish is cooked.

3 Mix the remaining lemon rind and juice with the remaining parsley in a small bowl, then season to taste with salt and pepper. Make a bed of plain boiled rice or noodles on each of four warmed serving plates and place two kebabs on each. Serve immediately with a green salad.

Cook's Tips
• *If you are using wooden kebab skewers, it is a good idea to soak them in cold water for 30 minutes to prevent them from charring during cooking.*
• *These kebabs are also ideal for cooking on the barbecue. Serve with baked potatoes or crusty bread and salad.*
• *If you are going to marinate the fish for longer than 30 minutes, place it in the refrigerator. Otherwise, simply leave it in a cool place.*

Fish Rolls Energy 139kcal/588kJ; Protein 15.5g; Carbohydrate 16.5g, of which sugars 5g; Fat 1.7g, of which saturates 0.3g; Cholesterol 32mg; Calcium 78mg; Fibre 2g; Sodium 217mg.
Mackerel Energy 265kcal/1100kJ; Protein 21.7g; Carbohydrate 1.5g, of which sugars 1.5g; Fat 19.1g, of which saturates 3.9g; Cholesterol 61mg; Calcium 44mg; Fibre 1.2g; Sodium 219mg.

Grilled Salmon Steaks with Fennel

Fennel grows wild all over the south of Italy where this dish originated. Its mild aniseed flavour goes well with fish.

Serves 4

juice of 1 lemon
45ml/3 tbsp chopped fresh
    fennel, or the green fronds from
    the top of a fennel bulb
5ml/1 tsp fennel seeds
45ml/3 tbsp olive oil
4 salmon steaks of the same
    thickness (about 700g/1½lb)
salt and ground black pepper
lemon wedges, to garnish

1 Combine the lemon juice, chopped fennel and fennel seeds with the olive oil in a non-metallic dish. Add the salmon steaks, turning them to coat them with the marinade. Sprinkle with salt and pepper. Cover with clear film (plastic wrap) and place in the refrigerator to marinate for about 2 hours.

2 Preheat the grill (broiler). Drain the fish and reserve the marinade. Place the salmon steaks in one layer on a grill (broiler) pan or shallow baking tray. Grill (broil) about 10cm/4in from the heat source for 3–4 minutes.

3 Turn the steaks over and spoon the remaining marinade over them. Grill for 3–4 minutes, or until the edges begin to brown. Serve immediately, garnished with lemon wedges.

> **Cook's Tips**
> • If you like, remove the skin from the salmon steaks before serving. Simply insert the prongs of a fork between the flesh and the skin at one end and roll the skin around the prongs in a fluid action.
> • Take care not to overcook the salmon. Although it is an oily fish, the flesh dries out very easily when subjected to fierce heat. If you're going to cook on the barbecue, raise the grill rack well above the coals before starting.

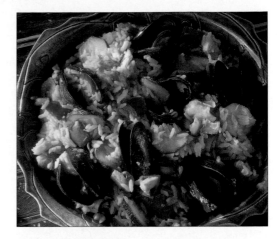

Seafood Pilaff

This one-pan dish makes a satisfying meal. For a special occasion, use dry white wine instead of orange juice.

Serves 4

10ml/2 tsp olive oil
250g/9oz/1⅓ cups long
    grain rice
5ml/1 tsp ground turmeric
1 fresh red (bell) pepper, seeded
    and diced
1 small onion, finely chopped
2 courgettes (zucchini), sliced
150g/5oz button (white)
    mushrooms, halved
350ml/12fl oz/1½ cups fish or
    chicken stock
150ml/¼ pint/⅔ cup orange
    juice
350g/12oz white fish fillets
12 fresh mussels, scrubbed
    and debearded
salt and ground black pepper
grated rind of 1 orange, to garnish

1 Heat the oil in a large non-stick frying pan over low heat. Add the rice and turmeric and cook, stirring frequently, for about 1 minute.

2 Add the red pepper, onion, courgettes and mushrooms and cook, stirring constantly, for 1 minute more, then increase the heat to medium, stir in the stock and orange juice and bring to the boil.

3 Lower the heat and add the fish. Cover with a tight-fitting lid and simmer gently for about 15 minutes, until the rice is tender and the liquid has been absorbed.

4 Stir in the mussels, re-cover the pan and cook for about 5 minutes until the shells have opened. Discard any mussels that remain closed. Adjust the seasoning, sprinkle with orange rind and serve immediately.

> **Variation**
> You can use cooked, shelled mussels, available from the chiller cabinets in supermarkets, instead of live. Add them in step 4 and simply heat through before serving.

Salmon Energy 395kcal/1639kJ; Protein 35.8g; Carbohydrate 0.8g, of which sugars 0.8g; Fat 27.6g, of which saturates 4.5g; Cholesterol 88mg; Calcium 47mg; Fibre 1.1g; Sodium 84mg.
Pilaff Energy 394kcal/1663kJ; Protein 28.7g; Carbohydrate 59g, of which sugars 12.5g; Fat 6.3g, of which saturates 0.5g; Cholesterol 46mg; Calcium 620mg; Fibre 2.3g; Sodium 115mg.

Grilled Fresh Sardines

Fresh sardines are flavoursome, firm-fleshed and rather different in taste and consistency from those canned in oil.

Serves 4–6
900kg/2lb fresh sardines, gutted and with heads removed

olive oil, for brushing
45ml/3 tbsp chopped fresh parsley
salt and ground black pepper
lemon wedges, to garnish

1 Preheat the grill (broiler). Rinse the sardines under cold running water. Pat dry with kitchen paper.

2 Brush the sardines lightly with olive oil and sprinkle generously with salt and pepper. Place the sardines in one layer in a grill (broiler) pan. Grill (broil) for about 3–4 minutes.

3 Turn, and cook for 3–4 minutes more, or until the skin begins to brown. Serve immediately, sprinkled with parsley and garnished with lemon wedges.

Cook's Tip
Frozen sardines are now available in supermarkets and will keep well in the freezer for six weeks. Thaw them in the refrigerator overnight. Scrape off the scales with your hands, working from tail to head, then use a sharp pointed knife to slit the belly, remove the innards and cut the heads off. For a fuller flavour and to make them less likely to fall apart when you turn them, you might like to leave them whole, as they do in some Mediterranean countries.

Variation
Substitute parsley butter for the fresh parsley. Simply beat chopped fresh parsley and lemon juice to taste into butter.

Red Mullet with Tomatoes

Red mullet is a popular fish in Italy, and in this recipe both its flavour and colour are accentuated.

Serves 4
4 red mullet or snapper (about 175–200g/6–7oz each)
450g/1lb tomatoes, peeled, or 400g/14oz can plum tomatoes

60ml/4 tbsp olive oil
60ml/4 tbsp finely chopped fresh parsley
2 garlic cloves, finely chopped
120ml/4fl oz/¹/₂ cup dry white wine
4 thin lemon slices, cut in half
salt and ground black pepper

1 Scale and gut the fish or ask your fish supplier to do this for you. Rinse well under cold running water and pat dry with kitchen paper.

2 Finely chop the tomatoes. Heat the oil in a pan or flameproof casserole large enough to hold the fish in one layer. Add the parsley and garlic, and cook, stirring, for 1 minute. Stir in the tomatoes and cook over medium heat, stirring occasionally, for 15–20 minutes. Season to taste with salt and pepper.

3 Add the fish to the tomato sauce and cook over medium to high heat for 5 minutes. Add the wine and the lemon slices. Bring the sauce back to the boil and cook for about 5 minutes more. Turn the fish over and cook for a further 4–5 minutes, until the fish flakes easily. Transfer the fish to a warmed serving platter and keep warm until required.

4 Boil the sauce for 3–4 minutes to reduce it slightly, then spoon it over the fish and serve immediately.

Cook's Tip
The liver of red mullet is regarded as a delicacy so you can leave it intact when you gut the fish or ask your fish supplier to keep it for you. This does not apply if you are preparing this dish with red snapper.

Middle Eastern Sea Bream

Buy the smallest sea bream you can find to cook whole, allowing a serving of one fish for two people.

Serves 4

1.75kg/4lb sea bream or porgy or 2 smaller sea bream or porgy
30ml/2 tbsp olive oil
75g/3oz/¾ cup pine nuts
1 large onion, finely chopped
450g/1lb ripe tomatoes, coarsely chopped
75g/3oz/½ cup raisins
2.5ml/½ tsp ground cinnamon
2.5ml/½ tsp mixed (apple pie) spice
45ml/3 tbsp chopped fresh mint
225g/8oz/generous 1 cup long grain rice
3 lemon slices
300ml/½ pint/1¼ cups fish stock

1 Trim the fins, scale the fish, then gut or ask your fish supplier to do this for you. Rinse well under cold running water and pat dry with kitchen paper. Meanwhile, preheat the oven to 175°C/350°F/Gas 4.

2 Heat the oil in a large, heavy pan over medium-low heat. Add the pine nuts and stir-fry for 1 minute. Add the onions and continue to stir-fry until softened but not coloured.

3 Add the tomatoes and simmer for 10 minutes, then stir in the raisins, half the cinnamon, half the mixed spice and the mint.

4 Add the rice and lemon slices. Transfer to a large roasting pan and pour the fish stock over the top.

5 Place the fish on top and cut several slashes in the skin. Sprinkle over a little salt, the remaining mixed spice and the remaining cinnamon and bake for 30–35 minutes for large fish or 20–25 minutes for smaller fish.

> **Variation**
> If you like, use almonds instead of pine nuts. Use the same quantity of blanched almonds and split them in half before stir-frying.

Salmon with Spicy Pesto

This pesto uses sunflower seeds and chilli as its flavouring rather than the classic basil and pine nuts.

Serves 4

4 salmon steaks (about 225g/8oz each)
30ml/2 tbsp sunflower oil
finely grated rind and juice of 1 lime
pinch of salt

For the pesto
6 mild fresh red chillies, seeded
2 garlic cloves
30ml/2 tbsp pumpkin or sunflower seeds
freshly grated rind and juice of 1 lime
75ml/5 tbsp olive oil
salt and ground black pepper

1 Insert a very sharp knife close to the top of the salmon's backbone. Working closely to the bone, cut your way to the end of the steak so one side of the steak has been released and one side is still attached. Repeat with the other side. Pull out any extra visible bones with a pair of tweezers.

2 Sprinkle a little salt on the surface and take hold of the end of the salmon, skin-side down. Insert a small sharp knife under the skin and, working away from you, cut off the skin, keeping as close to the skin as possible. Repeat with the three remaining pieces of fish.

3 Rub the sunflower oil into the boneless fish rounds and place in a non-metallic dish. Add the lime juice and rind, cover with clear film (plastic wrap) and place in the refrigerator to marinate for 2 hours.

4 To make the pesto, put the chillies, garlic, pumpkin or sunflower seeds, lime juice and rind in a food processor or blender and season with salt and pepper. Process until well mixed. With the motor running, gradually pour in the olive oil until the sauce has thickened and emulsified.

5 Preheat the grill (broiler). Drain the salmon from its marinade. Grill the fish steaks for about 5 minutes on each side and serve immediately with the spicy pesto.

Sea Bream Energy 562kcal/2348kJ; Protein 39.7g; Carbohydrate 46g, of which sugars 1.1g; Fat 24.1g, of which saturates 1.7g; Cholesterol 71mg; Calcium 89mg; Fibre 0.5g; Sodium 208mg.
Salmon Energy 653kcal/2719kJ; Protein 50.5g; Carbohydrate 1.4g, of which sugars 0.1g; Fat 49.6g, of which saturates 7.5g; Cholesterol 122mg; Calcium 60mg; Fibre 0.5g; Sodium 111mg.

Chicken with Lemon & Herbs

Chicken thighs tend to be overlooked when people are buying portions, yet the meat is full of flavour and two thighs will adequately serve one person.

Serves 2
50g/2oz/4 tbsp butter
2 spring onions, (scallions) white parts only, finely chopped
15ml/1 tbsp chopped fresh tarragon
15ml/1 tbsp chopped fresh fennel
juice of 1 lemon
4 chicken thighs
salt and ground black pepper
lemon slices and fresh herb sprigs, to garnish

1 Preheat the grill (broiler) to medium. Melt the butter in a small pan over low heat. Add the spring onions, tarragon, fennel and lemon juice and season with salt and pepper. Cook, stirring constantly, for 1 minute, then remove the pan from the heat.

2 Brush the chicken thighs generously with the herb mixture, then grill (broil), basting frequently with the herb mixture, for 10–12 minutes.

3 Turn the chicken over and baste again, then cook for a further 10–12 minutes, or until the chicken juices run clear when the thickest part of the thigh is pierced with the point of a knife.

4 Serve the chicken garnished with lemon slices and herb sprigs and accompanied by any remaining herb mixture.

Cook's Tip
Tarragon has a natural affinity with chicken. It is intensely aromatic with a hint of aniseed and so should be used sparingly. Make sure you buy French tarragon with its delicate leaves and fine flavour. Russian tarragon is virtually inedible. Fennel also has a strong aniseed flavour, so it too should be used with discretion.

Roast Chicken with Celeriac

Celeriac and brown breadcrumbs give the stuffing an unusual and delicious twist.

Serves 4
1.6kg/3½lb chicken
15g/½oz/1 tbsp butter

For the stuffing
450g/1lb celeriac, chopped
25g/1oz/2 tbsp butter
3 rashers (strips) bacon, chopped
1 onion, finely chopped
leaves from 1 fresh thyme sprig, chopped
leaves from 1 small fresh tarragon sprig, chopped
30ml/2 tbsp chopped fresh parsley
75g/3oz/1½ cups fresh brown breadcrumbs
dash of Worcestershire sauce
1 egg
salt and ground black pepper

1 To make the stuffing, cook the celeriac in a pan of boiling water until tender. Drain well and chop finely.

2 Melt the butter in a heavy pan over low heat. Add the bacon and onion and cook, stirring occasionally, for 5–7 minutes, until the onion is softened but not coloured.

3 Stir in the celeriac, thyme, tarragon and parsley and cook, stirring occasionally, for 2–3 minutes. Meanwhile, preheat the oven to 200°C/400°F/Gas 6.

4 Remove the pan from the heat and stir in the fresh breadcrumbs, Worcestershire sauce and sufficient egg to bind the mixture. Season with salt and pepper. Use this mixture to stuff the neck end of the chicken. Season the chicken all over with salt and pepper and then rub the butter into the skin with your fingertips.

5 Place the chicken in a roasting pan and roast, basting occasionally with the cooking juices, for 1¼–1½ hours, until the juices run clear when the thickest part of the leg is pierced with the point of a sharp knife. Turn off the oven, prop the door open slightly and leave the chicken to rest for about 10 minutes before removing from the oven and carving.

Roast Chicken Energy 507kcal/2116kJ; Protein 43.6g; Carbohydrate 16.8g, of which sugars 2.4g; Fat 30g, of which saturates 11.6g; Cholesterol 233mg; Calcium 99mg; Fibre 1.9g; Sodium 692mg.
Lemon Chicken Energy 406kcal/1692kJ; Protein 42.1g; Carbohydrate 0.5g, of which sugars 0.4g; Fat 26.2g, of which saturates 14.7g; Cholesterol 263mg; Calcium 23mg; Fibre 0.3g; Sodium 333mg.

Golden Parmesan Chicken

Served cold with the garlic mayonnaise, these morsels of chicken make fabulous picnic food.

Serves 4

4 skinless boneless chicken
　breast portions
75g/3oz/1½ cups fresh
　white breadcrumbs
40g/1½oz/½ cup finely grated
　Parmesan cheese
30ml/2 tbsp chopped
　fresh parsley
2 eggs, lightly beaten
50g/2oz/4 tbsp butter, melted
salt and ground black pepper
green salad, to serve

For the garlic mayonnaise

120ml/4fl oz/½ cup good-
　quality mayonnaise
120ml/4fl oz/½ cup fromage
　frais (farmer's cheese)
1–2 garlic cloves, crushed

1 Using a sharp knife, cut each chicken portion into four or five large pieces. Mix together the breadcrumbs, grated Parmesan cheese and parsley in a shallow dish and season with salt and pepper.

2 Dip the chicken pieces in the beaten egg, then into the breadcrumb mixture. Place in a single layer on a baking sheet and chill in the refrigerator for at least 30 minutes.

3 Meanwhile, make the garlic mayonnaise. Mix together the mayonnaise, fromage frais and garlic and season with pepper to taste. Spoon the mayonnaise into a small serving bowl, cover with clear film (plastic wrap) and chill in the refrigerator until ready to serve.

4 Preheat the oven to 180°C/350°F/Gas 4. Drizzle the melted butter over the chicken pieces and cook in the oven for about 20 minutes, until crisp and golden. Serve the chicken immediately with a crisp green salad and the garlic mayonnaise for dipping. Alternatively, transfer the chicken to a rack, using tongs, and leave to cool. Store in the refrigerator until required, then serve at room temperature with a green salad and the garlic mayonnaise.

Chicken with Peppers

This colourful and tasty dish comes from the south of Italy, where sweet peppers are plentiful.

Serves 4

1.5kg/3lb chicken, cut into
　serving pieces
90ml/6 tbsp olive oil
2 red onions, thinly sliced
2 garlic cloves, finely chopped
small piece of dried chilli,
　crumbled (optional)
120ml/4fl oz/½ cup dry
　white wine
3 large (bell) peppers (red, yellow
　or green), seeded and cut
　into strips
2 tomatoes, fresh or canned,
　peeled and chopped
45g/3 tbsp chopped fresh parsley
salt and ground black pepper

1 Trim any visible fat off the chicken with a sharp knife and remove all excess skin.

2 Heat half the oil in a large heavy pan or flameproof casserole over low heat. Add the onions and cook, stirring occasionally, for 5–7 minutes, until softened but not coloured. Transfer them to a plate.

3 Add the remaining oil to the pan and increase the heat to medium. Add the chicken pieces and cook, turning frequently, for 6–8 minutes, until browned on all sides. Return the onions to the pan and add the garlic and dried chilli, if using.

4 Pour in the wine and cook until it has reduced by about half. Add the peppers and stir well to coat. Season to taste with salt and pepper and cook for 3–4 minutes. Stir in the tomatoes, lower the heat, cover the pan with a tight-fitting lid and cook, stirring occasionally, for 25–30 minutes, until the peppers are soft and the chicken is cooked through. Stir in the chopped parsley and serve immediately.

Cook's Tip
For a more elegant version of this dish to serve at a dinner party, use skinless, boneless chicken breast portions.

Chicken in Green Sauce

Slow, gentle cooking makes the chicken in this dish very succulent and tender.

Serves 4

25g/1oz/2 tbsp butter
15ml/1 tbsp olive oil
4 chicken portions (legs, breast portions or quarters)
1 small onion, finely chopped
150ml/¼ pint/⅔ cup medium-bodied dry white wine
150ml/¼ pint/⅔ cup chicken stock
leaves from 2 fresh thyme sprigs and 2 fresh tarragon sprigs
175g/6oz watercress, leaves removed, or baby spinach leaves, trimmed
150ml/¼ pint/⅔ cup double (heavy) cream
salt and ground black pepper
watercress leaves or mizuna, to garnish

1 Heat the butter and oil in a frying pan over medium heat. Add the chicken portions and cook, turning frequently, for 8–10 minutes, until browned all over. Transfer the chicken to a plate using a slotted spoon and keep warm in the oven.

2 Lower the heat, add the onion to the pan and cook, stirring occasionally, for 5–7 minutes, until softened but not coloured. Stir in the wine, increase the heat to medium and bring to the boil. Boil for 2–3 minutes, then add the stock and bring the mixture back to the boil.

3 Return the chicken to the pan, lower the heat, cover with a tight-fitting lid and simmer very gently for about 30 minutes, until the chicken juices run clear when the thickest part of the meat is pierced with the point of a knife. Transfer the chicken to a warm dish, cover and keep warm.

4 Boil the cooking juices hard until they are reduced to about 60ml/4 tbsp. Add the thyme, tarragon and watercress or spinach leaves and stir in the cream. Simmer over medium heat until slightly thickened.

5 Return the chicken to the pan, season to taste with salt and pepper and heat through for a few minutes. Transfer to warmed serving plates, garnish with watercress or mizuna and serve.

Spatchcocked Devilled Poussin

"Spatchcock" – also known as "butterflied" – refers to birds that have been split and skewered flat. This shortens the cooking time considerably.

Serves 4

15ml/1 tbsp English (hot) mustard powder
15ml/1 tbsp paprika
15ml/1 tbsp ground cumin
20ml/4 tsp tomato ketchup
15ml/1 tbsp lemon juice
65g/2½oz/5 tbsp butter, melted
4 poussins (about 450g/1lb each)
salt

1 Mix together the mustard, paprika, cumin, ketchup, lemon juice and a pinch of salt in a bowl until smooth, then gradually stir in the butter.

2 Using game shears or strong kitchen scissors, split each poussin along one side of the backbone, then cut down the other side of the backbone and remove it.

3 Open out a poussin, skin-side uppermost, then press down firmly with the heel of your hand. Pass a long skewer through one leg and out through the other to secure the bird open and flat. Repeat with the remaining birds.

4 Spread the mustard mixture evenly over the skin of the birds. Cover loosely and leave in a cool place for at least 2 hours to marinate. Preheat the grill (broiler).

5 Place the birds, skin-side uppermost, under the grill and cook for about 12 minutes. Turn the birds over, baste with any juices in the grill (broiler) pan, and cook for a further 7 minutes, until the juices run clear when the thickest part is pierced with the point of a knife. Serve immediately.

> **Cook's Tip**
> For an al fresco meal in the summer, these spatchcocked poussins may be cooked on a barbecue.

Chicken Energy 502kcal/2089kJ; Protein 44.5g; Carbohydrate 3.3g, of which sugars 3g; Fat 32.1g, of which saturates 17.3g; Cholesterol 227mg; Calcium 114mg; Fibre 0.9g; Sodium 215mg.
Poussin Energy 659kcal/2742kJ; Protein 50.2g; Carbohydrate 3g, of which sugars 2.9g; Fat 49.8g, of which saturates 18.4g; Cholesterol 296mg; Calcium 22mg; Fibre 0.1g; Sodium 442mg.

Stoved Chicken

"Stoved" is derived from the French *étouffer*, meaning to cook in a covered pot.

Serves 4

1kg/2lb potatoes, cut into
5mm/¼in slices
2 large onions, thinly sliced
15ml/1 tbsp chopped fresh thyme
25g/1oz/2 tbsp butter
15ml/1 tbsp sunflower oil
2 large bacon rashers
(strips), chopped
4 large chicken portions, halved
1 bay leaf
600ml/1 pint/2½ cups chicken
stock
salt and ground black pepper

1 Preheat the oven to 150°C/300°F/Gas 2. Make a thick layer of half the potato slices in the base of a large, heavy, flameproof casserole, then cover with half the onion. Sprinkle with half the thyme and season with salt and pepper.

2 Heat the butter and oil in a large frying pan over medium heat. Add the bacon and chicken and cook, turning frequently, for 8–10 minutes, until the chicken is browned all over. Using a slotted spoon transfer the chicken and bacon to the casserole. Reserve the fat in the pan. Sprinkle the remaining thyme over the chicken and season with salt and pepper. Cover with the remaining onion, followed by a neat layer of overlapping potato slices. Season again with salt and pepper.

3 Pour the stock into the casserole, brush the potatoes with the reserved fat, then cover with a tight-fitting lid and cook in the oven for about 2 hours, until the chicken is tender.

4 Meanwhile, preheat the grill (broiler). Lift the casserole from the oven and remove the lid. Place under the grill and cook until the slices of potatoes are beginning to turn golden brown and crisp. Serve immediately.

> **Variation**
> Instead of using large chicken portions, use thighs or drumsticks, or a mixture of the two.

Chicken with Red Cabbage

Crushed juniper berries provide a distinctive flavour in this unusual casserole.

Serves 4

50g/2oz/¼ cup butter
4 large chicken portions, halved
1 onion, chopped
500g/1¼lb/5 cups finely
shredded red cabbage
4 juniper berries, crushed
12 cooked chestnuts
120ml/4fl oz/½ cup full-bodied
red wine
salt and ground black pepper

1 Melt the butter in a heavy, flameproof casserole over medium-low heat. Add the chicken pieces and cook, turning frequently, for 8–10 minutes, until lightly browned all over. Transfer the chicken to a plate using tongs.

2 Add the onion to the casserole and cook, stirring occasionally, for about 10 minutes, until softened and light golden brown. Stir the cabbage and juniper berries into the casserole, season with salt and pepper and cook over medium heat, stirring once or twice, for 6–7 minutes.

3 Stir the chestnuts into the casserole, then tuck the chicken pieces under the cabbage so that they are on the base of the casserole. Pour in the red wine.

4 Cover and cook gently for about 40 minutes, until the chicken juices run clear when the thickest part is pierced with the tip of a sharp knife and the cabbage is very tender. Taste and adjust the seasoning, if necessary, and serve immediately.

> **Cook's Tip**
> Red cabbage needs to be braised gently to be sure that it will be tender. Cooking it in red wine is a traditional accompaniment to game, but it works extremely well with chicken. The red wine helps to maintain the spectacular colour and you could also use ruby port for a slightly richer flavour. Juniper berries add a delightful resinous aroma to the dish.

Stoved Chicken Energy 524kcal/2206kJ; Protein 50.9g; Carbohydrate 48.2g, of which sugars 8.9g; Fat 15.5g, of which saturates 6g; Cholesterol 185mg; Calcium 53mg; Fibre 3.9g; Sodium 496mg.
With Red Cabbage Energy 405kcal/1697kJ; Protein 44.9g; Carbohydrate 18.6g, of which sugars 9.2g; Fat 14.9g, of which saturates 7.7g; Cholesterol 189mg; Calcium 94mg; Fibre 4.1g; Sodium 229mg.

Honey & Orange Glazed Chicken

This dish is popular in the United States and Australia and is ideal for an easy meal served with baked potatoes.

Serves 4
4 boneless chicken breast portions
  (about 175g/6oz each)
15ml/1 tbsp sunflower oil
4 spring onions (scallions),
  chopped
1 garlic clove, crushed
45ml/3 tbsp clear honey
60ml/4 tbsp fresh orange juice
1 orange, peeled and segmented
30ml/2 tbsp soy sauce
fresh lemon balm or flat leaf
  parsley, to garnish
baked potatoes and mixed salad,
  to serve

1 Preheat the oven to 190°C/375°F/Gas 5. Place the chicken portions, with skin still on, in a single layer in a shallow roasting pan and set aside.

2 Heat the sunflower oil in a small pan over low heat. Add the spring onions and garlic and cook, stirring occasionally, for about 2 minutes, until softened but not coloured.

3 Add the honey, orange juice, orange segments and soy sauce to the pan and cook, stirring constantly, until the honey has completely dissolved.

4 Pour the sauce over the chicken and bake, uncovered, for about 45 minutes, until the chicken is cooked, basting once or twice with the cooking juices. Check by piercing the thickest part with the point of a knife; the juices should run clear. Transfer the chicken to warmed individual plates, garnish with lemon balm or flat leaf parsley and serve immediately with baked potatoes and a salad.

> **Variation**
> *Create a slightly spicier version of this dish by substituting the same quantity of honey-flavoured mustard for the clear honey. Ensure the mustard has dissolved completely.*

Italian Chicken

Use chicken legs, breast portions or quarters in this colourful dish, and a different type of ribbon pasta if you like.

Serves 4
25g/1oz/¼ cup plain (all-
  purpose) flour
4 chicken portions
30ml/2 tbsp olive oil
1 onion, chopped
2 garlic cloves, chopped
1 red (bell) pepper, seeded
  and chopped
400g/14oz can chopped
  tomatoes
30ml/2 tbsp red pesto sauce
4 sun-dried tomatoes in oil,
  drained and chopped
150ml/¼ pint/⅔ cup chicken
  stock
5ml/1 tsp dried oregano
8 black olives, pitted
salt and ground black pepper
chopped fresh basil and whole
  basil leaves, to garnish
tagliatelle, to serve

1 Place the flour in a plastic bag and season with salt and pepper. Add the chicken portions and shake well until they are coated. Heat the oil in a flameproof casserole over medium heat. Add the chicken portions and cook, turning frequently, for 8–10 minutes, until browned all over. Remove with a slotted spoon and set aside.

2 Lower the heat, add the onion, garlic and red pepper and cook, stirring occasionally, for 5 minutes, until the onion is softened but not coloured.

3 Stir in the canned tomatoes, red pesto, sun-dried tomatoes, stock and oregano and bring to the boil.

4 Return the chicken portions to the casserole, season lightly with salt and pepper, cover with a tight-fitting lid and simmer gently for 30–35 minutes, until the chicken is cooked.

5 Add the black olives and simmer for a further 5 minutes. Transfer the chicken and vegetables to a warmed serving dish, sprinkle with the chopped basil and garnish with whole basil leaves. Serve immediately with hot tagliatelle.

Italian Chicken Energy 515kcal/2181kJ; Protein 51.6g; Carbohydrate 44.3g, of which sugars 39.1g; Fat 16g, of which saturates 3.5g; Cholesterol 162mg; Calcium 110mg; Fibre 12.7g; Sodium 345mg.
Glazed Chicken Energy 251kcal/1062kJ; Protein 42.4g; Carbohydrate 10.5g, of which sugars 10.5g; Fat 4.7g, of which saturates 0.9g; Cholesterol 123mg; Calcium 12mg; Fibre 0g; Sodium 642mg.

Moroccan Chicken Couscous

The combination of sweet and spicy flavours in the sauce and couscous makes this dish irresistible.

Serves 4

15g/1/2oz/1 tbsp butter
15ml/1 tbsp sunflower oil
4 chicken portions
2 onions, finely chopped
2 garlic cloves, crushed
2.5ml/1/2 tsp ground cinnamon
1.5ml/1/4 tsp ground ginger
1.5ml/1/4 tsp ground turmeric
30ml/2 tbsp orange juice
10ml/2 tsp clear honey
salt
fresh mint sprigs, to garnish

For the couscous

350g/12oz/2 1/4 cups couscous
5ml/1 tsp salt
10ml/2 tsp caster
   (superfine) sugar
15ml/1 tbsp sunflower oil
2.5ml/1/2 tsp ground cinnamon
pinch of grated nutmeg
15ml/1 tbsp orange
   blossom water
30ml/2 tbsp sultanas
   (golden raisins)
50g/2oz/1/2 cup chopped
   toasted almonds
45ml/3 tbsp chopped pistachios

1 Heat the butter and oil in a large pan over medium heat. Add the chicken portions, skin-side down, and cook, turning frequently, for 5–6 minutes, until golden. Turn them over. Add the onions, garlic, spices, a pinch of salt, the orange juice and 300ml/1/2 pint/1 1/4 cups water. Cover and bring to the boil, then lower the heat and simmer for about 30 minutes.

2 Mix the couscous with the salt and 350ml/12fl oz/1 1/2 cups water in a bowl. Leave for 5 minutes. Add the rest of the ingredients for the couscous.

3 Line a steamer with baking parchment and spoon in the couscous. Set the steamer over the pan of chicken and steam for 10 minutes.

4 Remove the steamer and keep covered. Stir the honey into the chicken liquid and boil rapidly for 3–4 minutes. Serve the chicken on a bed of couscous with some sauce spooned over it. Garnish with fresh mint and serve with the remaining sauce.

Creole Chicken Jambalaya

Clearly influenced by Spanish paella, this New Orleans speciality is probably the best-known dish of Creole cuisine.

Serves 4

1.2kg/2 1/2lb fresh chicken
1 1/2 onions
1 bay leaf
4 black peppercorns
30ml/2 tbsp vegetable oil
2 garlic cloves, chopped
1 green (bell) pepper, seeded
   and chopped
1 celery stick, chopped

225g/8oz/1 1/4 cups long
   grain rice
115g/4oz chorizo sausage, sliced
115g/4oz/1 cup chopped
   cooked ham
400g/14oz can
   chopped tomatoes
2.5ml/1/2 tsp hot chilli powder
2.5ml/1/2 tsp cumin seeds
2.5ml/1/2 tsp ground cumin
5ml/1 tsp dried thyme
115g/4oz/1 cup cooked peeled
   prawns (shrimp)
dash of Tabasco sauce
salt and ground black pepper
chopped fresh parsley, to garnish

1 Place the chicken in a flameproof casserole and pour in 600ml/1 pint/2 1/2 cups water. Add half an onion, the bay leaf and peppercorns and bring to the boil. Lower the heat, cover and simmer for 1 1/2 hours. Then lift the chicken out of the pan. Remove and discard the skin and bones and chop the meat. Strain the stock and reserve.

2 Chop the remaining whole onion. Heat the oil in a large frying pan over low heat. Add the onion, garlic, green pepper and celery and cook, stirring occasionally, for 5 minutes. Stir in the rice. Add the chorizo, ham and chicken and cook, stirring frequently, for 2–3 minutes.

3 Pour in the tomatoes and 300ml/1/2 pint/1 1/4 cups of the reserved stock and add the chilli, cumin and thyme. Bring to the boil, cover and simmer gently for 20 minutes, or until the rice is tender and the liquid absorbed.

4 Stir in the prawns and Tabasco. Cook for 5 minutes more, then season to taste with salt and pepper. Serve immediately, garnished with chopped fresh parsley.

Jambalaya Energy 802kcal/3340kJ; Protein 50.4g; Carbohydrate 59g, of which sugars 10.5g; Fat 40.5g, of which saturates 11.3g; Cholesterol 250mg; Calcium 104mg; Fibre 2.9g; Sodium 785mg.
Chicken Couscous Energy 630kcal/2639kJ; Protein 51.4g; Carbohydrate 64.1g, of which sugars 16.5g; Fat 20.2g, of which saturates 4.2g; Cholesterol 170mg; Calcium 91mg; Fibre 2.5g; Sodium 169mg.

Rabbit with Mustard

Farmed rabbit is now becoming increasingly available in larger supermarkets, ready prepared and cut into serving portions.

Serves 4

15g/¹/₂oz/2 tbsp plain (all-purpose) flour
15ml/1 tbsp English (hot) mustard powder
4 large rabbit portions
25g/1oz/2 tbsp butter
30ml/2 tbsp sunflower oil
1 onion, finely chopped

150ml/¹/₄ pint/²/₃ cup beer
300ml/¹/₂ pint/1¹/₄ cups chicken or veal stock
15ml/1 tbsp tarragon vinegar
25g/1oz/2 tbsp dark brown sugar
10–15ml/2–3 tsp prepared English mustard
salt and ground black pepper

To finish

50g/2oz/4 tbsp butter
30ml/2 tbsp sunflower oil
50g/2oz/1 cup fresh breadcrumbs
15ml/1 tbsp chopped fresh chives
15ml/1 tbsp chopped fresh tarragon

1 Preheat the oven to 160°C/325°F/Gas 3. Mix the flour and mustard powder together on a plate. Dip the rabbit portions in the flour mixture to coat. Reserve the excess flour.

2 Heat the butter and oil in a heavy, flameproof casserole over medium heat. Add the rabbit and cook, turning frequently, for 8–10 minutes, until browned all over. Transfer to a plate.

3 Lower the heat, add the onion to the pan and cook, stirring occasionally, for 5 minutes, until softened. Stir in any reserved flour mixture and cook, stirring, for 1 minute, then stir in the beer, stock and vinegar. Bring to the boil and add the sugar and black pepper. Simmer for 2 minutes. Return the rabbit and any juices that have collected to the casserole, cover with a tight-fitting lid and cook in the oven for 1 hour. Stir in the mustard and salt to taste, cover again and cook for a further 15 minutes.

4 To finish, heat together the butter and oil in a frying pan and fry the breadcrumbs, stirring frequently, until golden, then stir in the herbs. Transfer the rabbit to a warmed serving dish and sprinkle the breadcrumb mixture over the top.

Turkey Hot-pot

Turkey and sausages combine well with kidney beans and other vegetables in this hearty stew.

Serves 4

115g/4oz/scant ¹/₂ cup kidney beans, soaked overnight, drained and rinsed
40g/1¹/₂oz/3 tbsp butter
2 herb-flavoured pork sausages

450g/1lb turkey casserole meat
3 leeks, sliced
2 carrots, finely chopped
4 tomatoes, chopped
10–15ml/2–3 tsp tomato purée (paste)
1 bouquet garni
400ml/14fl oz/1¹/₂ cups chicken stock
salt and ground black pepper

1 Put the kidney beans in a pan, add water to cover and bring to the boil. Boil vigorously for 15 minutes, then drain and return to the pan. Add water to cover, bring to the boil, lower the heat and simmer for 40 minutes. Drain well and set aside.

2 Meanwhile, melt the butter in a flameproof casserole over medium-low heat. Add the sausages and cook, turning frequently, for 7–8 minutes, until browned all over and the fat runs. Remove from the casserole with tongs and drain well on kitchen paper.

3 Stir the turkey into the casserole and cook, stirring occasionally, for about 5 minutes, until lightly browned all over, then transfer to a bowl using a slotted spoon.

4 Stir the leeks and carrot into the casserole and cook, stirring occasionally, for about 8 minutes, until lightly browned. Add the chopped tomatoes and tomato purée and simmer gently for about 5 minutes.

5 Chop the sausages and return to the casserole with the beans, turkey, bouquet garni and stock and season to taste with salt and pepper. Lower the heat, cover with a tight-fitting lid and simmer gently for about 1¹/₄ hours, until the beans are tender and there is very little liquid. Spoon the stew on to warmed serving plates and serve immediately.

Rabbit Energy 531kcal/2209kJ; Protein 31.8g; Carbohydrate 21.3g, of which sugars 8.7g; Fat 35g, of which saturates 14.6g; Cholesterol 187mg; Calcium 48mg; Fibre 0.6g; Sodium 247mg.
Turkey Energy 474kcal/1994kJ; Protein 51.9g; Carbohydrate 27.9g, of which sugars 13.1g; Fat 18g, of which saturates 9g; Cholesterol 115mg; Calcium 116mg; Fibre 11.8g; Sodium 308mg.

Duck with Cumberland Sauce

A sophisticated dish: the sauce contains both port and brandy, making it very rich and quite delicious.

Serves 4
4 duck portions
grated rind and juice of 1 lemon
grated rind and juice of 1 large orange
60ml/4 tbsp redcurrant jelly
60ml/4 tbsp port
pinch of ground mace or ginger
15ml/1 tbsp brandy
salt and ground black pepper
orange slices, to garnish

1 Preheat the oven to 190°C/375°F/Gas 5. Place a rack in a roasting pan. Prick the skin of the duck portions all over and sprinkle with salt and pepper. Place on the rack and roast for 45–50 minutes, until the skin is crisp and the juices run clear when the thickest part is pierced with the point of a knife.

2 Meanwhile, simmer the lemon and orange rinds and juices together in a small pan for 5 minutes.

3 Add the redcurrant jelly and stir until melted, then stir in the port. Bring to the boil and add the mace or ginger and salt and pepper, to taste.

4 Transfer the duck to a serving platter and keep warm. Pour the fat from the roasting pan, leaving the cooking juices. Place the pan over low heat and stir in the brandy. Cook, scraping the sediment from the base of the pan, and bring to the boil. Stir in the port mixture and serve with the duck, garnished with orange slices.

> **Cook's Tip**
> Duck is well known for being a fatty bird. Pricking the skin helps to release the fat during cooking. A clean darning needle is ideal for this. You can also use a fork, but try not to pierce the flesh. If the duck is then roasted on a rack over a roasting pan, the fat will collect beneath the duck preventing it from sitting in a lake of grease.

Coronation Chicken

Created in 1953 in honour of the coronation of HM Queen Elizabeth II, this cold chicken dish with a mild, curry-flavoured sauce is ideal for summer lunch parties and picnics.

Serves 8
1/2 lemon
2.25kg/5lb chicken
1 onion, quartered
1 carrot, quartered
1 large bouquet garni
8 black peppercorns, crushed
pinch of salt
fresh watercress or parsley sprigs, to garnish

For the sauce
1 small onion, chopped
15g/1/2oz/1 tbsp butter
15ml/1 tbsp curry paste
15ml/1 tbsp tomato purée (paste)
120ml/4fl oz/1/2 cup red wine
1 bay leaf
juice of 1/2 lemon, or to taste
10–15ml/2–3 tsp apricot jam
300ml/1/2 pint/1 1/4 cups mayonnaise
120ml/4fl oz/1/2 cup whipping cream, whipped
salt and ground black pepper

1 Put the lemon half in the chicken cavity, then place the chicken in a pan that it just fits. Add the onion, carrot, bouquet garni, peppercorns and salt.

2 Add sufficient water to come two-thirds of the way up the chicken and bring to the boil, then lower the heat, cover and simmer for about 1 1/2 hours, until the chicken juices run clear.

3 Transfer the chicken to a large bowl, pour the cooking liquid over it and leave to cool. When cool, transfer the chicken to a board. Remove the skin and bones and chop the flesh.

4 To make the sauce, cook the onion in the butter until soft. Add the curry paste, tomato purée, wine, bay leaf and lemon juice, then cook for 10 minutes. Add the jam; sieve and cool.

5 Beat the sauce mixture into the mayonnaise. Fold in the cream, season to taste with salt and pepper and add the lemon juice, then stir in with the chicken. Garnish and serve.

Duck Energy 277kcal/1162kJ; Protein 29.7g; Carbohydrate 12.2g, of which sugars 12.2g; Fat 9.8g, of which saturates 3g; Cholesterol 165mg; Calcium 21mg; Fibre 0g; Sodium 170mg.
Chicken Energy 480kcal/1994kJ; Protein 30.9g; Carbohydrate 2.8g, of which sugars 2.5g; Fat 37.3g, of which saturates 9.4g; Cholesterol 135mg; Calcium 22mg; Fibre 0.2g; Sodium 265mg.

Tandoori Chicken Kebabs

This popular dish originates from the Punjab, where it is traditionally cooked in clay ovens known as *tandoors*.

Serves 4
4 skinless chicken breast fillets
    (about 175g/6oz each)
15ml/1 tbsp lemon juice
45ml/3 tbsp tandoori paste
45ml/3 tbsp natural (plain) yogurt

1 garlic clove, crushed
30ml/2 tbsp chopped fresh
    coriander (cilantro)
1 small onion, cut into wedges
    and separated into layers
vegetable oil, for brushing
salt and ground black pepper
fresh coriander sprigs, to garnish
pilau rice and naan bread,
    to serve

1 Chop the chicken fillets into 2.5cm/1in dice and place in a bowl. Add the lemon juice, tandoori paste, yogurt, garlic and coriander and season with salt and pepper. Cover with clear film (plastic wrap) and leave to marinate in the refrigerator, stirring occasionally, for 2–3 hours.

2 Preheat the grill (broiler). Thread alternate pieces of marinated chicken and onion on to four skewers.

3 Brush the onions with a little oil, lay on a grill (broiler) rack and cook under high heat for 10–12 minutes, turning once. Transfer the skewers to warmed plates, garnish the kebabs with fresh coriander and serve immediately with pilau rice and warm naan bread.

Cook's Tip
For a special occasion or when cooking these kebabs on a barbecue, serve with a yogurt dip. Mix together 250ml/8fl oz/ 1 cup natural (plain) yogurt, 30ml/2 tbsp double (heavy) cream, 30ml/2 tbsp chopped fresh mint and ½ peeled, seeded and finely chopped cucumber in a bowl. Season to taste with salt and pepper. Cover with clear film (plastic wrap) and chill in the refrigerator until ready to serve. As an alternative to the mint you could use chopped fresh coriander (cilantro).

Chinese Chicken with Cashew Nuts

The cashew nuts give this dish a delightful crunchy texture that contrasts well with the noodles.

Serves 4
4 skinless chicken breast fillets
    (about 175g/6oz each)
3 garlic cloves, crushed
60ml/4 tbsp soy sauce
30ml/2 tbsp cornflour
    (cornstarch)
225g/8oz/4 cups dried

egg noodles
45ml/3 tbsp groundnut (peanut)
    or sunflower oil
15ml/1 tbsp sesame oil
115g/4oz/1 cup roasted
    cashew nuts
6 spring onions (scallions), cut
    into 5cm/2in pieces and
    halved lengthways
spring onion curls and a little
    chopped fresh red chilli,
    to garnish

1 Slice the chicken into strips, place in a bowl and stir in the garlic, soy sauce and cornflour. Cover with clear film (plastic wrap) and chill in the refrigerator for about 30 minutes.

2 Meanwhile, bring a pan of water to the boil and add the egg noodles. Turn off the heat and leave to stand for 5 minutes. Drain well and reserve.

3 Heat the oils in a large frying pan or wok. Add the chilled chicken and marinade juices and stir-fry over high heat for 3–4 minutes, or until golden brown.

4 Add the cashew nuts and spring onions to the pan or wok and stir-fry for a further 2–3 minutes.

5 Add the drained noodles and stir-fry for 2 minutes more. Toss the noodles well and serve immediately, garnished with the spring onion curls and chopped chilli.

Cook's Tip
For a milder garnish, seed the red chilli before chopping or finely dice some red (bell) pepper instead.

Tandoori Energy 222kcal/937kJ; Protein 42.8g; Carbohydrate 2g, of which sugars 1.7g; Fat 4.8g, of which saturates 0.9g; Cholesterol 123mg; Calcium 34mg; Fibre 0.2g; Sodium 115mg.
Chinese Energy 717kcal/3007kJ; Protein 55.5g; Carbohydrate 54.3g, of which sugars 4.2g; Fat 32.3g, of which saturates 6.1g; Cholesterol 139mg; Calcium 44mg; Fibre 2.8g; Sodium 1363mg.

Duck, Avocado & Berry Salad

Duck breasts are roasted with a honey and soy glaze until crisp, then served warm with fresh raspberries and avocado.

Serves 4
4 small or 2 large duck breast
  portions, halved if large
15ml/1 tbsp clear honey
15ml/1 tbsp dark soy sauce
mixed chopped fresh salad leaves
  such as lamb's lettuce, radicchio
  or frisée

2 avocados, stoned (pitted),
  peeled and cut into chunks
115g/4oz/1 cup raspberries
salt and ground black pepper

For the dressing
60ml/4 tbsp olive oil
15ml/1 tbsp raspberry vinegar
15ml/1 tbsp redcurrant jelly

1 Preheat the oven to 220°C/425°F/Gas 7. Prick the skin of each duck breast portion with a fork. Blend the honey and soy sauce together in a small bowl, then brush the mixture all over the skins of the duck.

2 Place the duck breast portions on a rack set over a roasting pan and season with salt and pepper. Roast for 15–20 minutes, until the skins are crisp and the meat cooked.

3 Meanwhile, to make the dressing, put the oil, vinegar and redcurrant jelly in a small bowl, season with salt and pepper and whisk well until evenly blended.

4 Slice the duck breast portions diagonally and arrange on four individual plates with the salad leaves, avocados and raspberries. Spoon the dressing over the top and serve immediately.

> **Cook's Tip**
> *Small avocados contain the most flavour and have a good texture. They should be ripe but not too soft, so avoid any with skins that are turning black.*

Chinese-style Chicken Salad

For a variation and to add more colour, add some cooked, peeled prawns to this lovely salad.

Serves 4
4 chicken breast fillets (about
  175g/6oz each)
60ml/4 tbsp dark soy sauce
pinch of Chinese five-spice powder
squeeze of lemon juice
½ cucumber, peeled and cut into
  thin batons
5ml/1 tsp salt
45ml/3 tbsp sunflower oil
30ml/2 tbsp sesame oil

15ml/1 tbsp sesame seeds
30ml/2 tbsp Chinese rice wine or
  dry sherry
2 carrots, cut into thin batons
8 spring onions
  (scallions), shredded
75g/3oz/1 cup beansprouts

For the sauce
60ml/4 tbsp crunchy
  peanut butter
10ml/2 tsp lemon juice
10ml/2 tsp sesame oil
1.5ml/¼ tsp hot chilli powder
1 spring onion, finely chopped

1 Put the chicken into a pan and pour in water to cover. Add 15ml/1 tbsp of the soy sauce, the Chinese five-spice powder and lemon juice. Cover and bring to the boil, then lower the heat and simmer for 20 minutes. Drain the chicken and remove and discard the skin. Slice the flesh into thin strips.

2 Sprinkle the cucumber batons with salt, leave for 30 minutes, then rinse well and pat dry with kitchen paper.

3 Heat the oils in a small frying pan. Add the sesame seeds and cook for 30 seconds, then stir in the remaining soy sauce and the rice wine or sherry. Add the carrot batons and stir-fry for 2 minutes, then remove the pan from the heat.

4 Mix together the cucumber, spring onions, beansprouts, carrots, pan juices and chicken. Transfer to a shallow dish. Cover with clear film (plastic wrap) and chill in the refrigerator for 1 hour.

5 For the sauce, cream the first four ingredients together, then stir in the spring onion. Serve the chicken with the sauce.

Chicken Energy 452kcal/1886kJ; Protein 47g; Carbohydrate 4.1g, of which sugars 3g; Fat 27.2g, of which saturates 4.8g; Cholesterol 123mg; Calcium 53mg; Fibre 1.5g; Sodium 1720mg.
Duck Energy 345kcal/1438kJ; Protein 21.2g; Carbohydrate 8g, of which sugars 7.3g; Fat 27.2g, of which saturates 5g; Cholesterol 110mg; Calcium 26mg; Fibre 2.4g; Sodium 382mg.

Crumbed Turkey Steaks

The authentic Austrian dish, *wiener schnitzel*, uses veal escalopes, but turkey steaks make a tasty alternative.

Serves 4
4 turkey breast steaks (about 150g/5oz each)
40g/1½oz/⅓ cup plain (all-purpose) flour, seasoned
1 egg, lightly beaten
75g/3oz/1½ cups fresh white breadcrumbs
75ml/5 tbsp finely grated Parmesan cheese
25g/1oz/2 tbsp butter
45ml/3 tbsp sunflower oil
fresh parsley sprigs, to garnish
4 lemon wedges, to serve

1 Lay the turkey steaks between two sheets of clear film (plastic wrap). Beat each one with a rolling pin until flattened and even. Snip the edges of the steaks with kitchen scissors a few times to prevent them from curling during cooking.

2 Place the seasoned flour on one plate, the egg in a shallow bowl and the breadcrumbs and Parmesan mixed together on another plate.

3 Dip each side of the steaks into the flour and shake off any excess. Next, dip them into the egg and then gently press each side into the breadcrumbs and cheese until evenly coated.

4 Heat the butter and oil in a large frying pan over medium heat. Add the turkey steaks and cook for 2–3 minutes on each side, until golden. Transfer to warmed plates, garnish with fresh parsley sprigs and serve with lemon wedges.

Cook's Tip
The easiest way to make breadcrumbs is in a food processor. Tear the bread into 2.5cm/1in pieces and process in brief bursts with a metal blade. You can also use a blender in the same way, but work in small batches, emptying each one into a bowl before adding more bread. The traditional way is, of course, to use a grater, taking care not to damage your fingers.

Country Cider Hot-pot

Rabbit meat is now beginning to regain its popularity – it never lost it in some European countries – and, like all game, is a healthy, low-fat option.

Serves 4
25g/1oz/¼ cup plain (all-purpose) flour
4 boneless rabbit portions
25g/1oz/2 tbsp butter
15ml/1 tbsp vegetable oil
15 baby (pearl) onions
4 rashers (strips) streaky (fatty) bacon, chopped
10ml/2 tsp Dijon mustard
450ml/¾ pint/1¾ cups dry (hard) cider
3 carrots, chopped
2 parsnips, chopped
12 ready-to-eat prunes
1 fresh rosemary sprig
1 bay leaf
salt and ground black pepper
mashed potatoes, to serve (optional)

1 Preheat the oven to 160°C/325°F/Gas 3. Place the flour in a plastic bag, season with salt and pepper and shake to mix. Add the rabbit portions and shake until coated. Remove from the bag and set aside.

2 Heat the butter and oil in a flameproof casserole over medium-low heat. Add the onions and bacon and cook, stirring occasionally, for about 4 minutes, until the onions have softened. Remove with a slotted spoon and set aside.

3 Add the rabbit portions to the casserole and cook, turning frequently, for 8–10 minutes, until evenly browned all over. Spread a little of the mustard over the top of each portion.

4 Return the onions and bacon to the casserole, pour in the cider and add the carrots, parsnips, prunes, rosemary and bay leaf. Season generously with salt and pepper. Bring to the boil, then cover with a tight-fitting lid and transfer to the oven. Cook for about 1½ hours, until the meat is cooked through and the vegetables are tender.

5 Remove and discard the rosemary sprig and bay leaf and serve the rabbit hot with creamy mashed potatoes, if you like.

Turkey Energy 565kcal/2376kJ; Protein 64.9g; Carbohydrate 24.3g, of which sugars 0.7g; Fat 24g, of which saturates 9.4g; Cholesterol 191mg; Calcium 283mg; Fibre 0.8g; Sodium 538mg.
Hot-pot Energy 544kcal/2279kJ; Protein 41.1g; Carbohydrate 42.9g, of which sugars 32.2g; Fat 21g, of which saturates 8.2g; Cholesterol 136mg; Calcium 129mg; Fibre 8g; Sodium 488mg.

Turkey Pastitsio

A traditional Greek *pastitsio* is a rich, high-fat dish made with beef, but this lighter version is just as tasty.

Serves 4–6

450g/1lb lean minced (ground) turkey
1 large onion, finely chopped
60ml/4 tbsp tomato purée (paste)
250ml/8fl oz/1 cup red wine or chicken stock
5ml/1 tsp ground cinnamon
300g/11oz/3 cups macaroni
300ml/½ pint/1¼ cups skimmed milk
25g/1oz/2 tbsp sunflower margarine
25g/1oz/¼ cup plain (all-purpose) flour
5ml/1 tsp grated nutmeg
2 tomatoes, sliced
60ml/4 tbsp wholemeal (whole-wheat) breadcrumbs
salt and ground black pepper
green salad, to serve

1 Preheat the oven to 220°C/425°F/Gas 7. Fry the turkey and onion in a non-stick frying pan without adding any fat, stirring until the turkey is lightly browned.

2 Stir in the tomato purée, red wine or stock and cinnamon. Season with salt and pepper, then cover with a tight-fitting lid and simmer for 5 minutes.

3 Bring a pan of salted water to the boil, add the macaroni, bring back to the boil and cook for 8–10 minutes, until just tender. Drain well.

4 Spoon alternate layers of macaroni and the meat mixture into a wide ovenproof dish.

5 Place the milk, margarine and flour in a pan and whisk over medium heat until thickened and smooth. Add the nutmeg and season with salt and pepper to taste.

6 Pour the sauce evenly over the pasta and meat. Arrange the tomato slices on top and sprinkle lines of breadcrumbs over the surface. Bake for 30–35 minutes, or until golden brown and bubbling. Serve hot with a green salad.

Tuscan Chicken

A simple peasant casserole with all the flavours of Tuscan ingredients. The white wine can be replaced by chicken stock.

Serves 4

5ml/1 tsp olive oil
8 chicken thighs, skinned
1 onion, thinly sliced
2 red (bell) peppers, seeded and sliced
1 garlic clove, crushed
300ml/½ pint/1¼ cups passata (bottled strained tomatoes)
150ml/¼ pint/⅔ cup dry white wine
large fresh oregano sprig, or 5ml/1 tsp dried oregano
400g/14oz can cannellini beans, drained and rinsed
45ml/3 tbsp fresh breadcrumbs
salt and ground black pepper
fresh oregano or flat leaf parsley sprigs, to garnish

1 Heat the oil in a large, heavy pan over medium heat. Add the chicken and cook, turning frequently, for 8–10 minutes, until golden brown all over. Remove the chicken from the pan and keep hot.

2 Add the onion and red peppers to the pan, lower the heat and cook, stirring occasionally, for about 5 minutes, until softened but not coloured. Stir in the garlic.

3 Return the chicken to the pan and add the passata, wine and oregano. Season well with salt and pepper, bring to the boil, then cover the pan with a tight-fitting lid.

4 Lower the heat and simmer gently, stirring occasionally, for 30–35 minutes, or until the chicken is tender and the juices run clear when the thickest par is pierced with the point of a knife.

5 Preheat the grill (broiler). Stir in the cannellini beans and simmer for a further 5 minutes until heated through. Sprinkle with the breadcrumbs and cook under the grill for a few minutes, until golden brown.

6 Divide the chicken, beans and vegetables among warmed serving plates, garnish with herb sprigs and serve immediately.

Turkey Energy 406kcal/1716kJ; Protein 28.9g; Carbohydrate 56.8g, of which sugars 9.5g; Fat 5.5g, of which saturates 0.4g; Cholesterol 45mg; Calcium 117mg; Fibre 3.1g; Sodium 202mg.
Chicken Energy 379kcal/1599kJ; Protein 41.3g; Carbohydrate 35.8g, of which sugars 12.6g; Fat 6.2g, of which saturates 1.5g; Cholesterol 158mg; Calcium 118mg; Fibre 8.5g; Sodium 789mg.

Poussins with Grapes in Vermouth

This sauce could also be served with roast chicken, but poussins have the stronger flavour.

Serves 4
4 poussins (about 450g/1lb each)
50g/2oz/¼ cup butter, softened
2 shallots, chopped
60ml/4 tbsp chopped fresh parsley
225g/8oz/2 cups white grapes, preferably Muscatel, halved and seeded
150ml/¼ pint/⅔ cup white vermouth
5ml/1 tsp cornflour (cornstarch)
60ml/4 tbsp double (heavy) cream
30ml/2 tbsp pine nuts, toasted
salt and ground black pepper
watercress sprigs or mizuna, to garnish

1 Preheat the oven to 200°C/400°F/Gas 6. Spread the softened butter all over the poussins and put a hazelnut-sized piece in the cavity of each bird.

2 Mix together the shallots and parsley and place a quarter of the mixture inside each poussin. Put the poussins side by side in a large roasting pan and roast for 40–50 minutes, or until the juices run clear when the thickest part is pierced with the point of a sharp knife. Transfer the poussins to a warmed serving plate. Cover and keep warm.

3 Skim off most of the fat from the roasting pan, then add the grapes and vermouth. Place the pan over a low heat for a few minutes to warm and slightly soften the grapes. Lift the grapes out of the pan using a slotted spoon and place them around the poussins. Keep covered.

4 Stir the cornflour into the cream until smooth, then add to the pan juices. Cook gently, stirring constantly, for 3–4 minutes, until the sauce has thickened slightly. Season to taste with salt and pepper. Spoon the sauce around the poussins. Sprinkle with the toasted pine nuts and garnish with watercress sprigs or mizuna. Serve immediately.

Chicken Parcels with Herb Butter

These delightful individual filo pastry parcels contain a wonderfully moist and herb-flavoured filling.

Serves 4
4 skinless chicken breast fillets (about 175g/6oz each)
150g/5oz/generous ½ cup butter, softened, plus extra for greasing
90ml/6 tbsp mixed chopped fresh herbs, such as thyme, parsley, oregano and rosemary
5ml/1 tsp lemon juice
5 large sheets filo pastry, thawed if frozen
1 egg, beaten
30ml/2 tbsp freshly grated Parmesan cheese
salt and ground black pepper

1 Season the chicken fillets on both sides with salt and pepper. Melt 25g/1oz/2 tbsp of the butter in a frying pan over medium heat. Add the chicken and cook, turning once, for about 5 minutes, until lightly browned on both sides. Remove from the pan and leave to cool.

2 Preheat the oven to 190°C/375°F/Gas 5. Lightly grease a baking sheet with butter. Put the remaining measured butter, the herbs and lemon juice in a food processor or blender, season with salt and pepper and process until smooth. Melt half of this herb butter.

3 Take one sheet of filo pastry and brush with melted herb butter. Keep the other sheets covered with a damp dish towel. Fold the filo pastry sheet in half and brush again with butter. Place a chicken portion about 2.5cm/1in from the top end.

4 Dot the chicken with a quarter of the unmelted herb butter. Fold in the sides of the dough, then roll up to enclose the chicken completely. Place seam-side down on a lightly greased baking sheet. Repeat with the other chicken portions.

5 Brush the filo parcels with beaten egg. Cut the last sheet of filo into strips, then scrunch and arrange on top. Brush the parcels with the egg glaze, then sprinkle with Parmesan cheese. Bake for 35–50 minutes, until golden brown. Serve hot.

Poussins Energy 831kcal/3456kJ; Protein 52.1g; Carbohydrate 12.3g, of which sugars 11.1g; Fat 60.2g, of which saturates 21.8g; Cholesterol 308mg; Calcium 62mg; Fibre 1.2g; Sodium 270mg.
Chicken Energy 554kcal/2310kJ; Protein 42.5g; Carbohydrate 14.8g, of which sugars 0.5g; Fat 36.6g, of which saturates 22g; Cholesterol 240mg; Calcium 138mg; Fibre 0.6g; Sodium 417mg.

Pot-roast of Venison

The venison is marinated for 24 hours before preparation to give this rich dish an even fuller flavour.

Serves 4–5

1.75kg/4lb boned leg or shoulder of venison
75ml/5 tbsp sunflower oil
4 cloves
8 black peppercorns, lightly crushed
12 juniper berries, lightly crushed
250ml/8fl oz/1 cup full-bodied red wine
115g/4oz lightly smoked streaky (fatty) bacon, chopped
2 onions, finely chopped
2 carrots, chopped
150g/5oz large mushrooms, sliced
15g/½ oz/2 tbsp plain (all-purpose) flour
250ml/8fl oz/1 cup veal stock
30ml/2 tbsp redcurrant jelly
salt and ground black pepper

1 Put the venison in a bowl, add half the oil, the cloves, peppercorns, juniper berries and wine, cover with clear film (plastic wrap) and leave in a cold place or the refrigerator for 24 hours, turning the meat occasionally.

2 Preheat the oven to 160°C/325°F/Gas 3. Remove the venison from the bowl and pat dry. Reserve the marinade. Heat the remaining oil in a large shallow pan over medium heat. Add the venison and cook, turning once, for about 10 minutes, until evenly browned on both sides. Transfer to a plate.

3 Stir the bacon, onions, carrots and mushrooms into the pan and cook, stirring occasionally, for about 5 minutes. Stir in the flour and cook, stirring constantly, for 2 minutes, then remove the pan from the heat and gradually stir in the reserved marinade, stock and redcurrant jelly. Season with salt and pepper. Return the pan to the heat and bring to the boil, stirring constantly. Lower the heat and simmer for 2–3 minutes.

4 Transfer the venison and sauce to a casserole and cover with a tight-fitting lid. Cook in the oven, turning the the venison occasionally, for about 3 hours, until very tender. Remove the venison from the casserole and divide the sauce among warmed plates. Carve the venison and place on top. Serve.

Pheasant with Mushrooms

The wine and mushroom sauce in this recipe is given a lift by the inclusion of anchovy fillets.

Serves 4

1 pheasant, cut into portions
250ml/8fl oz/1 cup red wine
45ml/3 tbsp sunflower oil
60ml/4 tbsp Spanish sherry vinegar
1 large onion, chopped
2 rashers (strips) smoked bacon
350g/12oz chestnut (cremini) mushrooms, sliced
3 canned anchovy fillets, drained, soaked in water for 10 minutes and drained
350ml/12fl oz/1½ cups game, veal or chicken stock
1 bouquet garni
salt and ground black pepper

1 Place the pheasant portions in a dish. Add the wine, half the oil and half the vinegar, then sprinkle with half the onion. Season with salt and pepper. Cover the dish with clear film (plastic wrap) and leave in a cold place or the refrigerator, turning the pheasant portions occasionally, for 8–12 hours.

2 Preheat the oven to 160°C/325°F/Gas 3. Lift the pheasant portions from the dish and pat dry with kitchen paper. Reserve the marinade.

3 Heat the remaining oil in a flameproof casserole over medium heat. Add the pheasant portions and cook, turning frequently, for 8–10 minutes, until evenly browned all over. Transfer to a plate.

4 Cut the bacon into strips, then add to the casserole with the remaining onion. Cook over low heat, stirring occasionally, for 5 minutes, until the onion is softened but not coloured. Stir in the mushrooms and cook for about 3 minutes.

5 Stir in the anchovies and remaining vinegar and boil until reduced. Add the marinade, cook for 2 minutes, then add the stock and bouquet garni. Return the pheasant to the casserole, cover and bake for about 1½ hours. Transfer the pheasant to a serving dish. Boil the juices to reduce. Discard the bouquet garni, pour the juices over the pheasant and serve immediately.

Venison Energy 601kcal/2528kJ; Protein 83.1g; Carbohydrate 13g, of which sugars 9.6g; Fat 22.9g, of which saturates 5.9g; Cholesterol 187mg; Calcium 49mg; Fibre 1.9g; Sodium 566mg.
Pheasant Energy 457kcal/1910kJ; Protein 46.2g; Carbohydrate 6.4g, of which sugars 4.5g; Fat 23.1g, of which saturates 6.1g; Cholesterol 9mg; Calcium 102mg; Fibre 2g; Sodium 483mg.

Minty Yogurt Chicken

Marinated, grilled chicken thighs make a tasty light lunch or supper – and they are an economical buy, too.

Serves 4
8 chicken thigh portions

15ml/1 tbsp clear honey
30ml/2 tbsp lime juice
30ml/2 tbsp natural (plain) yogurt
60ml/4 tbsp chopped fresh mint
salt and ground black pepper
boiled new potatoes and tomato
salad, to serve (optional)

1 Skin the chicken thighs and slash the flesh at intervals with a sharp knife. Place them in a non-metal bowl. Mix together the honey, lime juice, yogurt and half the mint in another bowl and season with salt and pepper.

2 Spoon the marinade over the chicken, cover the bowl with clear film (plastic wrap) and leave to marinate in a cool place for 30 minutes.

3 Line a grill (broiler) pan with foil and preheat the grill (broiler). Remove the chicken from the marinade, place in the pan and cook, turning occasionally, for 15–20 minutes, until golden brown and the juices run clear when thickest part is pierced with point of a sharp knife.

4 Transfer the chicken thighs to warmed plates, sprinkle with the remaining mint and serve immediately with potatoes and tomato salad, if you like.

Cook's Tip
If you want to marinate the chicken for longer than 30 minutes, place the bowl in the refrigerator.

Variation
Substitute chicken drumsticks for the thighs and increase the cooking time by 5–10 minutes.

Mandarin Sesame Duck

The rind, juice and flesh of sweet mandarin oranges are used in this delightful dish.

Serves 4
4 duck leg or breast fillets
30ml/2 tbsp light soy sauce

45ml/3 tbsp clear honey
15ml/1 tbsp sesame seeds
4 mandarin oranges
5ml/1 tsp cornflour (cornstarch)
salt and ground black pepper

1 Preheat the oven to 180°C/350°F/Gas 4. Prick the duck skin all over. Slash the breast skin diagonally at intervals. Roast the duck for 1 hour. Mix 15ml/1 tbsp soy sauce with 30ml/2 tbsp honey and brush over the duck. Sprinkle with sesame seeds. Roast for a further 15 minutes.

2 Grate the rind from one mandarin and squeeze the juice from two. Place in a small pan and stir in the cornflour, remaining soy sauce and honey. Heat, stirring, until thickened and clear. Season with salt and pepper. Peel and slice the remaining mandarins. Serve the duck with the mandarin slices and sauce.

Sticky Ginger Chicken

For a fuller flavour, marinate the chicken drumsticks in the glaze for 30 minutes.

Serves 4
8 chicken drumsticks

30ml/2 tbsp lemon juice
25g/1oz light muscovado
(brown) sugar
5ml/1 tsp grated fresh root ginger
10ml/2 tsp soy sauce
ground black pepper

1 Slash the chicken drumsticks about three times through the thickest part of the flesh. Mix all the remaining ingredients in a bowl, then toss the drumsticks in the glaze.

2 Cook them under a hot grill (broiler) or on a barbecue, turning occasionally and brushing with the glaze, until golden and the juices run clear when the thickest part is pierced.

Minty Yogurt Energy 179kcal/752kJ; Protein 31.8g; Carbohydrate 3.4g, of which sugars 3.4g; Fat 4.3g, of which saturates 1.3g; Cholesterol 158mg; Calcium 25mg; Fibre 0g; Sodium 142mg.
Mandarin Duck Energy 254kcal/1066kJ; Protein 31g; Carbohydrate 12g, of which sugars 10.9g; Fat 12g, of which saturates 2.3g; Cholesterol 165mg; Calcium 55mg; Fibre 0.5g; Sodium 704mg.
Sticky Ginger Energy 234kcal/980kJ; Protein 29.2g; Carbohydrate 6.5g, of which sugars 6.5g; Fat 10.3g, of which saturates 2.7g; Cholesterol 155mg; Calcium 20mg; Fibre 0g; Sodium 145mg.

Oat-crusted Chicken with Sage

Oats make an excellent, crunchy coating for savoury foods, and offer a good way to add extra fibre.

Serves 4
45ml/3 tbsp milk
10ml/2 tsp English (hot) mustard
40g/1½oz/½ cup rolled oats
45ml/3 tbsp chopped fresh sage leaves
8 chicken thighs or drumsticks, skinned
120ml/4fl oz/½ cup fromage frais (farmer's cheese)
5ml/1 tsp wholegrain mustard
salt and ground black pepper
fresh sage leaves, to garnish

1 Preheat the oven to 200°C/400°F/Gas 6. Mix together the milk and mustard in a small bowl.

2 Mix the oats with 30ml/2 tbsp of the chopped sage on a plate and season with salt and pepper. Brush the chicken with the milk mixture and press into the oats to coat evenly.

3 Place the chicken on a baking sheet and bake for about 40 minutes, or until the juices run clear when the thickest part is pierced with the point of a sharp knife.

4 Meanwhile, mix together the fromage frais, wholegrain mustard and remaining sage in a bowl and season to taste with salt and pepper. Transfer to a small serving dish.

5 Place the chicken on warmed serving plates and garnish with fresh sage leaves. Serve immediately with the dish of sauce.

Cook's Tips
• If fresh sage is not available, choose another fresh herb, such as thyme, parsley or tarragon. Sage is one of those herbs that does not dry well, quickly becoming dusty and flavourless.
• These chicken thighs or drumsticks may be served hot or cold. They would be a good choice for a picnic. Pack the sauce separately in a plastic container or screw-top jar.
• If you find English (hot) mustard too spicy, substitute Dijon.

Chicken in Creamy Orange Sauce

The brandy adds a rich flavour to the sauce, but omit it if you prefer and use orange juice alone.

Serves 4
8 chicken thighs or drumsticks, skinned
45ml/3 tbsp brandy
300ml/½ pint/1¼ cups fresh orange juice
3 spring onions (scallions), chopped
10ml/2 tsp cornflour (cornstarch)
90ml/6 tbsp fromage frais (farmer's cheese)
salt and ground black pepper
boiled rice or pasta and green salad, to serve (optional)

1 Cook the chicken pieces in a non-stick or heavy frying pan, without any added fat, over medium-low heat for 8–10 minutes, turning frequently until evenly browned all over.

2 Stir in the brandy, orange juice and spring onions and bring to the boil. Lower the heat, cover and simmer gently for about 15 minutes, or until the chicken is tender and the juices run clear when the thickest part is pierced with the point of a sharp knife.

3 Blend the cornflour with a little water in a small bowl, then mix into the fromage frais. Stir this into a small pan and cook over medium heat until boiling.

4 Season the sauce to taste with salt and pepper. Spoon the chicken and cooking juices on to warmed plates, pour the sauce over it and serve with plain boiled rice or pasta and green salad, if you like.

Cook's Tip
For an even healthier version of this dish, suitable for those who are watching their weight or cholesterol levels, use low-fat fromage frais (farmer's cheese) which is virtually fat-free. The sauce will still be beautifully creamy and rich tasting.

Oat-crusted Energy 238kcal/997kJ; Protein 32.2g; Carbohydrate 3g, of which sugars 3g; Fat 10.9g, of which saturates 3.1g; Cholesterol 157mg; Calcium 66mg; Fibre 0g; Sodium 163mg.
In Orange Sauce Energy 306kcal/1287kJ; Protein 43.7g; Carbohydrate 10.1g, of which sugars 7.7g; Fat 7.5g, of which saturates 2.9g; Cholesterol 212mg; Calcium 50mg; Fibre 0.2g; Sodium 198mg.

Duck with Orange Sauce

This is a simple, yet more elegant-looking variation on the classic French whole duck.

Serves 4
4 duck breast portions
15ml/1 tbsp sunflower oil
2 oranges

150ml/¼ pint/⅔ cup fresh
   orange juice
15ml/1 tbsp port
30ml/2 tbsp Seville (Temple)
   orange marmalade
15g/½oz/1 tbsp butter
5ml/1 tsp cornflour (cornstarch)
salt and ground black pepper

1 Season the duck skin with salt and pepper. Heat the oil in a frying pan over a medium heat. Add the duck breast portions, skin-side down, cover and cook for 3–4 minutes, until just lightly browned. Turn the duck over, lower the heat slightly and cook, uncovered, for 5–6 minutes.

2 Peel the skin from the oranges and remove the white pith. Working over a bowl to catch any juice, slice either side of the membranes with a sharp knife to release the orange segments. Set the segments aside with the juice.

3 Remove the duck portions from the pan with a slotted spoon, drain on kitchen paper and keep warm in the oven while making the sauce.

4 Drain off the fat from the frying pan. Add the segmented oranges, all but 30ml/2 tbsp of the orange juice, the port and the orange marmalade. Bring to the boil and then reduce the heat slightly. Gradually whisk small knobs (pats) of the butter into the sauce, one piece at a time, and season to taste with salt and pepper.

5 Blend the cornflour with the reserved orange juice in a small bowl, pour into the pan and stir until the sauce has thickened slightly. Return the duck to the pan and cook over low heat for about 3 minutes. Remove the duck portions from the pan and cut into thick slices. Arrange them on warmed plates and spoon the sauce over them. Serve immediately.

Normandy Roast Chicken

The chicken is turned over halfway through roasting so that it cooks evenly and stays wonderfully moist.

Serves 4
50g/2oz/¼ cup butter, softened
30ml/2 tbsp chopped
   fresh tarragon

1 small garlic clove, crushed
1.5kg/3–3½lb fresh chicken
5ml/1 tsp plain (all-purpose) flour
150ml/¼ pint/⅔ cup double
   (heavy) cream
squeeze of lemon juice
salt and ground black pepper
fresh tarragon and lemon slices,
   to garnish

1 Preheat the oven to 200°C/400°F/Gas 6. Mix together the butter, 15ml/1 tbsp of the chopped tarragon and the garlic in a bowl and season with salt and pepper. Spoon half the butter mixture into the cavity of the chicken.

2 Carefully lift the skin at the neck end of the bird from the breast flesh on each side, then gently push a little of the butter mixture into each pocket and smooth it down over the breasts with your fingers.

3 Season the bird and lay it, breast-side down, in a roasting pan. Roast for 45 minutes, then turn the chicken over and baste with the cooking juices. Cook for a further 45 minutes, until the juices run clear when the thickest part of the chicken is pierced with the point of a sharp knife.

4 When the chicken is cooked, lift it to drain out any juices from the cavity into the pan, then transfer the bird to a warmed platter, cover and keep warm.

5 Place the roasting pan over low heat and heat until sizzling. Stir in the flour and cook, stirring constantly, for 1 minute, then stir in the cream, the remaining tarragon, 150ml/¼ pint/⅔ cup water and the lemon juice. Season to taste with salt and pepper. Bring to the boil and cook, stirring constantly, for 2–3 minutes, until thickened. Carve the chicken into slices and place them on warmed plates. Garnish with tarragon and lemon slices and serve with the sauce handed separately.

Roast Chicken Energy 491kcal/2038kJ; Protein 37.6g; Carbohydrate 1.2g, of which sugars 1.1g; Fat 37.3g, of which saturates 17.8g; Cholesterol 210mg; Calcium 71mg; Fibre 0.5g; Sodium 228mg.
Duck Breasts Energy 307kcal/1289kJ; Protein 30.6g; Carbohydrate 16.5g, of which sugars 15.4g; Fat 15.7g, of which saturates 4.2g; Cholesterol 173mg; Calcium 60mg; Fibre 1.3g; Sodium 201mg.

Pot-roast Poussin

This dish is inspired by the French method of cooking these birds. Pot-roasting keeps them beautifully moist and succulent.

Serves 4

15ml/1 tbsp olive oil
1 onion, sliced
1 large garlic clove, sliced
50g/2oz/⅓ cup diced smoked bacon
2 poussins (about 450g/1lb each)
30ml/2 tbsp melted butter
2 baby celery hearts, each cut into 4 pieces

8 baby carrots
2 small courgettes (zucchini), cut into chunks
8 small new potatoes
600ml/1 pint/2½ cups chicken stock
150ml/¼ pint/⅔ cup dry white wine
1 bay leaf
2 fresh thyme sprigs
2 fresh rosemary sprigs
15ml/1 tbsp butter, softened
15g/½oz/2 tbsp plain (all-purpose) flour
salt and ground black pepper
fresh herbs, to garnish

1 Preheat the oven to 190°C/375°F/Gas 5. Heat the olive oil in a large flameproof casserole over low heat. Add the onions, garlic and bacon and cook, stirring occasionally, for 5–6 minutes, until the onions have softened. Brush the poussins with half the melted butter and season with salt and pepper. Add to the casserole with the vegetables. Pour in the stock and wine and add the herbs. Cover and bake for 20 minutes.

2 Remove the lid and brush the birds with the remaining melted butter. Bake for a further 25–30 minutes, until golden. Transfer the poussins to a warmed serving platter and cut each in half with poultry shears or scissors. Remove the vegetables with a slotted spoon and arrange them around the birds. Cover with foil and keep warm.

3 Remove the herbs from the casserole and discard. Mix the butter and flour to a paste. Bring the cooking liquid to the boil, then whisk in spoonfuls of paste until thickened. Season with salt and pepper and serve with the poussins and vegetables, garnished with herbs.

Coq au Vin

Chicken is flamed in brandy, then braised in red wine with bacon, mushrooms and onions in this classic dish.

Serves 4

50g/2oz/½ cup plain (all-purpose) flour
1.5kg/3–3½ lb chicken, cut into 8 pieces
15ml/1 tbsp olive oil
65g/2½oz/5 tbsp butter
20 baby (pearl) onions

75g/3oz/½ cup diced streaky (fatty) bacon
about 20 button (white) mushrooms
30ml/2 tbsp brandy
1 bottle red Burgundy wine
bouquet garni
3 garlic cloves
5ml/1 tsp soft light brown sugar
salt and ground black pepper
15ml/1 tbsp chopped fresh parsley and croûtons, to garnish

1 Place 40g/1½oz/⅓ cup of the flour in a large plastic bag, season with salt and pepper and add the chicken pieces. Shake well to coat. Heat the oil and 50g/2oz/4 tbsp of the butter in a large flameproof casserole over low heat. Add the onions and bacon and cook, stirring occasionally, for about 10 minutes, until the onions have browned lightly. Add the mushrooms and cook for 2 minutes more. Remove with a slotted spoon and reserve.

2 Add the chicken pieces to the casserole, increase the heat to medium and cook, turning frequently, for about 5–6 minutes, until evenly browned all over. Add the brandy and, standing well back, ignite it with a match, then shake the casserole gently until the flames subside.

3 Add the wine, bouquet garni, garlic and sugar and season with salt and pepper. Bring to the boil, lower the heat, cover and simmer, stirring occasionally, for 1 hour. Add the onions, bacon and mushrooms, re-cover and cook for 30 minutes. Transfer the chicken, vegetables and bacon to a warmed dish.

4 Remove the bouquet garni and boil the liquid for 2 minutes. Cream the remaining butter and flour. Whisk in spoonfuls of the mixture to thicken the liquid. Pour the sauce over the chicken and serve garnished with parsley and croûtons.

Poussin Energy 549kcal/2290kJ; Protein 30.8g; Carbohydrate 25.8g, of which sugars 7.5g; Fat 34g, of which saturates 12.4g; Cholesterol 163mg; Calcium 76mg; Fibre 3.5g; Sodium 372mg.
Coq au Vin Energy 630kcal/2618kJ; Protein 42.8g; Carbohydrate 19.3g, of which sugars 7.4g; Fat 41g, of which saturates 17.3g; Cholesterol 209mg; Calcium 67mg; Fibre 2.6g; Sodium 480mg.

Moroccan Spiced Roast Poussin

The poussins are stuffed with a fruity and aromatic rice mixture and glazed with spiced yogurt in this flavoursome dish. One bird is sufficient for two servings.

Serves 4
75g/3oz/1 cup cooked long
   grain rice
1 small onion, chopped
finely grated rind and juice of
   1 lemon
30ml/2 tbsp chopped fresh mint
45ml/3 tbsp chopped
   dried apricots
30ml/2 tbsp natural
   (plain) yogurt
10ml/2 tsp ground turmeric
10ml/2 tsp ground cumin
2 poussins (about 450g/1lb each)
salt and ground black pepper
lemon slices and fresh mint
   sprigs, to garnish

1 Preheat the oven to 200°C/400°F/Gas 6. Mix together the rice, onion, lemon rind, mint and apricots in a bowl. Stir in half the lemon juice, half the yogurt, half the turmeric and half the cumin and season with salt and pepper.

2 Stuff the poussins with the rice mixture at the neck end only, taking care not to overfill them. Reserve the spare stuffing to be served separately. Place the poussins side by side on a rack in a roasting pan.

3 Mix together the remaining lemon juice, yogurt, turmeric and cumin in a small bowl, then brush this all over the poussins. Cover them loosely with foil and cook in the oven for 30 minutes.

4 Remove the foil and roast for a further 15 minutes, or until the poussins are golden brown and the juices run clear, when the thickest part is pierced with the point of a sharp knife.

5 Transfer both the poussins to a chopping board and cut them in half with a sharp knife or poultry shears. Place half a bird on each of four warmed plates. Garnish with slices of lemon and fresh mint sprigs and serve immediately with the remaining rice and apricot mixture.

Chilli Chicken Couscous

Couscous is a very easy alternative to rice and makes a good base for all kinds of ingredients.

Serves 4
225g/8oz/2 cups couscous
1 litre/1¼ pints/4 cups boiling
   water
5ml/1 tsp olive oil
400g/14oz skinless boneless
   chicken, diced
1 yellow (bell) pepper, seeded
   and sliced
2 large courgettes (zucchini),
   thickly sliced
1 small green chilli, thinly sliced, or
   5ml/1 tsp chilli sauce
1 large tomato, diced
425g/15oz can chickpeas,
   drained and rinsed
salt and ground black pepper
fresh coriander (cilantro) or
   parsley sprigs, to garnish

1 Place the couscous in a large bowl and pour the boiling water over it. Cover and leave to stand for 30 minutes.

2 Heat the oil in a large, non-stick frying pan over medium heat. Add the chicken and stir-fry quickly to seal, then reduce the heat to low.

3 Stir in the yellow pepper, courgettes and chilli or chilli sauce and cook, stirring occasionally, for about 10 minutes, until the vegetables are softened.

4 Stir in the tomato and chickpeas, then add the couscous. Season to taste with salt and pepper and cook over medium heat, stirring constantly, until hot. Serve immediately garnished with sprigs of fresh coriander or parsley.

> **Cook's Tip**
> You can use dried chickpeas in this recipe. Soak them overnight in cold water, then drain, place in a pan and add water to cover. Bring to the boil, then cook for 2–2½ hours, until tender. Drain well and add to the pan in step 4. Some cooks like to add a pinch of bicarbonate of soda (baking soda) to the water when cooking chickpeas, but this is not essential.

Poussin Energy 354kcal/1478kJ; Protein 27g; Carbohydrate 20.3g, of which sugars 5g; Fat 18.4g, of which saturates 5g; Cholesterol 131mg; Calcium 25mg; Fibre 0.9g; Sodium 92mg.
Chicken Energy 394kcal/1661kJ; Protein 36.8g; Carbohydrate 50.9g, of which sugars 5.2g; Fat 6.1g, of which saturates 0.9g; Cholesterol 70mg; Calcium 86mg; Fibre 6g; Sodium 299mg.

Mediterranean Turkey Skewers

These skewers are easy to assemble, and can be cooked under a grill or on a charcoal barbecue.

Serves 4

90ml/6 tbsp olive oil
45ml/3 tbsp lemon juice
1 garlic clove, finely chopped
30ml/2 tbsp chopped fresh basil
2 courgettes (zucchini)
1 long thin aubergine (eggplant)
300g/11oz skinless boneless
    turkey, cut into 5cm/2in cubes
12–16 baby onions
1 red or yellow (bell) pepper,
    seeded and cut into 5cm/
    2in squares
salt and ground black pepper

1 Mix the olive oil with the lemon juice, garlic and basil in a small bowl. Season with salt and pepper.

2 Slice the courgettes and aubergine lengthways into strips 5mm/¼in thick. Cut the strips crossways about two-thirds of the way along their length. Discard the shorter lengths. Wrap half the turkey pieces with the courgette slices and the other half with the aubergine slices.

3 Prepare the skewers by alternating the turkey, onions and pepper pieces. (If you are using wooden skewers, soak them in water first. This will prevent them from charring during cooking.) Lay the prepared skewers on a platter and sprinkle with the flavoured oil. Cover with clear film (plastic wrap) and leave to marinate in a cool place for at least 30 minutes. Preheat the grill (broiler).

4 Grill (broil), turning occasionally, for 10 minutes, until the vegetables are tender and the turkey is cooked through. Transfer the skewers to warmed plates and serve immediately.

> **Variation**
> For extra colour, substitute red and yellow cherry tomatoes for the pickled onions or simply add one tomato to each end of each skewer.

Duck with Chestnut Sauce

Chestnuts play an important role in Italian cooking. This autumnal dish makes use of the sweet chestnuts that are freely gathered in the woods there.

Serves 4–5

1 fresh rosemary sprig
1 garlic clove, sliced
30ml/2 tbsp olive oil
4 duck breast fillets, trimmed of
    visible fat

For the sauce

450g/1lb/4 cups chestnuts
5ml/1 tsp olive oil
350ml/12fl oz/1½ cups milk
1 small onion, finely chopped
1 carrot, finely chopped
1 small bay leaf
30ml/2 tbsp cream, warmed
salt and ground black pepper

1 Pull the needles from the sprig of rosemary. Combine them with the garlic and oil in a shallow bowl. Pat the duck breast fillets dry with kitchen paper. Brush them with the marinade and leave to stand for at least 2 hours before cooking.

2 Preheat the oven to 180°C/350°F/Gas 4. Cut a cross in the flat side of each chestnut with a sharp knife. Place the chestnuts on a baking sheet with the oil and shake the sheet until they are coated. Bake for 20 minutes, then remove from the oven and peel when they are cool enough to handle.

3 Place the chestnuts in a heavy pan with the milk, onion, carrot and bay leaf. Cook over low heat for 10–15 minutes, until the chestnuts are tender, then season with salt and pepper. Discard the bay leaf. Press the mixture through a sieve (strainer).

4 Return the sauce to the pan. Heat gently while the duck breasts are cooking. Just before serving, stir in the cream. If the sauce is too thick, add a little more cream. Preheat the grill (broiler) or prepare a barbecue.

5 Cook the duck breasts until medium-rare, for 6–8 minutes. They should be pink inside. Slice into rounds and arrange on warmed plates. Serve with the heated sauce.

Turkey Energy 315kcal/1311kJ; Protein 22.7g; Carbohydrate 16.1g, of which sugars 12.9g; Fat 18.2g, of which saturates 2.8g; Cholesterol 43mg; Calcium 70mg; Fibre 4.9g; Sodium 46mg.
Duck Energy 366kcal/1535kJ; Protein 25.9g; Carbohydrate 35.2g, of which sugars 8.2g; Fat 16.4g, of which saturates 3.5g; Cholesterol 135mg; Calcium 68mg; Fibre 4.2g; Sodium 148mg.

Turkey Spirals

These little spirals may look difficult, but they're easy to make, and a very good way to pep up plain turkey.

Serves 4
4 thinly sliced turkey breast steaks (about 90g/3½oz each)
20ml/4 tsp tomato purée (paste)
15g/½oz/¼ cup large fresh basil leaves
1 garlic clove, crushed
15ml/1 tbsp skimmed milk
25g/1oz/2 tbsp wholemeal (whole-wheat) flour
salt and ground black pepper
passata (bottled strained tomatoes) or fresh tomato sauce, pasta and fresh basil, to serve

1 Preheat the grill (broiler). Place the turkey steaks on a board. Cover with clear film (plastic wrap) and flatten them slightly by beating gently with the side of a rolling pin.

2 Spread each turkey breast steak with tomato purée, then top with a few leaves of basil and a little crushed garlic. Season with salt and pepper.

3 Roll up firmly around the filling and secure with a wooden cocktail stick (toothpick). Brush with milk and sprinkle with flour to coat lightly.

4 Place the turkey rolls on a foil-lined grill (broiler) pan. Cook under a moderately hot grill, turning them occasionally, for 15–20 minutes, until thoroughly cooked.

5 Transfer the rolls to a chopping board and cut them into slices. Place the slices on warmed plates and serve with a spoonful or two of passata or fresh tomato sauce and pasta, sprinkled with fresh basil.

Variation
This recipe is also suitable for pork and veal escalopes (US scallops) and chicken breast portions.

Caribbean Chicken Kebabs

These kebabs have a rich, sunshine Caribbean flavour and the marinade keeps them moist without the need for oil.

Serves 4
500g/1¼lb skinless chicken breast fillets
finely grated rind of 1 lime
30ml/2 tbsp lime juice
15ml/1 tbsp rum or sherry
15g/½oz/1 tbsp light muscovado (brown) sugar
5ml/1 tsp ground cinnamon
2 mangoes, peeled, stoned (pitted) and diced
rice and salad, to serve

1 Cut the chicken into bitesize chunks and place in a non-metallic bowl with the lime rind and juice, rum or sherry, sugar and cinnamon. Toss well, cover with clear film (plastic wrap) and place in the refrigerator to marinate for 1 hour.

2 Preheat the grill (broiler). Drain the chicken, reserving the marinade. Thread the chicken on to four wooden skewers, alternating with the mango cubes.

3 Cook the skewers under the grill, turning occasionally and basting with the reserved marinade, for 8–10 minutes, until the chicken is tender and golden brown. Transfer to warmed plates and serve immediately with rice and salad.

Cook's Tips
• Mangoes have a large, flat, central stone (pit). The easiest way to prepare them is to cut the thickest possible lengthways slice from each side of the stone, then cut through the flesh in an even criss-cross pattern, leaving the skin intact. Turn the slice inside out so that the flesh stands up and cut it off the skin or scoop off the cubes with a spoon.
• Use a dark rum for the marinade to give a really rich and exotic flavour. However, if you don't like it — or the alternative of sherry — you can omit it. The kebabs will still taste delicious.
• Skinless boneless chicken thighs are a more economical alternative to breast portions.

Spirals Energy 164kcal/696kJ; Protein 32.7g; Carbohydrate 4.9g, of which sugars 1g; Fat 1.7g, of which saturates 0.6g; Cholesterol 67mg; Calcium 13mg; Fibre 0.7g; Sodium 95mg.
Kebabs Energy 195kcal/826kJ; Protein 30.6g; Carbohydrate 14.6g, of which sugars 14.3g; Fat 1.5g, of which saturates 0.5g; Cholesterol 88mg; Calcium 18mg; Fibre 2g; Sodium 77mg.

Autumn Pheasant

Pheasant is worth buying as it is low in fat, full of flavour and never dry when cooked in this way.

Serves 4

1 oven-ready pheasant
2 small onions, quartered
3 celery sticks, thickly sliced
2 red eating apples, thickly sliced
120ml/4fl oz/½ cup stock
15ml/1 tbsp clear honey
30ml/2 tbsp Worcestershire sauce
pinch of freshly grated nutmeg
30ml/2 tbsp toasted hazelnuts
salt and ground black pepper

1 Preheat the oven to 180°C/350°F/Gas 4. Cook the pheasant without additional fat in a non-stick frying pan over medium-low heat, turning occasionally, for 8–10 minutes, until golden brown all over. Remove from the pan and keep hot.

2 Add the onions and celery to the pan, lower the heat and cook, stirring occasionally, for 8–10 minutes, until lightly browned. Spoon the vegetables into a casserole and place the pheasant on top. Tuck the apple slices around it.

3 Pour in the stock and add the honey and Worcestershire sauce. Sprinkle with nutmeg, season with salt and pepper, cover with a tight-fitting lid and bake for 1¼–1½ hours, or until tender. Sprinkle with the hazelnuts and serve immediately.

Cook's Tips
• Pheasant should be hung by the neck to develop its distinctive flavour for 7–14 days, depending on the degree of gaminess you like. After hanging, it must be plucked, cleaned and trussed.
• If you are buying the bird ready-prepared, it will almost certainly have already been hung. Make sure that all the tendons have been removed from the legs.
• This recipe provides an excellent method of cooking older cock birds, which tend to be rather tough and dry if they are just roasted. It is also a good choice for frozen birds as freezing has an adverse effect on their texture.

Chicken Stroganoff

This dish is based on the classic Russian dish (which is made with fillet of beef) and it is just as good.

Serves 4

4 skinless chicken breast fillets
45ml/3 tbsp olive oil
1 large onion, thinly sliced
225g/8oz mushrooms, sliced
300ml/½ pint/1¼ cups sour cream
salt and ground black pepper
15ml/1 tbsp chopped fresh parsley, to garnish

1 Divide the chicken into two natural fillets, place between two sheets of clear film (plastic wrap) and flatten each to a thickness of 5mm/¼in by beating lightly with the side of a rolling pin.

2 Remove the clear film and cut the meat into 2.5cm/1in strips diagonally across the fillets.

3 Heat 30ml/2 tbsp of the oil in a large frying pan over low heat. Add the onion and cook, stirring occasionally, for about 5 minutes, until softened but not coloured. Add the mushrooms and cook, stirring occasionally, for 5–8 minutes, until golden brown. Remove the onion and mushrooms and keep warm.

4 Increase the heat to medium and add the remaining oil to the pan. Add the chicken, in small batches, and cook, stirring frequently, for 3–4 minutes, until lightly coloured. Keep each batch warm while cooking the next.

5 Return all the chicken, onion and mushrooms to the pan and season with salt and pepper. Stir in the sour cream and bring to the boil. Sprinkle with fresh parsley and serve immediately.

Variation
Substitute smetana for the sour cream but do not let it boil as it will curdle. It is widely used in Russian cooking and is a good, low-fat substitute for cream.

Pheasant Energy 311kcal/1300kJ; Protein 30.6g; Carbohydrate 8.9g, of which sugars 8.4g; Fat 17.3g, of which saturates 4.6g; Cholesterol 230mg; Calcium 66mg; Fibre 1.4g; Sodium 169mg.
Stroganoff Energy 421kcal/1758kJ; Protein 40.7g; Carbohydrate 9.8g, of which sugars 7.4g; Fat 24.7g, of which saturates 10.8g; Cholesterol 146mg; Calcium 103mg; Fibre 2g; Sodium 118mg.

Chicken Tikka

The red food colourings give this dish its traditional bright colour. Serve with lemon wedges and a crisp mixed salad.

Serves 4

1.75kg/3½lb chicken
mixed fresh salad leaves such as
frisée, oakleaf lettuce or
radicchio, and lemon wedges
to serve

For the marinade

150ml/¼ pint/⅔ cup natural
(plain) yogurt
5ml/1 tsp ground paprika
10ml/2 tsp grated fresh
root ginger
1 garlic clove, crushed
10ml/2 tsp garam masala
2.5ml/½ tsp salt
red food colouring (optional)
juice of 1 lemon

1 Cut the chicken into eight even-size pieces, using a sharp knife or cleaver.

2 Mix all the marinade ingredients in a large dish, add the chicken pieces and turn to coat. Cover with clear film (plastic wrap) and leave in the refrigerator for 4 hours or overnight to allow the flavours to penetrate the flesh.

3 Preheat the oven to 200°C/400°F/Gas 6. Remove the chicken pieces from the marinade and arrange them in a single layer in a large ovenproof dish. Reserve the marinade. Bake the chicken, basting occasionally with the marinade, for 30–40 minutes, or until tender.

4 Arrange on a bed of salad leaves on individual plates, top with the chicken and serve immediately with lemon wedges. Alternatively, leave the chicken to cool, then serve cold on a bed of salad leaves.

Cook's Tip
This dish would also make an excellent appetizer. Cut the chicken into smaller pieces and reduce the cooking time slightly, then serve with lemon wedges and a simple salad garnish.

Simple Chicken Curry

Curry powder can be bought in three different strengths – mild, medium and hot. Use whichever type you prefer.

Serves 4

8 chicken legs, each piece
including thigh and drumstick
30ml/2 tbsp groundnut
(peanut) oil
1 onion, thinly sliced
1 garlic clove, crushed
15ml/1 tbsp medium
curry powder
25g/1oz/¼ cup plain (all-
purpose) flour
450ml/¾ pint/scant 2 cups
chicken stock
1 beefsteak tomato
15ml/1 tbsp mango chutney
15ml/1 tbsp lemon juice
salt and ground black pepper
boiled rice, to serve

1 Cut the chicken legs in half. Heat the oil in a large flameproof casserole over medium heat. Add the chicken pieces and cook, turning frequently, for 8–10 minutes, until evenly browned on both sides. Remove the chicken from the casserole and keep warm.

2 Add the onion and garlic to the casserole, lower the heat and cook, stirring occasionally, for about 5 minutes, until the onion is softened but not coloured. Stir in the curry powder and cook, stirring constantly, for a further 2 minutes.

3 Stir in the flour and cook, stirring constantly, for 1 minute, then gradually blend in the chicken stock, stirring well. Season with salt and pepper.

4 Bring to the boil, return the chicken pieces to the casserole, cover and simmer for 20–30 minutes, until tender.

5 Skin the beefsteak tomato by blanching in boiling water for about 15 seconds, then running it under cold water to loosen the skin. Peel and cut into small dice.

6 Add to the chicken with the mango chutney and lemon juice. Heat through gently and adjust the seasoning to taste. Serve with boiled rice and Indian accompaniments.

Tikka Energy 416kcal/1730kJ; Protein 46g; Carbohydrate 2.1g, of which sugars 0.2g; Fat 24.8g, of which saturates 8.5g; Cholesterol 203mg; Calcium 21mg; Fibre 0.5g; Sodium 173mg.
Curry Energy 571kcal/2392kJ; Protein 38.9g; Carbohydrate 78.9g, of which sugars 4g; Fat 10.8g, of which saturates 2g; Cholesterol 158mg; Calcium 43mg; Fibre 0.8g; Sodium 180mg.

Chicken Biryani

A biryani – from the Urdu – is a dish mixed with rice which resembles a risotto. It provides a one-pan meal.

Serves 4

275g/10oz/1½ cups basmati
  rice, rinsed and drained
2.5ml/½ tsp salt
5 cardamom pods
2–3 cloves
1 cinnamon stick
45ml/3 tbsp vegetable oil
3 onions, sliced
675g/1½lb skinless boneless
  chicken, diced
1.5ml/¼ tsp ground cloves
5 cardamom pods, seeds removed
  and ground
1.5ml/¼ tsp hot chilli powder
5ml/1 tsp ground cumin
5ml/1 tsp ground coriander
2.5ml/½ tsp ground black pepper
3 garlic cloves, finely chopped
5ml/1 tsp finely chopped fresh
  root ginger
juice of 1 lemon
4 tomatoes, sliced
30ml/2 tbsp chopped fresh
  coriander (cilantro)
150ml/¼ pint/⅔ cup natural
  (plain) yogurt
2.5ml/½ tsp saffron threads
  soaked in 10ml/2 tsp hot milk
45ml/3 tbsp toasted flaked
  (sliced) almonds and fresh
  coriander sprigs, to garnish
natural yogurt, to serve

1 Preheat the oven to 190°C/375°F/Gas 5. Bring a large pan of salted water to the boil and add the rice, salt, cardamom pods, cloves and cinnamon stick. Bring back to the boil and cook for 2 minutes. Drain, leaving the whole spices in the rice.

2 Heat the oil in a frying pan over low heat. Add the onions and cook, stirring occasionally, for about 10 minutes, until lightly browned. Add the chicken, ground spices, garlic, ginger and lemon juice and stir-fry for 5 minutes.

3 Transfer to a casserole and top with the tomatoes. Add the coriander, yogurt and rice in layers. Drizzle over the saffron and milk, then 150ml/¼ pint/⅔ cup water.

4 Cover and bake for 1 hour. Transfer to a warmed serving platter and remove the whole spices. Garnish with toasted almonds and coriander and serve with yogurt.

Spatchcock of Poussin

Also called spring chicken, poussins are between four and six weeks old and weigh 350–600g/12oz–1¼ lb. The very young, smallest birds make an attractive serving for one person.

Serves 4

4 poussins

15ml/1 tbsp mixed chopped fresh
  herbs, such as rosemary and
  parsley, plus extra to garnish
15ml/1 tbsp lemon juice
50g/2oz/¼ cup butter, melted
salt and ground black pepper
lemon slices, to garnish
boiled new potatoes and salad,
  to serve (optional)

1 Remove any trussing strings from the birds and, using a pair of kitchen scissors, cut down on either side of the backbone. Lay the poussins flat, skin-side up, and flatten with the help of a rolling pin or mallet, or use the heel of your hand.

2 Thread the legs and wings on to skewers to keep the poussins flat while they are cooking.

3 Brush both sides with melted butter and season with salt and pepper. Sprinkle with lemon juice and herbs.

4 Preheat the grill (broiler) and cook, skin-side uppermost, for 6 minutes, until golden brown. Turn over, brush with more melted butter and grill (broil) for a further 6–8 minutes, until the juices run clear when the thickest part is pierced with the point of a sharp knife.

5 Transfer the poussins to serving plates and remove the skewers. Garnish with chopped herbs and lemon slices and serve immediately with boiled new potatoes and salad.

> **Variation**
> *Squab, another very tender, young bird that provides an adequate single portion, is also ideal for this method of preparation and simple cooking.*

Biryani Energy 628kcal/2623kJ; Protein 41.5g; Carbohydrate 71.4g, of which sugars 13.4g; Fat 19.7g, of which saturates 2.9g; Cholesterol 642mg; Calcium 163mg; Fibre 3.6g; Sodium 174mg.
Poussin Energy 621kcal/2582kJ; Protein 50.1g; Carbohydrate 0.3g, of which sugars 0.3g; Fat 46.7g, of which saturates 16.4g; Cholesterol 288mg; Calcium 21mg; Fibre 0g; Sodium 256mg.

Chicken, Leek & Parsley Pie

A filling pie with a two-cheese sauce, this dish is ideal for serving on a cold winter's day.

Serves 4–6

3 skinless chicken breast fillets
I carrot, thickly sliced
I small onion, quartered
6 black peppercorns
I bouquet garni
450g/1lb shortcrust pastry dough, thawed if frozen
50g/2oz/¼ cup butter
2 leeks, thinly sliced
50g/2oz/¼ cup grated Cheddar cheese
25g/1oz/⅓ cup freshly grated Parmesan cheese
45ml/3 tbsp chopped fresh parsley
30ml/2 tbsp wholegrain mustard
5ml/1 tsp cornflour (cornstarch)
300ml/½ pint/1¼ cups double (heavy) cream
beaten egg, to glaze
salt and ground black pepper
mixed green salad leaves, to serve

1 Put the chicken, carrot, onion, peppercorns and bouquet garni in a shallow pan, add water and bring just to the boil. Lower the heat and poach gently, for 20–30 minutes, until tender. Leave to cool in the liquid, then drain and cut into strips.

2 Preheat the oven to 200°C/400°F/Gas 6. Divide the dough into two pieces, one slightly larger than the other. Use the larger piece to line an 18 x 28cm/7 x 11in baking tin (pan). Prick the base, bake for 15 minutes, then leave to cool.

3 Melt the butter in a frying pan over low heat. Add the leeks and cook, stirring occasionally, for 5–8 minutes, until soft. Stir in the cheeses and parsley.

4 Spread half the leek mixture over the pastry base, cover with the chicken strips, then top with the remaining leek mixture. Mix together the mustard, cornflour and cream in a bowl. Season with salt and pepper and pour into the pie.

5 Moisten the pastry base edges. Use the remaining pastry to cover the pie. Brush with beaten egg and bake for 30–40 minutes, until golden and crisp. Serve with salad.

Hampshire Farmhouse Flan

This English flan will satisfy even the heartiest appetite.

Serves 4

225g/8oz/2 cups wholemeal (whole-wheat) flour
50g/2oz/¼ cup butter, cubed
50g/2oz/¼ cup white cooking fat
5ml/1 tsp caraway seeds
5ml/1 tbsp vegetable oil
I onion, chopped
I garlic clove, crushed
225g/8oz/2 cups chopped cooked chicken
75g/3oz watercress or baby spinach leaves, chopped
grated rind of ½ lemon
2 eggs, lightly beaten
175ml/6fl oz/¾ cup double (heavy) cream
45ml/3 tbsp natural (plain) yogurt
large pinch of grated nutmeg
45ml/3 tbsp grated Caerphilly cheese
beaten egg, to glaze
salt and ground black pepper

1 Put the flour into a bowl with a pinch of salt. Add the butter and cooking fat and rub in with your fingertips until the mixture resembles breadcrumbs.

2 Stir in the caraway seeds and 45ml/3 tbsp iced water and mix to a firm dough. Knead until smooth, then use to line an 18 x 28cm/7 x 11 in loose-based flan tin (pan). Reserve the dough trimmings. Prick the base and chill for 20 minutes. Heat a baking sheet in the oven at 200°C/400°F/Gas 6.

3 Heat the oil in a frying pan over low heat. Add the onion and garlic and cook, stirring occasionally, for 5 minutes, until softened. Leave to cool. Meanwhile, line the pastry case (pie shell) with greaseproof (waxed) paper and baking beans. Bake for 10 minutes, remove the paper and beans and bake for a further 5 minutes.

4 Mix the onion mixture, chicken, watercress or spinach and lemon rind; spoon into the pastry case. Beat the eggs, cream, yogurt, nutmeg, cheese and seasoning; pour over the chicken mixture. Cut the pastry trimmings into 1cm/½in strips. Brush with egg, then twist and lay in a lattice over the flan. Press on the ends. Bake for 35 minutes, until golden.

Chicken Energy 620kcal/2584kJ; Protein 28.2g; Carbohydrate 39.4g, of which sugars 3.2g; Fat 39.7g, of which saturates 24.1g; Cholesterol 151mg; Calcium 237mg; Fibre 3.3g; Sodium 218mg.
Flan Energy 773kcal/3216kJ; Protein 28.2g; Carbohydrate 38g, of which sugars 2.9g; Fat 57.4g, of which saturates 30.2g; Cholesterol 244mg; Calcium 181mg; Fibre 5.6g; Sodium 247mg.

Chicken & Ham Pie

Chicken Charter Pie

This is a rich pie flavoured with fresh herbs and lightly spiced with mace – ideal for taking on a picnic.

Serves 8
400g/14oz shortcrust pastry
  dough, thawed if frozen
800g/1¾lb chicken breast
  portions
350g/12oz uncooked gammon
  (smoked or cured ham)
60ml/4 tbsp double
  (heavy) cream
6 spring onions (scallions),
  finely chopped
15ml/1 tbsp chopped
  fresh tarragon
10ml/2 tsp chopped fresh thyme
grated rind and juice of
  ½ large lemon
5ml/1 tsp ground mace
beaten egg or milk, to glaze
salt and ground black pepper

1 Preheat the oven to 190°C/375°F/Gas 5. Roll out one-third of the pastry dough and use it to line a 20cm/8in pie tin (pan), 5cm/2in deep. Place on a baking sheet.

2 Mince (grind) 115g/4oz of the chicken with the gammon, then mix with the cream, spring onions, herbs, lemon rind and 15ml/1 tbsp of the lemon juice in a bowl. Season lightly with salt and pepper. Cut the remaining chicken into 1cm/½in pieces and mix with the remaining lemon juice and the mace in another bowl and season with salt and pepper.

3 Make a layer of one-third of the gammon mixture in the pastry base, cover with half the chopped chicken, then add another layer of one-third of the gammon. Add all the remaining chicken followed by the remaining gammon.

4 Dampen the edges of the pastry base and roll out the remaining pastry to make a lid for the pie. Use the trimmings to make a lattice decoration. Make a small hole in the centre of the pie, then brush the top with beaten egg or milk.

5 Bake the pie for 20 minutes. Lower the oven temperature to 160°C/325°F/Gas 3 and bake for a further 1–1¼ hours, until the pastry is golden brown. Transfer the pie to a wire rack and leave to cool before serving.

Chicken Charter Pie

A light pie with a fresh taste; it is versatile enough to use for light meals or informal dinners.

Serves 4
50g/2oz/¼ cup butter
4 chicken legs
1 onion, finely chopped
150ml/¼ pint/⅔ cup milk
150ml/¼ pint/⅔ cup sour cream
4 spring onions (scallions), cut into
  quarters
20g/¾oz/⅓ cup fresh parsley
  leaves, finely chopped
225g/8oz puff pastry dough,
  thawed if frozen
120ml/4fl oz/½ cup double
  (heavy) cream
2 eggs, beaten, plus extra
  for glazing
salt and ground black pepper

1 Melt the butter in a frying pan over medium heat. Add the chicken legs and cook, turning frequently, for 8–10 minutes, until evenly browned all over. Transfer to a plate.

2 Add the onion to the pan, lower the heat and cook, stirring occasionally, for 5 minutes, until softened but not coloured. Stir the milk, sour cream, spring onions and parsley into the pan, season with salt and pepper and bring to the boil, then simmer for 2 minutes.

3 Return the chicken to the pan with any juices, cover and cook gently for 30 minutes. Transfer the chicken mixture to a 1.2 litre/2 pint/5 cup pie dish. Leave to cool.

4 Preheat the oven to 220°C/425°F/Gas 7. Place a narrow strip of pastry on the edge of the pie dish. Moisten the strip, then cover the dish with the pastry. Press the edges together. Make a hole in the centre of the pastry and insert a small funnel of foil. Brush the pastry with beaten egg to glaze, then bake for 15–20 minutes.

5 Lower the oven temperature to 180°C/350°F/Gas 4. Mix the cream and eggs, then pour into the pie through the funnel. Shake the pie to distribute the cream, then return to the oven for 5–10 minutes. Leave the pie in a warm place for about 5–10 minutes before serving, or cool completely.

Charter Pie Energy 713kcal/2967kJ; Protein 37.8g; Carbohydrate 25g, of which sugars 4.9g; Fat 52.6g, of which saturates 22.8g; Cholesterol 250mg; Calcium 154mg; Fibre 0.4g; Sodium 426mg.
Chicken & Ham Pie Energy 431kcal/1803kJ; Protein 34.8g; Carbohydrate 23.8g, of which sugars 0.8g; Fat 22.5g, of which saturates 8.3g; Cholesterol 98mg; Calcium 57mg; Fibre 1.1g; Sodium 647mg.

Venison with Cranberry Sauce

Venison steaks are now readily available. Lean and low in fat, they make a healthy and delicious choice for a special occasion.

Serves 4
1 orange
1 lemon
75g/3oz/³⁄₄ cup fresh or frozen unthawed cranberries
5ml/1 tsp grated fresh root ginger
1 fresh thyme sprig, plus extra to garnish
5ml/1 tsp Dijon mustard
60ml/4 tbsp redcurrant jelly
150ml/¹⁄₄ pint/²⁄₃ cup port
30ml/2 tbsp sunflower oil
4 venison steaks
2 shallots, finely chopped
salt and ground black pepper
fresh thyme sprigs, to garnish
mashed potatoes and steamed broccoli, to serve

1 Pare the rind from half the orange and half the lemon using a vegetable peeler, then cut into very fine strips. Blanch the strips in a small pan of boiling water for 5 minutes, until tender. Drain the strips and refresh under cold water.

2 Squeeze the juice from the orange and lemon and pour into a small pan. Add the cranberries, ginger, thyme sprig, mustard, redcurrant jelly and port. Cook over medium-low heat, stirring frequently, until the jelly has melted. Bring to the boil, stirring constantly, cover and lower the heat. Simmer gently for 15 minutes, until the cranberries are just tender.

3 Heat the oil in a large, heavy frying pan over a high heat. Add the venison steaks and cook for 2–3 minutes. Turn them over and add the shallots. Cook on the other side for 2–3 minutes, or until done to your taste. Just before the end of cooking, pour in the sauce and add the strips of orange and lemon rind. Leave the sauce to bubble for a few seconds to thicken slightly, then remove and discard the thyme sprig. Taste and adjust the seasoning, if necessary.

4 Transfer the venison steaks to warmed plates and spoon the sauce over them. Garnish with thyme sprigs and serve immediately accompanied by creamy mashed potatoes and steamed broccoli.

Turkey & Mangetout Stir-fry

Have all the ingredients prepared before you start cooking this dish, as it will be ready in minutes.

Serves 4
30ml/2 tbsp sesame oil
90ml/6 tbsp lemon juice
1 garlic clove, crushed
1cm/¹⁄₂in piece fresh root ginger, peeled and grated
5ml/1 tsp clear honey
450g/1lb turkey fillets, cut into strips
115g/4oz/1 cup mangetouts (snow peas), trimmed
30ml/2 tbsp groundnut (peanut) oil
50g/2oz/¹⁄₂ cup cashew nuts
6 spring onions (scallions), cut into strips
225g/8oz can water chestnuts, drained and thinly sliced
pinch of salt
saffron rice, to serve

1 Mix together the sesame oil, lemon juice, garlic, ginger and honey in a shallow non-metallic dish. Add the turkey and mix well. Cover and leave to marinate for 3–4 hours.

2 Blanch the mangetouts in boiling salted water for about 1 minute. Drain and refresh under cold running water.

3 Drain the turkey strips and reserve the marinade. Heat the groundnut oil in a wok or large frying pan, add the cashews and stir-fry for 1–2 minutes, until golden brown. Remove the nuts from the pan using a slotted spoon and set aside.

4 Add the turkey and stir-fry for 3–4 minutes, until golden brown. Add the spring onions, mangetouts, water chestnuts and reserved marinade. Cook for a few minutes, until the turkey is tender and the sauce is bubbling and hot. Stir in the cashew nuts and serve immediately with saffron rice.

> **Cook's Tip**
> This dish could be served on a bed of medium-width egg noodles for a quick meal.

Farmhouse Venison Pie

A simple and satisfying pie; the venison is cooked in a rich gravy, topped with potato and parsnip mash.

Serves 4

45ml/3 tbsp sunflower oil
1 onion, chopped
1 garlic clove, crushed
3 rashers (strips) rindless streaky (fatty) bacon, chopped
675g/1½lb minced (ground) venison
115g/4oz button (white) mushrooms, chopped
25g/1oz/¼ cup plain (all-purpose) flour
450ml/¾ pint/scant 2 cups beef stock
150ml/¼ pint/⅔ cup port
2 bay leaves
5ml/1 tsp chopped fresh thyme
5ml/1 tsp Dijon mustard
15ml/1 tbsp redcurrant jelly
675g/1½lb potatoes
450g/1lb parsnips
1 egg yolk
50g/2oz/¼ cup butter
pinch of freshly grated nutmeg
45ml/3 tbsp chopped fresh parsley
salt and ground black pepper
green vegetables, to serve (optional)

1 Heat the oil in a large frying pan over low heat. Add the onion, garlic and bacon and cook, stirring occasionally, for about 5 minutes, until the onion is softened. Add the venison and mushrooms and cook for a few minutes, stirring, until browned.

2 Stir in the flour and cook for 1–2 minutes, then add the stock, port, herbs, mustard and redcurrant jelly. Season with salt and pepper. Bring to the boil, cover with a tight-fitting lid and simmer for 30–40 minutes, until tender. Spoon into a large pie dish or four individual ovenproof dishes.

3 While the venison and mushroom mixture is cooking, preheat the oven to 200°C/400°F/Gas 6. Cut the potatoes and parsnips into large chunks. Cook together in salted boiling water for 20 minutes, or until tender. Drain and mash, then beat in the egg yolk, butter, nutmeg, parsley and seasoning.

4 Spread the potato and parsnip mixture over the meat and bake for 30–40 minutes, until hot and golden brown. Serve immediately with green vegetables, if you like.

Normandy Pheasant

Calvados, cider, apples and cream – the produce of Normandy – make this a rich and flavoursome dish.

Serves 4

2 oven-ready pheasants
15ml/1 tbsp olive oil
25g/1oz/2 tbsp butter
60ml/4 tbsp Calvados or applejack
450ml/¾ pint/scant 2 cups dry (hard) cider
1 bouquet garni
3 eating apples
150ml/¼ pint/⅔ cup double (heavy) cream
salt and ground black pepper
fresh thyme sprigs, to garnish

1 Preheat the oven to 160°C/325°F/Gas 3. Cut both pheasants into four pieces. Discard the backbones and knuckles.

2 Heat the oil and butter in a large flameproof casserole. Working in two batches, add the pheasant pieces to the casserole and brown them over a high heat. Return all the pheasant pieces to the casserole.

3 Standing well back, pour over the Calvados or applejack and ignite it with a match. Shake the casserole and when the flames have subsided, pour in the cider, then add the bouquet garni and season to taste with salt and pepper. Bring to the boil, cover with a tight-fitting lid and simmer for about 50 minutes.

4 Peel, core and thickly slice the apples. Tuck the apple slices around the pheasant. Cover and cook for 5–10 minutes, or until the pheasant is tender. Transfer the pheasant and apples to a warmed serving plate. Keep warm.

5 Remove and discard the bouquet garni, then boil the sauce rapidly to reduce by half to a syrupy consistency. Stir in the cream and simmer for a further 2–3 minutes, until thickened. Taste the sauce and adjust the seasoning, if necessary. Spoon the sauce over the pheasant pieces and serve immediately, garnished with fresh thyme sprigs.

Venison Energy 723kcal/3033kJ; Protein 48.5g; Carbohydrate 59.6g, of which sugars 20.4g; Fat 30.3g, of which saturates 11.2g; Cholesterol 174mg; Calcium 128mg; Fibre 9g; Sodium 447mg.
Pheasant Energy 805kcal/3347kJ; Protein 58.8g; Carbohydrate 8.1g, of which sugars 8.1g; Fat 52.9g, of which saturates 24.6g; Cholesterol 525mg; Calcium 91mg; Fibre 0.8g; Sodium 191mg.

Roast Beef with Yorkshire Pudding

This classic British dish is often served at Sunday lunch, accompanied by potatoes, mustard and horseradish sauce.

Serves 6
1.75kg/4lb rib of beef
30–60ml/2–4 tbsp vegetable oil
300ml/½ pint/1¼ cups vegetable
   or veal stock, wine or water
salt and ground black pepper

For the puddings
50g/2oz/½ cup plain (all-
   purpose) flour
1 egg, beaten
150ml/¼ pint/⅔ cup water
   mixed with milk
vegetable oil, for cooking

1 Weigh the beef and calculate the cooking time. Allow 15 minutes per 450g/1lb plus 15 minutes for rare meat, 20 minutes plus 20 minutes for medium, and 25–30 minutes plus 25 minutes for well-done.

2 Preheat the oven to 220°C/425°F/Gas 7. Heat the oil in a roasting pan. Place the meat on a rack, fat-side uppermost, then put the rack in the roasting pan. Baste the beef with the oil and cook for the required time, basting occasionally.

3 To make the Yorkshire puddings, stir the flour, salt and pepper together in a bowl and form a well in the centre. Pour the egg into the well, then slowly pour in the milk mixture, stirring in the flour to give a smooth batter. Leave to stand for 30 minutes.

4 A few minutes before the meat is ready, spoon a little oil in each of 12 patty tins (muffin pans) and place in the oven until very hot. Remove the meat, season, then cover loosely with foil and keep warm. Quickly divide the batter among the patty tins, then bake for 15–20 minutes, until well risen and brown.

5 Spoon off the fat from the roasting pan. Add the stock, wine or water and bring to the boil, stirring constantly. Cook for a few minutes, stirring. Season to taste with salt and pepper, then serve with the beef and Yorkshire puddings.

Beef Olives

So-called because of their shape, these beef rolls contain a delicious filling made with bacon, parsley and mushrooms.

Serves 4
25g/1oz/2 tbsp butter
2 rashers (strips) bacon,
   finely chopped
115g/4oz mushrooms, chopped
15ml/1 tbsp chopped
   fresh parsley

grated rind and juice of 1 lemon
115g/4oz/2 cups fresh
   white breadcrumbs
675g/1½lb topside (pot roast) of
   beef, cut into 8 thin slices
40g/1½oz/⅓ cup plain (all-
   purpose) flour
45ml/3 tbsp vegetable oil
2 onions, sliced
450ml/¾ pint/scant 2 cups
   brown veal stock
salt and ground black pepper

1 Preheat the oven to 160°C/325°F/Gas 3. Melt the butter in a pan over medium heat. Add the bacon and mushrooms and cook, stirring occasionally for 3 minutes. Mix them with the chopped parsley, lemon rind and juice and breadcrumbs in a bowl and season with salt and pepper.

2 Spread an equal quantity of the breadcrumb mixture evenly over the beef slices, leaving a narrow border clear around the edges. Roll up the slices and tie securely with fine string, then dip the beef rolls in the flour to coat lightly, shaking off any excess flour.

3 Heat the oil in a frying pan over medium heat. Add the beef rolls and cook, turning frequently, for 3–4 minutes, until evenly browned all over. Remove the rolls from the pan and keep warm. Add the onions and cook, stirring occasionally, for about 8 minutes, until browned. Stir in the remaining flour and cook until lightly browned. Pour in the stock, stirring constantly, bring to the boil, stirring, and simmer for 2–3 minutes.

4 Transfer the rolls to a casserole, pour the sauce over the top, then cover with a tight-fitting lid and cook in the oven for 2 hours. Lift out the "olives" using a slotted spoon and remove the string. Return them to the sauce and serve hot.

Roast Beef Energy 590kcal/2461kJ; Protein 68.5g; Carbohydrate 7.1g, of which sugars 0.7g; Fat 32g, of which saturates 11.9g; Cholesterol 202mg; Calcium 46mg; Fibre 0.3g; Sodium 204mg
Beef Olive Energy 519kcal/2181kJ; Protein 46.9g; Carbohydrate 38.1g, of which sugars 6.6g; Fat 21g, of which saturates 6.9g; Cholesterol 104mg; Calcium 90mg; Fibre 2.7g; Sodium 584mg

Lamb & Spring Vegetable Stew

Known as a *blanquette* in France, this stew may have blanched asparagus spears or green beans added.

Serves 4

65g/2¹/₂oz/5 tbsp butter
900g/2lb lean buned shoulder of lamb, cut into 4cm/1¹/₂in dice
600ml/1 pint/2¹/₂ cups lamb stock or water
150ml/¹/₄ pint/²/₃ cup dry white wine
1 onion, quartered
2 fresh thyme sprigs
1 bay leaf

225g/8oz baby (pearl) onions, halved
225g/8oz young carrots
2 small turnips, quartered
175g/6oz/³/₄ cup shelled broad (fava) beans
15g/¹/₂oz/2 tbsp plain (all-purpose) flour
1 egg yolk
45ml/3 tbsp double (heavy) cream
10ml/2 tsp lemon juice
salt and ground black pepper
30ml/2 tbsp chopped fresh parsley, to garnish

1 Melt 25g/1oz/2 tbsp of the butter in a pan over medium heat. Add the lamb and cook, stirring frequently, for 8 minutes, until browned. Add the stock or water and wine, bring to the boil and skim the surface. Add the quartered onion, thyme and bay leaf. Lower the heat, cover the pan and simmer for 1 hour.

2 Melt 15g/¹/₂oz/1 tbsp of the remaining butter in a frying pan over low heat. Add the baby onions and cook, stirring occasionally, for about 10 minutes, until lightly browned all over. Add to the lamb with the carrots and turnips. Simmer for a further 20 minutes. Add the beans and cook for 10 minutes.

3 Arrange the lamb and vegetables on a serving dish, discarding the onion quarters and herbs. Cover and keep warm. Strain the stock and skim off the fat. Bring to the boil and reduce the stock to 450ml/³/₄ pint/scant 2 cups. Mix the remaining butter and flour to a paste. Whisk into the stock, then simmer briefly.

4 Combine the egg yolk and cream. Add a little of the hot sauce, then stir into the pan. Do not boil. Add the lemon juice, and season. Pour the sauce over the lamb and garnish with parsley.

Beef Paprika with Roasted Peppers

This dish is perfect for family suppers – and roasting the peppers gives an added dimension.

Serves 4

30ml/2 tbsp olive oil
675g/1¹/₂lb braising steak, cut into 4cm/1¹/₂in dice
2 onions, chopped
1 garlic clove, crushed
15g/¹/₂oz/2 tbsp plain (all-purpose) flour

15ml/1 tbsp paprika, plus extra to garnish
400g/14oz can chopped tomatoes
2 red (bell) peppers, seeded and halved
150ml/¹/₄ pint/²/₃ cup crème fraîche
salt and ground black pepper
buttered noodles, to serve

1 Preheat the oven to 140°C/275°F/Gas 1. Heat the oil in a large flameproof casserole over medium heat. Add the meat, in batches, and cook, stirring frequently until evenly browned all over. Remove the meat from the casserole using a slotted spoon and set aside.

2 Add the onions and garlic and cook over low heat, stirring occasionally, for about 5 minutes, until softened but not coloured. Stir in the flour and paprika and cook, stirring constantly, for a further 1–2 minutes.

3 Return the meat and any juices that have collected on the plate to the casserole, then add the chopped tomatoes. Season with salt and pepper. Bring to the boil, stirring constantly, then cover with a tight-fitting lid and cook in the oven for 2¹/₂ hours.

4 Meanwhile, place the peppers, skin-side up, on a grill (broiler) rack and grill (broil) until the skins have blistered and charred. Cool, then peel off the skins. Cut the flesh into strips and add to the casserole. Re-cover the casserole and cook for a further 15–30 minutes, or until the meat is tender.

5 Stir in the crème fraîche and sprinkle with a little paprika. Serve hot with buttered noodles.

Lamb Energy 709kcal/2951kJ; Protein 50.2g; Carbohydrate 18.6g, of which sugars 9.5g; Fat 46.7g, of which saturates 24.4g; Cholesterol 271mg; Calcium 105mg; Fibre 5.7g; Sodium 321mg.
Beef Energy 562kcal/2338kJ; Protein 41.7g; Carbohydrate 16.5g, of which sugars 12.1g; Fat 37g, of which saturates 17.6g; Cholesterol 140mg; Calcium 62mg; Fibre 3.2g; Sodium 130mg.

Beef in Guinness

Guinness gives this stew a deep, rich flavour. Use Beamish or another stout if you prefer.

Serves 6

900g/2lb braising steak, cut into 4cm/1½in dice
plain (all-purpose) flour, for coating
45ml/3 tbsp vegetable oil
1 large onion, sliced
1 carrot, thinly sliced
2 celery sticks, thinly sliced
10ml/2 tsp sugar
5ml/1 tsp English (hot) mustard powder
15ml/1 tbsp tomato purée (paste)
2.5 x 7.5cm/1 x 3in strip orange rind
1 bouquet garni
600ml/1 pint/2½ cups Guinness
salt and ground black pepper

1 Toss the beef in flour to coat, shaking off any excess. Heat 30ml/2 tbsp of the oil in a large shallow pan over medium heat. Add the beef, in batches, and cook, stirring frequently, for 8–10 minutes, until lightly browned. Transfer to a bowl.

2 Add the remaining oil to the pan and lower the heat. Add the onion and cook, stirring occasionally, for about 8 minutes, until lightly browned. Add the carrot and celery and cook, stirring occasionally, for a further 5 minutes.

3 Stir in the sugar, mustard, tomato purée, orange rind and Guinness, season with salt and pepper, add the bouquet garni and bring to the boil.

4 Return the meat and any juices in the bowl to the pan. Add water, if necessary, so that the meat is covered. Cover the pan with a tight-fitting lid and simmer over low heat for 2–2½ hours, until the meat is very tender.

Cook's Tip
Like most stews, this can be prepared up to 2 days ahead and stored in the refrigerator, once cooled. The flavours and richness will intensify during this time.

Cottage Pie

This traditional dish is a favourite with adults and children alike.

Serves 4

30ml/2 tbsp vegetable oil
1 onion, finely chopped
1 carrot, finely chopped
115g/4oz chopped mushrooms
500g/1¼lb lean minced (ground) braising steak
300ml/½ pint/1¼ cups brown veal stock or water
15g/½oz/2 tbsp plain (all-purpose) flour
1 bay leaf
10–15ml/2–3 tsp Worcestershire sauce
15ml/1 tbsp tomato purée (paste)
675g/1½lb potatoes, boiled
25g/1oz/2 tbsp butter
45ml/3 tbsp hot milk
15ml/1 tbsp chopped fresh tarragon
salt and ground black pepper

1 Heat the oil in a pan over low heat. Add the onion, carrot and mushrooms and cook, stirring occasionally, for about 10 minutes, until the onion is softened and lightly browned. Stir the beef into the pan and cook, stirring to break up the lumps, for about 8 minutes, until lightly browned.

2 Blend a few spoonfuls of the stock or water with the flour, then stir into the pan. Stir in the remaining stock or water and bring to a simmer, stirring constantly.

3 Add the bay leaf, Worcestershire sauce and tomato purée, then cover with a tight-fitting lid and cook very gently for 1 hour, stirring occasionally. Uncover towards the end of cooking to allow any excess liquid to evaporate, if necessary.

4 Preheat the oven to 190°C/375°F/Gas 5. Gently heat the potatoes for a couple of minutes, then mash with the butter, milk and seasoning.

5 Add the tarragon to the meat mixture and season to taste with salt and pepper, then pour into a pie dish. Cover the meat with an even layer of mashed potatoes and mark the top of the pie with the prongs of a fork. Bake for about 25 minutes, until golden brown. Serve immediately.

Beef Energy 367kcal/1529kJ; Protein 35.3g; Carbohydrate 6.9g, of which sugars 5.7g; Fat 19.6g, of which saturates 6.4g; Cholesterol 87mg; Calcium 32mg; Fibre 1.2g; Sodium 119mg.
Cottage Pie Energy 281kcal/1179kJ; Protein 7.2g; Carbohydrate 34.6g, of which sugars 6.2g; Fat 13.7g, of which saturates 5.1g; Cholesterol 22mg; Calcium 50mg; Fibre 2.9g; Sodium 132mg.

Irish Stew

This wholesome and filling stew is given a slight piquancy by the inclusion of a little anchovy sauce.

Serves 4

4 rashers (strips) smoked streaky (fatty) bacon
2 celery sticks, chopped
2 large onions, sliced
8 middle neck (US shoulder) lamb chops (about 1kg/2¼lb total weight)
1kg/2¼lb potatoes, sliced
300ml/½ pint/1¼ cups brown veal stock
7.5ml/1½ tsp Worcestershire sauce
5ml/1 tsp anchovy sauce
salt and ground black pepper
fresh parsley, to garnish

1 Preheat the oven to 160°C/325°F/Gas 3. Dice the bacon and then cook in a heavy frying pan, without any added fat, over medium-low heat for 3–5 minutes, until the fat runs. Add the celery and one-third of the onions and cook, stirring occasionally, for about 10 minutes, until softened and browned.

2 Layer the lamb chops, potatoes, vegetable and bacon mixture and remaining onions in a heavy, flameproof casserole, seasoning each layer with salt and pepper as you go. Finish with a layer of potatoes.

3 Pour the veal stock, Worcestershire sauce and anchovy sauce into the bacon and vegetable cooking juices in the pan. Bring to the boil, stirring constantly. Pour the mixture into the casserole, adding water, if necessary, so that the liquid comes halfway up the sides of the casserole.

4 Cover the casserole with a tight-fitting lid, then cook in the oven for 3 hours, until the meat and vegetables are very tender. Return to the oven for longer if necessary. Serve immediately, sprinkled with chopped fresh parsley. Alternatively, leave to cool, then chill in the refrigerator overnight. Spoon off any fat that has solidified on the surface of the stew and reheat thoroughly in the oven or on the stove before serving.

Oatmeal & Herb Rack of Lamb

Ask the butcher to remove the chine bone that runs along the eye of the meat – this will make carving easier.

Serves 6

2 best end necks (cross rib) of lamb (about 900kg/2lb each)
finely grated rind of 1 lemon
60ml/4 tbsp medium oatmeal
50g/2oz/1 cup fresh white breadcrumbs
60ml/4 tbsp chopped fresh parsley
25g/1oz/2 tbsp butter, melted
30ml/2 tbsp clear honey
salt and ground black pepper
fresh herb sprigs, to garnish
roasted baby vegetables and gravy, to serve

1 Preheat the oven to 200°C/400°F/Gas 6. Using a small sharp knife, cut through the skin and meat of both pieces of lamb about 2.5cm/1in from the tips of the bones. Pull off the fatty meat to expose the bones, then scrape around each bone tip until completely clean.

2 Trim all the skin and most of the fat from the meat, then lightly score the remaining fat with a sharp knife. Repeat with the second rack.

3 Mix together the lemon rind, oatmeal, breadcrumbs and parsley in a bowl. Season with salt and pepper and stir in the melted butter until thoroughly combined.

4 Brush the fatty side of each rack of lamb with honey, then press the oatmeal mixture evenly over the surface with your fingers until well coated.

5 Place the racks in a roasting pan with the oatmeal sides uppermost. Roast for 40–50 minutes, depending on whether you like rare or medium lamb. Cover loosely with foil if browning too much.

6 To serve, slice each rack into three and place two chops on each of six warmed plates. Garnish with fresh herb sprigs and serve immediately with roasted baby vegetables and gravy made with the pan juices.

Stew Energy 823kcal/3453kJ; Protein 80g; Carbohydrate 50.3g, of which sugars 10.4g; Fat 34.9g, of which saturates 14.8g; Cholesterol 266mg; Calcium 137mg; Fibre 4.4g; Sodium 540mg.
Lamb Energy 719kcal/2979kJ; Protein 40g; Carbohydrate 15g, of which sugars 1.4g; Fat 55.9g, of which saturates 27.1g; Cholesterol 171mg; Calcium 59mg; Fibre 1.2g; Sodium 227mg.

Beef Wellington

This English dish is so-
named because of a
supposed resemblance in
shape and colour to the
Duke of Wellington's boot.

Serves 8
1.4kg/3lb fillet (tenderloin) of beef
15g/½oz/1 tbsp butter
30ml/2 tbsp vegetable oil

½ small onion, finely chopped
175g/6oz mushrooms, chopped
175g/6oz liver pâté
freshly squeezed lemon juice
a few drops of Worcestershire
    sauce
400g/14oz puff pastry dough,
    thawed if frozen
beaten egg, to glaze
salt and ground black pepper

1 Preheat the oven to 220°C/425°F/Gas 7. Season the beef
with pepper, then tie it at intervals with string.

2 Heat the butter and oil in a roasting pan over high heat.
Add the beef and cook, turning frequently, for 8–10 minutes,
until evenly browned all over. Transfer the roasting pan to the
oven and cook for 20 minutes. Remove the beef from the
oven, transfer to a plate and leave to cool. Remove and discard
the string.

3 Meanwhile, scrape the cooking juices into a pan, add the
onion and mushrooms and cook over low heat, stirring
occasionally, for about 5 minutes, until the onion is softened but
not coloured. Leave to cool, then mix with the pâté. Add the
lemon juice and Worcestershire sauce. Preheat the oven again
to 220°C/425°F/Gas 7.

4 Roll out the pastry dough to a large rectangle 5mm/¼in
thick. Spread the pâté mixture on the beef, then place it in the
centre of the dough. Dampen the edges of the dough, then fold
it over the beef to make a neat parcel, tucking in the ends tidily.
Press firmly to seal.

5 Place the parcel on a baking sheet with the join underneath
and brush with beaten egg. Bake in the oven for 25–45
minutes, depending how well done you like the beef. Serve in
generous slices.

Butterflied Cumin & Garlic Lamb

Ground cumin and garlic
give the lamb a wonderful
Middle-Eastern flavour.

Serves 6
1.75kg/4lb leg of lamb
60ml/4 tbsp extra virgin olive oil

30ml/2 tbsp ground cumin
4–6 garlic cloves, crushed
salt and ground black pepper
toasted almond and raisin rice,
    to serve
fresh coriander (cilantro) sprigs
    and lemon wedges, to garnish

1 To butterfly the lamb, cut away the meat from the bone using
a small sharp knife. Remove any excess fat and the thin,
parchment-like membrane. Flatten the meat with a rolling pin
to an even thickness, then prick the fleshy side of the lamb well
with the tip of a knife. Place the lamb in a large, shallow dish.

2 Mix together the olive oil, cumin and garlic in a bowl and
season with pepper. Spoon the mixture all over the lamb, then
rub it well into the crevices. Cover the dish with clear film
(plastic wrap) and place the lamb in the refrigerator to
marinate overnight.

3 Preheat the oven to 200°C/400°F/Gas 6. Spread the lamb,
skin side down, on a rack in a roasting pan. Season with salt and
roast for 45–60 minutes, until crusty brown on the outside but
still pink in the centre.

4 Remove the lamb from the roasting pan and place on a
board. Cover with foil and leave it to rest for about 10 minutes.
Cut into diagonal slices, place on warmed plates and serve
immediately with the toasted almond and raisin rice. Garnish
with fresh coriander sprigs and lemon wedges.

Cook's Tip
The lamb may be cooked on the barbecue rather than
roasted in the oven. Thread it on to two long skewers and
grill over hot coals for 20–25 minutes on each side, until it is
cooked to your liking.

Beef Energy 511kcal/2131kJ; Protein 41.7g; Carbohydrate 19.3g, of which sugars 1.2g; Fat 30.6g, of which saturates 7.2g; Cholesterol 128mg; Calcium 41mg; Fibre 0.4g; Sodium 320mg.
Lamb Energy 505kcal/2106kJ; Protein 59.8g; Carbohydrate 0g, of which sugars 0g; Fat 29.5g, of which saturates 12.8g; Cholesterol 225mg; Calcium 23mg; Fibre 0g; Sodium 128mg.

Somerset Pork with Apples

A creamy cider sauce accompanies tender pieces of pork and sliced apples to make a rich supper dish.

Serves 4

25g/1oz/2 tbsp butter
500g/1¼lb pork loin, cut into
  bitesize pieces
12 baby (pearl) onions, peeled
10ml/2 tsp grated lemon rind
300ml/½ pint/1¼ cups dry
  (hard) cider
150ml/¼ pint/⅔ cup veal stock
2 crisp eating apples such as
  Granny Smith, cored and sliced
45ml/3 tbsp chopped
  fresh parsley
100ml/3½fl oz/scant ½ cup
  whipping cream
salt and ground black pepper

1 Melt the butter in a large sauté or frying pan over medium heat. Add the pork, in batches, and cook, stirring frequently, for about 8 minutes, until browned all over. Transfer the pork to a bowl with a slotted spoon.

2 Add the onions to the pan and lower the heat. Cook, stirring occasionally, for 8–10 minutes, until lightly browned.

3 Stir in the lemon rind, cider and stock, bring to the boil and cook for about 3 minutes. Return all the pork to the pan, cover and simmer gently for about 25 minutes, until tender.

4 Add the apples to the pan and cook for a further 5 minutes. Using a slotted spoon, transfer the pork, onions and apples to a warmed serving dish, cover and keep warm.

5 Stir the parsley and cream into the pan and leave to bubble to thicken the sauce slightly. Season with salt and pepper, then pour over the pork and serve immediately.

> **Cook's Tip**
> *Veal stock is mellow in flavour and does not overpower other ingredients. The mainstay of restaurant kitchens, it's used less frequently at home. Chicken stock is a satisfactory alternative.*

Lamb with Mint Sauce

In this flavoursome dish, the classic British combination of lamb and mint is given an original twist.

Serves 4

8 lamb noisettes, 2–2.5cm/
  ¾–1in thick
30ml/2 tbsp vegetable oil
45ml/3 tbsp medium-bodied dry
  white wine, or vegetable or
  veal stock
salt and ground black pepper
fresh mint sprigs, to garnish

For the sauce
30ml/2 tbsp boiling water
5–10ml/1–2 tsp sugar
leaves from a small bunch of
  fresh mint, finely chopped
about 30ml/2 tbsp white
  wine vinegar

1 To make the sauce, stir the water and sugar together in a heatproof bowl, then add the mint and vinegar to taste. Season with salt and pepper. Leave to stand for 30 minutes.

2 Season the lamb with pepper. Heat the oil in a large, heavy frying pan. Add the lamb, in batches if necessary so that the pan is not crowded, and cook for about 3 minutes on each side for meat that is pink in the middle.

3 Transfer the lamb to a warmed plate and season with salt, then cover and keep warm.

4 Stir the wine or stock into the cooking juices, scraping up the sediment from the base of the pan, and bring to the boil. Leave to bubble for a couple of minutes, then pour over the lamb. Garnish the lamb noisettes with small sprigs of mint and serve hot with the mint sauce.

> **Cook's Tip**
> *In the past, cooks used more sugar to counteract the sharpness of the vinegar in the mint sauce. Add more to taste, if you like. It was also common to sprinkle the mint leaves with 5ml/1 tsp sugar before chopping them finely.*

Lamb Energy 332kcal/1384kJ; Protein 29.6g; Carbohydrate 1.6g, of which sugars 1.4g; Fat 22.3g, of which saturates 8.5g; Cholesterol 114mg; Calcium 22mg; Fibre 0g; Sodium 130mg.
Pork Energy 375kcal/1563kJ; Protein 28.7g; Carbohydrate 15g, of which sugars 12.7g; Fat 20.5g, of which saturates 11.3g; Cholesterol 118mg; Calcium 58mg; Fibre 2.2g; Sodium 141mg.

Pork with Plums

Plums poached in apple juice are used here to make a delightfully fruity sauce for pork chops.

Serves 4

450g/1lb ripe plums, halved and stoned (pitted)
300ml/½ pint/1¼ cups apple juice

40g/1½oz/3 tbsp butter
15ml/1 tbsp oil
4 pork chops (about 200g/7oz each)
1 onion, finely chopped
pinch of freshly ground mace
salt and ground black pepper
fresh sage leaves, to garnish

1 Put the plums and the apple juice in a pan and bring just to the boil. Lower the heat and simmer until tender. Strain off and reserve the juice. Place half the plums and a little of the juice in a food processor or blender and process to a purée.

2 Meanwhile, heat the butter and oil in a large frying pan over medium heat. Add the chops and cook for about 4 minutes on each side until evenly browned. Transfer them to a plate.

3 Add the onion to the frying pan and lower the heat. Cook, stirring occasionally, for about 5 minutes, until it is softened but not coloured.

4 Return the chops to the pan. Pour over the plum purée and all the reserved apple juice. Simmer, uncovered, for 10–15 minutes, until the chops are cooked through.

5 Add the remaining plums to the pan, then add the mace and season to taste with salt and pepper. Warm the sauce through over medium heat and serve garnished with fresh sage leaves.

> **Cook's Tip**
> When buying plums, look for firm fruit with a little "give" but avoid any that are squashy. Use within one or two days of purchase because they over-ripen very rapidly.

Lancashire Hot-pot

Browning the lamb and kidneys, plus the extra vegetables and herbs, adds flavour to the traditional basic ingredients.

Serves 4

45ml/3 tbsp vegetable oil
8 medium neck (US shoulder) lamb chops (about 900g/2lb total weight)
175g/6oz lamb's kidneys, cored and cut into large pieces

900g/2lb potatoes, thinly sliced
3 carrots, thickly sliced
450g/1lb leeks, sliced
3 celery sticks, sliced
15ml/1 tbsp chopped fresh thyme
30ml/2 tbsp chopped fresh parsley
small fresh rosemary sprig
600ml/1 pint/2½ cups veal or chicken stock
salt and ground black pepper

1 Preheat the oven to 170°C/325°F/Gas 3. Heat the oil in a frying pan over medium heat. Add the chops, in batches if necessary, and cook for 2–3 minutes on each side, until evenly browned. Transfer to a plate.

2 Add the kidneys to the pan, in batches if necessary, and cook for 1–2 minutes on each side, until evenly browned. Transfer to the plate with the chops. Reserve the fat in the pan.

3 Make alternate layers of lamb chops, kidneys, three-quarters of the potatoes and the carrots, leeks and celery. Sprinkle the herbs over each layer as you go and season each layer with salt and pepper. Tuck the rosemary sprig down the side.

4 Arrange the remaining potato slices on top to cover the meat and vegetables completely. Pour over the veal or chicken stock, brush the potato topping with the reserved fat from the frying pan, then cover the casserole with a tight-fitting lid and bake for 2½ hours.

5 Increase the oven temperature to 220°C/425°F/Gas 7. Uncover the casserole and cook for a further 30 minutes, until the potato topping is golden brown. Serve immediately straight from the casserole.

Pork Energy 620kcal/2595kJ; Protein 65.4g; Carbohydrate 17.4g, of which sugars 17.4g; Fat 32.6g, of which saturates 13.1g; Cholesterol 241mg; Calcium 40mg; Fibre 1.8g; Sodium 232mg.
Hot-Pot Energy 810kcal/3400kJ; Protein 76.7g; Carbohydrate 43.7g, of which sugars 9.3g; Fat 37.8g, of which saturates 13.2g; Cholesterol 363mg; Calcium 140mg; Fibre 6.2g; Sodium 285mg.

Pork Loin with Celery

Have a change from a plain Sunday roast and try this whole loin of pork in an unusual celery and cream sauce instead.

Serves 4

15ml/1 tbsp vegetable oil
50g/2oz/¼ cup butter
1kg/2¼lb boned, rolled loin
  of pork, rind removed
  and trimmed
1 onion, chopped
1 bouquet garni
3 fresh dill sprigs
150ml/¼ pint/⅔ cup dry
  white wine
150ml/¼ pint/⅔ cup water
sticks from 1 celery head, cut into
  2.5cm/1in lengths
25g/1oz/¼ cup plain (all-
  purpose) flour
150ml/¼ pint/⅔ cup double
  (heavy) cream
squeeze of lemon juice
salt and ground black pepper
chopped fresh dill, to garnish

1 Heat the oil and half the butter in a heavy flameproof casserole just large enough to hold the pork and celery. Add the pork and cook, turning frequently, for 8–10 minutes, until evenly browned. Transfer the pork to a plate.

2 Add the onion to the casserole, lower the heat and cook, stirring occasionally, for 5 minutes, until softened but not coloured. Add the bouquet garni and dill sprigs, place the pork on top and add any juices from the plate. Pour in the wine and water, season to taste, cover and simmer gently for 30 minutes.

3 Turn the pork, arrange the celery around it, cover again and cook for 40 minutes, until the pork and celery are tender. Transfer the pork and celery to a serving plate, cover and keep warm. Discard the bouquet garni and dill.

4 Cream the remaining butter with the flour, then whisk into the cooking liquid while it is barely simmering. Cook for 2–3 minutes, stirring occasionally. Stir the cream into the casserole, bring to the boil and add a squeeze of lemon juice.

5 Slice the pork, spoon a little sauce over the slices and garnish with dill. Serve with the remaining sauce handed separately.

Spiced Lamb with Apricots

Inspired by Middle Eastern cooking, this fruity, spicy casserole is simple to make yet looks impressive.

Serves 4

115g/4oz ready-to-eat
  dried apricots
50g/2oz/scant ½ cup seedless
  raisins
2.5ml/½ tsp saffron threads
150ml/¼ pint/⅔ cup orange
  juice
15ml/1 tbsp red wine vinegar
30–45ml/2–3 tbsp olive oil
1.5kg/3–3½ lb leg of lamb, boned
  and diced
1 onion, chopped
2 garlic cloves, crushed
10ml/2 tsp ground cumin
1.25ml/¼ tsp ground cloves
15ml/1 tbsp ground coriander
25g/1oz/¼ cup plain (all-
  purpose) flour
600ml/1 pint/2½ cups lamb or
  chicken stock
45ml/3 tbsp chopped fresh
  coriander (cilantro)
salt and ground black pepper
saffron rice mixed with toasted
  almonds and chopped fresh
  coriander, to serve

1 Mix together the dried apricots, raisins, saffron, orange juice and vinegar in a bowl. Cover with clear film (plastic wrap) and leave to soak for 2–3 hours.

2 Preheat the oven to 160°C/325°F/Gas 3. Heat 30ml/2 tbsp oil in a large flameproof casserole over medium heat. Add the lamb, in batches, and cook, stirring frequently, for 5–8 minutes, until evenly browned. Remove and set aside.

3 Add a little more oil to the casserole, if necessary, and lower the heat. Add the onion and garlic and cook, stirring occasionally, for 5 minutes, until softened but not coloured.

4 Stir in the spices and flour and cook for 1–2 minutes more. Return the meat to the casserole. Stir in the stock, fresh coriander and the soaked fruit with its liquid. Season to taste with salt and pepper, then bring to the boil. Cover the casserole with a tight-fitting lid and simmer for 1½ hours (adding extra stock if necessary), or until the lamb is tender. Serve with saffron rice mixed with toasted almonds and fresh coriander.

Pork Energy 669kcal/2783kJ; Protein 55.6g; Carbohydrate 8.1g, of which sugars 3g; Fat 43.5g, of which saturates 22.9g; Cholesterol 236mg; Calcium 105mg; Fibre 1.8g; Sodium 336mg.
Lamb Energy 765kcal/3192kJ; Protein 58.5g; Carbohydrate 27.5g, of which sugars 23.4g; Fat 47.5g, of which saturates 14.7g; Cholesterol 218mg; Calcium 53mg; Fibre 2.5g; Sodium 181mg.

Beef & Mushroom Burgers

It's worth making your own burgers to cut down on fat and for the added flavour – in this recipe the meat is extended with mushrooms for extra fibre.

Serves 4

1 small onion, coarsely chopped
150g/5oz/2 cups small
  cup mushrooms
450g/1lb lean minced
  (ground) beef
50g/2oz/1 cup fresh
  white breadcrumbs
5ml/1 tsp dried mixed herbs
15ml/1 tbsp tomato
  purée (paste)
plain (all-purpose) flour,
  for shaping
salt and ground black pepper

To serve
tomato or barbecue relish
salad
burger buns or pitta bread

1 Put the onion and mushrooms in a food processor and process until finely chopped. Add the beef, breadcrumbs, herbs and tomato purée and season with salt and pepper. Process until the mixture binds together but still has some texture.

2 Scrape the mixture into a bowl and divide into 8–10 pieces. Flour your hands and shape the pieces into patties. Place on a baking sheet or large plate, cover with clear film (plastic wrap) and chill in the refrigerator for 30 minutes.

3 Cook the burgers in a non-stick frying pan, without any added fat, or under a preheated grill (broiler), turning once, for 12–15 minutes, until evenly cooked. Serve immediately with relish and salad, in burger buns or pitta bread.

> **Cook's Tip**
> *Home-made burgers have a looser texture than the store-bought variety. It is useful to chill them before cooking as this helps the burgers to firm up, so they are less likely to disintegrate when turned during cooking. If you are grilling (broiling) them, don't transfer them from the baking sheet to the grill (broiler) pan.*

Ruby Bacon Chops

This dish can be prepared with minimal effort, yet still looks impressive.

Serves 4
1 ruby grapefruit
4 lean bacon loin chops
45ml/3 tbsp redcurrant jelly
ground black pepper
fresh vegetables, to serve

1 Cut off all the peel and pith from the grapefruit with a sharp knife. Cut out the segments, catching the juice in a bowl.

2 Fry the bacon chops in a non-stick frying pan without fat, turning them once, until golden. Add the reserved grapefruit juice and redcurrant jelly to the pan and stir until the jelly has melted. Add the grapefruit segments, season with pepper and serve hot with fresh vegetables.

Beef Strips with Orange & Ginger

Stir-frying is a good way of cooking with the minimum of fat, so it's one of the quickest as well as one of the healthiest ways to cook.

Serves 4
450g/1lb rump (round) steak, cut
  into strips
grated rind and juice of
  1 orange
15ml/1 tbsp soy sauce
1 tbsp cornflour (cornstarch)
2.5cm/1in fresh root ginger,
  finely chopped
10ml/2 tsp sesame oil
1 carrot, cut into small strips
2 spring onions, (scallions), sliced

1 Place the beef strips in a bowl and sprinkle with the orange rind and juice. Leave to marinate for 30 minutes. Drain the liquid and reserve, then mix the meat with the soy sauce, cornflour and ginger.

2 Heat the oil in a wok and stir-fry the beef for 1 minute. Add the carrot and stir-fry for 2–3 minutes. Stir in the spring onions and the reserved liquid, then boil, stirring, until thickened. Serve.

Bacon Energy 328kcal/1379kJ; Protein 47.7g; Carbohydrate 10.5g, of which sugars 10.5g; Fat 10.9g, of which saturates 3.5g; Cholesterol 129mg; Calcium 20mg; Fibre 0.5g; Sodium 92mg.
Beef Strips Energy 212kcal/885kJ; Protein 25.7g; Carbohydrate 3.8g, of which sugars 0.3g; Fat 10.5g, of which saturates 4.3g; Cholesterol 65mg; Calcium 7mg; Fibre 0g; Sodium 341mg.
Burgers Energy 266kcal/1115kJ; Protein 27.6g; Carbohydrate 14.3g, of which sugars 3.7g; Fat 11.3g, of which saturates 4.8g; Cholesterol 63mg; Calcium 44mg; Fibre 1.5g; Sodium 209mg.

Lamb Pie with Mustard Thatch

This makes a pleasant change from a classic shepherd's pie – and it is a healthier option, as well.

Serve 4

750g/1½lb potatoes, diced
30ml/2 tbsp skimmed milk
15ml/1 tbsp wholegrain or
  French mustard
450g/1lb lean minced
  (ground) lamb
1 onion, chopped
2 celery sticks, sliced
2 carrots, diced
150ml/¼ pint/⅔ cup beef stock
60ml/4 tbsp rolled oats
15ml/1 tbsp Worcestershire sauce
30ml/2 tbsp chopped fresh
  rosemary or 10ml/2 tsp
  dried rosemary
salt and ground black pepper
fresh vegetables, to serve

1 Cook the potatoes in boiling lightly salted water for about 20 minutes, until tender. Drain well and mash until smooth, then stir in the milk and mustard. Meanwhile, preheat the oven to 200°C/400°F/Gas 6.

2 Break up the lamb with a fork and cook without any additional fat in a non-stick pan until lightly browned. Add the onion, celery and carrots to the pan and cook for 2–3 minutes, stirring constantly.

3 Stir in the stock and rolled oats. Bring to the boil, then add the Worcestershire sauce and rosemary and season to taste with salt and pepper.

4 Turn the meat mixture into a 1.75 litre/3 pint/7½ cup ovenproof dish and spread the potato topping evenly over the top, swirling with the edge of a knife. Bake for 30–35 minutes, or until golden. Serve hot with fresh vegetables.

> **Variation**
> Substitute low-fat natural (plain) yogurt for the milk and 30ml/ 2 tbsp chopped fresh mint for the mustard for a herb-flavoured thatch that is still a healthy option.

Steak, Kidney & Mushroom Pie

If you prefer, you can omit the kidneys from this pie and substitute more braising steak in their place.

Serves 4

30ml/2 tbsp sunflower oil
1 onion, chopped
115g/4oz bacon, finely chopped
500g/1¼ lb braising steak, diced
25g/1oz/¼ cup plain (all-
  purpose) flour
115g/4oz lamb's kidneys
large bouquet garni
400ml/14fl oz/1¾ cups beef
  stock
115g/4oz button
  (white) mushrooms
225g/8oz puff pastry dough,
  thawed if frozen
beaten egg, to glaze
salt and ground black pepper

1 Preheat the oven to 160°C/325°F/Gas 3. Heat the oil in a heavy pan over low heat. Add the onion and bacon and cook, stirring occasionally, for about 8 minutes, until lightly browned.

2 Toss the steak in the flour. Stir the meat into the pan, in batches, and cook, stirring frequently, until evenly browned. Toss the kidneys in flour, add to the pan with the bouquet garni and cook briefly, stirring occasionally, until browned.

3 Transfer the meat and onions to a casserole, pour in the stock, cover with a tight-fitting lid and cook in the oven for 2 hours. Remove the casserole from the oven, stir in the mushrooms, season with salt and pepper and leave to cool.

4 Preheat the oven to 220°C/425°F/Gas 7. Roll out the pastry to 2cm/¾in larger than the top of a 1.2 litre/2 pint/5 cup pie dish. Cut off a pastry strip and fit it around the dampened rim of the dish. Brush the pastry strip with water.

5 Tip the meat mixture into the dish. Lay the pastry over the dish, press the edges together to seal, then knock them up with the back of a knife. Make a small slit in the pastry, brush with beaten egg and bake for 20 minutes. Lower the oven temperature to 180°C/350°F/Gas 4 and bake for a further 20 minutes, until the pastry is risen, golden and crisp.

Steak Energy 597kcal/2488kJ; Protein 42.5g; Carbohydrate 27g, of which sugars 1.7g; Fat 36.7g, of which saturates 7.5g; Cholesterol 178mg; Calcium 57mg; Fibre 0.7g; Sodium 742mg.
Lamb Energy 382kcal/1605kJ; Protein 25.9g; Carbohydrate 35.1g, of which sugars 6.8g; Fat 16.4g, of which saturates 7.6g; Cholesterol 89mg; Calcium 78mg; Fibre 2.9g; Sodium 169mg.

Sausage & Bean Ragoût

This is an economical and nutritious main course that children will love. Serve with warm garlic and herb bread, if you like.

Serves 4

350g/12oz/2 cups dried flageolet or cannellini beans, soaked overnight in cold water
45ml/3 tbsp olive oil
1 onion, finely chopped
2 garlic cloves, crushed
450g/1lb good-quality chunky sausages, skinned and thickly sliced
15ml/1 tbsp tomato purée (paste)
400g/14oz can chopped tomatoes
30ml/2 tbsp chopped fresh parsley
15ml/1 tbsp chopped fresh thyme
salt and ground black pepper
chopped fresh thyme and parsley, to garnish

1 Drain and rinse the soaked beans and place them in a pan with enough water to cover. Bring to the boil, cover the pan with a tight-fitting lid and simmer for about 1 hour, or until tender. Drain the beans and set aside.

2 Heat the oil in a frying pan over medium-low heat. Add the onion, garlic and sausages and cook, stirring and turning occasionally, until golden.

3 Stir in the tomato purée, tomatoes, chopped parsley and thyme. Season with salt and pepper, then bring to the boil.

4 Add the beans, lower the heat, cover with a lid and cook gently, stirring occasionally, for about 15 minutes, until the sausage slices are cooked through. Divide the ragoût among warmed plates, garnish with chopped fresh thyme and parsley and serve immediately.

Cook's Tip
For a spicier version, add some skinned, thinly sliced chorizo or kabanos sausage along with the cooked beans for the last 15 minutes of cooking.

Peppered Steaks with Madeira

This is a really easy dish for special occasions. Mixed peppercorns have an excellent flavour, although black pepper will do.

Serves 4

15ml/1 tbsp mixed dried peppercorns (green, pink and black)
4 fillet (beef tenderloin) or sirloin steaks (about 175g/6oz each)
15ml/1 tbsp olive oil, plus extra oil for pan-frying
1 garlic clove, crushed
60ml/4 tbsp Madeira
90ml/6 tbsp beef stock
150ml/¼ pint/⅔ cup double (heavy) cream
salt

1 Finely crush the peppercorns using a spice grinder, coffee grinder or mortar and pestle, then press them evenly on to both sides of the steaks.

2 Place the steaks in a shallow non-metallic dish, then add the olive oil, garlic and Madeira. Cover the dish with clear film (plastic wrap) and leave to marinate in a cold place or the refrigerator for at least 4–6 hours, or preferably overnight for a more intense flavour.

3 Remove the steaks from the dish, reserving the marinade. Brush a little olive oil over a large heavy frying pan and heat until it is hot.

4 Add the steaks to the pan and cook over high heat, according to taste. Allow about 3 minutes' cooking time per side for a medium steak or 2 minutes per side for rare. Remove the steaks from the frying pan and keep them warm.

5 Add the reserved marinade and the beef stock to the pan and bring to the boil, then leave the sauce to bubble gently until it is well reduced.

6 Add the double cream to the pan, season with salt to taste, and stir until the sauce has thickened slightly. Place the peppered steaks on warmed plates and serve immediately with the sauce handed separately.

Ragoût Energy 745kcal/3114kJ; Protein 32.3g; Carbohydrate 54.1g, of which sugars 8.2g; Fat 45.9g, of which saturates 15.2g; Cholesterol 53mg; Calcium 146mg; Fibre 15.6g; Sodium 889mg.
Steaks Energy 471kcal/1956kJ; Protein 41.8g; Carbohydrate 2.5g, of which sugars 2.5g; Fat 30.8g, of which saturates 16.4g; Cholesterol 141mg; Calcium 28mg; Fibre 0g; Sodium 131mg.

Pork with Mozzarella & Sage

Here is a variation of the famous dish *saltimbocca alla romana* – the mozzarella cheese adds a delicious creamy flavour.

Serves 2–3

225g/8oz pork fillet (tenderloin)
1 garlic clove, crushed
75g/3oz mozzarella cheese, cut into 6 slices
6 slices prosciutto
6 large sage leaves
25g/1oz/2 tbsp butter
salt and ground black pepper
potato wedges roasted in olive oil and green beans, to serve

1 Trim any excess fat from the pork, then cut the meat crossways into six pieces about 2.5cm/1in thick.

2 Stand each piece of pork on its end and flatten by beating with the side of a rolling pin. Rub each piece with garlic, place on a plate, cover with clear film (plastic wrap) and set aside for 30 minutes in a cool place.

3 Place a slice of mozzarella on top of each piece of pork and season with salt and pepper. Lay a slice of prosciutto on top of each, crinkling it a little to fit. Press a sage leaf on to each and secure with a wooden cocktail stick (toothpick).

4 Melt the butter in a large, heavy frying pan. Add the pieces of pork and cook for about 2 minutes on each side, until the mozzarella begins to melt. Remove and discard the cocktail sticks, divide the pork among warmed serving plates and serve immediately with roasted potatoes and green beans.

Cook's Tips
• The original *saltimbocca*, which means "jump in the mouth", was made with veal escalopes (US scallops) and there is no reason why you should not also use these for this variation.
• Try to find traditional mozzarella made with buffalo rather than cow's milk, as it has a better flavour and more delicate texture when melted.

Five-spice Lamb

This aromatic lamb casserole is a perfect dish to serve at an informal lunch or supper party.

Serves 4

30–45ml/2–3 tbsp vegetable oil
1.5kg/3–3½lb leg of lamb, boned and diced
1 onion, chopped
10ml/2 tsp grated fresh root ginger
1 garlic clove, crushed
5ml/1 tsp Chinese five-spice powder
30ml/2 tbsp hoisin sauce
15ml/1 tbsp soy sauce
300ml/½ pint/1¼ cups passata (bottled strained tomatoes)
250ml/8fl oz/1 cup lamb or chicken stock
1 red (bell) pepper, seeded and diced
1 yellow (bell) pepper, seeded and diced
30ml/2 tbsp chopped fresh coriander (cilantro)
15ml/1 tbsp sesame seeds, toasted
salt and ground black pepper
boiled rice, to serve

1 Preheat the oven to 160°C/325°F/Gas 3. Heat 30ml/2 tbsp of the oil in a large, flameproof casserole. Add the lamb, in batches, and cook over high heat, stirring frequently, until evenly browned. Remove to a plate and set aside.

2 Add the onion, ginger and garlic to the casserole with a little more of the oil, if necessary. Lower the heat and cook, stirring occasionally, for 5 minutes, until softened but not coloured.

3 Return the lamb to the casserole. Stir in the five-spice powder, hoisin sauce, soy sauce, passata and stock and season to taste with salt and pepper. Bring to the boil, then cover with a tight-fitting lid and cook in the oven for about 1¼ hours.

4 Remove the casserole from the oven and stir in the red and yellow peppers. Cover the casserole again and return to the oven for a further 15 minutes, or until the lamb is very tender.

5 Sprinkle with the chopped fresh coriander and toasted sesame seeds. Spoon on to warmed, individual plates and serve immediately accompanied by rice, if you like.

Pork Energy 245kcal/1018kJ; Protein 25.3g; Carbohydrate 0.3g, of which sugars 0.3g; Fat 15.8g, of which saturates 9.1g; Cholesterol 94mg; Calcium 99mg; Fibre 0g; Sodium 502mg.
Lamb Energy 453kcal/1892kJ; Protein 39.2g; Carbohydrate 9.4g, of which sugars 8.7g; Fat 29.1g, of which saturates 10.9g; Cholesterol 143mg; Calcium 59mg; Fibre 2.4g; Sodium 606mg.

Rich Beef Casserole

Use a full-bodied red wine such as a Burgundy to create the flavoursome sauce in this casserole.

Serves 4–6

900g/2lb braising steak steak, cut into cubes
2 onions, coarsely chopped
1 bouquet garni
6 black peppercorns
15ml/1 tbsp red wine vinegar
1 bottle red wine
45–60ml/3–4 tbsp olive oil
3 celery sticks, thickly sliced
50g/2oz/½ cup plain (all-purpose) flour
300ml/½ pint/1¼ cups beef stock
30ml/2 tbsp tomato purée (paste)
2 garlic cloves, crushed
175g/6oz chestnut (cremini) mushrooms, halved
400g/14oz can artichoke hearts, drained and halved
chopped fresh parsley and thyme, to garnish

1 Put the meat, onions, bouquet garni, peppercorns, vinegar and wine in a bowl. Cover with clear film (plastic wrap) and leave to marinate in the refrigerator overnight.

2 The next day, preheat the oven to 160°C/325°F/Gas 3. Drain the meat, reserving the marinade, and pat dry. Heat the oil in a large flameproof casserole. Add the meat and onions, in batches, and cook, stirring frequently, until the meat is evenly browned, adding a little more oil if necessary. Remove and set aside. Add the celery to the casserole and cook, stirring frequently, until browned, then remove and set aside.

3 Sprinkle the flour into the casserole and cook, stirring constantly, for 1 minute. Gradually add the reserved marinade and the stock, and bring to the boil, stirring constantly. Return the meat, onions and celery to the casserole, then stir in the tomato purée and garlic.

4 Cover the casserole with a tight-fitting lid and cook in the oven for about 2¼ hours. Stir in the mushrooms and artichokes, cover again and cook for a further 15 minutes, until the meat is tender. Garnish with parsley and thyme, and serve hot with creamy mashed potatoes, if you like.

Roast Pork with Sage & Onion

Pork roasted with a sage and onion stuffing makes a perfect Sunday lunch dish.

Serves 6–8

1.3–1.6kg/3–3½lb boneless loin of pork
60ml/4 tbsp fine, dry breadcrumbs
10ml/2 tsp chopped fresh sage
25ml/1½ tbsp plain (all-purpose) flour
300ml/½ pint/1¼ cups cider
150ml/¼ pint/⅔ cup hot water
5–10ml/1–2 tsp redcurrant jelly
salt and ground black pepper

For the stuffing

25g/1oz/2 tbsp butter
50g/2oz bacon, finely chopped
2 large onions, finely chopped
75g/3oz/1½ cups fresh white breadcrumbs
30ml/2 tbsp chopped fresh sage
5ml/1 tsp chopped fresh thyme
10ml/2 tsp grated lemon rind
1 small egg, beaten

1 Preheat the oven to 220°C/425°F/Gas 7. To make the stuffing, melt the butter in a heavy pan and fry the bacon until it begins to brown. Add the onions and cook gently until softened, but do not allow to brown. Mix with the breadcrumbs, sage, thyme, lemon rind and egg, then season well with salt and pepper.

2 Cut the rind off the joint of pork in one piece and score it well. Place the pork fat-side down and season. Add a layer of stuffing, then roll up and tie neatly. Lay the rind over the pork and rub in 5ml/1 tsp salt. Roast for 2–2½ hours, basting occasionally. Reduce the temperature to 190°C/375°F/Gas 5 after 20 minutes. Shape the remaining stuffing into balls and add to the roasting pan for the last 30 minutes.

3 Remove the rind from the pork. Increase the temperature to 220°C/425°F/Gas 7 and roast the rind for a further 20–25 minutes, until crisp. Mix the breadcrumbs and sage and press them into the pork fat. Cook the pork for 10 minutes, then cover and set aside in a warm place for 15–20 minutes.

4 Remove all but 30–45ml/2–3 tbsp of the fat from the pan. Place over medium heat, stir in the flour, the cider and water. Cook for 10 minutes. Strain the gravy into a clean pan, add the jelly and cook for 5 minutes. Serve with the pork and crackling.

Beef Energy 457kcal/1905kJ; Protein 36.8g; Carbohydrate 12.2g, of which sugars 4.7g; Fat 20g, of which saturates 6.5g; Cholesterol 87mg; Calcium 77mg; Fibre 2.3g; Sodium 169mg.
Pork Energy 446Kcal/1874kJ; Protein 52.8g; Carbohydrate 26.4g, of which sugars 5.1g; Fat 15.1g, of which saturates 6g; Cholesterol 185mg; Calcium 76mg; Fibre 1.7g; Sodium 479mg.

Beef Casserole & Dumplings

A traditional English recipe, this delicious casserole is topped with light herbed dumplings for a filling meal.

Serves 4
15ml/1 tbsp oil
450g/1lb minced (ground) beef
16 button (pearl) onions
2 carrots, thickly sliced
2 celery sticks, thickly sliced
25g/1oz/¼ cup plain (all-purpose) flour
600ml/1 pint/2½ cups beef stock
salt and ground black pepper
broccoli florets, to serve (optional)

For the dumplings
115g/4oz/1 cup shredded vegetable suet
50g/2oz/½ cup self-raising (self-rising) flour
15ml/1 tbsp chopped fresh parsley

1 Preheat the oven to 180°C/350°F/Gas 4. Heat the oil in a flameproof casserole over medium heat. Add the beef and cook, stirring frequently to break up the meat, for 5 minutes, until brown and sealed.

2 Add the onions and cook, stirring occasionally, for 5 minutes, until softened but not coloured.

3 Stir in the carrots, celery and flour and cook, stirring constantly, for 1 minute.

4 Gradually stir in the beef stock, season to taste with salt and pepper and bring to the boil. Cover with a tight-fitting lid and cook in the oven for 1¼ hours.

5 For the dumplings, mix together the suet, flour and parsley in a bowl. Stir in sufficient cold water to form a smooth dough and knead lightly.

6 Roll the dumpling mixture into eight equal-size balls between the palms of your hands and place them around the top of the casserole. Return the casserole, uncovered, to the oven for a further 20 minutes, until the dumplings are cooked. Serve with broccoli florets, if you like.

Stilton Burgers

This tasty recipe contains a delicious surprise: encased in the crunchy burger is lightly melted Stilton cheese.

Serves 4
450g/1lb minced (ground) beef
1 onion, finely chopped
1 celery stick, chopped
5ml/1 tsp mixed dried herbs
5ml/1 tsp mustard
50g/2oz/½ cup crumbled Stilton cheese
4 burger buns
salt and ground black pepper
burger buns, salad and mustard pickle, to serve

1 Preheat the grill (broiler). Place the minced beef in a bowl with the chopped onion and celery. Mix together, then season with salt and pepper.

2 Stir in the herbs and mustard, bringing all the ingredients together to form a firm mixture.

3 Divide the mixture into eight equal portions and roll them into balls between the palms of your hands. Place four on a chopping board and flatten each one slightly into a round.

4 Divide the crumbled cheese between the four rounds, placing a portion in the centre of each. Flatten the remaining balls into rounds and place on top, covering the cheese. Gently mould the mixture together, encasing the crumbled cheese completely, and shape into four burgers.

5 Grill (broil) under medium heat, turning once, for 10 minutes, or until cooked through. Split the burger buns and place a burger inside each. Serve with burger buns, a freshly made salad and some mustard pickle.

> **Cook's Tip**
> These burgers could be made with minced (ground) lamb or pork for a change, but make sure that they are thoroughly cooked and not pink inside.

Casserole Energy 619kcal/2567kJ; Protein 25.3g; Carbohydrate 25.5g, of which sugars 6.9g; Fat 46.8g, of which saturates 21.2g; Cholesterol 68mg; Calcium 68mg; Fibre 2.7g; Sodium 117mg.
Burgers Energy 519kcal/2177kJ; Protein 32.2g; Carbohydrate 42.8g, of which sugars 2.8g; Fat 25.5g, of which saturates 10.8g; Cholesterol 76mg; Calcium 156mg; Fibre 1.6g; Sodium 632mg.

Indian Curried Lamb Samosas

Authentic samosa pastry is difficult to make but these samosas work equally well using puff pastry.

Serves 4

15ml/1 tbsp vegetable oil
1 garlic clove, crushed
175g/6oz minced (ground) lamb
4 spring onions (scallions), finely chopped
10ml/2 tsp medium-hot curry paste
4 ready-to-eat dried apricots, chopped
1 small potato, diced
10ml/2 tsp apricot chutney
30ml/2 tbsp frozen peas
squeeze of lemon juice
15ml/1 tbsp chopped fresh coriander (cilantro)
225g/8oz puff pastry dough, thawed if frozen
beaten egg, to glaze
5ml/1 tsp cumin seeds
salt and ground black pepper
45ml/3 tbsp natural (plain) yogurt with chopped fresh mint, to serve
fresh mint sprigs, to garnish

1 Preheat the oven to 220°C/425°F/Gas 7 and dampen a large non-stick baking sheet. Heat the oil in a pan over medium heat and cook the garlic for 30 seconds, then add the lamb. Cook, stirring frequently, for about 5 minutes, until the meat is well browned.

2 Stir in the spring onions, curry paste, apricots and potato, and cook for 2–3 minutes. Then add the chutney, peas and 60ml/ 4 tbsp water. Cover and simmer for 10 minutes, stirring occasionally. Stir in the lemon juice and coriander, season to taste with salt and pepper, remove and leave to cool.

3 Roll out the pastry and cut into four 15cm/6in squares. Place a quarter of the curry mixture in the centre of each square and brush the edges with beaten egg. Fold over to make a triangle and seal the edges. Knock up the edges with the back of a knife and make a small slit in the top of each.

4 Brush each samosa with beaten egg and sprinkle with the cumin seeds. Place on the damp baking sheet and bake for about 20 minutes. Serve garnished with mint sprigs and with the minty yogurt handed separately.

Breton Pork & Bean Casserole

This is a traditional French dish, called *cassoulet*. There are many variations in the different regions of France.

Serves 4

30ml/2 tbsp olive oil
1 onion, chopped
2 garlic cloves, chopped
450g/1lb pork shoulder, diced
350g/12oz lean lamb (preferably leg), diced
225g/8oz coarse pork and garlic sausage, cut into chunks
400g/14oz can chopped tomatoes
30ml/2 tbsp red wine
15ml/1 tbsp tomato purée (paste)
1 bouquet garni
400g/14oz can cannellini beans, drained and rinsed
50g/2oz/1 cup fresh brown breadcrumbs
salt and ground black pepper
green salad and French bread, to serve

1 Preheat the oven to 160°C/325°F/Gas 3. Heat the oil in a large flameproof casserole over low heat. Add the onion and garlic and cook, stirring occasionally, for about 5 minutes, until softened but not coloured. Remove with a slotted spoon and set aside on a plate.

2 Add the pork, lamb and sausage chunks to the casserole, increase the heat to high and cook, stirring frequently, for about 8 minutes, until evenly browned. Return the onion and garlic to the casserole.

3 Stir in the chopped tomatoes, wine and tomato purée and add 300ml/½ pint/1¼ cups water. Season to taste with salt and pepper and add the bouquet garni. Cover with a tight-fitting lid and bring to the boil, then transfer the casserole to the oven and cook for 1½ hours.

4 Remove and discard the bouquet garni. Stir in the cannellini beans and sprinkle the breadcrumbs over the top. Return the casserole to the oven and cook, uncovered, for a further 30 minutes, until the meat is tender and the topping is golden brown. Serve immediately with a green salad and French bread to mop up the juices.

Samosas Energy 392kcal/1642kJ; Protein 13.7g; Carbohydrate 36.8g, of which sugars 12.4g; Fat 22.7g, of which saturates 3.2g; Cholesterol 34mg; Calcium 66mg; Fibre 2.3g; Sodium 212mg.
Casserole Energy 724kcal/3030kJ; Protein 56.6g; Carbohydrate 37.7g, of which sugars 9.2g; Fat 39g, of which saturates 14g; Cholesterol 164mg; Calcium 138mg; Fibre 8.1g; Sodium 1086mg.

Pan-fried Mediterranean Lamb

The warm, summery flavours of the Mediterranean are combined for a simple weekday meal.

Serves 4
8 lean lamb cutlets
 (US rib chops)
1 onion, thinly sliced
2 red (bell) peppers, seeded
 and sliced
400g/14oz can plum tomatoes
1 garlic clove, crushed
45ml/3 tbsp chopped fresh basil
30ml/2 tbsp chopped pitted
 black olives
salt and ground black pepper
pasta, to serve (optional)

1 Trim any excess fat from the lamb, then cook in a non-stick frying pan, without any added fat, turning frequently, for 4–5 minutes, until golden brown all over.

2 Add the onion and red peppers to the pan. Cook, stirring, for a few minutes to soften, then add the plum tomatoes, garlic and fresh basil leaves.

3 Cover and simmer for 20 minutes, or until the lamb is tender. Stir in the olives, season to taste with salt and pepper and serve hot, with pasta if you like.

> **Cook's Tip**
> *Lamb cutlets (US rib chops) are much thinner than chops taken from the loin and it is necessary to cut off the fat before cooking. However, they are less expensive than chops and the meat has a very sweet flavour.*

> **Variations**
> • *The red (bell) peppers give this dish a slightly sweet taste. If you prefer, use green peppers for a more savoury stew.*
> • *Substitute sliced green olives stuffed with pimiento for the chopped black ones.*

Greek Lamb Pie

Ready-made filo pastry is so easy to use and gives a most professional look to this lamb and spinach pie.

Serves 4
sunflower oil, for brushing
450g/1lb minced (ground) lamb
1 onion, sliced
1 garlic clove, crushed
400g/14oz can plum tomatoes
30ml/2 tbsp chopped fresh mint
5ml/1 tsp freshly grated nutmeg
350g/12oz young spinach leaves
275g/10oz filo pastry, thawed if
 frozen
5ml/1 tsp sesame seeds
salt and ground black pepper
green salad or vegetables,
 to serve (optional)

1 Preheat the oven to 200°C/400°F/Gas 6. Lightly oil a 22cm/8½in round springform tin (pan).

2 Cook the lamb and onion, without any added fat, in a non-stick pan over medium heat, stirring frequently, for about 5 minutes, until the meat is golden brown.

3 Stir in the garlic, tomatoes with their can juices, mint and nutmeg and season with salt and pepper. Bring to the boil, stirring occasionally. Lower the heat and simmer gently, stirring occasionally, until most of the liquid has evaporated. Remove the pan from the heat and leave to cool.

4 Wash the spinach and remove any tough stalks, then cook in a large pan with only the water clinging to the leaves for about 2 minutes, until just wilted. Drain well, squeezing out as much liquid as possible.

5 Lightly brush each sheet of filo pastry with oil and lay in overlapping layers in the prepared tin, leaving enough pastry overhanging the sides to wrap over the top.

6 Spoon in the meat mixture and spinach, then wrap the pastry over to enclose, scrunching it slightly. Lightly brush the top of the pie with oil, sprinkle with sesame seeds and bake for about 25–30 minutes, or until golden and crisp. Serve hot, with a green salad or vegetables.

Pan-Fried Energy 637kcal/2634kJ; Protein 23.9g; Carbohydrate 9.9g, of which sugars 9.3g; Fat 56g, of which saturates 27.3g; Cholesterol 117mg; Calcium 33mg; Fibre 2.8g; Sodium 272mg.
Lamb Pie Energy 446kcal/1872kJ; Protein 29.2g; Carbohydrate 39.7g, of which sugars 5.9g; Fat 20g, of which saturates 7.7g; Cholesterol 87mg; Calcium 248mg; Fibre 4.5g; Sodium 211mg.

Cheese Pasta Bolognese

If you like lasagne, you will love this dish. It is especially popular with children too.

Serves 4
30ml/2 tbsp olive oil
1 onion, chopped
1 garlic clove, crushed
1 carrot, diced
2 celery sticks, chopped
2 rashers (strips) streaky (fatty) bacon, finely chopped
5 button (white) mushrooms, chopped
450g/1lb lean minced (ground) beef
120ml/4fl oz/½ cup red wine
15ml/1 tbsp tomato purée (paste)
200g/7oz can chopped tomatoes
fresh thyme sprig
225g/8oz/2 cups dried penne pasta
300ml/½ pint/1¼ cups milk
25g/1oz/2 tbsp butter
25g/1oz/¼ cup plain (all-purpose) flour
150g/5oz/ mozzarella cheese, diced
60ml/4 tbsp freshly grated Parmesan cheese
salt and ground black pepper
fresh basil sprigs, to garnish

1 Heat the oil in a pan over low heat. Add the onion, garlic, carrot and celery and cook, stirring occasionally, for 5 minutes, until softened. Add the bacon and cook for 3–4 minutes. Add the mushrooms and cook for 2 minutes. Add the beef and cook, stirring frequently, for 5–6 minutes, until well browned.

2 Add the wine, tomato purée, 45ml/3 tbsp water, the tomatoes and thyme sprig. Bring to the boil, cover, and simmer gently for 30 minutes.

3 Preheat the oven to 200°C/400°F/Gas 6. Cook the pasta. Meanwhile, place the milk, butter and flour in a pan and heat gently, whisking until thickened. Stir in the mozzarella and half the Parmesan. Season with salt and pepper.

4 Drain the pasta and stir into the cheese sauce. Uncover the Bolognese sauce and boil rapidly for 2 minutes. Spoon the sauce into an ovenproof dish, top with the pasta mixture and sprinkle with the remaining Parmesan. Bake for 25 minutes, or until golden. Garnish with basil and serve hot.

Corned Beef & Egg Hash

This classic American hash is a perennially popular brunch dish and should be served with chilli sauce for an authentic touch.

Serves 4
30ml/2 tbsp vegetable oil
25g/1oz/2 tbsp butter
1 onion, finely chopped
1 small green (bell) pepper, seeded and diced
2 large boiled potatoes, diced
350g/12oz can corned beef, diced
1.5ml/¼ tsp freshly grated nutmeg
1.5ml/¼ tsp paprika
4 eggs
salt and ground black pepper
chopped fresh parsley, to garnish
chilli sauce, to serve

1 Heat the oil and butter in a large frying pan. Add the onion and cook, stirring occasionally, for 5–6 minutes until softened.

2 Mix together the green pepper, potatoes, corned beef, nutmeg and paprika in a bowl. Season with salt and pepper. Add to the pan and toss gently. Press down lightly and cook over a medium heat for 3–4 minutes, until a golden brown crust has formed on the underside.

3 Stir the mixture to distribute the crust, then repeat the process twice, until the mixture is well browned.

4 Make four wells in the hash and crack an egg into each one. Cover and cook gently for 4–5 minutes, until the egg whites are just set.

5 Sprinkle with chopped parsley and cut the hash into quarters. Serve immediately with chilli sauce.

> **Cook's Tip**
> Put the can of corned beef in the refrigerator for 30 minutes before using. It will firm up and you will be able to cut it into cubes more easily than if it is used at room temperature.

Pasta Energy 806kcal/3369kJ; Protein 46.1g; Carbohydrate 54.6g, of which sugars 9.6g; Fat 44.1g, of which saturates 21.1g; Cholesterol 122mg; Calcium 461mg; Fibre 3.3g; Sodium 503mg.
Hash Energy 403kcal/1683kJ; Protein 30.4g; Carbohydrate 13g, of which sugars 5.1g; Fat 26.1g, of which saturates 10.5g; Cholesterol 277mg; Calcium 64mg; Fibre 1.4g; Sodium 868mg.

MEAT

Best-ever American Burgers

These meaty quarter-pounders are far superior in both taste and texture to any burgers you can buy ready-made.

Makes 4 burgers
15ml/1 tbsp vegetable oil
1 small onion, chopped
450g/1lb minced (ground) beef
1 large garlic clove, crushed
5ml/1 tsp ground cumin
10ml/2 tsp ground coriander
30ml/2 tbsp tomato purée
  (paste) or ketchup

5ml/1 tsp wholegrain mustard
dash of Worcestershire sauce
30ml/2 tbsp mixed chopped fresh
  herbs, such as parsley, thyme
  and oregano or marjoram
15ml/1 tbsp lightly beaten egg
salt and ground black pepper
plain (all purpose) flour,
  for shaping
vegetable oil, for frying (optional)
burger buns, mixed salad, chips
  (French fries) and relish, to
  serve

1 Heat the oil in a frying pan. Add the onion and cook, stirring occasionally, for 5 minutes, until softened. Remove from the pan, drain on kitchen paper and leave to cool.

2 Mix together the beef, garlic, spices, tomato purée or ketchup, mustard, Worcestershire sauce, herbs, beaten egg and seasoning in a bowl. Stir in the cooled onions.

3 Sprinkle a board with flour and shape the mixture into four burgers with floured hands and a spatula. Cover and chill in the refrigerator for 15 minutes.

4 Heat a little oil in a pan and fry the burgers over medium heat for about 5 minutes each side, depending on how rare you like them. Alternatively, cook under a medium grill (broiler) for the same time. Serve with buns, salad, chips and relish.

Cook's Tip
If you prefer, make eight smaller burgers to serve in buns, with melted cheese and tomato slices.

Bacon & Sausage Sauerkraut

Juniper berries and crushed coriander seeds flavour this traditional dish from Alsace.

Serves 4
30ml/2 tbsp vegetable oil
1 large onion, thinly sliced
1 garlic clove, crushed
450g/1lb bottled sauerkraut,
  rinsed and drained
1 eating apple, cored
  and chopped

5 juniper berries
5 coriander seeds, crushed
450g/1lb piece of lightly smoked
  bacon loin roast
225g/8oz whole smoked pork
  sausage, pricked
175ml/6fl oz/³/₄ cup unsweetened
  apple juice
150ml/¹/₄ pint/²/₃ cup chicken
  stock
1 bay leaf
8 small salad potatoes

1 Preheat the oven to 180°C/350°F/Gas 4. Heat the oil in a flameproof casserole over medium heat. Add the onion and garlic and cook, stirring occasionally, for 3–4 minutes, until softened but not coloured. Stir in the sauerkraut, apple, juniper berries and coriander seeds.

2 Lay the piece of bacon loin and the sausage on top of the sauerkraut, pour in the apple juice and stock, and add the bay leaf. Cover and bake in the oven for about 1 hour.

3 Remove from the oven and put the potatoes in the casserole. Add a little more stock if necessary, cover and bake for a further 30 minutes, or until the potatoes are tender.

4 Just before serving, lift out the bacon and sausages on to a board and slice. Spoon the sauerkraut on to a warmed platter, top with the meat and surround with the potatoes.

Cook's Tip
Sauerkraut is finely sliced, salted and fermented white cabbage. It is available in bottles and cans and, as it is pasteurized, it does not require the very long cooking times traditionally associated with this speciality.

Burger Energy 298kcal/1237kJ; Protein 23.5g; Carbohydrate 2.3g, of which sugars 1.9g; Fat 21.7g, of which saturates 8.3g; Cholesterol 91mg; Calcium 20mg; Fibre 0.4g; Sodium 117mg.
Sauerkraut Energy 562kcal/2347kJ; Protein 42.6g; Carbohydrate 31.8g, of which sugars 14.4g; Fat 30.2g, of which saturates 10g; Cholesterol 49mg; Calcium 118mg; Fibre 5.1g; Sodium 2352mg.

Ginger Pork with Black Bean Sauce

Preserved black beans provide a unique flavour in this dish. Look for them in specialist Chinese grocers.

Serves 4

350g/12oz pork fillet (tenderloin)
1 garlic clove, crushed
15ml/1 tbsp grated fresh
   root ginger
90ml/6 tbsp chicken stock
30ml/2 tbsp dry sherry
15ml/1 tbsp light soy sauce
5ml/1 tsp sugar
10ml/2 tsp cornflour (cornstarch)
45ml/3 tbsp groundnut
   (peanut) oil
2 yellow (bell) peppers, seeded
   and cut into strips
2 red (bell) peppers, seeded and
   cut into strips
1 bunch of spring onions
   (scallions), sliced diagonally
45ml/3 tbsp preserved black
   beans, coarsely chopped
fresh coriander (cilantro) sprigs,
   to garnish

1 Cut the pork into thin slices across the grain of the meat. Put the slices into a dish and mix them with the garlic and ginger. Cover with clear film (plastic wrap) and leave to marinate at room temperature for 15 minutes.

2 Blend together the stock, sherry, soy sauce, sugar and cornflour in a small bowl, then set the sauce mixture aside.

3 Heat the oil in a wok or large frying pan. Add the pork slices and stir-fry for 2–3 minutes. Add the yellow and red peppers and spring onions and stir-fry for a further 2 minutes.

4 Add the beans and sauce mixture and cook, stirring constantly, until thick. Serve immediately, garnished with the fresh coriander sprigs.

> **Cook's Tip**
> If you cannot find preserved black beans, use the same amount of black bean sauce instead.

Golden Pork & Apricot Casserole

The rich golden colour and warm spicy flavour of this simple casserole make it ideal for a chilly winter's day.

Serves 4

4 lean pork loin chops
1 onion, thinly sliced
2 yellow (bell) peppers, seeded
   and sliced
10ml/2 tsp medium curry powder
15g/½ oz/2 tbsp plain (all-
   purpose) flour
250ml/8fl oz/1 cup chicken stock
115g/4oz ready-to-eat
   dried apricots
30ml/2 tbsp wholegrain mustard
salt and ground black pepper
boiled rice or new potatoes, to
   serve (optional)

1 Trim the excess fat from the pork. Cook the chops, without any additional fat, in a large heavy or non-stick pan over medium heat for about 6 minutes, until lightly browned.

2 Lower the heat, add the onion and yellow peppers to the pan and cook, stirring frequently, for about 5 minutes, until softened but not coloured.

3 Stir in the curry powder and the flour and cook, stirring constantly, for 1 minute.

4 Gradually stir in the stock, then add the apricots and mustard and bring to the boil over medium heat. Cover with a tight-fitting lid, lower the heat and simmer gently for 25–30 minutes, until the chops are cooked through and tender. Season to taste with salt and pepper and serve immediately, with boiled rice or new potatoes, if you like.

> **Variations**
> • This recipe also works well with chicken breast portions – with or without the skin – instead of pork chops. However, you will need to heat 15ml/1 tbsp sunflower oil in the pan for the initial browning in step 1.
> • Substitute the same quantity of ready-to-eat prunes for the apricots and use red (bell) peppers instead of yellow.

Ginger Pork Energy 302kcal/1263kJ; Protein 23.8g; Carbohydrate 22.1g, of which sugars 13.4g; Fat 12.8g, of which saturates 3.1g; Cholesterol 55mg; Calcium 41mg; Fibre 4.1g; Sodium 341mg.
Golden Pork Energy 281kcal/1181kJ; Protein 34.9g; Carbohydrate 20.9g, of which sugars 16.7g; Fat 6.9g, of which saturates 2.2g; Cholesterol 95mg; Calcium 64mg; Fibre 4.1g; Sodium 124mg.

Sukiyaki-style Beef

This dish incorporates all the traditional Japanese elements – meat, vegetables, noodles and tofu.

Serves 4

450g/1lb thick rump
    (round) steak
200g/7oz/3½ cups Japanese
    rice noodles
15ml/1 tbsp shredded suet
200g/7oz firm tofu, cut into dice

8 shiitake mushrooms, trimmed
2 leeks, sliced into 2.5cm/
    1in lengths
90g/3½ oz/scant 1 cup baby
    spinach, to serve

For the stock

15g/½oz/1 tbsp caster
    (superfine) sugar
90ml/6 tbsp rice wine
45ml/3 tbsp dark soy sauce
120ml/4fl oz/½ cup water

1 If there is time, chill the steak in the freezer for 30 minutes to make it easier to slice thinly. Cut the steak into thin even-size slices with a very sharp knife.

2 Blanch the rice noodles in a large pan of boiling water for 2 minutes, then drain well.

3 Mix together all the ingredients for the stock in a bowl, stirring until the sugar has dissolved. Set aside.

4 Heat a wok, then add the suet. When the suet has melted, add the steak and stir-fry for 2–3 minutes, until it is cooked but still pink in colour.

5 Pour the stock over the beef and add the tofu, mushrooms and leeks. Cook, stirring occasionally, for 4 minutes, until the leeks are tender. Divide the different ingredients equally among individual plates, spoon the stock over them and serve immediately with a few baby spinach leaves each.

> **Cook's Tip**
> Add a touch of authenticity and serve this complete meal with chopsticks and a porcelain spoon to collect the stock juices.

Stir-fried Pork with Mustard

Fry the apple for this dish very carefully, because it will disintegrate if it is overcooked.

Serves 4

500g/1¼lb pork fillet (tenderloin)
1 tart eating apple, such as
    Granny Smith
40g/1½oz/3 tbsp unsalted
    (sweet) butter
15g/½oz/1 tbsp caster
    (superfine) sugar

1 small onion, finely chopped
30ml/2 tbsp Calvados or brandy
15ml/1 tbsp Meaux or coarse
    grain mustard
15ml/¼ pint/⅔ cup double
    (heavy) cream
30ml/2 tbsp chopped
    fresh parsley
salt and ground black pepper
fresh flat leaf parsley sprigs,
    to garnish

1 Cut the pork fillet into thin even size slices with a sharp knife. Peel and core the apple, then cut it into thick slices.

2 Heat a wok, then add half the butter. When the butter is hot, add the apple slices, sprinkle the sugar over them and stir-fry for 2–3 minutes. Remove the apple from the wok and set aside. Wipe out the wok with kitchen paper.

3 Reheat the wok, then add the remaining butter and stir-fry the pork fillet and onion together for 2–3 minutes, until the pork is golden and the onion has begun to soften.

4 Stir in the Calvados or brandy, bring to the boil and cook until it has reduced by about half. Stir in the mustard.

5 Add the cream and simmer gently for about 1 minute, then stir in the parsley. Transfer to warmed plates, divide the apple among them and serve garnished with sprigs of flat leaf parsley.

> **Cook's Tip**
> If you haven't got a wok, use a large frying pan, preferably with deep, sloping sides.

Beef Energy 489kcal/2044kJ; Protein 34.7g; Carbohydrate 49g, of which sugars 6.9g; Fat 16.7g, of which saturates 6.5g; Cholesterol 68mg; Calcium 328mg; Fibre 2.4g; Sodium 916mg.
Pork Energy 278kcal/1162kJ; Protein 27.5g; Carbohydrate 7.8g, of which sugars 7.4g; Fat 15.4g, of which saturates 8.2g; Cholesterol 105mg; Calcium 42mg; Fibre 1.2g; Sodium 154mg.

Hungarian Beef Goulash

Spicy beef stew served with caraway flavoured dumplings will satisfy even the hungriest Hungarian.

Serves 4
30ml/2 tbsp vegetable oil
1 kg/2lb braising steak, diced
2 onions, chopped
1 garlic clove, crushed
15g/¹⁄₂oz/2 tbsp plain (all-
　purpose) flour
10ml/2 tsp paprika
5ml/1 tsp caraway seeds
400g/14oz can
　chopped tomatoes

300ml/¹⁄₂ pint/1¹⁄₄ cups beef
　stock
1 large carrot, chopped
1 red (bell) pepper, seeded
　and chopped
salt and ground black pepper
sour cream, to serve
pinch of paprika, to garnish

For the dumplings
115g/4oz/1 cup self-raising (self-
　rising) flour
40g/2oz/¹⁄₂ cup shredded suet
15ml/1 tbsp chopped
　fresh parsley
2.5ml/¹⁄₂ tsp caraway seeds

1 Heat the oil in a flameproof casserole over high heat. Add the meat and cook, stirring frequently, for 5 minutes, until evenly browned. Remove with a slotted spoon.

2 Lower the heat, add the onions and garlic and cook, stirring occasionally, for about 5 minutes, until softened but not coloured. Stir in the flour, paprika and caraway seeds and cook, stirring constantly, for 2 minutes.

3 Return the meat to the casserole and stir in the tomatoes and stock. Bring to the boil, cover and simmer for 2 hours.

4 To make the dumplings, sift the flour and seasoning into a bowl, add the suet, parsley, caraway seeds and 45–60ml/ 3–4 tbsp water and mix to a soft dough. Divide into eight pieces and roll into balls. Cover and set aside.

5 After 2 hours, stir the carrot and red pepper into the goulash, and season. Drop the dumplings into the casserole, cover and simmer for a further 25 minutes. Serve in bowls topped with a spoonful of sour cream sprinkled with paprika.

Pork Satay with Peanut Sauce

These delightful little satay sticks from Thailand make a good light meal or a drinks party snack.

Makes 8
¹⁄₂ small onion, chopped
2 garlic cloves, crushed
30ml/2 tbsp lemon juice
15ml/1 tbsp soy sauce
5ml/1 tsp ground coriander
2.5ml/¹⁄₂ tsp ground cumin
5ml/1 tsp ground turmeric
30ml/2 tbsp vegetable oil
450g/1lb pork fillet (tenderloin)
salt and ground black pepper
fresh coriander (cilantro) sprigs,
　to garnish
boiled rice, to serve

For the sauce
150ml/¹⁄₄ pint/²⁄₃ cup coconut
　cream
60ml/4 tbsp crunchy
　peanut butter
15ml/1 tbsp lemon juice
2.5ml/¹⁄₂ tsp ground cumin
2.5ml/¹⁄₂ tsp ground coriander
5ml/1 tsp soft brown sugar
15ml/1 tbsp soy sauce
1–2 dried red chillies, seeded
　and chopped
15ml/1 tbsp chopped
　fresh coriander

For the salad
¹⁄₂ small cucumber, peeled
　and diced
15ml/1 tbsp white wine vinegar
15ml/1 tbsp chopped
　fresh coriander

1 Put the onion, garlic, lemon juice, soy sauce, ground coriander, cumin, turmeric and oil in a food processor and process until smooth. Cut the pork into strips, mix with the spice marinade in a bowl, cover with clear film (plastic wrap) and chill.

2 Preheat the grill (broiler). Thread two or three pork pieces on to each of eight soaked wooden skewers and grill (broil) for 2–3 minutes on each side, basting with the marinade.

3 To make the sauce, put all the ingredients into a pan, bring to the boil, stirring constantly, and simmer for 5 minutes.

4 Mix together all the salad ingredients. Arrange the satay sticks on a platter, garnish with coriander sprigs and season. Serve immediately with the sauce and boiled rice.

Goulash Energy 751kcal/3136kJ; Protein 62.1g; Carbohydrate 41.2g, of which sugars 13.2g; Fat 38.9g, of which saturates 15.4g; Cholesterol 153mg; Calcium 159mg; Fibre 4.6g; Sodium 282mg.
Satay Energy 189kcal/784kJ; Protein 14.5g; Carbohydrate 2.9g, of which sugars 2.2g; Fat 13.3g, of which saturates 5.8g; Cholesterol 35mg; Calcium 25mg; Fibre 0.9g; Sodium 70mg.

Stir-fried Pork with Lychees

No extra oil or fat is needed to cook this dish, as the pork produces enough on its own.

Serves 4

450g/1lb fatty pork, such as belly pork, with the skin on or off

30ml/2 tbsp hoisin sauce
4 spring onions (scallions), sliced diagonally
175g/6oz lychees, peeled, stoned (pitted) and cut into slivers
salt and ground black pepper
fresh lychees and parsley sprigs, to garnish

1 Cut the pork into bitesize pieces and place in a dish. Pour the hoisin sauce over it and toss to coat. Cover with clear film (plastic wrap) and leave to marinate in a cool place for at least 30 minutes.

2 Heat a wok, then add the pork and stir-fry for 5 minutes, until crisp and golden. Add the spring onions and stir-fry for a further 2 minutes.

3 Sprinkle the lychee slivers over the pork, and season well with salt and pepper. Transfer to warmed plates, garnish with lychees and parsley sprigs and serve immediately.

Cook's Tip
Lychees have a very pretty pink skin which cracks easily when the fruit is pressed between finger and thumb, making them easy to peel. The fruit is a soft, fleshy berry and contains a long, shiny, brown seed. This is inedible and must be removed. The sweet flesh is pearly white and fragrant, similar in texture to a grape. When buying lychees, avoid any that are turning brown, as they will be over-ripe. Equally, avoid under-ripe lychees with green or beige skins. Look for fruit with as much red or pink in the skins as possible. Fresh lychees are delicate and should be used as soon after purchase as possible, but can be stored in the refrigerator for up to a week. If you cannot buy the fresh fruit, you could use drained canned lychees, but they do not have the same fragrance or flavour.

Sizzling Beef with Celeriac Straw

The crisp celeriac batons look like fine pieces of straw when cooked and have a mild celery-like flavour.

Serves 4

450g/1lb celeriac
150ml/¼ pint/⅔ cup vegetable oil
1 red (bell) pepper
6 spring onions (scallions)
450g/1lb rump (round) steak
60ml/4 tbsp beef stock
30ml/2 tbsp sherry vinegar
10ml/2 tsp Worcestershire sauce
10ml/2 tsp tomato purée (paste)
salt and ground black pepper

1 Peel the celeriac and then cut it into fine batons, using a cleaver if you have one or a large sharp knife.

2 Heat a wok, then add two-thirds of the oil. When the oil is hot, add the celeriac batons, in batches, and stir-fry until golden brown and crisp. Drain well on kitchen paper. Discard the oil.

3 Seed the red pepper and cut it and the spring onions into 2.5cm/1in lengths, cutting diagonally. Cut the steak into strips, across the grain of the meat.

4 Heat the wok again, then add the remaining oil. When the oil is hot, add the red pepper and spring onions and stir-fry for 2–3 minutes.

5 Add the steak strips and stir-fry for a further 3–4 minutes, until well browned. Add the stock, vinegar, Worcestershire sauce and tomato purée. Season well with salt and pepper and serve with the celeriac "straw".

Cook's Tip
The Chinese use a large cleaver for preparing most vegetables. With a little practice, you will discover that it is the ideal kitchen utensil for cutting fine vegetable batons and chopping thin strips of meat.

Pork Energy 465kcal/1926kJ; Protein 17.9g; Carbohydrate 8.7g, of which sugars 8.6g; Fat 40.1g, of which saturates 14.8g; Cholesterol 81mg; Calcium 17mg; Fibre 0.5g; Sodium 206mg.
Beef Energy 318kcal/1324kJ; Protein 26.2g; Carbohydrate 5g, of which sugars 4.8g; Fat 21.6g, of which saturates 3.9g; Cholesterol 66mg; Calcium 66mg; Fibre 2.2g; Sodium 174mg.

Turkish Lamb & Apricot Stew

Couscous flavoured with almonds and parsley accompanies this rich and delicious stew of lamb, apricots and chickpeas.

Serves 4

1 large aubergine
(eggplant), diced
30ml/2 tbsp sunflower oil
1 onion, chopped
1 garlic clove, crushed
5ml/1 tsp ground cinnamon
3 cloves
450g/1lb boned leg of lamb, diced
400g/14oz can
chopped tomatoes
115g/4oz ready-to-eat
dried apricots
115g/4oz/1 cup canned
chickpeas, drained and rinsed
5ml/1 tsp clear honey
salt and ground black pepper

To serve

400g/14oz/2 cups couscous,
prepared
30ml/2 tbsp olive oil
30ml/2 tbsp chopped almonds,
fried in a little oil
30ml/2 tbsp chopped
fresh parsley

1 Place the diced aubergine in a colander, sprinkle with salt and leave for about 30 minutes. Heat the oil in a large flameproof casserole. Add the onion and garlic and cook, stirring occasionally, for about 5 minutes, until softened.

2 Stir in the cinnamon and cloves and cook, stirring constantly, for 1 minute. Add the lamb and cook, stirring frequently, for 5–6 minutes, until evenly browned.

3 Rinse, drain and pat dry the aubergine with kitchen paper, add to the casserole and cook, stirring constantly, for 3 minutes. Add the tomatoes, 300ml/½ pint/1¼ cups water and the apricots, and season to taste with salt and pepper. Bring to the boil, then lower the heat, cover with a tight-fitting lid and simmer gently for about 45 minutes.

4 Stir the chickpeas and honey into the stew and cook for a final 15–20 minutes, or until the lamb is tender. Serve the dish accompanied by couscous with the olive oil, fried almonds and chopped parsley stirred into it.

Curried Lamb & Lentils

This colourful curry is packed with protein and low in fat, so it makes a tasty yet healthy meal.

Serves 4

8 lean boned lamb leg steaks
(about 500g/1¼lb
total weight)
1 onion, chopped
2 carrots, diced
1 celery stick, chopped
15ml/1 tbsp hot curry paste
30ml/2 tbsp tomato
purée (paste)
475ml/16fl oz/2 cups chicken or
veal stock
175g/6oz/1 cup green lentils
salt and ground black pepper
fresh coriander (cilantro) leaves,
to garnish
boiled rice, to serve

1 Cook the lamb steaks in a large, non-stick frying pan, without any added fat, for 2–3 minutes on each side, until browned.

2 Add the onion, carrots and celery and cook, stirring occasionally, for 2 minutes, then stir in the curry paste, tomato purée, stock and lentils.

3 Bring to the boil, lower the heat, cover with a tight-fitting lid and simmer gently for 30 minutes, until tender. Add some extra stock, if necessary.

4 Season to taste with salt and pepper. Spoon the curry on to warmed plates and serve immediately, garnished with coriander and accompanied by rice.

Cook's Tip
Lentils are one of the few pulses (legumes) that do not require prolonged soaking in cold water before cooking. However, just like dried beans and peas, they should not be seasoned with salt until after cooking or their skins will become unpleasantly tough. Both green and brown lentils keep their shape well, as do the rather more expensive small Puy lentils. Red and yellow lentils are not suitable for this recipe as they tend to disintegrate during cooking.

Turkish Lamb Energy 462kcal/1931kJ; Protein 28.5g; Carbohydrate 23.2g, of which sugars 17.6g; Fat 29.1g, of which saturates 7.8g; Cholesterol 86mg; Calcium 77mg; Fibre 5.8g; Sodium 114mg.
Curried Lamb Energy 381kcal/1600kJ; Protein 35.5g; Carbohydrate 28.4g, of which sugars 4.3g; Fat 14.7g, of which saturates 6.6g; Cholesterol 95mg; Calcium 47mg; Fibre 3.2g; Sodium 144mg.

Middle-Eastern Lamb Kebabs

Skewered, grilled meats are a staple of Middle Eastern cooking. Here, marinated lamb is grilled with a colourful mix of vegetables.

Makes 4

450g/1lb boned leg of lamb, diced
75ml/5 tbsp olive oil
15ml/1 tbsp chopped fresh
  oregano or thyme, or
  10ml/2 tsp dried oregano
15ml/1 tbsp chopped
  fresh parsley
juice of ½ lemon
½ small aubergine (eggplant),
  thickly sliced and quartered
4 baby (pearl) onions, halved
2 tomatoes, quartered
4 fresh bay leaves
salt and ground black pepper
pitta bread and natural (plain)
  yogurt, to serve

1 Place the lamb in a non-metallic bowl. Mix together the olive oil, oregano or thyme, parsley and lemon juice in a jug (pitcher) and season with salt and pepper. Pour over the lamb and mix well. Cover with clear film (plastic wrap) and leave to marinate in the refrigerator for about 1 hour.

2 Preheat the grill (broiler). Thread the marinated lamb, aubergine, onions, tomatoes and bay leaves alternately on to four large skewers. (If using wooden skewers, soak them first.) Reserve the marinade.

3 Place the kebabs on a grill (broiler) rack and brush the vegetables liberally with the reserved marinade. Cook the kebabs under medium heat for 8–10 minutes on each side, basting once or twice with the juices that have collected in the bottom of the pan. Serve the kebabs immediately, accompanied by hot pitta bread and yogurt.

Cook's Tips
• For a more piquant marinade, add one or two peeled and crushed garlic cloves.
• These kebabs can also be cooked for the same length of time on a barbecue.

Mexican Spiced Roast Leg of Lamb

Make sure you push the garlic slices deeply into the meat or they will burn and develop a bitter flavour.

Serves 4

1 small leg or half leg of lamb
  (about 1.25kg/2½lb)
15ml/1 tbsp dried oregano
5ml/1 tsp ground cumin
5ml/1 tsp hot chilli powder
2 garlic cloves
45ml/3 tbsp olive oil
30ml/2 tbsp red wine vinegar
300ml/½ pint/1¼ cups chicken
  or veal stock
salt and ground black pepper
fresh oregano sprigs, to garnish

1 Preheat the oven to 220°C/425°F/Gas 7. Place the leg of lamb on a large chopping board.

2 Place the oregano, cumin and chilli powder in a bowl. Crush one of the garlic cloves and add it to the bowl. Pour in half the olive oil and mix well to form a paste.

3 Using a sharp knife, make a criss-cross pattern of fairly deep slits going through the skin and just into the meat of the leg of lamb. Press the spice paste into the slits with the back of a round-bladed knife. Peel and thinly slice the remaining garlic clove, then cut each slice in half. Push the pieces of garlic deeply into the slits made in the meat.

4 Place the lamb in a roasting pan. Mix together the vinegar and remaining oil in a bowl and pour over the meat. Season with salt and pepper.

5 Roast the lamb for about 15 minutes, then lower the oven temperature to 180°C/350°F/Gas 4 and roast for a further 1¼ hours (or a little longer if you like your meat well done).

6 Transfer the lamb to a carving board, cover with foil and leave to stand. Place the roasting pan over medium heat, pour in the stock and bring to the boil, scraping up the sediment from the base of the pan. Cook, stirring constantly, for 2–3 minutes, until slightly thickened. Carve the lamb and serve, garnished with oregano sprigs and accompanied by the gravy.

Kebabs Energy 339kcal/1409kJ; Protein 22.6g; Carbohydrate 2.7g, of which sugars 2.4g; Fat 26.5g, of which saturates 7.9g; Cholesterol 86mg; Calcium 16mg; Fibre 0.7g; Sodium 102mg.
Roast Leg Energy 733kcal/3073kJ; Protein 94.8g; Carbohydrate 4.1g, of which sugars 0.4g; Fat 37.8g, of which saturates 13.1g; Cholesterol 313mg; Calcium 27mg; Fibre 1g; Sodium 198mg.

Boeuf Bourguignon

This French classic is named after the region it comes from, Burgundy, where the local red wine is used to flavour it.

Serves 4
30ml/2 tbsp olive oil
225g/8oz piece streaky (fatty)
    bacon, diced
12 baby (pearl) onions
900g/2lb braising steak, cut into
    5cm/2in cubes
1 large onion, thickly sliced
15g/½oz/2 tbsp plain (all-
    purpose) flour
about 450ml/¾ pint/scant 2 cups
    red Burgundy wine
1 bouquet garni
1 garlic clove
225g/8oz button (white)
    mushrooms, halved
salt and ground black pepper
chopped fresh parsley, to garnish

1 Heat the oil in a flameproof casserole over low heat. Add the bacon and baby onions and cook, stirring occasionally, for 7–8 minutes, until the onions are evenly browned and the bacon fat has become translucent. Remove with a slotted spoon and set aside on a plate.

2 Add the beef to the casserole, increase the heat to medium and cook, stirring frequently, until evenly browned all over. Add the sliced onion and cook, stirring occasionally for a further 4–5 minutes.

3 Sprinkle in the flour and cook, stirring constantly, for 1 minute. Gradually stir in the wine, add the bouquet garni and garlic and season with salt and pepper. Bring to the boil, then lower the heat, cover with a tight-fitting lid and simmer gently for about 2 hours.

4 Stir in the baby onions and bacon and add a little extra wine, if necessary. Add the mushrooms. Replace the lid of the casserole and cook for a further 30 minutes, or until the meat is very tender. Remove and discard the bouquet garni and garlic. Taste and adjust the seasoning, if necessary, then ladle the stew on to warmed plates, garnish with chopped fresh parsley and serve immediately.

Spiced Lamb Bake

A delicious shepherd's pie from South Africa. The recipe was originally poached from the Afrikaners' Malay slaves.

Serves 4
15ml/1 tbsp vegetable oil
1 onion, chopped
675g/1½lb minced (ground)
    lamb
30ml/2 tbsp medium curry paste
30ml/2 tbsp mango chutney
30ml/2 tbsp freshly squeezed
    lemon juice
60ml/4 tbsp chopped,
    blanched almonds
30ml/2 tbsp sultanas
    (golden raisins)
200ml/7fl oz/scant 1 cup coconut
    cream
2 eggs
2 bay leaves
salt and ground black pepper
broccoli florets, to serve (optional)

1 Preheat the oven to 180°C/350°F/Gas 4. Heat the oil in a large, heavy frying pan over low heat. Add the onion and cook, stirring occasionally, for 5–6 minutes, until softened but not coloured.

2 Add the minced lamb, increase the heat to medium and cook, stirring frequently to break up the lumps, for 6–8 minutes, until evenly browned.

3 Stir in the curry paste, mango chutney, lemon juice, almonds and sultanas, season well with salt and pepper and cook, stirring occasionally, for about 5 minutes.

4 Transfer the mixture to an ovenproof dish and cook in the oven, uncovered, for 10 minutes.

5 Meanwhile, beat the coconut cream with the eggs in a bowl and season with salt and pepper.

6 Remove the dish from the oven and pour the coconut custard over the meat mixture. Lay the bay leaves on the top and return the dish to the oven for 30–35 minutes, or until the top is set and golden. Spoon the bake on to warmed plates and serve immediately with cooked broccoli if you like.

Boeuf Energy 749kcal/3117kJ; Protein 63.3g; Carbohydrate 15.2g, of which sugars 8.8g; Fat 40.3g, of which saturates 14g; Cholesterol 167mg; Calcium 69mg; Fibre 2.8g; Sodium 868mg.
Lamb Energy 657kcal/2732kJ; Protein 40.1g; Carbohydrate 12.5g, of which sugars 11.7g; Fat 50.1g, of which saturates 23.4g; Cholesterol 225mg; Calcium 94mg; Fibre 1.6g; Sodium 243mg.

Bacon Koftas

These easy koftas are good for barbecues and summer grills, served with lots of fresh salad.

Serves 4

225g/8oz lean smoked back bacon, coarsely chopped
75g/3oz/1½ cups fresh wholemeal (whole-wheat) breadcrumbs
2 spring onions (scallions), chopped
15ml/1 tbsp chopped fresh parsley
finely grated rind of 1 lemon
1 egg white
pinch of paprika
ground black pepper
lemon rind and fresh parsley leaves, to garnish
rice, to serve (optional)

1 Preheat the grill (broiler). Place the bacon in a food processor with the breadcrumbs, spring onions, parsley, grated lemon rind and egg white and season with pepper. Process the mixture until it is finely chopped and is beginning to bind together. Alternatively, use a mincer (meat grinder).

2 Scrape the bacon mixture into a bowl and divide into eight even-size pieces. Shape the pieces into long ovals around eight soaked wooden or bamboo skewers.

3 Sprinkle the koftas with paprika and cook under a hot grill, turning occasionally, for 8–10 minutes, until evenly browned all over and cooked through. Alternatively, cook them on a barbecue in the same way. Garnish with lemon rind and parsley leaves, then serve hot with cooked rice, if you like.

Cook's Tips
• This is a good way to spread a little meat a long way as each portion requires only 50g/2oz bacon. Use good quality bacon, preferably dry cured, for this recipe.
• Bacon is a very useful stand-by, as it will keep for up to 3 weeks if stored in the coolest part of the refrigerator. If you buy pre-packed bacon, take note of the "use by" date printed on the packaging.

Greek Pasta Bake

Another excellent main meal (called *pastitsio* in Greece), this recipe is both economical and filling.

Serves 4

15ml/1 tbsp olive oil
450g/1lb minced (ground) lamb
1 onion, chopped
2 garlic cloves, crushed
30ml/2 tbsp tomato purée (paste)
25g/1oz/¼ cup plain (all-purpose) flour
300ml/½ pint/1¼ cups lamb or chicken stock
2 large tomatoes
115g/4oz cup pasta shapes
450g/1lb tub Greek (US strained plain) yogurt
2 eggs, lightly beaten
salt and ground black pepper
green salad, to serve

1 Preheat the oven to 190°C/375°F/Gas 5. Heat the oil in a large pan over medium heat. Add the lamb and cook, stirring frequently, for 5 minutes. Add the onion and garlic and cook, stirring occasionally, or a further 5 minutes.

2 Stir in the tomato purée and flour. Cook, stirring constantly, for 1 minute, then gradually stir in the stock and season to taste with salt and pepper. Bring to the boil, then lower the heat and simmer for 20 minutes.

3 Slice the tomatoes, spoon the meat mixture into an ovenproof dish and arrange the tomatoes on top.

4 Bring a pan of salted water to the boil and cook the pasta shapes for 8–10 minutes until just tender. Drain well.

5 Mix together the pasta, yogurt and eggs in a bowl. Spoon the mixture on top of the tomatoes and bake for 1 hour. Serve immediately with a crisp green salad.

Cook's Tip
Choose open pasta shapes for this dish rather than tubes, so the sauce coats the pasta all over. Try shells, spirals or bows.

Pasta Energy 555kcal/2321kJ; Protein 36.9g; Carbohydrate 33g, of which sugars 7.5g; Fat 32.8g, of which saturates 14.1g; Cholesterol 182mg; Calcium 230mg; Fibre 2.2g; Sodium 219mg.
Koftas Energy 194kcal/813kJ; Protein 13g; Carbohydrate 14.7g, of which sugars 0.6g; Fat 9.7g, of which saturates 3.5g; Cholesterol 30mg; Calcium 30mg; Fibre 0.5g; Sodium 1040mg.

Peking Beef & Pepper Stir-fry

Once the steak has marinated, this colourful dish can be prepared in just a few minutes.

Serves 4

350g/12oz rump (round) or
    sirloin steak, sliced into strips
30ml/2 tbsp soy sauce
30ml/2 tbsp medium sherry
15ml/1 tbsp cornflour
    (cornstarch)
5ml/1 tsp brown sugar
15ml/1 tbsp sunflower oil

15ml/1 tbsp sesame oil
1 garlic clove, finely chopped
15ml/1 tbsp grated fresh
    root ginger
1 red (bell) pepper, seeded
    and sliced
1 yellow (bell) pepper, seeded
    and sliced
115g/4oz/1 cup sugar snap peas
4 spring onions (scallions), cut into
    5cm/2in pieces
30ml/2 tbsp oyster sauce
hot noodles, to serve

1 Mix together the steak strips, soy sauce, sherry, cornflour and brown sugar in a bowl. Cover with clear film (plastic wrap) and leave in a cool place to marinate for 30 minutes.

2 Heat a wok or large frying pan and add the sunflower and sesame oils. When the oils are hot add the garlic and ginger and stir-fry for about 30 seconds.

3 Add the red and yellow peppers, sugar snap peas and spring onions and stir-fry over high heat for 3 minutes.

4 Add the steak with the marinade juices to the wok or frying pan and stir-fry for a further 3–4 minutes.

5 Finally, pour in the oyster sauce and 60ml/4 tbsp water and cook, stirring constantly, until the sauce has thickened slightly. Serve immediately with hot noodles.

Cook's Tip
Although it is made from oysters, plus other ingredients, oyster sauce will not impart a fishy flavour to the meat.

Texan Barbecued Ribs

This barbecue or oven-roast dish of pork spare ribs cooked in a sweet and sour sauce is a favourite in the United States.

Serves 4

1.5kg/3lb (about 16) lean pork
    spare ribs
1 onion, finely chopped
1 large garlic clove, crushed
120ml/4fl oz/½ cup tomato
    purée (paste)

30ml/2 tbsp orange juice
30ml/2 tbsp red wine vinegar
5ml/1 tsp mustard
10ml/2 tsp clear honey
25g/1oz/2 tbsp soft light
    brown sugar
dash of Worcestershire sauce
30ml/2 tbsp vegetable oil
salt and ground black pepper
chopped fresh parsley, to garnish

1 Preheat the oven to 200°C/400°F/Gas 6. Place the pork spare ribs in a single layer in a large, shallow roasting pan and bake for 20 minutes.

2 Meanwhile, mix together the onion, garlic, tomato purée, orange juice, wine vinegar, mustard, clear honey, brown sugar, Worcestershire sauce and oil in a pan and season with salt and pepper. Bring to the boil, then lower the heat and simmer for about 5 minutes.

3 Remove the ribs from the oven and reduce the oven temperature to 180°C/350°F/Gas 4. Spoon half the sauce over the ribs, covering them well and bake for 20 minutes. Turn them over, baste with the remaining sauce and cook for 25 minutes.

4 Sprinkle the spare ribs with parsley before serving and allow three or four ribs per person.

Cook's Tip
Use American mustard for an authentic flavour. It is sweet and mild with a very soft consistency. Otherwise, Dijon mustard, which is sharper and hotter, would work well.

Stir-Fry Energy 225kcal/940kJ; Protein 22.7g; Carbohydrate 11.9g, of which sugars 8.9g; Fat 9.9g, of which saturates 2.4g; Cholesterol 52mg; Calcium 23mg; Fibre 3g; Sodium 713mg.
Ribs Energy 664kcal/2761kJ; Protein 56.5g; Carbohydrate 14.6g, of which sugars 14.2g; Fat 42.4g, of which saturates 13.8g; Cholesterol 199mg; Calcium 41mg; Fibre 1.1g; Sodium 258mg.

Skewers of Lamb with Mint

For a more substantial meal, you could serve these skewers on a bed of flavoured rice or couscous.

Serves 4
300ml/½ pint/1¼ cups Greek (US strained plain) yogurt
½ garlic clove, crushed
generous pinch of saffron powder
30ml/2 tbsp chopped fresh mint
30ml/2 tbsp clear honey
45ml/3 tbsp olive oil
3 lamb neck (US shoulder) fillets (about 675g/1½ lb total)
1 aubergine (eggplant), cut into 2.5cm/1in cubes
2 small red onions, quartered
salt and ground black pepper
small fresh mint leaves, to garnish
mixed salad and hot pitta bread, to serve

1 Mix together the yogurt, garlic, saffron, mint, honey and oil in a shallow dish and season with pepper.

2 Trim the lamb and cut into 2.5cm/1in cubes. Add to the marinade and stir until well coated. Cover with clear film (plastic wrap) and leave to marinate in the refrigerator for at least 4 hours or preferably overnight.

3 Blanch the diced aubergine in a pan of salted boiling water for 1–2 minutes. Drain well and pat dry on kitchen paper.

4 Preheat the grill (broiler). Drain the lamb and reserve the marinade. Thread the lamb, aubergine and onion pieces alternately on to skewers. (If you are using wooden skewers, soak them in water for 30 minutes first to prevent them from charring during cooking.)

5 Grill (broil) for 10–12 minutes, turning and basting occasionally with the reserved marinade, until the lamb and vegetables are tender. Alternatively, cook the kebabs on the barbecue for the same length of time.

6 Transfer the skewers to plates and serve immediately, garnished with mint leaves and accompanied by a mixed salad and hot pitta bread.

Beef Stew with Red Wine

A slow-cooked casserole of tender beef in a red wine and tomato sauce, with black olives and red pepper.

Serves 6
75ml/5 tbsp olive oil
1.2kg/2½lb braising steak, cut into 3cm/1½in cubes
1 onion, very thinly sliced
2 carrots, chopped
45ml/3 tbsp finely chopped fresh parsley
1 garlic clove, chopped
1 bay leaf
a few fresh thyme sprigs
pinch of freshly ground nutmeg
250ml/8fl oz/1 cup red wine
400g/14oz can plum tomatoes, chopped, with their juice
120ml/4fl oz/½ cup beef or chicken stock
about 15 black olives, pitted and halved
salt and ground black pepper
1 large red (bell) pepper, seeded and cut into strips

1 Preheat the oven to 180°C/350°F/Gas 4. Heat 45ml/3 tbsp of the oil in a large heavy flameproof casserole over medium heat. Add the meat, in batches, and cook, stirring frequently, until evenly browned all over. Remove to a side plate as the meat is browned and set aside until needed.

2 Add the remaining oil, the onion and carrots to the casserole and lower the heat. Cook, stirring occasionally, for about 5 minutes, until the onion has softened but not coloured. Add the parsley and garlic and cook, stirring occasionally, for a further 3–4 minutes.

3 Return the meat to the casserole, increase the heat and stir well to mix the vegetables with the meat. Stir in the bay leaf, thyme and nutmeg. Add the wine, bring to the boil and cook, stirring constantly, for 4–5 minutes. Stir in the tomatoes, stock and olives and mix well. Season to taste with salt and pepper. Cover the casserole with a tight-fitting lid and transfer to the oven. Bake for 1½ hours.

4 Remove the casserole from the oven. Stir in the strips of pepper. Return the casserole to the oven and cook, uncovered, for 30 minutes more, or until the beef is tender.

Lamb Energy 526kcal/2194kJ; Protein 39.7g; Carbohydrate 15.4g, of which sugars 13.4g; Fat 35.4g, of which saturates 14g; Cholesterol 128mg; Calcium 155mg; Fibre 3.1g; Sodium 204mg.
Beef Energy 464kcal/1929kJ; Protein 42.7g; Carbohydrate 4.5g, of which sugars 4.1g; Fat 27.5g, of which saturates 8.3g; Cholesterol 106mg; Calcium 44mg; Fibre 1.8g; Sodium 321mg.

Vegetable & Tofu Kebabs

A colourful mixture of vegetables and tofu, skewered, glazed and grilled until tender.

Serves 4
1 yellow (bell) pepper
2 small courgettes (zucchini)
225g/8oz piece of firm tofu
8 cherry tomatoes
6 button (white) mushrooms
15ml/1 tbsp wholegrain mustard
15ml/1 tbsp clear honey
30ml/2 tbsp olive oil
salt and ground black pepper
lime wedges and flat leaf parsley, to garnish
cooked mixed rice and wild rice, to serve

1 Preheat the grill (broiler). Cut the pepper in half and remove the seeds. Cut each half into quarters and then cut each quarter in half.

2 Trim the courgettes and then cut each courgette into seven or eight chunks.

3 Cut the tofu into 4cm/1½in pieces. Use a sharp knife to avoid squashing it and breaking it up.

4 Thread the pepper pieces, courgette chunks, tofu, cherry tomatoes and mushrooms alternately on to four long or eight shorter metal or bamboo skewers. (If you are using bamboo skewers, soak them in a bowl of cold water first. This will prevent them from charring during cooking.)

5 Whisk together the mustard, honey and olive oil in a small bowl. Season to taste with salt and pepper.

6 Put the kebabs on to a baking sheet. Brush them with the mustard and honey glaze. Cook under the grill for 8 minutes, turning once or twice during cooking and brushing with any remaining glaze.

7 Transfer the skewers to warmed plates and garnish with lime wedges and flat leaf parsley. Serve immediately with a mixture of long grain and wild rice.

Grilled Mixed Peppers

Soft smoky grilled peppers make a lovely combination with the slightly tart salsa.

Serves 4
4 medium (bell) peppers in different colours
45ml/3 tbsp chopped fresh flat leaf parsley

For the salsa
45ml/3 tbsp chopped fresh dill
45ml/3 tbsp chopped fresh mint
1 small red onion, finely chopped
15ml/1 tbsp capers, rinsed and coarsely chopped
50g/2oz/¼ cup Greek olives, pitted and sliced
1 fresh green chilli, seeded and finely chopped
60g/4 tbsp pistachios, chopped
75ml/5 tbsp extra virgin olive oil
45ml/3 tbsp fresh lime juice
115g/4oz medium-fat feta cheese, crumbled
25g/1oz gherkins, finely chopped

1 Preheat the grill (broiler). Place the whole peppers on a baking sheet and grill (broil), turning occasionally with tongs, until charred and blistered.

2 Using tongs transfer the peppers to a plastic bag, tie the top and leave to cool.

3 When the peppers are cool enough to handle, peel and seed them and cut the flesh into even strips.

4 To make the salsa, mix all the ingredients together in a bowl and stir in the pepper strips. Serve at room temperature. If you are not going to serve immediately, cover the bowl with clear film (plastic wrap) and store in the refrigerator.

Cook's Tip
Placing the charred (bell) peppers in a sealed plastic bag to cool causes condensation, which helps to loosen the skins. An equally good method is to place the charred peppers in a bowl, cover with crumpled kitchen paper and leave to cool. If you are in a hurry, you can peel them as soon as they're cool enough to handle – it's just a bit more awkward.

Peppers Energy 364kcal/1504kJ; Protein 9.8g; Carbohydrate 13.6g, of which sugars 12.6g; Fat 30.3g, of which saturates 7.4g; Cholesterol 20mg; Calcium 193mg; Fibre 5.4g; Sodium 790mg.
Kebabs Energy 139kcal/575kJ; Protein 7.1g; Carbohydrate 8.7g, of which sugars 8.2g; Fat 8.6g, of which saturates 1.3g; Cholesterol 0mg; Calcium 318mg; Fibre 1.9g; Sodium 8mg.

Cheese Bubble & Squeak

This London breakfast dish was originally made on Mondays with leftover vegetables from the previous Sunday's lunch.

Serves 4

about 450g/1lb/3 cups mashed potatoes

about 225g/8oz/4 cups shredded cooked cabbage or kale

1 egg, lightly beaten

115g/4oz/1 cup grated Cheddar cheese

pinch of freshly grated nutmeg

salt and ground black pepper

plain (all-purpose) flour, for coating

vegetable oil, for frying

1 Mix together the mashed potatoes, cabbage or kale, egg, cheese and nutmeg in a bowl and season with salt and pepper. Divide the mixture into eight pieces and shape into patties.

2 Place the patties on a large plate, cover with clear film (plastic wrap) and chill in the refrigerator for 1 hour or more, if possible, as this helps firm up the mixture.

3 Gently toss the patties in the flour to coat lightly. Heat about 1cm/½in oil in a frying pan until it is quite hot.

4 Carefully slide the patties into the oil and cook for about 3 minutes on each side, until golden and crisp. Remove with a slotted spatula, drain on kitchen paper and serve hot and crisp.

> **Variation**
> For traditional bubble and squeak, heat 30ml/2 tbsp vegetable oil in a frying pan. Add 1 finely chopped onion and cook over low heat, stirring occasionally, for about 5 minutes, until softened but not coloured. Using a slotted spoon, transfer the onion to a bowl and mix with the other ingredients in step 1, omitting the cheese and using finely chopped cooked cabbage or Brussels sprouts. Use the same frying pan, with additional oil, for cooking the patties in step 4.

Soufflé Omelette

This delectable fluffy omelette is light and delicate enough to melt in the mouth.

Serves 1

2 eggs, separated

30ml/2 tbsp cold water

15ml/1 tbsp chopped fresh coriander (cilantro)

7.5ml/1½ tsp olive oil

30ml/2 tbsp mango chutney

25g/1oz/¼ cup grated Jarlsberg cheese

salt and ground black pepper

1 Beat the egg yolks together with the cold water and coriander in a bowl and season with salt and pepper.

2 Whisk the egg whites in another grease-free bowl until stiff peaks form, then gently fold them into the egg yolk mixture with a rubber spatula.

3 Heat the oil in a frying pan, pour in the egg mixture and reduce the heat. Do not stir. Cook until the omelette becomes puffy and golden brown on the underside (carefully lift one edge with a spatula to check).

4 Spoon the chutney over the omelette and sprinkle with the Jarlsberg. Fold over and slide on to a warmed plate. Serve immediately. (If you like, place the pan under a hot grill/broiler to set the top before adding the chutney and cheese.)

> **Cook's Tip**
> If there is any trace of grease – and that includes any yolk – egg whites will not foam when whisked. It's best to use a glass, china or metal bowl. Plastic is easily scratched and then traces of grease are almost impossible to remove. The perfect choice is a copper bowl as the egg whites react with the metal to create a full and stable foam. However, do not leave the whisked whites to stand in a copper bowl, as they will turn grey. Whatever the material, the bowl should be a generous size to allow plenty of room for whisking.

Omelette Energy 377kcal/1570kJ; Protein 19g; Carbohydrate 14.9g, of which sugars 14.8g; Fat 27g, of which saturates 9.2g; Cholesterol 405mg; Calcium 249mg; Fibre 0.3g; Sodium 648mg.
Bubble & Squeak Energy 281kcal/1175kJ; Protein 11.6g; Carbohydrate 21g, of which sugars 4.3g; Fat 16.7g, of which saturates 7.4g; Cholesterol 75mg; Calcium 254mg; Fibre 2.3g; Sodium 242mg.

Aubergine & Red Pepper Pâté

This simple pâté of baked
aubergine, pink peppercorns
and red peppers has more
than a hint of garlic.

Serves 4
3 aubergines (eggplants)

2 large red (bell) peppers
5 garlic cloves, unpeeled
7.5ml/1½ tsp pink peppercorns
   in brine, drained and crushed
30ml/2 tbsp chopped fresh
   coriander (cilantro)
mixed salad leaves, to serve

1 Preheat the oven to 200°C/400°F/Gas 6. Arrange the whole
aubergines, peppers and garlic cloves on a baking sheet and
bake for 10 minutes. Transfer the garlic cloves to a chopping
board. Turn over the aubergines and peppers and return them
to the oven for a further 20 minutes.

2 Meanwhile, peel the garlic cloves and place them in a blender
or food processor.

3 When the peppers are blistered and charred, use tongs to
transfer them to a plastic bag, tie the top and leave to cool.
Return the aubergines to the oven for a further 10 minutes.

4 Remove the aubergines from the oven. Split them in half and
scoop the flesh into a sieve (strainer) placed over a bowl. Press
the flesh with a spoon to remove the bitter juices.

5 Add the aubergine flesh to the garlic and process until
smooth. Place in a large mixing bowl.

6 Peel and seed the red peppers and chop the flesh. Stir it into
the aubergine mixture. Mix in the pink peppercorns and
chopped fresh coriander and serve immediately on a bed of
mixed salad leaves.

> **Cook's Tip**
> Serve the pâté with Melba toast, oatcakes, fingers of olive
> focaccia or mini pitta breads.

Red Pepper Watercress Parcels

The peppery watercress
flavour contrasts delightfully
with sweet red pepper in
these crisp filo parcels.

Makes 8
3 red (bell) peppers
175g/6oz watercress or
   rocket (arugula)

225g/8oz 1 cup ricotta cheese
50g/2oz/½ cup toasted,
   chopped almonds
8 sheets filo pastry, thawed
   if frozen
30ml/2 tbsp olive oil
salt and ground black pepper

1 Preheat the oven to 190°C/375°F/Gas 5 and preheat the grill
(broiler). Place the red peppers on a baking sheet and grill
(broil), turning occasionally with tongs, until blistered and
charred. Use tongs to transfer to a plastic bag, tie the top and
leave to cool.

2 When the peppers are cool enough to handle, peel and seed
them. Pat dry with kitchen paper.

3 Place the peppers and watercress or rocket in a food
processor and pulse until coarsely chopped. Spoon the mixture
into a bowl. Stir in the ricotta and almonds and season to taste
with salt and pepper.

4 Working with one sheet of filo pastry at a time and keeping
the others covered, cut out two 18cm/7in and two 5cm/2in
squares from each sheet. Brush one large square with a little
olive oil and place a second large square at an angle of
45 degrees to form a star shape.

5 Place one of the smaller squares in the centre of the star
shape, brush lightly with olive oil and top with the second
small square.

6 Top with one-eighth of the red pepper mixture. Bring the
edges together to form a purse shape and twist to seal. Place
on a lightly greased baking sheet and cook for 25–30 minutes,
until golden. Serve immediately.

Pâté Energy 51kcal/213kJ; Protein 2.2g; Carbohydrate 8.9g, of which sugars 8.4g; Fat 1g, of which saturates 0.2g; Cholesterol 0mg; Calcium 22mg; Fibre 4.4g; Sodium 7mg.
Parcels Energy 163kcal/677kJ; Protein 5.9g; Carbohydrate 10.9g, of which sugars 5.7g; Fat 10.9g, of which saturates 3.4g; Cholesterol 12mg; Calcium 67mg; Fibre 2.1g; Sodium 15mg.

Nutty Cheese Balls

An extremely quick and simple recipe. Try making smaller portions to serve as canapés at a drinks party.

Serves 4

225g/8oz/1 cup low-fat soft (farmer's) cheese
50g/2oz/1/2 cup Dolcelatte or Gorgonzola cheese
15ml/1 tbsp finely chopped onion
15ml/1 tbsp finely chopped celery
15ml/1 tbsp finely chopped fresh parsley
15ml/1 tbsp finely chopped gherkin
5ml/1 tsp brandy or port (optional)
pinch of paprika
50g/2oz/1/2 cup walnuts, coarsely chopped
90ml/6 tbsp chopped fresh chives
salt and ground black pepper

To serve
crusty bread
mixed salad leaves
sliced radishes

1 Put the soft cheese and Dolcelatte or Gorgonzola in a bowl and beat with a spoon until combined and quite smooth.

2 Add the onion, celery, parsley, gherkin, brandy or port, if using, paprika and walnuts, season with salt and pepper and stir well to combine.

3 Divide the mixture into 12 pieces and roll each piece into a ball between the palms of your hands.

4 Roll each ball gently in the chopped chives and place on a plate. Cover with clear film (plastic wrap) or foil, and chill in the refrigerator for about 1 hour. Serve with crusty bread, mixed salad leaves and sliced radishes.

Variation
For an alternative look, mix the chives with the rest of the ingredients in step 2 but omit the walnuts. Instead, chop the walnuts very finely and use to coat the cheese balls in step 4. For a larger number of guests make one batch of each type and serve a mixture of the two.

Fried Tomatoes with Polenta Crust

This recipe works well with green tomatoes freshly picked from the garden or greenhouse.

Serves 4

4 large firm under-ripe tomatoes
115g/4oz/scant 1 cup polenta or coarse cornmeal
5ml/1 tsp dried oregano or marjoram
2.5ml/1/2 tsp garlic powder
1 egg
plain (all-purpose) flour, for dredging
vegetable oil, for deep-frying
salt and ground black pepper
salad, to serve

1 Cut the tomatoes into thick slices. Mix the polenta or cornmeal with the oregano or marjoram and garlic powder in a shallow bowl.

2 Lightly beat the egg in another shallow bowl and season with salt and pepper. Put the flour in a third shallow bowl. Dip the tomato slices first into the flour, then into the egg and finally into the polenta or cornmeal mixture.

3 Fill a shallow frying pan one-third full of vegetable oil and heat steadily until quite hot.

4 Slip the tomato slices into the oil carefully, a few at a time, and fry on each side until crisp. Remove with a slotted spoon and drain well on kitchen paper. Repeat with the remaining tomatoes, reheating the oil in between each batch. Serve immediately with salad.

Variations
• This is also a tasty way to cook mushrooms. Coat 450g/1lb whole button (white) mushrooms with flour, seasoned egg and the polenta mixture and deep-fry until crisp.
• Substitute goat's cheese or mozzarella for the tomatoes. Cut 225–275g/8–10oz cheese into fairly thick slices, then coat and cook as in the recipe. Bocconcini, bitesize balls of mozzarella, would be perfect for this treatment.

Cheese Balls Energy 213kcal/883kJ; Protein 13.4g; Carbohydrate 4g, of which sugars 3.5g; Fat 16.9g, of which saturates 6g; Cholesterol 23mg; Calcium 170mg; Fibre 1.4g; Sodium 409mg.
Tomatoes Energy 215kcal/897kJ; Protein 5g; Carbohydrate 24.1g, of which sugars 3.1g; Fat 10.9g, of which saturates 1.5g; Cholesterol 48mg; Calcium 15mg; Fibre 1.6g; Sodium 27mg.

Bean Purée with Grilled Vegetables

The slightly bitter radicchio and chicory make a wonderful marriage with the creamy citrus bean purée.

Serves 4
400g/14oz can cannellini beans
45ml/3 tbsp low-fat fromage blanc (farmer's cheese)
finely grated rind and juice of 1 large orange
15ml/1 tbsp finely chopped fresh rosemary
4 heads of chicory (Belgian endive)
2 radicchio
15ml/1 tbsp walnut oil

1 Preheat the grill (broiler). Drain the beans, rinse, and drain again. Put the beans, cheese, half the orange rind, the orange juice and rosemary in a food processor or blender and process until combined. Set aside.

2 Cut the heads of chicory in half lengthways. Cut each radicchio into eight wedges.

3 Spread out the chicory and radicchio on a baking sheet and brush with walnut oil. Grill (broil) for 2–3 minutes. Serve the leaves with the bean purée, sprinkled with the remaining orange rind.

Variations
• For a Middle Eastern flavour, substitute 30ml/2 tbsp tahini, also known as sesame seed paste, for the orange juice and omit the orange rind. Add 4 chopped spring onions (scallions) to the mixture in the food processor or blender and substitute chopped fresh mint for the rosemary. If the mixture seems too thick, add 15ml/1 tbsp olive oil. Garnish with fresh mint sprigs.
• For a North African flavour, substitute canned broad (fava) beans for the cannellini beans, 1½ lemons for the orange and 5ml/1 tsp ground cumin for the rosemary.
• For a Tex-Mex treat, substitute canned red kidney beans for the cannellini beans, 2 limes for the orange and 2–3 seeded and finely chopped fresh red chillies for the rosemary.

Broccoli & Chestnut Terrine

Served hot or cold, this versatile terrine is just as suitable for a dinner party as for a picnic.

Serves 4–6
450g/1lb/4 cups broccoli florets
225g/8oz/2 cups cooked chestnuts, coarsely chopped
50g/2oz/1 cup fresh wholemeal (whole-wheat) breadcrumbs
60ml/4 tbsp low-fat natural (plain) yogurt
30ml/2 tbsp finely grated Parmesan cheese
pinch of freshly grated nutmeg
2 eggs, lightly beaten
salt and ground black pepper
boiled new potatoes and mixed salad leaves, to serve

1 Preheat the oven to 180°C/350°F/Gas 4. Base-line a 900g/2lb non-stick loaf tin (pan) with baking parchment.

2 Blanch or steam the broccoli for 3–4 minutes, until just tender. Drain well. Reserve a quarter of the smallest florets and chop the rest finely.

3 Mix together the chestnuts, breadcrumbs, yogurt, Parmesan and nutmeg and season to taste with salt and pepper. Fold in the chopped broccoli, reserved florets and the beaten eggs.

4 Spoon the broccoli mixture into the prepared tin. Place in a roasting pan and pour in boiling water to come about halfway up the sides of the loaf tin. Bake for 20–25 minutes.

5 Remove the terrine from the oven and invert on to a warmed plate or tray. Cut into even slices and serve immediately with new potatoes and salad leaves. Alternatively, leave the terrine in the loaf tin to cool completely, then turn out and serve cold.

Cook's Tip
If you do not have a non-stick loaf tin (pan), grease it lightly with olive or sunflower oil after base-lining.

Baked Squash with Parmesan

Spaghetti squash is an unusual vegetable – when baked, the flesh separates into long strands.

Serves 2
1 spaghetti squash
115g/4oz/½ cup butter
45ml/3 tbsp mixed chopped fresh
  herbs such as parsley, chives
  and oregano
1 garlic clove, crushed
1 shallot, chopped
5ml/1 tsp lemon juice
50g/2oz/⅔ cup freshly grated
  Parmesan cheese
salt and ground black pepper

1 Preheat the oven to 180°C/350°F/Gas 4. Cut the squash in half lengthways. Place the halves, cut-sides down, in a roasting pan. Pour a little water around them, then bake for about 40 minutes, until tender.

2 Meanwhile, put the butter, herbs, garlic, shallot and lemon juice in a food processor or blender and process until thoroughly blended and creamy in consistency. Season to taste with salt and pepper.

3 When the squash is tender, scrape out and discard any seeds, then cut a thin slice from the base of each half, so that they will sit level. Place the squash halves on warmed serving plates.

4 Using a fork, pull out a few of the spaghetti-like strands in the centre of each. Add a spoonful of herb butter, then sprinkle with a little of the grated Parmesan. Serve the remaining herb butter and Parmesan separately, adding them as you pull out more strands.

Cook's Tip
Spaghetti squash is also good served with simple garlic butter. If you don't want to bother making a herb butter of any sort, serve with a dish of ready-made pesto.

Asparagus Rolls with Herb Sauce

For a taste sensation, try tender asparagus spears wrapped in crisp filo pastry served with a rich, buttery herb sauce.

Serves 2
50g/2oz/¼ cup butter, plus extra
  for greasing
5 sheets filo pastry
10 asparagus spears
salad, to garnish (optional)

For the sauce
2 shallots, finely chopped
1 bay leaf
150ml/¼ pint/⅔ cup dry
  white wine
175g/6oz/¾ cup butter, softened
15ml/1 tbsp chopped fresh
  herbs, such as parsley, basil
  and thyme
salt and ground black pepper
chopped fresh chives, to garnish

1 Preheat the oven to 200°C/400°F/Gas 6. Grease a baking sheet. Melt the ¼ cup butter. Cut the filo pastry sheets in half. Brush a half sheet with melted butter. Fold one corner of the sheet down to the bottom edge to give a wedge shape.

2 Trim the asparagus, then lay a spear on top at the longest pastry edge and roll up towards the shortest edge. Make nine more rolls in the same way.

3 Lay the rolls on the prepared baking sheet. Brush with the remaining melted butter. Bake in the preheated oven for about 8 minutes, until golden.

4 Meanwhile, put the shallots, bay leaf and wine into a pan. Cover with a tight-fitting lid and cook over high heat until the wine is reduced to 45–60ml/3–4 tbsp.

5 Strain the wine mixture into a bowl. Whisk in the ¾ cup butter, a little at a time, until the sauce is smooth and glossy.

6 Stir in the herbs and season to taste with salt and pepper. Return to the pan and keep the sauce warm. Serve the asparagus rolls on warmed individual plates with a salad garnish, if you like. Sprinkle the butter sauce with a few chopped chives and hand around separately.

Squash Energy 597kcal/2467kJ; Protein 13g; Carbohydrate 10.4g, of which sugars 8g; Fat 56.2g, of which saturates 35.5g; Cholesterol 148mg; Calcium 420mg; Fibre 3.9g; Sodium 622mg.
Asparagus Energy 986kcal/4066kJ; Protein 5.1g; Carbohydrate 20.7g, of which sugars 4.6g; Fat 93.4g, of which saturates 58.7g; Cholesterol 240mg; Calcium 121mg; Fibre 3g; Sodium 694mg.

Multi-mushroom Stroganoff

A pan-fry of sliced mushrooms swirled with sour cream makes a delicious accompaniment to pasta or rice.

Serves 3–4
45ml/3 tbsp olive oil
450g/1lb fresh mixed wild and
   cultivated mushrooms such as
   ceps, shiitakes or oysters, sliced
3 spring onions (scallions), sliced
2 garlic cloves, crushed
30ml/2 tbsp dry sherry
   or vermouth
300ml/½ pint/1¼ cups sour
   cream or crème fraîche
15ml/1 tbsp chopped fresh
   marjoram or thyme leaves
chopped fresh parsley, to garnish
rice, pasta or potatoes, to serve

1 Heat the oil in a large frying pan over low heat. Add the mushrooms and cook, stirring occasionally, for about 5 minutes, until they are softened and just cooked.

2 Add the spring onions, garlic and sherry or vermouth and cook for 1 minute more. Season well with salt and pepper.

3 Stir in the sour cream or crème fraîche and heat to just below boiling point. Stir in the marjoram or thyme, then sprinkle over the parsley. Serve with rice, pasta or boiled new potatoes.

> **Cook's Tips**
> • To create the most interesting flavour in this dish, use at least three different varieties of mushroom, preferably incorporating some woodland or wild mushrooms.
> • It is important not to let the mixture boil after adding the cream. Like single (light) cream, sour cream and crème fraîche have a tendency to curdle when heated even though they both contain slightly more butterfat (single cream 19 per cent, sour cream 20 per cent, crème fraîche 15–40 per cent). Curdling is also much more likely to occur if the other ingredients in the pan include something acidic, such as lemon juice or, as in this case, sherry or vermouth.

Ratatouille with Cheese Croûtons

Crunchy croûtons and creamy Camembert cheese provide a tasty topping on hot, bought or home-made ratatouille.

Serves 2
3 thick slices white bread
225g/8oz firm
   Camembert cheese
60ml/4 tbsp olive oil
1 garlic clove, chopped
400g/14oz can ratatouille
fresh parsley sprigs, to garnish

1 Trim the crusts from the bread slices and discard. Cut the bread into 2.5cm/1in squares. Cut the Camembert cheese into 2.5cm/1in cubes.

2 Heat 45ml/3 tbsp of the oil in a frying pan. Add the bread cubes and cook over a high heat, stirring constantly, for about 5 minutes, until golden all over. Reduce the heat, add the garlic and cook for 1 minute more. Remove the croûtons with a slotted spoon and drain on kitchen paper.

3 Put the ratatouille in a pan and place over medium heat, stirring occasionally, until hot.

4 Heat the remaining oil in the frying pan. Add the cheese cubes and sear over high heat for 1 minute. Divide the hot ratatouille between two serving bowls, spoon the croûtons and cheese on top, garnish with parsley and serve immediately.

> **Cook's Tip**
> To make your own ratatouille, heat 45ml/3 tbsp olive oil in a heavy pan and add the following vegetables sequentially: 3 sliced aubergines (eggplants), 1 seeded green (bell) pepper, cut into strips, 3 peeled and chopped tomatoes, 1 sliced onion, 2 chopped garlic cloves and 3 sliced courgettes (zucchini). Add a bouquet garni, season with salt and pepper, cover and cook over very low heat for 30 minutes. Add 30ml/2 tbsp olive oil, cover and simmer for a further 30–40 minutes.

Stroganoff Energy 253kcal/1044kJ; Protein 4.4g; Carbohydrate 3.6g, of which sugars 3.4g; Fat 23.8g, of which saturates 10.7g; Cholesterol 45mg; Calcium 80mg; Fibre 1.4g; Sodium 38mg.
Ratatouille Energy 829kcal/3442kJ; Protein 28.5g; Carbohydrate 26.2g, of which sugars 8.2g; Fat 66.2g, of which saturates 25.2g; Cholesterol 105mg; Calcium 374mg; Fibre 2.6g; Sodium 861mg.

Tofu & Crunchy Vegetables

High protein tofu is nicest if it is marinated lightly before it is cooked.

Serves 4

2 x 225g/8oz packets
  smoked tofu, diced
45ml/3 tbsp soy sauce
30ml/2 tbsp dry sherry
  or vermouth
15ml/1 tbsp sesame oil
45ml/3 tbsp groundnut (peanut)
  or sunflower oil
2 leeks, thinly sliced
2 carrots, cut into batons
1 large courgette (zucchini),
  thinly sliced
115g/4oz baby corn, halved
115g/4oz button (white) or
  shiitake mushrooms, sliced
15ml/1 tbsp sesame seeds
cooked noodles dressed with
  sesame oil, to serve (optional)

1 Place the tofu in a shallow dish. Mix together the soy sauce, sherry or vermouth and sesame oil and pour over the tofu. Cover with clear film (plastic wrap) and leave to marinate in a cool place for at least 30 minutes. Drain the tofu cubes and reserve the marinade.

2 Heat a wok or large, heavy frying pan and add the groundnut oil. When the oil is hot, add the tofu cubes and stir-fry until browned all over. Remove the tofu from the pan.

3 Add the leeks, carrots, courgette and baby corn to the pan and stir-fry for about 2 minutes. Add the mushrooms and cook for 1 minute more.

4 Return the tofu to the pan and pour in the reserved marinade. Heat, stirring gently, until bubbling, then sprinkle with the sesame seeds. Serve immediately with hot cooked noodles dressed with a little sesame oil, if you like.

> **Cook's Tip**
> *The actual cooking of this dish takes just a few minutes, so have all the ingredients prepared before you start.*

Sprouting Beans & Pak Choi

Stir-frying is a great way to cook vegetables as they retain their colour, texture and most of their nutrients.

Serves 4

45ml/3 tbsp groundnut
  (peanut) oil
3 spring onions (scallions), sliced
2 garlic cloves, cut into slivers
2.5cm/1in piece fresh root ginger,
  cut into slivers
1 carrot, cut into thick batons
150g/5oz/scant 1 cup sprouting
  beans (lentils, mung beans,
  chickpeas)
200g/7oz pak choi (bok
  choy), shredded
50g/2oz/½ cup unsalted cashew
  nuts or halved almonds

For the sauce

45ml/3 tbsp light soy sauce
30ml/2 tbsp dry sherry
15ml/1 tbsp sesame oil
150ml/¼ pint/⅔ cup cold water
5ml/1 tsp cornflour (cornstarch)
5ml/1 tsp clear honey
salt and ground black pepper

1 Heat a large wok and add the oil. When the oil is hot add the spring onions, garlic, ginger and carrot and stir-fry over medium heat for 2 minutes.

2 Add the sprouting beans and stir-fry for a further 2 minutes. Add the pak choi and cashew nuts or almonds and stir-fry until the leaves are just wilting.

3 Mix all the sauce ingredients together in a jug (pitcher) and pour into the wok, stirring constantly.

4 When all the vegetables are coated in a thin glossy sauce season with salt and pepper. Serve immediately.

> **Variation**
> *You can use a variety of other Chinese greens besides pak choi (bok choy). Try Chinese leaves (Chinese cabbage), Chinese flowering cabbage, Chinese spinach, also known as callalo, or Chinese water spinach.*

Tofu Energy 251kcal/1040kJ; Protein 12.6g; Carbohydrate 7.2g, of which sugars 5.8g; Fat 18.3g, of which saturates 2.4g; Cholesterol 0mg; Calcium 578mg; Fibre 3.8g; Sodium 877mg.
Pak Choi Energy 230kcal/954kJ; Protein 5g; Carbohydrate 11.3g, of which sugars 7.6g; Fat 17.7g, of which saturates 3.3g; Cholesterol 0mg; Calcium 46mg; Fibre 2.4g; Sodium 848mg.

Tomato Omelette Envelopes

These delicious chive omelettes are folded and filled with tomato and melting Camembert cheese.

Serves 2
1 small onion
4 tomatoes
30ml/2 tbsp vegetable oil
4 eggs
30ml/2 tbsp chopped fresh chives
115g/4oz Camembert cheese, rinded and diced
salt and ground black pepper
lettuce leaves and Granary (whole-wheat) bread, to serve (optional)

1 Cut the onion in half and cut each half into thin wedges. Cut the tomatoes into wedges of similar size.

2 Heat 15ml/1 tbsp of the oil in a frying pan. Add the onion and cook over medium heat for 2 minutes. Increase the heat, add the tomatoes and cook for a further 2 minutes, then remove the pan from the heat.

3 Beat the eggs with the chives in a bowl and season with salt and pepper. Heat the remaining oil in an omelette pan. Add half the egg mixture and tilt the pan to spread thinly. Cook for 1 minute. Flip the omelette over and cook for 1 minute more. Remove from the pan and keep hot. Make a second omelette with the remaining egg mixture.

4 Return the tomato mixture to high heat. Add the cheese and toss the mixture over the heat for 1 minute.

5 Divide the mixture between the omelettes and fold them over. Serve immediately with crisp lettuce leaves and chunks of Granary bread, if you like.

> **Variation**
> Add 2–3 sliced mushrooms to the tomato-onion filling. For a mushroom omelette, substitute 6–8 button (white) mushrooms for the tomato. They will need a slightly longer cooking time.

Curried Eggs

Hard-boiled eggs are served on a mild creamy sauce with just a hint of curry.

Serves 2
4 eggs
15ml/1 tbsp sunflower oil
1 small onion, chopped
2.5cm/1in piece of fresh root ginger, grated
2.5ml/½ tsp ground cumin
2.5ml/½ tsp garam masala
22.5ml/1½ tbsp tomato purée (paste)
10ml/2 tsp tandoori paste
10ml/2 tsp freshly squeezed lemon juice
50ml/2fl oz/¼ cup single (light) cream
15ml/1 tbsp finely chopped fresh coriander (cilantro)
salt and ground black pepper
fresh coriander sprigs, to garnish

1 Put the eggs in a pan of water. Bring to the boil, lower the heat and simmer for 10 minutes.

2 Meanwhile, heat the oil in a frying pan over medium heat. Add the onion and cook, stirring occasionally, for 2–3 minutes. Add the ginger and cook, stirring constantly, for 1 minute more.

3 Stir in the ground cumin, garam masala, tomato purée, tandoori paste, lemon juice and cream. Cook for 1–2 minutes more, but do not allow the mixture to boil. Stir in the chopped coriander and season to taste with salt and pepper.

4 Drain the eggs, remove the shells and cut each egg in half. Spoon the sauce into a serving bowl, top with the eggs and garnish with fresh coriander. Serve immediately.

> **Cook's Tip**
> It is recommended that you store eggs in the refrigerator for health reasons. Do not wash them, but equally do not use dirty eggs. Store eggs pointed ends downwards, and remove from the refrigerator about 30 minutes before you want to cook them to allow them to come to room temperature. This will help prevent them from cracking.

Potatoes with Blue Cheese

So often served as a mere accompaniment, potatoes also make a satisfying main dish, as here.

Serves 4

450g/1lb small new potatoes
small head of celery, sliced
small red onion, thinly sliced
115g/4oz blue cheese, mashed
150ml/¼ pint/⅔ cup single (light) cream
90g/3½ oz/scant 1 cup walnut pieces
30ml/2 tbsp chopped fresh parsley
salt and ground black pepper

1 Put the potatoes in a pan, add water to cover and bring to the boil. Cook for about 15 minutes, adding the sliced celery and onion to the pan for the last 5 minutes or so.

2 Drain the vegetables well and put them into a warmed, shallow serving dish, making sure that they are evenly distributed. Keep warm.

3 Put the cheese and cream in a small pan and melt over low heat, stirring frequently. Do not allow the mixture to boil, but heat it until it scalds.

4 Season the sauce to taste with salt and pepper, bearing in mind that the cheese will already be quite salty. Pour it over the vegetables and sprinkle the walnuts and chopped parsley over the top. Serve immediately.

> **Cook's Tip**
> Choose any blue cheese you like, such as Stilton, Danish blue, Blue Vinney or blue Brie.

> **Variation**
> Substitute a thinly sliced fennel bulb for the celery if you like its distinctive aniseed-like flavour.

Greek Spinach & Cheese Pies

These individual spinach, feta and Parmesan cheese pies are easy to make using ready-made filo pastry.

Makes 4

15ml/1 tbsp olive oil
1 small onion, finely chopped
275g/10oz/2½ cups spinach, stalks removed
50g/2oz/4 tbsp butter, melted
4 sheets filo pastry
1 egg
large pinch of freshly grated nutmeg
75g/3oz/¾ cup crumbled feta cheese
15ml/1 tbsp freshly grated Parmesan cheese
salt and ground black pepper

1 Preheat the oven to 190°C/375°F/Gas 5. Heat the oil in a large pan over low heat. Add the onion and cook, stirring occasionally, for 5–6 minutes, until softened. Add the spinach leaves and cook, stirring, until the spinach has wilted and most of the liquid has evaporated. Remove from the heat and leave to cool completely.

2 Brush four 10cm/4in diameter loose-based tartlet tins (muffin pans) with melted butter. Cut two sheets of filo into eight 14cm/4½in squares each.

3 Brush four squares at a time with melted butter. Line the first tartlet tin with one square, gently easing it into the base and up the sides. Leave the edges overhanging. Lay the remaining squares on top of the first, turning them so the corners form a star shape. Repeat for the remaining tins.

4 Beat the egg with the nutmeg and seasoning, then stir in the cheeses and spinach. Divide the mixture among the tins and smooth level. Fold the overhanging pastry over the filling.

5 Cut the third pastry sheet into eight 10cm/4in rounds. Brush with butter and place two on top of each tartlet. Press around the edges to seal. Brush the last pastry sheet with butter and cut into strips. Gently twist each strip and lay them on top of the tartlets. Bake for 30–35 minutes, until golden brown. Serve the pies hot or cold.

Potatoes Energy 419kcal/1744kJ; Protein 13.3g; Carbohydrate 22g, of which sugars 4.8g; Fat 31.6g, of which saturates 11.4g; Cholesterol 42mg; Calcium 261mg; Fibre 3.6g; Sodium 439mg.
Cheese Pies Energy 287kcal/1191kJ; Protein 9.9g; Carbohydrate 17.2g, of which sugars 2.5g; Fat 20.3g, of which saturates 10.7g; Cholesterol 91mg; Calcium 269mg; Fibre 2.2g; Sodium 502mg.

Chilli Beans with Basmati Rice

Red kidney beans, chopped tomatoes and hot chilli make a great combination in this colourful dish.

Serves 4
350g/12oz/2 cups basmati rice
30ml/2 tbsp olive oil
1 large onion, chopped
1 garlic clove, crushed
15ml/12 tbsp hot chilli powder
15g/1⁄2oz/2 tbsp plain (all-purpose) flour
15ml/1 tbsp tomato purée (paste)
400g/14oz can chopped tomatoes
400g/14oz can red kidney beans, drained
150ml/1⁄4 pint/2⁄3 cup hot vegetable stock
salt and ground black pepper
chopped fresh parsley, to garnish

1 Wash the rice several times under cold running water. Drain well. Bring a large pan of water to the boil. Add the rice and cook for 10–12 minutes, until tender. Meanwhile, heat the oil in a frying pan over low heat. Add the onion and garlic and cook, stirring occasionally, for about 2 minutes.

2 Stir the chilli powder and flour into the onion and garlic mixture and cook, stirring frequently, for 2 minutes more.

3 Stir in the tomato purée and chopped tomatoes. Rinse and drain the kidney beans well and add to the pan with the hot vegetable stock. Cover and simmer gently, stirring occasionally, for 12 minutes.

4 Season the chilli sauce to taste with salt and pepper. Drain the rice and serve immediately with the chilli beans, garnished with a little chopped fresh parsley.

Cook's Tip
You can also serve the chilli beans with pasta, such as penne or conchiglie, or with hot pitta bread. They also make a really scrumptious filling for baked potatoes.

Lentil Stir-fry

Mushrooms, artichoke hearts, sugar snap peas and green lentils make a satisfying stir-fry supper.

Serves 2–3
115g/4oz/1 cup sugar snap peas
25g/1oz/2 tbsp butter
1 small onion, chopped
115g/4oz cup brown cap (cremini) mushrooms, sliced
400g/14oz can artichoke hearts, drained and halved
400g/14oz can green lentils, drained and rinsed
60ml/4 tbsp single (light) cream
25g/1oz/1⁄4 cup flaked (sliced) almonds, toasted
salt and ground black pepper
French bread, to serve

1 Bring a pan of salted water to the boil, add the sugar snap peas and cook for about 4 minutes, until just tender. Drain, refresh under cold running water, then drain again. Pat the peas dry with kitchen paper and set aside.

2 Melt the butter in a frying pan. Add the onion and cook over medium heat, stirring occasionally, for 2–3 minutes.

3 Add the mushrooms to the pan. Stir until well combined, then cook for 2–3 minutes, until just tender.

4 Add the artichoke hearts, sugar snap peas and lentils to the pan and cook, stirring constantly, for 2 minutes.

5 Stir in the cream and almonds and cook for 1 minute, but do not allow the mixture to come to the boil. Season to taste with salt and pepper. Spoon the stir-fry on to warmed plates and serve immediately with chunks of French bread.

Cook's Tip
Use dried green lentils if you prefer. Cook them in a pan of boiling water for 30–45 minutes first (without adding any salt), then drain well and add them to the stir-fry with the artichokes and sugar snap peas.

Chilli Beans Energy 523kcal/2194kJ; Protein 15.5g; Carbohydrate 100.1g, of which sugars 11.5g; Fat 7.1g, of which saturates 1g; Cholesterol 0mg; Calcium 120mg; Fibre 8.5g; Sodium 410mg.
Lentil Energy 345kcal/1443kJ; Protein 18.4g; Carbohydrate 30.9g, of which sugars 4.7g; Fat 17.3g, of which saturates 7.4g; Cholesterol 29mg; Calcium 139mg; Fibre 9.7g; Sodium 144mg.

Arabian Spinach

Stir-fry spinach with onions and spices, then mix in a can of chickpeas and you have a quick, delicious main meal.

Serves 4

30ml/2 tbsp olive or sunflower oil
1 onion, sliced
2 garlic cloves, crushed
5ml/1 tsp cumin seeds
400g/14oz/3½ cups spinach, washed and shredded
425g/15oz can chickpeas, drained and rinsed
knob (pat) of butter
salt and ground black pepper

1 Heat the oil in a large frying pan or wok over low heat. Add the onion and cook, stirring occasionally, for about 5 minutes, until softened but not coloured. Add the garlic and cumin seeds and cook, stirring constantly, for another minute.

2 Add the spinach, in batches, stirring until the leaves begin to wilt. Fresh spinach leaves collapse down dramatically on cooking and they will all fit into the pan.

3 Stir in the chickpeas and butter and season to taste with salt and pepper. Reheat until just bubbling, then serve immediately. Drain off any pan juices, if you like, but this dish is rather good served with a little sauce.

> **Cook's Tip**
> Always use spinach within a day of purchase as it does not keep well and quickly becomes slimy. Store it in a cool place and wash thoroughly and spin dry before cooking.

> **Variations**
> • You can use other canned pulses (legumes) besides chickpeas for this dish. Ful medames, for example, would be a good choice, as their nutty flavour goes particularly well with cumin.
> • For a more substantial dish, top with hot, quartered hard-boiled eggs.

Courgettes en Papillote

An impressive dinner party side dish, these puffed paper parcels should be broken open at the table.

Serves 4

2 courgettes (zucchini)
1 leek
225g/8oz young asparagus, trimmed
4 fresh tarragon sprigs
4 garlic cloves, unpeeled
1 egg, beaten
salt and ground black pepper

1 Preheat the oven to 200°C/400°F/Gas 6. Using a vegetable peeler, slice the courgettes lengthways into thin strips.

2 Cut the leek into very fine julienne strips and cut the asparagus evenly into 5cm/2in lengths.

3 Cut out four sheets of greaseproof (waxed) paper measuring about 30 x 38cm/12 x 15in and fold in half. Draw a large curve to make a heart shape when unfolded. Cut along the inside of the line and open out.

4 Divide the courgettes, leek and asparagus evenly among each paper heart, positioning the filling on one side of the fold line, and topping each with a sprig of fresh tarragon and an unpeeled garlic clove. Season to taste with salt and pepper.

5 Brush the edges lightly with the beaten egg and fold over. Pleat the edges together so that each parcel is completely sealed. Lay the parcels on a baking sheet and bake for about 10 minutes. Serve immediately.

> **Variation**
> Experiment with other combinations of vegetables and herbs such as sugar snap peas or mangetouts (snow peas) and mint; baby carrots and rosemary; fine green beans or baby broad (fava) beans and savory; asparagus and basil – the possibilities are almost endless. Always include a member of the onion family, preferably one with a mild flavour.

Spinach Energy 201kcal/841kJ; Protein 11.4g; Carbohydrate 21g, of which sugars 3.4g; Fat 8.4g, of which saturates 1g; Cholesterol 0mg; Calcium 220mg; Fibre 6.6g; Sodium 146mg.
Courgettes Energy 60kcal/249kJ; Protein 5.7g; Carbohydrate 4.2g, of which sugars 3.7g; Fat 2.4g, of which saturates 0.6g; Cholesterol 48mg; Calcium 58mg; Fibre 2.8g; Sodium 20mg.

Green Lentil & Cabbage Salad

This warm crunchy salad makes a satisfying meal if served with crusty French bread or wholemeal rolls.

Serves 4–6
225g/8oz/1 cup Puy lentils
1.3 litres/2¼ pints/6 cups cold
  water
3 garlic cloves
1 bay leaf
1 small onion, peeled and studded
  with 2 cloves
15ml/1 tbsp olive oil
1 red onion, thinly sliced
15ml/1 tbsp fresh thyme leaves
350g/12oz/3 cups finely
  shredded cabbage
finely grated rind and juice of
  1 lemon
15ml/1 tbsp raspberry vinegar
salt and ground black pepper

1 Rinse the lentils in cold water and place in a large pan with the water, 1 peeled garlic clove, bay leaf and clove-studded onion. Bring to the boil and cook for about 10 minutes. Reduce the heat, cover the pan with a tight-fitting lid and simmer gently for 15–20 minutes. Drain well. Remove and discard the onion, garlic and bay leaf.

2 Heat the oil in a large pan over low heat. Add the red onion, 2 crushed garlic cloves and thyme and cook, stirring occasionally, for 5 minutes, until the onion has softened.

3 Add the shredded cabbage and cook, stirring occasionally, for 3–5 minutes, until just cooked but still crunchy.

4 Stir in the cooked lentils, grated lemon rind and juice and the raspberry vinegar. Season with salt and pepper to taste and serve immediately.

> **Variation**
> This recipe works equally well with other types of cabbage. Choose whatever is in season: white cabbage or Savoy, or try fresh spring greens (collards) instead.

Tomato & Basil Tart

You could make individual tartlets instead of one large tart if you prefer, but reduce the baking time slightly.

Serves 6–8
175g/6oz/1½ cups plain (all-
  purpose) flour
2.5ml/½ tsp salt
115g/4oz/½ cup butter or
  margarine, chilled
45–75ml/3–5 tbsp water
salt and ground black pepper

For the filling
30ml/2 tbsp extra virgin olive oil
175g/6oz mozzarella cheese,
  thinly sliced
12 fresh basil leaves
  6 coarsely torn
4–5 tomatoes, cut into
  5mm/¼in slices
60ml/4 tbsp freshly grated
  Parmesan cheese

1 Sift the flour and salt into a bowl, then rub in the butter until the mixture resembles breadcrumbs. Add 45ml/3 tbsp water and combine with a fork until the dough holds together. Mix in more water if necessary. Gather the dough into a ball, wrap in baking parchment and chill in the refrigerator for 40 minutes. Preheat the oven to 190°C/375°F/Gas 5.

2 Roll out the dough to a thickness of 5mm/¼in and use to line a 28cm/11in fluted loose-based flan tin (pan). Prick the base all over and chill in the refrigerator for 20 minutes.

3 Line the pastry case (pie shell) with a sheet of baking parchment and fill with dried beans. Place the flan tin on a baking sheet and bake blind for 15 minutes. Remove from the oven but leave the oven switched on.

4 Remove the beans and paper. Brush the pastry case with oil. Line with the mozzarella. Sprinkle the torn basil over the top.

5 Arrange the tomato slices over the cheese. Dot with the whole basil leaves. Season with salt and pepper, and sprinkle with Parmesan and oil. Bake for 35 minutes. If the cheese exudes a lot of liquid during baking, tilt the tin and spoon it off to keep the crust crisp. Serve hot or at room temperature.

Salad Energy 151kcal/638kJ; Protein 10.2g; Carbohydrate 22.8g, of which sugars 4.4g; Fat 2.7g, of which saturates 0.3g; Cholesterol 0mg; Calcium 60mg; Fibre 4.9g; Sodium 9mg.
Tart Energy 307kcal/1279kJ; Protein 9.6g; Carbohydrate 19g, of which sugars 2.4g; Fat 21.9g, of which saturates 12.5g; Cholesterol 51mg; Calcium 207mg; Fibre 1.3g; Sodium 262mg.

Spinach & Potato Galette

Creamy layers of potato, spinach and fresh herbs make a warming and filling supper dish.

Serves 6
900g/2lb large potatoes
450g/1lb/4 cups spinach
400g/14oz/1¾ cups low-fat cream cheese
15ml/1 tbsp wholegrain mustard
2 eggs
50g/2oz mixed chopped fresh herbs, such as chives, parsley, chervil or sorrel
salt and ground black pepper

1 Preheat the oven to 180°C/350°F/Gas 4. Base-line a deep 23cm/9in round cake tin (pan) with baking parchment.

2 Place the potatoes in a large pan and add cold water to cover. Bring to the boil, cover and cook for 10 minutes. Drain well and leave to cool slightly before slicing thinly.

3 Wash the spinach and place in another large pan with only the water that is clinging to the leaves. Cover and cook, stirring once, until the spinach has just wilted. Drain well in a sieve (strainer) and squeeze out the excess moisture with the back of a spoon. Chop the spinach finely.

4 Beat together the cream cheese, mustard and eggs in a bowl, then stir in the chopped spinach and fresh herbs.

5 Place a layer of the sliced potatoes in the lined tin, arranging them in concentric circles. Top with a spoonful of the cream cheese mixture and spread out. Continue layering, seasoning with salt and pepper as you go, until all the potatoes and the cream cheese mixture are used up.

6 Cover the tin with a piece of foil, scrunched around the edge, and place in a roasting pan.

7 Pour boiling water into the roasting pan to come about halfway up the sides and cook the galette in the oven for 45–50 minutes. Turn out on to a plate and serve immediately or leave to cool completely and serve cold.

Cowboy Hot-pot

A great dish to serve as a children's main meal, which adults will enjoy too – if they are allowed to join the posse.

Serves 4–6
45ml/3 tbsp sunflower oil
1 onion, sliced
1 red (bell) pepper, seeded and sliced
1 sweet potato or 2 carrots, chopped
115g/4oz/scant ½ cup chopped green beans
400g/14oz can baked beans
200g/7oz can corn
15ml/1 tbsp tomato purée (paste)
5ml/1 tsp barbecue spice seasoning
115g/4oz cheese (preferably smoked), diced
450g/1lb potatoes, thinly sliced
25g/1oz/2 tbsp butter, melted
salt and ground black pepper

1 Preheat the oven to 190°C/375°F/Gas 5. Heat the oil in a frying pan over low heat. Add the onion, red pepper and sweet potato or carrots and cook, stirring occasionally, for about 5 minutes, until softened but not coloured.

2 Increase the heat to medium and stir in the green beans, baked beans, corn (and liquid), tomato purée and barbecue spice seasoning. Bring to the boil, then lower the heat and simmer for 5 minutes.

3 Transfer the vegetable mixture to an ovenproof dish and stir in the diced cheese.

4 Cover the vegetable and cheese mixture with the potato slices, brush generously with the melted butter and season with salt and pepper. Bake the hot-pot for 30–40 minutes, until golden brown on top and the potato is cooked. Serve immediately straight from the dish.

Cook's Tip
Use any vegetable mixture you like in this versatile hot-pot, depending on what you have to hand.

Galette Energy 239kcal/1004kJ; Protein 16.9g; Carbohydrate 27.9g, of which sugars 5.6g; Fat 8.4g, of which saturates 4.2g; Cholesterol 79mg; Calcium 240mg; Fibre 3.5g; Sodium 440mg.
Hot-pot Energy 351kcal/1470kJ; Protein 12g; Carbohydrate 40.1g, of which sugars 11.1g; Fat 16.6g, of which saturates 7.3g; Cholesterol 27mg; Calcium 199mg; Fibre 5.7g; Sodium 503mg.

Quorn with Ginger, Chilli & Leeks

Quorn easily absorbs different flavours and retains a good firm texture, making it ideal for stir-frying.

Serves 4

225g/8oz packet Quorn, diced
45ml/3 tbsp dark soy sauce
30ml/2 tbsp dry sherry
  or vermouth
10ml/2 tsp clear honey
150ml/¼ pint/⅔ cup vegetable
  stock
10ml/2 tsp cornflour (cornstarch)
45ml/3 tbsp sunflower or
  groundnut (peanut) oil
3 leeks, thinly sliced
1 red chilli, seeded and sliced
2.5cm/1in piece fresh root
  ginger, shredded
salt and ground black pepper
rice or egg noodles, to serve

1 Toss the Quorn in the soy sauce and sherry or vermouth in a bowl until well coated. Leave to marinate for 30 minutes.

2 Drain the Quorn and reserve the marinade in a jug (pitcher). Mix the marinade with the honey, vegetable stock and cornflour to make a paste.

3 Heat the oil in a wok or large frying pan and, when hot, add the Quorn and stir-fry until it is crisp on the outside. Remove the Quorn and set aside.

4 Reheat the oil. Add the leeks, chilli and ginger and stir-fry for about 2 minutes, until they are just soft. Season to taste with salt and pepper.

5 Return the Quorn to the pan, together with the marinade mixture, and stir well until the liquid is thick and glossy. Serve immediately with rice or egg noodles.

Cook's Tip
Quorn is a versatile, mycoprotein food, now available in most supermarkets. If you cannot find it, you could use tofu instead.

Chinese Potatoes with Chilli Beans

This Chinese-inspired dish is made particularly appealing by its tasty sauce.

Serves 4

4 potatoes, cut into thick chunks
30ml/2 tbsp sunflower or
  groundnut (peanut) oil
3 spring onions (scallions), sliced
1 large chilli, seeded and sliced
2 garlic cloves, crushed
400g/14oz can red kidney
  beans, drained
30ml/2 tbsp dark soy sauce
15ml/1 tbsp sesame oil
salt and ground black pepper
15ml/1 tbsp sesame seeds,
  to sprinkle
chopped fresh coriander (cilantro)
  or parsley, to garnish

1 Put the potatoes in a pan, add cold water to cover and bring to the boil. Cover and cook for about 15 minutes, until they are just tender but still firm. Take care not to overcook them. Drain well and set aside.

2 Heat the oil in a wok or large, heavy frying pan. Add the spring onions and chilli and stir-fry over a medium heat for about 1 minute, then add the garlic and stir-fry for a few seconds longer.

3 Rinse and drain the kidney beans, then add them to the pan with the potatoes, stirring well. Finally, stir in the soy sauce and sesame oil.

4 Season to taste with salt and pepper and cook the vegetables until they are well heated through. Sprinkle with the sesame seeds and serve immediately, garnished with the chopped fresh coriander or parsley.

Cook's Tip
Coriander (cilantro) is also known as Chinese parsley and Greek parsley and it does resemble flat leaf parsley in appearance. However, the flavour is quite different. It is intensely aromatic, almost spicy, and goes especially well with chillies. It is one of those herbs that you either love or loathe.

Quorn Energy 158kcal/657kJ; Protein 8.6g; Carbohydrate 5.1g, of which sugars 3.8g; Fat 10.6g, of which saturates 1.4g; Cholesterol 0mg; Calcium 27mg; Fibre 4.9g; Sodium 939mg.
Potatoes Energy 272kcal/1141kJ; Protein 9.7g; Carbohydrate 34.8g, of which sugars 5.7g; Fat 11.4g, of which saturates 1.6g; Cholesterol 0mg; Calcium 107mg; Fibre 7.6g; Sodium 936mg.

Corn & Bean Tamale Pie

This hearty dish has a cheese-flavoured polenta topping which covers corn and kidney beans in a rich hot sauce. It is substantial enough for meat-eaters.

Serves 4

2 corn on the cob
30ml/2 tbsp vegetable oil
I onion, chopped
2 garlic cloves, crushed
I red (bell) pepper, seeded and chopped
2 green chillies, seeded and chopped
10ml/2 tbsp ground cumin
450g/1lb ripe tomatoes, peeled, seeded and chopped

15ml/1 tbsp tomato purée (paste)
425g/15oz can red kidney beans, drained and rinsed
15ml/1 tbsp chopped fresh oregano
oregano leaves, to garnish

For the topping

115g/4oz/scant I cup polenta
15g/¹/₂oz/2 tbsp plain (all-purpose) flour
2.5ml/¹/₂ tsp salt
10ml/2 tsp baking powder
I egg, lightly beaten
120ml/4fl oz/¹/₂ cup milk
15g/¹/₂oz/1 tbsp butter, melted
50g/2oz/¹/₂ cup grated smoked Cheddar cheese

1 Preheat the oven to 220°C/425°F/Gas 7. Husk the corn on the cob, then par-boil for 8 minutes. Drain well, leave to cool slightly, then remove the kernels with a sharp knife.

2 Heat the oil in a large pan. Add the onion, garlic and red pepper and cook over low heat, stirring occasionally, for about 5 minutes, until softened. Add the chillies and cumin and cook, stirring constantly, for 1 minute. Stir in the tomatoes, tomato purée, beans, corn kernels and oregano. Season with salt and pepper. Simmer, uncovered, for 10 minutes.

3 To make the topping, mix the polenta, flour, salt, baking powder, egg, milk and butter to form a thick batter.

4 Transfer the bean mixture to an ovenproof dish, spoon the polenta mixture over and spread evenly. Bake for 30 minutes. Remove from the oven, sprinkle the cheese over the top, then bake for a further 5–10 minutes, until golden.

Pepper & Potato Tortilla

A traditional Spanish dish, tortilla is best eaten cold in chunky wedges and makes an ideal picnic food.

Serves 4

2 potatoes
45ml/3 tbsp olive oil
I large onion, thinly sliced
2 garlic cloves, crushed

I green (bell) pepper, seeded and thinly sliced
I red (bell) pepper, seeded and thinly sliced
6 eggs, beaten
115g/4oz/1 cup grated mature (sharp) Cheddar or Mahón cheese
salt and ground black pepper

1 Do not peel the potatoes, but scrub them well under cold running water. Par-boil them for about 10 minutes, then drain and, when they are cool enough to handle, slice them thickly. Preheat the grill (broiler).

2 Heat the oil in a large non-stick or well seasoned frying pan. Add the onion, garlic and green and red peppers and cook over medium heat, stirring occasionally, for about 5 minutes, until softened but not coloured.

3 Add the potatoes, lower the heat and cook, stirring occasionally, until the potatoes are completely cooked and the vegetables are soft. Add a little extra olive oil if the pan seems too dry.

4 Pour in half the beaten eggs, then sprinkle over half the grated cheese. Add the rest of the eggs. Season with salt and pepper and sprinkle with the remaining cheese.

5 Continue to cook over low heat, without stirring, half covering the pan with a lid to help set the eggs.

6 When the mixture is firm, place the pan under the hot grill for a few seconds to seal the top lightly. Leave the tortilla in the pan to cool. This helps it firm up further and makes it easier to turn out. Cut into generous wedges or squares and serve at room temperature.

Pie Energy 513kcal/2154kJ; Protein 19.5g; Carbohydrate 71.1g, of which sugars 19.8g; Fat 17.6g, of which saturates 6.4g; Cholesterol 69mg; Calcium 233mg; Fibre 10.2g; Sodium 758mg.
Tortilla Energy 321kcal/1333kJ; Protein 13.1g; Carbohydrate 19.6g, of which sugars 10.2g; Fat 21.1g, of which saturates 8.3g; Cholesterol 123mg; Calcium 256mg; Fibre 3g; Sodium 254mg.

Chickpea Stew

This hearty chickpea and vegetable stew is delicious served with garlic-flavoured mashed potato.

Serves 4
30ml/2 tbsp olive oil
1 small onion, finely chopped
225g/8oz carrots, halved
   lengthways and thinly
   sliced
2.5ml/½ tsp ground cumin
5ml/1 tsp ground coriander

25g/1oz/¼ cup plain (all-
   purpose) flour
225g/8oz courgettes
   (zucchini), sliced
200g/7oz can corn, drained
400g/14oz can chickpeas,
   drained and rinsed
30ml/2 tbsp tomato
   purée (paste)
200ml/7fl oz/scant 1 cup hot
   vegetable stock
salt and ground black pepper
mashed potato, to serve

1 Heat the olive oil in a frying pan. Add the onion and carrots and cook over medium heat, stirring occasionally, for about 5 minutes, until the onion has softened but not coloured.

2 Add the ground cumin, coriander and flour and cook, stirring constantly, for 1 minute more.

3 Cut the courgette slices in half and add to the pan with the corn, chickpeas, tomato purée and vegetable stock. Stir well. Cook for 10 minutes, stirring frequently.

4 Season the stew to taste with salt and pepper. Spoon on to warmed plates and serve immediately with mashed potato.

Cook's Tip
To make garlic mash, add 4–6 finely chopped or crushed garlic cloves to the potatoes about 15 minutes after they began boiling. Reserve 30–45ml/2–3 tbsp of the cooking liquid when you drain the potatoes. Heat a little milk with the reserved liquid, add a little butter and remove the pan from the heat. Add the potatoes and garlic and mash well with a potato masher. Beat with a wooden spoon and season with salt and pepper.

Potato & Broccoli Stir-fry

This wonderful stir-fry combines potato, broccoli and red pepper with just a hint of fresh ginger.

Serves 2
450g/1lb potatoes
45ml/3 tbsp groundnut
   (peanut) oil

50g/2oz/4 tbsp butter
1 small onion, chopped
1 red (bell) pepper, seeded
   and chopped
225g/8oz broccoli, broken
   into florets
2.5cm/1in piece of fresh root
   ginger, grated
salt and ground black pepper

1 Peel the potatoes and cut them into 1cm/½in dice. Heat the oil in a large frying pan. Add the potatoes and cook over a high heat, stirring and tossing frequently, for about 8 minutes, until browned and just tender.

2 Drain off the oil from the pan. Add the butter to the potatoes in the pan. As soon as it melts, add the onion and red pepper and stir-fry for 2 minutes.

3 Add the broccoli florets and ginger to the pan. Stir-fry for a further 2–3 minutes, taking care not to break up the potatoes. Season to taste with salt and pepper and serve immediately.

Cook's Tip
Always use a vegetable peeler with a swivel blade for peeling potatoes. As most of the nutrients are directly beneath the skin, it is important to peel them as thinly as possible.

Variations
• Substitute 1 finely chopped celery stick and 1 thinly sliced carrot for the red (bell) pepper.
• For a milder tasting dish, omit the ginger, replace the broccoli with peeled, seeded and diced tomatoes and flavour with torn fresh basil leaves.

Stew Energy 288kcal/1211kJ; Protein 11.2g; Carbohydrate 42g, of which sugars 12.3g; Fat 9.5g, of which saturates 1.3g; Cholesterol 0mg; Calcium 88mg; Fibre 7.3g; Sodium 388mg.
Stir-fry Energy 2442kcal/10069kJ; Protein 10.2g; Carbohydrate 46.4g, of which sugars 11.8g; Fat 247.4g, of which saturates 55.9g; Cholesterol 53mg; Calcium 96mg; Fibre 7g; Sodium 190mg.

Vegetables with Lentil Bolognese

Instead of the more traditional cheese sauce, it makes a pleasant change to top lightly steamed vegetables with a delicious lentil sauce.

Serves 6
1 small cauliflower broken into florets
225g/8oz/2 cups broccoli florets
2 leeks, thickly sliced
225g/8oz Brussels sprouts, halved if large

For the lentil Bolognese sauce
45ml/3 tbsp olive oil
1 onion, chopped
2 garlic cloves, crushed
2 carrots, coarsely grated
2 celery sticks, chopped
115g/4oz/½ cup red lentils
400g/14oz can chopped tomatoes
30ml/2 tbsp tomato purée (paste)
450ml/¾ pint/2 cups vegetable stock
15ml/1 tbsp fresh marjoram, chopped, or 5ml/1 tsp dried marjoram
salt and ground black pepper

1 First make the lentil Bolognese sauce. Heat the oil in a large pan over low heat. Add the onion, garlic, carrots and celery and cook, stirring occasionally, for about 5 minutes, until softened but not coloured.

2 Increase the heat to medium and add the lentils, tomatoes, tomato purée, stock and marjoram. Bring the mixture to the boil, then lower the heat, partially cover the pan with a lid and simmer gently for 20–30 minutes, until the sauce is thick and soft. Season to taste with salt and pepper.

3 Meanwhile, place the cauliflower, broccoli, leeks and Brussels sprouts in a steamer set over a pan of boiling water, cover and cook for 8–10 minutes, until all the vegetables are just tender but still have a little crunch.

4 Drain the vegetables and place in a warmed, shallow serving dish. Spoon the lentil Bolognese sauce on top, stir lightly to mix and serve immediately.

Black Bean & Vegetable Stir-fry

This colourful and very flavoursome vegetable mixture is coated in a classic Chinese sauce.

Serves 4
8 spring onions (scallions)
225g/8oz button (white) mushrooms
1 red (bell) pepper
1 green (bell) pepper
2 large carrots
60ml/4 tbsp sesame oil
2 garlic cloves, crushed
60ml/4 tbsp black bean sauce
90ml/6 tbsp warm water
225g/8oz/scant 3 cups beansprouts
salt and ground black pepper

1 Thinly slice the spring onions and button mushrooms. Set aside in separate bowls.

2 Cut both the peppers in half, remove and discard the seeds and slice the flesh into thin strips.

3 Cut the carrots in half. Cut each half into thin strips lengthways. Stack the slices and cut through them to make very fine strips.

4 Heat the oil in a large wok or frying pan until very hot. Add the spring onions and garlic and stir-fry for 30 seconds.

5 Add the mushrooms, peppers and carrots. Stir-fry over high heat for a further 5–6 minutes, until just beginning to soften.

6 Mix the black bean sauce with the water. Add to the wok or frying pan and cook for a further 3–4 minutes. Stir in the beansprouts and stir-fry for a final 1 minute, until all the vegetables are coated in the sauce. Season to taste with salt and pepper. Serve immediately.

Cook's Tip
Black bean sauce is available in jars and cans. Once opened it should be stored in the refrigerator.

Bolognese Energy 195kcal/817kJ; Protein 11.8g; Carbohydrate 20.5g, of which sugars 8.8g; Fat 7.8g, of which saturates 1.3g; Cholesterol 0mg; Calcium 83mg; Fibre 7.2g; Sodium 46mg.
Stir-fry Energy 196kcal/817kJ; Protein 6.5g; Carbohydrate 16.1g, of which sugars 9.4g; Fat 12.2g, of which saturates 1.9g; Cholesterol 0mg; Calcium 45mg; Fibre 4.6g; Sodium 19mg.

Tomato & Okra Stew

Okra is an unusual and delicious vegetable. It releases a sticky sap when cooked, which helps to thicken the stew.

Serves 4

15ml/1 tbsp olive oil
1 onion, chopped
400g/14oz can pimientos, drained
2 x 400g/14oz cans chopped tomatoes
275g/10oz okra
30ml/2 tbsp chopped fresh parsley
salt and ground black pepper

1 Heat the oil in a pan over medium heat. Add the onion and cook, stirring occasionally, for 2–3 minutes, until it is just beginning to soften.

2 Coarsely chop the pimientos and add to the onion. Add the tomatoes with their can juices and mix well.

3 Cut the tops off the okra and cut into halves or quarters if large. Add them to the pan. Season to taste with plenty of salt and pepper.

4 Bring the vegetable stew to the boil, then lower the heat, cover the pan with a tight-fitting lid and simmer gently for about 12 minutes, until all the vegetables are tender and the sauce has thickened. Stir in the chopped parsley, transfer to a warmed serving dish and serve immediately.

Cook's Tip
Okra, also known as bhindi, gumbo and ladies' fingers, is now available all year round. Do not buy pods any longer than 7.5–10cm/3–4in as larger ones tend to be fibrous. Look for clean, dark green pods – a brown tinge indicates staleness. They should feel firm and slightly springy when squeezed and should snap easily, not bend. Store them in the salad drawer of the refrigerator where they will keep for a few days. When preparing, if the ridges look tough or damaged, scrape them with a sharp knife.

Chunky Vegetable Paella

This Spanish rice dish is now enjoyed the world over. This version includes aubergine and chickpeas.

Serves 6

large pinch of saffron threads
1 aubergine (eggplant), cut into thick chunks
90ml/6 tbsp olive oil
1 large onion, thickly sliced
3 garlic cloves, crushed
1 yellow (bell) pepper, seeded and sliced
1 red (bell) pepper, seeded and sliced
10ml/2 tsp paprika
225g/8oz/1¼ cups Valencia or risotto rice
600ml/1 pint/2½ cups vegetable stock
450g/1lb fresh tomatoes, peeled and chopped
115g/4oz mushrooms, sliced
115g/4oz/scant ½ cup cut green beans
400g/14oz can chickpeas

1 Place the saffron in a small bowl, add 45ml/3 tbsp hot water and set aside to steep.

2 Place the aubergine chunks in a colander, sprinkle with salt and leave to drain for 30 minutes. Rinse thoroughly under cold running water and pat dry with kitchen paper.

3 Heat the oil in a large paella or frying pan over low heat. Add the onion, garlic, yellow and red peppers and aubergine and cook, stirring occasionally, for about 5 minutes, until the onion has softened but not coloured. Sprinkle in the paprika and stir well.

4 Increase the heat to medium and mix in the rice, then pour in the vegetable stock and add the tomatoes. Stir in the saffron with its soaking water. Season well with salt and pepper. Bring the mixture to the boil, then lower the heat and simmer gently for about 15 minutes, uncovered, shaking the pan frequently and stirring occasionally.

5 Stir in the mushrooms, green beans and chickpeas with their can juices. Simmer gently for a further 10 minutes, then serve hot, direct from the pan.

Stew Energy 122kcal/515kJ; Protein 4.8g; Carbohydrate 16.7g, of which sugars 15.6g; Fat 4.6g, of which saturates 0.9g; Cholesterol 0mg; Calcium 152mg; Fibre 7g; Sodium 97mg.
Paella Energy 385kcal/1610kJ; Protein 11g; Carbohydrate 54.5g, of which sugars 12g; Fat 14.2g, of which saturates 2g; Cholesterol 0mg; Calcium 79mg; Fibre 7.7g; Sodium 160mg.

Onion & Gruyère Tart

The secret of this tart is to cook the onions very slowly until they almost caramelize.

Serves 4

175g/6oz/1½ cups plain (all-purpose) flour
pinch of salt
75g/3oz/6 tbsp butter, diced
1 egg yolk

For the filling
50g/2oz/4 tbsp butter

450g/1lb onions, thinly sliced
15–30ml/1–2 tbsp wholegrain mustard
2 eggs, plus 1 egg yolk
300ml/½ pint/1 cup double (heavy) cream
75g/3oz/¾ cup grated Gruyère cheese
pinch of freshly grated nutmeg
salt and ground black pepper

1 To make the pastry, sift the flour and salt into a bowl. Add the butter and rub it into the flour with your fingertips until the mixture resembles fine breadcrumbs. Add the egg yolk and 15ml/1 tbsp cold water and mix to a firm dough. Chill in the refrigerator for 30 minutes.

2 Preheat the oven to 200°C/400°F/Gas 6. Knead the dough, then roll it out on a lightly floured work surface and use to line a 23cm/9in loose-based flan tin (pan). Prick the base all over with a fork, line the pastry case (pie shell) with baking parchment and fill with baking beans.

3 Bake the pastry case blind for 15 minutes. Remove the paper and beans and bake for a further 10–15 minutes, until the pastry case is crisp. Meanwhile, melt the butter in a pan, add the onions, cover with a tight-fitting lid and cook over low heat, stirring occasionally, for 20 minutes, until golden.

4 Reduce the oven temperature to 180°C/350°F/Gas 4. Spread the pastry case with mustard and top with the onions. Mix together the eggs, egg yolk, cream, cheese and nutmeg and season with salt and pepper. Pour over the onions. Bake for 30–35 minutes, until golden. Remove the tart from the oven and leave to cool slightly. Serve warm.

Potato & Spinach Gratin

Pine nuts add a satisfying crunch to this gratin of wafer-thin potato slices and spinach in a wonderfully creamy cheese sauce.

Serves 2

450g/1lb potatoes
1 garlic clove, crushed
3 spring onions (scallions), thinly sliced

150ml/¼ pint/⅔ cup single (light) cream
250ml/8fl oz/1 cup milk
225g/8oz frozen chopped spinach, thawed
115g/4oz/1 cup grated mature (sharp) Cheddar cheese
25g/1oz/¼ cup pine nuts
salt and ground black pepper
lettuce and tomato salad, to serve

1 Peel the potatoes and cut them carefully into wafer-thin slices. This is most easily done with a mandoline or the slicing attachment of a food processor. Spread the slices out in a large, heavy, non-stick frying pan.

2 Sprinkle the crushed garlic and sliced spring onions evenly over the potatoes.

3 Mix together the cream and milk in a jug (pitcher) and pour the mixture over the potatoes. Place the pan over low heat, cover with a tight-fitting lid and cook for 8 minutes, or until the potatoes are tender.

4 Drain the spinach thoroughly, then, using both hands, squeeze it as dry as possible. Add the spinach to the potatoes, mixing lightly. Cover the pan with a tight-fitting lid and cook for 2 minutes more.

5 Season to taste with salt and pepper, then spoon the mixture into a gratin dish. Preheat the grill (broiler).

6 Sprinkle the grated cheese and pine nuts evenly over the potato and spinach mixture. Lightly toast under the grill for 2–3 minutes, until the cheese has melted and the topping is golden brown. Serve the gratin immediately with a lettuce and tomato salad.

Tart Energy 904kcal/3746kJ; Protein 15g; Carbohydrate 36.7g, of which sugars 3g; Fat 78.2g, of which saturates 47g; Cholesterol 384mg; Calcium 272mg; Fibre 1.6g; Sodium 383mg.
Gratin Energy 527kcal/2212kJ; Protein 28.1g; Carbohydrate 45.3g, of which sugars 11.7g; Fat 27.3g, of which saturates 11.6g; Cholesterol 79mg; Calcium 413mg; Fibre 5.1g; Sodium 183mg.

Stuffed Peppers

Sweet peppers filled with a tasty anchovy and tomato-flavoured rice stuffing, then baked until meltingly tender, make an irresistible light meal. A fresh-tasting tomato sauce makes a perfect accompaniment to the dish.

Serves 6
6 red and yellow (bell) peppers
200g/7oz/generous 1 cup rice
60ml/4 tbsp olive oil

1 large onion, chopped
3 anchovy fillets, chopped
2 garlic cloves, finely chopped
3 tomatoes, peeled and
    finely diced
60ml/4 tbsp white wine
45ml/3 tbsp finely chopped
    fresh parsley
115g/4oz/scant ½ cup
    mozzarella cheese, grated
90ml/6 tbsp freshly grated
    Parmesan cheese
salt and ground black pepper

1 Cut off the tops of the peppers. Scoop out the seeds and the cores. Blanch the pepper shells in a large pan of boiling water for 3–4 minutes. Remove and stand upside down on wire racks to drain thoroughly.

2 Boil the rice according to the packet instructions, but drain and rinse it in cold water for 3 minutes before the recommended cooking time has elapsed. Drain again.

3 Heat the oil in a pan, add the onion and sauté until soft. Mash in the anchovies and garlic. Add the tomatoes and wine and cook for 5 minutes, stirring frequently.

4 Preheat the oven to 190°C/375°F/Gas 5. Remove the tomato mixture from the heat, then stir in the rice, parsley, mozzarella and 60ml/4 tbsp of the Parmesan cheese. Season to taste with salt and pepper.

5 Pat the insides of the peppers dry with kitchen paper, then sprinkle with salt and pepper. Carefully spoon the rice mixture into the peppers. Sprinkle the tops with the remaining Parmesan and a little oil. Arrange the peppers in a shallow baking dish. Pour in enough water to come 1cm/½in up the sides of the peppers. Bake for 25 minutes. Serve immediately.

Broccoli & Ricotta Cannelloni

A vegetarian version of an Italian favourite, this pasta dish is the perfect dish for an informal gathering.

Serves 4
12 dried cannelloni tubes,
    7.5cm/3in long
450g/1lb/4 cups broccoli florets
75g/3oz/1½ cups fresh
    breadcrumbs
150ml/¼ pint/⅔ cup milk
60ml/4 tbsp olive oil, plus extra
    for brushing
225g/8oz/1 cup ricotta cheese
pinch of freshly grated nutmeg

90ml/6 tbsp freshly grated
    Parmesan or Pecorino cheese
salt and ground black pepper
30ml/2 tbsp pine nuts,
    for sprinkling

For the tomato sauce
1 onion, finely chopped
1 garlic clove, crushed
30ml/2 tbsp olive oil
2 x 400g/14oz cans chopped
    tomatoes
15ml/1 tbsp tomato purée
    (paste)
4 black olives, pitted and chopped
5ml/1 tsp dried thyme

1 Preheat the oven to 190°C/375°F/Gas 5 and grease an ovenproof dish. Bring a pan of water to the boil, add a little olive oil and simmer the pasta, uncovered, until nearly cooked.

2 Meanwhile, boil the broccoli until tender. Drain the pasta and rinse under cold water. Drain the broccoli, then process in a food processor or blender until smooth.

3 Mix together the breadcrumbs, milk and oil in a bowl. Add the ricotta, broccoli purée, nutmeg and 60ml/4 tbsp Parmesan cheese. Season to taste with salt and pepper.

4 To make the sauce, fry the onions and garlic in the oil for 5 minutes. Stir in the tomatoes, tomato purée, olives, thyme and seasoning. Simmer for 2 minutes, then pour into the dish.

5 Open the pasta tubes and, holding them upright on the work surface, pipe in the filling using a 1cm/½in piping nozzle. Arrange in the dish on top of the sauce. Brush with olive oil, then sprinkle over the remaining cheese and the pine nuts. Bake for 30 minutes, or until golden on top. Serve immediately.

Peppers Energy 354kcal/1474kJ; Protein 14.9g; Carbohydrate 41.4g, of which sugars 13.2g; Fat 13.7g, of which saturates 6.5g; Cholesterol 27mg; Calcium 304mg; Fibre 3.9g; Sodium 313mg.
Cannelloni Energy 808kcal/3387kJ; Protein 33.6g; Carbohydrate 80.8g, of which sugars 12.9g; Fat 41.2g, of which saturates 13.4g; Cholesterol 48mg; Calcium 436mg; Fibre 7.1g; Sodium 501mg.

Pasta Carbonara

This classic Roman dish is traditionally made with spaghetti, but is equally good with fresh egg tagliatelle.

Serves 4
350–450g/12oz–1lb fresh
    tagliatelle pasta
15ml/1 tbsp olive oil
225g/8oz piece of ham or bacon,
    cut into 2.5cm/1in sticks
115g/4oz button mushrooms,
    sliced
4 eggs, lightly beaten
75ml/5 tbsp single (light) cream
30ml/2 tbsp finely grated
    Parmesan cheese
salt and ground black pepper
fresh basil sprigs, to garnish

1 Bring a large pan of lightly salted water to the boil, add a little oil and cook the tagliatelle for 6–8 minutes or until *al dente*.

2 Meanwhile, heat the oil in a frying pan and cook the ham for 3–4 minutes, then add the mushrooms and fry for a further 3–4 minutes. Turn off the heat and set the pan aside. Lightly beat the eggs and cream together in a bowl and season well with salt and pepper.

3 When the pasta is cooked, drain it well and return to the pan. Add the ham, mushrooms and any pan juices and stir well into the pasta.

4 Pour in the egg and cream mixture, together with half the Parmesan cheese. Stir well – as you do this the eggs will cook in the heat of the pasta. Pile on to warmed serving plates, sprinkle with the remaining Parmesan and garnish with basil leaves. Serve immediately.

Cook's Tip
For an authentic Italian flavour, use slices of pancetta. Made from pork belly, it is cured in salt and spices to give it a delicious taste. Pancetta is sold at Italian delicatessens and is now increasingly available from larger supermarkets.

Pasta with Spring Vegetables

Pasta tossed with broccoli, leeks, asparagus and fennel makes an attractive dish, bursting with fresh flavours.

Serves 4
115g/4oz/1 cup broccoli florets
115g/4oz baby leeks
225g/8oz asparagus
1 small fennel bulb
115g/4oz/1 cup fresh or frozen
    peas
40g/1½ oz/3 tbsp butter
1 shallot, chopped
45ml/3 tbsp mixed chopped fresh
    herbs, such as parsley, thyme
    and sage
300ml/½ pint/1¼ cups double
    (heavy) cream
350g/12oz/3 cups dried penne
    pasta
salt and ground black pepper
freshly grated Parmesan cheese,
    to serve

1 Divide the broccoli florets into tiny sprigs. Cut the leeks and asparagus diagonally into 5cm/2in lengths. Trim the fennel bulb and remove any tough outer leaves. Cut into wedges, leaving the layers attached at the root ends so the pieces stay intact.

2 Cook each vegetable separately in boiling salted water until just tender – use the same water for each vegetable. Drain well and keep warm.

3 Melt the butter in a separate pan, add the chopped shallot and cook, stirring occasionally, until softened but not browned. Stir in the herbs and cream and cook for a few minutes, until slightly thickened.

4 Meanwhile, bring a large pan of lightly salted water to the boil and cook the penne for 10 minutes or until *al dente*. Drain well and add to the cream sauce with all the vegetables. Toss gently to combine and season to taste with plenty of pepper. Serve immediately, with plenty of grated Parmesan cheese.

Cook's Tip
If you are not keen on the aniseed taste of fennel, you can use a small onion instead. Prepare in the same way.

Vegetables Energy 767kcal/3196kJ; Protein 16.5g; Carbohydrate 64g, of which sugars 7.8g; Fat 51.3g, of which saturates 30.6g; Cholesterol 124mg; Calcium 138mg; Fibre 7.8g; Sodium 93mg.
Carbonara Energy 535kcal/2257kJ; Protein 31.7g; Carbohydrate 66g, of which sugars 4g; Fat 18.1g, of which saturates 6.6g; Cholesterol 241mg; Calcium 165mg; Fibre 3.2g; Sodium 838mg.

Spinach & Hazelnut Lasagne

Hazelnuts add a delicious crunchy texture to the spinach layer of this wholesome lasagne.

Serves 4
900g/2lb/8 cups fresh spinach
300ml/½ pint/1¼ cups vegetable stock
1 onion, finely chopped
1 garlic clove, crushed
75g/3oz/¾ cup hazelnuts
30ml/2 tbsp chopped fresh basil
6 sheets no pre-cook lasagne
400g/14oz can chopped tomatoes
250ml/8fl oz/1 cup mascarpone or fromage frais
salt and ground black pepper
flaked hazelnuts and chopped fresh parsley

1 Preheat the oven to 200°C/400°F/Gas 6. Wash the spinach and place in a pan with just the water that clings to the leaves. Cook over high heat for 2 minutes until wilted. Drain well.

2 Heat 30ml/2 tbsp of the stock in a pan and simmer the onion and garlic until soft. Stir in the spinach, hazelnuts and chopped fresh basil.

3 Arrange a layer of the spinach mixture in a large rectangular ovenproof dish. Top with a layer of lasagne, then a layer of chopped tomatoes, seasoning with salt and pepper as you work. Continue in this way, finishing with a layer of pasta.

4 Pour in the remaining stock, then spread the mascarpone or fromage frais over the top. Bake for 45 minutes. Serve hot, sprinkled with hazelnuts and chopped parsley.

> **Cook's Tip**
> If you're short of time, use frozen spinach instead of fresh – you will need 450g/1lb.

Tagliatelle with Hazelnut Pesto

Hazelnuts are used instead of pine nuts in this pesto sauce, providing a healthier, lower-fat option.

Serves 4
2 garlic cloves, crushed
25g/1oz fresh basil leaves
25g/1oz/¼ cup chopped hazelnuts
200g/7oz/scant 1 cup soft cheese
225g/8oz tagliatelle
ground black pepper

1 Place the garlic, basil, hazelnuts and cheese in a food processor or blender and process to a thick paste.

2 Bring a large pan of lightly salted water to the boil and cook the tagliatelle until *al dente*. Drain well.

3 Spoon the sauce into the hot pasta, tossing until melted. Sprinkle with pepper and serve immediately.

Spaghetti with Tuna Sauce

Tuna is combined with tomatoes, garlic and chilli to make a great piquant sauce for pasta.

Serves 4
225g/8oz dried spaghetti or 450g/1lb fresh spaghetti
400g/14oz can chopped tomatoes
1 garlic clove
425g/15oz canned tuna
4 black olives
2.5ml/½ tsp chilli sauce (optional)
salt and ground black pepper

1 Bring a large pan of lightly salted water to the boil and cook the spaghetti until *al dente*. Drain well and keep hot.

2 Place the chopped tomatoes in a pan with the garlic and simmer for 2–3 minutes. Add the tuna, olives and chilli sauce, if using, and heat well. Toss with the spaghetti and heat through. Season to taste with salt and pepper and serve immediately.

Lasagne Energy 442kcal/1853kJ; Protein 19.6g; Carbohydrate 48.8g, of which sugars 12.3g; Fat 19.9g, of which saturates 4.8g; Cholesterol 5mg; Calcium 501mg; Fibre 8.6g; Sodium 350mg.
Tagliatelle Energy 392kcal/1642kJ; Protein 12.1g; Carbohydrate 42.2g, of which sugars 2.3g; Fat 20.6g, of which saturates 10.1g; Cholesterol 45mg; Calcium 90mg; Fibre 2.4g; Sodium 169mg.
Spaghetti Energy 413kcal/1748kJ; Protein 36.3g; Carbohydrate 44.8g, of which sugars 5g; Fat 11.2g, of which saturates 1.9g; Cholesterol 53mg; Calcium 36mg; Fibre 2.7g; Sodium 386mg.

Penne with Broccoli & Chilli

Simple to make, yet filled with tasty flavours, this dish is ideal for an easy midweek meal. Try using other pasta shapes, such as fusilli spirals.

Serves 4
350g/12oz/3 cups penne pasta
450g/1lb/4 cups small broccoli florets
30ml/2 tbsp stock
1 garlic clove, crushed
1 small red chilli, finely sliced, or 2.5ml/½ tsp chilli sauce
60ml/4 tbsp natural (plain) low-fat yogurt
30ml/2 tbsp toasted pine nuts or cashew nuts
salt and ground black pepper

1 Bring a large pan of lightly salted water to the boil, add the pasta and return to the boil. Place the broccoli in a steamer basket over the top. Cover and cook for 8–10 minutes, until both are just tender. Drain.

2 Heat the stock in a pan and add the crushed garlic and chilli or chilli sauce. Stir over a low heat for 2–3 minutes.

3 Stir in the broccoli, pasta and yogurt. Season to taste with salt and pepper, then sprinkle with nuts and serve immediately.

Cook's Tips
• For the best results, it is important that the broccoli is very fresh – it should be bright green and firm, not limp. Cut the florets into bite-size pieces, removing any woody stem.
• To toast pine nuts for sprinkling on top, heat a dry heavy frying pan, add the pine nuts and toss quickly over medium heat until they turn pale golden. Do not allow them to brown, otherwise they will taste bitter.

Variation
For a milder sauce you could omit the chilli. Instead, add some diced ham with the garlic to give extra flavour and texture.

Linguine with Pesto Sauce

Pesto, the famous Italian basil sauce, originates in Liguria, where the sea breezes are said to give the local basil a particularly fine flavour. Pesto is traditionally made with a pestle and mortar, but it is easier to make in a food processor or blender.

Serves 5–6
65g/2½ oz fresh basil leaves
3–4 garlic cloves, peeled
45ml/3 tbsp pine nuts
75ml/5 tbsp extra virgin olive oil
50g/2oz/scant ¾ cup freshly grated Parmesan cheese
60ml/4 tbsp freshly grated Pecorino cheese
salt and ground black pepper
500g/1¼ lb linguine pasta

1 Place the basil leaves, garlic cloves, pine nuts, 2.5ml/½ tsp salt and olive oil in a food processor or blender and process until smooth. Transfer to a bowl.

2 Stir in the Parmesan and Pecorino cheeses and stir to combine thoroughly. Season to taste with salt and pepper.

3 Bring a large pan of lightly salted water the boil and cook the linguine until it is *al dente*. Just before draining the pasta, take out about 60ml/4 tbsp of the cooking water and stir it into the pesto sauce.

4 Drain the pasta and toss with the sauce. Serve at once, with extra cheese if wished.

Cook's Tip
• Pecorino cheese is not as widely available as Parmesan. If you cannot find it, use all Parmesan instead. For the best flavour, buy a piece of Parmesan and grate it yourself.
• Pesto sauce is handy to have as a standby in the freezer. It's a good idea to freeze the pesto in an ice cube tray so that you can use as little or as much as you like. Freeze at the end of step 1, before adding the cheese.

Penne Energy 397kcal/1678kJ; Protein 17.3g; Carbohydrate 68.3g, of which sugars 6g; Fat 7.9g, of which saturates 0.8g; Cholesterol 0mg; Calcium 114mg; Fibre 5.6g; Sodium 24mg.
Linguine Energy 476kcal/2000kJ; Protein 17.6g; Carbohydrate 56.1g, of which sugars 2.9g; Fat 21.7g, of which saturates 5.6g; Cholesterol 18mg; Calcium 258mg; Fibre 2.6g; Sodium 217mg.

Spaghetti with Herb Sauce

Fresh herbs make a wonderful aromatic sauce – the heat from the pasta releases their flavour to delicious effect. Serve with chunks of warm ciabatta.

Serves 4
50g/2oz chopped mixed fresh
  herbs such as parsley, basil
  and thyme
2 garlic cloves, crushed
60ml/4 tbsp pine nuts, toasted
150ml/¼ pint/⅔ cup olive oil
350g/12oz dried spaghetti
60ml/4 tbsp freshly grated
  Parmesan cheese
salt and ground black pepper
fresh basil leaves, to garnish

1 Put the herbs, garlic and half the pine nuts into a food processor or blender. With the machine running slowly, add the oil and process to form a thick purée.

2 Bring a large pan of lightly salted water to the boil and cook the spaghetti until *al dente*. Drain thoroughly.

3 Transfer the herb purée to a large warm bowl, then add the spaghetti and Parmesan. Toss well to coat the pasta with the sauce. Season with salt and pepper.

4 Sprinkle the remaining pine nuts and the basil leaves over the pasta and serve immediately.

> **Cook's Tip**
> When cooking long strands of pasta like spaghetti, drop one end of the pasta into the boiling water and, as it softens, push it down gently until it bends in the middle and is completely immersed. Refer to the packet instructions for cooking times as these can vary from type to type. As a general rule, dried pasta needs 8–10 minutes. Do not be tempted to overcook pasta; it should be cooked until al dente, *that is, until is it is tender but still firm to the bite.* Always test pasta for doneness just before you think it should be ready, to avoid overcooking.

Tagliatelle with Saffron Mussels

Mussels bathed in a delicate saffron and cream sauce are served with tagliatelle for a simple, yet sophisticated, lunch or supper dish.

Serves 4
1.8kg/4–4½lb live mussels in
  the shell
150ml/¼ pint/⅔ cup dry white
  wine
2 shallots, finely chopped
350g/12oz dried tagliatelle
25g/1oz/2 tbsp butter
2 garlic cloves, crushed
250ml/8fl oz/1 cup double
  (heavy) cream
large pinch of saffron threads
1 egg yolk
salt and ground black pepper
30ml/2 tbsp chopped fresh
  parsley, to garnish

1 Scrub the mussels well under cold running water. Remove the "beards" and discard any mussels that are open.

2 Place the mussels in a large pan with the white wine and chopped shallots. Cover with a tight-fitting lid and cook over high heat for 5–8 minutes, shaking the pan occasionally, until the mussels have opened.

3 Drain the mussels, reserving the cooking liquid. Discard any mussels that remain closed. Shell all but a few of the mussels and keep warm. Bring the reserved cooking liquid to the boil, then reduce by half. Strain into a jug (cup).

4 Bring a large pan of lightly salted water to the boil and cook the tagliatelle for 10 minutes or until *al dente*.

5 Meanwhile, melt the butter in a frying pan and fry the garlic for 1 minute. Pour in the reduced mussel liquid, cream and saffron threads. Heat gently until the sauce thickens slightly.

6 Remove the pan from the heat and stir in the egg yolk and shelled mussels. Season to taste with salt and pepper.

7 Drain the tagliatelle and transfer to warmed serving bowls. Spoon the sauce over and sprinkle with chopped parsley. Garnish with the mussels in shells and serve immediately.

Spaghetti Energy 699kcal/2924kJ; Protein 18.9g; Carbohydrate 65.8g, of which sugars 3.8g; Fat 41.9g, of which saturates 7.5g; Cholesterol 15mg; Calcium 229mg; Fibre 3.5g; Sodium 171mg.
Tagliatelle Energy 803kcal/3366kJ; Protein 34.8g; Carbohydrate 67.6g, of which sugars 5.3g; Fat 43.1g, of which saturates 24.7g; Cholesterol 152mg; Calcium 339mg; Fibre 3.3g; Sodium 335mg.

Macaroni Cheese with Mushrooms

An old favourite is given a new twist with the addition of mushrooms and a light sprinkling of pine nuts. It is finished off under the grill to give a glorious golden top.

Serves 4
450g/1lb/4 cups quick-cooking
   dried elbow macaroni
45ml/3 tbsp olive oil
225g/8oz button (white)
   mushrooms, sliced
2 fresh thyme sprigs
50g/2oz/4 tbsp plain
   (all-purpose) flour
1 vegetable stock cube
600ml/1 pint/2½ cups milk
2.5ml/½ tsp celery salt
5ml/1 tsp Dijon mustard
175g/6oz/1½ cups grated
   Cheddar cheese
25g/1oz/⅓ cup freshly grated
   Parmesan cheese
25g/1oz/¼ cup pine nuts
salt and ground black pepper

1 Bring a large pan of lightly salted water to the boil and cook the macaroni until *al dente*.

2 Meanwhile, heat the oil in a heavy pan, add the mushrooms and thyme, cover and cook over gentle heat for 2–3 minutes. Stir in the flour and remove from the heat. Add the stock cube and stir continuously until evenly blended. Stir in the milk a little at a time, stirring after each addition.

3 Add the celery salt, mustard and Cheddar cheese and season to taste with salt and pepper. Stir to combine well, then simmer for about 1–2 minutes, stirring continuously, until the sauce has thickened.

4 Preheat the grill (broiler) to medium. Drain the macaroni well, toss into the sauce and turn into four individual dishes or one large flameproof gratin dish. Scatter with grated Parmesan cheese and pine nuts, then grill (broil) until brown and bubbly.

> **Variation**
> *Add 115g/4oz crisply fried bacon pieces and a handful of fresh spinach to the sauce just before adding the macaroni.*

Pasta Rapido with Parsley Pesto

This fresh, lively sauce will stir the appetite and pep up any pasta supper. Made with parsley and almonds, it makes a tasty change from the more familiar basil and pine nut pesto.

Serves 4–6
450g/1lb/4 cups dried pasta
75g/3oz/¾ cup whole almonds
50g/2oz/½ cup flaked (sliced)
   almonds toasted
25g/1oz/⅓ cup freshly grated
   Parmesan cheese
pinch of salt

For the sauce
40g/1½oz fresh flat leaf parsley
2 garlic cloves, crushed
45ml/3 tbsp olive oil
45ml/3 tbsp lemon juice
5ml/1 tsp sugar
250ml/8fl oz/1 cup boiling water

1 Bring a large pan of lightly salted water to the boil and cook the pasta until *al dente*.

2 Meanwhile, toast the whole and flaked almonds separately under a medium grill (broiler) until golden brown. Set the flaked almonds aside.

3 To make the sauce, chop the parsley finely in a food processor. Add the whole almonds and reduce to a fine consistency. Add the garlic, olive oil, lemon juice, sugar and water. Process to make a sauce.

4 Drain the pasta and transfer to a warmed serving bowl. Add half of the sauce and toss to combine well. (Keep the rest of the sauce for another dish.) Top with freshly grated Parmesan cheese and the reserved flaked almonds, and serve.

> **Cook's Tip**
> *The unused parsley pesto sauce will keep in a screw-top jar in the refrigerator for up to ten days. Serve it with any type of cooked pasta or try using the sauce as a topping for lightly cooked broccoli or grilled chicken thighs.*

Pasta Energy 688kcal/2894kJ; Protein 23.1g; Carbohydrate 87.3g, of which sugars 6.4g; Fat 29.9g, of which saturates 4.1g; Cholesterol 6mg; Calcium 199mg; Fibre 6.2g; Sodium 79mg.
Macaroni Energy 831kcal/3497kJ; Protein 35.2g; Carbohydrate 100.7g, of which sugars 11.4g; Fat 33.9g, of which saturates 14.2g; Cholesterol 58mg; Calcium 628mg; Fibre 4.4g; Sodium 456mg.

Pasta with Roasted Pepper Sauce

A touch of chilli powder gives this delicious pepper and tomato sauce a slight kick. Serve with a rocket salad for a tasty supper.

Serves 4

2 red (bell) peppers
2 yellow (bell) peppers
45ml/3 tbsp olive oil
1 onion, sliced
2 garlic cloves, crushed
2.5ml/½ tsp mild chilli powder
400g/14oz can chopped plum
    tomatoes
450g/1lb/4 cups dried pasta
    shells or spirals
salt and ground black pepper
freshly grated Parmesan cheese,
    to serve

1 Preheat the oven to 200°C/400°F/Gas 6. Place the peppers on a baking sheet and bake for about 20 minutes, or until they are beginning to char and blister. Alternatively, grill (broil) the peppers, turning them from time to time.

2 Rub the skins off the peppers under cold water, or place the charred peppers in a bowl, cover with kitchen paper and leave to cool for 10 minutes, then peel off the skins. Halve the skinned peppers, remove the seeds and roughly chop the flesh.

3 Heat the oil in a pan and cook the onion and garlic gently for 5 minutes, until soft and golden.

4 Stir in the chilli powder, cook for 2 minutes, then add the tomatoes and peppers. Bring to the boil and simmer for about 10–15 minutes, until slightly thickened and reduced. Season with salt and pepper to taste.

5 Bring a large pan of lightly salted water to the boil and cook the pasta until *al dente*. Drain well and toss with the sauce. Serve piping hot with lots of freshly grated Parmesan cheese.

> **Variation**
> *Add other vegetables such as French beans or courgettes (zucchini) or even chickpeas to make the dish more substantial.*

Stir-fried Vegetables with Pasta

This is a colourful oriental-style dish, easily prepared using pasta instead of Chinese noodles.

Serves 4

1 carrot
175g/6oz small courgettes
    (zucchini)
175g/6oz runner or other green
    beans
175g/6oz baby corn on the cob
450g/1lb dried ribbon pasta such
    as tagliatelle
pinch of salt
30ml/2 tbsp corn oil, plus extra
    for tossing the pasta
1cm/½ in piece fresh root ginger,
    peeled and finely chopped
2 garlic cloves, finely chopped
90ml/6 tbsp yellow bean sauce
6 spring onions (scallions), sliced
    into 2.5cm/1in lengths
30ml/2 tbsp dry sherry
5ml/1 tsp sesame seeds

1 Slice the carrot and courgettes diagonally into chunks. Slice the beans diagonally, then cut the baby corn on the cob diagonally in half.

2 Bring a large pan of lightly salted water to the boil and cook the pasta until *al dente*. Drain, then rinse under hot water. Toss in a little oil.

3 Heat 30ml/2 tbsp oil in a wok or frying pan until smoking and add the ginger and garlic. Stir-fry for 30 seconds, then add the carrots, courgettes and beans.

4 Stir-fry for 3–4 minutes then stir in the yellow bean sauce. Stir-fry for 2 minutes, add the spring onions, sherry and pasta and stir-fry for a further 1 minute until piping hot. Sprinkle with sesame seeds and serve immediately.

> **Variation**
> *You can vary the vegetables as you wish. Try strips of red (bell) pepper, sugar snap peas, button mushrooms and beansprouts. Make sure the wok is very hot before adding the vegetables.*

Pasta Energy 537kcal/2273kJ; Protein 16.1g; Carbohydrate 98.9g, of which sugars 18.3g; Fat 11.3g, of which saturates 1.7g; Cholesterol 0mg; Calcium 53mg; Fibre 7.3g; Sodium 20mg.
Stir-fried Vegetables Energy 560kcal/2370kJ; Protein 21.6g; Carbohydrate 100g, of which sugars 8g; Fat 9.1g, of which saturates 1.3g; Cholesterol 0mg; Calcium 86mg; Fibre 7.5g; Sodium 513mg.

Tagliatelle with Gorgonzola Sauce

Gorgonzola, the Italian creamy blue cheese, is used to create a mouthwatering sauce for pasta. Serve with a mixed green salad as a foil to the richness of the dish.

Serves 4

25g/1oz/2 tbsp butter, plus extra
  for tossing the pasta
225g/8oz Gorgonzola cheese
150ml/¼ pint/⅔ cup double
  (heavy) or whipping cream
30ml/2 tbsp dry vermouth
5ml/1 tsp cornflour (cornstarch)
30ml/1 tbsp chopped fresh sage
450g/1lb dried tagliatelle
salt and ground black pepper
sage leaves, to garnish (optional)

1 Melt the butter in a heavy pan (it needs to be thick-based to prevent the cheese from burning). Stir in 175g/6oz/1½ cups crumbled Gorgonzola cheese and stir over very gentle heat for 2–3 minutes, until the cheese has melted.

2 Pour in the cream, vermouth and cornflour, whisking well to amalgamate. Stir in the chopped sage, then season to taste with salt and pepper. Cook, whisking all the time, until the sauce boils and thickens. Set aside.

3 Bring a large pan of lightly salted water to the boil and cook the tagliatelle until al dente. Drain well and toss with a little butter to coat evenly.

4 Reheat the sauce gently, whisking well. Divide the pasta among four serving bowls, top with the sauce and sprinkle over the remaining cheese. Garnish with sage leaves, if using, then serve immediately.

Cook's Tip
If you do not have vermouth, you can use a good quality dry sherry in its place very successfully. The Gorgonzola can be substituted by another well-flavoured, creamy blue cheese such as Danish Blue or Pipo Crème.

Rigatoni with Garlic Crumbs

A spicy treat: pasta tubes coated in a chilli-flavoured tomato sauce, topped with crunchy garlicky crumbs.

Serves 4–6

45ml/3 tbsp olive oil
2 shallots, chopped
8 streaky (fatty) bacon rashers
  (strips), chopped
10ml/2 tsp crushed dried chillies
400g/14oz can chopped
  tomatoes with herbs
6 slices white bread, crusts
  removed
115g/4oz/½ cup butter
2 garlic cloves, chopped
450g/1lb/4 cups dried rigatoni
salt and ground black pepper
fresh herbs sprigs, to garnish

1 Heat the oil in a pan and fry the shallots and bacon gently for 6–8 minutes until golden. Add the dried chillies and chopped tomatoes, half-cover with a lid and simmer for about 20 minutes, stirring occasionally.

2 Meanwhile, place the bread in a blender or food processor and process to fine crumbs. Heat the butter in a frying pan and stir-fry the garlic and breadcrumbs until golden and crisp. (Be careful not to let the crumbs catch and burn.)

3 Bring a large pan of lightly salted water to the boil and cook the rigatoni until al dente. Drain well.

4 Toss the pasta with the tomato sauce and divide among four bowls. Sprinkle with the crumbs and garnish with herbs.

Cook's Tip
To keep the breadcrumbs crisp and dry after frying, drain them on kitchen paper and place in a low oven until ready to use.

Variation
To make this dish suitable for vegetarians, leave out the bacon, or replace it with sliced mushrooms.

Tagliatelle Energy 746kcal/3131kJ; Protein 26.1g; Carbohydrate 86g, of which sugars 5.2g; Fat 34.7g, of which saturates 24.2g; Cholesterol 58mg; Calcium 334mg; Fibre 3.3g; Sodium 750mg.
Rigatoni Energy 645kcal/2708kJ; Protein 18.4g; Carbohydrate 75g, of which sugars 6.1g; Fat 32.3g, of which saturates 14.1g; Cholesterol 65mg; Calcium 68mg; Fibre 3.5g; Sodium 771mg.

Pasta Spirals with Pepperoni

A warming supper dish, this tangy pepperoni and tomato sauce could be served on any type of pasta.

Serves 4
1 red (bell) pepper
1 green (bell) pepper
30ml/2 tbsp olive oil, plus extra
   for tossing the pasta
1 onion, chopped
800g/1¾ lb canned chopped
   tomatoes
30ml/2 tbsp tomato purée
   (paste)
10ml/2 tsp paprika
175g/6oz pepperoni or chorizo
45ml/3 tbsp chopped fresh
   parsley
450g/1lb/4 cups dried long pasta
   spirals
salt and ground black pepper

1 Cut the peppers in half, then remove the seeds and cores. Cut the flesh into dice.

2 Heat the oil in a pan, add the onion and cook for about 2 minutes, until beginning to colour. Stir in the peppers, tomatoes, tomato purée and paprika, then bring to the boil and simmer uncovered for 15–20 minutes, until the sauce is reduced and thickened.

3 Slice the sausage and stir into the sauce with about half the chopped parsley. Season to taste with salt and pepper and continue to simmer until the sausage is cooked through.

4 While the sauce is simmering, cook the pasta in plenty of lightly salted boiling water until *al dente*. Drain well.

5 Toss the pasta with the remaining parsley mixed with a little extra olive oil. Divide the pasta among warmed bowls and top with the sauce. Serve immediately.

> **Cook's Tip**
> *All types of sausage are suitable to include in this dish. If using fresh, raw sausages, cook them first, then cut up and add to the sauce, or cook thoroughly with the onion in step 2.*

Pasta with Tomatoes & Rocket

This pretty-coloured pasta dish relies for its success on the slightly peppery taste of the rocket. It is deliciously fresh tasting. Serve it with chunks of rustic bread and a glass of dry white wine for a perfect lunch dish.

Serves 4
450g/1lb/4 cups dried conchiglie
450g/1lb ripe cherry tomatoes
75g/3oz fresh rocket
45ml/3 tbsp olive oil
salt and ground black pepper
Parmesan cheese shavings,
   to serve

1 Bring a large pan of lightly salted water to the boil and cook the pasta until *al dente*.

2 Meanwhile, halve the tomatoes. Wash and dry the rocket.

3 Heat the oil in a large pan and gently cook the tomatoes for barely 1 minute. The tomatoes should only just be heated through and not be allowed to disintegrate.

4 Drain the pasta and add to the pan, then add the rocket. (Roughly tear any rocket leaves that are over-large.) Carefully stir to mix and heat through. Season to taste with salt and pepper. Serve hot, with plenty of shaved Parmesan cheese.

> **Cook's Tip**
> *Rocket has a distinctive peppery taste that is useful for adding character to all sorts of salad dishes. It is increasingly available in supermarkets. However, if you have difficulty finding it, why not grow your own: it is very easy to grow in the garden or even in a window-box, and this will ensure that you have a plentiful supply to hand.*

> **Variation**
> *Add a crushed garlic clove to the pan with the tomatoes, or just add a dash of balsamic vinegar for added flavour.*

Tomatoes & Rocket Energy 483kcal/2044kJ; Protein 14.8g; Carbohydrate 87.2g, of which sugars 7.5g; Fat 10.8g, of which saturates 1.5g; Cholesterol 0mg; Calcium 68mg; Fibre 4.8g; Sodium 40mg.
Pasta Spirals Energy 610kcal/2579kJ; Protein 22.5g; Carbohydrate 100.4g, of which sugars 17.9g; Fat 16g, of which saturates 3.6g; Cholesterol 50mg; Calcium 87mg; Fibre 8g; Sodium 402mg.

Pasta Bows with Smoked Salmon

For a quick dish with a touch of luxury, this recipe is hard to beat – a divine combination of creamy smoked salmon sauce and pretty pasta shapes.

Serves 4
6 spring onions (scallions), sliced
50g/2oz/¼ cup butter
90ml/6 tbsp dry white wine or vermouth
450ml/¾ pint/scant 2 cups double (heavy) cream
a pinch of freshly grated nutmeg
225g/8oz smoked salmon
30ml/2 tbsp chopped fresh dill or 15ml/1 tbsp dried dill
freshly squeezed lemon juice
450g/1lb/4 cups dried farfalle
salt and ground black pepper

1 Slice the spring onions finely. Melt the butter in a pan and fry the spring onions for about 1 minute until they begin to soften.

2 Add the wine or vermouth and boil hard to reduce to about 30ml/2 tbsp. Stir in the cream and add salt, pepper and nutmeg to taste. Bring to the boil and simmer for about 2–3 minutes, until slightly thickened.

3 Cut the smoked salmon into 2.5cm/1in squares and stir into the sauce with the dill. Taste and add a little lemon juice. Keep the sauce warm.

4 Bring a large pan of lightly salted water to the boil and cook the pasta until al dente. Drain well and toss with the sauce.

Cook's Tip
Smoked salmon trimmings are perfectly adequate for this dish.

Variation
This dish could also be prepared with canned salmon, broken into bitesize pieces, if you prefer.

Pasta with Tuna & Capers

A piquant sauce of tuna, capers, anchovies and fresh basil combines brilliantly with pasta, creating an easy dish full of punchy flavours.

Serves 4
400g/14oz can tuna in oil
30ml/2 tbsp olive oil
2 garlic cloves, crushed
800g/1¾ lb canned chopped tomatoes
6 canned anchovy fillets, drained
30ml/2 tbsp capers in vinegar, drained
30ml/2 tbsp chopped fresh basil
450g/1lb/4 cups dried garganelle, penne or rigatoni
salt and ground black pepper
fresh basil sprigs, to garnish

1 Drain the oil from the tuna into a pan, add the olive oil and heat gently until it stops spitting.

2 Add the garlic and fry until golden. Stir in the tomatoes and simmer for 25 minutes until thickened.

3 Flake the tuna and cut the anchovies in half. Stir into the sauce with the capers and chopped basil. Season to taste with salt and pepper.

4 Bring a large pan of lightly salted water to the boil and cook the pasta until al dente. Drain well and toss with the sauce. Garnish with fresh basil sprigs and serve immediately.

Cook's Tip
Tubular pasta is particularly good with this sauce as the tasty bits get trapped in the tube cavities. Other hollow shapes, such as conchiglie (shells) and lumache (snails), will also work well.

Variation
This piquant sauce could be made without the addition of tomatoes – just heat the oil, add the other ingredients and heat through gently before tossing with the pasta.

Tuna & Capers Energy 666kcal/2817kJ; Protein 43.1g; Carbohydrate 89.6g, of which sugars 9.9g; Fat 17.6g, of which saturates 2.8g; Cholesterol 53mg; Calcium 68mg; Fibre 5.3g; Sodium 488mg.
Pasta Bows Energy 1144kcal/4770kJ; Protein 30g; Carbohydrate 86.5g, of which sugars 6.8g; Fat 75.3g, of which saturates 44.8g; Cholesterol 201mg; Calcium 104mg; Fibre 3.5g; Sodium 1165mg.

Pasta with Prawns & Feta Cheese

Pasta tubes tossed with fresh prawns and sharp-tasting feta cheese is a winning combination. Serve with a mixed salad for an impressive light meal.

Serves 4

450g/1lb/4 cups medium raw
   prawns (shrimp)
6 spring onions (scallions)
50g/2oz/4 tbsp butter
225g/8oz feta cheese
small bunch fresh chives
450g/1lb/4 cups dried penne,
   garganelle or rigatoni
salt and ground black pepper

1 Remove the heads from the prawns by twisting and pulling off. Peel the prawns and discard the shells. With a sharp knife, remove the black intestinal vein running down the back of larger prawns and discard. Chop the spring onions.

2 Melt the butter in a frying pan and cook the prawns until they turn pink, then add the spring onions and cook gently for a further 1 minute.

3 Cut the feta cheese into 1cm/½in dice. Stir the cheese into the prawn mixture and season to taste with pepper.

4 Cut the chives into 2.5cm/1in lengths and stir half into the prawn mixture.

5 Bring a large pan of lightly salted water to the boil and cook the pasta until al dente. Drain well, pile into a warmed serving dish and top with the sauce. Scatter with the remaining chives and serve immediately.

Cook's Tips
• Substitute goat's cheese for the feta cheese if you like; prepare the dish in the same way.
• If raw prawns are unavailable, use cooked prawns but cook the spring onions first, then add the prawns to heat through.

Tagliatelle with Prosciutto & Parmesan

Consisting of a few prime Italian ingredients, this pasta dish is simplicity itself to make yet tastes wonderful. Serve with a tomato salad and chunks of ciabatta.

Serves 4

115g/4oz prosciutto
450g/1lb tagliatelle
75g/3oz/6 tbsp butter
50g/2oz/1½ cup grated Parmesan
   cheese
salt and ground black pepper
a few fresh sage leaves, to garnish

1 Cut the prosciutto into strips of the same width as the tagliatelle. Bring a large pan of lightly salted water to the boil and cook the tagliatelle until al dente.

2 Meanwhile, melt the butter gently in a pan, stir in the prosciutto strips and heat through over very gently heat, being careful not to let them colour.

3 Drain the tagliatelle well and pile into a warm serving dish. Sprinkle all the Parmesan cheese over the top.

4 Pour the buttery prosciutto over the top of the tagliatelle and Parmesan. Season well with pepper and garnish with the sage leaves.

Cook's Tips
• Buy Parmesan cheese in a block and grate it yourself. The flavour is far superior to that of ready-grated Parmesan cheese.
• Prosciutto, the Italian cured ham, is available from Italian delicatessens and supermarkets. The famous Parma ham is a superior type, coming from the Parma region of Italy.
• Both fresh and dried tagliatelle are good with this sauce. For a change, use green spinach-flavoured tagliatelle, or try a mix of green and white ribbons – bundles of these are called paglia e fieno, which means "straw and hay" in Italian.

Prawns & Feta Energy 707kcal/2980kJ; Protein 42.5g; Carbohydrate 84.7g, of which sugars 5.1g; Fat 24.4g, of which saturates 14.6g; Cholesterol 285mg; Calcium 328mg; Fibre 3.5g; Sodium 1104mg.
Tagliatelle Energy 612kcal/2576kJ; Protein 23.8g; Carbohydrate 83.8g, of which sugars 4.1g; Fat 22.5g, of which saturates 12.9g; Cholesterol 69mg; Calcium 184mg; Fibre 3.3g; Sodium 598mg.

Cannelloni al Forno

This recipe provides a lighter, healthier alternative to the usual beef-filled, béchamel-coated version.

Serves 4–6
450g/1lb boned chicken breast, skinned and cooked
225g/8oz mushrooms
2 garlic cloves, crushed
30ml/2 tbsp chopped fresh parsley
15ml/1 tbsp chopped fresh tarragon
1 egg, beaten
squeeze of lemon juice
12–18 cannelloni tubes
butter, for greasing
1 jar passata (bottled strained tomatoes)
50g/2oz/scant ¾ cup freshly grated Parmesan cheese
salt and ground black pepper
fresh parsley sprigs, to garnish

1 Preheat the oven to 200°C/400°F/Gas 6. Place the chicken in a food processor and blend until finely minced. Transfer to a bowl and set aside.

2 Place the mushrooms, garlic, parsley and tarragon in the food processor and blend until finely minced. Beat the mushroom mixture into the chicken with the egg, and season with salt and pepper and lemon juice to taste.

3 Bring a large pan of lightly salted water to the boil and cook the cannelloni until al dente. Drain well on a clean dish towel.

4 Place the filling in a piping bag fitted with a large plain nozzle. Use this to fill each tube of cannelloni.

5 Lay the filled cannelloni tightly together in a single layer in a buttered shallow ovenproof dish. Spoon over the passata and sprinkle with Parmesan cheese. Bake in the oven for 30 minutes or until brown and bubbling. Garnish with sprigs of parsley.

> **Cook's Tip**
> *Passata is sieved (strained) ripe tomatoes and is a convenient store-cupboard item. It is available from larger supermarkets.*

Fettuccine all'Alfredo

A classic from Rome, this dish is simply pasta tossed with cream, butter and freshly grated Parmesan cheese. It makes a great supper dish, served with a crisp green salad to cut through the richness.

Serves 4
25g/1oz/2 tbsp butter
150ml/¼ pint/⅔ cup double (heavy) cream, plus 60ml/4 tbsp extra
450g/1lb dried fettuccine
50g/2oz/scant ¾ cup freshly grated Parmesan cheese, plus extra to serve
pinch of freshly grated nutmeg
salt and ground black pepper

1 Place the butter and 150ml/¼ pint/⅔ cup cream in a heavy pan. Bring to the boil, then simmer for 1 minute until the mixture has slightly thickened.

2 Bring a large pan of lightly salted water to the boil and cook the fettuccine until it is al dente – it should still be a little firm to the bite.

3 Drain the pasta very thoroughly and return to the pan with the cream sauce.

4 Place the pan on the heat and turn the pasta in the sauce to coat it evenly.

5 Add the remaining cream, the Parmesan cheese, salt and pepper to taste and a little grated nutmeg. Toss until well coated and heated through. Serve immediately with some extra grated Parmesan cheese sprinkled on top.

> **Variations**
> *For a little extra colour, fresh or frozen peas make an attractive addition to the sauce. You could also try stirring in thin strips of ham if you are not catering for vegetarians. The fettuccine ribbons can be replaced by spaghetti very successfully.*

Cannelloni Energy 375kcal/1589kJ; Protein 31.8g; Carbohydrate 51.8g, of which sugars 4.5g; Fat 6g, of which saturates 2.4g; Cholesterol 93mg; Calcium 151mg; Fibre 3.2g; Sodium 308mg.
Fettuccine Energy 674kcal/2830kJ; Protein 19.1g; Carbohydrate 84g, of which sugars 4.4g; Fat 31.4g, of which saturates 18.6g; Cholesterol 77mg; Calcium 198mg; Fibre 3.3g; Sodium 186mg.

Onion & Gorgonzola Pizzas

These small pizzas are good for snacks or party food.

Serves 4
1 quantity Basic Pizza Dough (see below)
30ml/2 tbsp garlic oil

2 small red onions
150g/5oz Gorgonzola cheese, rind removed and diced
2 garlic cloves, cut into strips lengthways
10ml/2 tsp chopped fresh sage
pinch of black pepper

1 Preheat the oven to 220°C/425°F/Gas 7. Divide the dough into eight pieces and roll out to small ovals about 5mm/¼in thick. Place well apart on two greased baking sheets and prick with a fork. Brush well with 15ml/1 tbsp of the garlic oil.

2 Halve, then slice the onions into thin wedges. Scatter over the pizza bases. Sprinkle with the cheese, then the garlic and sage. Drizzle the remaining oil on top and grind over plenty of pepper. Bake for 10–15 minutes until crisp and golden.

Basic Pizza Dough

Making your own pizza base is easy – and it tastes great.

Makes one 25–30cm/10–12in round pizza base
175g/6oz/1½ cups strong white flour

1.25ml/¼ tsp salt
5ml/1 tsp easy-blend (rapid-rise) dried yeast
120–150ml/4–5fl oz/½–¾ cup lukewarm water
15ml/1 tbsp olive oil

1 Sift the flour and salt into a large mixing bowl and stir in the yeast. Make a well in the centre and pour in the water and oil. Mix to a soft dough. Knead the dough on a lightly floured board for 10 minutes until smooth and elastic.

2 Place in a greased bowl, cover with clear film (plastic wrap) and leave to double in size for about 1 hour. Turn out on to a floured surface; knead gently for 2–3 minutes. Use as required.

Feta & Roasted Garlic Pizzettes

These pizzettes are for garlic lovers. Mash down the cloves as you eat them – they should be meltingly soft and sweet-tasting.

Serves 4
1 garlic bulb, unpeeled
45ml/3 tbsp olive oil
1 red (bell) pepper, seeded and quartered
1 yellow (bell) pepper, seeded and quartered
2 plum tomatoes
1 quantity Basic Pizza Dough (see below left)
175g/6oz/1½ cups crumbled feta cheese
pinch of black pepper
15–30ml/1–2 tbsp chopped fresh oregano, to garnish

1 Preheat the oven to 220°C/425°F/Gas 7. Break the garlic into cloves, discarding the outer papery layers. Toss in 15ml/1 tbsp of the olive oil.

2 Place the peppers skin-side up on a baking sheet and grill (broil), turning them until the skins are evenly charred. Place in a covered bowl for 10 minutes, then peel off the skins. Cut the flesh into strips.

3 Make a slash in the skin of each tomato, then put them in a bowl and pour over boiling water. Leave for 30 seconds, then plunge into cold water. Peel, seed and roughly chop the flesh.

4 Divide the pizza dough into four pieces and roll out each one on a lightly floured surface to an equal-sized circle of about 13cm/5in diameter. Place the dough circles well apart on two greased baking sheets, then push up the dough edges to form a thin rim around the dough circles.

5 Brush the dough circles with half the remaining oil and scatter over the chopped tomatoes. Top with the peppers, crumbled feta cheese and garlic cloves. Drizzle over the remaining oil and season to taste with pepper.

6 Bake in the oven for 15–20 minutes until crisp and golden. Garnish with chopped oregano and serve immediately.

Onion Energy 371kcal/1550kJ; Protein 12.5g; Carbohydrate 38g, of which sugars 3.5g; Fat 19.8g, of which saturates 8.5g; Cholesterol 28mg; Calcium 263mg; Fibre 2.2g; Sodium 461mg.
Pizza Dough Energy 696kcal/2944kJ; Protein 16.4g; Carbohydrate 136g, of which sugars 2.6g; Fat 13.3g, of which saturates 1.9g; Cholesterol 0mg; Calcium 245mg; Fibre 5.4g; Sodium 5mg.
Feta & Garlic Energy 419kcal/1751kJ; Protein 14.1g; Carbohydrate 45.9g, of which sugars 8.6g; Fat 21.1g, of which saturates 7.8g; Cholesterol 31mg; Calcium 234mg; Fibre 4.3g; Sodium 640mg.

Wild Mushroom Pizzas

With their delicate earthy flavour, wild mushrooms make a delicious topping for these little pizzas. Serve as an unusual starter or for a stylish light meal.

Serves 4

45ml/3 tbsp olive oil
350g/12oz fresh mixed wild
  mushrooms, washed and sliced
2 shallots, chopped
2 garlic cloves, finely chopped
30ml/2 tbsp chopped fresh mixed
  thyme and flat leaf parsley
1 quantity Basic Pizza Dough
  (see page 158)
40g/1½ oz/generous ¼ cup
  grated Gruyère cheese
30ml/2 tbsp freshly grated
  Parmesan cheese
salt and ground black pepper

1 Preheat the oven to 220°C/425°F/Gas 7. Heat 30ml/2 tbsp of the oil in a frying pan and fry the mushrooms, shallots and garlic over medium heat, stirring occasionally, until all the juices have evaporated.

2 Stir in half the herbs and season with salt and pepper then set aside to cool.

3 Divide the dough into four pieces and roll out each one on a lightly floured surface to a 13cm/5in circle. Place well apart on two greased baking sheets, then push up the dough edges to form a thin rim around the dough circles.

4 Brush the pizza bases with the remaining oil and spoon the wild mushrooms on top. Mix together the Gruyère and Parmesan, then sprinkle over the mushroom mixture.

5 Bake the pizza for 15–20 minutes until crisp and golden. Remove from the oven and scatter over the remaining herbs.

Cook's Tip
Fresh wild mushrooms add a distinctive flavour to the topping, but if they are unavailable, a mixture of cultivated mushrooms, such as shiitake, oyster and chestnut, would do just as well.

Mussel & Leek Pizzas

Serve these lovely little seafood pizzas with a crisp green salad for a light lunch.

Serves 4

450g/1lb live mussels in the shell
120ml/4fl oz/½ cup dry white
  wine
1 quantity Basic Pizza Dough (see
  page 158)
15ml/1 tbsp olive oil
50g/2oz Gruyère cheese
50g/2oz mozzarella cheese
2 small leeks, thinly sliced
salt and ground black pepper

1 Preheat the oven to 220°C/425°F/Gas 7. Place the mussels in a bowl of cold water to soak, then scrub well. Remove the beards, and discard any mussels that are open.

2 Place the mussels in a pan. Pour over the dry white wine, cover with a tight-fitting lid and cook over high heat, shaking the pan occasionally, for 5–10 minutes until the mussels open.

3 Drain off the cooking liquid. Remove the mussels from their shells, discarding any that remain closed. Leave to cool.

4 Divide the dough into four pieces and roll out each one on a lightly floured surface to a 13cm/5in circle. Place well apart on two greased baking sheets, then push up the dough edges to form a thin rim around the dough circles.

5 Brush the pizza bases with the oil. Grate the cheeses and sprinkle half evenly over the bases. Arrange the leeks over the cheese. Bake for 10 minutes, then remove from the oven.

6 Arrange the mussels on top. Season with salt and pepper and sprinkle over the remaining cheese. Bake for a further 5–10 minutes until crisp and golden. Serve immediately.

Cook's Tip
Frozen or canned mussels can also be used but will give a different flavour and texture to these pizzettes.

Mussel & Leek Energy 343kcal/1441kJ; Protein 16.3g; Carbohydrate 35.6g, of which sugars 2g; Fat 13.6g, of which saturates 5.5g; Cholesterol 33mg; Calcium 280mg; Fibre 2.5g; Sodium 214mg.
Mushroom Energy 340kcal/1425kJ; Protein 11.4g; Carbohydrate 35.6g, of which sugars 1.7g; Fat 17.8g, of which saturates 5.5g; Cholesterol 17mg; Calcium 234mg; Fibre 2.5g; Sodium 160mg.

Ham, Pepper & Mozzarella Pizzas

Succulent roasted peppers, salty proscuitto and creamy mozzarella make a delicious topping for these pizzas.

Serves 2
1 red (bell) pepper
1 yellow (bell) pepper
4 thick slices ciabatta bread
4 slices proscuitto, cut into thick strips
75g/3oz mozzarella cheese
ground black pepper
tiny fresh basil leaves, to garnish

1 Place the peppers skin-side up on a baking sheet and grill (broil), turning them until the skins are evenly charred. Place in a bowl, cover with a cloth and leave for 10 minutes. Peel the skins from the peppers and remove the seeds and cores. Cut the flesh into thick strips.

2 Lightly toast the slices of ciabatta bread on both sides until they are golden.

3 Arrange the strips of pepper on the toasted bread with the strips of proscuitto.

4 Thinly slice the mozzarella and arrange on top. Grind over plenty of pepper. Place under a hot grill (broiler) for 2–3 minutes until the cheese is bubbling.

5 Garnish each pizza with basil leaves and serve immediately.

Cook's Tip
For added flavour, cut a garlic clove in half and rub the cut side over the toasted bread before adding the topping.

Variation
Try using pieces of sun-dried tomato in oil instead of the peppers and use Emmenthal cheese instead of mozzarella.

Fruity French Bread Pizza

Using a base of French bread, these pizzas are quick and easy to make. Perfect for all the family.

Serves 4
2 small baguettes
1 jar ready-made tomato sauce or pizza topping
75g/3oz sliced cooked ham
4 rings canned pineapple, drained and chopped
1/2 small green (bell) pepper, seeded and cut into thin strips
75g/3oz mature Cheddar cheese
salt and ground black pepper

1 Preheat the oven to 200°C/400°F/Gas 6. Cut the baguettes in half lengthways and toast the outsides under a grill (broiler) until crisp and golden.

2 Spread the tomato sauce or pizza topping over the toasted baguette halves.

3 Cut the ham into strips and arrange on the baguettes with the pineapple and pepper. Season with salt and pepper.

4 Grate the Cheddar and sprinkle over the top of the pineapple and pepper. Bake in the oven for 15–20 minutes until crisp and golden. Serve immediately.

Cook's Tip
These pizzas may be grilled (broiled) instead of baked in the oven. Cook them for the same length of time under a medium grill (broiler) but check that they do not burn.

Variation
If you have time, make your own tomato sauce. Soften a sliced garlic clove and small onion in olive oil. Add a handful of herbs and 400g/14oz can tomatoes with 15ml/1 tbsp sun-dried tomato paste and a splash of wine. Simmer for 30 minutes.

Ham, Pepper Energy 466kcal/1965kJ; Protein 26.3g; Carbohydrate 63.6g, of which sugars 14.2g; Fat 13.6g, of which saturates 6.4g; Cholesterol 45mg; Calcium 274mg; Fibre 5.1g; Sodium 1173mg.
French Bread Energy 420kcal/1779kJ; Protein 18.3g; Carbohydrate 67.4g, of which sugars 13g; Fat 10.1g, of which saturates 5.1g; Cholesterol 31mg; Calcium 281mg; Fibre 4g; Sodium 1056mg.

Marinara Pizza

The combination of garlic, good quality olive oil and oregano gives this pizza an unmistakably Italian flavour.

Serves 2–3
1 quantity Basic Pizza Dough
   (see page 158)

675g/1½ lb ripe plum tomatoes
60ml/4 tbsp extra virgin olive oil
4 garlic cloves, cut into slivers
15ml/1 tbsp chopped fresh
   oregano
salt and ground black pepper

1 Roll out the pizza dough to a 25–30cm/10–12in circle and place on a greased baking sheet. Push up the edge of the dough to form a thin rim around the dough circle.

2 Make a slash in the skin of each tomato, then put them all in a heatproof bowl and pour over boiling water. Leave for 30 seconds, then plunge the tomatoes into cold water. Peel and seed, then roughly chop the flesh.

3 Preheat the oven to 220°C/425°F/Gas 7. Heat 30ml/2 tbsp of the oil in a pan. Add the tomatoes and cook, stirring frequently, for about 5 minutes until soft.

4 Place the tomatoes in a metal sieve (strainer) and leave them to drain for about 5 minutes. Transfer the tomatoes to a food processor or blender and purée until smooth.

5 Brush the pizza base with half the remaining oil. Spoon over the tomatoes and sprinkle with garlic and oregano. Drizzle over the remaining oil and season to taste.

6 Bake for 15–20 minutes until crisp. Serve immediately.

> **Cook's Tip**
> Ready-made pizza bases are handy if you are short of time. They are available from most supermarkets and come in a range of sizes. It is useful to keep a few in the freezer.

Quattro Formaggi

Rich and cheesy, these individual pizzas are quick to make, and the aroma of melting cheese is irresistible.

Serves 4
1 quantity Basic Pizza Dough
   (see page 158)
15ml/1 tbsp garlic oil
½ small red onion, very thinly
   sliced

50g/2oz Dolcelatte cheese
50g/2oz mozzarella cheese
50g/2oz/½ cup grated Gruyère
   cheese
30ml/2 tbsp freshly grated
   Parmesan cheese
15ml/1 tbsp chopped fresh thyme
ground black pepper

1 Preheat the oven to 220°C/425°F/Gas 7. Divide the dough into four pieces and roll out each one on a lightly floured surface into a 13cm/5in circle. Place well apart on two greased baking sheets, then push up the dough edges to make a thin rim. Brush with garlic oil and top with the red onion.

2 Cut the Dolcelatte and mozzarella cheeses into dice and arrange over the bases. Mix together the Gruyère, Parmesan and thyme and sprinkle over the pizzas.

3 Grind plenty of pepper over the pizzas. Bake for 15–20 minutes until the base is crisp and golden and the cheeses are bubbling. Serve immediately.

> **Cook's Tip**
> To make garlic oil, put 3–4 peeled garlic cloves in a jar and pour in 120ml/4fl oz/½ cup olive oil. Cover tightly and store in the refrigerator for up to 1 month.

> **Variation**
> Any variety of cheese that melts readily can be used, but a mixture of soft and hard cheeses gives the best result.

Marinara Energy 415kcal/1742kJ; Protein 8.1g; Carbohydrate 54.5g, of which sugars 8.1g; Fat 19.8g, of which saturates 3g; Cholesterol 0mg; Calcium 100mg; Fibre 4.6g; Sodium 23mg.
Formaggi Energy 397kcal/1661kJ; Protein 14.6g; Carbohydrate 39.7g, of which sugars 3.9g; Fat 20.8g, of which saturates 9.3g; Cholesterol 37mg; Calcium 283mg; Fibre 2.3g; Sodium 405mg.

Rocket & Tomato Pizza

Peppery rocket leaves and aromatic basil add colour and flavour to this pizza.

Serves 2
10ml/2 tsp olive oil, plus extra
   for oiling and drizzling
1 garlic clove, crushed
150g/5oz/1 cup canned chopped
   tomatoes
2.5ml/½ tsp sugar
30ml/2 tbsp torn basil leaves
2 tomatoes, seeded and chopped

150g/5oz/⅔ cup mozzarella
   cheese, sliced
20g/¾oz/1 cup rocket leaves
rock salt and ground black pepper

For the pizza base
225g/8oz/2 cups strong white
   bread flour, sifted
5ml/1 tsp salt
2.5ml/½ tsp easy-blend
   (rapid-rise) dried yeast
15ml/1 tbsp olive oil
150ml/¼ pint/⅔ cup warm water

1 To make the pizza base, place the flour, salt and yeast in a bowl. Make a well in the centre and add the oil and warm water. Mix to form a soft dough.

2 Turn out the dough on to a lightly floured work surface and knead for 5 minutes. Cover with the upturned bowl and leave to rest for about 5 minutes, then knead for a further 5 minutes until the dough is smooth and elastic. Place in a lightly oiled bowl and cover with clear film (plastic wrap). Leave in a warm place for about 45 minutes until doubled in size.

3 Preheat the oven to 220°C/425°F/Gas 7. To make the topping, heat the oil in a frying pan and fry the garlic for 1 minute. Add the tomatoes and sugar and cook for 5–7 minutes until reduced and thickened. Stir in the basil and season to taste with salt and pepper. Set aside.

4 Knead the risen dough lightly, then roll out to form a rough 30cm/12in round. Place on a lightly oiled baking sheet and push up the edges of the dough to form a shallow, even rim. Spoon the tomato mixture over the pizza base, then top with the fresh tomatoes and mozzarella. Adjust the seasoning and drizzle with a little olive oil. Bake for 10–12 minutes until crisp and golden. Arrange the rocket over the pizza just before serving.

Four Seasons Pizza

The topping on this pizza is divided into four quarters, one for each "season", creating a colourful effect.

Serves 4
450g/1lb peeled plum tomatoes,
   weighed whole (or canned
   without their juice)
75ml/5 tbsp olive oil
115g/4oz mushrooms, thinly
   sliced
1 garlic clove, finely chopped

1 quantity Basic Pizza Dough
   (see page 158)
350g/12oz/scant 2½ cups diced
   mozzarella cheese
4 thin slices of ham, cut into
   5cm/2in squares
32 black olives, pitted and halved
8 artichoke hearts, preserved in
   oil, drained and cut in half
5ml/1 tsp oregano leaves, fresh or
   dried
salt and ground black pepper

1 Preheat the oven to 240°C/475°F/Gas 9 for at least 20 minutes before baking the pizza. Strain the tomatoes through the medium holes of a food mill placed over a bowl, scraping in all the pulp.

2 Heat 30ml/2 tbsp of the oil in a pan and lightly sauté the mushrooms. Stir in the garlic and set aside.

3 Roll out the pizza dough to a 25–30cm/10–12in circle and place on a greased baking sheet. Push up the edge of the dough to form a thin rim around the dough circle.

4 Spread the puréed tomatoes on the prepared pizza dough, up to the rim. Sprinkle evenly with the mozzarella cheese. Spread the mushrooms over one quarter of the pizza.

5 Arrange the ham on one quarter and the olives on another quarter. Arrange the artichoke hearts on the remaining quarter.

6 Sprinkle the whole of the pizza with oregano and season with salt and pepper. Sprinkle over the remaining olive oil. Immediately place the pizza in the oven and bake for about 15–20 minutes, or until the crust is golden brown and the topping is bubbling.

Rocket Energy 735Kcal/3087kJ; Protein 26.1g; Carbohydrate 93g, of which sugars 7.3g; Fat 31.3g, of which saturates 12.7g; Cholesterol 44mg; Calcium 459mg; Fibre 5.5g; Sodium 330mg.
Four Seasons Energy 586kcal/2442kJ; Protein 24.3g; Carbohydrate 37.9g, of which sugars 4.5g; Fat 38.5g, of which saturates 15.2g; Cholesterol 58mg; Calcium 410mg; Fibre 3.7g; Sodium 1080mg.

Fiorentina Pizza

Fresh spinach is the star ingredient of this pizza. A grating of nutmeg heightens its flavour.

Serves 2–3

1 quantity Basic Pizza Dough (see page 158)
175g/6oz/1½ cups fresh spinach
45ml/3 tbsp olive oil
1 small red onion, thinly sliced
1 jar ready-made tomato sauce or pizza topping
pinch of freshly grated nutmeg
150g/5oz mozzarella cheese
1 egg
25g/1oz/¼ cup grated Gruyère cheese

1 Preheat the oven to 220°C/425°F/Gas 7. Roll out the pizza dough to a 25–30cm/10–12in circle and place on a greased baking sheet. Push up the edge of the dough to form a thin rim.

2 Remove the stalks from the spinach and wash the leaves in plenty of cold water. Drain well and pat dry with kitchen paper.

3 Heat 15ml/1 tbsp of the oil in a large frying pan and fry the onion until softened. Add the spinach and continue to fry until just wilted. Drain off any excess liquid.

4 Brush the pizza base with half the remaining oil. Spread over the tomato sauce or pizza topping, then top with the spinach mixture. Grate over some nutmeg.

5 Thinly slice the mozzarella cheese and arrange over the spinach. Drizzle over the remaining oil. Bake for 10 minutes, then remove from the oven.

6 Make a small well in the centre of the pizza and drop the egg into the hole. Sprinkle over the Gruyère and return to the oven for a further 5–10 minutes until crisp and golden.

> **Cook's Tip**
> The egg adds the finishing touch to this spinach pizza. Try not to overcook it, as it is best when the yolk is still slightly soft.

Chilli Beef Pizza

Minced beef and red kidney beans combined with oregano, cumin and chillies turn this pizza into a Mexican extravaganza.

Serves 4

1 quantity Basic Pizza Dough (see page 158)
30ml/2 tbsp olive oil
1 red onion, finely chopped
1 garlic clove, crushed
½ red (bell) pepper, seeded and finely chopped
175g/6oz/¾ cup lean minced (ground) beef
2.5ml/½ tsp ground cumin
2 fresh red chillies, seeded and chopped
115g/4oz/scant ½ cup (drained weight) canned red kidney beans, rinsed
1 jar ready-made tomato sauce or pizza topping
15ml/1 tbsp chopped fresh oregano
50g/2oz/½ cup grated mozzarella cheese
75g/3oz/¾ cup grated oak-smoked Cheddar cheese
salt and ground black pepper

1 Preheat the oven to 220°C/425°F/Gas 7. Roll out the pizza dough to a 25–30cm/10–12in circle and place on a greased baking sheet. Push up the edge of the dough to form a thin rim.

2 Heat 15ml/1 tbsp of the oil in a frying pan and gently fry the onion, garlic and pepper until soft. Increase the heat, add the beef and brown well, stirring constantly.

3 Add the cumin and chillies and continue to cook, stirring, for about 5 minutes. Add the kidney beans and season with salt and pepper. Remove from the heat.

4 Spread the tomato sauce over the pizza base. Spoon the beef mixture over the top, then sprinkle with the oregano.

5 Arrange over the mozzarella and Cheddar cheeses on top, then sprinkle with the remaining olive oil. Immediately place the pizza in the oven and bake for about 15–20 minutes, or until the crust is golden brown and the topping is bubbling.

Fiorentina Energy 515kcal/2150kJ; Protein 20.9g; Carbohydrate 40.8g, of which sugars 5.2g; Fat 30.8g, of which saturates 11.4g; Cholesterol 104mg; Calcium 415mg; Fibre 3.2g; Sodium 634mg.
Chilli Beef Energy 494kcal/2067kJ; Protein 22.7g; Carbohydrate 43.9g, of which sugars 5g; Fat 26.1g, of which saturates 10.6g; Cholesterol 54mg; Calcium 280mg; Fibre 4.1g; Sodium 411mg.

Tuna, Anchovy & Caper Pizza

Packed with Italian flavours, this substantial pizza is great for an informal gathering.

Serves 2–3
115g/4oz/1 cup self-raising
    (self-rising) flour
115g/4oz/1 cup self-raising
    wholemeal (self-rising whole-
    wheat) flour
pinch of salt
50g/2oz/¼ cup butter, diced
about 150ml/¼ pint/⅔ cup milk

For the topping
30ml/2 tbsp olive oil
1 jar ready-made tomato sauce or
    pizza topping
1 small red onion
200g/7oz can tuna, drained
15ml/1 tbsp capers
12 black olives, pitted
45ml/3 tbsp freshly grated
    Parmesan cheese
50g/2oz can anchovy fillets,
    drained and halved lengthways
ground black pepper

1 Place the flours and salt in a bowl and rub in the butter until the mixture resembles fine breadcrumbs. Add the milk and mix to a soft dough with a wooden spoon. Knead on a lightly floured surface until smooth.

2 Preheat the oven to 220°C/425°F/Gas 7. Roll out the dough on a lightly floured surface to a 25cm/10in circle. Place on a greased baking sheet and brush with 15ml/1 tbsp of the oil. Spread the tomato sauce or pizza topping evenly over the dough, leaving the edge uncovered.

3 Cut the onion into thin wedges and arrange on top. Roughly flake the tuna with a fork and scatter over the onion. Sprinkle over the capers, black olives and Parmesan cheese.

4 Place the anchovy fillets over the top of the pizza in a criss-cross pattern. Drizzle over the remaining oil, then grind over plenty of pepper. Bake for 15–20 minutes until crisp and golden. Serve immediately.

Variation
If you have time, make your own herb-flavoured tomato sauce.

Salmon & Avocado Pizza

Smoked and fresh salmon make a delicious and luxurious pizza topping when mixed with avocado.

Serves 3–4
150g/5oz salmon fillet
120ml/4fl oz/½ cup dry white
    wine
1 quantity Basic Pizza Dough
    (see page 158)
15ml/1 tbsp olive oil
400g/14oz can chopped
    tomatoes, drained well

115g/4oz/scant 1 cup grated
    mozzarella
1 small avocado
10ml/2 tsp lemon juice
30ml/2 tbsp crème fraîche
75g/3oz smoked salmon, cut into
    strips
15ml/1 tbsp capers
30ml/2 tbsp snipped fresh chives,
    to garnish
ground black pepper

1 Place the salmon fillet in a frying pan, pour over the wine and season with pepper. Bring slowly to the boil over gentle heat, remove from the heat, cover with a tight-fitting lid and leave to cool. (The fish will cook in the cooling liquid.) Skin and flake the salmon into small pieces, removing any bones.

2 Preheat the oven to 220°C/425°F/Gas 7. Roll out the pizza dough to a 25–30cm/10–12in circle and place on a greased baking sheet. Push up the edge of the dough to form a thin rim.

3 Brush the pizza base with the oil and spread the drained tomatoes over the top. Sprinkle half the mozzarella. Bake for 10 minutes, then remove from the oven.

4 Meanwhile, halve, stone and peel the avocado. Cut the flesh into small dice and toss in the lemon juice.

5 Dot teaspoonfuls of the crème fraîche over the pizza base. Arrange the fresh and smoked salmon, avocado, capers and remaining mozzarella on top. Season to taste with pepper.

6 Bake for 5–10 minutes until crisp and golden. Sprinkle over the chives and serve immediately.

Tuna Energy 713kcal/2985kJ; Protein 37.8g; Carbohydrate 58.5g, of which sugars 3.8g; Fat 38.1g, of which saturates 15g; Cholesterol 97mg; Calcium 328mg; Fibre 5.7g; Sodium 1518mg.
Salmon Energy 451kcal/1884kJ; Protein 22g; Carbohydrate 31g, of which sugars 5.3g; Fat 25.3g, of which saturates 8.6g; Cholesterol 53mg; Calcium 193mg; Fibre 3.3g; Sodium 282mg.

Mushroom & Pancetta Pizzas

Try to use a mix of wild and cultivated mushrooms to give these individual pizzas lots of earthy flavour.

Serves 4
1 quantity Basic Pizza Dough (see page 158)
60ml/4 tbsp olive oil
2 garlic cloves, crushed
225g/8oz fresh mixed ceps and chestnut mushrooms, roughly chopped
75g/3oz pancetta, roughly chopped
15ml/1 tbsp chopped fresh oregano
45ml/3 tbsp freshly grated Parmesan cheese
salt and ground black pepper

1 Preheat the oven to 220°C/425°F/Gas 7. Divide the dough into four pieces and roll out each one on a lightly floured surface to a 13cm/5in circle. Place well apart on two greased baking sheets.

2 Heat 30ml/2 tbsp of the olive oil in a frying pan and fry the garlic and mushrooms gently until the mushrooms are tender and the juices have evaporated. Season to taste with salt and pepper, then cool.

3 Brush the pizza bases with 15ml/1 tbsp oil, then spoon over the mushrooms. Scatter over the pancetta and oregano.

4 Sprinkle the toppings with grated Parmesan cheese and drizzle over the remaining oil. Bake for 10–15 minutes, until crisp. Serve immediately.

> **Cook's Tip**
> • Pancetta is available in larger supermarkets and Italian delicatessens. If you have difficulty finding it, use chopped slices of streaky (fatty) bacon in its place.
> • If fresh ceps are not available, you can add extra flavour to cultivated mushrooms by adding some dried porcini mushrooms, which are sold in larger supermarkets. Soak them in hot water for 20 minutes until soft before adding to the pan in step 2.

Pepperoni Pizza

This classic pizza is sure to go down well with family and friends alike. Who can resist a slice of home-made pizza, topped with a luscious combination of tangy pepperoni, sweet pepper and lashings of cheese?

Serves 4
For the sauce
30ml/2 tbsp olive oil
1 onion, finely chopped
1 garlic clove, crushed
400g/14oz can chopped tomatoes with herbs
15ml/1 tbsp tomato purée (paste)

For the pizza base
275g/10oz/2½ cups plain (all-purpose) flour
2.5ml/½ tsp salt
5ml/1 tsp easy-blend (rapid-rise) dried yeast
30ml/2 tbsp olive oil

For the topping
½ each red, yellow and green (bell) pepper, sliced into rings
150g/5oz mozzarella cheese, sliced
75g/3oz pepperoni sausage, thinly sliced
8 black olives, pitted
3 sun-dried tomatoes, chopped
2.5ml/½ tsp dried oregano
olive oil, for drizzling

1 To make the sauce, heat the oil and fry the onions and garlic until softened. Add the tomatoes and tomato purée, then boil rapidly for 5 minutes until reduced slightly. Leave to cool.

2 To make the pizza base, sift the flour and salt into a bowl. Sprinkle over the yeast and make a well in the centre. Pour in 175ml/6fl oz/¾ cup warm water and the olive oil. Mix to a soft dough. Knead the dough on a lightly floured surface for about 5–10 minutes until smooth. Roll out to a 25cm/10in round, press up the edges slightly and place on a greased baking sheet.

3 Spread over the tomato sauce and top with the peppers, mozzarella, pepperoni, olives and sun-dried tomatoes. Sprinkle over the oregano and drizzle with olive oil.

4 Cover loosely and leave in a warm place for 30 minutes. Meanwhile, preheat the oven to 220°C/425°F/ Gas 7. Bake for 25–30 minutes, then serve.

Mushroom Energy 344kcal/1435kJ; Protein 12g; Carbohydrate 27g, of which sugars 1.7g; Fat 21.6g, of which saturates 5.5g; Cholesterol 23mg; Calcium 180mg; Fibre 1.6g; Sodium 488mg.
Pepperoni Energy 521kcal/2184kJ; Protein 17.5g; Carbohydrate 62.4g, of which sugars 8.6g; Fat 24g, of which saturates 8.2g; Cholesterol 43mg; Calcium 256mg; Fibre 4.7g; Sodium 484mg.

Farmhouse Pizza

This is the ultimate party pizza. Served cut into fingers, it is ideal for a large and hungry gathering.

Serves 8
90ml/6 tbsp olive oil
225g/8oz button (white) mushrooms, sliced
2 quantities Basic Pizza Dough (see page 158)
1 jar ready-made tomato sauce or pizza topping
300g/10oz mozzarella cheese, thinly sliced

115g/4oz wafer-thin smoked ham slices
6 bottled artichoke hearts in oil, drained and sliced
50g/2oz can anchovy fillets, drained and halved lengthways
10 black olives, pitted and halved
30ml/2 tbsp chopped fresh oregano
15ml/3 tbsp freshly grated Parmesan cheese
ground black pepper

1 Preheat the oven to 220°C/425°F/Gas 7. In a large frying pan, heat 30ml/2 tbsp of the oil. Gently fry the mushrooms for 5 minutes until all the juices have evaporated. Remove from the heat and leave to cool.

2 Roll out the dough on a lightly floured surface to make a 30 x 25cm/12 x 10in rectangle. Transfer to a greased baking sheet, then push up the dough edges to form a thin rim. Brush with 30ml/2 tbsp of the oil.

3 Spread the tomato sauce or pizza topping over the dough, then arrange the sliced mozzarella over the sauce.

4 Scrunch up the ham and arrange on top with the artichoke hearts, mushrooms and anchovies.

5 Dot with the black olives, then sprinkle over the chopped oregano and grated Parmesan. Drizzle over the remaining oil and season to taste with pepper.

6 Bake for about 25 minutes until the pizza crust is crisp and golden. Serve immediately.

Crab & Parmesan Calzonelli

These calzonelli – purses of pizza dough filled with a luxurious creamy crab filling – make attractive and impressive party food.

Makes 10–12
1 quantity Basic Pizza Dough (see page 158)
115g/4oz mixed prepared crab meat, defrosted if frozen

15ml/1 tbsp double (heavy) cream
30ml/2 tbsp freshly grated Parmesan cheese
30ml/2 tbsp chopped fresh parsley
1 garlic clove, crushed
salt and ground black pepper
fresh parsley sprigs, to garnish

1 Preheat the oven to 200°C/400°F/Gas 6. Roll out the pizza dough on a lightly floured surface to 3mm/⅛in thick. Using a 7.5cm/3in plain round pastry cutter, stamp out ten to twelve circles of dough.

2 In a bowl, mix the crab meat with the cream, Parmesan cheese, parsley and garlic. Season to taste with salt and pepper.

3 Spoon a little of the filling on to one half of each circle. Dampen the edges of the dough with water and fold over to enclose the filling.

4 Seal the edges by pressing with a fork. Place well apart on two greased baking sheets. Bake for 10–15 minutes until golden. Garnish with parsley sprigs.

> **Cook's Tip**
> Make sure that the pizza dough is rolled out thinly and evenly.

> **Variation**
> If you prefer, use prawns (shrimp) instead of crab meat. If buying frozen prawns, make sure they are fully defrosted first.

Farmhouse Energy 412kcal/1725kJ; Protein 17.2g; Carbohydrate 36.4g, of which sugars 2g; Fat 23g, of which saturates 8g; Cholesterol 38mg; Calcium 259mg; Fibre 2.4g; Sodium 822mg.
Calzonelli Energy 84kcal/354kJ; Protein 4.2g; Carbohydrate 11.4g, of which sugars 0.3g; Fat 2.7g, of which saturates 1.1g; Cholesterol 11mg; Calcium 68mg; Fibre 0.6g; Sodium 82mg.

Aubergine & Shallot Calzone

Aubergines, shallots and sun-dried tomatoes make an unusual filling for calzone.

Serves 2

4 baby aubergines (eggplants)
45ml/3 tbsp olive oil
3 shallots, chopped
1 garlic clove, chopped
6 pieces sun-dried tomatoes in oil, drained and chopped
1.5ml/¼ tsp dried red chilli flakes
10ml/2 tsp chopped fresh thyme
1 quantity Basic Pizza Dough (see page 158)
75g/3oz/generous ½ cup diced mozzarella cheese
salt and ground black pepper
15–30ml/1–2 tbsp freshly grated Parmesan cheese, to serve

1 Preheat the oven to 220°C/425°F/Gas 7. Trim the baby aubergines, then cut into small dice.

2 Heat 30ml/2 tbsp oil in a heavy frying pan. Add the shallots and fry over low heat, stirring occasionally, for 5 minutes until softened by not browned.

3 Add the aubergines, garlic, sun-dried tomatoes, red chilli flakes and thyme to the shallots and season with salt and pepper. Cook for 4–5 minutes, stirring frequently, until the aubergine is beginning to soften.

4 Divide the dough in half and roll out each piece on a lightly floured surface to an 18cm/7in circle. Spread the aubergine mixture over half of each circle, leaving a 2.5cm/1in border, then arrange the mozzarella on top.

5 Dampen the edges with water, then fold the dough over to enclose the filling. Press the edges firmly together to seal. Place on two greased baking sheets.

6 Brush with half the remaining oil and make a small hole in the top of each to allow the steam to escape. Bake for about 15–20 minutes until golden. Remove from the oven and brush with the remaining oil. Sprinkle over the Parmesan and serve the calzone immediately.

Ham & Mozzarella Calzone

A calzone is a kind of "inside-out" pizza – the dough is on the outside and the filling on the inside. This is particulary good food for eating al fresco.

Serves 2

1 quantity Basic Pizza Dough (see page 158)
115g/4oz/½ cup ricotta cheese
30ml/2 tbsp freshly grated Parmesan cheese
1 egg yolk
30ml/2 tbsp chopped fresh basil
75g/3oz cooked ham, finely chopped
75g/3oz mozzarella cheese, cut into small dice
olive oil, for brushing
salt and ground black pepper

1 Preheat the oven to 220°C/425°F/Gas 7. Divide the dough in half and roll out each piece on a lightly floured surface to an 18cm/7in circle.

2 In a bowl, mix together the ricotta and Parmesan cheeses, then stir in the egg yolk and basil. Season with salt and pepper.

3 Spread the mixture over half of each circle, leaving a 2.5cm/1in border, then arrange the ham and mozzarella on top.

4 Dampen the edges with water, then fold over the dough to enclose the filling.

5 Press the edges firmly together to seal. Place on two greased baking sheets. Brush with oil and make a small hole in the top of each to allow the steam to escape.

6 Bake for 15–20 minutes until golden. Serve immediately.

Cook's Tips
• For a vegetarian version, replace the ham with fried mushrooms or chopped cooked spinach.
• For a decorative finishing touch, seal the edges of the uncooked dough circles by pressing with a fork.

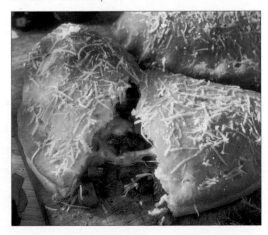

Mozzarella Energy 686kcal/2877kJ; Protein 34.8g; Carbohydrate 70.2g, of which sugars 3.5g; Fat 31.5g, of which saturates 15.6g; Cholesterol 183mg; Calcium 453mg; Fibre 2.7g; Sodium 769mg.
Aubergine Energy 672kcal/2814kJ; Protein 20.5g; Carbohydrate 75.6g, of which sugars 7.8g; Fat 34.1g, of which saturates 10.3g; Cholesterol 29mg; Calcium 378mg; Fibre 7.4g; Sodium 240mg.

Root Vegetable Couscous

Harissa is a very fiery Tunisian chilli sauce which is now available ready-made from larger supermarkets.

Serves 4
350g/12oz/2¼ cups couscous
45ml/3 tbsp olive oil
4 baby onions, halved
675g/1½lb fresh mixed root
    vegetables such as carrots, swede
    (ratabega), turnip, celeriac and
    sweet potatoes, cubed
2 garlic cloves, crushed
pinch of saffron threads
2.5ml/½ tsp each ground
    cinnamon and ginger
2.5ml/½ tsp ground turmeric
5ml/1 tsp each ground cumin and
    coriander

15ml/1 tbsp tomato purée
    (paste)
450ml/¾ pint/scant 2 cups hot
    vegetable stock
1 small fennel bulb, quartered
115g/4oz/1 cup cooked or
    canned chickpeas
50g/2oz/½ cup seedless raisins
30ml/2 tbsp chopped fresh
    coriander (cilantro)
30ml/2 tbsp chopped fresh flat
    leaf parsley
salt and ground black pepper

For the spiced sauce
15ml/1 tbsp olive oil
15ml/1 tbsp lemon juice
15ml/1 tbsp chopped fresh
    coriander (cilantro)
2.5–5ml/½–1 tsp harissa

1 Put the couscous in a bowl, cover with hot water, then drain. Heat the oil in a frying pan and gently fry the onions for 3 minutes. Add the root vegetables and fry for 5 minutes. Add the garlic and spices and cook for 1 minute, stirring.

2 Transfer the vegetable mixture to a large deep pan. Stir in the tomato purée, stock, fennel, chickpeas, raisins, chopped coriander and flat leaf parsley. Bring to the boil. Put the couscous into a muslin-lined steamer and place this over the vegetable mixture. Cover and simmer for 20 minutes, or until the vegetables are tender.

3 To make the sauce, put 250ml/8fl oz/1 cup of the vegetable liquid in a bowl and mix with all of the sauce ingredients.

4 Spoon the couscous on to a plate and pile the vegetables on top. Serve at once, handing round the sauce separately.

Risotto with Mushrooms

The addition of wild mushrooms gives a lovely woody flavour to this dish.

Serves 4
25g/1oz dried wild mushrooms,
    preferably porcini
350ml/12fl oz/1½ cups warm
    water
900ml/1½ pints/3¾ cups meat
    or chicken stock
175g/6oz fresh cultivated
    mushrooms

juice of ½ lemon
75g/3oz/6 tbsp butter
30ml/2 tbsp finely chopped fresh
    parsley
30ml/2 tbsp olive oil
1 small onion, finely chopped
275g/10oz/1½ cups arborio
    risotto rice
120ml/4fl oz/½ cup dry white
    wine
45ml/3 tbsp freshly grated
    Parmesan cheese
salt and ground black pepper

1 Place the dried mushrooms in a small bowl with the warm water. Leave to soak for at least 40 minutes. Remove the mushrooms and rinse, then filter the soaking water through a sieve (strainer) lined with kitchen paper into a pan. Add the stock and leave to simmer until needed.

2 Slice the fresh mushrooms. Toss with the lemon juice. Melt a third of the butter in a large frying pan. Stir in the mushrooms and cook until they begin to brown. Stir in the parsley, cook for 30 seconds more, then transfer to a side dish.

3 Heat another third of the butter with the olive oil in the mushroom pan and cook the onion until golden. Add the rice and stir for 1–2 minutes. Add all the mushrooms. Pour in the wine and cook until it has evaporated.

4 Add a ladleful of the hot stock and stir gently until it has been absorbed. Continue adding a ladleful of stock at a time, until all the stock has been absorbed and the rice is tender and creamy.

5 Remove the risotto pan from the heat. Stir in the remaining butter and the Parmesan. Grind in a little pepper, and taste again for salt; adjust if necessary. Allow the risotto to rest for 3–4 minutes before serving.

Couscous Energy 444kcal/1855kJ; Protein 9.5g; Carbohydrate 75.1g, of which sugars 24.2g; Fat 13.5g, of which saturates 1.8g; Cholesterol 0mg; Calcium 115mg; Fibre 7.5g; Sodium 131mg.
Risotto Energy 518kcal/2150kJ; Protein 10.6g; Carbohydrate 56.5g, of which sugars 1.2g; Fat 25.2g, of which saturates 12.9g; Cholesterol 51mg; Calcium 161mg; Fibre 0.7g; Sodium 240mg.

Tomato Risotto

This pretty risotto makes a lovely summery meal, served with a chilled white wine.

Serves 4
675g/1½ lb firm ripe tomatoes
50g/2oz/¼ cup butter
1 onion, finely chopped
1.2 litres/2 pints/5 cups vegetable stock
275g/10oz/1½ cups arborio rice
400g/14oz can cannellini beans, drained
50g/2oz/½ cup finely grated Parmesan cheese
salt and ground black pepper
10–12 fresh basil leaves, shredded and freshly grated Parmesan cheese, to serve

1 Halve the tomatoes and scoop out the seeds into a sieve (strainer) placed over a bowl. Press the seeds with a spoon to extract all the juice. Set the juice aside.

2 Grill (broil) the tomatoes skin-side up until evenly charred and blistered. Rub off the skins and dice the flesh.

3 Melt the butter in a large frying pan and cook the onion for 5 minutes until beginning to soften. Add the tomatoes and the reserved juice. Season with salt and pepper, then cook, stirring occasionally, for about 10 minutes. Meanwhile, bring the vegetable stock to the boil in another pan.

4 Add the rice to the tomatoes and stir to coat, then add a ladleful of the stock and stir gently until it has been absorbed. Continue adding a ladleful of stock at a time, until all the stock has been absorbed and the rice is tender and creamy.

5 Stir in the cannellini beans and grated Parmesan and heat through for a few minutes. Just before serving the risotto, sprinkle each portion with shredded basil leaves and Parmesan.

> **Cook's Tip**
> If possible, use plum tomatoes in this dish, as they have a fresh, vibrant flavour and meaty texture.

Grilled Polenta with Peppers

Golden slices of herby polenta taste delicious topped with yellow and red pepper strips, heightened with balsamic vinegar.

Serves 4
2 red (bell) peppers
2 yellow (bell) peppers
115g/4oz/scant 1 cup polenta
25g/1oz/2 tbsp butter
15–30ml/1–2 tbsp mixed chopped herbs such as parsley, thyme and sage
melted butter, for brushing
60ml/4 tbsp olive oil
1–2 garlic cloves, cut into slivers
15ml/1 tbsp balsamic vinegar
salt and ground black pepper
fresh herb sprigs, to garnish

1 Preheat the oven to 200°C/400°F/Gas 6. Place the peppers on a baking sheet and bake for about 20 minutes or until they are beginning to char and blister.

2 Put the charred peppers in a bowl, cover and leave to cool for 10 minutes, then peel off the skins. Remove the seeds and cores, then cut the flesh into strips. Set aside.

3 Bring 600ml/1 pint/2½ cups salted water to the boil in a heavy pan. Trickle in the polenta, beating continuously, then cook gently for 15–20 minutes, stirring occasionally, until the mixture is no longer grainy and comes away from the sides of the pan.

4 Remove the pan from the heat and beat in the butter, chopped herbs and plenty of pepper. Pour the polenta into a pudding bowl, smooth the surface and leave until cold and firm.

5 Turn out the polenta on to a board and cut into thick slices. Brush the polenta slices with melted butter and grill (broil) each side for about 4–5 minutes, until golden brown.

6 Meanwhile, heat the olive oil in a frying pan, add the garlic and peppers and stir-fry for 1–2 minutes. Stir in the balsamic vinegar and season with salt and pepper.

7 Spoon the pepper mixture over the polenta slices and garnish with fresh herb sprigs. Serve immediately.

Risotto Energy 531kcal/2220kJ; Protein 18.4g; Carbohydrate 79.2g, of which sugars 9.8g; Fat 15.9g, of which saturates 9.4g; Cholesterol 39mg; Calcium 252mg; Fibre 8.1g; Sodium 618mg.
Polenta Energy 309kcal/1280kJ; Protein 4.6g; Carbohydrate 32.5g, of which sugars 10.7g; Fat 17.8g, of which saturates 5g; Cholesterol 13mg; Calcium 16mg; Fibre 3.5g; Sodium 45mg.

Okra Fried Rice

This spicy rich dish gains its creamy consistency from the natural juices of the sliced okra.

Serves 3–4

30ml/2 tbsp vegetable oil
15g/½ oz/1 tbsp butter or
  margarine
1 garlic clove, crushed
½ red onion, finely chopped
115g/4oz okra, topped and tailed

30ml/2 tbsp diced green and red
  (bell) peppers
2.5ml/½ tsp dried thyme
2 green chillies, finely chopped
2.5ml/½ tsp five-spice powder
1 vegetable stock cube
30ml/2 tbsp soy sauce
15ml/1 tbsp chopped fresh
  coriander (cilantro)
225g/8oz/2½ cups cooked rice
salt and ground black pepper
fresh coriander sprigs, to garnish

1 Heat the oil and butter or margarine in a frying pan or wok and cook the garlic and onion over medium heat for 5 minutes until softened.

2 Thinly slice the okra, add to the pan or wok and sauté gently for 6–7 minutes.

3 Add the green and red peppers, thyme, chillies and five-spice powder. Cook gently for 3 minutes, then crumble in the vegetable stock cube.

4 Add the soy sauce, coriander and rice and heat through, stirring well. Season to taste with salt and pepper. Serve hot, garnished with coriander sprigs.

Cook's Tips
• Okra is a five-sided green pod with a tapering end. When buying okra, choose small firm pods that are brightly coloured. Avoid any that are bendy and browning at the edges or tips.
• When preparing chillies, wear rubber gloves if possible, as chillies contain a substance that burns sensitive skin. Wash the knife, board and your hands (if not protected) after preparation. Never rub your eyes or touch your lips after handling chillies.

Asparagus & Cheese Risotto

It's important to use arborio rice for this Italian dish in order to achieve the creamy texture that is characteristic of an authentic risotto.

Serves 4

1.5ml/¼ tsp saffron threads
750ml/1¼ pints/3 cups hot
  chicken stock
25g/1oz/2 tbsp butter
30ml/2 tbsp olive oil
1 large onion, finely chopped

2 garlic cloves, finely chopped
225g/8oz/1¼ cups arborio
  risotto rice
300ml/½ pint/1¼ cups dry white
  wine
225g/8oz asparagus tips, cooked
75g/3oz/1 cup freshly grated
  Parmesan cheese
salt and ground black pepper
fresh Parmesan cheese shavings,
  to garnish
ciabatta bread rolls and green
  salad, to serve

1 Sprinkle the saffron over the stock and leave to infuse for 5 minutes. Heat the butter and oil in a frying pan and fry the onion and garlic for about 6 minutes until softened.

2 Add the rice and stir-fry for 1–2 minutes to coat the grains with the butter and oil. Pour on 300ml/½ pint/1¼ cups of the stock and saffron. Cook gently, stirring frequently, until the liquid is absorbed. Repeat with another 300ml/½ pint/1¼ cups stock. When that is absorbed, add the wine and continue to cook, stirring, until the rice has a creamy consistency.

3 Add the asparagus and remaining stock, and stir until the liquid is absorbed and the rice is tender. Stir in the Parmesan cheese and season to taste with salt and pepper.

4 Spoon the risotto on to warmed plates and garnish with the Parmesan cheese shavings. Serve immediately with hot ciabatta rolls and a mixed green salad.

Cook's Tip
If preferred, you can use whole asparagus spears, cut into 5cm/2in lengths, but the stems should not be too thick.

Indian Pilau Rice

Basmati rice is simply flavoured with aromatic spices and seeds to create a delightfully fragrant dish.

Serves 4
225g/8oz/1¼ cups basmati rice, rinsed well
30ml/2 tbsp vegetable oil
1 small onion, finely chopped
1 garlic clove, crushed
5ml/1 tsp fennel seeds
15ml/1 tbsp sesame seeds
2.5ml/½ tsp ground turmeric
5ml/1 tsp ground cumin
1.5ml/¼ tsp salt
2 whole cloves
4 green cardamom pods, lightly crushed
5 black peppercorns
450ml/¾ pint/scant 2 cups chicken stock
15ml/1 tbsp ground almonds
fresh coriander (cilantro) sprigs, to garnish

1 Soak the rice in water for 30 minutes. Heat the oil in a pan, and fry the onions and garlic gently for 5–6 minutes, until soft.

2 Stir in the fennel and sesame seeds, the turmeric, cumin, salt, cloves, cardamom pods and peppercorns and cook for about 1 minute. Drain the rice well, add to the pan and stir-fry for a further 3 minutes.

3 Pour on the chicken stock. Bring to the boil, then cover with a tight-fitting lid, reduce the heat to very low and simmer gently for 20 minutes, without removing the lid, until all the liquid has been absorbed.

4 Remove from the heat and leave to stand for 2–3 minutes. Fluff up the rice with a fork and stir in the ground almonds. Garnish with coriander sprigs and serve immediately.

> **Cook's Tips**
> • Basmati rice is the most popular choice for Indian dishes, but you could use long grain rice instead.
> • Green cardamoms are more suitable for this dish than the black variety as they are more delicate in flavour and texture.

Louisiana Rice

Minced pork and chicken livers with mixed vegetables make a tasty dish that is a meal in itself.

Serves 4
60ml/4 tbsp vegetable oil
1 small aubergine (eggplant), diced
225g/8oz minced (ground) pork
1 green (bell) pepper, seeded and chopped
2 celery sticks, chopped
1 onion, chopped
1 garlic clove, crushed
5ml/1 tsp cayenne pepper
5ml/1 tsp paprika
5ml/1 tsp ground black pepper
2.5ml/½ tsp salt
5ml/1 tsp dried thyme
2.5ml/½ tsp dried oregano
475ml/16fl oz/2 cups chicken stock
225g/8oz chicken livers, minced (ground)
150g/5oz/¾ cup long grain rice
1 bay leaf
45ml/3 tbsp chopped fresh parsley
celery leaves, to garnish

1 Heat the oil in a frying pan until really hot, then stir-fry the aubergine for about 5 minutes. Add the pork and cook for about 6–8 minutes, until browned, using a wooden spoon to break up any lumps.

2 Add the green pepper, celery, onion, garlic, cayenne pepper, paprika, black pepper, salt, thyme and oregano. Cover and cook over high heat for 5–6 minutes, stirring frequently from the bottom to scrape up and distribute the crispy bits of pork.

3 Pour on the chicken stock and stir, scraping the bottom of the pan clean. Readuce the heat to medium, cover the pan and cook for 6 minutes. Stir in the chicken livers, cook for a further 2 minutes, then stir in the rice and add the bay leaf.

4 Reduce the heat, cover and simmer for about 6–7 minutes more. Turn off the heat and leave to stand for a further 10–15 minutes until the rice is tender.

5 Remove the bay leaf and stir in the chopped parsley. Serve the rice hot, garnished with the celery leaves.

Louisiana Rice Energy 406kcal/1690kJ; Protein 24.7g; Carbohydrate 35.2g, of which sugars 4.7g; Fat 18.4g, of which saturates 3.8g; Cholesterol 251mg; Calcium 34mg; Fibre 2.1g; Sodium 92mg.
Pilau Rice Energy 302kcal/1258kJ; Protein 5.8g; Carbohydrate 46.4g, of which sugars 1g; Fat 10.1g, of which saturates 1.1g; Cholesterol 0mg; Calcium 49mg; Fibre 0.8g; Sodium 2mg.

Chinese Special Fried Rice

This staple of Chinese cuisine consists of a mixture of chicken, shrimps and vegetables with fried rice.

Serves 4

200g/7oz/1 cup long grain white rice
45ml/3 tbsp groundnut (peanut) oil
1 garlic clove, crushed
4 spring onions (scallions), finely chopped
115g/4oz/1 cup diced cooked chicken
115g/4oz/1 cup peeled, cooked shrimps
50g/2oz/½ cup frozen peas
1 egg, beaten with a pinch of salt
50g/2oz/1 cup finely shredded lettuce
30ml/2 tbsp light soy sauce
pinch of caster (superfine) sugar
salt and ground black pepper
15ml/1 tbsp chopped, roasted cashew nuts, to garnish

1 Rinse the rice in two to three changes of warm water to wash away some of the starch. Drain well.

2 Put the rice in a pan and add 15ml/1 tbsp of the oil and 350ml/12fl oz/1½ cups water. Cover and bring to the boil, stir once, then cover and simmer for 12–15 minutes, until nearly all the water has been absorbed. Turn off the heat, cover and leave to stand for 10 minutes. Fluff up with a fork and leave to cool.

3 Heat the remaining oil in a wok or frying pan and stir-fry the garlic and spring onions for 30 seconds.

4 Add the chicken, shrimps and peas and stir-fry for about 1–2 minutes, then add the cooked rice and stir-fry for a further 2 minutes. Pour in the egg and stir-fry until just set. Stir in the lettuce, soy sauce, sugar and salt and pepper to taste.

5 Transfer to a warmed serving bowl, sprinkle with the chopped cashew nuts and serve immediately.

> **Cook's Tip**
> When using a wok, preheat it before adding the oil. Swirl the oil around the sides and heat it up before adding the ingredients.

Lemony Bulgur Wheat Salad

This Middle-Eastern salad, called *tabbouleh,* is delicious as an accompaniment to grilled meats or fish, or on its own as a light snack.

Serves 4

2 tomatoes, peeled and chopped
225g/8oz/1½ cups bulgur wheat
4 spring onions (scallions), finely chopped
75ml/5 tbsp chopped fresh mint
75ml/5 tbsp chopped fresh parsley
15ml/1 tbsp chopped fresh coriander (cilantro)
juice of 1 lemon
75ml/5 tbsp olive oil
salt and ground black pepper
fresh mint sprigs, to garnish

1 Make a slash in the skin of each tomato, then put them all in a heatproof bowl and pour over boiling water. Leave for 30 seconds, then plunge the tomatoes into cold water. Peel and seed, then roughly chop the flesh. Set aside.

2 Place the bulgur wheat in a bowl, pour on enough boiling water to cover and leave to soak for 20 minutes.

3 Line a colander with a clean dish towel. Turn the soaked bulgur wheat into the centre, let it drain, then gather up the sides of the dish towel and squeeze out any remaining liquid. Turn the bulgur wheat into a large bowl.

4 Add the spring onions, mint, parsley, coriander and tomatoes. Mix well, then pour over the lemon juice and olive oil. Season generously with salt and pepper, then toss so that all the ingredients are combined.

5 Chill in the refrigerator for a couple of hours before serving, garnished with mint.

> **Variation**
> Add some pitted, halved black olives to the salad just before serving for extra tangy flavour.

Fried Rice Energy 343kcal/1434kJ; Protein 20.2g; Carbohydrate 40.5g, of which sugars 4.2g; Fat 11.2g, of which saturates 1.6g; Cholesterol 124mg; Calcium 91mg; Fibre 2.4g; Sodium 632mg.
Wheat Salad Energy 194kcal/811kJ; Protein 4.3g; Carbohydrate 31.2g, of which sugars 2.3g; Fat 6.5g, of which saturates 0.9g; Cholesterol 0mg; Calcium 56mg; Fibre 1.6g; Sodium 12mg.

Tanzanian Vegetable Rice

This light, fluffy dish of steamed rice flavoured with colourful vegetables makes a versatile accompaniment.

Serves 4–6
350g/12oz/2 cups basmati rice
45ml/3 tbsp vegetable oil

1 onion, chopped
750ml/1¼ pints/3 cups vegetable stock or water
2 garlic cloves, crushed
115g/4oz/1 cup sweetcorn
½ fresh red or green (bell) pepper, chopped
1 large carrot, grated

1 Rinse the rice in a sieve (strainer) under cold water, then leave to drain for about 15 minutes.

2 Heat the oil in a large pan, add the onion and fry for a few minutes over medium heat until just softened.

3 Add the rice and stir-fry for about 10 minutes, taking care to stir continuously so that the rice does not stick to the bottom of the pan.

4 Add the stock or water and the garlic and stir well. Bring to the boil and cook over high heat for 5 minutes, then reduce the heat, cover with a tight-fitting lid and leave the rice to cook for 20 minutes.

5 Scatter the corn over the rice, then spread the pepper on top and lastly sprinkle over the grated carrot.

6 Cover tightly and continue to steam over low heat until the rice is cooked. Gently fork through the rice to fluff up and serve immediately.

Variation
Vary the vegetables according to what you have to hand. Sliced courgettes (zucchini) or small broccoli florets would work well, while frozen peas make an easy, colourful addition. Defrost them before adding to the rice.

Rice with Seeds & Spices

A change from plain boiled rice, this spicy dish makes a colourful accompaniment to curries.

Serves 4
5ml/1 tsp sunflower oil
2.5ml/½ tsp ground turmeric
6 green cardamom pods, lightly crushed
5ml/1 tsp coriander seeds, lightly crushed

1 garlic clove, crushed
200g/7oz/1 cup basmati rice
400ml/14fl oz/1⅔ cups stock
120ml/4fl oz/½ cup natural (plain) yogurt
15ml/1 tbsp toasted sunflower seeds
15ml/1 tbsp toasted sesame seeds
salt and ground black pepper
fresh coriander (cilantro) leaves, to garnish

1 Heat the oil in a non-stick frying pan and fry the spices and garlic for about 1 minute, stirring constantly.

2 Add the rice and stock and stir to mix. Bring to the boil, then cover and simmer for 15 minutes or until just tender.

3 Stir in the yogurt and the toasted sunflower and sesame seeds. Season with salt and pepper to taste and serve immediately, garnished with coriander leaves.

Cook's Tips
• *If you have time, soak the rice for 30 minutes in cold water before cooking.*
• *Although basmati rice gives the best texture and flavour, you could substitute ordinary long grain rice if you prefer.*

Variation
You can always add some unsalted nuts to the dish, to give interesting texture. Shelled pistachios would be a good choice, as they add extra colour, but peanuts, almonds and cashews will all taste just as delicious.

Tanzanian Energy 449kcal/1877kJ; Protein 8.1g; Carbohydrate 83g, of which sugars 7.7g; Fat 9.3g, of which saturates 1.1g; Cholesterol 0mg; Calcium 30mg; Fibre 1.8g; Sodium 85mg.
Seeds & Spices Energy 248kcal/1035kJ; Protein 6.6g; Carbohydrate 42.2g, of which sugars 2.3g; Fat 5.7g, of which saturates 0.9g; Cholesterol 0mg; Calcium 117mg; Fibre 0.6g; Sodium 27mg.

Lemon & Herb Risotto Cake

This unusual rice dish can be served as a light main course with salad, or as a satisfying side dish.

Serves 4

1 small leek, thinly sliced
600ml/1 pint/2¹⁄₂ cups chicken or vegetable stock
225g/8oz/1¹⁄₄ cups risotto rice
finely grated rind of 1 lemon
30ml/2 tbsp chopped fresh chives
30ml/2 tbsp chopped fresh parsley
75g/3oz/generous ¹⁄₂ cup grated mozzarella cheese
salt and ground black pepper
fresh parsley and lemon wedges, to garnish

1 Preheat the oven to 200°C/400°F/Gas 6. Lightly oil a 22cm/8¹⁄₂in round loose-bottomed cake tin (pan).

2 Put the sliced leek in a large pan with 45ml/3 tbsp of the stock. Cook over medium heat, stirring occasionally, for about 5 minutes until softened. Add the rice and the remaining stock.

3 Bring to the boil. Lower the heat, cover the pan with a tight-fitting lid and simmer gently, stirring occasionally, for about 20 minutes, or until all the liquid has been absorbed.

4 Stir in the lemon rind, chives, chopped parsley and grated mozzarella cheese and season with salt and pepper to taste. Spoon into the tin, cover with foil and bake for 30–35 minutes or until lightly browned.

5 Carefully turn out the risotto cake and cut into slices. Serve immediately, garnished with parsley and lemon wedges.

Cook's Tips
• This risotto cake is equally delicious served cold, so it makes ideal picnic food. Chill until needed, then pack layered with kitchen foil or baking parchment.
• If you cannot obtain risotto rice, use short grain rice – the type normally used for puddings – instead.

Bulgur & Lentil Pilaff

Many of the ingredients for this tasty, aromatic dish can be found in a well-stocked store cupboard.

Serves 4

5ml/1 tsp olive oil
1 large onion, thinly sliced
2 garlic cloves, crushed
5ml/1 tsp ground coriander
5ml/1 tsp ground cumin
5ml/1 tsp ground turmeric
2.5ml/¹⁄₂ tsp ground allspice
225g/8oz/1¹⁄₄ cups bulgur wheat
about 750ml/1¹⁄₄ pints/3 cups vegetable stock or water
115g/4oz/1¹⁄₂ cups sliced button (white) mushrooms
115g/4oz/¹⁄₂ cup green lentils
cayenne pepper
salt and ground black pepper
fresh parsley sprigs, to garnish

1 Heat the oil in a non-stick pan and fry the onion, garlic, ground coriander, cumin, turmeric and allspice and fry over low heat, stirring constantly, for 1 minute.

2 Stir in the bulgur wheat and cook, stirring constantly, for about 2 minutes, until lightly browned. Add the stock or water, mushrooms and lentils.

3 Bring to the boil, cover, then simmer over very low heat for 25–30 minutes, until the bulgur wheat and lentils are tender and all the liquid has been absorbed. Add more stock or water during cooking, if necessary.

4 Season well with salt, black pepper and cayenne pepper. Transfer to a warmed serving dish and serve immediately, garnished with parsley sprigs.

Cook's Tips
• Bulgur wheat is very easy to cook and can be used in almost any way you would normally use rice – hot or cold. Some of the finer grades need hardly any cooking, so check the packet instructions for cooking times.
• Green lentils can be cooked without presoaking. They cook quite quickly and keep their shape.

Risotto Energy 260kcal/1086kJ; Protein 8.4g; Carbohydrate 46g, of which sugars 0.9g; Fat 4.4g, of which saturates 2.6g; Cholesterol 11mg; Calcium 110mg; Fibre 1.2g; Sodium 79mg.
Pilaff Energy 242kcal/1016kJ; Protein 11.3g; Carbohydrate 47g, of which sugars 3.2g; Fat 2.1g, of which saturates 0.2g; Cholesterol 0mg; Calcium 45mg; Fibre 3.6g; Sodium 7mg.

Creole Jambalaya

A fusion of exciting flavours, this colourful dish of chicken thighs, vegetables and rice is very enticing. Serve this nourishing dish surrounded by fresh frisée salad leaves.

Serves 6

4 chicken thighs, boned, skinned and diced
about 300ml/½ pint/1¼ cups chicken stock
1 large green (bell) pepper, seeded and sliced
3 celery sticks, sliced
4 spring onions (scallions), sliced
400g/14oz can tomatoes
5ml/1 tsp ground cumin
5ml/1 tsp ground allspice
2.5ml/½ tsp cayenne pepper
5ml/1 tsp dried thyme
300g/10oz/1½ cups long grain rice
200g/7oz/scant 2 cups peeled, cooked prawns (shrimp)
salt and ground black pepper

1 Fry the chicken in a non-stick pan without fat, turning occasionally, until golden brown.

2 Add 15ml/1 tbsp stock to the pan with the sliced green pepper, celery stick and spring onions. Cook for a few minutes, stirring occasionally, until softened, then stir in the tomatoes, cumin, allspice, cayenne pepper and thyme.

3 Stir in the rice and the remaining stock. Bring to the boil, then reduce the heat, cover tightly and simmer for about 20 minutes, stirring occasionally, until the rice is tender. Add more stock during cooking, if necessary.

4 Stir the peeled prawns into the rice, then return to low heat to warm through the prawns. Season to taste with salt and pepper and serve immediately.

Variation
Traditionally, Jambalayas are made with ham, so try adding 115g/4oz diced cooked ham with the vegetables.

Minted Couscous Castles

These pretty little timbales are perfect for serving as part of a summer lunch. They are virtually fat-free, so you can happily indulge yourself without feeling remotely guilty.

Serves 6
225g/8oz/1¼ cups couscous
475ml/16fl oz/2 cups boiling vegetable stock
15ml/1 tbsp lemon juice
2 tomatoes, diced
30ml/2 tbsp chopped fresh mint
oil, for brushing
salt and ground black pepper
fresh mint sprigs, to garnish

1 Place the couscous in a bowl and pour over the boiling stock. Cover the bowl and leave to stand for 30 minutes, until all the stock has been absorbed and the grains are tender.

2 Stir in the lemon juice with the tomatoes and chopped mint. Adjust the seasoning with salt and pepper.

3 Brush the insides of four cups or individual moulds lightly with oil. Spoon in the couscous mixture and pack down firmly. Chill for several hours.

4 Invert the castles on to a platter and serve cold, garnished with mint. Alternatively, cover and heat gently in a low oven, then turn out and serve hot.

Cook's Tip
You will need the "instant" type of couscous for this dish, which is now widely available from most supermarkets. However, this type of quick couscous is not always immediately distinguishable from traditional couscous, which requires steaming first, so always check the instructions on the packet before buying. Only Moroccan couscous is produced in this "instant" form. The grains of traditional couscous can vary in size depending on the country of origin; the grains of Moroccan couscous are small, whereas Lebanese couscous is about the size of chickpeas.

Red Fried Rice

In this delicious version of egg fried rice, the vibrant colours of red onion, red pepper and cherry tomatoes add lots of eye appeal. An ideal dish for a quick supper.

Serves 2
115g/4oz/¾ cup basmati rice

30ml/2 tbsp groundnut (peanut) oil
1 small red onion, chopped
1 red (bell) pepper, seeded and chopped
225g/8oz cherry tomatoes, halved
2 eggs, beaten
salt and ground black pepper

1 Rinse the rice several times under cold running water. Drain well. Bring a large pan of water to the boil, add the rice and cook for 10–12 minutes.

2 Meanwhile, heat the oil in a wok until very hot and stir-fry the onion and red pepper for 2–3 minutes. Add the cherry tomatoes and stir-fry for a further 2 minutes.

3 Pour in the beaten eggs all at once. Cook for 30 seconds without stirring, then stir to break up the eggs as they set.

4 Drain the cooked rice thoroughly, add to the wok and toss it over the heat with the vegetable and egg mixture for 3 minutes. Season the fried rice with salt and pepper to taste.

Cook's Tips
• Basmati rice is good for this dish as its slightly crunchy texture complements the softness of the egg.
• It is possible to stir-fry in a frying pan, if you don't have a wok. However, the heat will be less evenly distributed and it is harder to toss the ingredients.

Variation
Add diced cooked ham or chicken with dashes of soy sauce.

Fruity Brown Rice

An oriental-style dressing gives this colourful rice salad extra piquancy.

Serves 4
115g/4oz/²⁄₃ cup brown rice
1 small red (bell) pepper, seeded and diced
200g/7oz can sweetcorn kernels, drained
45ml/3 tbsp sultanas (golden raisins)

225g/8oz can pineapple pieces in fruit juice
15ml/1 tbsp light soy sauce
15ml/1 tbsp sunflower oil
15ml/1 tbsp hazelnut oil
1 garlic clove, crushed
5ml/1 tsp finely chopped fresh root ginger
salt and ground black pepper
4 spring onions (scallions), diagonally sliced, to garnish

1 Bring a large pan of lightly salted water to the boil and cook the brown rice for about 30 minutes, or until it is just tender. Drain thoroughly, rinse under cold water and drain again. Set aside to cool.

2 Turn the rice into a large serving bowl and add the red pepper, sweetcorn and sultanas. Drain the pineapple pieces, reserving the juice, then add to the rice mixture and toss lightly.

3 Pour the reserved pineapple juice into a clean screw-top jar. Add the soy sauce, sunflower and hazelnut oils, garlic and chopped root ginger. Season to taste with salt and pepper. Close the jar tightly and shake vigorously to combine.

4 Pour the dressing over the salad and toss well. Scatter the spring onions over the top and serve.

Cook's Tip
• Hazelnut oil gives a distinctive flavour to any salad dressing. Like olive oil, it contains mainly mono-unsaturated fats.
• Brown rice is often mistakenly called wholegrain. In fact, the outer husk is completely inedible and is removed from all rice, but the bran layer is left intact on brown rice.

Red Rice Energy 437kcal/1821kJ; Protein 12.6g; Carbohydrate 57.4g, of which sugars 10.5g; Fat 17.6g, of which saturates 3.1g; Cholesterol 190mg; Calcium 62mg; Fibre 3g; Sodium 85mg.
Fruity Rice Energy 189kcal/797kJ; Protein 3g; Carbohydrate 35.5g, of which sugars 14.4g; Fat 4.8g, of which saturates 0.6g; Cholesterol 0mg; Calcium 18mg; Fibre 1.9g; Sodium 272mg.

Nut Pilaff with Omelette Rolls

This pilaff fuses together a wonderful mixture of textures – soft fluffy rice with crunchy nuts and omelette rolls.

Serves 2
175g/6oz/1 cup basmati rice
15ml/1 tbsp sunflower oil
1 small onion, chopped
1 red (bell) pepper, finely diced
350ml/12fl oz/1½ cups hot
   vegetable stock
2 eggs
25g/1oz/¼ cup salted peanuts
15ml/1 tbsp soy sauce
salt and ground black pepper
fresh parsley sprigs, to garnish

1 Rinse the rice several times under cold running water. Drain thoroughly and set aside.

2 Heat half the oil in a large frying pan and fry the onion and red pepper for 2–3 minutes, then stir in the rice and stock. Bring to the boil, lower the heat slightly and simmer for 10 minutes until the rice is tender.

3 Meanwhile, beat the eggs lightly and season to taste with salt and pepper. Heat the remaining oil in a second large frying pan. Pour in the eggs and tilt the pan to cover the base thinly. Cook the omelette for 1 minute, then flip it over and cook the other side for 1 minute.

4 Slide the omelette on to a clean board and roll it up tightly. Cut the omelette roll into eight slices.

5 Stir the peanuts and the soy sauce into the pilaff and add black pepper to taste. Turn the pilaff into a serving dish, then carefully arrange the omelette rolls on top and garnish with the parsley. Serve immediately.

> **Variation**
> To ring the changes, try salted cashew nuts or toasted flaked almonds instead of the peanuts.

Aubergine Pilaff

This hearty dish is made with bulgur wheat and aubergine, flavoured with fresh mint. It is a perfect choice for a midweek supper as it can be prepared within 15 minutes.

Serves 2
2 aubergines (eggplants)
60–90ml/4–6 tbsp sunflower oil
1 small onion, finely chopped
175g/6oz/1 cup bulgur wheat
450ml/¾ pint/scant 2 cups
   vegetable stock
30ml/2 tbsp pine nuts, toasted
15ml/1 tbsp chopped fresh mint
salt and ground black pepper

For the garnish
lime wedges
lemon wedges
fresh mint sprigs

1 Trim the ends from the aubergines, then slice them lengthways. Cut each slice into neat sticks and then into 1cm/½in dice.

2 Heat 60ml/4 tbsp of the oil in a large heavy frying pan, add the onion and fry over medium heat for 1 minute. Add the the diced aubergine. Increase the heat to high and cook, stirring frequently, for about 4 minutes until just tender. Add the remaining oil if needed.

4 Stir in the bulgur wheat, mixing well, then pour in the vegetable stock. Bring to the boil, then lower the heat and simmer for 10 minutes or until all the liquid has evaporated. Season to taste with salt and pepper.

5 Stir in the pine nuts and mint, then spoon the pilaff on to individual plates. Garnish each portion with lime and lemon wedges. Sprinkle with torn mint leaves for extra colour and serve immediately.

> **Variation**
> Use courgettes (zucchini) instead of aubergine, or for something completely different, substitute pumpkin or acorn squash.

Nut Energy 550kcal/2292kJ; Protein 17.4g; Carbohydrate 80g, of which sugars 8.4g; Fat 17.7g, of which saturates 3.4g; Cholesterol 190mg; Calcium 69mg; Fibre 2.6g; Sodium 609mg.
Aubergine Energy 542kcal/2248kJ; Protein 9.6g; Carbohydrate 52.2g, of which sugars 5.3g; Fat 34g, of which saturates 3.5g; Cholesterol 0mg; Calcium 83mg; Fibre 3.7g; Sodium 7mg.

Winter Vegetable Salad

This simple side salad is guaranteed to brighten up a winter menu. Made of leeks, cauliflower and celery, it is subtly flavoured with white wine, chopped herbs and juniper berries.

Serves 4
175ml/6 fl oz/³⁄₄ cup white wine
5ml/1 tsp olive oil
30ml/2 tbsp lemon juice

2 bay leaves
1 fresh thyme sprig
4 juniper berries
450g/1lb leeks, trimmed and cut
   into 2.5cm/1in lengths
1 small cauliflower, broken into
   florets
4 celery sticks, sliced on the
   diagonal
30ml/2 tbsp chopped fresh
   parsley
salt and ground black pepper

1 Put the wine, olive oil, lemon juice, bay leaves, thyme and juniper berries into a large, heavy pan and bring to the boil. Cover and leave to simmer 20 minutes.

2 Add the leeks, cauliflower and celery. Simmer very gently for 5–6 minutes, or until just tender.

3 Remove the vegetables with a slotted spoon and transfer them to a serving dish. Briskly boil the cooking liquid remaining in the pan for 15–20 minutes, or until reduced by half. Strain through a sieve (strainer).

4 Stir the parsley into the liquid and season to taste with salt and pepper. Pour over the vegetables and leave to cool. Chill for at least 1 hour before serving.

> **Cook's Tips**
> • Using the stock as a dressing, and adding only a tiny amount of oil, means that this dish is ideal for anyone on a low-fat diet.
> • Do not overcook the cauliflower: it should still feel firm to the bite. Remove the vegetables from the pan as they are done.
> • Vary the vegetables for this salad according to taste: the cauliflower with broccoli and the celery with carrot sticks.

Braised Red Cabbage

Lightly spiced with a sharp-sweet flavour, this dish goes well with roast pork, duck and game dishes.

Serves 4–6
1kg/2lb red cabbage
2 onions, chopped
2 cooking apples, peeled, cored
   and grated

5ml/1 tsp freshly grated nutmeg
1.5ml/¼ tsp ground cloves
1.5ml/¼ tsp ground cinnamon
15g/½ oz/1 tbsp soft dark brown
   sugar
45ml/3 tbsp red wine vinegar
25g/1oz/2 tbsp butter or
   margarine, diced
salt and ground black pepper

1 Preheat the oven to 160°C/325°F/Gas 3. Cut away and discard the large white ribs from the outer cabbage leaves using a large sharp knife, then finely shred the cabbage.

2 Layer the shredded cabbage in a large ovenproof dish with the onions, apples, spices and sugar, seasoning with salt and pepper. Pour over the red wine vinegar and add the diced butter or margarine.

3 Cover the ovenproof dish and cook in the oven for about 1½ hours, stirring a couple of times, until the cabbage is very tender. Serve immediately.

> **Cook's Tips**
> • This recipe can be cooked in advance. Bake the cabbage for 1½ hours, then cool. To complete the cooking, oven bake at the same temperature for about 30 minutes, stirring occasionally.
> • Add a splash of red wine if the dish starts to look dry during cooking, then add a little extra sugar to taste.

> **Variation**
> Try adding a strip of orange rind to the dish before cooking, then remove before serving.

Ratatouille

Bursting with Mediterranean flavours, this tasty dish may be served hot or cold, as a tasty starter, side dish or vegetarian main course.

Serves 4
2 large aubergines (eggplants), roughly chopped
150ml/¼ pint/⅔ cup olive oil
2 onions, sliced
2 garlic cloves, chopped
4 courgettes (zucchini), roughly chopped
1 large red (bell) pepper, seeded and roughly chopped
2 large yellow (bell) peppers, seeded and roughly chopped
1 fresh rosemary sprig
1 fresh thyme sprig
5ml/1 tsp coriander seeds, crushed
3 plum tomatoes, peeled, seeded and chopped
8 basil leaves, roughly torn
salt and ground black pepper
fresh parsley or basil sprigs, to garnish

1 Place the aubergines in a colander, sprinkle with salt and place a plate with a weight on top. Leave for 30 minutes to extract the bitter juices.

2 Heat the olive oil in a large pan and gently fry the onions for about 6–7 minutes until just softened. Add the garlic and cook for a further 2 minutes, stirring frequently.

3 Rinse the aubergines under cold running water, then drain and pat dry with kitchen paper. Add the aubergines to the pan of onions, together with the courgettes and peppers. Increase the heat and sauté for a few minutes until just turning brown.

4 Add the rosemary, thyme and coriander seeds, then cover the pan and cook gently for about 30 minutes.

5 Add the tomatoes and season to taste with salt and pepper. Cook gently for a further 10 minutes, until the vegetables are soft but not too mushy.

6 Remove the sprigs of herbs. Stir in the torn basil leaves and adjust the seasoning. Leave to cool slightly and serve warm or cold, garnished with sprigs of parsley or basil.

Lemony Carrots

The carrots are cooked until just tender in a lemony stock which is then thickened to make a light tangy sauce.

Serves 4
450g/1lb carrots, thinly sliced
bouquet garni
15ml/1 tbsp freshly squeezed lemon juice
pinch of freshly grated nutmeg
20g/¾ oz/1½ tbsp butter
15ml/½ oz/1 tbsp plain (all-purpose) flour
salt and ground black pepper

1 Bring 600ml/1 pint/2½ cups water to the boil in a large pan, then add the carrots, bouquet garni and lemon juice. Add a pinch of nutmeg and season to taste with salt and pepper.

2 Bring back to the boil, then lower the heat slightly and simmer until the carrots are tender. Remove the carrots using a slotted spoon, then keep warm.

3 Boil the cooking liquid hard until it has reduced to about 300ml/½ pint/1¼ cups. Discard the bouquet garni.

4 Mash 15g/½oz/1 tbsp of the butter and all of the flour together, then gradually whisk into the simmering reduced cooking liquid, whisking well after each addition. Continue to simmer for about 3 minutes, stirring frequently, until the sauce has thickened.

5 Return the carrots to the pan, heat through in the sauce, then remove from the heat. Stir in the remaining butter and serve immediately.

Cook's Tip
A bouquet garni is a small bunch of herbs, usually bay leaves, parsley and thyme, tied together with string or in a muslin bag. If you make your own, you can add different herbs to suit a dish. Dried bouquet garnis are sold in supermarkets.

Carrots Energy 89kcal/372kJ; Protein 1.1g; Carbohydrate 11.8g, of which sugars 8.4g; Fat 4.5g, of which saturates 2.7g; Cholesterol 11mg; Calcium 34mg; Fibre 2.8g; Sodium 59mg.
Ratatouille Energy 349kcal/1442kJ; Protein 6.4g; Carbohydrate 21.6g, of which sugars 19.1g; Fat 26.9g, of which saturates 4g; Cholesterol 0mg; Calcium 82mg; Fibre 7.3g; Sodium 18mg.

Fried Spring Greens

Nutrient-rich leafy vegetables make a healthy side dish.

Serves 4

15ml/1 tbsp olive oil
75g/3oz rindless smoked streaky (fatty) bacon, chopped
1 large onion, thinly sliced
2 garlic cloves, finely chopped
900g/2lb spring greens (collards), shredded
salt and ground black pepper

1 Heat the oil in a frying pan and fry the bacon for 2 minutes. Add the onion and garlic and fry for 3 minutes until softened.

2 Reduce the heat, add the spring greens and season with salt and pepper. Cook, covered, over gentle heat for about 15 minutes until the greens are tender. Serve immediately.

Parsnips with Almonds

Parsnips are sweetly spiced to bring out their flavour.

Serves 4

450g/1lb small parsnips
35g/1¼ oz/scant 3 tbsp butter
25g/1oz/¼ cup flaked (sliced) almonds
15g/½ oz/1 tbsp soft light brown sugar
pinch of ground mixed spice
15ml/1 tbsp lemon juice
salt and ground black pepper
chopped fresh chervil or parsley, to garnish

1 Cook the parsnips in boiling salted water until almost tender. Drain well. When the parsnips are cool enough to handle, cut each in half across its width, then quarter lengthways.

2 Melt the butter in a pan. Gently cook the parsnips and almonds, stirring and turning until they are lightly flecked with brown.

3 Mix together the sugar and spice, sprinkle over the parsnips and stir to mix. Trickle over the lemon juice. Season to taste with salt and pepper and heat for 1 minute. Garnish with herbs.

Turnips with Orange

Turnips coated in a delicious orange-flavoured buttery sauce make a wonderful alternative to the more usual potato side dish.

Serves 4

50g/2oz/¼ cup butter
15ml/1 tbsp vegetable oil
1 small shallot, finely chopped
450g/1lb small turnips, peeled and quartered
300ml/½ pint/1¼ cups freshly squeezed orange juice
salt and ground black pepper
roughly torn fresh flat leaf parsley, to garnish

1 Heat the butter and oil in a pan and cook the shallot gently, stirring occasionally, until softened but not coloured.

2 Add the turnips to the shallot and cook over medium heat, shaking the pan frequently, until the turnips start to absorb the butter and oil.

3 Pour the orange juice on to the turnips, turn to coat well, then simmer gently for about 30 minutes, until the turnips are tender and the orange juice is reduced to a buttery sauce. Season with salt and pepper, if required, then garnish with parsley and serve immediately.

Cook's Tips
• Sprinkle toasted nuts, such as flaked (sliced) almonds or chopped walnuts, over the turnips to add a contrast in textures.
• Use tender, young turnips, available in early summer. They have creamy coloured flesh and skins tinged with purple or green.

Variation
Use a mixture of parsnips and carrots; cut into large chunks and add 10ml/2 tsp soft light brown sugar with the orange juice to bring out the sweetness of the vegetables.

Spring Greens Energy 156kcal/644kJ; Protein 9.9g; Carbohydrate 8.2g, of which sugars 6.9g; Fat 9.5g, of which saturates 2.2g; Cholesterol 12mg; Calcium 478mg; Fibre 7.9g; Sodium 282mg.
Parsnips Energy 190kcal/794kJ; Protein 3.4g; Carbohydrate 18.5g, of which sugars 10.7g; Fat 11.9g, of which saturates 5.1g; Cholesterol 19mg; Calcium 65mg; Fibre 5.7g; Sodium 66mg.
Turnips Energy 176kcal/732kJ; Protein 1.7g; Carbohydrate 13.2g, of which sugars 12.6g; Fat 13.5g, of which saturates 6.9g; Cholesterol 27mg; Calcium 68mg; Fibre 3g; Sodium 101mg.

Red Cabbage with Pears & Nuts

A sweet and sour, spicy red cabbage dish, with the added juiciness of pears and extra crunch of walnuts.

Serves 6

15ml/1 tbsp walnut oil
1 onion, sliced
2 whole star anise
5ml/1 tsp ground cinnamon
pinch of ground cloves

450g/1lb red cabbage, finely shredded
25g/1oz/2 tbsp soft dark brown sugar
45ml/3 tbsp red wine vinegar
300ml/½ pint/1¼ cups red wine
150ml/¼ pint/⅔ cup port
2 pears, cut into 1cm/½in cubes
115g/4oz/⅔ cup raisins
115g/4oz/1 cup walnut halves
salt and ground black pepper

1 Heat the oil in a large heavy pan. Add the sliced onion and cook over low heat, stirring occasionally, for about 5 minutes until softened.

2 Add the star anise, cinnamon, cloves and cabbage and cook for about 3 minutes more.

3 Stir in the sugar, vinegar, red wine and port. Cover the pan and simmer gently for 10 minutes, stirring occasionally.

4 Stir in the cubed pears and raisins and cook without replacing the lid for a further 10 minutes, or until the cabbage is tender. Season to taste with salt and pepper. Mix in the walnut halves and serve immediately.

Cook's Tip
The vinegar and wine help to preserve the beautiful colour of the cabbage as well as adding to the flavour.

Variation
Omit the star anise and cinnamon and add 15ml/1 tbsp juniper berries with the ground cloves.

Swiss Soufflé Potatoes

A fabulous combination of rich and satisfying ingredients – cheese, eggs, cream, butter and potatoes. This is the perfect dish for cold-weather entertaining.

Serves 4

4 baking potatoes, about 900g/2lb total weight
115g/4oz/1 cup grated Gruyère cheese
115g/4oz/½ cup herb butter
60ml/4 tbsp double (heavy) cream
2 eggs, separated
salt and ground black pepper
snipped fresh chives, to garnish

1 Preheat the oven to 220°C/425°F/Gas 7. Scrub the potatoes, then prick them all over with a fork. Bake for 1–1½ hours until tender. Remove them from the oven and reduce the temperature to 180°C/350°F/Gas 4.

2 Cut each potato in half and scoop out the flesh into a bowl. Place the potato shells on a baking sheet and return them to the oven to crisp up while you are making the filling.

3 Mash the potato flesh, then add the Gruyère cheese, herb butter, cream and egg yolks. Beat well until smooth, then season to taste with salt and pepper.

4 Whisk the egg whites until stiff peaks form, then carefully fold into the potato mixture. Pile the mixture into the potato shells and bake for 20–25 minutes until risen and golden brown.

5 Transfer the potatoes to a warmed serving dish, garnish with chives and serve immediately.

Cook's Tip
To make the herb butter, mix 45ml/3 tbsp finely chopped fresh parsley and 10ml/2 tsp finely chopped fresh dill with 115g/4oz/½ cup softened butter. Season with a little salt.

Red Cabbage Energy 202kcal/847kJ; Protein 1.8g; Carbohydrate 30.1g, of which sugars 29.8g; Fat 2.1g, of which saturates 0.2g; Cholesterol 0mg; Calcium 60mg; Fibre 3.2g; Sodium 23mg.
Potatoes Energy 585kcal/2431kJ; Protein 14.3g; Carbohydrate 32.7g, of which sugars 3.1g; Fat 44.5g, of which saturates 27.2g; Cholesterol 205mg; Calcium 251mg; Fibre 2g; Sodium 443mg.

Thai Vegetables with Noodles

This dish makes a delicious vegetarian supper on its own, or it could be served as an accompaniment.

Serves 4
225g/8oz/4 cups egg noodles
15ml/1 tbsp sesame oil
45ml/3 tbsp groundnut (peanut) oil
2 garlic cloves, thinly sliced
2.5cm/1in piece fresh root ginger, finely chopped
2 fresh red chillies, seeded and sliced
115g/4oz/1 cup broccoli florets
115g/4oz baby corn on the cob
175g/6oz shiitake or oyster mushrooms, sliced
1 bunch spring onions (scallions), sliced
115g/4oz pak choi (bok choy) or Chinese leaves (Chinese cabbage), shredded
115g/4oz/generous 1 cup beansprouts
15–30ml/1–2 tbsp dark soy sauce
salt and ground black pepper

1 Bring a pan of salted water to the boil and cook the egg noodles according to the instructions on the packet. Drain well and toss in the sesame oil. Set aside.

2 Heat the groundnut oil in a wok or large frying pan and stir-fry the garlic and ginger for 1 minute. Add the chillies, broccoli, baby corn on the cob and mushrooms and stir-fry for a further 2 minutes.

3 Add the spring onions, shredded pak choi or Chinese leaves and beansprouts and stir-fry for another 2 minutes. Toss in the drained noodles, adding soy sauce and pepper to taste.

4 Continue to cook over high heat, stirring, for a further 2–3 minutes, until the ingredients are well mixed and warmed through. Serve immediately.

> **Variation**
> This is a very versatile dish – you can vary the vegetables as you wish. Try replacing the broccoli with asparagus tips or use mangetouts (snow peas) instead of the Chinese leaves.

Cauliflower with Three Cheeses

The mingled flavours of three cheeses give a new twist to cauliflower cheese. Serve with roasted cherry tomatoes and chunks of hot olive bread for an elegant meat-free meal.

Serves 4
4 baby cauliflowers
250ml/8fl oz/1 cup single (light) cream
75g/3oz dolcelatte cheese, diced
75g/3oz mozzarella cheese, diced
45ml/3 tbsp freshly grated Parmesan cheese
pinch of freshly grated nutmeg
ground black pepper
toasted breadcrumbs, to garnish

1 Cook the cauliflowers in a large pan of boiling salted water for 8–10 minutes until just tender.

2 Meanwhile, put the cream in a small pan with the cheeses. Heat gently until the cheeses have melted, stirring occasionally. Season to taste with nutmeg and pepper.

3 When the cauliflowers are cooked, drain them thoroughly and place one on each of four warmed plates.

4 Carefully spoon a little of the cheese sauce over each cauliflower and sprinkle each with a few of the toasted breadcrumbs. Serve immediately.

> **Cook's Tips**
> • For a more economical dish or if baby cauliflowers are not available, use one large cauliflower instead. Cut it into quarters with a large sharp knife and remove the central core.
> • The luxurious sauce is very simple to make as it does not use a butter and flour base like a conventional cheese sauce. To make the sauce slightly less rich, replace the cream with milk.
> • To make the toasted breadcrumbs, use bread that is a couple of days old and turn into crumbs in a food processor. Toast until golden, shaking often. You could also use chopped nuts instead.

Thai Vegetables Energy 364kcal/1528kJ; Protein 12g; Carbohydrate 44.3g, of which sugars 4g; Fat 16.7g, of which saturates 3.4g; Cholesterol 17mg; Calcium 102mg; Fibre 4.7g; Sodium 744mg.
Cauliflower Energy 318kcal/1318kJ; Protein 17.4g; Carbohydrate 4.4g, of which sugars 3.9g; Fat 25.8g, of which saturates 16.3g; Cholesterol 71mg; Calcium 371mg; Fibre 1.8g; Sodium 453mg.

Winter Vegetable Hot-pot

Made with a variety of root vegetables, this one-pot dish is richly flavoured, and substantial enough to make a vegetarian main course.

Serves 4
2 onions, sliced
4 carrots, sliced
1 small swede, sliced
2 parsnips, sliced
3 small turnips, sliced
1/2 celeriac, cut into matchsticks
2 leeks, thinly sliced
30ml/2 tbsp mixed chopped fresh herbs, such as parsley and thyme
1 garlic clove, chopped
1 bay leaf, crumbled
300ml/1/2 pint/1 1/4 cups vegetable stock
15g/1/2 oz/1 tbsp plain (all-purpose) flour
675g/1 1/2 lb red-skinned potatoes, scrubbed and thinly sliced
50g/2oz/1/4 cup butter
salt and ground black pepper

1 Preheat the oven to 190°C/375°F/Gas 5. Arrange all the vegetables, except the potatoes, in layers in a large casserole with a tight-fitting lid, seasoning them lightly with salt and pepper and sprinkling them with chopped fresh herbs, garlic and crumbled bay leaf as you go.

2 Blend the vegetable stock into the flour and pour over the vegetables. Arrange the potatoes in overlapping layers on top. Dot with butter and cover tightly.

3 Cook in the oven for 1 1/4 hours, or until the vegetables are tender. Remove the lid from the casserole and cook for a further 15–20 minutes until the top layer of potatoes is golden and crisp at the edges. Serve immediately.

> **Cook's Tips**
> • Make sure the root vegetables are cut into even-size slices so they cook uniformly.
> • For cheesy toasts to serve with the hot-pot, toast slices of French bread on one side. Turn over and sprinkle the other side with grated Gruyère cheese, then grill (broil) until golden.

Potato Gnocchi with Hazelnut Sauce

These delicate Italian potato dumplings are dressed with a wonderful, creamy-tasting hazelnut sauce.

Serves 4
675g/1 1/2 lb large potatoes
115g/4oz/1 cup plain (all-purpose) flour, plus extra for dusting

For the hazelnut sauce
115g/4oz/1/2 cup hazelnuts, roasted
1 garlic clove, roughly chopped
1/2 tsp grated lemon rind
1/2 tsp lemon juice
30ml/2 tbsp sunflower oil
150g/5oz/3/4 cup low-fat fromage frais
salt and ground black pepper

1 To make the sauce, put just over half of the hazelnuts in a blender or food processor with the garlic, grated lemon rind and juice. Process until coarsely chopped. With the motor running, gradually add the oil until the mixture is smooth. Spoon into a heatproof bowl and mix in the fromage frais. Season to taste with salt and pepper.

2 Put the potatoes in a pan of cold water. Bring to the boil and cook for 20–25 minutes. Drain well. When cool enough to handle, peel them and pass through a food mill into a bowl.

3 Add the flour a little at a time, until the mixture is smooth and slightly sticky. Add salt to taste. Roll out the mixture on to a floured board to form a sausage 1cm/1/2in in diameter. Cut into 2cm/3/4in lengths. Roll one piece at at time on a floured fork to make the characteristic ridges. Flip on to a floured plate or tray.

4 Cook a batch of gnocchi in a large pan of boiling water for 3–4 minutes. Lift out with a slotted spoon and keep hot while cooking the rest of the gnocchi in the same way.

5 To heat the sauce, place the bowl over a pan of simmering water and heat gently, being careful not to let it curdle. Pour the sauce over the gnocchi. Roughly chop the remaining hazelnuts, scatter them over the top and serve immediately.

Gnocchi Energy 495kcal/2071kJ; Protein 11.9g; Carbohydrate 52.9g, of which sugars 5.3g; Fat 27.6g, of which saturates 4.3g; Cholesterol 3mg; Calcium 132mg; Fibre 4.5g; Sodium 35mg.
Hot-Pot Energy 367kcal/1542kJ; Protein 8.5g; Carbohydrate 58.2g, of which sugars 24.5g; Fat 12.8g, of which saturates 7g; Cholesterol 27mg; Calcium 203mg; Fibre 13.1g; Sodium 178mg.

Vegetable Ribbons

This elegant vegetable side dish looks very impressive.

Serves 4
3 carrots
3 courgettes (zucchini)
120ml/4fl oz/1/2 cup chicken stock
30ml/2 tbsp freshly chopped parsley
salt and ground black pepper

1 Using a vegetable peeler or sharp knife, cut the carrots and courgettes into thin ribbons.

2 Bring the chicken stock to the boil in a pan and add the carrots. Return the stock to the boil, then add the courgettes. Boil rapidly for 2–3 minutes, or until the vegetable ribbons are just tender. Stir in the chopped parsley, season lightly with salt and ground black pepper and serve immediately.

Runner Beans with Tomatoes

Try to use tender young beans for this dish. If you use older ones, you will need to remove the "strings" down the sides before cooking.

Serves 4
675g/1½ lb/2 cups sliced runner (green) beans
40g/1½oz/3 tbsp butter
4 ripe tomatoes, peeled and chopped
salt and ground black pepper
chopped fresh tarragon, to garnish

1 Bring a pan of water to the boil, add the beans, return to the boil and cook for 3 minutes. Drain well.

2 Heat the butter in a pan, add the tomatoes and beans and season with salt and pepper. Cover the pan with a tight-fitting lid and simmer gently for about 10–15 minutes until tender.

3 Turn the beans and tomatoes into a warm serving dish, garnish with tarragon and serve immediately.

Rosemary Roasties

Theses potatoes are roasted with their skins on, giving them far more flavour than traditional roast potatoes. They are the ideal accompaniment to roast lamb.

Serves 4
1kg/2lb small red potatoes
30ml/2 tbsp olive oil
30ml/2 tbsp fresh rosemary leaves
pinch of paprika
salt

1 Leave the potatoes whole with the skins on, or if large, cut in half. Place the potatoes in a large pan of cold water and bring to the boil, then drain immediately.

2 Meanwhile, preheat the oven to 240°C/475°F/Gas 9.

3 Return the potatoes to the pan and drizzle the oil over them. Shake the pan to coat the potatoes evenly in the oil.

4 Transfer the potatoes to a roasting pan. Sprinkle with the rosemary, paprika and salt, then roast in the oven for 30 minutes, until the potatoes are golden brown and crisp; turn them once during cooking so that they brown evenly.

5 Remove the roasties from the oven, drain on kitchen paper and serve immediately.

Cook's Tip
The potatoes can be cut into smaller wedges, in which case the boiling stage can be omitted. Serve wedges with mayonnaise as an alternative to chips, or offer as canapés with drinks.

Variation
Add about 10 unpeeled garlic cloves to the roasting pan with the potatoes, adding a little extra oil and tossing well to coat. Roast the garlic with the potatoes; they will develop a sweet taste.

Ribbons Energy 42kcal/175kJ; Protein 2g; Carbohydrate 7.4g, of which sugars 6.9g; Fat 0.7g, of which saturates 0.2g; Cholesterol 0mg; Calcium 39mg; Fibre 2.5g; Sodium 183mg.
Runner Beans Energy 129kcal/536kJ; Protein 3.5g; Carbohydrate 8.6g, of which sugars 7.9g; Fat 9.2g, of which saturates 5.5g; Cholesterol 21mg; Calcium 65mg; Fibre 4.4g; Sodium 70mg.
Roasties Energy 189kcal/801kJ; Protein 4.3g; Carbohydrate 40.3g, of which sugars 3.3g; Fat 2.3g, of which saturates 0.4g; Cholesterol 0mg; Calcium 15mg; Fibre 2.5g; Sodium 28mg.

Courgette & Tomato Bake

In this tasty French dish, the vegetables are baked with bacon, rice and cheese.

Serves 4

45ml/3 tbsp olive oil
1 onion, chopped
1 garlic clove, crushed
3 rashers (strips) lean bacon, chopped
4 courgettes (zucchini), grated
2 tomatoes, peeled, seeded and chopped
115g/4oz/scant ¾ cup cooked long grain rice
10ml/2 tsp chopped fresh thyme
15ml/1 tbsp chopped fresh parsley
60ml/4 tbsp grated Parmesan cheese
2 eggs, lightly beaten
15ml/1 tbsp fromage frais or mascarpone
salt and ground black pepper

1 Preheat the oven to 180°C/350°F/Gas 4. Grease a shallow ovenproof dish with a little olive oil.

2 Heat the oil in a frying pan and fry the onion and garlic for 5 minutes until softened.

3 Add the bacon and fry for 2 minutes, then stir in the courgettes and fry for a further 8 minutes, stirring from time to time and allowing some of the liquid to evaporate. Remove the pan from the heat.

4 Add the tomatoes, cooked rice, herbs, 30ml/2 tbsp of the Parmesan cheese, the eggs and fromage frais or mascarpone, then season to taste with salt and pepper. Mix together well.

5 Spoon the mixture into the dish and sprinkle over the remaining Parmesan. Bake for 45 minutes until set and golden.

> **Cook's Tip**
> *For a dinner party, divide the mixture among four lightly greased individual gratin dishes and bake at the same temperature for about 25 minutes until set and golden.*

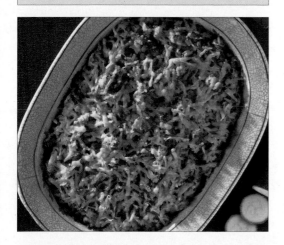

Spanish Green Beans with Ham

Spanish raw-cured Serrano ham is now increasingly available in supermarkets, but if you have difficulty finding it, you can use Parma ham or bacon instead.

Serves 4

450g/1lb green beans
45ml/3 tbsp olive oil
1 onion, thinly sliced
2 garlic cloves, finely chopped
75g/3oz Serrano ham, chopped
salt and ground black pepper

1 Top and tail the beans, then cook them in boiling salted water for about 5–6 minutes until they are just tender.

2 Meanwhile, heat the oil in a pan, add the onion and fry for 5 minutes until softened and translucent. Add the garlic and ham and cook for a further 1–2 minutes.

3 Drain the beans, then add them to the pan and cook, stirring occasionally, for 2–3 minutes. Season well with salt and pepper.

Tomato & Aubergine Gratin

This tasty Mediterranean dish is perfect with plainly cooked meat or poultry.

Serves 6

2 aubergines (eggplants), thinly sliced
45ml/3 tbsp olive oil
400g/14oz ripe tomatoes, sliced
40g/1½oz/½ cup freshly grated Parmesan cheese
salt and ground black pepper

1 Preheat the grill (broiler). Arrange the aubergines on a foil-lined grill rack. Brush with olive oil and grill (broil) for 15–20 minutes until golden, turning once and brushing with more oil.

2 Preheat the oven to 200°C/400°F/Gas 6. Toss the aubergine and tomato slices together with salt and pepper and put in a shallow ovenproof dish. Sprinkle with the cheese. Bake for 20 minutes, until the vegetables are hot and the top is golden.

Courgette Energy 302kcal/1255kJ; Protein 16.4g; Carbohydrate 14.6g, of which sugars 5.2g; Fat 20.2g, of which saturates 6.5g; Cholesterol 120mg; Calcium 249mg; Fibre 2.1g; Sodium 495mg.
Spanish Beans Energy 127kcal/523kJ; Protein 5.8g; Carbohydrate 5g, of which sugars 3.6g; Fat 9.5g, of which saturates 1.5g; Cholesterol 11mg; Calcium 46mg; Fibre 2.7g; Sodium 226mg.
Gratin Energy 101kcal/420kJ; Protein 3.7g; Carbohydrate 3.5g, of which sugars 3.4g; Fat 8.1g, of which saturates 2.3g; Cholesterol 7mg; Calcium 91mg; Fibre 2g; Sodium 80mg.

Sweet Potatoes with Bacon

This sweet potato dish is often served for Thanksgiving in North America to celebrate the settlers' first harvest.

Serves 4
2 large sweet potatoes (about 450g/1lb each), washed
50g/2oz/½ cup soft light brown sugar
30ml/2 tbsp lemon juice
40g/1½ oz/3 tbsp butter, plus extra for greasing
4 rashers (strips) smoked streaky (fatty) bacon, cut into thin strips
salt and ground black pepper
sprig of flat leaf parsley, to garnish

1 Preheat the oven to 190°C/375°F/Gas 5 and lightly butter a shallow ovenproof dish. Cut the unpeeled sweet potatoes crossways into four and place the pieces in a pan of boiling water. Cover with a tight-fitting lid and cook for about 25 minutes until just tender.

2 Drain the potatoes and, when cool enough to handle, peel and slice quite thickly. Place in a single layer in the prepared dish, arranging so that each slice overlaps one another.

3 Sprinkle over the sugar and lemon juice and dot with butter. Top with the bacon and season with salt and pepper.

4 Bake, uncovered, for 35–40 minutes, basting once or twice, until the potatoes are tender.

5 Preheat the grill (broiler) to high. Grill (broil) the potatoes for about 2–3 minutes, until they are browned and the bacon crispy. Garnish with parsley and serve immediately.

Cook's Tip
Sweet potatoes are now widely available in supermarkets. The orange-fleshed variety not only looks attractive but tastes delicious, particularly when the sweetness is enhanced, as here.

Potatoes Baked with Tomatoes

This dish from the south of Italy is utterly delicious, yet simplicity itself to make – mouthwatering layers of vegetables and cheese, baked until meltingly tender.

Serves 6
2 large red or yellow onions, thinly sliced
900g/2¼ lb potatoes, thinly sliced
450g/1lb fresh tomatoes, or canned, with their juice, sliced
90ml/6 tbsp olive oil
115g/4oz/1 cup freshly grated Parmesan or mature Cheddar cheese
few sprigs of fresh basil
salt and ground black pepper

1 Preheat the oven to 180°C/350°F/Gas 4. Brush a large baking dish generously with oil.

2 Arrange a layer of onions in the dish, followed by layers of potatoes and tomatoes. Pour on a little of the oil and sprinkle with cheese. Season with salt and pepper.

3 Repeat until the vegetables are used up, ending with an overlapping layer of potatoes and tomatoes. Tear the basil leaves into pieces, then add them here and there among the vegetables. Sprinkle the top with cheese and a little oil.

4 Pour on 50ml/2fl oz/¼ cup water. Bake for 1 hour, or until tender. If the top begins to brown too much, place a sheet of foil on top of the dish during cooking.

Cook's Tip
When ripe, flavourful tomatoes are available, use these instead of the canned variety; the resulting dish will be delicious and have a more authentic Italian flavour.

Variation
Add chopped, fried smoked bacon to the layer of onions.

Stuffed Onions

Roasted onions, filled with a ham and cheese stuffing, make a winning lunch dish. If you use small onions, they also made a tasty side dish.

Serves 6
6 large onions
75g/3oz/scant ½ cup ham, cut into small dice
1 egg
50g/2oz/½ cup dried breadcrumbs
45ml/3 tbsp finely chopped fresh parsley
1 garlic clove, chopped
pinch of freshly grated nutmeg
75g/3oz/¾ cup freshly grated cheese such as Parmesan or mature Cheddar
90ml/6 tbsp olive oil
salt and ground black pepper

1 Peel the onions without cutting through the bases. Cook them in a large pan of boiling water for about 20 minutes. Drain, then refresh in plenty of cold water.

2 Using a small sharp knife, cut around and scoop out each central section. Remove about half the inside (save it for soup). Lightly sprinkle the empty cavities with salt and leave the onions to drain upside down.

3 Preheat the oven to 200°C/400°F/Gas 6. Beat the ham into the egg in a small bowl. Stir in the breadcrumbs, parsley, garlic, nutmeg and all but 45ml/3 tbsp of the grated cheese. Add 45ml/3 tbsp of the oil, then season with salt and pepper.

4 Pat the insides of the onions dry with kitchen paper. Using a small spoon, fill them with the stuffing. Arrange the onions in a single layer in an oiled baking dish.

5 Sprinkle the tops with the remaining cheese and then with oil. Bake for 45 minutes, or until the onions are tender and golden on top. Serve immediately.

> **Cook's Tip**
> *These are particularly good with a home-made tomato sauce.*

Aubergine Baked with Cheeses

The key to this speciality of southern Italy is a good home-made tomato sauce.

Serves 4–6
900g/2lb aubergines (eggplants), thinly sliced
flour, for coating
olive oil, for frying and greasing
40g/1½ oz/½ cup freshly grated Parmesan cheese
400g/14oz mozzarella cheese, sliced very thinly
salt and ground black pepper

For the tomato sauce
60ml/4 tbsp olive oil
1 onion, very finely chopped
1 garlic clove, chopped
450g/1lb fresh tomatoes, or canned, chopped, with the juice
few fresh basil or parsley sprigs

1 Layer the aubergine slices in a colander, sprinkling each layer with a little salt. Leave to drain for about 20 minutes, then rinse under cold running water and pat dry with kitchen paper.

2 To make the tomato sauce, cook the onion in the oil until translucent. Stir in the garlic and the tomatoes (if using fresh tomatoes, add 45ml/3 tbsp water). Season to taste with salt and pepper, then add the basil or parsley. Simmer gently for 30 minutes, stirring occasionally. Purée in a food mill, if you wish.

3 Pat the aubergine slices dry, then coat them lightly in flour. Heat a little oil in a large non-stick frying pan. Add a single layer of aubergines, cover and cook over low to medium heat until softened. Turn and cook on the other side. Remove from the pan with a slotted spoon and repeat with the remaining slices.

4 Preheat the oven to 180°C/350°F/Gas 4. Grease a wide shallow baking dish. Spread a little tomato sauce in the base. Cover with a layer of aubergine. Sprinkle with a few teaspoons of Parmesan, season to taste with salt and pepper, and cover with a layer of mozzarella. Spoon on some tomato sauce.

5 Repeat until all the ingredients are used up, ending with a covering of the tomato sauce and a sprinkling of Parmesan. Sprinkle with a little olive oil, and bake for about 45 minutes until golden and bubbling.

Aubergine Energy 345kcal/1433kJ; Protein 17.2g; Carbohydrate 7.7g, of which sugars 5.9g; Fat 27.6g, of which saturates 12.3g; Cholesterol 45mg; Calcium 347mg; Fibre 3.9g; Sodium 346mg.
Stuffed Onions Energy 140kcal/584kJ; Protein 8.7g; Carbohydrate 13.4g, of which sugars 5.2g; Fat 5.9g, of which saturates 3.1g; Cholesterol 51mg; Calcium 145mg; Fibre 1.7g; Sodium 320mg.

Mushrooms with Chipotle Chillies

Chipotle chillies are *jalapeños* that have been smoke-dried. They are the perfect foil for the mushrooms in this simple warm salad. Serve with lots of warm bread to soak up the tasty juices.

Serves 6
2 chipotle chillies
450g/1lb/6 cups button (white) mushrooms
60ml/4 tbsp vegetable oil
1 onion, finely chopped
2 garlic cloves, chopped
fresh coriander (cilantro), to garnish

1 Soak the dried chillies in a bowl of hot water for about 10 minutes. Drain, then trim and remove the seeds. Chop finely.

2 Cut the mushrooms in half, if large. Heat the oil in a large frying pan. Add the onion, garlic, chillies and mushrooms and stir to coat in the oil. Fry for 6–8 minutes until the onion has softened. Transfer to a warmed dish. Chop some of the coriander, leaving some whole leaves, and use to garnish.

Baked Fennel with Parmesan

The delicate aniseed flavour of fennel is delicious with the sharpness of Parmesan cheese. Try serving with pasta dishes and risottos.

Serves 4–6
900g/2lb fennel bulbs, washed and cut in half
50g/2oz/¼ cup butter
40g/1½ oz/½ cup freshly grated Parmesan cheese

1 Cook the fennel bulbs in a large pan of boiling water until softened but not mushy. Drain well. Preheat the oven to 200°C/400°F/Gas 6.

2 Cut the fennel bulbs lengthways into four or six pieces. Place them in a buttered baking dish. Dot with butter, then sprinkle with the grated Parmesan. Bake in the oven for about 20 minutes until the cheese is golden brown. Serve immediately.

Courgettes with Sun-dried Tomatoes

Sun-dried tomatoes have a concentrated sweet flavour that goes particularly well with courgettes.

Serves 6
10 sun-dried tomatoes, dry or preserved in oil and drained
175ml/6fl oz/¾ cup warm water

75ml/5 tbsp olive oil
1 large onion, finely sliced
2 garlic cloves, finely chopped
900g/2lb courgettes (zucchini), cut into thin strips
salt and ground black pepper

1 Slice the sun-dried tomatoes into thin strips. Place in a bowl with the warm water. Allow to stand for 20 minutes.

2 Heat the oil in a large frying pan or pan, add the onion and cook over low to medium heat, stirring, until it has softened and turned translucent.

3 Stir in the garlic and the courgettes. Cook for about a further 5 minutes, continuing to stir the mixture.

4 Stir in the tomatoes and their soaking liquid. Season to taste with salt and pepper. Increase the heat slightly and cook until the courgettes are just tender. Serve hot or cold.

Cook's Tip
Sprinkle with grated Parmesan just before serving, if you wish.

Variation
For courgettes in rich tomato sauce, cook the courgettes up to the end of step 3, then add one 400g/14oz can drained chopped tomatoes and 4 peeled and chopped fresh tomatoes. Stir in 5ml/1 tsp vegetable bouillon powder and 30ml/2tbsp tomato purée (paste). Simmer for 10–15 minutes, until the sauce has thickened. Season with salt and pepper and serve.

Mushrooms Energy 83kcal/341kJ; Protein 2g; Carbohydrate 1.2g, of which sugars 0.8g; Fat 7.8g, of which saturates 0.9g; Cholesterol 0mg; Calcium 12mg; Fibre 1g; Sodium 5mg.
Baked Fennel Energy 96kcal/397kJ; Protein 3g; Carbohydrate 0.7g, of which sugars 0.6g; Fat 9.1g, of which saturates 5.7g; Cholesterol 24mg; Calcium 90mg; Fibre 0.8g; Sodium 127mg.
Courgettes Energy 141kcal/580kJ; Protein 3.2g; Carbohydrate 5.9g, of which sugars 4.9g; Fat 11.7g, of which saturates 1.7g; Cholesterol 0mg; Calcium 47mg; Fibre 2g; Sodium 4mg.

Broccoli Cauliflower Gratin

Broccoli and cauliflower look and taste good when served together, and this dish is much lighter than a classic cauliflower cheese.

Serves 4
1 small cauliflower (weighing about 250g/9oz)
1 head broccoli (weighing about 250g/9oz)
120ml/4fl oz/½ cup natural (plain) low-fat yogurt
75g/3oz/¼ cup grated reduced-fat Cheddar cheese
5ml/1 tsp wholegrain mustard
30ml/2 tbsp wholemeal (whole-wheat) breadcrumbs
salt and ground black pepper

1 Break the cauliflower and broccoli into florets and cook in lightly salted boiling water for 8–10 minutes, until just tender. Drain well and arrange in a flameproof dish.

2 Preheat the grill (broiler) to medium hot. Mix together in a bowl the yogurt, grated cheese and mustard. Season the mixture to taste with pepper and spoon over the cauliflower and broccoli florets.

3 Sprinkle the breadcrumbs over the top of the dish and place under the grill until golden brown. Serve immediately.

Cook's Tip
When preparing the cauliflower and broccoli, discard the tougher parts of the stalks, then break the florets into even-size pieces so they will cook evenly.

Variations
Chopped nuts make a good alternative to breadcrumbs in this light dish; almonds, hazelnuts or walnuts would all be suitable. Alternatively, add chopped ham to the dish before topping with the sauce, but this will increase the saturated fat content.

Tex-Mex Baked Potatoes with Chilli

A great way to spice up baked potatoes – top them with a chilli bean sauce then serve with sour cream.

Serves 4
2 large potatoes
15ml/1 tbsp oil, plus extra for rubbing
1 garlic clove, crushed
1 small onion, chopped
½ small red (bell) pepper, seeded and chopped
225g/8oz/1 cup lean minced (ground) beef
½ small fresh red chilli, seeded and chopped
5ml/1 tsp ground cumin
pinch of cayenne pepper
200g/7oz can chopped tomatoes
30ml/2 tbsp tomato purée (paste)
2.5ml/½ tsp dried oregano
2.5ml/½ tsp dried marjoram
200g/7oz can red kidney beans, drained and rinsed
15ml/1 tbsp chopped fresh coriander (cilantro)
60ml/4 tbsp sour cream
salt and ground black pepper
chopped fresh parsley, to garnish

1 Preheat the oven to 220°C/425°F/Gas 7. Rub the potatoes with a little oil and pierce with a skewer. Bake them on the top shelf for about 1 hour until cooked through.

2 Meanwhile, heat the oil in a pan and fry the garlic, onion and pepper gently for 4–5 minutes, until softened.

3 Add the beef and cook over medium heat, stirring, until browned all over. Stir in the chilli, cumin, cayenne pepper, tomatoes, tomato purée, oregano and marjoram, then add 60ml/4 tbsp water.

4 Cover the pan with a tight-fitting lid and simmer for about 25 minutes, stirring occasionally.

5 Remove the lid, stir in the kidney beans and cook for 5 minutes. Turn off the heat and stir in the chopped fresh coriander. Season to taste with salt and pepper and set aside.

6 Cut the baked potatoes in half and place them in serving bowls. Top with the chilli mixture and a dollop of soured cream, then garnish with chopped fresh parsley. Serve immediately.

Gratin Energy 137kcal/573kJ; Protein 13.5g; Carbohydrate 11.1g, of which sugars 5g; Fat 4.5g, of which saturates 2.3g; Cholesterol 8mg; Calcium 273mg; Fibre 2.9g; Sodium 218mg.
Tex-Mex Energy 327kcal/1369kJ; Protein 17.7g; Carbohydrate 30.6g, of which sugars 8.2g; Fat 15.7g, of which saturates 6.4g; Cholesterol 43mg; Calcium 71mg; Fibre 5.2g; Sodium 277mg.

VEGETABLES & SALADS

Spanish Chilli Potatoes

The Spanish name for this dish, *patatas bravas*, means fierce, hot potatoes. Reduce the amount of chilli if you find it too fiery.

Serves 4

900g/2lb new or salad potatoes
60ml/4 tbsp olive oil
1 onion, finely chopped
2 garlic cloves, crushed
15ml/1 tbsp tomato purée (paste)
200g/7oz can chopped tomatoes
15ml/1 tbsp red wine vinegar
2–3 small dried red chillies, seeded and chopped finely, or 5–10ml/1–2 tsp hot chilli powder
5ml/1 tsp paprika
salt and ground black pepper
fresh flat leaf parsley sprig, to garnish

1 Cook the potatoes in their skins in boiling water for 10–12 minutes, or until just tender. Drain them well and leave to cool, then cut in half and set aside.

2 Heat the oil in a large pan and fry the onion and garlic for 5–6 minutes until just softened. Stir in the tomato purée, tomatoes, vinegar, chilli and paprika and simmer for about 5 minutes.

3 Add the potatoes and mix into the sauce mixture to coat. Cover with a tight-fitting lid and simmer gently for about 8–10 minutes, or until the potatoes are tender.

4 Season well with salt and pepper, then transfer to a warmed serving dish. Serve, garnished with a sprig of flat leaf parsley.

Cook's Tip
Dried chillies will last for years, but they lose their savour over time, so buy only small quantities as you need them.

Variation
Stir in a few spoonfuls of sour cream at the end of step 3.

Bombay Spiced Potatoes

A delicately aromatic mixture of whole and ground spices are used to flavour the potatoes in this classic Indian dish.

Serves 4

4 large potatoes (Maris Piper or King Edward), diced
60ml/4 tbsp sunflower oil
1 garlic clove, finely chopped
10ml/2 tsp brown mustard seeds
5ml/1 tsp black onion seeds (optional)
5ml/1 tsp ground turmeric
5ml/1 tsp ground cumin
5ml/1 tsp ground coriander
5ml/1 tsp fennel seeds
generous squeeze of lemon juice
salt and ground black pepper
chopped fresh coriander (cilantro) and lemon wedges, to garnish

1 Bring a pan of salted water to the boil, add the potatoes and simmer for about 4 minutes until just tender. Drain well.

2 Heat the oil in a large frying pan and add the garlic along with all the whole and ground spices. Stir-fry gently for 1–2 minutes until the mustard seeds start to pop.

3 Add the potatoes and stir-fry over medium heat for about 5 minutes, or until they are heated through and well coated with the spicy oil.

4 Season well with salt and pepper, then sprinkle over the lemon juice. Garnish with coriander and lemon wedges.

Cook's Tip
Keep an eye open for black onion seeds – kalonji – in Indian or Pakistani food stores.

Variation
For spiced potatoes and spinach, blanch about 450g/1lb fresh young spinach in boiling water for 2 minutes, then drain and squeeze dry. Add with the potatoes in step 3.

Bombay Spiced Energy 260kcal/1091kJ; Protein 4.8g; Carbohydrate 35.2g, of which sugars 2.8g; Fat 12.1g, of which saturates 1.5g; Cholesterol 0mg; Calcium 39mg; Fibre 3.4g; Sodium 40mg.
Spanish Chilli Energy 273kcal/1148kJ; Protein 4.6g; Carbohydrate 39.5g, of which sugars 5.9g; Fat 11.9g, of which saturates 1.9g; Cholesterol 0mg; Calcium 22mg; Fibre 3.1g; Sodium 39mg.

Florets Polonaise

Steamed vegetables make a delicious and extremely healthy accompaniment.

Serves 6
500g/1¼lb cauliflower and broccoli

finely grated rind of ½ lemon
1 large garlic clove, crushed
25g/1oz/½ cup wholegrain breadcrumbs, lightly baked or grilled (broiled) until crisp
2 eggs, hard-boiled and shelled
salt and ground black pepper

1 Trim the cauliflower and broccoli and break into florets, then place in a steamer over a pan of boiling water and steam for about 12 minutes. (If you prefer, boil the vegetables in salted water for 5–7 minutes, until just tender.) Drain the vegetables well and transfer to a warmed serving dish.

2 Meanwhile, make the topping. In a bowl, combine the lemon rind with the garlic and breadcrumbs. Finely chop the eggs and stir into the breadcrumb mixture. Season with salt and black pepper to taste, then sprinkle over the cooked vegetables.

Two Beans Provençal

This would make a tasty side dish for any main course.

Serves 4
5ml/1 tsp olive oil
1 small onion, finely chopped
1 garlic clove, crushed

225g/8oz/scant 1 cup green beans
225g/8oz/scant 1 cup runner (green) beans
2 tomatoes, peeled and chopped
salt and ground black pepper

1 Heat the oil in a heavy or non-stick frying pan, add the onion and sauté over medium heat until softened but not browned.

2 Add the garlic, both beans and the tomatoes. Season well with salt and pepper, then cover tightly. Cook over fairly low heat, shaking the pan from time to time, for about 30 minutes, or until the beans are tender. Serve immediately.

Spicy Jacket Potatoes

These lightly spiced potatoes make a glorious snack, light lunch or accompaniment to a meal.

Serves 2–4
2 large baking potatoes
5ml/1 tsp sunflower oil
1 small onion, chopped

2.5cm/1in piece fresh root ginger, grated
5ml/1 tsp ground cumin
5ml/1 tsp ground coriander
2.5ml/½ tsp ground turmeric
generous pinch of garlic salt
natural (plain) yogurt and fresh coriander (cilantro) sprigs, to serve

1 Preheat the oven to 220°C/425°F/Gas 7. Scrub the potatoes, then prick them all over with a fork. Bake for 1–1½ hours until tender. Remove them from the oven and reduce the temperature to 180°C/350°F/Gas 4.

2 Cut each potato in half and scoop out the flesh into a bowl. Place the potato shells on a baking sheet and return them to the oven to crisp up while you are making the filling.

3 Heat the oil in a non-stick frying pan, add the onion and fry for a few minutes until softened. Stir in the ginger, cumin, coriander and turmeric.

4 Stir over gentle heat for about 2 minutes, then add the potato flesh and garlic salt to taste. Mix well. Continue to cook the potato mixture gently for a further 2 minutes, stirring occasionally.

5 Remove the potato shells from the oven. Carefully spoon the potato mixture back into the shells and top each with a spoonful of natural yogurt and a sprig or two of fresh coriander. Serve immediately.

Cook's Tip
For the best results, choose a floury variety of potato, such as King Edward or Maris Piper.

Spicy Potatoes Energy 85kcal/361kJ; Protein 2g; Carbohydrate 17.6g, of which sugars 2.2g; Fat 1.2g, of which saturates 0.2g; Cholesterol 0mg; Calcium 18mg; Fibre 1.5g; Sodium 17mg.
Two Beans Energy 47kcal/195kJ; Protein 2.5g; Carbohydrate 6.3g, of which sugars 5.3g; Fat 1.4g, of which saturates 0.3g; Cholesterol 0mg; Calcium 46mg; Fibre 3.1g; Sodium 5mg.

VEGETABLES & SALADS

Chinese Crispy Seaweed

In northern China, a special kind of seaweed is used for this dish, but spring greens make a very successful alternative. Serve as part of a Chinese spread.

Serves 4
225g/8oz spring greens (collards)
groundnut (peanut) or sunflower
    oil, for deep-frying
1.5ml/¼ tsp salt
10ml/2 tsp soft light brown sugar
30–45ml/2–3 tbsp toasted,
    flaked (sliced) almonds

1 Cut out and discard any tough stalks from the spring greens. Place about six leaves on top of each other, then roll them up into a tight roll.

2 Using a sharp knife, slice across into thin shreds. Lay on a tray and leave to dry for about 2 hours.

3 Heat about 5–7.5cm/2–3in of oil in a wok or pan to 190°C/375°F. Carefully place a handful of the leaves into the oil – it will bubble and spit for the first 10 seconds and then die down. Deep-fry for about 45 seconds, or until a slightly darker green: do not let the leaves burn.

4 Remove with a slotted spoon, drain on kitchen paper and transfer to a serving dish. Keep warm in the oven while frying the remainder.

5 When you have fried all the shredded leaves, sprinkle with the salt and sugar and toss lightly. Garnish with the toasted almonds and serve immediately.

Cook's Tips
• *Make sure that your deep frying pan is deep enough to allow the oil to bubble up during cooking. The pan should be less than half full.*
• *The sugar gives the "seaweed" its characteristic sweet flavour; add to taste.*

Leek & Parsnip Purée

This vegetable purée makes a delectable accompaniment to roasted meat or chicken.

Serves 4
2 large leeks, sliced
3 parsnips, sliced
knob (pat) of butter
45ml/3 tbsp top of the milk or
    single (light) cream
30ml/2 tbsp fromage frais or
    cream cheese
generous squeeze of lemon juice
salt and ground black pepper
large pinch of freshly grated
    nutmeg, to garnish

1 Steam or boil the leeks and parsnips together for about 15 minutes until tender. Drain well, then place in a food processor or blender.

2 Add the remaining ingredients and process until really smooth, then season with salt and pepper to taste. Transfer to a warmed bowl and garnish with a sprinkling of nutmeg.

Mexican-style Green Peas

This is a great way to make the most of fresh peas.

Serves 4
15ml/1 tbsp olive oil
2 garlic cloves, halved
1 onion, halved and thinly sliced
2 tomatoes, peeled, seeded and
    chopped into dice
400g/14oz/scant 3 cups shelled
    fresh peas
salt and ground black pepper
fresh chives, to garnish

1 Heat the oil in a pan and cook the garlic until golden. Scoop it out with a slotted spoon and discard. Add the onion to the pan and fry until translucent. Add the tomatoes and peas.

2 Pour 30ml/2 tbsp water into the pan and stir to mix. Lower the heat and cover the pan tightly. Cook for about 10 minutes, until the peas are cooked. Season with plenty of salt and pepper, then transfer the mixture to a heated dish. Garnish with fresh chives and serve immediately.

Crispy Seaweed Energy 171kcal/707kJ; Protein 3.3g; Carbohydrate 4.4g, of which sugars 3.9g; Fat 15.7g, of which saturates 1.7g; Cholesterol 0mg; Calcium 137mg; Fibre 2.5g; Sodium 13mg.
Leek Purée Energy 98kcal/413kJ; Protein 3.9g; Carbohydrate 13.3g, of which sugars 7.5g; Fat 3.6g, of which saturates 1.7g; Cholesterol 6mg; Calcium 75mg; Fibre 5.7g; Sodium 32mg.
Mexican Peas Energy 130kcal/541kJ; Protein 7.8g; Carbohydrate 15.6g, of which sugars 6.3g; Fat 4.6g, of which saturates 0.8g; Cholesterol 0mg; Calcium 32mg; Fibre 5.9g; Sodium 11mg.

Middle-Eastern Vegetable Stew

This spiced dish of mixed vegetables can be served as a side dish or as a vegetarian main course.

Serves 4–6

45ml/3 tbsp vegetable or chicken stock
1 green (bell) pepper, seeded and sliced
2 courgettes (zucchini), sliced
2 carrots, sliced
2 celery sticks, sliced
2 potatoes, diced
400g/14oz can chopped tomatoes
5ml/1 tsp chilli powder
30ml/2 tbsp chopped fresh mint
15ml/1 tbsp ground cumin
400g/14oz can chickpeas, drained
salt and ground black pepper
fresh mint sprigs, to garnish

1 Heat the vegetable or chicken stock in a large flameproof casserole until boiling, then add the sliced pepper, courgettes, carrots and celery. Stir over high heat for 2–3 minutes, until the vegetables are just beginning to soften.

2 Add the potatoes, tomatoes, chilli powder, mint and cumin. Add the chickpeas and bring to the boil.

3 Reduce the heat, cover the casserole with a tight-fitting lid and simmer for 30 minutes, or until all the vegetables are tender. Season to taste with salt and pepper and serve hot, garnished with mint leaves.

> **Cook's Tip**
> As a vegetarian main course, this dish is delicious with a couscous accompaniment. Soak 275g/10oz/1⅔ cups couscous in boiling vegetable stock for 10 minutes. Fluff up with a fork, then add about 15 pitted black olives, 2 small courgettes (zucchini) cut into strips and some toasted flaked (sliced) almonds. Whisk together 60ml/4 tbsp olive oil, 15ml/1 tbsp lemon juice and 15ml/1 tbsp each chopped coriander (cilantro) and parsley. Whisk in a pinch of cumin, cayenne pepper and salt. Pour the dressing over the salad and toss to mix.

Summer Vegetable Braise

Tender young vegetables are ideal for quick cooking in a minimum of liquid.

Serves 4

175g/6oz baby carrots
175g/6oz/1½ cups sugar snap peas or mangetouts (snow peas)
115g/4oz baby corn
90ml/6 tbsp vegetable stock
10ml/2 tsp lime juice
salt and ground black pepper
chopped fresh parsley and snipped fresh chives, to garnish

1 Place the baby carrots, peas and baby corn in a large heavy pan with the vegetable stock and lime juice. Bring to the boil.

2 Cover the pan and reduce the heat, then simmer for about 6–8 minutes, shaking the pan occasionally, until the vegetables are just tender.

3 Season the vegetables to taste with salt and pepper, then stir in the chopped fresh parsley and snipped chives. Cook the vegetables for a few seconds more, stirring them once or twice until the herbs are well mixed, then serve.

> **Cook's Tip**
> This dish would be excellent for anyone on a low-fat diet.

> **Variations**
> • Mix and match the summer vegetables as you wish: asparagus and young broad beans would make good additions.
> • You can cook a winter version of this dish using seasonal root vegetables. Cut the peeled vegetables into even-size chunks and cook for slightly longer.

Vegetable Stew Energy 149kcal/630kJ; Protein 7.8g; Carbohydrate 24.9g, of which sugars 6.8g; Fat 2.7g, of which saturates 0.4g; Cholesterol 0mg; Calcium 66mg; Fibre 5.7g; Sodium 172mg.
Summer Braise Energy 36kcal/151kJ; Protein 2.7g; Carbohydrate 5.9g, of which sugars 5.1g; Fat 0.3g, of which saturates 0.1g; Cholesterol 0mg; Calcium 33mg; Fibre 2.5g; Sodium 340mg.

Sautéed Wild Mushrooms

This is a quick dish to prepare and makes an ideal side dish for all kinds of grilled and roast meats.

Serves 6
900g/2lb fresh mixed wild and cultivated mushrooms such as morels, porcini, chanterelles, oyster or shiitake

30ml/2 tbsp olive oil
25g/1oz/2 tbsp unsalted (sweet) butter
2 garlic cloves, chopped
3 or 4 shallots, finely chopped
45–60ml/3–4 tbsp chopped fresh parsley, or a mixture of different chopped fresh herbs
salt and ground black pepper

1 Wash and carefully dry the mushrooms. Trim the stems and cut the mushrooms into quarters, or slice if they are very large.

2 Heat the oil in a large frying pan over medium-hot heat. Add the butter and swirl to melt, then stir in the mushrooms and cook for 4–5 minutes until beginning to brown.

3 Add the garlic and shallots to the pan and cook for a further 4–5 minutes until the mushrooms are tender and any liquid given off has evaporated. Season to taste with salt and pepper and stir in the parsley or mixed herbs and serve hot.

Cook's Tip
Use as many different varieties of cultivated and wild mushrooms as you can find for a maximum taste.

Variation
For marinated mushrooms, fry 1 small chopped onion and 1 garlic clove in 30ml/2 tbsp olive oil. Stir in 15ml/1 tbsp tomato purée (paste) and 50ml/2fl oz/¼ cup dry white wine and a pinch of saffron threads. Season, cover and simmer gently for 45 minutes. Add 225g/8oz mushrooms, cover and cook for 5 minutes. Cool, still covered, then chill before serving.

Straw Potato Cake

This potato cake is so-named in France because of its resemblance to a woven straw doormat. But, of course, it tastes mouthwateringly good.

Serves 4
450g/1lb baking potatoes
22.5ml/1½ tbsp melted butter
15ml/1 tbsp vegetable oil
salt and ground black pepper

1 Peel the baking potatoes and grate them coarsely, then immediately toss them with the melted butter and season well with salt and pepper.

2 Heat the oil in a large frying pan. Add the potato mixture and press down to form an even layer that covers the base of the pan. Cook over medium heat for 7–10 minutes until the underside is well browned.

3 Loosen the potato cake by shaking the pan or running a thin palette knife under it.

4 To turn it over, invert a large baking sheet over the frying pan and, holding it tightly against the pan, turn them both over. Lift off the frying pan, return it to the heat and add a little more oil if it looks dry. Slide the potato cake into the frying pan and continue cooking until it is crisp and browned on the second side. Serve immediately.

Cook's Tip
Make several small potato cakes instead of one large one, if you prefer. Simply adjust the cooking time.

Variation
Replace some of the potato with grated carrot or parsnip, or add some grated cheese and a pinch of freshly grated nutmeg to the raw potato and butter mix.

Potato Cake Energy 145kcal/609kJ; Protein 2g; Carbohydrate 18.2g, of which sugars 1.5g; Fat 7.7g, of which saturates 3.4g; Cholesterol 12mg; Calcium 8mg; Fibre 1.1g; Sodium 47mg.
Wild Mushrooms Energy 92kcal/381kJ; Protein 3.2g; Carbohydrate 2.2g, of which sugars 1.4g; Fat 8g, of which saturates 2.9g; Cholesterol 9mg; Calcium 29mg; Fibre 2.3g; Sodium 36mg.
Celeriac (opposite) Energy 41kcal/171kJ; Protein 1g; Carbohydrate 1.7g, of which sugars 1.7g; Fat 3.5g, of which saturates 2g; Cholesterol 8mg; Calcium 78mg; Fibre 2.1g; Sodium 135mg.

Cannellini Bean Purée

This easy dish is wonderful with warm pitta bread.

Serves 4

400g/14oz can cannellini beans, rinsed and drained
45ml/3tbsp fromage frais or cream cheese
grated rind and juice of 1 large orange
15ml/1 tbsp finely chopped fresh rosemary
4 heads chicory (Belgian endive), halved lengthways
2 radicchio, cut into 8 wedges
15ml/1 tbsp walnut oil

1 Purée the drained beans in a blender or food processor with the fromage frais, orange rind and juice and the rosemary.

2 Lay the chicory and radicchio on a baking tray and brush with the walnut oil. Grill (broil) for 2–3 minutes until beginning to brown. Serve immediately with the purée.

Creamy Spinach Purée

Crème fraîche or béchamel sauce usually gives this dish its creamy richness. Here is a quick light alternative.

Serves 4

675g/1½lb/6 cups leaf spinach, stems removed
115g/4oz/½ cup full or medium-fat soft cheese
milk (if required)
pinch of freshly grated nutmeg
salt and ground black pepper

1 Rinse the spinach, shake lightly and place in a deep frying pan or wok. Cook over medium heat for about 3–4 minutes until wilted. Drain in a colander, pressing with the back of a spoon. The spinach does not need to be completely dry.

2 Process the spinach and soft cheese in a food processor or blender to form a purée, then transfer to a bowl. If the purée is too thick, add a little milk. Season to taste with salt, pepper and nutmeg. Transfer to a heavy pan and reheat gently to serve.

Celeriac Purée

Many chefs add potato to celeriac purée, but this recipe highlights the pure flavour of the vegetable.

Serves 4

1 large celeriac (about 800g/1¾ lb), peeled
15g/½ oz/1 tbsp butter
pinch of grated nutmeg
salt and ground black pepper

1 Cut the celeriac into large dice, put in a pan with enough cold water to cover and add a little salt. Bring to the boil over medium-hot heat and cook gently for about 10–15 minutes until tender.

2 Drain the celeriac, reserving a little of the cooking liquid, and place in a food processor fitted with a metal blade or a blender. Process until smooth, adding a little of the cooking liquid if the purée needs thinning.

3 Stir in the butter and season to taste with salt, pepper and nutmeg. Reheat, if necessary, before serving.

Hummus

This popular dish is widely available in supermarkets, but nothing compares to the home-made variety. It is very easy to make.

Serves 4–6

175g/6oz/1 cup cooked chickpeas
120ml/4fl oz/½ cup tahini paste
3 garlic cloves
juice of 2 lemons
45–60ml/3–4 tbsp water
salt and ground black pepper

1 Place the chickpeas, tahini paste, garlic, lemon juice, seasoning and a little of the water in a blender or food processor. Process until smooth, adding a little more water, if necessary. Chill before serving.

Hummus Energy 303kcal/1282kJ; Protein 18.5g; Carbohydrate 44.7g, of which sugars 5.2g; Fat 6.9g, of which saturates 1.2g; Cholesterol 0mg; Calcium 88mg; Fibre 7.2g; Sodium 16mg.
Cannellini Energy 143kcal/602kJ; Protein 8.2g; Carbohydrate 20.5g, of which sugars 6.3g; Fat 3.6g, of which saturates 0.4g; Cholesterol 0mg; Calcium 96mg; Fibre 6.7g; Sodium 397mg.
Spinach Energy 94kcal/388kJ; Protein 7.4g; Carbohydrate 3.6g, of which sugars 3.4g; Fat 5.5g, of which saturates 2.8g; Cholesterol 12mg; Calcium 287mg; Fibre 3.6g; Sodium 236mg.

Frankfurter Salad

A last-minute salad you can throw together using store-cupboard ingredients.

Serves 4
675g/1½ lb new potatoes
2 eggs
350g/12oz frankfurters
1 round (butterhead) lettuce, leaves separated
225g/8oz young spinach
30–45ml/2–3 tbsp oil and vinegar dressing
salt and ground black pepper

1 Boil the new potatoes in lightly salted water for 20 minutes. Drain, cover and keep warm.

2 Hard-boil the eggs for 12 minutes, then shell and quarter. Score the skins of the frankfurters cork-screw fashion, cover with boiling water and simmer for 5 minutes. Drain; keep warm.

3 Distribute the lettuce and spinach leaves among 4 plates, moisten the potatoes and frankfurters with dressing and arrange over the salad. Top with the eggs. Season with salt and pepper.

New Potato & Chive Salad

The secret is to add the dressing while the potatoes are still hot so that they absorb all the flavours.

Serves 4–6
675g/1½ lb new potatoes
45ml/3 tbsp olive oil
15ml/1 tbsp white wine vinegar
4ml/¾ tsp Dijon mustard
4 spring onions (scallions), finely chopped
175ml/6fl oz/¾ cup good quality mayonnaise
45ml/3 tbsp snipped fresh chives
salt and ground black pepper

1 Cook the potatoes, unpeeled, in boiling salted water until tender. Meanwhile, whisk together the oil, vinegar and mustard.

2 Drain the potatoes well, then immediately toss lightly with the vinegar mixture and spring onions and leave to cool. Stir in the mayonnaise and chives, season to taste and chill.

Watercress Potato Salad Bowl

New potatoes tossed with watercress, tomatoes and pumpkin seeds make a colourful, nutritious salad.

Serves 4
450g/1lb small new potatoes, unpeeled
1 bunch watercress
200g/7oz cherry tomatoes, halved
30ml/2 tbsp pumpkin seeds
45ml/3 tbsp low-fat fromage frais or natural (plain) yogurt
15ml/1 tbsp cider vinegar
5ml/1 tsp soft light brown sugar
salt and paprika

1 Cook the potatoes in lightly salted boiling water until just tender, then drain and leave to cool.

2 Toss together the potatoes, watercress, tomatoes and pumpkin seeds. Whisk together the fromage frais, vinegar, sugar, salt and paprika and, just before serving, toss with the salad.

Mixed Leafy Salad

This flavourful salad makes an ideal side dish for serving with meat and fish.

Serves 4
15g/1oz/½ cup mixed fresh herbs, such as chervil, tarragon (use sparingly), dill, basil, marjoram (use sparingly), flat leaf parsley, mint, sorrel, fennel and coriander (cilantro)
350g/12oz mixed salad leaves, such as rocket (arugula), radicchio, chicory (Belgian endive), watercress, frisée, baby spinach and oakleaf lettuce

For the dressing
50ml/2fl oz/¼ cup extra virgin olive oil
15ml/1 tbsp cider vinegar
salt and ground black pepper

1 Wash the herbs and salad leaves, then dry in a salad spinner, or use two clean, dry dish towels to pat them dry.

2 To make the dressing, blend together the olive oil and vinegar in a small bowl and season with salt and pepper to taste. Place all the leaves in a salad bowl. Toss with the dressing and serve.

Frankfurter Energy 472kcal/1969kJ; Protein 20g; Carbohydrate 30.9g, of which sugars 5g; Fat 29.3g, of which saturates 9.7g; Cholesterol 162mg; Calcium 146mg; Fibre 3.5g; Sodium 998mg.
Chive Salad Energy 334kcal/1385kJ; Protein 2.6g; Carbohydrate 19g, of which sugars 2.2g; Fat 28g, of which saturates 4.2g; Cholesterol 22mg; Calcium 27mg; Fibre 1.6g; Sodium 147mg.
Watercress Energy 152kcal/644kJ; Protein 6.1g; Carbohydrate 23.1g, of which sugars 5.2g; Fat 4.6g, of which saturates 0.7g; Cholesterol 0mg; Calcium 114mg; Fibre 2.8g; Sodium 45mg.

Fresh Tuna Salad Niçoise

Fresh tuna transforms this classic colourful salad from the south of France into something really special.

Serves 4

4 tuna steaks, about 150g/5oz each
30ml/2 tbsp olive oil
225g/8oz fine French beans, trimmed
1 small cos lettuce or 2 Little Gem lettuces
4 new potatoes, boiled
4 ripe tomatoes, or 12 cherry tomatoes
2 red peppers, seeded and cut into thin strips
4 hard-boiled eggs, sliced
8 drained anchovy fillets in oil, halved lengthways
16 large black olives
salt and ground black pepper
12 fresh basil leaves, to garnish

For the dressing
15ml/1 tbsp red wine vinegar
90ml/6 tbsp olive oil
1 fat garlic clove, crushed

1 Brush the tuna on both sides with a little olive oil and season. Heat a ridged grill (broiler) pan or the grill until very hot, then grill (broil) the tuna steaks for 1–2 minutes on each side.

2 Cook the beans in a pan of lightly salted boiling water for 4–5 minutes or until crisp-tender. Drain, refresh under cold water and drain again.

3 Separate the lettuce leaves and wash and dry them. Arrange them on four individual serving plates. Slice the potatoes and tomatoes, if large (leave cherry tomatoes whole) and divide them among the plates. Arrange the fine French beans and red pepper strips over them.

4 Shell the hard-boiled eggs, then cut them into thick slices. Place two half eggs on each plate with an anchovy fillet draped over. Arrange four olives on to each plate.

5 To make the dressing, whisk together the vinegar, olive oil and garlic and season to taste. Drizzle over the salads, arrange the tuna steaks on top, sprinkle over the basil and serve.

Caesar Salad

A famous and popular combination of crisp lettuce, crunchy croûtons and Parmesan cheese in a tasty egg dressing.

Serves 4

1 large cos or romaine lettuce
4 thick slices white or granary bread, without crusts
45ml/3 tbsp olive oil
1 garlic clove, crushed
75ml/5 tbsp freshly grated Parmesan cheese

For the dressing
1 egg
1 garlic clove, chopped
30ml/2 tbsp lemon juice
dash of Worcestershire sauce
3 anchovy fillets, chopped
120ml/4fl oz/½ cup olive oil

1 Preheat the oven to 220°C/425°F/Gas 7. Separate, rinse and dry the lettuce leaves. Tear the outer leaves roughly and chop the heart. Arrange the lettuce in a large salad bowl.

2 Dice the bread and mix with the olive oil and garlic in a separate bowl until the bread has soaked up the oil. Lay the bread dice on a baking sheet and place in the oven for about 6–8 minutes until golden. Remove and leave to cool.

3 To make the dressing, break the egg into the bowl of a food processor or blender and add the garlic, lemon juice, Worcestershire sauce and one of the anchovy fillets. Process until smooth.

4 With the motor running, pour in the olive oil in a thin stream until the dressing has the consistency of thin cream. Season to taste with salt and pepper, if needed.

5 Pour the dressing over the salad leaves and toss well, then toss in the garlic croûtons, Parmesan cheese and finally the remaining anchovies and serve immediately.

> **Cook's Tip**
> *Keep an eye on the croûtons in the oven; don't let them burn.*

Leafy Salad (opposite) Energy 92kcal/380kJ; Protein 0.8g; Carbohydrate 1.6g, of which sugars 1.6g; Fat 9.2g, of which saturates 1.4g; Cholesterol 0mg; Calcium 32mg; Fibre 1g; Sodium 4mg.
Niçoise Energy 578kcal/2408kJ; Protein 46.4g; Carbohydrate 15g, of which sugars 10.6g; Fat 37.5g, of which saturates 7.1g; Cholesterol 235mg; Calcium 127mg; Fibre 4.7g; Sodium 585mg.
Caesar Energy 420kcal/1740kJ; Protein 12.2g; Carbohydrate 13.6g, of which sugars 1.9g; Fat 35.6g, of which saturates 8.2g; Cholesterol 68mg; Calcium 288mg; Fibre 1.1g; Sodium 443mg.

Grilled Pepper Salad

This tangy salad hails from southern Italy where all the ingredients thrive in the Mediterranean sun. Serve as a colourful side salad for a cold spread, or as a fresh-tasting starter, topped with a sprinkling of basil.

Serves 6
4 large (bell) peppers, red or
   yellow or a combination of both

30ml/2 tbsp capers in salt,
   vinegar or brine, rinsed
18–20 black or green olives

For the dressing
90ml/6 tbsp extra virgin olive oil
2 garlic cloves, chopped
30ml/2 tbsp balsamic or wine
   vinegar
salt and ground black pepper

1 Place the whole peppers under a hot grill (broiler) and grill (broil), turning occasionally, until they are beginning to char and blister on all sides.

2 Put the charred peppers in a bowl, cover with kitchen paper and leave to cool for 10 minutes, then peel off the skins. Remove the seeds and cores, then cut the flesh into quarters.

3 Cut the peppers into strips and arrange them in a serving dish. Distribute the capers and olives evenly over them.

4 To make the dressing, mix the oil and garlic together in a small bowl, crushing the garlic with a spoon to release as much flavour as possible. Mix in the vinegar and season to taste with salt and pepper.

5 Pour the dressing over the salad, mix well and allow to stand for at least 30 minutes before serving.

> **Cook's Tip**
> *Charring the peppers under the grill helps to bring out their delicious sweet flavour. It also lifts the skin from the pepper flesh, making peeling easy.*

Tuna & Bean Salad

This popular salad makes a good light meal, and can be very quickly assembled from store-cupboard ingredients.

Serves 4–6
2 x 400g/14oz cans cannellini or
   borlotti beans
2 x 200g/7oz cans tuna fish,
   drained

60ml/4 tbsp extra virgin olive oil
30ml/2 tbsp lemon juice
15ml/1 tbsp chopped fresh
   parsley
3 spring onions (scallions), thinly
   sliced
salt and ground black pepper
fresh parsley sprigs, to garnish
   (optional)

1 Pour the beans into a large sieve (strainer) and rinse under cold running water. Drain well. Place in a serving dish.

2 Break the tuna into fairly large flakes with a fork and arrange over the beans.

3 Make the dressing by combining the oil with the lemon juice in a small bowl. Season with salt and pepper, and stir in the parsley. Mix well. Pour the dressing over the beans and tuna.

4 Sprinkle the sliced spring onions over the salad and toss well. Garnish with parsley, if using, and serve immediately.

> **Cook's Tip**
> *If you prefer a milder onion flavour, gently sauté the spring onions in a little oil until softened, before adding to the salad.*

> **Variation**
> *For a vegetarian version, roast, peel and dice 2 red (bell) peppers, saving any juices. Fry 1 large crushed garlic clove in 30ml/2 tbsp olive oil until soft, then add a handful of chopped parsley, the pepper and juices, plus 15ml/1 tbsp balsamic vinegar. Pour over the beans, toss together, season and serve.*

Bean Salad Energy 294kcal/1235kJ; Protein 27.4g; Carbohydrate 23.9g, of which sugars 4.9g; Fat 10.5g, of which saturates 1.7g; Cholesterol 33mg; Calcium 105mg; Fibre 8.4g; Sodium 714mg.
Pepper Salad Energy 148kcal/612kJ; Protein 1.5g; Carbohydrate 8g, of which sugars 7.2g; Fat 12.4g, of which saturates 1.8g; Cholesterol 0mg; Calcium 15mg; Fibre 2.3g; Sodium 192mg.

Warm Chicken Liver & Tomato Salad

Warm salads are especially welcome during the autumn months when the evenings are growing shorter and cooler. Serve with French bread for mopping up the delicious juices.

Serves 4

225g/8oz/4 cups young spinach, stems removed
1 frisée lettuce

105ml/7 tbsp groundnut (peanut) or sunflower oil
175g/6oz rindless bacon, cut into strips
3 slices day-old bread, without crusts, cut into short fingers
450g/1lb chicken livers
115g/4oz cherry tomatoes
salt and ground black pepper

1 Wash the spinach and the frisée lettuce leaves, then dry thoroughly in a salad spinner Place in a salad bowl.

2 Heat 60ml/4 tbsp of the oil in a large frying pan and cook the bacon for 3–4 minutes until crisp and brown. Remove the bacon with a slotted spoon and leave to drain on a piece of kitchen paper.

3 To make the croûtons, fry the bread in the bacon-flavoured oil, tossing until crisp and golden. Drain on kitchen paper.

4 Heat the remaining 45ml/3 tbsp of oil in the frying pan and fry the chicken livers briskly for 2–3 minutes. Transfer the livers and pan juices to the salad leaves in the bowl, add the fried bacon, croûtons and cherry tomatoes. Season with salt and pepper, toss gently and serve.

Cook's Tip
Although fresh chicken livers are preferable, frozen ones could be used in this salad. It is important to make sure they are completely thawed before cooking.

Maryland Salad

A harmonious blend of sweet and savoury flavours, this salad makes a stunning main-course salad.

Serves 4

4 free-range chicken breast fillets
olive oil, for brushing
225g/8oz rindless unsmoked bacon
4 corn on the cob
40g/1½oz/3 tbsp butter, softened
4 ripe bananas, peeled and halved
4 firm tomatoes, halved

4 escarole or round (butterhead) lettuces
1 bunch watercress, weighing about 115g/4oz
salt and ground black pepper

For the dressing

75ml/5 tbsp groundnut (peanut) oil
15ml/1 tbsp white wine vinegar
5ml/1 tsp maple syrup
10ml/2 tsp mild mustard

1 Season the chicken fillets with salt and pepper, brush with oil and barbecue or grill (broil) for 15 minutes, turning once, until cooked through. Keep warm.

2 Barbecue or grill the bacon for 8–10 minutes or until crisp. Keep warm.

3 Bring a large pan of salted water to the boil. Trim and husk the corn on the cob, then add to the boiling water and cook for 20 minutes. Brush with butter and brown over the barbecue or under the grill.

4 Barbecue or grill the bananas and tomatoes for 6–8 minutes, brushing with butter, if you wish.

5 To make the dressing, combine the oil, vinegar, maple syrup and mustard with 15ml/1 tbsp water in a screw-top jar and shake well. Put the lettuce leaves in a bowl with the watercress, then toss with the dressing.

6 Divide the salad leaves among four large plates. Slice the chicken and arrange over the leaves with the bacon, banana, corn and tomatoes. Serve immediately.

Chicken Liver Energy 441kcal/1834kJ; Protein 31g; Carbohydrate 11.7g, of which sugars 3.5g; Fat 30.3g, of which saturates 6g; Cholesterol 451mg; Calcium 149mg; Fibre 2.4g; Sodium 934mg.
Maryland Energy 613kcal/2562kJ; Protein 48.9g; Carbohydrate 29.3g, of which sugars 26.8g; Fat 34.1g, of which saturates 12.2g; Cholesterol 156mg; Calcium 102mg; Fibre 3.3g; Sodium 1193mg.

Leeks with Mustard Dressing

Leeks are turned into an unusual and truly delicious salad when married with a mustardy dressing.

Serves 4

8 slim leeks, each about
   13cm/5in long
5–10/1–2 tsp Dijon mustard
10ml/2 tsp white wine vinegar
1 hard-boiled egg, halved
   lengthways
75ml/5 tbsp light olive oil
10ml/2 tsp chopped fresh parsley
salt and ground black pepper

1 Place the leeks in a steamer over a pan of boiling water and cook until they are just tender.

2 Meanwhile, stir together the mustard and vinegar in a bowl. Scoop the egg yolk into the bowl and, using a fork, mash thoroughly into the vinegar mixture.

3 Gradually work in the oil to make a smooth sauce, then season to taste with salt and pepper.

4 Lift the leeks out of the steamer and place on several layers of kitchen paper, then cover the leeks with several more layers of kitchen paper and dry.

5 Transfer the leeks to a serving dish while still warm, spoon the dressing over them and allow to cool. Finely chop the egg white using a large sharp knife, then mix with the chopped fresh parsley and scatter over the leeks. Chill before serving.

Cook's Tips
• Pencil-slim baby leeks are increasingly available nowadays, and are beautifully tender. Use three or four of these smaller leeks per serving.
• It is important that the leeks are thoroughly dried before placing in the serving dish, and they should still be warm when the dressing is added so that they absorb all the flavours.

Lettuce, Cucumber & Herb Salad

For a really quick salad, look out for pre-packed bags of mixed baby lettuce leaves in the supermarket.

Serves 4

½ cucumber
mixed lettuce leaves
1 bunch watercress, weighing
   about 115g/4oz
1 chicory (Belgian endive)
   head, sliced
45ml/3 tbsp mixed chopped fresh
   herbs such as parsley, thyme,
   tarragon, chives and chervil

For the dressing
15ml/1 tbsp white wine vinegar
5ml/1 tsp Dijon mustard
75ml/5 tbsp olive oil
salt and ground black pepper

1 Peel the cucumber, if you wish, then cut it in half lengthways and scoop out the seeds. Thinly slice the flesh. Tear the lettuce leaves into bite-size pieces.

2 Toss the cucumber, lettuce, watercress, chicory and herbs together in a large salad bowl, or arrange them in the bowl in layers, if you prefer.

3 To make the dressing, mix the vinegar and mustard together, then whisk in the oil and season with salt and pepper.

4 Stir the dressing and pour over the salad. Toss lightly to coat the salad vegetables and leaves and serve immediately.

Cook's Tip
Do not dress the salad until just before serving, otherwise the lettuce leaves will wilt.

Variation
To turn the salad into a light lunch dish, toss in some crisply fried bacon pieces and toasted pine nuts.

Leeks Energy 162kcal/670kJ; Protein 3.1g; Carbohydrate 2.5g, of which sugars 1.9g; Fat 15.7g, of which saturates 2.4g; Cholesterol 48mg; Calcium 48mg; Fibre 2.2g; Sodium 23mg.
Lettuce Energy 149kcal/612kJ; Protein 2.1g; Carbohydrate 2.7g, of which sugars 2.1g; Fat 14.6g, of which saturates 2.2g; Cholesterol 0mg; Calcium 100mg; Fibre 2g; Sodium 21mg.

Goat's Cheese Salad

The robust flavours of the goat's cheese and buckwheat combine especially well with figs and walnuts in this salad.

Serves 4
175g/6oz/1 cup couscous
30ml/2 tbsp toasted buckwheat
1 hard-boiled egg
4 ripe figs
30ml/2 tbsp chopped fresh parsley
60ml/4 tbsp olive oil, preferably Sicilian
45ml/3 tbsp walnut oil
115g/4oz rocket (arugula)
½ frisée lettuce, separated into leaves
175g/6oz crumbly white goat's cheese
50g/2oz/½ cup broken walnuts, toasted

1 Place the couscous and buckwheat in a bowl, cover with boiling water and leave to soak for 15 minutes. Place in a sieve (strainer), if necessary, to drain off any remaining water, then spread out on a metal tray and allow to cool.

2 Shell the hard-boiled egg and pass it through a fine grater. Trim the figs and almost cut each into four, leaving the pieces joined at the base.

3 Toss together the egg, parsley and couscous in a bowl. Mix together the two oils and use half to moisten the couscous and buckwheat mixture.

4 Put the lettuce leaves in a bowl and dress with the remaining oil, then divide among four large plates.

5 Pile the couscous into the centre of the leaves, crumble on the goat's cheese, scatter with toasted walnuts, and add the trimmed figs. Serve immediately.

Cook's Tip
Serve this strongly flavoured salad with a gutsy red wine from the Rhône or South of France.

Sweet Potato & Carrot Salad

A medley of colours, this warm salad not only looks great but has a fabulous sweet-and-sour flavour.

Serves 4
1 sweet potato
2 carrots, cut into thick diagonal slices
3 tomatoes
8–10 iceberg lettuce leaves
75g/3oz/½ cup canned chickpeas, drained

For the dressing
15ml/1 tbsp clear honey
90ml/6 tbsp natural (plain) yogurt
2.5ml/½ tsp salt
5ml/1 tsp ground black pepper

For the garnish
15ml/1 tbsp walnuts
15ml/1 tbsp sultanas (golden raisins)
1 small onion, cut into rings

1 Peel the sweet potato and cut roughly into cubes. Boil it until it is soft but not mushy, then drain and set aside.

2 Boil the carrots for just a few minutes, making sure that they remain crunchy. Drain the carrots and mix with the sweet potato in a large bowl.

3 Slice the tops off the tomatoes, then scoop out the seeds with a spoon and discard. Roughly chop the flesh. Slice the lettuce into strips across the leaves.

4 Line a salad bowl with the shredded lettuce leaves. Mix the chickpeas and tomatoes with the sweet potato and carrots, then place in the centre of the lettuce.

5 To make the dressing, put the honey and yogurt in a bowl with salt and pepper to taste, then mix well, using a fork. Garnish the salad with the walnuts, sultanas and onion rings. Pour the dressing over the top just before serving.

Variation
Use baby new potatoes instead of the sweet potato cubes.

Goat's Cheese Energy 595kcal/2469kJ; Protein 18g; Carbohydrate 38.7g, of which sugars 12.3g; Fat 41.8g, of which saturates 11.3g; Cholesterol 88mg; Calcium 243mg; Fibre 3.3g; Sodium 381mg.
Sweet Potato Energy 158kcal/669kJ; Protein 4.8g; Carbohydrate 27.7g, of which sugars 16.6g; Fat 4g, of which saturates 0.6g; Cholesterol 0mg; Calcium 94mg; Fibre 4.4g; Sodium 101mg.

Wild Rice with Grilled Vegetables

A colourful array of summer vegetables, served on wild and white rice tossed in a garlicky dressing, provides a lovely main-course salad.

Serves 4
225g/8oz/1¼ cups wild and long grain rice mixture
1 large aubergine (eggplant), thickly sliced
1 red, 1 yellow and 1 green (bell) pepper, seeded and cut into quarters
2 red onions, sliced
225g/8oz brown cap or shiitake mushrooms
2 small courgettes (zucchini), cut in half lengthways
olive oil, for brushing
30ml/2 tbsp chopped fresh thyme

For the dressing
90ml/6 tbsp extra virgin olive oil
30ml/2 tbsp balsamic vinegar
2 garlic cloves, crushed
salt and ground black pepper

1 Put the rice mixture in a pan of cold salted water. Bring to the boil, reduce the heat, cover with a tight-fitting lid and cook gently for 30–40 minutes or according to the packet instructions, until all the grains are tender.

2 To make the dressing, mix together the olive oil, vinegar, garlic and salt and pepper to taste in a small bowl or screw-top jar until well blended. Set aside while you cook the vegetables.

3 Arrange the vegetables on a grill (broiler) rack. Brush with olive oil and grill (broil) for 8–10 minutes, until tender and well browned, turning them occasionally and brushing again with oil.

4 Drain the rice and toss in half the dressing. Turn into a serving dish and arrange the grilled vegetables on top. Pour over the remaining dressing and sprinkle over the chopped fresh thyme.

Cook's Tip
Wild rice is not a rice at all, but is actually a type of wild grass. It has a wonderfully nutty flavour and also adds attractive texture when mixed with long grain rice.

Baby Leaf Salad with Croûtons

Crispy croûtons, made from Italian ciabatta bread, give a lovely crunch to this mixed leaf and avocado salad.

Serves 4
15ml/1 tbsp olive oil
1 garlic clove, crushed
15ml/1 tbsp freshly grated Parmesan cheese
15ml/1 tbsp chopped fresh parsley
4 slices ciabatta bread, crusts removed, cut into small dice
1 large bunch watercress
1 large handful of rocket (arugula)
1 bag mixed baby salad leaves, including oakleaf and cos lettuce
1 ripe avocado

For the dressing
45ml/3 tbsp olive oil
15ml/1 tbsp walnut oil
juice of ½ lemon
2.5ml/½ tsp Dijon mustard
salt and ground black pepper

1 Preheat the oven to 190°C/375°F/Gas 5. Put the oil, garlic, Parmesan, parsley and bread in a bowl and toss to coat well. Spread out the diced bread on a baking sheet and bake for about 8 minutes until crisp. Leave to cool.

2 Remove any coarse or discoloured stalks or leaves from the watercress and place in a serving bowl with the rocket and baby salad leaves.

3 Halve the avocado and remove the stone (pit). Peel and cut into chunks, then add it to the salad bowl.

4 To make the dressing, mix together the oils, lemon juice, mustard and salt and pepper to taste in a small bowl or screw-top jar until evenly blended. Pour over the salad and toss well. Sprinkle over the croûtons and serve at once.

Cook's Tip
Walnut oil adds a lovely nutty flavour to the dressing, but if you do not have any, just use olive oil only and add 15ml/1 tbsp balsamic vinegar instead of the lemon juice, if you prefer.

Baby Leaf Energy 334kcal/1397kJ; Protein 9.7g; Carbohydrate 26.9g, of which sugars 2.1g; Fat 21.6g, of which saturates 4g; Cholesterol 4mg; Calcium 238mg; Fibre 3.2g; Sodium 348mg.
Wild Rice Energy 438kcal/1824kJ; Protein 8.6g; Carbohydrate 60.3g, of which sugars 13.6g; Fat 18.1g, of which saturates 2.7g; Cholesterol 0mg; Calcium 56mg; Fibre 5.1g; Sodium 12mg.

Fresh Spinach & Avocado Salad

Young, tender spinach leaves make a change from lettuce. They are delicious served with avocado, cherry tomatoes and radishes in an unusual tofu sauce.

Serves 4–6

1 large avocado
juice of 1 lime
225g/8oz/4 cups baby spinach
   leaves
115g/4oz cherry tomatoes
4 spring onions (scallions), sliced
½ cucumber
50g/2oz radishes, sliced

For the dressing
115g/4oz soft silken tofu
45ml/3 tbsp milk
10ml/2 tsp mustard
2.5ml/½ tsp white wine vinegar
cayenne pepper
salt and ground black pepper
radish roses and fresh herb sprigs,
   to garnish

1 Cut the avocado in half, remove the stone and strip off the skin. Cut the flesh into slices. Transfer to a plate, drizzle over the lime juice and set aside.

2 Rinse and thoroughly dry the baby spinach leaves. Put them in a mixing bowl.

3 Cut the larger cherry tomatoes in half and add all the tomatoes to the mixing bowl with the spring onions. Cut the cucumber into even-size chunks and add to the bowl with the sliced radishes.

4 To make the dressing, put the silken tofu, milk, mustard, wine vinegar and a pinch of cayenne in a food processor or blender. Add salt and pepper to taste, then process for 30 seconds until the dressing is smooth.

5 Scrape the dressing into a bowl and add a little extra milk if you like a thinner consistency. Sprinkle with a little extra cayenne, garnish with radish roses and herb sprigs.

6 Arrange the avocado slices with the spinach salad on a serving dish and serve immediately, with the tofu dressing handed round separately.

Russian Salad

This hearty salad became fashionable in the hotel dining rooms of Europe in the 1920s and 1930s.

Serves 4

115g/4oz large button (white)
   mushrooms
120ml/4fl oz/½ cup mayonnaise
15ml/1 tbsp lemon juice
350g/12oz peeled, cooked
   prawns (shrimp)
1 large dill pickle, finely chopped,
   or 30ml/2 tbsp capers
115g/4oz broad (fava) beans
115g/4oz small new potatoes,
   scrubbed or scraped
115g/4oz young carrots, trimmed
   and peeled
115g/4oz baby sweetcorn
115g/4oz baby turnips, trimmed
15ml/1 tbsp olive oil, preferably
   French or Italian
4 hard-boiled eggs, shelled
salt and ground black pepper
25g/1oz canned anchovy fillets,
   cut into fine strips, to garnish
paprika, to garnish

1 Slice the mushrooms thinly, then cut into matchsticks. Combine the mayonnaise and lemon juice. Fold the mayonnaise into the mushrooms and prawns, add the dill pickle or capers, then season to taste with salt and pepper.

2 Bring a large pan of salted water to the boil, add the broad beans and cook for 3 minutes. Drain and cool under running water, then pinch the beans between thumb and forefinger to release them from their tough skins.

3 Boil the potatoes for 20 minutes and the remaining vegetables for 6 minutes. Drain and cool under running water.

4 Toss the vegetables with the olive oil and divide among four shallow bowls. Spoon on the dressed prawns and place a hard-boiled egg in the centre. Garnish the egg with strips of anchovy and sprinkle with paprika. Serve immediately.

> **Cook's Tip**
> It's worth the effort of removing the broad bean skins, as the bright green beans beneath are exceptionally tender.

Russian Energy 455kcal/1890kJ; Protein 28.1g; Carbohydrate 12.8g, of which sugars 5g; Fat 32.8g, of which saturates 5.7g; Cholesterol 387mg; Calcium 162mg; Fibre 4.3g; Sodium 963mg.
Spinach Energy 71kcal/293kJ; Protein 2.8g; Carbohydrate 2g, of which sugars 1.6g; Fat 5.7g, of which saturates 1.2g; Cholesterol 0mg; Calcium 135mg; Fibre 1.7g; Sodium 46mg.

Pear & Roquefort Salad

The partnership of blue cheese with sweet fruit and crunchy nuts is magical.

Serves 4
50g/2oz/1½ cup hazelnuts
3 ripe pears
lemon juice
about 175g/6oz mixed fresh
    salad leaves
175g/6oz Roquefort cheese

For the dressing
30ml/2 tbsp hazelnut oil
45ml/3 tbsp olive oil
15ml/1 tbsp cider vinegar
5ml/1 tsp Dijon mustard
salt and ground black pepper

1 Toast the hazelnuts in a dry frying pan over low heat for about 2 minutes until golden, tossing frequently to prevent them from burning. Chop the nuts and set aside.

2 To make the dressing, mix together the oils, vinegar and mustard in a bowl or place in a screw-top jar and shake to combine. Season to taste with salt and pepper.

3 Peel, core and slice the pears, then toss them in the lemon juice to prevent them from discolouring.

4 Divide the salad leaves among four serving plates, then place the pears on top. Crumble the cheese and scatter over the salad along with the toasted hazelnuts. Spoon over the dressing and serve immediately.

Cook's Tip
Choose ripe but firm Comice or Williams' pears for this salad. Toss the pears, cheese and nuts with the leaves, if you prefer.

Variation
Replace the hazelnuts with walnuts, and use watercress instead of mixed salad – the peppery leaves go well with the pears.

Mediterranean Mixed Pepper Salad

This Italian-style salad is great to serve as part of a cold lunch spread, with salamis, hams and chunks of warm ciabatta bread.

Serves 4
2 red (bell) peppers, halved and
    seeded
2 yellow (bell) peppers, halved
    and seeded
150ml/¼ pint/⅔ cup olive oil
1 onion, thinly sliced
2 garlic cloves, crushed
generous squeeze of lemon juice
chopped fresh parsley, to garnish

1 Place the peppers, skin-side up, under a hot grill (broiler) and grill (broil) until beginning to char and blister. Put the pepper pieces in a bowl, cover with kitchen paper and leave to cool for 10 minutes,

2 Meanwhile, heat 30ml/2 tbsp of the olive oil in a frying pan and fry the onion for about 5–6 minutes over medium heat, stirring occasionally, until softened and translucent. Remove from the heat and reserve.

3 Remove the peppers from the bowl, then peel off and discard the skins. Slice each pepper half into fairly thin strips.

4 Place the peppers, cooked onion and any oil from the pan into a bowl. Add the crushed garlic and pour in the remaining olive oil. Add a generous squeeze of lemon juice and season to taste with salt and pepper. Mix well, cover and marinate for 2–3 hours, stirring the mixture once or twice.

5 Just before serving, garnish the pepper salad with chopped fresh parsley.

Variation
Add 4 peeled and halved tomatoes to the pepper and onion mixture. Use a red onion and finish off with a sprinkling of black olive halves and torn basil leaves.

Pear Energy 381kcal/1579kJ; Protein 11.4g; Carbohydrate 12.8g, of which sugars 12.5g; Fat 31.9g, of which saturates 10.3g; Cholesterol 33mg; Calcium 256mg; Fibre 3.7g; Sodium 539mg.
Mixed Pepper Energy 299kcal/1233kJ; Protein 2.9g; Carbohydrate 14.4g, of which sugars 11.7g; Fat 25.8g, of which saturates 3.8g; Cholesterol 0mg; Calcium 20mg; Fibre 3.5g; Sodium 8mg.

Californian Salad

Full of vitality and vitamins, this is a lovely light and healthy salad for sunny summer days.

Serves 4
1 small crisp lettuce, torn into pieces
225g/8oz/4 cups young spinach leaves
2 carrots, coarsely grated
115g/4oz cherry tomatoes, halved
2 celery sticks, thinly sliced
75g/3oz/1/2 cup raisins
50g/2oz/1/2 cup blanched almonds or unsalted cashew nuts, halved
30ml/2 tbsp sunflower seeds
30ml/2 tbsp sesame seeds, lightly toasted

For the dressing
45ml/3 tbsp extra virgin olive oil
30ml/2 tbsp cider vinegar
10ml/2 tsp clear honey
juice of 1 small orange
salt and ground black pepper

1 Put the lettuce, spinach, carrots, tomatoes and celery in a large bowl. Add the raisins, almonds and the sunflower and sesame seeds.

2 Put all the dressing ingredients in a screw-top jar and shake well to combine, then pour over the salad.

3 Toss the salad thoroughly and divide among four small salad bowls. Season with salt and pepper and serve immediately.

Cook's Tips
• For tomato and mozzarella toasts to serve with the salad, cut French bread diagonally into slices, then toast lightly on both sides. Spread some sun-dried tomato paste on one side of each slice. Cut some mozzarella into small pieces and arrange over the tomato paste. Put on baking sheets, sprinkle with chopped herbs and black pepper to taste and drizzle with olive oil. Bake in a hot oven for 5 minutes or until the mozzarella has melted. Leave to settle for a few minutes before serving.
• If the tomatoes are hard and tasteless, try roasting them in the oven with a little olive oil, then add to the salad.

Scandinavian Cucumber & Dill

This refreshing salad is good with hot and spicy food.

Serves 4
2 cucumbers
30ml/2 tbsp snipped fresh chives
30ml/2 tbsp chopped fresh dill
150ml/1/4 pint/2/3 cup sour cream or fromage frais
salt and ground black pepper

1 Slice the cucumbers as thinly as possible, preferably in a food processor or with a slicer. Place the slices in layers in a colander (strainer), sprinkling each layer evenly, but not too heavily, with salt. Set over a plate to catch the juices.

2 Leave the cucumber to drain for up to 2 hours, then lay out the slices on a clean dish towel and pat them dry. Mix the cucumber with the herbs, cream or fromage frais and plenty of pepper. Serve immediately.

Spinach & Roast Garlic Salad

This salad makes the most of the health-giving qualities of spinach and garlic.

Serves 4
12 garlic cloves, unpeeled
60ml/4 tbsp extra virgin olive oil
450g/1lb/8 cups baby spinach leaves
50g/2oz/1/2 cup pine nuts, lightly toasted
juice of 1/2 lemon
salt and ground black pepper

1 Preheat the oven to 190°C/375°F/Gas 5. Place the unpeeled garlic cloves in a small roasting pan, drizzle over 30ml/2 tbsp of the olive oil and toss to coat. Bake for about 15 minutes until slightly charred.

2 Place the garlic cloves, still in their skins, in a salad bowl. Add the spinach, pine nuts, lemon juice and remaining olive oil. Toss well and season with salt and pepper. Serve immediately, gently squeezing the softened garlic purée out of the skins to eat.

Californian Energy 319kcal/1327kJ; Protein 7.9g; Carbohydrate 23.5g, of which sugars 21.7g; Fat 22.1g, of which saturates 2.6g; Cholesterol 0mg; Calcium 205mg; Fibre 5g; Sodium 114mg.
Scandinavian Energy 88kcal/361kJ; Protein 1.9g; Carbohydrate 2.8g, of which sugars 2.7g; Fat 7.7g, of which saturates 4.7g; Cholesterol 23mg; Calcium 69mg; Fibre 1g; Sodium 21mg.
Spinach Energy 222kcal/915kJ; Protein 5.1g; Carbohydrate 4g, of which sugars 3.5g; Fat 20.7g, of which saturates 2.3g; Cholesterol 0mg; Calcium 238mg; Fibre 4.1g; Sodium 23mg.

Chicory, Fruit & Nut Salad

Mildly bitter chicory is wonderful with sweet fruit, and is delicious when complemented by a creamy curry sauce.

Serves 4
45ml/3 tbsp mayonnaise
15ml/1 tbsp Greek-style (US strained, plain) yogurt
15ml/1 tbsp mild curry paste
90ml/6 tbsp single (light) cream
½ iceberg lettuce
2 heads chicory (Belgian endive)
50g/2oz/1 cup flaked coconut
50g/2oz/½ cup cashew nuts
2 red eating apples
75g/3oz/½ cup currants

1 Mix together the mayonnaise, Greek-style yogurt, curry paste and single cream in a small bowl. Cover and chill until required.

2 Tear the iceberg lettuce into even-size pieces and put into a salad bowl.

3 Cut the root end off each head of chicory and discard. Slice the chicory, or separate the leaves, and add to the salad bowl. Preheat the grill (broiler).

4 Spread out the coconut flakes on a baking sheet. Grill (broil) for 1 minute until golden. Turn into a bowl and set aside. Toast the cashew nuts for 2 minutes until golden.

5 Quarter the apples and cut out the cores. Slice the apple quarters and add to the lettuce with the toasted coconut, cashew nuts and currants.

6 Stir up the chilled dressing and pour over the salad. Toss lightly together and serve immediately.

Cook's Tip
Choose a sweet, well-flavoured variety of red apple for this salad, such as Royal Gala. Leave on the skins to provide added colour and texture.

Spicy Sweetcorn Salad

This brilliant, sweet-flavoured salad is served warm with a delicious, spicy dressing.

Serves 4
30ml/2 tbsp vegetable oil
450g/1lb drained canned sweetcorn, or frozen sweetcorn, thawed
1 green (bell) pepper, seeded and diced
1 small red chilli, seeded and finely diced
4 spring onions (scallions), sliced
45ml/3 tbsp chopped fresh parsley
225g/8oz cherry tomatoes, halved
salt and ground black pepper

For the dressing
2.5ml/½ tsp sugar
30ml/2 tbsp white wine vinegar
2.5ml/½ tsp Dijon mustard
15ml/1 tbsp chopped fresh basil
15ml/1 tbsp mayonnaise
1.5ml/¼ tsp chilli sauce

1 Heat the oil in a frying pan. Add the sweetcorn, green pepper, chilli and spring onions. Cook over medium heat for about 5 minutes, until softened, stirring frequently.

2 Transfer the vegetables to a salad bowl. Stir in the parsley and the cherry tomatoes.

3 To make the dressing, combine all the ingredients in a small bowl and whisk together.

4 Pour the dressing over the sweetcorn mixture. Season with salt and pepper to taste. Toss well to combine, then serve immediately, while the salad is still warm.

Cook's Tip
Don't touch your eyes with your hands while preparing the chilli.

Variation
If serving the salad to children, you can make the flavour milder by omitting the fresh chilli and the chilli sauce.

Fennel & Orange Salad

This light and refreshing salad originated in Sicily, following the old custom of serving fennel at the end of a meal, to help digestion. The delicate aniseed flavour of the fennel marries well with sweet oranges.

Serves 4
2 large fennel bulbs (about 675g/1½ lb total)
2 sweet oranges
2 spring onions (scallions), to garnish

For the dressing
60ml/4 tbsp extra virgin olive oil
30ml/2 tbsp fresh lemon juice
salt and ground black pepper

1 Wash the fennel bulbs and remove any brown or stringy outer leaves. Slice the bulbs and stems into thin pieces. Place in a shallow serving bowl.

2 Peel the oranges with a sharp knife, cutting away the white pith. Slice thinly. Cut each slice into thirds. Arrange over the fennel, adding any juice from the oranges.

3 To make the dressing, mix the oil and lemon juice together. Season with salt and pepper. Pour the dressing over the salad and mix well.

4 Slice the white and green sections of the spring onions thinly. Sprinkle over the salad and serve immediately.

Cook's Tips
• For a delicate orange rind garnish to enhance the flavour of the salad, use a vegetable peeler to cut thin strips of rind from the unpeeled oranges, leaving the pith behind. Then cut the pieces into thin matchstick strips and cook in a small pan of boiling water for 2–3 minutes. Drain and dry on kitchen paper, then sprinkle on top of the salad before serving.
• When buying fennel, choose firm round bulbs. The outer layers should be crisp and white, with the texture of green celery.

Tomato & Bread Salad

This salad is a traditional peasant dish from Tuscany and was created to use up bread that was several days old. The success of the dish depends on the quality of the tomatoes – they must be ripe and well flavoured. Serve with a green salad for a good contrast in colour and texture.

Serves 4
400g/14oz stale white or brown bread or rolls
4 large tomatoes
1 large red onion, or 6 spring onions (scallions)
a few fresh basil leaves, to garnish

For the dressing
60ml/4 tbsp extra virgin olive oil
30ml/2 tbsp white wine vinegar
salt and ground black pepper

1 Cut the bread or rolls into thick slices. Place in a shallow bowl and add enough cold water to soak the bread. Leave for at least 30 minutes.

2 Cut the tomatoes into chunks and place in a serving bowl. Finely slice the onion or spring onions and add them to the tomatoes. Squeeze as much water out of the bread as possible. Add the bread to the vegetables.

3 To make the dressing, whisk the olive oil with the vinegar, then season with salt and pepper.

4 Pour the dressing over the salad and mix well. Decorate with the basil leaves. Allow to stand in a cool place for a least 2 hours before serving.

Cook's Tip
Tomatoes left to ripen on the vine will have the best flavour so try to buy "vine-ripened" varieties. If you can only find unripened tomatoes, you can help them along by putting them in a paper bag with a ripe tomato or leaving them in a fruit bowl with a banana; the gases the ripe fruits give off will ripen them, but, unfortunately, this process cannot improve the flavour.

Tomato Energy 369kcal/1557kJ; Protein 9.7g; Carbohydrate 56.4g, of which sugars 8.5g; Fat 13.3g, of which saturates 1.7g; Cholesterol 0mg; Calcium 130mg; Fibre 3.2g; Sodium 531mg.
Fennel Energy 148kcal/614kJ; Protein 2.5g; Carbohydrate 9.6g, of which sugars 9.4g; Fat 11.4g, of which saturates 1.6g; Cholesterol 0mg; Calcium 78mg; Fibre 5.4g; Sodium 23mg.

Parmesan & Poached Egg Salad

Soft poached eggs, hot croûtons and cool crisp salad leaves make a lively and unusual combination.

Serves 2

½ small loaf white bread
75ml/5 tbsp extra virgin olive oil
2 eggs
115g/4oz mixed salad leaves
2 garlic cloves, crushed
10ml/½ tbsp white wine vinegar
30ml/2 tbsp freshly shaved Parmesan cheese
ground black pepper

1 Remove the crust from the bread and discard it. Cut the bread into 2.5cm/1in cubes.

2 Heat 30ml/2 tbsp of the oil in a large frying pan. Add the bread cubes and cook for about 5 minutes, tossing the cubes occasionally, until they are crisp and golden brown all over.

3 Bring a pan of water to the boil. Break the eggs into separate cups, then carefully slide into the water. Gently poach the eggs for about 4 minutes until they are lightly cooked.

4 Meanwhile, divide the salad leaves between two plates. Remove the croûtons from the pan and arrange over the leaves. Wipe the frying pan clean with kitchen paper.

5 Heat the remaining oil in the frying pan and cook the garlic and vinegar over high heat for about 1 minute. Pour the warm dressing over the salad leaves and croûtons. Place a poached egg on each salad. Scatter with shavings of Parmesan cheese and a little freshly ground black pepper.

Cook's Tip
Add a dash of vinegar to the water before poaching the eggs. This helps to keep the whites together. To ensure that a poached egg has a good shape, swirl the water with a spoon before sliding in the egg.

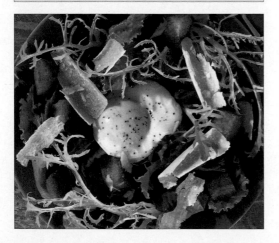

Classic Greek Salad

Anyone who has spent a holiday in Greece will have eaten a version of this salad – the Greek equivalent to a mixed salad.

Serves 4

1 cos lettuce
½ cucumber, halved lengthways
4 tomatoes
8 spring onions (scallions)
75g/3oz Greek black olives
115g/4oz feta cheese
90ml/6 tbsp white wine vinegar
150ml/¼ pint/⅔ cup extra virgin olive oil
salt and ground black pepper
rustic bread, to serve (optional)

1 Tear the lettuce leaves into pieces and place them in a large serving bowl. Slice the cucumber and add to the bowl.

2 Cut the tomatoes into wedges and put them into the bowl.

3 Slice the spring onions. Add them to the bowl along with the olives and toss well.

4 Cut the feta cheese into dice and add to the salad.

5 Put the vinegar and olive oil into a small bowl and season to taste with salt and pepper. Whisk well. Pour the dressing over the salad and toss to combine. Serve at once with extra olives and chunks of bread, if you wish.

Cook's Tips
• This salad can be assembled in advance, but should only be dressed just before serving. Keep the dressing at room temperature as chilling deadens its flavours.
• The success of this salad relies on using the freshest of ingredients and a good olive oil.

Variation
The lettuce can be left out for a salad with a bit more bite.

Poached Egg Energy 632kcal/2641kJ; Protein 21g; Carbohydrate 50.3g, of which sugars 3.6g; Fat 40.1g, of which saturates 8.6g; Cholesterol 205mg; Calcium 335mg; Fibre 2g; Sodium 755mg.
Greek Salad Energy 347kcal/1433kJ; Protein 6.3g; Carbohydrate 5.4g, of which sugars 5.3g; Fat 33.5g, of which saturates 8g; Cholesterol 20mg; Calcium 148mg; Fibre 2.5g; Sodium 849mg.

Avocado, Tomato & Mozzarella

This popular, attractive salad is made from ingredients representing the colours of the Italian flag – a sunny, cheerful dish! The addition of pasta turns it into a main course for a light lunch.

Serves 4
175g/6oz/1½ cups farfalle
6 ripe red tomatoes
225g/8oz mozzarella cheese
1 large ripe avocado

30ml/2 tbsp chopped fresh basil
30ml/2 tbsp pine nuts, toasted
fresh basil sprig, to garnish

For the dressing
90ml/6 tbsp olive oil
30ml/2 tbsp wine vinegar
5ml/1 tsp balsamic vinegar
   (optional)
5ml/1 tsp wholegrain mustard
pinch of sugar
salt and ground black pepper

1 Bring a large pan of lightly salted water to the boil and cook the pasta bows until *al dente*.

2 Slice the tomatoes and mozzarella cheese into thin rounds. Halve the avocado, remove the stone (pit) and peel off the skin. Slice the flesh lengthways.

3 Place the dressing ingredients in a small bowl and whisk together to combine.

4 Arrange the tomato, mozzarella and avocado slices in overlapping slices around the edge of a flat serving plate.

5 Toss the pasta with half of the dressing and the chopped basil. Pile into the centre of the plate. Pour over the remaining dressing, scatter over the pine nuts and garnish with basil.

Cook's Tip
The pale green flesh of the avocado quickly discolours once it is cut. Prepare it at the last minute and place immediately in dressing. If you must prepare it ahead, squeeze lemon juice over the cut side and cover with clear film (plastic wrap).

Pear & Pecan Nut Salad

Toasted pecan nuts have a special affinity with crisp white pears. Their robust flavours combine well with a rich Blue Cheese and Chive dressing to make this a salad to remember.

Serves 4
75g/3oz/½ cup shelled pecan
   nuts, roughly chopped

3 crisp pears
175g/6oz/3 cups young spinach,
   stems removed
1 escarole or round (butterhead)
   lettuce
1 radicchio
salt and ground black pepper
crusty bread, to serve

1 Toast the pecan nuts under a medium grill (broiler) to bring out their flavour.

2 Cut the pears into quarters and remove the cores, but leave the skins intact. Cut into even slices.

3 Place the spinach, lettuce and radicchio leaves in a large bowl. Add the sliced pears and toasted pecans, then pour over the dressing and toss well.

4 Divide the salad among four plates and season with salt and pepper. Serve the salad with warm crusty bread.

Cook's Tip
• The pecan nuts will burn very quickly under the grill, so keep constant watch over them and remove them as soon as they change colour.
• To make 350ml/12 fl oz/1½ cups of Blue Cheese and Chive Dressing: remove the rind from 75g/3 oz blue cheese (Stilton, Bleu d'Auvergne or Gorgonzola) and combine with a third of 150ml/¼ pint/⅔ cup natural (plain) yogurt. Then add the remaining yogurt, 45ml/3 tbsp of olive oil and 30ml/1 tbsp lemon juice, and mix well. Stir in 15ml/1 tbsp chopped chives and season to taste with ground black pepper.

Avocado Energy 612kcal/2552kJ; Protein 18.8g; Carbohydrate 38.3g, of which sugars 6.6g; Fat 43.7g, of which saturates 12.7g; Cholesterol 33mg; Calcium 231mg; Fibre 4.6g; Sodium 240mg.
Pear Energy 227kcal/939kJ; Protein 3.9g; Carbohydrate 14.6g, of which sugars 14.2g; Fat 17.3g, of which saturates 1.2g; Cholesterol 3mg; Calcium 117mg; Fibre 4.7g; Sodium 150mg.

Queen of Puddings

This great hot pudding was developed from a seventeenth-century recipe by Queen Victoria's chefs at Buckingham Palace.

Serves 4
75g/3oz/1½ cups fresh breadcrumbs

50g/2oz/¼ cup caster (superfine) sugar, plus about 5ml/1 tsp for sprinkling
5ml/1 tsp grated lemon rind
600ml/1 pint/2½ cups milk
4 eggs
butter, for greasing
45ml/3 tbsp raspberry jam, warmed

1 Stir the breadcrumbs, 25g/1oz/2 tbsp of the sugar and the lemon rind together in a heatproof bowl. Bring the milk to the boil in a pan, then stir into the breadcrumbs.

2 Separate three of the eggs and beat the yolks with the whole egg. Stir into the breadcrumb mixture, pour into a buttered baking dish and leave to stand for 30 minutes. Meanwhile, preheat the oven to 160°C/325°F/Gas 3. Bake the pudding for 50–60 minutes, until set.

3 Whisk the egg whites in a large, clean grease-free bowl until stiff but not dry, then gradually whisk in 25g/1oz/2 tbsp caster sugar until the mixture is thick and glossy, taking care not to overwhisk.

4 Spread the raspberry jam over the set pudding, then spoon over the meringue to cover the top completely.

5 Evenly sprinkle about 5ml/1tsp sugar over the meringue, then bake for a further 15 minutes, until the meringue is beginning to turn a light golden colour.

> **Variation**
> Ring the changes by using another flavoured jam or a layer of fruit purée – poach the fruit with a little sugar and water, then purée in a blender or food processor and strain, if necessary.

Pear & Blackberry Brown Betty

Very easy to make, this delicious fruity pudding simply consists of layers of golden breadcrumbs and fresh fruit. Just the thing for feeding family and friends, it is lovely served with hot home-made custard, pouring cream or ice cream.

175g/6oz/3 cups fresh breadcrumbs
450g/1lb ripe pears
450g/1lb/4 cups blackberries
grated rind and juice of 1 small orange
115g/4oz/½ cup demerara (raw) sugar, plus extra for sprinkling

Serves 4–6
75g/3oz/6 tbsp butter, diced, plus extra for greasing

1 Preheat the oven to 180°C/350°F/Gas 4. Heat the butter in a heavy frying pan over medium heat and add the fresh breadcrumbs. Stir until golden, then remove from the heat.

2 Peel and core the pears, then cut them into thick slices and mix with the blackberries, orange rind and juice.

3 Mix the demerara sugar with the breadcrumbs, then layer with the fruit in a 900ml/1½ pint/3¾ cup buttered baking dish, beginning and ending with a layer of sugared breadcrumbs.

4 Sprinkle the extra demerara sugar over the top. Cover the baking dish, then bake the pudding for 20 minutes.

5 Uncover the pudding, then bake for a further 30–35 minutes, until the fruit is cooked and the top is brown and crisp.

> **Cook's Tip**
> This is a great way to use up slightly stale bread; just process the crustless bread in a blender or food processor to form crumbs. Flavour the breadcrumbs with a little ground cinnamon and grated nutmeg for a touch of added spice.

Queen Energy 293kcal/1238kJ; Protein 13.7g; Carbohydrate 43.7g, of which sugars 29.7g; Fat 8.5g, of which saturates 3.2g; Cholesterol 199mg; Calcium 242mg; Fibre 0.4g; Sodium 281mg.
Brown Betty Energy 324kcal/1362kJ; Protein 4.5g; Carbohydrate 54.8g, of which sugars 32.9g; Fat 11.1g, of which saturates 6.5g; Cholesterol 27mg; Calcium 90mg; Fibre 4.6g; Sodium 303mg.

Kentish Cherry Batter Pudding

Kent, known as the "Garden of England", is particularly well known for cherries and the dishes made from them. This method of baking the fruit in batter is an absolute winner.

Serves 4

45ml/3 tbsp Kirsch (optional)
450g/1lb dark cherries, pitted
50g/2oz/½ cup plain
   (all-purpose) flour
50g/2oz/¼ cup caster
   (superfine) sugar
2 eggs, separated
300ml/½ pint/1¼ cups milk
75g/3oz/6 tbsp butter, melted
caster (superfine) sugar,
   for sprinkling

1 Sprinkle the Kirsch, if using, over the cherries in a small bowl and leave them to soak for about 30 minutes.

2 Mix the flour and sugar together, then slowly stir in the egg yolks and milk to make a smooth batter. Stir in half the butter and set aside for 30 minutes.

3 Preheat the oven to 220°C/425°F/Gas 7, then pour the remaining butter into a 600ml/1 pint/2½ cup baking dish and put in the oven to heat.

4 Whisk the egg whites until stiff peaks form, then fold into the batter with the cherries and Kirsch, if using. Pour into the dish and bake for 15 minutes.

5 Reduce the oven temperature to 180°C/350°F/Gas 4 and bake for 20 minutes, or until golden and set in the centre. Serve sprinkled with sugar.

> **Cook's Tip**
> It is worth the effort of pitting the cherries as it makes the dish easier to eat. Use a cherry stoner (pitter) or slit each fruit with the point of a small sharp knife and prise out the stones (pits).

Baked Stuffed Apples

When apples are plentiful, this traditional pudding is a popular and easy choice. The filling of dried apricots, honey and ground almonds gives a new twist to an old favourite.

Serves 4

75g/3oz/scant 1 cup ground
   almonds
25g/1oz/2 tbsp butter, softened
5ml/1 tsp clear honey
1 egg yolk
50g/2oz dried apricots, chopped
4 cooking apples, preferably
   Bramleys

1 Preheat the oven to 200°C/400°F/Gas 6. Beat together the almonds, butter, honey, egg yolk and apricots.

2 Stamp out the cores from the cooking apples using a large apple corer, then score a line with the point of a sharp knife around the circumference of each apple.

3 Lightly grease a shallow baking dish, then arrange the cooking apples in the dish.

4 Using a small spoon, divide the apricot mixture among the cavities in the apples, then bake in the oven for 45–60 minutes, until the apples are fluffy.

> **Cook's Tip**
> Scoring the apples around the middle helps to prevent them from bursting during cooking.

> **Variations**
> To ring the changes, replace the dried apricots with seedless raisins or sultanas (golden raisins). Alternatively, fill the cored apples with chopped dates, mixed with finely chopped walnuts and little soft light brown sugar, then top each with a knob (pat) of butter and bake as above.

Baked Apples Energy 237kcal/989kJ; Protein 5.5g; Carbohydrate 16.3g, of which sugars 15.8g; Fat 17.2g, of which saturates 4.5g; Cholesterol 64mg; Calcium 65mg; Fibre 3.8g; Sodium 47mg.
Pudding Energy 357kcal/1493kJ; Protein 8g; Carbohydrate 39.4g, of which sugars 29.8g; Fat 19.8g, of which saturates 11.4g; Cholesterol 140mg; Calcium 147mg; Fibre 1.4g; Sodium 183mg.

Sticky Toffee Pudding

Filling, warming and packed with calories, this delightfully gooey steamed pudding is still a firm favourite.

Serves 6
115g/4oz/1 cup toasted walnuts, chopped
175g/6oz/³⁄₄ cup butter, plus extra for greasing
175g/6oz/1 cup soft brown sugar
60ml/4 tbsp double (heavy) cream
30ml/2 tbsp lemon juice
2 eggs, beaten
115g/4oz/1 cup self-raising (self-rising) flour

1 Grease a 900ml/1½ pint/3¾ cup heatproof deep bowl and add half the chopped nuts.

2 Heat 50g/2oz/¼ cup of the butter with 50g/2oz/¼ cup of the sugar, the cream and 15ml/1 tbsp of the lemon juice in a small pan, stirring until smooth. Pour half into the greased bowl, then swirl to coat it a little way up the sides. Reserve the rest of the sauce for serving.

3 Beat the remaining butter and sugar until light and fluffy, then gradually beat in the eggs. Fold in the flour and the remaining nuts and lemon juice and spoon into the bowl.

4 Cover the bowl with greaseproof (waxed) paper with a pleat folded in the centre, then tie securely with string.

5 Place the bowl in a pan with enough water to come halfway up the sides of the bowl. Cover with a lid and bring to the boil. Keep the water boiling gently and steam the pudding for 1¼ hours, topping up the water as required, until the pudding is completely set in the centre. Alternatively, steam the pudding in a steamer.

6 Just before serving, gently warm the reserved sauce. To serve, run a knife around the edge of the pudding to loosen it, then turn out on to a warm plate. Pour the warm sauce over the pudding and serve immediately.

Easy Chocolate & Orange Soufflé

The base of this delicious soufflé is a simple semolina mixture, rather than the thick white sauce of most sweet soufflés. The finished dish looks most impressive.

Serve 4
butter, for greasing
600ml/1 pint/2½ cups milk
50g/2oz/scant ½ cup semolina
50g/2oz/¼ cup soft light brown sugar
grated rind of 1 orange
90ml/6 tbsp fresh orange juice
3 eggs, separated
65g/2½oz plain (semisweet) chocolate, grated
icing (confectioners') sugar, for sprinkling
pouring (half-and-half) cream, to serve (optional)

1 Preheat the oven to 200°C/400°F/Gas 6. Butter a shallow 1.75 litre/3 pint/7½ cup ovenproof dish.

2 Pour the milk into a heavy pan, sprinkle over the semolina and brown sugar, then heat, stirring the mixture constantly, until boiling and thickened.

3 Remove the pan from the heat; beat in the orange rind and juice, egg yolks and all but 15ml/1 tbsp of the chocolate.

4 Whisk the egg whites until stiff but not dry, then lightly fold one-third into the semolina mixture. Fold in the remaining egg white in two batches.

5 Spoon the mixture into the dish and bake for about 30 minutes until just set in the centre and risen.

6 Sprinkle the top with the remaining chocolate and icing sugar, then serve immediately with pouring cream, if you wish.

> **Variation**
> For a sophisticated touch, replace 15ml/1 tbsp of the orange juice with the same amount of orange-flavoured liqueur, such as Cointreau or Grand Marnier.

Toffee Energy 603kcal/2510kJ; Protein 7.2g; Carbohydrate 46.4g, of which sugars 31.6g; Fat 44.6g, of which saturates 20.2g; Cholesterol 139mg; Calcium 80mg; Fibre 1.3g; Sodium 206mg.
Chocolate Energy 308kcal/1300kJ; Protein 12.1g; Carbohydrate 42.1g, of which sugars 32.3g; Fat 11.5g, of which saturates 5.5g; Cholesterol 153mg; Calcium 218mg; Fibre 0.7g; Sodium 123mg.

Plum & Walnut Crumble

Walnuts add a lovely crunch to the fruit layer in this rich and warming crumble. Serve with dollops of whipped cream for a tasty dessert.

Serves 4–6

75g/3oz/³/4 cup walnut pieces
900g/2lb plums
175g/6oz/1 cup demerara (raw) sugar
75g/3oz/6 tbsp butter or hard margarine, cut into dice
175g/6oz/1½ cups plain (all-purpose) flour

1 Preheat the oven to 180°C/350°F/Gas 4. Spread the nuts on a baking sheet and place in the oven for 8–10 minutes until evenly coloured.

2 Butter a 1.2 litre/2 pint/5 cup baking dish. Halve and stone (pit) the plums, then put them into the dish and stir in the nuts and half of the demerara sugar.

3 Rub the butter or margarine into the flour until the mixture resembles coarse crumbs. Stir in the remaining sugar and continue to rub in until fine crumbs are formed.

4 Cover the fruit with the crumb mixture and press it down lightly. Bake the pudding for about 45 minutes, until the top is golden brown and the fruit tender.

Cook's Tip
For speed, use a food processor to rub the butter into the flour.

Variations
• *To make an oat and cinnamon crumble, substitute rolled oats for half the flour in the crumble mixture and add 2.5–5ml/ ½ –1 tsp ground cinnamon, to taste.*
• *Try replacing the walnuts with hazelnuts or almonds.*

Baked Rice Pudding

Ready-made rice pudding simply cannot compare with this creamy home-made version, especially if you like the golden skin.

Serves 4

50g/2oz/¼ cup short grain pudding rice
25g/1oz/2 tbsp soft light brown sugar
50g/2oz/¼ cup butter, plus extra for greasing
900ml/1½ pints/3¾ cups milk
small strip of lemon rind
pinch of freshly grated nutmeg
fresh mint sprigs, to decorate
raspberries, to serve

1 Preheat the oven to 150°C/300°F/Gas 2, then butter a 1.2 litre/2 pint/5 cup shallow baking dish.

2 Put the rice, sugar and butter into the prepared dish, then stir in the milk and lemon rind. Sprinkle a little nutmeg over the surface of the mixture.

3 Bake the rice pudding in the oven for about 2½ hours, stirring after 30 minutes and another couple of times during the next 2 hours until the rice is tender and the pudding has a thick and creamy consistency.

4 If you like skin on top, leave the rice pudding undisturbed for the final 30 minutes of cooking (otherwise, stir it again). Serve the rice pudding immediately, decorated with fresh mint sprigs and raspberries.

Variations
• *Use 1.5ml/¼ tsp ground cinnamon or mixed spice instead of the grated nutmeg for a change of flavour.*
• *Baked rice pudding is even more delicious with fruit. Add some sultanas (golden raisins), raisins or chopped ready-to-eat dried apricots to the pudding, or serve it alongside sliced fresh peaches or nectarines, or whole fresh strawberries.*

Crumble Energy 325kcal/1361kJ; Protein 4.1g; Carbohydrate 36.5g, of which sugars 26.9g; Fat 19.2g, of which saturates 7.2g; Cholesterol 27mg; Calcium 58mg; Fibre 3.2g; Sodium 81mg.
Pudding Energy 266kcal/1114kJ; Protein 8.7g; Carbohydrate 27.2g, of which sugars 17.2g; Fat 14.2g, of which saturates 8.9g; Cholesterol 40mg; Calcium 278mg; Fibre 0g; Sodium 173mg.

Floating Islands in Plum Sauce

This unusual dessert is simpler to make than it looks, and is quite delicious. It also has the added bonus of being low in fat.

Serves 4
450g/1lb red plums
300ml/½ pint/1¼ cups apple juice
2 egg whites
30ml/2 tbsp concentrated apple juice syrup
pinch of freshly grated nutmeg (optional)

1 Halve the plums and remove the stones (pits). Place them in a wide pan with the apple juice.

2 Bring to the boil, then cover with a tight-fitting lid and leave to simmer gently until the plums are tender.

3 Meanwhile, place the egg whites in a grease-free, dry bowl and whisk until stiff peaks form.

4 Gradually whisk in the apple juice syrup, whisking until the meringue holds fairly firm peaks.

5 To make the "islands", use a tablespoon to scoop the meringue mixture carefully into the gently simmering plum sauce. (You may need to cook them in two batches.)

6 Cover again and allow to simmer gently for 2–3 minutes, until the meringues are just set. Serve immediately, sprinkled with a little freshly grated nutmeg.

Cook's Tip
• A bottle of concentrated apple juice is a useful store-cupboard sweetener, but if you don't have any, just use a little honey instead.
• This is useful for entertaining as the plum sauce can be made in advance and reheated just before you cook the meringues.

Souffléed Rice Pudding

The fluffy egg whites in this unusually light rice pudding make the portions seem much more substantial, without adding lots of extra unwanted fat.

Serves 4
65g/2½ oz/⅓ cup short grain pudding rice
45ml/3 tbsp clear honey
750ml/1¼ pints/3 cups semi-skimmed milk
1 vanilla pod (bean) or 2.5ml/½ tsp vanilla extract
2 egg whites
5ml/1 tsp finely grated nutmeg

1 Place the pudding rice, clear honey and the milk in a heavy or non-stick pan and bring to the boil. Add the vanilla pod, if using.

2 Lower the heat and cover with a tight-fitting lid. Leave to simmer gently for about 1–1¼ hours, stirring occasionally to prevent sticking, until most of the liquid has been absorbed.

3 Remove the vanilla pod from the pan, or if using vanilla extract, add this to the rice mixture now. Set aside so that the mixture cools slightly. Preheat the oven to 220°C/425°F/Gas 7.

4 Place the egg whites in a clean dry bowl and whisk until stiff peaks form.

5 Using a metal spoon or spatula, fold the egg whites evenly into the rice mixture and turn into a 1 litre/1¾ pint/4 cup ovenproof dish.

6 Sprinkle with grated nutmeg and bake for 15–20 minutes, until the pudding is well risen and golden brown.

Cook's Tip
You can use skimmed milk instead of semi-skimmed if you like, but take care when it is simmering as, with so little fat, it tends to boil over very easily.

Islands Energy 94kcal/406kJ; Protein 2.2g; Carbohydrate 22.5g, of which sugars 22.5g; Fat 0.2g, of which saturates 0g; Cholesterol 0mg; Calcium 22mg; Fibre 1.8g; Sodium 38mg.
Pudding Energy 183kcal/773kJ; Protein 9.1g; Carbohydrate 30.4g, of which sugars 17.4g; Fat 3.3g, of which saturates 2g; Cholesterol 11mg; Calcium 230mg; Fibre 0g; Sodium 112mg.

Cabinet Pudding

Rich custard is baked with dried fruit and sponge cake to make a delightful old-fashioned dessert that is sure to cause a stir.

Serves 4

25g/1oz/2½ tbsp raisins, chopped
30ml/2 tbsp brandy (optional)
25g/1oz glacé (candied) cherries, halved
25g/1oz angelica, chopped
2 trifle sponge (pound) cakes
50g/2oz ratafias (almond macaroons)
2 eggs
2 egg yolks
25g/1oz/2 tbsp sugar
450ml/¾ pint/1¾ cups single (light) cream or milk
few drops of vanilla extract

1 Soak the raisins in the brandy, if using, for several hours.

2 Butter a 750ml/1¼ pint/3 cup charlotte mould and arrange some of the cherries and angelica in the base.

3 Dice the sponge cakes and crush the ratafias. Mix with the remaining cherries and angelica, raisins and brandy, if using, and spoon into the mould.

4 Lightly whisk together the eggs, egg yolks and sugar. Bring the cream or milk just to the boil, then stir into the egg mixture with the vanilla extract.

5 Strain the egg mixture into the mould, then set aside for 15–30 minutes. Preheat the oven to 160°C/325°F/Gas 3.

6 Place the mould in a roasting pan. Cover with baking parchment and pour boiling water into the roasting pan. Bake for 1 hour, or until set. Leave for 2–3 minutes, then loosen the edge with a knife and turn out on to a warmed plate.

> **Cook's Tip**
> If you do not have a traditional charlotte mould, you can use a deep round cake tin (pan) instead.

Eve's Pudding

The apples beneath the topping are the reason for this pudding's name.

Serves 4–6

115g/4oz/½ cup butter, softened
115g/4oz/generous ½ cup caster (superfine) sugar
2 eggs, beaten
grated rind and juice of 1 lemon
90g/3½ oz/scant 1 cup self-raising (self-rising) flour
40g/1½ oz/generous ¼ cup ground almonds
115g/4oz/½ cup soft brown sugar
500–675g/1¼–1½ lb cooking apples, cored and thinly sliced
25g/1oz/¼ cup flaked (sliced) almonds
ready-made fresh custard or single (light) cream, to serve

1 Beat together the butter and caster sugar in a large mixing bowl until the mixture is very light and fluffy.

2 Gradually beat the eggs into the butter mixture, beating well after each addition, then fold in the lemon rind, flour and ground almonds.

3 Mix the brown sugar with the apples and lemon juice in a bowl, then turn into an ovenproof dish. Spoon the topping mixture on top of the apples, levelling the surface, then sprinkle with the flaked almonds.

4 Bake for 40–45 minutes, until golden. Serve immediately with fresh custard or cream.

> **Variations**
> • To ring the changes, replace half the apples with fresh blackberries. Halved apricots and sliced peaches can also be used instead of the apples.
> • To vary the topping, leave out the ground and flaked almonds and use demerara (raw) sugar instead of the caster sugar, then serve sprinkled with icing (confectioners') sugar.

Cabinet Energy 424kcal/1769kJ; Protein 10.5g; Carbohydrate 31.3g, of which sugars 23.1g; Fat 29.5g, of which saturates 16.2g; Cholesterol 286mg; Calcium 160mg; Fibre 0.5g; Sodium 128mg.
Eve's Energy 697kcal/2926kJ; Protein 9.5g; Carbohydrate 90g, of which sugars 72.4g; Fat 35.9g, of which saturates 16.5g; Cholesterol 156mg; Calcium 126mg; Fibre 3.9g; Sodium 218mg.

Strawberry & Apple Crumble

A high-fibre, low-fat version of the classic apple crumble that will appeal to both children and adults alike.

Serves 4
450g/1lb cooking apples
150g/5oz/1¼ cups strawberries, hulled
30ml/2 tbsp caster (superfine) sugar
2.5ml/½ tsp ground cinnamon
30ml/2 tbsp orange juice
natural (plain) yogurt, to serve (optional)

For the crumble
45ml/3 tbsp plain wholemeal (whole-wheat) flour
50g/2oz/⅔ cup rolled oats
30ml/2 tbsp low-fat spread

1 Preheat the oven to 180°C/350°F/Gas 4. Peel, core and cut the apples into approximately 5mm/¼in size slices. Halve the strawberries.

2 Toss together the apples, strawberries, sugar, cinnamon and orange juice. Transfer the mixture to a 1.2 litre/2 pint/5 cup ovenproof dish.

3 To make the crumble, combine the flour and oats in a bowl and mix in the low-fat spread with a fork.

4 Sprinkle the crumble evenly over the fruit. Bake for 40–45 minutes, until golden brown and bubbling. Serve warm, with yogurt, if you like.

Cook's Tip
Use cooking apples rather than eating ones, as their soft cooked texture combines well with the crunchy topping.

Variation
Blackberries, raspberries or redcurrants can be used instead of the strawberries very successfully.

Castle Puddings with Custard Sauce

These attractive sponge puddings make a lovely finale to a dinner party.

Serves 4
about 45ml/3 tbsp blackcurrant, strawberry or raspberry jam
115g/4oz/½ cup butter, softened, plus extra for greasing
115g/4oz/generous ½ cup caster (superfine) sugar
2 eggs, beaten
few drops of vanilla extract
130g/4½ oz/generous 1 cup self-raising (self-rising) flour
mint sprigs, to decorate

For the custard sauce
4 eggs
15–25g/½ –1oz/1–2 tbsp sugar
450ml/¾ pint/scant 2 cups milk
few drops of vanilla extract

1 Preheat the oven to 180°C/350°F/Gas 4. Butter eight dariole moulds. Put about 10ml/2 tsp of your chosen jam in the base of each mould.

2 Beat the butter and sugar together until light and fluffy, then gradually beat in the eggs, beating well after each addition, and add the vanilla extract towards the end. Lightly fold in the flour, then divide the mixture among the moulds. Bake the puddings for about 20 minutes until well risen and a light golden colour.

3 To make the custard, whisk the eggs and sugar together. Bring the milk to the boil in a heavy, preferably non-stick, pan, then slowly pour on to the egg mixture, stirring constantly.

4 Return the milk mixture to the pan and heat very gently, stirring, until it thickens enough to coat the back of a spoon; do not allow to boil. Cover the pan and remove from the heat.

5 Remove the moulds from the oven. Leave to stand for a few minutes, then turn the puddings out on to warmed individual plates. Decorate with mint and serve with the custard.

Cook's Tip
If you do not have dariole moulds, use ramekin dishes instead.

Crumble Energy 200kcal/846kJ; Protein 3.8g; Carbohydrate 38.7g, of which sugars 21g; Fat 4.4g, of which saturates 0.9g; Cholesterol 0mg; Calcium 41mg; Fibre 3.4g; Sodium 59mg.
Puddings Energy 644kcal/2701kJ; Protein 16.7g; Carbohydrate 72.5g, of which sugars 47.7g; Fat 34.3g, of which saturates 18.6g; Cholesterol 353mg; Calcium 247mg; Fibre 1g; Sodium 334mg.

Bread & Butter Pudding

An unusual version of a classic recipe, this pudding is made with French bread and mixed dried fruit. As a finishing touch, it is served with a whisky-flavoured cream

Serves 4–6

4 ready-to-eat dried apricots, finely chopped
15ml/1 tbsp raisins
30ml/2 tbsp sultanas (golden raisins)
15ml/1 tbsp chopped mixed (candied) peel
1 French loaf (about 200g/7oz), thinly sliced
50g/2oz/¼ cup butter, melted, plus extra for greasing

450ml/¾ pint/scant 2 cups milk
150ml/¼ pint/⅔ cup double (heavy) cream
115g/4oz/½ cup caster (superfine) sugar
3 eggs
2.5ml/½ tsp vanilla extract
30ml/2 tbsp whisky

For the cream

150ml/¼ pint/⅔ cup double (heavy) cream
30ml/2 tbsp Greek-style (US strained, plain) yogurt
15–30ml/1–2 tbsp whisky
15g/½oz/1 tbsp caster (superfine) sugar

1 Preheat the oven to 180°C/350°F/Gas 4. Butter a deep 1.5 litre/2½ pint/6¼ cup ovenproof dish. Mix together the dried fruits. Brush the bread on both sides with butter.

2 Fill the dish with alternate layers of bread and dried fruit, starting with fruit and finishing with bread. Heat the milk and cream in a pan until just boiling. Whisk together the sugar, eggs and vanilla extract.

3 Whisk the milk mixture into the eggs, then strain into the dish. Sprinkle the whisky over the top. Press the bread down, cover with foil and leave to stand for 20 minutes.

4 Place the foil-covered dish in a roasting pan, half filled with water, and bake for 1 hour, or until the custard is just set. Remove the foil and cook for 10 minutes more until golden.

5 Just before serving, heat all the cream ingredients in a small pan, stirring. Serve with the hot pudding.

Chocolate Amaretti Peaches

This dessert is quick and easy to prepare, yet sophisticated enough to serve at the most elegant dinner party.

Serves 4

115g/4oz amaretti, crushed
50g/2oz plain (semisweet) chocolate, chopped

grated rind of ½ orange
15ml/1 tbsp clear honey
1.5ml/¼ tsp ground cinnamon
1 egg white, lightly beaten
4 firm ripe peaches
butter, for greasing
150ml/¼ pint/⅔ cup white wine
15g/½ oz/1 tbsp caster (superfine) sugar
whipped cream, to serve

1 Preheat the oven to 190°C/375°F/Gas 5. Mix together the crushed amaretti, chocolate, orange rind, honey and cinnamon in a bowl. Add the beaten egg white and mix to bind the mixture together.

2 Halve and stone (pit) the peaches and fill the cavities with the chocolate mixture, mounding it up slightly.

3 Arrange the stuffed peaches in a lightly buttered shallow ovenproof dish which will just hold the fruit comfortably. Pour the wine into a measuring jug and stir in the sugar.

4 Pour the wine mixture around the peaches. Bake for 30–40 minutes, until the peaches are tender. Serve with a little of the cooking juices spooned over and the whipped cream.

> **Cook's Tip**
> Italian amaretti are crisp little cookies, flavoured with bitter almonds. They are now available from supermarkets.

> **Variation**
> This dessert can also be prepared using fresh nectarines or apricots instead of peaches. Use 2 apricots per person.

Pudding Energy 622kcal/2597kJ; Protein 10.5g; Carbohydrate 55.6g, of which sugars 37.8g; Fat 39g, of which saturates 23g; Cholesterol 186mg; Calcium 203mg; Fibre 1.6g; Sodium 350mg.
Peaches Energy 275kcal/1163kJ; Protein 4g; Carbohydrate 45.3g, of which sugars 32.7g; Fat 7.4g, of which saturates 3.8g; Cholesterol 1mg; Calcium 55mg; Fibre 2.2g; Sodium 114mg.

Warm Autumn Compôte

This is a simple yet sophisticated dessert featuring succulent ripe autumnal fruits. Serve with vanilla-flavoured cream and thin, crisp cookies.

Serves 4
75g/3oz/generous ¼ cup caster (superfine) sugar
1 bottle red wine
1 vanilla pod (bean), split
1 strip pared lemon rind
4 pears
2 purple figs, quartered
225g/8oz/2 cups raspberries
lemon juice, to taste

1 Put the caster sugar and red wine in a large pan and heat gently until the sugar has completely dissolved. Add the vanilla pod and lemon rind and bring to the boil. Reduce the heat and simmer for 5 minutes.

2 Peel and halve the pears, then scoop out the cores, using a melon baller or teaspoon. Add the pears to the syrup and poach for about 15 minutes, turning them several times so they colour evenly.

3 Add the quartered figs and poach for a further 5 minutes, until the fruits are tender.

4 Transfer the poached pears and figs to a serving bowl using a slotted spoon, then scatter over the raspberries.

5 Return the syrup to the heat and boil rapidly to reduce slightly and concentrate the flavour. Add a little lemon juice to taste. Strain the syrup over the fruits and serve warm.

> **Cook's Tip**
> Serve with vanilla cream: using 300ml/½ pint/1¼ cups double (heavy) cream, place half in a pan with a vanilla pod (bean). Bring almost to the boil, then cool for 30 minutes. Remove the pod, mix with the remaining cream and add sugar to taste.

Apple Soufflé Omelette

Apples sautéed until they are slightly caramelized make a delicious autumn filling for this sweet, light-as-air omelette.

Serves 2
4 eggs, separated
30ml/2 tbsp single (light) cream
15g/½oz/1 tbsp caster (superfine) sugar

15g/½ oz/1 tbsp butter
sifted icing (confectioners') sugar, for dredging

For the filling
1 eating apple, peeled, cored and sliced
25g/1oz/2 tbsp butter
25g/1oz/2 tbsp soft light brown sugar
45ml/3 tbsp single (light) cream

1 To make the filling, sauté the apple slices in the butter and sugar until just tender. Stir in the cream and keep warm, while making the omelette.

2 Place the egg yolks in a bowl with the cream and sugar and beat well. Whisk the egg whites until stiff peaks form, then fold into the yolk mixture.

3 Melt the butter in a large heavy frying pan, then pour in the soufflé mixture and spread evenly. Cook for 1 minute until golden underneath, then place under a hot grill (broiler) to brown the top.

4 Slide the omelette on to a plate, spoon the apple mixture on to one side, then fold over. Dredge the icing sugar over thickly, then quickly mark in a criss-cross pattern with a hot metal skewer. Serve immediately.

> **Cook's Tips**
> • When cooking the top, remove the omelette as soon as it is browned. Do not overcook at this stage otherwise the light texture of the omelette will be damaged.
> • You can replace the apples with fresh raspberries or strawberries when they are in season.

Warm Lemon & Syrup Cake

This simple cake is made special by the lemony syrup which is poured over it when baked.

Serves 8
3 eggs
175g/6oz/³/4 cup butter, softened
175g/6oz/scant 1 cup caster (superfine) sugar
175g/6oz/1½ cups self-raising (self-rising) flour
50g/2oz/½ cup ground almonds
1.5ml/¼ tsp freshly grated nutmeg
50g/2oz candied lemon peel, finely chopped
grated rind of 1 lemon
30ml/2 tbsp freshly squeezed lemon juice
poached pears, to serve

For the syrup
175g/6oz/scant 1 cup caster (superfine) sugar
juice of 3 lemons

1 Preheat the oven to 180°C/350°F/Gas 4. Lightly grease and base-line a deep round 20cm/8in cake tin (pan).

2 Place all the cake ingredients in a large bowl and beat well for 2–3 minutes until light and fluffy.

3 Turn the mixture into the prepared tin, spread level and bake for 1 hour, or until golden and firm to the touch.

4 To make the syrup, put the caster sugar, lemon juice and 75ml/5 tbsp water in a pan. Place over low heat and stir until the sugar has completely dissolved, then boil, without stirring, for 1–2 minutes.

5 Turn out the cake on to a plate with a rim. Prick the surface of the cake all over with a fork, then pour over the hot syrup. Leave to soak for about 30 minutes. Serve the cake warm with thin wedges of poached pears.

> **Cook's Tip**
> To speed up the preparation, mix the ingredients together in a food processor, but take care not to overbeat.

Papaya & Pineapple Crumble

Fruit crumbles are always popular with children and adults, but you can ring the changes with this great exotic variation.

Serves 4–6
175g/6oz/1½ cups plain (all-purpose) flour
75g/3oz/6 tbsp butter, diced
75g/3oz/generous ¼ cup caster (superfine) sugar
75g/3oz/½ cup mixed chopped nuts

For the filling
1 medium-ripe pineapple
1 large ripe papaya
15g/½ oz/1 tbsp caster (superfine) sugar
5ml/1 tsp mixed (apple pie) spice
grated rind of 1 lime
natural (plain) yogurt, to serve

1 Preheat the oven to 180°C/350°F/Gas 4. To make the topping, sift the flour into a bowl and rub in the butter until the mixture resembles breadcrumbs. Stir in the caster sugar and mixed chopped nuts.

2 To make the filling, peel the pineapple, remove the eyes, then cut in half. Cut away the core and cut the flesh into bitesize chunks. Halve the papaya and scoop out the seeds using a spoon. Peel, then cut the flesh into similar size pieces.

3 Put the pineapple and papaya chunks into a large ovenproof dish. Sprinkle over the sugar, mixed spice and lime rind and toss gently to mix.

4 Spoon the crumble topping over the fruit and spread out evenly with a fork, but don't press it down. Bake in the oven for 45–50 minutes, until golden brown. Serve the crumble hot or warm with natural yogurt.

> **Variation**
> If unavailable, the papaya can be replaced with fresh mango.

Syrup Cake Energy 488kcal/2047kJ; Protein 6g; Carbohydrate 66.5g, of which sugars 50.1g; Fat 23.9g, of which saturates 12.3g; Cholesterol 118mg; Calcium 138mg; Fibre 1.4g; Sodium 259mg.
Crumble Energy 403kcal/1690kJ; Protein 5.5g; Carbohydrate 54.8g, of which sugars 32.5g; Fat 19.5g, of which saturates 7.3g; Cholesterol 27mg; Calcium 96mg; Fibre 4g; Sodium 84mg.

Zabaglione

A much-loved simple Italian dessert traditionally made with Marsala, an Italian fortified wine.

Serves 4
4 egg yolks
50g/2oz/¼ cup (superfine) sugar
60ml/4 tbsp Marsala
amaretti, to serve

1 Half fill a medium pan with water and bring to a simmer.

2 Place the egg yolks and caster sugar in a large heatproof bowl and whisk with an electric whisk until the mixture turns pale yellow and thick.

3 Gradually add the Marsala, about 15ml/1 tbsp at a time, whisking well after each addition (at this stage the mixture will be quite runny).

4 Place the bowl over the pan of gently simmering water and continue to whisk for at least 5–7 minutes, until the mixture becomes thick and mousse-like; when the beaters are lifted they should leave a thick trail on the surface of the mixture. (If you don't beat the mixture for long enough, the zabaglione will be too runny and will probably separate.)

5 Pour into four warmed stemmed glasses and serve immediately with the amaretti for dipping.

> **Cook's Tip**
> If you don't have any Marsala, substitute Madeira, a medium-sweet sherry or a dessert wine.

> **Variation**
> For chocolate zabaglione, whisk in 20ml/4 tsp unsweetened cocoa powder with the Marsala at step 3.

Thai-fried Bananas

In this very easy dessert, bananas are simply fried in butter, sugar and lime juice.

Serves 4
40g/1½ oz/3 tbsp unsalted (sweet) butter
4 large slightly under-ripe bananas
15ml/1 tbsp desiccated (dry unsweetened shredded) coconut
50g/2oz/¼ cup soft light brown sugar
60ml/4 tbsp lime juice
2 lime slices, to decorate
thick and creamy natural (plain) yogurt, to serve

1 Heat the butter in a large frying pan or wok and fry the bananas for 1–2 minutes on each side until golden. Meanwhile, dry-fry the coconut in a small frying pan until golden; reserve.

2 Sprinkle the sugar into the pan with the bananas, add the lime juice and cook, stirring, until dissolved. Sprinkle the coconut over the bananas, decorate with lime and serve with yogurt.

Hot Spiced Bananas

Bananas baked in a rum and fruit syrup are perfect for impromptu entertaining.

Serves 6
6 ripe bananas
butter, for greasing
200g/7oz/1 cup light muscovado (brown) sugar
250ml/8fl oz/1 cup unsweetened pineapple juice
120ml/4fl oz/½ cup dark rum
2 cinnamon sticks
12 whole cloves

1 Preheat the oven to 180°C/350°F/Gas 4. Cut the bananas, at a slant, into 2.5cm/1in pieces. Arrange in a greased baking dish.

2 Mix the sugar and pineapple juice in a pan. Heat gently until the sugar has dissolved, stirring occasionally. Add the rum, cinnamon sticks and cloves. Bring to the boil, then remove from the heat. Pour over the bananas and bake for 25–30 minutes until the bananas are hot and tender.

Zabaglione Energy 134kcal/561kJ; Protein 3g; Carbohydrate 14.9g, of which sugars 14.9g; Fat 5.5g, of which saturates 1.6g; Cholesterol 202mg; Calcium 31mg; Fibre 0g; Sodium 10mg.
Thai-fried Energy 241kcal/1013kJ; Protein 1.5g; Carbohydrate 36.6g, of which sugars 34.3g; Fat 10.9g, of which saturates 7.3g; Cholesterol 21mg; Calcium 15mg; Fibre 1.6g; Sodium 64mg.
Hot Spiced Energy 288kcal/1221kJ; Protein 1.5g; Carbohydrate 62.4g, of which sugars 60.1g; Fat 0.3g, of which saturates 0.1g; Cholesterol 0mg; Calcium 27mg; Fibre 1.1g; Sodium 6mg.

Crêpes Suzette

This dish is a classic of French cuisine and still enjoys worldwide popularity.

Makes 8
115g/4oz/1 cup plain
   (all-purpose) flour
pinch of salt
1 egg
1 egg yolk
300ml/½ pint/1¼ cups
   semi-skimmed milk
15g/½ oz/1 tbsp butter, melted,
   plus extra, for shallow frying

For the sauce
2 large oranges
50g/2oz/¼ cup butter
50g/2oz/¼ cup soft light brown
   sugar
15ml/1 tbsp Grand Marnier
15ml/1 tbsp brandy

1 Sift the flour and salt into a bowl and make a well in the centre. Crack the egg and extra yolk into the well. Stir the eggs to incorporate all the flour. When the mixture thickens, gradually pour in the milk, beating well after each addition, until a smooth batter is formed. Stir in the butter, transfer to a jug, cover and chill for 30 minutes.

2 Heat a shallow frying pan, add a little butter and melt until sizzling. Pour in a little batter, tilting the pan to cover the base. Cook over medium heat for 1–2 minutes until lightly browned underneath, then flip and cook for a further minute. Make eight crêpes and stack them on a plate.

3 Pare the rind from one of the oranges and reserve about 5ml/1 tsp. Squeeze the juice from both oranges.

4 To make the sauce, melt the butter in a large frying pan and heat the sugar with the orange rind and juice until dissolved and gently bubbling. Fold each crêpe into quarters. Add to the pan one at a time, coat in the sauce and fold in half again. Move to the side of the pan to make room for the others.

5 Pour on the Grand Marnier and brandy and cook gently for 2–3 minutes, until the sauce has slightly caramelized. Sprinkle with the reserved orange rind and serve immediately.

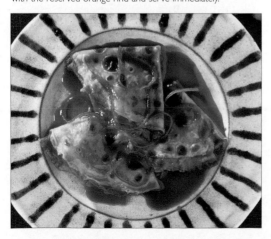

Bananas with Dark Rum & Raisins

A classic way of serving bananas, the rum is set alight just before serving. This gives the fruit a wonderful flavour, making an irresistible dish.

Serves 4
40g/1½ oz/scant ¼ cup seedless
   raisins
75ml/5 tbsp dark rum
50g/2oz/4 tbsp unsalted (sweet)
   butter
50g/2oz/¼ cup soft light brown
   sugar
4 bananas, halved lengthways
1.5ml/¼ tsp grated nutmeg
1.5ml/¼ tsp ground cinnamon
30ml/2 tbsp slivered almonds,
   toasted
chilled cream or vanilla ice cream,
   to serve (optional)

1 Put the raisins in a bowl with the rum. Leave them to soak for about 30 minutes to plump up.

2 Melt the butter in a frying pan, add the sugar and stir until completely dissolved. Add the bananas and cook for a few minutes until tender.

3 Sprinkle the spices over the bananas, then pour over the soaked raisins and rum. Carefully set alight using a long taper and stir gently to mix.

4 Scatter over the slivered almonds and serve immediately with chilled cream or vanilla ice cream, if you wish.

> **Cook's Tips**
> • Chose almost-ripe bananas with evenly coloured skins, either all yellow or just green at the tips. Over-ripe bananas will not hold their shape as well when cooked.
> • Setting light to the rum – known as flambéeing – dispels most of the alcohol content, but gives the bananas an intense flavour. Stand well back when you set the rum alight and shake the pan gently until the flames subside.

Crêpes Energy 195kcal/818kJ; Protein 4.4g; Carbohydrate 23.8g, of which sugars 12.8g; Fat 8.9g, of which saturates 5.1g; Cholesterol 69mg; Calcium 100mg; Fibre 1.3g; Sodium 79mg.
Bananas Energy 352kcal/1474kJ; Protein 3.1g; Carbohydrate 43.8g, of which sugars 41.3g; Fat 14.8g, of which saturates 7g; Cholesterol 27mg; Calcium 38mg; Fibre 1.9g; Sodium 85mg.

Orange Rice Pudding

In Spain, Greece, Italy and Morocco creamy rice puddings are a favourite dish, especially when sweetened with honey. This version is enhanced with a fresh orange flavour.

Serves 4
50g/2oz/¼ cup short grain pudding rice
600ml/1 pint/2½ cups milk

30–45ml/2–3 tbsp clear honey, to taste
finely grated rind of ½ small orange
150ml/¼ pint/⅔ cup double (heavy) cream
15ml/1 tbsp chopped pistachios, toasted

1 Mix the rice with the milk, honey and orange rind in a pan and bring to the boil, then reduce the heat, cover the pan with a tight-fitting lid and simmer very gently for about 1¼ hours, stirring regularly.

2 Remove the lid and continue cooking and stirring for about 15–20 minutes, until the rice is creamy.

3 Pour in the cream and simmer for 5–8 minutes longer. Serve the rice sprinkled with the chopped toasted pistachios in individual warmed bowls.

Cook's Tip
Make sure you use short grain rice for this recipe; the small chalky grains absorb liquid well, producing a creamy texture.

Variation
For a more fragrant version, omit the grated orange rind and stir in 15ml/1 tbsp orange flower water, 15ml/1 tbsp ground almonds and 5ml/1tsp almond extract at step 3, along with the cream. Serve sprinkled with chopped dates and pistachios.

Apple & Blackberry Nut Crumble

This much-loved dish of apples and blackberries is topped with a golden, sweet crumble. The addition of nuts gives an extra-delicious crunchy texture.

Serves 4
900g/2lb (about 4 medium) cooking apples, peeled, cored and sliced
115g/4oz/½ cup butter, diced, plus extra for greasing

115g/4oz/½ cup soft light brown sugar
175g/6oz/1½ cups blackberries
75g/3oz/¾ cup wholemeal (whole-wheat) flour
75g/3oz/¾ cup plain (all-purpose) flour
2.5ml/½ tsp ground cinnamon
45ml/3 tbsp chopped mixed nuts, toasted
custard, cream or ice cream, to serve

1 Preheat the oven to 180°C/350°F/Gas 4. Lightly butter a 1.2 litre/2 pint/5 cup ovenproof dish.

2 Place the apples in a pan with 25g/1oz/2 tbsp of the butter, 25g/1oz/2 tbsp of the sugar and 15ml/1 tbsp water. Cover with a tight-fitting lid and cook gently for about 10 minutes, until the apples are just tender but still holding their shape.

3 Remove from the heat and gently stir in the blackberries. Spoon the mixture into the ovenproof dish and set aside while you make the topping.

4 To make the crumble topping, sift the flours and cinnamon into a bowl, tipping in any of the bran left in the sieve (strainer). Add the remaining 75g/3oz/6 tbsp butter and rub into the flour with your fingertips until the mixture resembles fine breadcrumbs. Alternatively, you can use a food processor to do this stage for you.

5 Stir in the remaining sugar and the nuts and mix well. Sprinkle the crumble topping over the fruit.

6 Bake the crumble for 35–40 minutes until the top is golden brown. Serve immediately with custard, cream or ice cream.

Pudding Energy 355kcal/1477kJ; Protein 7.4g; Carbohydrate 26.6g, of which sugars 16.5g; Fat 24.8g, of which saturates 14.4g; Cholesterol 60mg; Calcium 206mg; Fibre 0.2g; Sodium 94mg.
Crumble Energy 573kcal/2398kJ; Protein 6.8g; Carbohydrate 68.3g, of which sugars 42.3g; Fat 32.2g, of which saturates 15.7g; Cholesterol 61mg; Calcium 86mg; Fibre 5.6g; Sodium 181mg.

Banana, Maple & Lime Crêpes

Crêpes are a treat any day of the week, and they can be made in advance and stored in the freezer for convenience.

Serves 4
115g/4oz/1 cup plain
  (all-purpose) flour
1 egg white

250ml/8fl oz/1 cup skimmed milk
sunflower oil, for frying

For the filling
4 bananas, sliced
45ml/3 tbsp maple or golden
  (light corn) syrup
30ml/2 tbsp freshly squeezed
  lime juice
strips of lime rind, to decorate

1 Beat together the flour, egg white, milk and 50ml/2f oz/¼ cup water until the mixture is smooth and bubbly. Chill in the refrigerator until ready to use.

2 Heat a small amount of oil in a non-stick frying pan and pour in enough batter just to coat the base. Swirl it around the pan to coat evenly.

3 Cook until golden, then toss or turn and cook the other side. Place on a plate, cover with foil and keep hot while making the remaining pancakes.

4 To make the filling, place the bananas, syrup and lime juice in a pan and simmer gently for 1 minute. Spoon into the pancakes and fold into quarters. Sprinkle with shreds of lime rind to decorate. Serve immediately.

> **Cook's Tip**
> To freeze the crêpes, interleaf them with baking parchment and seal in a plastic bag. They should be used within 3 months.

> **Variation**
> Use strawberries instead of bananas, and orange in place of lime.

Apple Strudel

This great Austrian dessert is traditionally made with strudel pastry, but it is just as good prepared with ready-made filo pastry.

Serves 4–6
75g/3oz/¾ cup hazelnuts,
  chopped and roasted
30ml/2 tbsp nibbed almonds,
  roasted
50g/2oz/4 tbsp demerara (raw)
  sugar

2.5ml/½ tsp ground cinnamon
grated rind and juice of ½ lemon
2 large cooking apples, peeled,
  cored and chopped
50g/2oz/⅓ cup sultanas (golden
  raisins)
4 large sheets filo pastry
50g/2oz/4 tbsp unsalted (sweet)
  butter, melted
sifted icing (confectioners') sugar,
  for dusting
cream, custard or yogurt, to serve

1 Preheat the oven to 190°C/375°F/Gas 5. In a bowl mix together the hazelnuts, almonds, sugar, cinnamon, lemon rind and juice, apples and sultanas. Set aside.

2 Lay one sheet of filo pastry on a clean dish towel and brush with melted butter. Lay a second sheet on top and brush again with melted butter. Repeat with the remaining two sheets.

3 Spread the fruit and nut mixture over the pastry, leaving a 7.5cm/3in border at each of the shorter ends. Fold the pastry ends in over the filling. Roll up from one long edge to the other, using the dish towel to help.

4 Carefully transfer the strudel to a greased baking sheet, placing it seam-side down. Brush all over with butter and bake for 30–35 minutes until golden and crisp. Dust the strudel generously with icing sugar and serve while still hot with cream, custard or yogurt.

> **Cook's Tip**
> Chilled filo pastry sheets are available from most supermarkets. Work quickly with the thin sheets as they dry out rapidly.

Spiced Pears in Cider

A cider sauce, delicately flavoured with cinnamon and lemon, transforms pears into an elegant dessert.

Serves 4
4 medium-firm pears
250ml/8fl oz/1 cup dry cider
thinly pared strip of lemon rind
1 cinnamon stick
25g/1oz/2 tbsp light muscovado (brown) sugar
5ml/1 tsp arrowroot
blanched shreds of lemon rind, to decorate

1 Peel the pears thinly, leaving them whole with the stalks on. Place in a pan with the cider, lemon rind and cinnamon. Cover and simmer gently, turning the pears occasionally, for 15–20 minutes, or until tender.

2 Lift out the pears with a slotted spoon. Boil the syrup, uncovered, to reduce by about half. Remove the lemon rind and cinnamon stick, then stir in the sugar.

3 Mix the arrowroot with 15ml/1 tbsp cold water in a small bowl until smooth, then stir into the syrup. Bring to the boil and stir over medium heat until thickened and clear.

4 Pour the sauce over the pears and sprinkle with lemon rind shreds. Leave to cool slightly, before serving.

Cook's Tips
• Any variety of pear can be used for cooking, but choose a firm variety such as Conference for this recipe.
• Using whole pears looks impressive but if you prefer they can be halved and cored before cooking. This will shorten the cooking time slightly.

Variation
The cider can be substituted with red wine for pink-tinted pears.

Fruity Bread Pudding

A delicious old-fashioned family favourite with a lighter, healthier touch for today. The perfect way to round off a family meal.

Serves 4
75g/3oz/2/3 cup mixed dried fruit
150ml/1/4 pint/2/3 cup apple juice
115g/4oz stale brown or white bread, diced
5ml/1 tsp mixed (apple pie) spice
1 large banana, sliced
150ml/1/4 pint/2/3 cup skimmed milk
15g/1/2 oz/1 tbsp demerara (raw) sugar
natural (plain) yogurt, to serve

1 Preheat the oven to 200°C/400°F/Gas 6. Place the mixed dried fruit in a small pan with the apple juice and bring to the boil over medium heat.

2 Remove the pan from the heat and stir in the diced bread, mixed spice and banana. Spoon the mixture into a shallow 1.2 litre/2 pint/5 cup ovenproof dish, then pour over the milk.

3 Sprinkle with demerara sugar and bake for about 25–30 minutes, until the pudding is firm and golden brown. Serve immediately with natural yogurt.

Cook's Tips
• Different types of bread will absorb varying amounts of liquid, so you may need to reduce the amount of milk used to allow for this.
• This is a good way to use up stale, leftover bread. Any type of bread is suitable, but wholemeal (whole-wheat) gives a healthier slant to the dish. Remove the crusts before cutting into dice.

Variation
You can experiment as much as you like with the dried fruit. A mix of raisins, sultanas (golden raisins) and chopped ready-to-eat apricots or dates works well.

Pears Energy 107kcal/454kJ; Protein 0.5g; Carbohydrate 23.2g, of which sugars 23.2g; Fat 0.2g, of which saturates 0g; Cholesterol 0mg; Calcium 25mg; Fibre 3.3g; Sodium 9mg.
Pudding Energy 178kcal/759kJ; Protein 4.4g; Carbohydrate 40.9g, of which sugars 27g; Fat 0.8g, of which saturates 0.1g; Cholesterol 1mg; Calcium 97mg; Fibre 1.1g; Sodium 176mg.

Apple Couscous Pudding

Couscous makes a delicious and healthy family pudding.

Serves 4

600ml/1 pint/2½ cups apple juice
115g/4oz/⅔ cup couscous
40g/1½ oz/scant ¼ cup sultanas (golden raisins)
2.5ml/½ tsp mixed spice
1 large cooking apple, peeled, cored and sliced
25g/1oz/2 tbsp light brown sugar

1 Preheat the oven to 200°C/400°F/Gas 6. Place the apple juice, couscous, sultanas and spice in a pan and bring to the boil, stirring. Cover. Simmer for 10–12 minutes to absorb the liquid.

2 Spoon half the mixture into a 1.2 litre/1 pint/5 cup ovenproof dish and top with half the apple slices. Top with the remaining couscous. Arrange the remaining apple slices overlapping on the top and sprinkle with the sugar. Bake for 25–30 minutes, or until the apples are golden brown. Serve immediately.

Crunchy Gooseberry Crumble

Gooseberries make the perfect filling for this extra special crumble.

Serves 4

500g/1¼ lb/4¼ cups gooseberries
50g/2oz/¼ cup caster (superfine) sugar
75g/3oz/1 cup rolled oats
75g/3oz/1 cup wholemeal (whole-wheat) flour
60ml/4 tbsp sunflower oil
50g/2oz/¼ cup demerara (raw) sugar
30ml/2 tbsp chopped walnuts
natural (plain) yogurt, to serve

1 Preheat the oven to 200°C/400°F/Gas 6. Place the gooseberries in a pan with the caster sugar. Cover the pan and cook over low heat for 10 minutes, until the gooseberries are just tender. Transfer to an ovenproof dish.

2 To make the crumble, place the oats, flour and oil in a bowl and stir with a fork until evenly mixed. Stir in the demerara sugar and walnuts, then spread evenly over the gooseberries. Bake for 25–30 minutes, or until golden. Serve with yogurt.

Gingerbread Upside-down Pudding

A proper pudding goes down well on a cold winter's day. This one is quite quick to make and looks very impressive.

Serves 4–6

sunflower oil, for brushing
15g/½ oz/1 tbsp light soft brown sugar
4 peaches, halved and stoned (pitted), or canned peach halves, drained
8 walnut halves

For the base

130g/4½ oz/1 cup wholemeal (whole-wheat) flour
2.5ml/½ tsp bicarbonate of soda (baking soda)
7.5ml/1½ tsp ground ginger
5ml/1 tsp ground cinnamon
115g/4oz/½ cup muscovado (molasses) sugar
1 egg
120ml/4fl oz/½ cup skimmed milk
50ml/2fl oz/¼ cup sunflower oil

1 Preheat the oven to 180°C/350°F/Gas 4. Brush the base and sides of a 23cm/9in round springform cake tin (pan) with oil. Sprinkle the soft brown sugar evenly over the base.

2 Arrange the peaches, cut-side down, in the tin with a walnut half in each.

3 To make the base, sift together the flour, bicarbonate of soda, ginger and cinnamon, then stir in the sugar. Beat together the egg, milk and oil, then mix into the dry ingredients until smooth.

4 Pour the mixture evenly over the peaches and bake for 35–40 minutes, until firm to the touch. Turn out on to a serving plate. Serve hot with yogurt or custard, if you like.

> **Cook's Tips**
> • *To turn out the pudding successfully, run the point of a sharp knife round the edge of the pudding, then place a serving plate upside-down on top. Holding the plate and tin together firmly, invert. Release the sides and remove the tin.*
> • *The soft brown sugar caramelizes during baking, creating a delightfully sticky topping.*

Couscous Energy 180kcal/767kJ; Protein 2.2g; Carbohydrate 44.6g, of which sugars 29.8g; Fat 0.5g, of which saturates 0g; Cholesterol 0mg; Calcium 26mg; Fibre 0.5g; Sodium 6mg.
Crumble Energy 591kcal/2496kJ; Protein 18.1g; Carbohydrate 84.5g, of which sugars 60.7g; Fat 22.8g, of which saturates 2.1g; Cholesterol 0mg; Calcium 352mg; Fibre 30.3g; Sodium 27mg.
Gingerbread Energy 274kcal/1155kJ; Protein 6.6g; Carbohydrate 42.7g, of which sugars 29.3g; Fat 9.8g, of which saturates 1.1g; Cholesterol 32mg; Calcium 62mg; Fibre 3.3g; Sodium 24mg.

Lemon Meringue Pie

In this popular dish, a light meringue topping crowns a delicious citrus-filled pie.

Serves 4
50g/2oz/¼ cup butter, diced
115g/4oz/1 cup plain
    (all-purpose) flour
25g/1oz/3 tbsp ground almonds
25g/1oz/2 tbsp caster (superfine)
    sugar
1 egg yolk

For the filling
juice of 3 lemons
finely grated rind of 2 lemons
45ml/3 tbsp cornflour
    (cornstarch)
75g/3oz/generous ¼ cup caster
    (superfine) sugar
2 egg yolks
15g/½oz/1 tbsp butter

For the meringue
2 egg whites
115g/4oz/½ cup caster
    (superfine) sugar

1 Rub the butter into the flour until the mixture resembles breadcrumbs. Stir in the almonds and sugar, then add the egg yolk and 30ml/2 tbsp cold water. Mix until the pastry comes together. Knead on a lightly floured surface, then wrap in cling film (plastic wrap) and chill for about 30 minutes.

2 Preheat a baking sheet at 200°C/400°F/Gas 6. Roll out the pastry and use to line a 18.5cm/7½in fluted loose-based flan tin (pan). Prick the base. Line with baking parchment and fill with baking beans. Place the tin on the baking sheet and bake blind for 12 minutes. Remove the paper and beans and bake for a further 5 minutes. Allow to cool. Reduce the temperature to 150°C/300°F/Gas 2.

3 To make the filling, blend the lemon juice, rind and cornflour. Pour into a pan and add 150ml/¼ pint/⅔ cup water. Bring to the boil, stirring until smooth and thickened. Remove and beat in the sugar and egg yolks, then add the butter. Spoon into the pastry case (pie shell).

4 To make the meringue, whisk the egg whites until stiff, then gradually whisk in the sugar until thick and glossy. Pile on top of the filling. Bake for 30–35 minutes, or until golden.

Apple & Orange Pie

A tasty variation of an old favourite, this easy-to-make two-fruit pie will be a big hit. Make sure you choose really juicy oranges or even blood oranges for succulent results. It's delicious served with lashings of cream.

Serves 4
400g/14oz ready-made shortcrust
    (unsweetened) pastry
3 oranges, peeled
900g/2lb cooking apples, cored
    and thickly sliced
25g/1oz/2 tbsp demerara (raw)
    sugar
beaten egg, to glaze
caster (superfine) sugar,
    for sprinkling

1 Roll out the pastry on a lightly floured surface to about 2cm/¾in larger than the top of a 1.2 litre/2 pint/5 cup pie dish. Cut off a narrow strip around the edge of the pastry and fit on the rim of the pie dish.

2 Preheat the oven to 190°C/375°F/Gas 5. Hold one orange at a time over a bowl to catch the juice, and cut down between the membranes to remove the segments.

3 Mix the orange segments and juice, the apples and sugar in the pie dish. Place a pie funnel in the centre of the dish.

4 Dampen the pastry strip. Cover the dish with the rolled out pastry and press the edges to the pastry strip. Brush the top with beaten egg, then bake for 35–40 minutes, until lightly browned. Sprinkle with caster sugar before serving.

> **Cook's Tip**
> If you have time, make your own shortcrust pastry. Sift 225g/8oz/2 cups plain (all-purpose) flour and a pinch of salt into a bowl. Add 115g/4oz/½ cup diced butter and rub in with your fingertips until the mixture resembles breadcrumbs. Mix to a dough with about 45ml/3 tbsp cold water, then wrap and chill for 30 minutes before rolling out as above.

Meringue Energy 2180kcal/9185kJ; Protein 29.4g; Carbohydrate 357.5g, of which sugars 227.8g; Fat 80.2g, of which saturates 38.4g; Cholesterol 542mg; Calcium 403mg; Fibre 5.5g; Sodium 577mg.
Orange Pie Energy 610kcal/2566kJ; Protein 8.1g; Carbohydrate 86.1g, of which sugars 40.2g; Fat 28.5g, of which saturates 8.8g; Cholesterol 14mg; Calcium 168mg; Fibre 8.1g; Sodium 413mg.

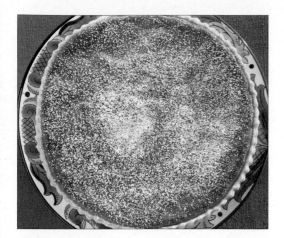

Yorkshire Curd Tart

The distinguishing characteristic of this old-fashioned tart is the allspice, or "clove pepper" as it was once known locally. The tart is quite delicious, without tasting too sweet.

Serves 8
225g/8oz/2 cups plain
  (all-purpose) flour
115g/4oz/1/2 cup butter, diced
1 egg yolk
15–30ml/1–2 tbsp chilled water

For the filling
large pinch of allspice
90g/3 1/2 oz/scant 1/2 cup soft
  light brown sugar
3 eggs, beaten
grated rind and juice of 1 lemon
40g/1 1/2 oz/3 tbsp butter, melted
450g/1lb/2 cups curd cheese
75g/3oz/1/2 cup raisins or
  sultanas (golden raisins)
single (thin) cream, to serve
  (optional)

1 To make the pastry, place the flour in a mixing bowl. Add the butter and rub it into the flour with your fingertips until the mixture resembles breadcrumbs. Stir the egg yolk into the flour mixture with just enough of the water to bind to a dough.

2 Turn the dough on to a lightly floured surface, knead lightly and briefly, then form into a ball. Roll out the pastry thinly and use to line a 20cm/8in fluted loose-based flan tin (pan). Chill for 15 minutes in the refrigerator.

3 Meanwhile, preheat the oven to 190°C/375°F/Gas 5. To make the filling, mix the allspice with the sugar, then stir in the eggs, lemon rind and juice, melted butter, curd cheese and raisins.

4 Pour the filling into the pastry case (pie shell), then bake for about 40 minutes until the pastry is cooked and the filling is lightly set and golden. Serve warm, with cream, if you wish.

> **Cook's Tip**
> Although it is not traditional, mixed (apple pie) spice would make a good substitute for the ground allspice.

Bakewell Tart

This classic tart, with its crisp pastry base and delicious almond sponge filling, is always popular.

Serves 4
225g/8oz ready-made puff pastry
30ml/2 tbsp raspberry or
  apricot jam
2 eggs
2 egg yolks
115g/4oz/1/2 cup caster
  (superfine) sugar
115g/4oz/1/2 cup butter, melted
50g/2oz/2/3 cup ground almonds
few drops of almond extract
sifted icing (confectioners') sugar,
  for dredging

1 Preheat the oven to 200°C/400°F/Gas 6. Roll out the pastry on a lightly floured surface and use it to line an 18cm/7in pie plate or fluted loose-based flan tin (pan). Spread the jam over the base of the pastry case (pie shell).

2 Whisk the eggs, egg yolks and sugar together in a large bowl until thick and pale.

3 Gently stir the butter, ground almonds and almond extract into the egg mixture.

4 Pour the mixture into the pastry case and bake for about 30 minutes until the filling is just set and browned. Dredge with icing sugar before eating hot, warm or cold.

> **Cook's Tips**
> • Since the pastry case isn't baked blind first, place a baking sheet in the oven while it preheats, then place the pie dish or flan tin on the hot sheet. This will ensure that the base of the pastry case cooks through.
> • Fresh, ready-made puff pastry is sold in the chilled section of supermarkets. Rich and buttery, puff pastry takes time and patience to make, as the method involves a drawn-out folding and rolling process. The ready-made version is more practical.
> • Although the pastry base technically makes this a tart, the original recipe refers to it as a pudding.

Bakewell Energy 701kcal/2922kJ; Protein 10.8g; Carbohydrate 57.1g, of which sugars 36.7g; Fat 50g, of which saturates 17.1g; Cholesterol 260mg; Calcium 110mg; Fibre 0.9g; Sodium 395mg.
Curd Tart Energy 480kcal/2005kJ; Protein 16.2g; Carbohydrate 48.2g, of which sugars 23.7g; Fat 27g, of which saturates 15.8g; Cholesterol 173mg; Calcium 153mg; Fibre 1.2g; Sodium 451mg.

HOT DESSERTS

American Spiced Pumpkin Pie

This spicy sweet pie is traditionally served at Thanksgiving in the United States and Canada, when pumpkins are plentiful.

Serves 4–6
175g/6oz/1½ cups plain
  (all-purpose) flour
pinch of salt
75g/3oz/6 tbsp unsalted butter
15g/½ oz/1 tbsp caster
  (superfine) sugar

For the filling
450g/1lb peeled fresh pumpkin,
  diced, or 400g/14oz canned
  pumpkin, drained
115g/4oz/1 cup soft light brown
  sugar
1.5ml/¼ tsp salt
1.5ml/¼ tsp allspice
2.5ml/½ tsp ground cinnamon
2.5ml/½ tsp ground ginger
2 eggs, lightly beaten
120ml/4fl oz/½ cup double
  (heavy) cream
whipped cream, to serve

1 To make the pastry, place the flour in a bowl with a pinch of salt. Rub in the butter with your fingertips until the mixture resembles breadcrumbs. Add the sugar and 30–45ml/2–3 tbsp water, then mix to a soft dough. Knead briefly, flatten into a round, wrap in cling film (plastic wrap) and chill for 1 hour.

2 Preheat the oven to 200°C/400°F/Gas 6 with a baking sheet inside the oven. If using fresh pumpkin, steam for 15 minutes, then cool. Process in a food processor or blender to form a smooth purée.

3 Line a deep pie tin (pan) with the pastry. Prick the base. Cut out leaf shapes from the excess pastry and mark veins with the back of a knife. Brush the edges with water and stick on the leaves to overlap around the pastry edge. Chill.

4 Mix together the pumpkin purée, sugar, salt, spices, eggs and cream and pour into the pastry case (pie shell).

5 Place on the preheated baking sheet and bake for 15 minutes. Then reduce the temperature to 180°C/350°F/Gas 4 and cook for a further 30 minutes, or until the filling is set and the pastry golden. Serve warm with whipped cream.

Pear & Blueberry Pie

Pears combine brilliantly with blueberries to create a lovely fruit pie that is just as delicious served cold as it is warm.

Serves 4
225g/8oz/2 cups plain
  (all-purpose) flour
pinch of salt
50g/2oz/¼ cup lard (shortening),
  diced

50g/2oz/¼ cup butter, diced
675g/1½ lb/4½ cups blueberries
25g/1oz/2 tbsp caster
  (superfine) sugar, plus extra for
  sprinkling
15ml/1 tbsp arrowroot
2 ripe but firm pears, peeled,
  cored and sliced
2.5ml/½ tsp ground cinnamon
grated rind of ½ lemon
beaten egg, to glaze
crème fraîche, to serve (optional)

1 Sift the flour and salt into a bowl. Rub in the fats with your fingertips until the mixture resembles fine breadcrumbs. Mix to a dough with 45ml/3 tbsp cold water. Chill for 30 minutes.

2 Place 225g/8oz/2 cups of the blueberries in a pan with the sugar. Cover with a lid and cook gently until the blueberries have softened. Press through a nylon sieve (strainer). Return the puréed blueberries to the pan.

3 Blend the arrowroot with 30ml/2 tbsp cold water and add to the blueberries in the pan. Bring to the boil, stirring until thickened. Allow to cool slightly.

4 Preheat the oven to 190°C/375°F/Gas 5 with a baking sheet inside the oven. Roll out just over half the pastry on a lightly floured surface and use to line a 20cm/8in shallow pie dish.

5 Mix together the remaining blueberries, the pears, ground cinnamon and lemon rind and spoon into the dish. Pour over the blueberry purée.

6 Use the remaining pastry to cover the pie. Make a slit in the centre. Brush with egg and sprinkle with caster sugar. Bake on the baking sheet for 40–45 minutes, until golden. Serve warm, with crème fraîche, if you wish.

Pumpkin Energy 411kcal/1721kj; Protein 5.9g; Carbohydrate 47.4g, of which sugars 24.8g; Fat 23.4g, of which saturates 13.8g; Cholesterol 117mg; Calcium 96mg; Fibre 1.7g; Sodium 106mg.
Blueberry Energy 493kcal/2063kj; Protein 7.1g; Carbohydrate 66.4g, of which sugars 23.6g; Fat 23.8g, of which saturates 11.7g; Cholesterol 38mg; Calcium 162mg; Fibre 8.6g; Sodium 84mg.

Mississippi Pecan Pie

This fabulous dessert
started life in the United
States but has become an
international favourite.

Serves 4–6
115g/4oz/1 cup plain
  (all-purpose) flour
50g/2oz/¼ cup butter, diced
25g/1oz/2 tbsp caster
  (superfine) sugar
1 egg yolk

For the filling
175g/6oz/5 tbsp golden
  (light corn) syrup
50g/2oz/¼ cup dark muscovado
  (molasses) sugar
50g/2oz/¼ cup butter
3 eggs, lightly beaten
2.5ml/½ tsp vanilla extract
150g/5oz/1¼ cups pecan nuts
cream or ice cream, to serve

1 Place the flour in a bowl. Rub the butter into the flour with
your fingertips until the mixture resembles breadcrumbs.
(Alternatively use a food processor.) Stir in the sugar, egg yolk
and about 30ml/2 tbsp cold water. Mix to a dough and knead
on a lightly floured surface until smooth.

2 Roll out the pastry and use to line a 20cm/8in fluted
loose-based flan tin (pan). Prick the base, then line with baking
parchment and fill with baking beans. Chill for 30 minutes.
Meanwhile, preheat the oven to 200°C/400°F/Gas 6.

3 Bake the pastry case blind for 10 minutes. Remove the paper
and beans and continue to bake for 5 more minutes. Reduce
the oven temperature to 180°C/350°F/Gas 4.

4 To make the filling, heat the syrup, sugar and butter in a pan
until the sugar dissolves. Remove from the heat and cool
slightly. Whisk in the eggs and vanilla extract and stir in the nuts.
Pour into the pastry case (pie shell) and bake for 35–40
minutes, until the filling is set. Serve with cream or ice cream.

Variation
Use maple syrup instead of golden syrup.

Upside-down Apple Tart

Cox's Pippin apples are
perfect to use in this tart
because they hold their
shape so well.

Serves 4
50g/2oz/¼ cup butter, softened
40g/1½ oz/3 tbsp caster
  (superfine) sugar
1 egg
115g/4oz/1 cup plain
  (all-purpose) flour

pinch of salt
whipped cream, to serve

For the apple layer
75g/3oz/6 tbsp butter, softened,
  plus extra for greasing
75g/3oz/scant ½ cup soft light
  brown sugar
10 eating apples, peeled, cored
  and thickly sliced

1 To make the pastry, beat together the butter and sugar until
pale and creamy. Beat in the egg, then sift in the flour and salt
and mix to a soft dough. Knead, wrap in cling film (plastic wrap)
and chill for 1 hour.

2 For the apple layer, grease a 23cm/9in cake tin (pan), then
add 50g/2oz/¼ cup of the butter. Place over low heat to melt
the butter. Remove from the heat and sprinkle over 50g/2oz/
¼ cup of the sugar. Arrange the apple slices on top, sprinkle
with the remaining sugar and dot with the remaining butter.

3 Preheat the oven to 230°C/450°F/Gas 8. Place the cake tin
on the hob again over low to medium heat for about
15 minutes, until a light golden caramel forms on the base.

4 Roll out the pastry on a lightly floured surface to around the
same size as the tin and lay it on top of the apples. Tuck the
pastry edges down around the sides of the apples.

5 Bake for about 20–25 minutes until the pastry is golden.
Remove from the oven and leave to stand for 5 minutes.

6 Place an upturned plate on top of the tin and, holding the
two together with a dish towel, turn the apple tart out on to
the plate. Serve while still warm with whipped cream.

Pie Energy 373kcal/1563kJ; Protein 5.7g; Carbohydrate 51.1g, of which sugars 36.5g; Fat 17.6g, of which saturates 9.8g; Cholesterol 164mg; Calcium 59mg; Fibre 0.6g; Sodium 218mg.
Tart Energy 550kcal/2310kJ; Protein 5.4g; Carbohydrate 74.8g, of which sugars 52.9g; Fat 27.7g, of which saturates 16.7g; Cholesterol 114mg; Calcium 78mg; Fibre 4.9g; Sodium 215mg.

Gooseberry & Elderflower Cream

Fresh-tasting gooseberries and fragrant elderflowers give this dessert an attractive flavour. For the best presentation, serve the cream in individual dishes, prettily decorated with sprigs of mint.

Serves 4
500g/1¼ lb/4¼ cups gooseberries
300ml/½ pint/1¼ cups double (heavy) cream
about 115g/4oz/1 cup sifted icing (confectioners') sugar, to taste
30ml/2 tbsp elderflower cordial
fresh mint sprigs, to decorate
amaretti, to serve

1 Place the gooseberries in a heavy pan, cover and cook over low heat, shaking the pan occasionally, until the gooseberries are tender. Turn the gooseberries into a bowl, crush them, then leave to cool completely.

2 Whip the cream until soft peaks form, then fold in half of the crushed gooseberries. Sweeten with icing sugar and add elderflower cordial to taste. Sweeten the remaining gooseberries with icing sugar.

3 Layer the cream mixture and the crushed gooseberries in four dessert dishes or tall glasses, then cover and chill. Decorate the dessert with the fresh mint sprigs and serve with amaretti.

Cook's Tips
• If you prefer, the cooked gooseberries can be puréed and sieved (strained) instead of crushed.
• When elderflowers are in season, instead of using the cordial, cook two or three elderflower heads with the gooseberries.

Variation
The elderflower cordial can be replaced by orange flower water to produce a delicately fragrant dessert.

Eton Mess

This dish traditionally forms part of the picnic meals enjoyed by parents and pupils at Eton school. Extremely simple to make, it is a great way to serve succulent strawberries.

Serves 4
500g/1¼ lb/4¼ cups strawberries, roughly chopped
45–60ml/3–4 tbsp Kirsch
300ml/½ pint/1¼ cups double (heavy) cream
6 small white meringues
fresh mint sprigs, to decorate

1 Put the strawberries in a bowl, sprinkle over the Kirsch, then cover and chill in the refrigerator for 2–3 hours.

2 Whip the cream until soft peaks form, then gently fold in the strawberries with their juices.

3 Crush the meringues into rough chunks, then scatter over the strawberry mixture and fold in gently.

4 Spoon the strawberry mixture into a glass serving bowl, decorate with the fresh mint sprigs and serve immediately.

Cook's Tip
Home-made meringues taste even better. Whisk 3 egg whites until stiff, then gradually whisk in 75g/3oz/6 tbsp caster (superfine) sugar. Fold in another 75g/3oz/6 tbsp caster sugar. Spoon into small mounds on two baking sheets lined with non-stick baking parchment. Bake at 110°C/225°F/Gas ¼ for 2½–3 hours until firm and crisp, but still white.

Variation
If you would prefer to make a less rich version of this dessert, use Greek (US strained plain) or thick and creamy natural (plain) yogurt instead of part or all of the cream. Beat the yogurt gently before adding the strawberries.

Gooseberry Energy 509kcal/2115kJ; Protein 2.7g; Carbohydrate 35.1g, of which sugars 35.1g; Fat 40.8g, of which saturates 25.1g; Cholesterol 103mg; Calcium 87mg; Fibre 3g; Sodium 21mg.
Eton Mess Energy 526kcal/2182kJ; Protein 3.5g; Carbohydrate 32.8g, of which sugars 32.8g; Fat 40.4g, of which saturates 25.1g; Cholesterol 103mg; Calcium 60mg; Fibre 1.4g; Sodium 53mg.

Old English Trifle

This old-fashioned dessert never fails to please. If you are making it for children, replace the sherry and brandy with orange juice.

Serves 6

75g/3oz day-old sponge (pound) cake, broken into bitesize pieces
8 ratafia biscuits (almond macaroons), broken into halves
100ml/3½fl oz/⅓ cup medium sherry
30ml/2 tbsp brandy
350g/12oz/3 cups prepared fruit such as raspberries, peaches or strawberries

300ml/½ pint/1¼ cups double (heavy) cream
40g/1½oz/scant ½ cup toasted flaked (sliced) almonds, to decorate
strawberries, to decorate

For the custard
4 egg yolks
25g/1oz/2 tbsp caster (superfine) sugar
450ml/¾ pint/scant 2 cups single (light) or whipping cream
a few drops of vanilla extract

1 Put the sponge cake and ratafias in a glass serving dish, then sprinkle over the sherry and brandy and leave until they have been absorbed.

2 To make the custard, whisk the egg yolks and caster sugar together. Bring the cream to the boil in a heavy pan, then pour on to the egg yolk mixture, stirring constantly.

3 Return the mixture to the pan and heat very gently, stirring all the time with a wooden spoon, until the custard thickens enough to coat the back of the spoon; do not allow to boil. Stir in the vanilla extract. Leave to cool, stirring occasionally.

4 Put the fruit in an even layer over the sponge cake and ratafias in the serving dish, then strain the custard over the fruit and leave to set.

5 Lightly whip the cream, then spread it evenly over the custard. Chill the trifle well. Decorate with flaked almonds and strawberries just before serving.

Cranachan

Crunchy toasted oatmeal and soft raspberries combine to give this Scottish dessert a lovely texture, while whisky adds a touch of punchy taste.

Serves 4

60ml/4 tbsp clear honey
45ml/3 tbsp whisky
50g/2oz/¾ cup medium oatmeal
300ml/½ pint/1¼ cups double (heavy) cream
350g/12oz/2 cups raspberries
fresh mint sprigs, to decorate

1 Put the honey in a small pan with the whisky. Heat gently to warm the honey in the whisky, then leave to cool.

2 Preheat the grill (broiler). Spread the oatmeal in a very shallow layer in the grill pan and toast, stirring occasionally, until browned. Leave to cool.

3 Whip the cream in a large bowl until soft peaks form, then gently stir in the oatmeal and the honey and whisky mixture until well combined.

4 Reserve a few raspberries for decoration, then layer the remainder with the oat mixture in four stemmed glasses. Cover and chill for 2 hours.

5 About 30 minutes before serving, remove the glasses from the refrigerator to bring to room temperature. Decorate with the reserved raspberries and mint sprigs.

Cook's Tip
For finger biscuits to serve with the dessert, cream 150g/5oz/ 10 tbsp butter with 75g/3oz/6 tbsp caster (superfine) sugar until light and fluffy, then beat in an egg, a few drops of almond extract and 225g/8oz/2 cups plain (all-purpose) flour. Spoon into a piping (pastry) bag, fitted with a plain nozzle, and pipe 7.5cm/3in fingers on to baking sheets lined with baking parchment. Bake at 230°C/450°F/Gas 8 for 5 minutes. Cool.

Cranachan Energy 512kcal/2126kJ; Protein 4g; Carbohydrate 25.9g, of which sugars 16.8g; Fat 41.6g, of which saturates 25.1g; Cholesterol 103mg; Calcium 66mg; Fibre 3.1g; Sodium 25mg.
Trifle Energy 764kcal/3160kJ; Protein 7.7g; Carbohydrate 23.2g, of which sugars 17.4g; Fat 68.9g, of which saturates 38.1g; Cholesterol 296mg; Calcium 135mg; Fibre 2.2g; Sodium 106mg.

Cherry Syllabub

This recipe follows the style of the earliest syllabubs from the sixteenth and seventeenth centuries, producing a frothy creamy layer over a liquid one. It's easy to make and delicious.

Serves 4
225g/8oz/2 cups ripe dark cherries, stoned (pitted) and chopped

30ml/2 tbsp Kirsch
2 egg whites
30ml/2 tbsp lemon juice
150ml/¼ pint/⅔ cup sweet white wine
75g/3oz/generous ¼ cup caster (superfine) sugar
300ml/½ pint/1¼ cups double (heavy) cream

1 Divide the chopped cherries among six tall dessert glasses and sprinkle over the Kirsch.

2 Whisk the egg whites in a clean, grease-free bowl until stiff peaks form. Gently fold in the lemon juice, wine and sugar.

3 In a separate bowl (but using the same whisk), lightly beat the cream, then fold into the egg white mixture.

4 Spoon the cream mixture over the cherries, then chill overnight. Serve straight from the refrigerator.

> **Cook's Tip**
> Be careful not to overbeat the egg whites otherwise they will separate, which will spoil the consistency of the dessert. Whip the cream until it just forms soft peaks.

> **Variation**
> To ring the changes, try using crushed fresh raspberries or chopped ripe peaches instead of the cherries. Ratafia biscuits (almond macaroons) are the perfect accompaniment.

Damask Cream

It is important not to move this elegant dessert while it is setting, or it will separate.

Serves 4
600ml/1 pint/2½ cups milk
40g/1½ oz/3 tbsp caster (superfine) sugar

several drops of triple-strength rose water
10ml/2 tsp rennet
60ml/4 tbsp double (heavy) cream
sugared rose petals, to decorate (optional)

1 Gently heat the milk and 25g/1oz/2 tbsp of the sugar, stirring, until the sugar has melted and the temperature of the mixture feels neither hot nor cold. Stir rose water to taste into the milk, then remove the pan from the heat and stir in the rennet.

2 Pour the milk into a serving dish and leave undisturbed for 2–3 hours, until set. Stir the remaining sugar into the cream, then carefully spoon over the junket. Decorate with sugared rose petals, if you wish.

Mandarins in Orange-flower Syrup

Mandarins, tangerines, clementines, mineolas: any of these citrus fruits are suitable to use in this refreshing recipe.

Serves 4
11 mandarins
15ml/1 tbsp icing (confectioners') sugar
10ml/2 tsp orange-flower water

1 Pare some rind from one mandarin and cut it into fine shreds for decoration. Squeeze the juice from two mandarins and reserve it. Peel eight further mandarins, removing the white pith. Arrange the whole fruit in a wide dish.

2 Mix the reserved juice with the icing sugar and orange-flower water and pour over the fruit. Cover and chill. Blanch the rind in boiling water for 30 seconds. Drain, cool and sprinkle over the mandarins, with pistachio nuts if you wish.

Syllabub Energy 531kcal/2201kJ; Protein 3.3g; Carbohydrate 29.6g, of which sugars 29.6g; Fat 40.3g, of which saturates 25.1g; Cholesterol 103mg; Calcium 60mg; Fibre 0.5g; Sodium 54mg.
Damask Energy 183kcal/767kJ; Protein 5.4g; Carbohydrate 17.8g, of which sugars 17.8g; Fat 10.6g, of which saturates 6.6g; Cholesterol 29mg; Calcium 193mg; Fibre 0g; Sodium 69mg.
Mandarins Energy 61kcal/261kJ; Protein 1.2g; Carbohydrate 14.8g, of which sugars 14.8g; Fat 0.1g, of which saturates 0g; Cholesterol 0mg; Calcium 41mg; Fibre 1.5g; Sodium 5mg.

Chocolate Blancmange

An old-fashioned dessert that deserves a revival! Serve with thin cream for a touch of luxury.

Serves 4

60ml/4 tbsp cornflour (cornstarch)
600ml/1 pint/2½ cups milk
40g/1½ oz/3 tbsp caster (superfine) sugar
50–115g/2–4oz plain (semi-sweet) chocolate, chopped
vanilla extract, to taste
white and plain (semisweet) chocolate curls, to decorate

1 Rinse a 750ml/1¼ pint/3 cup fluted mould with cold water and leave it upside down to drain. Blend the cornflour to a smooth paste with a little of the milk.

2 Bring the remaining milk to the boil, preferably in a non-stick pan, then pour on to the blended mixture, stirring constantly.

3 Pour all the milk back into the pan and bring slowly to the boil over low heat, stirring constantly until the mixture boils and thickens. Remove the pan from the heat, then add the sugar, chopped chocolate and a few drops of vanilla extract. Stir until the chocolate has melted.

4 Pour the chocolate mixture into the mould and leave in a cool place for several hours to set.

5 To unmould the blancmange, place a large serving plate on top, then, holding the plate and mould firmly together, invert them. Give both plate and mould a gentle but firm shake to loosen the blancmange, then lift off the mould. Scatter white and plain chocolate curls over the top of the blancmange to decorate, and serve at once.

> **Cook's Tip**
> For a special dinner party, flavour the chocolate mixture with crème de menthe or orange-flavoured liqueur instead of vanilla, and set the blancmange in individual moulds.

Yogurt Ring with Tropical Fruit

An impressive, light and colourful dessert with a truly tropical flavour, combining a magical mix of exotic fruits.

Serves 6

175ml/6fl oz/¾ cup tropical fruit juice
15ml/1 tbsp powdered gelatine
3 egg whites
150ml/¼ pint/⅔ cup low-fat natural (plain) yogurt
finely grated rind of 1 lime

For the filling
1 mango
2 kiwi fruit
10–12 physalis (Cape gooseberries), plus extra to decorate
juice of 1 lime

1 Pour the tropical fruit juice into a small pan and sprinkle the powdered gelatine over the surface. Heat gently until the gelatine has dissolved.

2 Whisk the egg whites in a clean, grease-free bowl until they hold soft peaks. Continue whisking hard, gradually adding the yogurt and lime rind.

3 Continue whisking hard and pour in the hot gelatine mixture in a steady stream, until evenly mixed.

4 Quickly pour the mixture into a 1.5 litre/2½ pint/6¼ cup ring mould. Chill the mould until the mixture has set. The mixture will separate into two layers.

5 To make the filling, halve, stone (pit), peel and dice the mango. Peel and slice the kiwi fruit. Remove the husks from the physalis and cut the fruit in half. Toss all the fruits together in a bowl and stir in the lime juice.

6 Run a knife around the edge of the ring to loosen the mixture. Dip the mould quickly into hot water, then place a serving plate on top. Holding the plate and mould firmly together, invert them, then lift off the mould. Spoon all the prepared fruit into the centre of the ring, decorate with extra physalis and serve immediately.

Blancmange Energy 225kcal/954kJ; Protein 5.9g; Carbohydrate 39.2g, of which sugars 25.3g; Fat 6.2g, of which saturates 3.7g; Cholesterol 10mg; Calcium 192mg; Fibre 0.3g; Sodium 74mg.
Yogurt Ring Energy 63kcal/267kJ; Protein 5.4g; Carbohydrate 10.1g, of which sugars 10g; Fat 0.4g, of which saturates 0.2g; Cholesterol 0mg; Calcium 59mg; Fibre 1.1g; Sodium 55mg.

Peach Melba

The original dish created for the opera singer Dame Nellie Melba had peaches and ice cream served in grand style upon an ice swan.

Serves 4

300g/11oz/scant 2 cups fresh
   raspberries
squeeze of lemon juice
icing (confectioners') sugar,
   to taste
2 large ripe peaches or
   425g/15oz can sliced peaches
8 scoops vanilla ice cream

1 Press the raspberries through a non-metallic sieve (strainer) to form a purée.

2 Add a little lemon juice to the raspberry purée and sweeten to taste with icing sugar.

3 If using fresh peaches, cover them with boiling water for 4–5 seconds, then slip off the skins. Halve the peaches along the indented line, then slice neatly. If using canned peaches, place them in a strainer and drain them well.

4 Place two scoops of ice cream in each of 4 individual glass dishes, top with peach slices, then pour over the raspberry purée. Serve immediately.

Cook's Tip
For homemade vanilla ice cream, put 300ml/½ pint/1¼ cups milk in a heavy pan, with a split vanilla pod (bean). Bring to the boil, then remove from the heat and leave for 15 minutes. Remove the pod and scrape the seeds into the milk. Whisk 4 egg yolks with 75g/3oz/6 tbsp caster (superfine) sugar and 5ml/1tsp cornflour (cornstarch) until thick and foamy. Gradually whisk in the hot milk. Return to the pan and cook, stirring, until thick. Cool. Whip 300ml/½ pint/1¼ cups double (heavy) cream until thick; fold into the custard. Pour into a freezer container. Freeze for 6 hours or until firm, beating twice during this time.

Summer Pudding

Unbelievably simple to make and totally delicious, this is a real warm weather classic. It's also a productive way of using up leftover bread.

Serves 4

about 8 thin slices white bread,
   at least one day old
800g/1¾lb mixed summer fruits
about 30ml/2 tbsp granulated
   sugar

1 Remove the crusts from the bread. Cut a round from one slice of bread to fit in the base of a 1.2 litre/2 pint/5 cup round, deep bowl and place in position. Cut strips of bread about 5cm/2in wide and use to line the sides of the bowl, overlapping the strips as you work.

2 Place the fruit, sugar and 30ml/2 tbsp water in a large heavy pan and heat gently, shaking the pan occasionally, until the fruit juices begin to run.

3 Reserve about 45ml/3 tbsp fruit juice, then spoon the fruit and remaining juice into the prepared bowl, taking care not to dislodge the bread lining.

4 Cut the remaining bread to fit entirely over the fruit. Stand the bowl on a plate and cover with a saucer or small plate that will just fit inside the top of the bowl. Place a heavy weight on top. Chill the pudding and the reserved fruit juice overnight.

5 Run a knife carefully around the inside of the bowl rim, then invert the pudding on to a cold serving plate. Pour over the reserved juice, making sure that all the bread is completely covered, and serve.

Cook's Tips
• Use a good mix of summer fruits for this pudding – red and blackcurrants, raspberries, strawberries and loganberries.
• Summer pudding freezes well so make an extra one to enjoy during the winter.

Peach Melba Energy 256kcal/1078kJ; Protein 6.1g; Carbohydrate 32.9g, of which sugars 31.6g; Fat 10.6g, of which saturates 7.4g; Cholesterol 29mg; Calcium 144mg; Fibre 3g; Sodium 75mg.
Pudding Energy 206kcal/872kJ; Protein 6.2g; Carbohydrate 45.2g, of which sugars 19.9g; Fat 1.2g, of which saturates 0g; Cholesterol 0mg; Calcium 95mg; Fibre 3g; Sodium 293mg.

Raspberries with Fruit Purée

Three colourful fruit purées, swirled together, make a kaleidoscopic garnish for a nest of raspberries.

Serves 4–6
200g/7oz/1¼ cups raspberries
120ml/4fl oz/½ cup red wine
icing (confectioners') sugar,
    for dusting

For the decoration
1 large mango, peeled and
    chopped
400g/14oz kiwi fruit, peeled and
    chopped
200g/7oz/1¼ cups raspberries
icing (confectioners') sugar,
    to taste
hazlenut cookies, to serve

1 Place the raspberries in a bowl with the red wine and allow to macerate for about 2 hours.

2 To make the decoration, purée the mango in a food processor, adding water if necessary. Press through a sieve (strainer) into a bowl. Purée the kiwi fruit in the same way, then make a third purée from the remaining raspberries. Sweeten the purées with sifted icing sugar, if necessary.

3 Spoon each purée on to a serving plate, separating the kiwi and mango with the raspberry purée as if creating a four-wedged pie. Gently tap the plate on the work surface to settle the purées against each other.

4 Using a skewer, draw a spiral outwards from the centre of the plate to the rim. Drain the macerated raspberries, pile them in the centre, and dust them heavily with icing sugar.

> **Cook's Tip**
> For hazelnut bites, cream 115g/4oz/½ cup butter with 75g/3oz/⅔ cup icing (confectioners') sugar until light and fluffy. Beat in 115g/4oz/1 cup flour, 75g/3oz/¾ cup ground hazelnuts and 1 egg yolk. Shape into small balls and place on lined baking sheets. Press a hazelnut into the centre of each. Bake at 180°C/350°F/Gas 4 for 10 minutes and allow to cool.

Apricot & Orange Jelly

This refreshing jelly is the perfect way to round off a summer. Decorate with slivers of fresh apricot or blanched orange rind shreds, if you prefer.

Serves 4
350g/12oz well-flavoured fresh
    ripe apricots, stoned (pitted)

50–75g/2–3oz/about ⅓ cup
    sugar
about 300ml/½ pint/1¼ cups
    freshly squeezed orange juice
15ml/1 tbsp powdered gelatine
single (light) cream, to serve
finely chopped candied orange
    peel, to decorate

1 Heat the apricots, sugar and 120ml/4fl oz/½ cup of the orange juice, stirring until the sugar has dissolved. Simmer gently until the apricots are tender.

2 Press the apricot mixture through a nylon sieve (strainer) into a small measuring jug (cup).

3 Pour 45ml/3 tbsp of the orange juice into a small heatproof bowl, sprinkle over the gelatine and leave for about 5 minutes, until spongy.

4 Place the bowl over a pan of hot water and heat until the gelatine has dissolved. Slowly pour into the apricot mixture, stirring, constantly. Make up to 600ml/1 pint/2½ cups with the remaining orange juice.

5 Pour the apricot mixture into four individual dishes and chill in the refrigerator until set.

6 Just before serving, pour a thin layer of cream over the surface of the jellies and decorate with candied orange peel.

> **Variation**
> You could also make this light dessert with nectarines or peaches instead of the apricots.

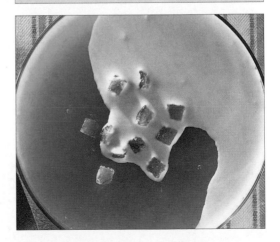

Fruit Purée Energy 69kcal/294kJ; Protein 1.7g; Carbohydrate 11.9g, of which sugars 11.7g; Fat 0.5g, of which saturates 0.1g; Cholesterol 0mg; Calcium 34mg; Fibre 3.3g; Sodium 6mg.
Orange Jelly Energy 116kcal/496kJ; Protein 4.4g; Carbohydrate 26g, of which sugars 26g; Fat 0.2g, of which saturates 0g; Cholesterol 0mg; Calcium 27mg; Fibre 1.6g; Sodium 10mg.

Summer Berry Medley with Red Sauce

Make the most of seasonal fruits in this refreshing, easy-to-make dessert.

Serves 4–6
450–675g/1–1½ lb/4½ cups
fresh mixed soft summer fruits
such as strawberries,
raspberries, blueberries,
redcurrants and blackcurrants
vanilla ice cream or crème
fraîche, to serve

For the sauce
175g/6oz/1½ cups redcurrants,
stripped from their stalks
175g/6oz/1 cup raspberries
50g/2oz/¼ cup caster (superfine)
sugar
30–45ml/2–3 tbsp crème de
framboise

1 To make the sauce, place the redcurrants in a bowl with the raspberries, caster sugar and crème de framboise. Cover and leave to macerate for 1–2 hours.

2 Put the macerated fruit, together with its juices, in a pan and cook over a low heat for 5–6 minutes, stirring occasionally, until the fruit is just tender.

3 Pour the fruit into a blender or food processor and process until smooth. Press through a nylon sieve (strainer) to remove any pips (seeds). Leave to cool, then chill.

4 Divide the mixed soft fruit among four individual dishes and pour over the sauce. Serve immediately with vanilla ice cream or crème fraîche.

> **Cook's Tips**
> • The red sauce is also good swirled into mascarpone or plain yogurt. Try it as a topping for peaches or bananas and cream.
> • Crème de framboise is raspberry-flavoured liqueur. You could use Kirsch or an orange-flavoured liqueur instead.

Brown Bread Ice Cream

This delicious textured ice cream is irresistible served with a blackcurrant sauce.

Serves 6
50g/2oz/½ cup roasted and
chopped hazelnuts, ground
75g/3oz/1½ cups wholemeal
(whole-wheat) breadcrumbs
50g/2oz/¼ cup demerara (raw)
sugar
3 egg whites

115g/4oz/generous ⅔ cup caster
(superfine) sugar
300ml/½ pint/1¼ cups double
(heavy) cream
a few drops of vanilla extract

For the sauce
225g/8oz/2 cups blackcurrants
75g/3oz/generous ⅓ cup caster
(superfine) sugar
15ml/1 tbsp crème de cassis
fresh mint sprigs, to decorate

1 Combine the hazelnuts and breadcrumbs on a baking sheet, then sprinkle over the demerara sugar. Place under a medium grill (broiler) and cook until crisp and browned.

2 Whisk the egg whites in a clean, grease-free bowl until stiff, then gradually whisk in the caster sugar until thick and glossy. Whip the cream until soft peaks form and fold into the meringue with the breadcrumb mixture and vanilla extract.

3 Spoon the mixture into a 1.2 litre/2 pint/5 cup loaf tin (pan). Smooth the top level, then cover and freeze until firm.

4 To make the sauce, put the blackcurrants in a small bowl with the sugar. Toss gently to mix and leave for about 30 minutes. Purée the blackcurrants in a food processor or blender, then press through a nylon sieve (strainer) until smooth. Add the crème de cassis and chill.

5 To serve, arrange a slice of ice cream on a plate, spoon over a little sauce and decorate with fresh mint sprigs.

> **Cook's Tip**
> Crème de cassis is the famous French blackcurrant liqueur.

Berry Medley Energy 85kcal/361kJ; Protein 1.3g; Carbohydrate 16.5g, of which sugars 16.5g; Fat 0.2g, of which saturates 0g; Cholesterol 0mg; Calcium 41mg; Fibre 2.6g; Sodium 7mg.
Ice Cream Energy 526kcal/2198kJ; Protein 5.4g; Carbohydrate 55.3g, of which sugars 45.8g; Fat 32.4g, of which saturates 17.1g; Cholesterol 69mg; Calcium 97mg; Fibre 2.2g; Sodium 141mg.

Raspberry Meringue Gâteau

A rich, hazelnut meringue sandwiched with whipped cream and raspberries is the ultimate in elegance.

Serves 6
4 egg whites
225g/8oz/1 cup caster (superfine) sugar
a few drops of vanilla extract
5ml/1 tsp distilled malt vinegar
115g/4oz/1 cup roasted and chopped hazelnuts, ground

300ml/½ pint/1¼ cups double (heavy) cream
350g/12oz/2 cups raspberries
icing (confectioners') sugar, for dusting
fresh mint sprigs, to decorate

For the sauce
225g/8oz/1½ cups raspberries
45–60ml/3–4 tbsp icing (confectioners') sugar, sifted
15ml/1 tbsp orange liqueur

1 Preheat the oven to 180°C/350°F/Gas 4. Grease two 20cm/8in sandwich tins (layer cake pans) and line the bases with baking parchment.

2 Whisk the egg whites in a large clean bowl until they hold stiff peaks, then gradually whisk in the caster sugar a tablespoon at a time, whisking well after each addition. Continue whisking the meringue mixture for a minute of two until very stiff, then fold in the vanilla extract, vinegar and ground hazelnuts.

3 Divide the meringue mixture between the prepared tins and spread level. Bake for 50–60 minutes until crisp. Remove the meringues from the tins and leave them to cool on a wire rack.

4 Meanwhile, make the sauce. Process the raspberries with the icing sugar and liqueur in a blender or food processor, then press through a sieve (strainer) to remove seeds. Chill the sauce.

5 Whip the cream until it forms soft peaks, then gently fold in the raspberries. Sandwich the meringue rounds together with the raspberry cream.

6 Dust the top of the gâteau with icing sugar. Decorate with mint sprigs and serve with the raspberry sauce.

Iced Chocolate & Nut Gâteau

Autumn hazelnuts add crunchiness to this popular iced dinner-party dessert.

Serves 6–8
75g/3oz/¾ cup shelled hazelnuts
about 32 sponge (lady fingers) fingers
150ml/¼ pint/⅔ cup cold strong black coffee

30ml/2 tbsp Cognac or other brandy
450ml/¾ pint/scant 2 cups double (heavy) cream
75g/3oz/⅔ cup icing (confectioners') sugar, sifted
150g/5oz plain (semisweet) chocolate
icing (confectioners') sugar and unsweetened cocoa powder, for dusting

1 Preheat the oven to 200°C/400°F/Gas 6. Spread out the hazelnuts on a baking sheet and toast them in the oven for 5 minutes until golden. Transfer the nuts to a clean dish towel and rub off the skins. Cool, then chop finely.

2 Line a 1.2 litre/2 pint/5 cup loaf tin (pan) with clear film (plastic wrap) and cut the sponge fingers to fit the base and sides. Reserve the remaining fingers.

3 Mix the coffee with the Cognac or other brandy in a shallow dish. Dip the sponge fingers briefly into the coffee mixture and return to the tin, sugary-side down.

4 Whip the cream with the icing sugar until it holds soft peaks. Roughly chop 75g/3oz of the chocolate, and fold into the cream with the hazelnuts.

5 Melt the remaining chocolate in a heatproof bowl set over a pan of barely simmering water. Cool, then fold into the cream mixture. Spoon into the tin.

6 Moisten the remaining sponge fingers in the coffee mixture and lay over the filling. Wrap and freeze until firm.

7 Remove the gâteau from the freezer 30 minutes before serving. Turn out and dust with icing sugar and cocoa powder.

Raspberry Energy 434kcal/1799kJ; Protein 6.8g; Carbohydrate 14.3g, of which sugars 13.9g; Fat 39.3g, of which saturates 17.7g; Cholesterol 69mg; Calcium 81mg; Fibre 3.7g; Sodium 56mg.
Iced Chocolate Energy 631kcal/2628kJ; Protein 8.2g; Carbohydrate 49.7g, of which sugars 38.3g; Fat 44.9g, of which saturates 23.3g; Cholesterol 192mg; Calcium 90mg; Fibre 1.5g; Sodium 57mg.

Blackberry Brown Sugar Meringue

A rich dessert which is elegant enough to be served at an autumnal dinner party.

Serves 6
For the meringue
175g/6oz/¾ cup soft light brown sugar
3 egg whites
5ml/1 tsp distilled malt vinegar
2.5ml/½ tsp vanilla extract

For the filling
350–450g/12oz–1lb/3–4 cups blackberries
30ml/2 tbsp crème de cassis
300ml/½ pint/1¼ cups double (heavy) cream
15ml/1 tbsp icing (confectioners') sugar, sifted
small blackberry leaves, to decorate (optional)

1 Preheat the oven to 160°C/325°F/Gas 3. Draw a 20cm/8in circle on a sheet of non-stick baking parchment, turn over and place on a baking sheet. Spread the brown sugar out on a baking sheet, dry in the oven for 8–10 minutes, then sieve (sift).

2 Whisk the egg whites in a clean, grease-free bowl until stiff. Add half the dried brown sugar, 15g/½oz/1 tbsp at a time, whisking well after each addition. Add the vinegar and vanilla extract, then fold in the remaining sugar.

3 Spoon the meringue on to the drawn circle on the paper, making a hollow in the centre. Bake for 45 minutes, then turn off the oven and leave the meringue in the oven with the door slightly open, until cold. Meanwhile, place the blackberries in a bowl, sprinkle over the crème de cassis and leave to macerate for 30 minutes.

4 When the meringue is cold, carefully peel off the baking parchment and transfer to a serving plate. Lightly whip the cream with the icing sugar and spoon into the centre. Top with the blackberries and decorate with blackberry leaves, if you like.

Variation
Fill with a mix of raspberries, strawberries and red currants.

Clementines in Cinnamon Caramel

The combination of sweet yet sharp clementines and caramel sauce, flavoured with a hint of spice, is divine. Serve with thick yogurt or crème fraîche to make a delicious dessert for family and friends.

Serves 4–6
8–12 clementines
225g/8oz/generous 1 cup sugar
300ml/½ pint/1¼ cups warm water
2 cinnamon sticks
30ml/2 tbsp orange-flavoured liqueur
25g/1oz/¼ cup shelled pistachio nuts

1 Using a vegetable peeler, pare the rind from two clementines, and cut it into fine strips. Set aside.

2 Peel the clementines, removing all the pith but keeping them intact. Put the fruits in a serving bowl.

3 Gently heat the sugar in a pan until it melts and turns a rich golden brown. Immediately turn off the heat.

4 Cover your hand with a dish towel and pour in the warm water (the mixture will bubble violently). Bring slowly to the boil, stirring until the caramel has dissolved. Add the shredded rind and whole cinnamon sticks, then simmer for 5 minutes. Stir in the orange-flavoured liqueur.

5 Leave the syrup to cool for about 10 minutes, then pour over the clementines. Cover the bowl and chill for several hours or overnight.

6 Blanch the pistachios in boiling water. Drain, cool and remove the dark outer skins. Scatter over the clementines and serve.

Variation
Use oranges instead of clementines: using a sharp knife, remove the rind and pith, cutting downwards, then slice horizontally.

Meringue Energy 404kcal/1684kJ; Protein 2.9g; Carbohydrate 36.9g, of which sugars 36.9g; Fat 27g, of which saturates 16.7g; Cholesterol 69mg; Calcium 66mg; Fibre 1.8g; Sodium 45mg.
Clementines Energy 215kcal/912kJ; Protein 1.7g; Carbohydrate 46.8g, of which sugars 46.7g; Fat 2.4g, of which saturates 0.3g; Cholesterol 0mg; Calcium 50mg; Fibre 1.3g; Sodium 28mg.

Chocolate Chestnut Roulade

Don't worry if this moist sponge cracks as you roll it up – this is the sign of a good roulade.

Serves 8

175g/6oz plain (semisweet) chocolate
30ml/2 tbsp strong black coffee
5 eggs, separated
175g/6oz/scant 1 cup caster (superfine) sugar
250ml/8fl oz/1 cup double (heavy) cream
225g/8oz unsweetened chestnut purée
45–60ml/3–4 tbsp icing (confectioners') sugar, plus extra for dusting
single (light) cream, to serve

1 Preheat the oven to 180°C/350°F/Gas 4, then line and oil a 33 × 23cm/13 × 9in Swiss roll tin (jell roll pan); use non-stick baking parchment. Melt the chocolate in a bowl over gently simmering water, then stir in the coffee. Leave to cool slightly.

2 Whisk the egg yolks and caster sugar together until thick and light, then stir in the cooled chocolate mixture. Whisk the egg whites in another clean bowl until stiff. Stir a spoonful into the chocolate mixture to lighten it, then gently fold in the rest.

3 Pour the mixture into the prepared tin and spread level. Bake for 20 minutes. Remove from the oven, cover with a dish towel and leave to cool in the tin for several hours.

4 Whip the double cream until soft peaks begin to form. Mix together the chestnut purée and icing sugar, then fold into the whipped cream.

5 Dust a sheet of greaseproof (waxed) paper with icing sugar. Turn out the roulade on to this paper and peel off the lining paper. Trim the sides. Gently spread the chestnut cream evenly over the roulade to within 2.5cm/1in of the edges. Using the greaseproof paper to help you, carefully roll up the roulade as tightly and evenly as possible.

6 Chill the roulade for about 2 hours, then dust liberally with icing sugar. Serve cut into thick slices with cream poured over.

Pasta Timbales with Apricot Sauce

This unusual dessert is made like a rice pudding, but uses tiny pasta shapes instead of the rice. It looks very attractive.

Serves 4

100g/4oz/1 cup orzo or other small soup pasta
75g/3oz/⅓ cup caster (superfine) sugar
pinch of salt
25g/1oz/2 tbsp butter
1 vanilla pod (bean), split
750ml/1¼ pints/3 cups milk
300ml/½ pint/1¼ cups ready-made custard
45ml/3 tbsp Kirsch
15ml/1 tbsp powdered gelatine
oil, for greasing
400g/14oz can apricots in juice
lemon juice to taste
fresh flowers, to decorate (optional)

1 Place the pasta, sugar, pinch of salt, butter, vanilla pod and milk into a heavy pan and bring to the boil. Turn down the heat and simmer for 25 minutes until the pasta is tender and most of the liquid is absorbed. Stir frequently to prevent it from sticking.

2 Remove the vanilla pod and transfer the pasta to a bowl to cool. Stir in the custard and add 30ml/2 tbsp of the kirsch.

3 Sprinkle the gelatine over 45ml/2 tbsp water in a small bowl set in a pan of barely simmering water. Allow to become spongy and heat gently to dissolve. Stir into the pasta.

4 Lightly oil 4 timbale moulds and spoon in the pasta. Chill for 2 hours until set.

5 Meanwhile, purée the apricots in a food processor or blender, then pass through a sieve (strainer) and add lemon juice and Kirsch to taste. Dilute with a little water if too thick.

6 Run a knife around the edge of each timbale to loosen the mixture. To turn out, place an individual plate on the top of each mould, then holding the plate and mould firmly together, invert them. Serve with apricot sauce and decorated with fresh flowers if you wish.

Roulade Energy 469kcal/1961kJ; Protein 6.2g; Carbohydrate 53.5g, of which sugars 44.9g; Fat 27.1g, of which saturates 15.2g; Cholesterol 163mg; Calcium 68mg; Fibre 1.7g; Sodium 57mg.
Timbales Energy 425kcal/1797kJ; Protein 12g; Carbohydrate 67.6g, of which sugars 47.3g; Fat 10.2g, of which saturates 5.3g; Cholesterol 26mg; Calcium 332mg; Fibre 1.7g; Sodium 156mg.

Coffee Jellies with Amaretti Cream

This impressive dessert is very easy to prepare. For the best results, use a high-roasted Arabica bean for the coffee.

Serves 4
75g/3oz/generous ⅓ cup caster
    (superfine) sugar
450ml/¾ pint/1¾ cups hot
    strong coffee
30–45ml/2–3 tbsp dark rum or
    coffee liqueur
20ml/4 tsp powdered gelatine

For the amaretti cream
150ml/¼ pint/⅔ cup double
    (heavy) cream
15ml/1 tbsp icing (confectioners')
    sugar, sifted
10–15ml/2–3 tsp instant coffee
    granules dissolved in
    15ml/1 tbsp hot water
6 large amaretti, crushed

1 Put the sugar in a pan with 75ml/5 tbsp water and stir over low heat until the sugar has dissolved. Increase the heat and boil the syrup steadily, without stirring, for about 3–4 minutes.

2 Stir the hot coffee and rum or coffee liqueur into the syrup, then sprinkle the gelatine over the top and stir the mixture until it is completely dissolved.

3 Carefully pour the coffee jelly mixture into four wetted 150ml/¼ pint/⅔ cup moulds, allow to cool and then leave in the refrigerator for several hours until set.

4 To make the amaretti cream, lightly whip the cream with the icing sugar until the mixture holds stiff peaks. Stir in the dissolved coffee, then gently fold in all but 30ml/2 tbsp of the crushed amaretti.

5 To turn out, first quickly dip the moulds in hot water, then place an individual plate on the top of each mould. Holding each plate and mould firmly together, invert them.

6 Spoon a little of the amaretti cream beside each jelly. Dust over the reserved amaretti crumbs and serve immediately.

Chocolate Date Torte

A stunning cake that tastes wonderful. Rich and gooey – it's a chocoholic's delight!

Serves 8
4 egg whites
115g/4oz/generous ⅔ cup caster
    (superfine) sugar
200g/7oz plain (semisweet)
    chocolate
175g/6oz Medjool dates, stoned
    (pitted) and chopped

175g/6oz/1½ cups walnuts or
    pecan nuts, chopped
5ml/2 tsp vanilla extract, plus a
    few extra drops

For the frosting
200g/7oz/scant 1 cup fromage
    frais
200g/7oz/scant 1 cup
    mascarpone
icing (confectioners') sugar,
    to taste

1 Preheat the oven to 180°C/350°F/Gas 4. Lightly grease and base-line a 20cm/8in springform cake tin (pan).

2 To make the frosting, mix together the fromage frais and mascarpone, and a few drops of vanilla extract and icing sugar to taste, then set aside.

3 Whisk the egg whites in a clean, grease-free bowl until stiff peaks form. Whisk in 30ml/2 tbsp of the caster sugar until the meringue is thick and glossy, then fold in the remainder.

4 Chop 175g/6oz of the chocolate. Carefully fold into the meringue with the dates, nuts and 5ml/1 tsp vanilla extract. Pour into the prepared tin, level the surface and bake for about 45 minutes, until risen around the edges.

5 Allow the torte to cool in the tin for about 10 minutes, then turn out on to a wire rack. Peel off the lining paper and leave until completely cold. When cool, swirl the frosting over the top of the torte.

6 Melt the remaining chocolate in a bowl set over hot water. Spoon into a small paper piping (icing) bag, snip off the top and drizzle the chocolate over the torte. Chill in the refrigerator before serving, cut into wedges.

Jellies Energy 355kcal/1480kJ; Protein 5.5g; Carbohydrate 32.1g, of which sugars 27.7g; Fat 21.5g, of which saturates 13.1g; Cholesterol 51mg; Calcium 43mg; Fibre 0.2g; Sodium 43mg.
Torte Energy 427kcal/1784kJ; Protein 9.2g; Carbohydrate 41.5g, of which sugars 40.9g; Fat 26g, of which saturates 7.8g; Cholesterol 12mg; Calcium 57mg; Fibre 2.1g; Sodium 41mg.

Crème Caramel

This creamy, caramel-flavoured custard from France is popular worldwide.

Serves 4–6

115g/4oz/generous ½ cup granulated (white) sugar
300ml/½ pint/1¼ cups milk
300ml/½ pint/1¼ cups single (light) cream
6 eggs
75g/3oz/generous ¼ cup caster (superfine) sugar
2.5ml/½ tsp vanilla extract

1 Preheat the oven to 150°C/300°F/Gas 2 and half-fill a large roasting pan with water.

2 Place the granulated sugar in a pan with 60ml/4 tbsp water and heat gently, swirling the pan occasionally, until the sugar has dissolved. Increase the heat and boil for a good caramel colour. Immediately pour the caramel into an ovenproof soufflé dish. Place in the roasting pan and set aside.

3 To make the egg custard, heat the milk and cream together in a pan until almost boiling. Meanwhile, beat the eggs, caster sugar and vanilla extract together in a mixing bowl using a large balloon whisk.

4 Whisk the hot milk into the eggs and sugar, then strain the liquid through a sieve (strainer) into the soufflé dish, on top of the cooled caramel base.

5 Transfer the tin to the centre of the oven and bake for about 1½–2 hours (topping up the water level after 1 hour), or until the custard has set in the centre. Lift the dish carefully out of the water and leave to cool, then cover and chill overnight.

6 Run a knife around the edge of the chilled custard, then place an inverted plate (large enough to hold the caramel sauce that will flow out as well) on top of the dish. Holding the dish and plate together, turn upside down. Give both plate and dish a gentle but firm shake to loosen the crème caramel, then lift off the mould. Serve immediately.

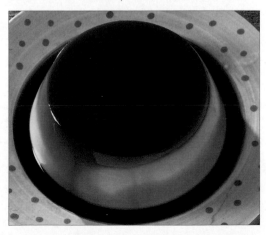

Australian Hazelnut Pavlova

A hazelnut meringue base is topped with orange cream, nectarines and raspberries in this famous dessert.

Serves 4–6

3 egg whites
175g/6oz/1 cup caster (superfine) sugar
5ml/1 tsp cornflour (cornstarch)
5ml/1 tsp white wine vinegar
40g/1½ oz/generous ¼ cup chopped roasted hazelnuts
250ml/8fl oz/1 cup double (heavy) cream
15ml/1 tbsp orange juice
30ml/2 tbsp natural (plain) thick and creamy yogurt
2 ripe nectarines, stoned (pitted) and sliced
225g/8oz/2 cups raspberries, halved
15–30ml/1–2 tbsp redcurrant jelly, warmed

1 Preheat the oven to 140°C/275°F/Gas 1. Lightly grease a baking sheet. Draw a 20cm/8in circle on a sheet of baking parchment. Place pencil-side down on the baking sheet.

2 Place the egg whites in a clean, grease-free bowl and whisk until stiff peaks form. Whisk in the caster sugar 15g/½oz/1 tbsp at a time, whisking well after each addition.

3 Add the cornflour, vinegar and hazelnuts and fold in carefully with a large metal spoon.

4 Spoon the meringue on to the marked circle and spread out to the edges, making a dip in the centre. Bake for about 1¼–1½ hours, until crisp. Cool completely; transfer to a serving platter.

5 Whip the double cream and orange juice until the mixture is just thick, stir in the yogurt and spoon on to the meringue. Top with the prepared fruit and drizzle over the warmed redcurrant jelly. Serve immediately.

> **Variation**
> *For extra colour, add a couple of peeled and sliced kiwi fruit.*

Caramel Energy 318kcal/1335kJ; Protein 9.8g; Carbohydrate 36.6g, of which sugars 36.6g; Fat 16g, of which saturates 8.2g; Cholesterol 221mg; Calcium 150mg; Fibre 0g; Sodium 108mg.
Pavlova Energy 427kcal/1783kJ; Protein 5g; Carbohydrate 44.1g, of which sugars 43.2g; Fat 26.9g, of which saturates 14.3g; Cholesterol 57mg; Calcium 71mg; Fibre 2.2g; Sodium 50mg.

Chocolate Eclairs

These choux pastry éclairs are filled with a luscious vanilla-flavoured cream.

Serves 12
300ml/½ pint/1¼ cups double (heavy) cream
10ml/2 tsp icing (confectioners') sugar, sifted
1.5ml/¼ tsp vanilla extract

115g/4oz plain (semisweet) chocolate
25g/1oz/2 tbsp butter

For the pastry
65g/2½oz/9 tbsp plain (all-purpose) flour
pinch of salt
50g/2oz/¼ cup butter, diced
2 eggs, lightly beaten

1 Preheat the oven to 200°C/400°F/Gas 6. Grease a large baking sheet and line with baking parchment.

2 To make the pastry, sift the flour and salt on to a small sheet of baking parchment. Very gently heat the butter and 150ml/¼ pint/⅔ cup water in a pan until the butter has melted. Bring to a rolling boil, then remove from the heat and immediately tip in all the flour. Beat vigorously to mix well. Return the pan to a low heat. Beat the mixture until it leaves the sides of the pan and forms a ball. Set aside and allow to cool for 2–3 minutes.

3 Beat in the eggs, a little at a time, to form a smooth, shiny paste. Spoon into a piping (pastry) bag fitted with a 2.5cm/1in plain nozzle. Pipe 10cm/4in lengths on to the baking sheet.

4 Bake for 25–30 minutes, or until the pastries are well risen and golden brown. Make a neat slit along the side of each to release the steam. Lower the temperature to 180°C/350°F/Gas 4 and bake for a further 5 minutes. Cool on a wire rack.

5 To make the filling, whip the cream with the icing sugar and vanilla until it just holds its shape. Pipe into the éclairs.

6 Place the chocolate and 30ml/2 tbsp water in a small bowl set over a pan of hot water. Melt, stirring, then remove from the heat and gradually stir in the butter. Use the chocolate mixture to coat the éclairs. Place on a wire rack and leave to set.

Apricot & Almond Jalousie

Jalousie means "shutter", and the slatted pastry topping of this pie looks exactly like French window shutters. The dish not only looks attractive, but tastes wonderful, too.

Serves 4
225g/8oz ready-made puff pastry
a little beaten egg
90ml/6 tbsp apricot conserve
25g/1oz/2 tbsp caster (superfine) sugar
30ml/2 tbsp flaked almonds
cream, to serve

1 Preheat the oven to 220°C/425°F/Gas 7. Roll out the pastry on a lightly floured surface and cut into a square measuring 30cm/12in. Cut in half to make two rectangles.

2 Place one piece of pastry on a wetted baking sheet and brush all round the edges with beaten egg. Spread the apricot conserve over the unbrushed part of the rectangle.

3 Fold the remaining rectangle in half lengthways and cut about eight diagonal slits from the centre fold to within about 1cm/½in from the edge all the way along.

4 Unfold the cut pastry and lay it on top of the pastry on the baking sheet. Press the pastry edges together well to seal and knock them up with the back of a knife.

5 Brush the slashed pastry with water and sprinkle over the caster sugar and flaked almonds.

6 Bake in the oven for 25–30 minutes, until well risen and golden brown. Remove the jalousie from the oven and leave to cool. Serve sliced, accompanied by cream.

> **Cook's Tip**
> *Make smaller individual jalousies and serve them with morning coffee, if you like. Use other flavours of fruit conserve to ring the changes – a summer berry conserve would be delicious.*

Eclairs Energy 253Kcal/1046kJ; Protein 2.7g; Carbohydrate 10.8g, of which sugars 6.5g; Fat 22.4g, of which saturates 13.5g; Cholesterol 86mg; Calcium 30mg; Fibre 0.4g; Sodium 58mg.
Jalousie Energy 339kcal/1423kJ; Protein 4.9g; Carbohydrate 43.5g, of which sugars 23.2g; Fat 18g, of which saturates 0.3g; Cholesterol 0mg; Calcium 56mg; Fibre 0.6g; Sodium 186mg.

Mango Ice Cream

Canned mangoes are used to make a deliciously rich and creamy ice cream, with a delicate oriental flavour.

Serves 4–6
2 x 425g/15oz cans sliced
mango, drained

50g/2oz/¹⁄₄ cup caster (superfine)
sugar
30ml/2 tbsp lime juice
45ml/3 tbsp hot water
15ml/1 tbsp powdered gelatine
350ml/12fl oz/1¹⁄₂ cups double
(heavy) cream, lightly whipped
fresh mint sprigs, to decorate

1 Reserve four slices of mango for decoration and chop the remainder. Place the chopped mango pieces in a bowl with the caster sugar and lime juice.

2 Put the hot water in a small heatproof bowl and sprinkle over the gelatine. Place the bowl over a pan of gently simmering water and stir until the gelatine has dissolved. Pour on to the mango mixture and mix well.

3 Add the lightly whipped cream and fold into the mango mixture. Pour the mixture into a plastic freezer container and freeze until half frozen.

4 Place the half-frozen ice cream in a food processor or blender and process until smooth. Spoon back into the container and return to the freezer to freeze completely.

5 Remove from the freezer 10 minutes before serving and place in the refrigerator. Serve scoops of ice cream decorated with pieces of the reserved sliced mango and fresh mint sprigs.

> **Cook's Tip**
> • Transferring the ice cream to the refrigerator for a short time before serving allows it to soften slightly, making scooping easier and helping the flavour to be more pronounced.
> • Use a metal scoop to serve the ice cream, dipping the scoop briefly in warm water between servings. Or simply slice, if easier.

Baked American Cheesecake

The lemon-flavoured cream cheese provides a subtle filling for this classic dessert.

Makes 9 squares
175g/6oz/1¹⁄₂ cups crushed digestive
biscuits (graham crackers)
40g/1¹⁄₂ oz/3 tbsp butter, melted,
plus extra for greasing

For the topping
450g/1lb/2¹⁄₂ cups curd (farmer's)
cheese or full-fat soft (cream)
cheese

115g/4oz/generous ¹⁄₂ cup caster
(superfine) sugar
3 eggs
finely grated rind of 1 lemon
15ml/1 tbsp lemon juice
2.5ml/¹⁄₂ tsp vanilla extract
15ml/1 tbsp cornflour
(cornstarch)
30ml/2 tbsp sour cream
150ml/¹⁄₄ pint/²⁄₃ cup sour cream
and 1.5ml/¹⁄₄ tsp ground
cinnamon, to decorate

1 Preheat the oven to 170°C/325°F/Gas 3. Lightly grease an 18cm/7in square loose-based cake tin (pan), then line the base with baking parchment.

2 Place the crushed biscuits and butter in a bowl and mix well. Turn into the base of the prepared cake tin and press down firmly with a potato masher.

3 To make the topping, place the curd or soft cheese in a mixing bowl, add the sugar and beat well until smooth. Add the eggs one at a time, beating well after each addition.

4 Stir in the lemon rind and juice, the vanilla extract, cornflour and 30ml/2 tbsp sour cream. Beat until the mixture is smooth. Pour the mixture on to the biscuit base and level the surface.

5 Bake for 1¹⁄₄ hours, or until the cheesecake has set in the centre. Turn off the oven but leave the cheesecake inside until completely cold.

6 Remove the cheesecake from the tin, top with the sour cream and swirl with the back of a spoon. Sprinkle with cinnamon and serve cut into squares.

Cheesecake Energy 311kcal/1302kJ; Protein 11.4g; Carbohydrate 30.8g, of which sugars 18.5g; Fat 17.4g, of which saturates 9.7g; Cholesterol 105mg; Calcium 112mg; Fibre 0.4g; Sodium 396mg.
Ice Cream Energy 409kcal/1701kJ; Protein 1.4g; Carbohydrate 32.4g, of which sugars 32.3g; Fat 31.3g, of which saturates 19.5g; Cholesterol 80mg; Calcium 44mg; Fibre 0.9g; Sodium 17mg.

Berry Frozen Yogurt

A super-easy iced dessert, using frozen summer fruits.

Serves 6
350g/12oz/3 cups frozen
summer fruits

200l/7fl oz/scant 1 cup Greek
(US strained plain) yogurt
25g/1oz/¼ cup icing
(confectioners') sugar

1 Put all the ingredients into a food processor and process until combined but still quite chunky. Spoon into six 150ml/¼ pint/⅔ cup ramekin dishes. Cover with cling film (plastic wrap) and freeze for 2 hours until firm.

2 To turn out, dip briefly in hot water and invert on to individual plates, tapping the bases of the dishes to release the desserts.

Rippled Chocolate Ice Cream

Rich, smooth and packed with chocolate, this heavenly ice cream is a real treat.

Serves 4
60ml/4 tbsp chocolate and
hazelnut spread

450ml/¾ pint/scant 2 cups
double (heavy) cream
15ml/1 tbsp icing (confectioners')
sugar
50g/2oz plain (semisweet)
chocolate, chopped
chocolate curls, to decorate

1 Mix together the chocolate and hazelnut spread and 75ml/5 tbsp of the double cream in a bowl.

2 Place the remaining cream in another bowl, sift in the icing sugar and beat until softly whipped. Lightly fold in the chocolate and hazelnut mixture with the chopped chocolate until the mixture is rippled. Transfer to a plastic freezer container and freeze for 3–4 hours, until firm.

3 Remove from the freezer about 10 minutes before serving. Serve in scoops, topped with a few chocolate curls.

Fruited Rice Ring

This unusual chilled rice pudding ring is topped with a tasty mix of dried fruits that have been simmered until meltingly soft. The delicious combination of the fruits and rice makes this a truly healthy dish.

Serves 4
65g/2½ oz/¼ cup short grain
pudding rice
900ml/1½ pints/3¾ cups semi-
skimmed (low-fat) milk
1 cinnamon stick
175g/6oz mixed dried fruit
175ml/6fl oz/¾ cup orange juice
40g/1½oz/3 tbsp caster
(superfine) sugar
finely grated rind of 1 small
orange

1 Place the rice, milk and cinnamon stick in a large pan and bring to the boil. Cover and simmer, stirring occasionally, for about 1½ hours, until all the liquid has been absorbed.

2 Meanwhile, place the dried fruit and orange juice in a pan and bring to the boil. Cover and simmer very gently for about 1 hour, until tender and all the liquid has been absorbed.

3 Remove the cinnamon stick from the rice and discard. Stir in the caster sugar and orange rind.

4 Carefully spoon the cooked fruit into the base of a lightly oiled 1.5 litre/2½ pint/6¼ cup ring mould. Spoon the rice over the fruit, smoothing it down firmly. Chill.

5 Run a knife around the edge of the mould and turn out the rice carefully on to a serving plate.

Cook's Tip
Rather than using a ring mould and turning out the dish, you may prefer to serve the dessert straight from individual small dishes. In this case, spoon the cooked rice into 6 dishes, then top with the cooked fruit. Chill well before serving.

Yogurt Energy 71kcal/295kJ; Protein 2.6g; Carbohydrate 8.5g, of which sugars 8.5g; Fat 3.5g, of which saturates 1.7g; Cholesterol 0mg; Calcium 62mg; Fibre 0.7g; Sodium 28mg.
Chocolate Energy 719kcal/2971kJ; Protein 3.4g; Carbohydrate 22.9g, of which sugars 22.6g; Fat 68.9g, of which saturates 41.2g; Cholesterol 155mg; Calcium 81mg; Fibre 0.4g; Sodium 33mg.
Rice Ring Energy 334kcal/1418kJ; Protein 10.1g; Carbohydrate 67.6g, of which sugars 54.7g; Fat 4.1g, of which saturates 2.4g; Cholesterol 13mg; Calcium 315mg; Fibre 1g; Sodium 123mg.

Apricot Mousse

Dried apricots are used to flavour this delightful, light and airy dessert. Serve in dainty stemmed glass dishes for a pretty effect.

Serves 4

300g/10oz ready-to-eat dried apricots

300ml/½ pint/1¼ cups fresh orange juice
200g/7oz/¾ cup low-fat Greek (US strained plain) yogurt
2 egg whites
fresh mint sprigs, to decorate

1 Place the apricots in a pan with the orange juice and heat gently until boiling. Cover the pan and gently simmer the apricots for 3 minutes.

2 Cool slightly, then place in a food processor or blender and process until smooth. Stir in the Greek yogurt.

3 Whisk the egg whites in a clean, grease-free bowl until stiff enough to hold soft peaks, then fold gently into the puréed apricot mixture.

4 Spoon the mousse into four stemmed glasses or one large serving dish. Chill in the refrigerator before serving, decorated with sprigs of fresh mint.

> **Cook's Tips**
> • This fluffy dessert can be made with any dried fruits instead of apricots – try dried peaches, prunes or apples.
> • When folding in whisked egg whites, always use a large metal spoon, and employ a light cutting action.

> **Variation**
> To make a speedier, fool-type dessert, omit the egg whites and simply swirl together the apricot mixture and the yogurt.

Apple Foam with Blackberries

A light-as-air dessert, with lots of contrast in colour, flavour and texture, this is the perfect dish for people wanting to cut down on their fat intake.

Serves 4
225g/8oz/2 cups blackberries
150ml/¼ pint/⅔ cup apple juice
5ml/1 tsp powdered gelatine
15ml/1 tbsp clear honey
2 egg whites

1 Place the blackberries in a pan with 60ml/4 tbsp of the apple juice and heat gently until the fruit is soft. Remove from the heat, cool, then chill in the refrigerator.

2 Sprinkle the gelatine over the remaining apple juice in a small pan and stir over gentle heat until dissolved. Stir in the honey.

3 Whisk the egg whites in a clean, grease-free bowl until stiff peaks form. Continue whisking hard and gradually pour in the hot gelatine mixture until well mixed.

4 Quickly spoon the foam into rough mounds on individual plates. Chill. To serve, spoon the blackberries and juice around the foam rounds.

> **Cook's Tips**
> • Make sure you dissolve the gelatine over very low heat. It must not boil, otherwise it will lose its setting ability.
> • Use a balloon, rotary or electric whisk to whisk the egg whites, or use an electric whisk. The bowl must be completely clean, otherwise, if there is any grease in the bowl, the egg whites will not achieve optimum volume. Do not overbeat the egg whites, as this makes them dry and they will not fold in evenly.

> **Variation**
> Any seasonal soft fruit can be used to accompany the apple foam if blackberries are not available.

Mousse Energy 180kcal/768kJ; Protein 8.7g; Carbohydrate 37.4g, of which sugars 37.4g; Fat 0.6g, of which saturates 0.1g; Cholesterol 1mg; Calcium 107mg; Fibre 4.8g; Sodium 65mg.
Apple Foam Energy 49kcal/209kJ; Protein 3.1g; Carbohydrate 9.5g, of which sugars 9.5g; Fat 0.2g, of which saturates 0g; Cholesterol 0mg; Calcium 27mg; Fibre 1.8g; Sodium 33mg.

Raspberry Passion Fruit Swirls

If passion fruit is not available, this simple dessert can be made with raspberries alone.

Serves 4
300g/11oz/generous 2½ cups raspberries

2 passion fruit
350ml/12fl oz/1½ cups Greek (US strained plain) yogurt
25g/1oz/2 tbsp caster (superfine) sugar
raspberries and sprigs of fresh mint, to decorate

1 Mash the raspberries in a small bowl with a fork until the juice runs. Scoop out the passion fruit pulp into a separate bowl, add the yogurt and sugar and mix well.

2 Spoon alternate spoonfuls of the raspberry pulp and the yogurt mixture into stemmed glasses or one large serving dish, stirring lightly to create a swirled effect.

3 Decorate the desserts with whole raspberries and sprigs of fresh mint. Serve chilled.

Frudités with Honey Dip

A colourful and tasty variation on the popular savoury crudités, this dessert is great fun for impromptu entertaining. Use any combination of fresh fruit you wish.

Serves 4
225g/8oz/1 cup Greek (US strained plain) yogurt
45ml/3 tbsp clear honey
selection of fruits such as apples, grapes, strawberries, peaches and cherries, for dipping

1 Place the yogurt in a dish, beat until smooth, then stir in the honey, leaving a marbled effect.

2 Cut a selection of fruits into wedges or bitesize pieces or leave whole, depending on your choice. Arrange on a platter with the bowl of dip in the centre. Chill before serving.

Creamy Mango Cheesecake

This low-fat cheesecake is as creamy as any other, but makes a healthier dessert option – so there's no need to hold back!

Serves 4
115g/4oz/1¼ cups rolled oats
40g/1½ oz/3 tbsp sunflower margarine
30ml/2 tbsp clear honey

1 large ripe mango
300g/10oz/1¼ cups low-fat soft cheese
150ml/¼ pint/⅔ cup low-fat natural (plain) yogurt
finely grated rind of 1 small lime
45ml/3 tbsp apple juice
20ml/4 tsp powdered gelatine
fresh mango and lime slices, to decorate

1 Preheat the oven to 200°C/400°F/Gas 6. Place the rolled oats in a mixing bowl and add the margarine and honey. Mix well together, then press into the base of a 20cm/8in loose-bottomed cake tin (pan).

2 Bake the oat base for 12–15 minutes, then remove the tin from the oven and leave to cool.

3 Peel, stone (pit) and roughly chop the mango. Place in a food processor or blender with the cheese, yogurt and lime rind and process until smooth.

4 Put the apple juice in a small pan and place over heat until boiling. Remove from the heat, sprinkle the gelatine over the apple juice, then stir until dissolved. Stir into the mango and cheese mixture.

5 Pour into the tin and chill until set. Remove from the tin and decorate with mango and lime slices.

> **Cook's Tip**
> For a richer, no-cook base, process 150g/5oz/1½ cups digestive biscuits (graham crackers) to form crumbs. Melt 40g/1½oz/ 3 tbsp butter, stir in the crumbs, then press into the tin and chill.

Swirls Energy 97kcal/414kJ; Protein 8g; Carbohydrate 16.4g, of which sugars 16.4g; Fat 0.4g, of which saturates 0.2g; Cholesterol 1mg; Calcium 99mg; Fibre 2.1g; Sodium 33mg.
Frudités Energy 97kcal/407kJ; Protein 3.7g; Carbohydrate 9.7g, of which sugars 9.7g; Fat 5.7g, of which saturates 2.9g; Cholesterol 0mg; Calcium 85mg; Fibre 0g; Sodium 41mg.
Cheesecake Energy 373kcal/1567kJ; Protein 21.2g; Carbohydrate 38.6g, of which sugars 17.6g; Fat 17.1g, of which saturates 4.1g; Cholesterol 19mg; Calcium 180mg; Fibre 2.9g; Sodium 451mg.

Strawberry & Blueberry Tart

This tart works equally well using either autumn or winter fruits as long as there is a riot of colour.

Serves 6–8

For the pastry
225g/8oz/2 cups plain (all-purpose) flour
pinch of salt
75g/3oz/⅔ cup icing (confectioners') sugar
150g/5oz/generous ½ cup unsalted (sweet) butter
1 egg yolk

For the filling
350g/12oz/1¾ cups mascarpone
30ml/2 tbsp icing (confectioners') sugar
few drops of vanilla extract
finely grated rind of 1 orange
450–675g/1–1½ lb/4½ cups fresh mixed strawberries and blueberries
90ml/6 tbsp redcurrant jelly
30ml/2 tbsp orange juice

1 Sift the flour, salt and sugar into a bowl. Dice the butter and rub it in until the mixture resembles coarse breadcrumbs. Mix in the egg yolk and 10ml/2 tsp cold water. Gather the dough together, knead lightly, wrap and chill for 1 hour.

2 Preheat the oven to 190°C/375°F/Gas 5. Roll out the pastry and use to line a 25cm/10in fluted flan tin (pan). Prick the base and chill for 15 minutes.

3 Line the chilled pastry case (pie shell) with baking parchment and baking beans, then bake blind for 15 minutes. Remove the paper and beans and bake for a further 15 minutes, until crisp and golden. Leave to cool in the tin.

4 To make the filling, beat together the mascarpone, sugar, vanilla extract and orange rind in a mixing bowl until smooth.

5 Remove the pastry case from the tin, then spoon in the filling and pile the fruits on top.

6 Heat the redcurrant jelly with the orange juice until runny, sieve, then brush over the fruit to form a glaze.

Boston Banoffee Pie

This dessert's rich, creamy, toffee-style filling just can't be resisted – but who cares!

Serves 4–6

For the pastry
150g/5oz/1¼ cups plain (all-purpose) flour
115g/4oz/½ cup butter, diced
50g/2oz/¼ cup caster (superfine) sugar

For the filling
115g/4oz/½ cup butter, diced
½ x 400g/14oz can skimmed, sweetened condensed milk
115g/4oz/⅔ cup soft light brown sugar
30ml/2 tbsp golden (light corn) syrup
2 small bananas, sliced
a little lemon juice
whipped cream and grated chocolate, to decorate

1 Preheat the oven to 160°C/325°F/Gas 3. To make the pastry, put the flour in a bowl and rub in the butter until the mixture resembles coarse breadcrumbs. Stir in the caster sugar and squeeze together to form a dough.

2 Press into the base of a 20cm/8in loose-based fluted flan tin (pan). Chill for 15 minutes.

3 Line the chilled pastry case (pie shell) with baking parchment and baking beans, then bake blind for 15 minutes. Remove the paper and beans and bake for a further 15 minutes, until crisp and golden. Leave to cool in the tin.

4 To make the filling, put the butter, condensed milk, brown sugar and syrup into a non-stick pan and heat gently, stirring, until the butter has melted and the sugar has dissolved.

5 Bring to a gentle boil and cook for 7 minutes, stirring constantly, until the mixture thickens and turns a light caramel colour. Pour into the cooled pastry case and leave until cold.

6 Sprinkle the bananas with lemon juice and arrange in overlapping circles on top of the caramel filling, leaving a gap in the centre. Pipe a swirl of whipped cream in the centre and sprinkle with grated chocolate.

Pie Energy 582kcal/2437kJ; Protein 5.8g; Carbohydrate 74g, of which sugars 58.8g; Fat 31.2g, of which saturates 19.6g; Cholesterol 80mg; Calcium 161mg; Fibre 0.9g; Sodium 293mg.
Tart Energy 419kcal/1753kJ; Protein 7.8g; Carbohydrate 48.5g, of which sugars 27.1g; Fat 22.9g, of which saturates 14g; Cholesterol 84mg; Calcium 63mg; Fibre 1.5g; Sodium 123mg.

Strawberries in Spiced Grape Jelly

Strawberries set in a fruity jelly delicately flavoured with cinnamon makes this the ideal dessert to serve after a filling main course.

Serves 4
450ml/³/4 pint/scant 2 cups red grape juice
1 cinnamon stick
1 small orange
15ml/1 tbsp powdered gelatine
225g/8oz/2 cups strawberries, chopped, plus extra to decorate

1 Place the grape juice in a pan with the cinnamon stick. Thinly pare the rind from the orange. Add most of it to the pan, but shred some pieces and set them aside for the decoration.

2 Place the pan over very low heat heat for 10 minutes, then remove the cinnamon stick and orange rind.

3 Squeeze the juice from the orange into a bowl and sprinkle over the powdered gelatine. Stir into the grape juice until the gelatine has completely dissolved. Allow to cool until just starting to set.

4 Stir in the strawberries, then quickly turn the mixture into a 1 litre/1¾ pint/4 cup mould or serving dish. Chill until set.

5 To serve, dip the mould quickly into hot water and turn the jelly out on to a serving plate. Decorate with whole strawberries and the reserved shreds of orange rind.

Cook's Tip
Do not wash the strawberries until just before you hull them. Dip them quickly in water, then pat dry on kitchen paper.

Variation
Use a different flavoured fruit juice, such as cranberry juice.

Plum & Port Sorbet

This sophisticated sorbet is deliciously refreshing.

Serves 4
900g/2lb ripe red plums, stoned (pitted) and halved
75g/3oz/6 tbsp caster (superfine) sugar
45ml/3 tbsp ruby port or red wine
crisp sweet cookies, to serve

1 Place the plums in a pan with the sugar and 45ml/3 tbsp water. Stir over low heat until the sugar has melted. Cover and simmer gently for about 5 minutes until the fruit is soft.

2 Turn into a food processor or blender and purée until smooth, then stir in the port or red wine. Cool completely, then turn into a plastic freezer container and freeze until the sorbet is firm around the edges. Process until smooth. Spoon back into the freezer container and freeze until solid.

3 Allow to soften slightly at room temperature for about 15–20 minutes before serving in scoops, with sweet cookies.

Quick Apricot Blender Whip

This is one of the quickest desserts you could make and also one of the prettiest. Decorate with lightly toasted slivered almonds if you like.

Serves 4
400g/14oz can apricot halves
15ml/1 tbsp Grand Marnier or brandy
175ml/6fl oz/³/4 cup Greek (US plain strained) yogurt

1 Drain the juice from the apricot halves and place the fruit in a blender or food processor with the Grand Marnier or brandy. Process until smooth.

2 Spoon the fruit purée and the yogurt in alternate spoonfuls into four tall glasses, swirling them together slightly to give a marbled effect. Serve immediately.

Grape Jelly Energy 80kcal/338kJ; Protein 4g; Carbohydrate 16.6g, of which sugars 16.6g; Fat 0.2g, of which saturates 0g; Cholesterol 0mg; Calcium 31mg; Fibre 0.6g; Sodium 11mg.
Sorbet Energy 173kcal/738kJ; Protein 1.5g; Carbohydrate 40.8g, of which sugars 40.8g; Fat 0.2g, of which saturates 0g; Cholesterol 0mg; Calcium 40mg; Fibre 3.6g; Sodium 6mg.
Apricot Whip Energy 117kcal/491kJ; Protein 5.4g; Carbohydrate 11.9g, of which sugars 11.7g; Fat 4.9g, of which saturates 0.6g; Cholesterol 1mg; Calcium 140mg; Fibre 2.3g; Sodium 50mg.

Tofu Berry Brulée

If you feel that classic brulée is too rich for you, then this lighter variation is a must. Made from tofu, it is low in fat yet tastes great. Use any soft fruits that are in season.

Serves 4
225g/8oz/2 cups red berry fruits
   such as strawberries,
   raspberries and redcurrants
300g/11oz packet silken tofu
45ml/3 tbsp icing (confectioners')
   sugar
65g/2½ oz/¼ cup demerara
   (raw) sugar

1 Halve or quarter any large strawberries, but leave the smaller ones whole. Mix with the other chosen berries.

2 Place the tofu and icing sugar in a food processor or blender and process until smooth.

3 Stir in the fruits and spoon into a flameproof dish with a 900ml/1½ pint/3¾ cup capacity. Sprinkle the top with enough demerara sugar to cover evenly.

4 Place under a very hot grill (broiler) until the sugar melts and caramelizes. Chill well before serving.

Cook's Tips
• Choose silken tofu rather than firm tofu as it gives a smoother texture in this type of dish. Firm tofu is better for cooking in chunks.
• Tofu is make from soya beans and is a popular vegetarian ingredient as it is a good source of protein. It is bland in taste, but absorbs other flavours well.

Variation
For a more indulgent version, replace the tofu with double (heavy) cream and add a few drops of vanilla extract.

Peach & Ginger Pashka

A low-fat version of the Russian Easter favourite – a glorious cheese dessert flavoured with peaches and preserved stem ginger.

2 pieces preserved stem ginger in
   syrup, drained and chopped,
   plus 30ml/2 tbsp syrup from
   the jar
2.5ml/½ tsp vanilla extract

Serves 4
350g/12oz/1½ cups low-fat
   cottage cheese
2 peaches or nectarines, peeled
90g/3½oz/scant ½ cup low-fat
   natural (plain) yogurt

To decorate
1 peach or nectarine, peeled and
   sliced
10ml/2 tsp slivered almonds,
   toasted

1 Drain the cottage cheese and rub it through a fine sieve (strainer) into a bowl. Remove the stones (pits) from the peaches or nectarines and roughly chop.

2 Mix together the chopped peaches or nectarines in a large bowl with the low-fat cottage cheese, yogurt, preserved stem ginger and syrup and vanilla extract.

3 Line a new, clean flower pot or a strainer with a piece of clean, fine cloth, such as muslin (cheesecloth).

4 Add the cheese mixture and wrap over the cloth to cover. Place a saucer on top and weigh down. Stand over a bowl in a cool place and leave to drain overnight.

5 To serve, unwrap the cloth and turn the pashka out on to a serving plate. Decorate the pashka with peach or nectarine slices and toasted almonds.

Cook's Tip
Rather than making one large pashka, line 4 to 6 cups or ramekins with a clean cloth or muslin and divide the mixture evenly among them.

Brulée Energy 178kcal/754kJ; Protein 6.7g; Carbohydrate 32.7g, of which sugars 32.4g; Fat 3.2g, of which saturates 0.4g; Cholesterol 0mg; Calcium 406mg; Fibre 0.6g; Sodium 8mg.
Pashka Energy 79kcal/334kJ; Protein 9.3g; Carbohydrate 8.6g, of which sugars 8.6g; Fat 1.1g, of which saturates 0.7g; Cholesterol 3mg; Calcium 116mg; Fibre 0.8g; Sodium 197mg.

Pecan Cake

This delicious cake is an example of the French influence on Mexican cooking. Serve with a few redcurrants for a splash of uplifting colour.

Serves 8–10

115g/4oz/1 cup pecan nuts
115g/4oz/¼ cup butter, softened
115g/4oz/½ cup soft light brown sugar
5ml/1 tsp vanilla extract

4 large eggs, separated
75g/3oz/⅔ cup plain (all-purpose) flour
pinch of salt
12 whole pecan nuts, to decorate
whipped cream or crème fraîche, to serve

For drizzling
50g/2oz/¼ cup butter
120ml/4fl oz/scant ½ cup clear honey

1 Preheat the oven to 180°C/350°F/Gas 4. Grease a 20cm/8in round cake tin (pan). Toast the nuts in a dry frying pan for 5 minutes, shaking frequently. Grind finely and place in a bowl.

2 Cream the butter with the sugar in a mixing bowl, then beat in the vanilla extract and egg yolks.

3 Add the flour to the ground nuts and mix well. Whisk the egg whites with the salt in a clean, grease-free bowl until soft peaks form. Fold the whites into the butter mixture, then gently fold in the flour and nut mixture.

4 Spoon the mixture into the cake tin and bake for 30 minutes or until a skewer inserted in the centre comes out clean.

5 Cool the cake in the tin for 5 minutes, then remove the sides of the tin. Stand the cake on a wire rack until cold.

6 Remove the cake from the base of the tin if necessary, then return it to the rack and arrange the pecans on top. Transfer to a plate. Melt the butter for drizzling in a small pan, add the honey and bring to the boil, stirring. Lower the heat and simmer for 3 minutes, then pour over the cake. Serve with whipped cream or crème fraîche.

Chilled Chocolate Slice

This is a very rich family pudding, but it is also designed to use up the occasional leftover.

Serves 6–8
115g/4oz/½ cup butter, melted
225g/8oz ginger nut biscuits (gingersnaps), finely crushed
50g/2oz stale sponge cake crumbs

60–75ml/4–5 tbsp orange juice
115g/4oz stoned (pitted) dates
25g/1oz/¼ cup finely chopped nuts
175g/6oz dark (bittersweet) chocolate
300ml/½ pint/1¼ cups whipping cream
grated chocolate and icing (confectioners') sugar, to decorate

1 Mix together the butter and ginger nut biscuit crumbs, then pack around the sides and base of an 18cm/7in loose-based flan tin (pan). Chill while making the filling.

2 Put the cake crumbs into a large bowl with the orange juice and leave to soak. Warm the dates thoroughly, then mash and blend into the cake crumbs along with the nuts.

3 Melt the chocolate with 45–60ml/3–4 tbsp of the cream. Softly whip the rest of the cream, then fold in the melted chocolate mixture.

4 Stir the cream and chocolate mixture into the crumbs and mix well. Pour into the prepared tin, mark into portions with a sharp knife and leave to set.

5 Scatter the grated chocolate over the top and dust with icing sugar. Serve cut into wedges.

> **Cook's Tip**
> This dessert is delicious served with slices of fresh fruit, such as peaches, mango or pineapple. Alternatively, offer plums or nectarines poached in a little wine and sugar, or try orange segments in a syrup made from sugar, water and orange juice.

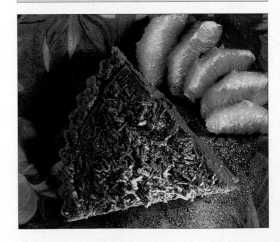

Pecan Cake Energy 428Kcal/1785kJ; Protein 6.2g; Carbohydrate 34.7g, of which sugars 27.4g; Fat 30.5g, of which saturates 12.5g; Cholesterol 158mg; Calcium 51mg; Fibre 1g; Sodium 170mg.
Chocolate Slice Energy 545kcal/2269kJ; Protein 4.8g; Carbohydrate 45.8g, of which sugars 32g; Fat 39.3g, of which saturates 22.6g; Cholesterol 85mg; Calcium 80mg; Fibre 1.4g; Sodium 198mg.

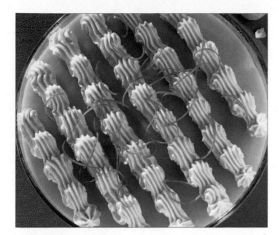

Blackberry & Apple Romanoff

The unbeatable combination of blackberries and apples gives this rich iced dessert delicious flavour. Surprisingly easy to make, the dish offers a stunning finale to a meal.

Serves 6–8
350g/12oz sharp eating apples, peeled, cored and chopped
40g/1½ oz/3 tbsp caster (superfine) sugar
250ml/8fl oz/1 cup whipping cream
5ml/1 tsp grated lemon rind
90ml/6 tbsp Greek (US strained plain) yogurt
50g/2oz (about 4–6) crisp meringues, roughly crumbled
225g/8oz/2 cups blackberries (fresh or frozen)
whipped cream, a few blackberries and fresh mint leaves, to decorate

1 Line a 900ml–1.2 litre/1½–2 pint/4–5 cup round, deep freezerproof bowl with clear film (plastic wrap). Toss the chopped apples into a pan with 1oz/2 tbsp sugar and cook for 2–3 minutes until softened. Mash with a fork and leave to cool.

2 Whip the cream and fold in the lemon rind, yogurt, the remaining sugar, the mashed apples and the meringues.

3 Gently stir in the blackberries, then turn the mixture into the prepared bowl and freeze for 1–3 hours.

4 Loosen the edges with a knife, then turn out on to a plate and remove the clear film. Decorate with whirls of whipped cream, blackberries and mint leaves.

Cook's Tip
If you would prefer a more fruity decoration, try serving with a blackberry sauce. Put 225g/8oz blackberries in a pan with a little sugar and cook over low heat for about 5 minutes until just soft. Press half through a sieve (strainer), then mix the purée with the rest of the berries. Cool. Add a splash of crème de cassis liqueur, if you wish. Spoon a little over the dessert and serve the rest as an accompanying sauce.

Tangerine Trifle

An unusual variation on a traditional trifle – of course, you can add a little alcohol if you wish.

Serves 4
5 trifle sponges, halved lengthways
30ml/2 tbsp apricot jam
15–20 ratafia biscuits (almond macaroons)
142g/4¾oz packet tangerine jelly (gelatine)
300g/11oz can mandarin oranges, drained, reserving juice
600ml/1 pint/2½ cups ready-made custard
whipped cream and shreds of orange rind, to decorate
caster (superfine) sugar, for sprinkling

1 Spread the halved sponge cakes with apricot jam and arrange in the base of a deep serving bowl or glass dish. Sprinkle the ratafias over the top.

2 Break up the jelly into a heatproof measuring jug (cup), add the juice from the canned mandarins and dissolve in a pan of hot water or in the microwave. Stir until the liquid is clear.

3 Make up to 600ml/1 pint/2½ cups with ice-cold water, stir well and leave to cool for up to 30 minutes. Scatter the mandarin oranges over the cake and ratafias.

4 Pour the jelly over the mandarin oranges, cake and ratafias and chill for 1 hour or more.

5 When the jelly has set, pour the custard over the top and chill again in the refrigerator.

6 When ready to serve, pipe the whipped cream over the custard. Wash the orange rind shreds, sprinkle them with caster sugar and use to decorate the trifle.

Cook's Tip
For an even better flavour, why not make your own custard?

Trifle Energy 566kcal/2392kJ; Protein 12.9g; Carbohydrate 106.7g, of which sugars 74.2g; Fat 11g, of which saturates 3.2g; Cholesterol 116mg; Calcium 244mg; Fibre 1.4g; Sodium 240mg.
Romanoff Energy 198kcal/825kJ; Protein 2.1g; Carbohydrate 17.6g, of which sugars 17.6g; Fat 13.8g, of which saturates 8.5g; Cholesterol 33mg; Calcium 52mg; Fibre 1.6g; Sodium 25mg.

Apple & Hazelnut Shortcake

This is a variation on the classic strawberry shortcake and is equally delicious.

Serves 8–10
3 sharp eating apples
5ml/1 tsp lemon juice
15–25g/½–1oz/1–2 tbsp caster (superfine) sugar
15ml/1 tbsp chopped fresh mint, or 5ml/1 tsp dried mint
250ml/8fl oz/1 cup whipping cream
a few drops of vanilla extract
a few fresh mint leaves and whole hazelnuts, to decorate

For the hazelnut shortcake
150g/5oz/1¼ cups plain wholemeal (whole-wheat) flour
50g/2oz/½ cup ground hazelnuts
50g/2oz/½ cup icing (confectioners') sugar, sifted
150g/5oz/generous 1 cup unsalted butter

1 To make the hazelnut shortcake, process the flour, ground hazelnuts and icing sugar with the butter in a food processor in short bursts, until they come together. Bring the dough together, adding a very little iced water if needed. Knead briefly, wrap and chill for 30 minutes.

2 Preheat the oven to 160°C/325°F/Gas 3. Cut the dough in half and roll out each half to an 18cm/7in round. Place on baking parchment on baking sheets. Bake for 40 minutes, or until crisp. Allow to cool.

3 Peel, core and chop the apples into a pan with the lemon juice. Add sugar to taste, then cook for 2–3 minutes, until just soft. Mash the apple gently with the mint and leave to cool.

4 Whip the cream with the vanilla extract. Place one shortbread base on a serving plate. Spread half the apple and half the cream on top.

5 Place the second shortcake on top, then spread over the remaining apple and cream, swirling the top layer of cream gently. Decorate the top with mint leaves and a few whole hazelnuts, then serve at once.

Lemon Cheesecake

A lovely light cream cheese filling is presented on an elegant brandy snap base.

Serves 8
½ x 142g/4¾oz packet lemon jelly (gelatine)
45–60ml/3–4 tbsp boiling water
50g/1lb/2 cups low-fat cream cheese
10ml/2 tsp grated lemon rind
75–115g/3–4oz/about ½ cup caster (superfine) sugar
a few drops of vanilla extract
150ml/¼ pint/⅔ cup Greek (US strained plain) yogurt
8 brandy snaps
a few fresh mint leaves and icing sugar, to decorate

1 Dissolve the jelly in the boiling water in a heatproof measuring jug (cup) and, when clear, add enough cold water to make up to 150ml/¼ pint/⅔ cup. Chill until the jelly begins to thicken. Meanwhile, line a 450g/1lb loaf tin (pan) with clear film (plastic wrap).

2 Cream the cheese with the lemon rind, sugar and vanilla and beat until light and smooth. Then fold in the thickening lemon jelly and the yogurt. Spoon into the prepared tin and chill until set. Preheat the oven to 160°C/325°F/Gas 3.

3 Place two or three brandy snaps at a time on a baking sheet. Place in the oven for no more than 1 minute, until soft enough to unroll and flatten out completely. Leave on a cold plate or tray to harden again. Repeat with the remaining brandy snaps.

4 To serve, turn the cheesecake out on to a board with the help of the clear film. Cut into eight slices and place one slice on each brandy snap base. Decorate with mint leaves and dust with icing sugar before serving.

> **Variation**
> Use a packet of orange jelly instead of lemon and use grated orange rind instead of the lemon. Omit the vanilla extract and decorate with pared orange rind shreds in place of mint.

Shortcake Energy 333kcal/1386kJ; Protein 3.3g; Carbohydrate 23.1g, of which sugars 13.8g; Fat 25.9g, of which saturates 14.4g; Cholesterol 58mg; Calcium 36mg; Fibre 2.2g; Sodium 99mg.
Cheesecake Energy 237kcal/1000kJ; Protein 10.9g; Carbohydrate 36.3g, of which sugars 33.9g; Fat 7.2g, of which saturates 3g; Cholesterol 14mg; Calcium 119mg; Fibre 0.1g; Sodium 299mg.

Frozen Strawberry Mousse Cake

Children love this cake because it is pink and pretty, and it is just like an ice cream treat.

Serves 4–6
425g/15oz can strawberries
  in syrup
15ml/1 tbsp powdered gelatine

6 trifle sponges
45ml/3 tbsp strawberry conserve
200ml/7fl oz/scant 1 cup crème
  fraîche
200ml/7fl oz/scant 1 cup
  whipped cream, to decorate

1 Strain the syrup from the strawberries into a large heatproof jug (cup). Sprinkle over the gelatine and stir well. Stand the jug in a pan of hot water and stir until the gelatine has dissolved.

2 Leave to cool, then chill in the refrigerator for just under 1 hour, until beginning to set. Meanwhile, cut the sponge cake in half lengthways, then spread the cut surfaces evenly with the strawberry conserve.

3 Slowly whisk the crème fraîche into the strawberry jelly, then whisk in the canned strawberries. Line a deep 20cm/8in loose-based cake tin (pan) with non-stick baking parchment.

4 Pour half the strawberry mousse mixture into the tin, arrange the sponge cakes over the surface and then spoon over the remaining mousse mixture, pushing down any sponge cakes which rise up.

5 Freeze for 1–2 hours until firm. Unmould the cake and carefully remove the lining paper. Transfer to a serving plate. Decorate with whirls of cream, a few strawberry leaves and a fresh strawberry, if you have them.

> **Cook's Tip**
> For a glamorous finishing touch, spoon the whipped cream into a piping (pastry) bag fitted with a star nozzle and pipe swirls.

Frozen Lemon Soufflé with Blackberry Sauce

This tangy iced dessert is complemented wonderfully by the richly coloured blackberry sauce.

Serves 6
grated rind of 1 lemon and juice
  of 2 lemons
15ml/1 tbsp powdered gelatine
5 eggs, separated
150g/5oz/1¼ cups caster
  (superfine) sugar

a few drops of vanilla extract
400ml/14fl oz/1⅔ cups whipping
  cream

For the sauce
175g/6oz/1½ cups blackberries
  (fresh or frozen)
25–40g/1–1½oz/2–3 tbsp caster
  (superfine) sugar
a few fresh blackberries and
  blackberry leaves, to decorate

1 Place the lemon juice in a small pan and heat through. Sprinkle on the gelatine and leave to dissolve, or gently heat further until clear. Allow to cool.

2 Put the lemon rind, egg yolks, sugar and vanilla extract into a large bowl and whisk until the mixture is very thick, pale and really creamy.

3 Whisk the egg whites in a clean, grease-free bowl until almost stiff. Whip the cream until stiff.

4 Stir the gelatine mixture into the yolk mixture, then fold in the whipped cream and lastly the egg whites. When lightly but thoroughly blended, turn into a 1.5 litre/2½ pint/6¼ cup soufflé dish and freeze for about 2 hours.

5 To make the sauce, place the blackberries in a pan with the sugar and cook for 4–6 minutes until the juices begin to run and all the sugar has dissolved. Pass through a nylon sieve (strainer) to remove the seeds, then chill until ready to serve.

6 When the soufflé is almost frozen, scoop or spoon out on to individual plates and serve with the blackberry sauce.

Mousse Cake Energy 419kcal/1746kJ; Protein 5.1g; Carbohydrate 36.5g, of which sugars 29.1g; Fat 29.1g, of which saturates 18.1g; Cholesterol 148mg; Calcium 73mg; Fibre 0.8g; Sodium 54mg.
Soufflé Energy 438kcal/1821kJ; Protein 7g; Carbohydrate 33.8g, of which sugars 33.8g; Fat 31.6g, of which saturates 18.1g; Cholesterol 229mg; Calcium 90mg; Fibre 0.9g; Sodium 77mg.

Index

NOTES

NOTES

NOTES

Notes

NOTES

NOTES

NOTES

NOTES